... Vase ...	Bleu Celeste fleurs		384.
2 g.e v g.e	g.e	288.	576.
1. Cuvette à fleurs verdun. g.e Enfans Colorés	....	"	600.
1. g.e à fleurs unie Lapis mosaique Enf Camay	....	"	300.
2 Vases Canelés 1.e g.e fleurs Guirlandes	....	300.	600.
2 g.e à Dauphin Bleu Celeste Enf Colorés	....	600	1200.
2 g.e à oreilles 4 g.e g.e " g.e		132.	264.
2 g.e ... g.e oiseaux		120.	240.
2 Caisses v.e g.e .... Enfans Camay	....	48.	96.
1. Vase à l'Holandoise v.e g.e Enf Colorés emadrés		"	300.
1 Cuvette à fleurs unie Lapis fleur	....	"	216.
2 Vazes à oreilles v.e g.e Bleu Celeste Enf Colorés	432.	864.
2 Pots pourri Pompad. 4e g.e Enf Camayeux			
Chaines Colorées emadrés	....	144.	288.
2 Caisses 4.e g.e Bleu Celeste Enfans Camayeux	96.	192.
2 Vazes canelés v.e g.e Lapis mosaique fleur —			
Guirlande	....	300.	600.
11. Beignoires d'yeux fleurs	....	6.	66.
2 Pots à pommade 1.e g.e blanc et or	....	9	18.
1 fontaine .... fleurs Guirlande			
1 Cuvette ... g.e	}	"	600.
1 Pannier 8 g.e .... Bleu Celeste filet d'or	....	"	360.
3 Boëttes à fiches mosaique g.e fleurs	....	g.e	288.
1 Platteau à fromage .... fleur filet bleu	....	"	72.
1 Pot à sucre ... g.e	....	"	18.
1 platteau hebert ... g.e			
1 Gobelet ... g.e			
1 Sorcoupe g.e ... g.e	}	"	120.
1 pot à sucre ... g.e			
1 Pot à Lait ... g.e			
1 Gobelet Couvert ... g.e			
1 Sorcoupe ... g.e	}	"	15.
1 fontaine Enfans Cam. Chaines Colo. emadrés	}	"	600.
1 Jatte g.e ... g.e			
1272 pieces			62375 64 .... 62375. "

French Eighteenth-Century Porcelain

at the Wadsworth Atheneum

The J. Pierpont Morgan Collection

Linda H. Roth

Clare Le Corbeiller

Wadsworth Atheneum

Support for the research for this book was
provided by:

   The National Endowment for the Arts

   The Samuel H. Kress Foundation

   The Florence J. Gould Foundation

Support for the publication of this book was
provided by:

   William and Norma Horvitz

   The Florence Gould Foundation

   The Ceramica-Stiftung, Basle, Switzerland

   The Wadsworth Atheneum

Library of Congress Catalogue Number 00-132655

Editing and project management by John Adamson,
90 Hertford Street, Cambridge CB4 3AQ, England

Set in Granjon and designed by James Shurmer,
24 Ollard's Grove, Loughton, Essex, IG10 4DW, England

Printed in Italy by Conti Tipocolor on Parilux 150 gsm
matt white

ISBN 0 918333 16 4

Published in 2000 by the Trustees of the Wadsworth
Atheneum

Copyright © 2000

Frontispiece: pot-pourri vase (*pot-pourri à jour*),
Vincennes, c. 1752–1753, catalogue no. 56

Endpapers: pages from the sales ledgers at Sèvres, Vy 1,
fols. 118v–119, 1 October–31 December 1755, referring
to the fountain and basin (*fontaine unie et cuvette*),
catalogue no. 151

Contents

Acknowledgements

I have benefited throughout from Bernard Dragesco's courtesy, considered opinions, and generously offered information. Geneviève Le Duc also contributed essential support, and her death before she would have reviewed certain passages is a loss to the subject as well as a personal one. I am especially grateful to Letitia Roberts for giving me free rein of the invaluable photo archives of Sotheby's Porcelain Department. For advice and assistance I am indebted to Anthony du Boulay, Donna Corbin, J. D. van Dam, Aileen Dawson, James David Draper, Antoinette Hallé, Penelope Hunter-Stiebel, Oliver Impey, C. J. A. Jörg, Pamela Klaber, Wolfram Koeppe, Jennifer Komar, C. Jubert, Laurence Libin, John Mallet, Errol Manners, Chantal Meslin-Perrier, Susan Miller, Christina Nelson, Tamara Préaud, Bertrand Rondot, William R. Sargent, Clare Vincent, Jody Wilkie, and the late Bernard Watney.

To Linda Roth I owe my deepest thanks for the invitation to work with this material, and for her unfailing enthusiasm and support.

Clare Le Corbeiller

This catalogue was conceived just over ten years ago. During this period, several people have been indispensable to me, giving generously of their time, knowledge, and support. I owe the utmost thanks to Tamara Préaud, archiviste de la Manufacture nationale de Sèvres, who guided me through the factory documents with unending generosity, encouragement, and patience. Madame Préaud also read all of the Vincennes and Sèvres entries while in manuscript form, provided valuable suggestions, and checked archival citations for accuracy. Special thanks also go to Antoine d'Albis, Chief Scientist, Manufacture nationale de Sèvres, who examined the collection in detail, provided invaluable assistance with technical history and analysis, and reviewed the manuscript along with Madame Préaud. I would also like to express my profound gratitude to Bernard Dragesco, who examined the collection with me on several occasions, answered countless inquiries, facilitated access to collections and scholars in France, shared his photographic archives, and reviewed many entries for content. To Rosalind Savill and Sir Geoffrey de Bellaigue, I would like to say thank you for encouraging me to undertake this project, and for kind and helpful information and suggestions all along the way. I owe Sir Geoffrey a particular thanks for introducing me to the wonder of Sèvres porcelain during a visit to the Wadsworth Atheneum almost twenty years ago, and for setting the stage for this catalogue with his work on the collection and his contribution to the Museum's exhibition catalogue, *J. Pierpont Morgan, Collector: European Decorative Arts from the Wadsworth Atheneum*, published in 1987. Bertrand Rondot and Antoinette Faÿ-Hallé granted me repeated access to the important collections at the Musée des Arts décoratifs and the Musée national de Céramique, Sèvres. David Peters was extremely helpful concerning marks and service pieces, and read many of the entries in advance. Theodore Dell gave valuable advice regarding the gilt-bronze mounts.

Many others kindly assisted me with inquiries for information and photographs. They are: Armin Allen, Liana Paredes Arend, Jonas Gramkow Barlyng, Christian Baulez, Shelley Bennett, Michelle Beiny, Terry Bloxham, Dr. Dale Brent, Maureen Cassidy-Geiger, Yveline de Chavagnac, Meredith Chilton, Claudine P. Colombo, Donna Corbin, Howard Coutts, Didier Cramoisan, Leon Dalva, Aileen Dawson, Pierre-François Dayot, Theodore Dell, the late Geneviève Le Duc, Pierre Ennès, Dr. Sabine Glaser, Alden Gordon, Alain Gruber, Oliver Impey, Christopher Hartop, Henry Hawley, James Higgenbothen, Robin Hildyard, William Johnston, Christian Jörg, Ulrich Leben, Thomas Lemann, Andrew McClellan, Bet McLeod, Errol Manners, Dr. Markus Miller, Jeffrey Munger, Christina Nelson, Robert E. Parks, Elizabeth Pergam, Robert Pirie, Maxime Préaud, Letitia Roberts, Marie-Laure de Rochebrune, Judy Rudoe, William Sargent, Carolyn Sargentson, Adrian Sassoon, Selma Schwartz, William Stout, Jean Strouse, Sheila Tabakoff, Sylvie Wallez, Jeffrey Weaver, Beth Carver-Wees, Richard Wenger, John Whitehead, Jodie Wilkie, Gillian Wilson, David Wright, Hilary Young, Ghenete Zelleke.

Naturally, the staff at the Wadsworth Atheneum deserves much credit and many thanks. I would like to thank former directors Patrick McCaughey and then Peter Sutton for allowing me to undertake and complete the project, and committing the Museum's resources to this purpose. My dear friend and colleague Jean Cadogan offered early support and much-needed cheerleading. Cindy Roman was unfailing in her assistance, especially with the arduous tasks of organizing the photography of the collection, and supervising a host of interns who checked references, page numbers, and remeasured objects. Other staff, volunteers, and interns who provided assistance are: Cecil Adams, Christy Anderson, Peter Barberie, Gertrud Bourgoyne, Zenon Ganszinec, John Gay, Amy Larkin Gelbach, Amber Woods Germano, Mark Guiliano, Alison Hewey, Stephen Kornhauser, Lynn Mervosh, Kristin Shanksy, Jack Tracz, Steve Winot, and Mark Zuroli.

Joseph Szaszfai and David Stansbury did an admirable job photographing this challenging material.

Support during the research phase of this project was given by: The National Endowment for the Arts, The Samuel H. Kress Foundation, and The Florence J. Gould Foundation. J. Taylor Crandall and the Bell and Howell Corporation generously donated a microfilm reader-printer to the Museum, enabling me to consult critical documents from the Sèvres Archives at my convenience.

I would especially like to thank Clare Le Corbeiller for agreeing to catalogue the Saint-Cloud, Villeroy, Mennecy, and Chantilly pieces, and for her sage advice concerning all aspects of this project. John Adamson, as editor, indexer, and publishing consultant, worked tirelessly to insure that the book was coherent, accessible to a varied audience, as well as beautifully produced. Finally, I owe all of my family my unfailing gratitude for their support and unending patience.

Linda H. Roth

Director's Foreword

The origins of the Wadsworth Atheneum's collections of European decorative arts lie in the 1917 gift of over one thousand objects from the collection of J. Pierpont Morgan. Four years after his father's death, J.P. Morgan, Jr., honored his father's will by distributing his art collections among the Morgan Library, the Metropolitan Museum of Art, and the Wadsworth Atheneum. The Atheneum received ancient bronzes, Renaissance majolica, baroque ivory and silver-gilt pieces, and rare eighteenth-century porcelains. These treasures were highlighted in a major traveling exhibition titled *J. Pierpont Morgan, Collector*, organized by Linda Roth and the Wadsworth Atheneum in 1987. The large collection of French eighteenth-century porcelain formed by Morgan remains to this day among the chief highlights of the Wadsworth Atheneum, and it now receives its due attention with the publication of this detailed scholarly catalogue.

Over a decade ago, Linda Roth, Charles C. and Eleanor Lamont Cunningham Curator of European Decorative Arts, undertook the Herculean task of cataloguing this extensive collection. In the subsequent years, she has demonstrated both great scholarship and a deep commitment to revealing to the public the importance of this distinct collection of over 250 objects. Her dedicated research has yielded many new discoveries and has resulted in a catalogue that makes major contributions to both the study of patronage and to the field of French porcelain.

The Wadsworth Atheneum takes great pride in this publication and in Linda Roth's achievements. This undertaking exemplifies one of the most important and fundamental responsibilities of the art museum: to make widely available to scholars, students and the general public the most up-to-date information, historical knowledge and visual record of its collections.

This labor of love has been generously supported by a number of foundations and individuals. The Wadsworth Atheneum expresses its gratitude to the National Endowment for the Arts; the Kress Foundation; the Florence J. Gould Foundation; Ceramica Stiftung, Basle, Switzerland; and William and Norma Horvitz. We appreciate all of the funders' generosity and patience, as Linda Roth successfully completed this major undertaking.

Finally, the Wadsworth Atheneum wishes to thank the many scholars and institutions who have assisted in this ambitious project, in particular, Clare Le Corbeiller (Emeritus Curator of European Sculpture and Decorative Arts), Metropolitan Museum of Art, who has made a significant contribution to the catalogue. Many members of the Atheneum's staff ably assisted in the production of this publication and are to be thanked. We share with them and all lovers of French decorative arts a sense of institutional pride in presenting this important publication to the public.

Elizabeth Mankin Kornhauser
Acting Director
Wadsworth Atheneum Museum of Art

Note to the Reader

Unless otherwise stated, all the porcelain in this catalogue was collected by J. Pierpont Morgan and, following his wishes, given to the Wadsworth Atheneum by his son, J.P. Morgan, Jr. in 1917, four years after the elder Morgan's death. All other details of known provenance are given in each entry, and a summary of all provenances (other than J. Pierpont Morgan) is given in the index under provenance.

Many of the objects will be known by their accession numbers. A separate concordance of the accession numbers and their corresponding catalogue numbers is provided at the back of the book.

Most decipherable marks (factory, painters', gilders', *répareurs'*, unattributed and hitherto unrecorded) that appear on the objects are illustrated. Where the same mark occurs on more than one object in a set or group, the mark is only shown once. A summary of all the marks is provided within the index under marks.

The objects in this catalogue have been grouped by factory and then by function. For ease of access, the entries for Vincennes-Sèvres porcelain are divided into subheadings of model, function, commentary and condition.

Throughout this catalogue all quotations from the French are given with their original spelling and any grammatical infelicities. The Sèvres names of some of the objects reflect accepted norms of pronunciation and spelling of the eighteenth century, such as *vase hollandois* or *marronnière à ozier*. As elsewhere in literature on Sèvres porcelain, these differences from modern French have been retained in the nomenclature.

The terms *père* and *fils*, denoting the elder and younger (father and son) or *aîné* and *cadet*, the older and younger of two siblings have also been retained.

Quotations from the Sèvres archives are given in italics. Other quoted material is given within quotation marks.

The glossary provides background information on the materials, process, decoration, sale and distribution of porcelain in the eighteenth century, with particular emphasis on the Vincennes-Sèvres factory. It contains an explanation of the dating system used in this catalogue.

Neither the objects nor the marks are shown to scale. However, the size of all objects is given in inches (rounded up to the next 1/16 inch). The equivalent in centimeters (to one decimal place) is given in parentheses. For ease of reference sizes of objects given elsewhere in the literature in centimeters only are also given in inches.

Abbreviations

D.	depth
DIAM.	diameter
H.	height
L.	length
W.	width

Abbreviations used in the endnotes

AMNS	Archives de la Manufacture Nationale de Sèvres
AN	Archives nationales
APML	Archives of the Pierpont Morgan Library, New York
IF	Institut de France
MAD	Musée des Arts décoratifs, Paris
MFA	Museum of Fine Arts, Boston
MMA	The Metropolitan Museum of Art, New York
MNC	Musée national de Céramique, Sèvres
V&A	Victoria and Albert Museum, London

J. Pierpont Morgan and the French Porcelain at the Wadsworth Atheneum

The collection of French eighteenth-century porcelain at the Wadsworth Atheneum was largely formed by John Pierpont Morgan and comprises works from the major soft-paste factories of the period, notably Saint-Cloud, Chantilly, Villeroy, Mennecy, Vincennes, and Sèvres. In 1917 approximately 290 pieces from a collection of about 330 objects were donated to the Museum by Morgan's son, J.P. Morgan, Jr.

John Pierpont Morgan was one of the world's great art collectors (fig. 1). He collected on a modest scale as a young man, but began buying art in earnest in 1890, when his father Junius Spencer Morgan died, leaving him considerable wealth and in charge of a powerful financial organization.[1] His success in business provided him with the means to surround himself and his family with beautiful works of art. And yet in this pursuit he was also motivated by the desire for American culture to reach a level worthy of its economic and political stature. In twenty-three years he amassed a collection of over 20,000 works of art, valued in 1912 at about 50 million dollars.[2]

The range of objects he collected was vast, and included antiquities, medieval silver gilt and ivories, Limoges enamels, Renaissance bronzes and maiolica, Renaissance and Baroque silver gilt, ivories, and glass, watches and clocks, jewelry, rock crystal, and amber, sculpture, miniatures, Meissen porcelain, Old Master paintings, and drawings, books, and illuminated manuscripts. However, the vast majority of Morgan's collection consisted of decorative arts, for which he seemed to have a special affinity. French decorative arts, including eighteenth-century gold boxes, Beauvais and Gobelins tapestries, carpets, furniture, and French porcelain, constituted an important part of this collection.

Morgan was born in Hartford, Connecticut, in 1837. He was the eldest of five children, son of Junius Spencer and Juliet Pierpont Morgan. Morgan lived in Hartford until he was fourteen, at which time he moved to Boston with his parents, and then three years later to London. He attended private school in Vevey, Switzerland (1854–55), and then the University of Göttingen in Germany (1856–57). He learned German and French during these years, and began collecting stained glass fragments and autographs. He remained in touch with his friends and family in Hartford, especially James Goodwin. The Goodwin family was actively supporting the Wadsworth Atheneum in the late nineteenth century.

During the 1870s and 1880s Morgan was busy raising his family, and building his career, becoming one of the great financiers of the late nineteenth and early twentieth centuries. He was to be instrumental in reorganizing the American railroad and shipping industries, in the growth of the steel industry, and provided much-needed

Fig. 1 J. Pierpont Morgan, Edward Steichen, photograph, 1903

capital and security for both private industry and the United States Government. While the quest to attain money and position played an important role in his business life, he was also motivated by the desire to help his young nation to become a new economic and political power.

Morgan's interest in the Wadsworth Atheneum began to manifest itself in the 1890s. In 1893 he began buying land adjacent to the Museum, and was already thinking of building an addition to the Museum. It took him until 1905 to assemble enough land finally to begin planning the Morgan Memorial, which he dedicated to his father. Construction began in 1908, and the building opened in 1910. At this time, twenty-one new galleries to the east of the Memorial were begun. These opened in 1915, two years after Morgan's death.

Morgan was also active in the Metropolitan Museum of Art in New York. He was president of its board from 1904, and gave important parts of his decorative arts collections to that museum beginning in 1897. Several segments of his collection were given to the Metropolitan after his death as well.

From the turn of the century, Morgan spent more and more of his time devoted to buying art. The collection was divided between his house and library in New York, and the houses he inherited from his father at Princes Gate, London and in the English countryside at Roehampton. While many objects were loaned to museums in England, predominantly the South Kensington Museum (now the Victoria and Albert Museum), Morgan's collections, especially of eighteenth-century decorative arts, were an integral part of his domestic environment, and kept where he could enjoy them all the time. A brief description by a friend, Bishop Lawrence, gives an idea of how the collections were displayed at Princes Gate:

Glancing at two glorious Turners, one at each side of the large door, we passed into the next room, a perfect example of Louis XVI, walls, rugs, furniture and ornaments of the richest of that day. Across the hall ... we entered the Fragonard Room, whose walls were drawn in by the builder to meet the exact dimension and designs of the panels. In the centre stood a table covered with a glass cabinet filled with beautiful jewelled boxes. A glimpse of the portrait of the most attractive boy that one has ever seen, probably by Velasquez, drew one into the Louis XV Room, where were beautiful cabinets and examples of Sevres (fig. 2).[3]

Morgan's interest in the French *ancien régime* was not confined to works of art, but extended to historical material, including autograph letters by Madame de Maintenon, Madame de Pompadour, Marie-Antoinette, as well as marriage contracts for the French kings from Louis XIII to Louis XVIII.[4]

It is difficult to document Morgan's collecting before 1896, as invoices for his purchases do not survive before that year. Furthermore, few letters from Morgan survive, so there is little written evidence of his tastes and motivations. Still, much can be gleaned not only from the invoices from dealers, but also from the collections themselves. Among the dealers he bought French porcelain from were Durlacher Brothers, Cartier et Fils, Charles Wertheimer, Jacques Seligmann, A.B. Daniell & Sons, Duveen Brothers, and Edouard Chappey. Occasionally he bought at auction, usually through one of his favorite dealers. He did not buy his French porcelain or furniture en bloc from earlier collectors. For French porcelain he relied on the advice of the collector/dealer J.H. Fitzhenry, and the scholar/collector the comte de Chavagnac.

Reviewing extant invoices and letters in the archives of the Morgan Library allows one to track many of Morgan's purchases over seventeen years, from 1896 until his death in 1913. According to a recent scholar, his love for French decorative arts seems to have stemmed from the purchase of Fragonard's panels known as *The Progress of Love*, in 1898 (described by Bishop Lawrence above).[5] In this year he bought a Sèvres biscuit bust of Louis XVI for $125, and the following year a Riesener *commode* and *secrétaire* from Duveen. In 1899 he also spent a staggering £11,550 for the celebrated "Coventry Vases," which included a Sèvres *pot-pourri à vaisseau* (now at the J. Paul Getty Museum, California), and a pair of *vases hollandois* (Museum of Fine Arts, Boston).[6]

In 1900 Morgan bought the wonderful *bleu turquin* marble table by Gouthière now in the Frick Collection, New York.[7] This same year he bought three glazed white Vincennes figures of *Le Jaloux*, *Les Mangeurs de raisins*, and *Le Flûteur* for $2,500 (catalogue nos. 170–72). He also bought the extraordinary Meissen basket with Vincennes flowers and French ormolu mounts (catalogue no. 55). Incorrectly thinking the mounts had been regilded, Jacques Seligmann only charged him $500 for the ensemble. Again, in 1900, Morgan bought a garniture of three *bleu céleste vases hollandois* with Teniers subjects by the Sèvres painter Dodin for £8,000, and a Sèvres inkstand with celestial and terrestrial globes and a bust in the center, for £132. He also bought a chinoiserie figure from Cartier in Paris, then thought to be either Chantilly or Saint-Cloud, as well as a Sèvres tray, two orange tubs, and a small, green-ground service. This is the year that the Wallace Collection at Hertford House, London opened to the public. Filled with paintings, tapestries, Renaissance bronzes, maiolica, miniatures, arms and armor, gold- and silversmith's works, ivories, and eighteenth-century furniture and porcelain, this collection must also have had a profound effect on Morgan.[8]

The year 1901 saw the purchase of French furniture, sculpture, gold boxes, and porcelain, along with Meissen porcelain, Renaissance bronzes, Gainsborough's *Duchess of Devonshire*,[9] and the Garland collection of Chinese porcelain (for the Metropolitan Museum of Art).[10] From Duveen came a yellow-ground tea service, as well as other small pieces of Sèvres.[11] The large pink-ground Sèvres *déjeuner Courteille* (catalogue no. 83) and the important Vincennes *pots-pourris à jour* (catalogue no. 56) were bought from A.B. Daniell & Sons, London, the former for £2,145 and the latter for £2,200. From Cartier in Paris came a number of pieces of French porcelain, from cups and saucers, toilet pots, teapots, broth basins, trays, to a water jug and basin for 25,000 francs, and a five-piece garniture (including the Atheneum's *bleu lapis vase hollandois* and *pots-pourris*

Fig. 2 Morgan's "Louis XVI"
drawing room at 13 Princes
Gate, London, watercolor,
Claire de Chavagnac

Pompadour, catalogue nos. 63–64) for 60,000 francs.[12] During the same year Morgan also bought sculptures by Clodion, Houdon, Pigalle, and Falconet.[13]

Morgan's collection of French decorative arts continued to grow in 1902, with the purchase of a Louis XVI regulator clock from Seligmann, and pair of candelabra now attributed to Thomire. Today they reside in the Frick Collection.[14] From Duveen Morgan bought a number of pieces of Sèvres porcelain, including then popular yellow and pink-ground objects.[15] Cartier continued to be one of his preferred sources for French porcelain, supplying Morgan with the white-ground chestnut basket in the Atheneum's collection (catalogue no. 135), as well as a large late tea service (catalogue no. 130). The large pair of *vases ferrés* (catalogue no. 69) with a green ground and figures was bought from Charles Wertheimer for $10,000.

Important pieces of French porcelain came into Morgan's collection in 1903, including the Vincennes fountain and basin (catalogue no. 151) thought to have been bought by either the Dauphin or the Dauphine in 1756. This ensemble was sold by Seligmann, along with a pair of *vases à oreilles* (catalogue no. 60), a *bleu céleste* garniture of *cuvettes à tombeau* (catalogue no. 70), and yellow-ground service pieces from the 1790s decorated with Buffon birds (catalogue nos. 145–46). Cartier continued to furnish Morgan with Vincennes and Sèvres, as well as with a Mennecy group of musicians.[16]

The year 1904 was important for Morgan's collection. At this time he doubled his space at Princes Gate by buying the townhouse next door. From this time Morgan began buying furniture with specific destinations for each piece, as well as the entire ensemble in mind.[17] During the next two years he increased his expenditures markedly, in order to furnish the new addition. The dealers Duveen and A.B. Daniell both helped, and their dual role is reflected in the fact that Morgan had two accounts with Daniell, one for fine arts and one for household items. A single invoice dated January 1906 from Duveen shows that Morgan spent more than $131,000 over the course of 1905 with this dealer alone.[18] An October 1906 bill from Duveen summarizing several earlier purchases is divided up room by room, indicating that Morgan was thinking thematically about his new space, although an examination of the specific purchases for each room reveals that there was little rigidity in adhering to these themes.[19] The "new French rooms" included the Regency Room, the Louis XV Sitting Room, the Louis XVI Drawing Room, the Louis XVI Room, the Louis XVI Marble Hall, and the Fragonard Room.[20]

In the category of French porcelain, a number of objects were bought during these two years. Domestic wares continued to enter the collection, as did decorative figures and vases. In 1905 Morgan bought from J. & S. Goldschmidt in Frankfurt-am-Main the very important mounted vase with the statuette of Louis XV inside (catalogue no. 65). This object must not have been terribly fashionable for it only cost $1,500, compared to the $18,500 for a "garniture" of three vases (*vase Bachelier à anses tortillées* and two *vases chinois*, catalogue nos. 71–72) purchased from Wertheimer in 1906. Morgan also began buying furniture with Sèvres plaques during these years, which was destined for the Louis XVI drawing room. An invoice from Duveen lists a writing table and two *guéridons*,[21] and Wertheimer sold him a small Louis XVI table and a tripod worktable with porcelain plaques as well.[22] Morgan seems to have begun buying from the collector/dealer Edouard Chappey in 1904, and continued with this dealer for the next two years. Among the pieces of French porcelain coming from this source are the rare hard-paste *Boy with a Tambourine* (catalogue no. 178), the Vincennes biscuit *L'Amitié au cœur* (catalogue no. 176), the white-ground *déjeuner à baguettes* with gold decoration (catalogue no. 104), and the green inkstand from Madame de Pompadour's collection (catalogue no. 152). In 1906 Morgan bought the Hoentschel collection of French *boiseries* and decorative furniture for the Metropolitan Museum of Art. This was meant to be the nucleus of a decorative arts collection for the young museum.[23]

In 1907 Morgan did not seem to buy very much French furniture or porcelain, perhaps due to his purchase of a group of paintings from the Rodolfe Kann collection for over £225,000.[24] In 1908 Morgan bought the monumental white glazed porcelain bust of *Louis XV* made at Chantilly (then attributed to Mennecy) for 25,300 francs (catalogue no. 20), and in 1909 a pair of Chantilly candelabra with figures, perhaps the Atheneum's chinoiserie *Puppeteers* (catalogue no. 18).

In 1910 Morgan published privately a catalogue of his French porcelain collection written by one of the leading experts on the subject, the comte de Chavagnac. According to Bishop Lawrence, Chavagnac was told to sell any piece that was not of the rarest quality.[25]

This same year he bought the Gaston Lebreton *faïence* collection for the Metropolitan Museum in New York.[26] This included Medici porcelain and Saint-Porchaire ceramics. Morgan also purchased the Atheneum's important Saint-Cloud green-ground ewer and basin (catalogue no. 8), although it originally was catalogued as Mennecy. This was the second of this unusual type of green-ground piece to enter his collection.[27]

The following year Morgan bought a round worktable with a yellow-ground Sèvres porcelain plaque depicting mythological subjects, table by Martin Carlin. It is now in the Frick Art Museum, Pittsburgh.[28] He also bought a small square Louis XVI table with a Sèvres plaque. Both were bought from Wertheimer's executors.[29] From then the pace of acquisitions seems to have slowed, evidenced by fewer invoices in the files of the Morgan Library.

In 1912 Morgan was occupied with shipping his collections from Europe to New York and negotiating with New York to build a new wing to house much of his collection at the Metropolitan Museum.[30] The city did not want to pay for a new wing, and Morgan simultaneously made it clear to the Metropolitan that he, in fact, did not intend to leave the whole collection to that museum.[31] His intentions never were clarified and therefore few specific provisions for placing his collections were made in his will. He did specify that some of his collections were to go to the Wadsworth Atheneum.

I have been greatly interested for many years in gathering my collections of paintings, miniatures, porcelains and other works of art, and it has been my desire and intention to make some suitable disposition of them or of such portions of them as I might determine, which would render them permanently available for the instruction and pleasure of the American people ... It would be agreeable to me to have "The Morgan Memorial" which forms a portion of the property of the Wadsworth Athenaeum at Hartford, Connecticut, utilized to effectuate a part of this purpose.[32]

Morgan died in Europe in 1913. His collections were left to his son, J.P. Morgan, Jr., to distribute, according to the instructions in his will, or to sell. Much of the collection was given to the Metropolitan Museum of Art, including the many pieces that had been bought directly for the museum. The Pierpont Morgan Library retained the works on paper, books, and manuscripts, as well as the decorative objects and paintings that were part of the Library's furnishings and decoration. Owing to financial considerations imposed by heavy estate taxes, large segments of the collection were sold. This included much of the French furniture collection, many pieces subsequently bought by Henry Clay Frick. Frick also purchased Fragonard's series *The Progress of Love*. Approximately three-quarters of the French porcelain was given to the Wadsworth Atheneum in

Hartford, the remaining works staying in his son's collection until his death in 1943. Several auctions in New York and London in 1944 dispersed these pieces, and many now reside in other American museums.[33]

The Wadsworth Atheneum received important pieces of French porcelain from other collectors, some before and some after Morgan, which are included in this catalogue. Among the most important are from the collection of Forsyth Wickes (1876–1965). While Wickes bequeathed most of his porcelain to the Museum of Fine Arts in Boston, along with furniture, painting, and other French decorative objects, he did present the Wadsworth Atheneum with three objects, a Chantilly *cup and saucer* (catalogue no. 13), a Saint-Cloud *covered jar* (catalogue no. 7), and the lovely Mennecy figure of *Amphitrite* (catalogue no. 37).

NOTES

1 According to Strouse (p. 281), Morgan received £600,000 outright, the capital his father had in J.S. Morgan & Co., his father's houses in London and Roehampton, England, investments, personal effects, and several paintings. Strouse estimates that, excluding the art, the inheritance was worth nearly $15 million, which in 1990s dollars equals roughly 225 million. There was no inheritance tax in 1890.

2 For Morgan's history as an art collector, see Roth, "Morgan," pp. 26–42 (with selected bibliography, p. 205). For the most recent and thorough biography of Morgan see Strouse, passim.

3 Lawrence, p. 52 (see Roth, "Morgan," p. 31).

4 Strouse, p. 382. According to Strouse (p. 430), Morgan's mistress, Adelaide Douglas, must have encouraged his interest in eighteenth-century French decorative arts. In 1901 Mrs. Douglas moved to 46th Street in New York and in the years following this move, Morgan bought her several objects from this period, including Riesener furniture, Sèvres porcelain, and a "coffret de mariage de Marie-Antoinette."

5 Dell, p. 26.

6 No. 75.DE.11, see Sassoon, pp. 49–56, no. 10; No. 65.1799ab, see Munger, *Wickes*, pp. 174–75, no. 121.

7 No. 15.5.59, see Dell, p. 27.

8 Strouse, p. 486; Dell, p. 26.

9 Strouse, p. 412.

10 Ibid., p. 494.

11 APML, Duveen file, invoice 18 September 1901.

12 Ibid., Cartier file, invoice 24 May 1901. Also included in this purchase were a broth basin and stand, probably cat. no. 150, a green butter dish (cat. no. 143), two *plateaux losange* (cat. no. 89 and perhaps cat. no. 92), and a "*ravier*," probably the *plateau porte huilier* (cat. no. 82).

13 Ibid., Duveen file.

14 Dell, p. 26.

15 APML, Duveen file, invoices for 11 April and 11 July 1902. Included in the April invoice were pink-ground pieces that may correspond to the Museum's redecorated salt cellars (cat. no. 193) and two *compotiers ovales* (cat. no. 141). The July invoice lists a pair of ormolu-mounted yellow vases that probably are the Museum's redecorated toilet pots (cat. no. 197).

16 Ibid., Cartier file, invoice 31 December 1903, covering purchases for that year. Also listed are the Museum's yellow milk jug (cat. no. 78) and redecorated yellow sugar bowl (cat. no. 183).

17 Dell, p. 26.

18 APML, Duveen file, invoice 4 January 1906.

19 Ibid., 4 October 1906 (summarized in Dell, pp. 26–27).

20 Strouse, pp. 502–3.

21 Dell, p. 27, citing invoice of 8 July 1905. According to Dell, this table is now in the Frick Art Museum, Pittsburgh.

22 Ibid., pp. 27, 30, fig. 7. This table is in the Philadelphia Museum of Art, Rice Bequest.

23 Roth, "Morgan," p. 36; Dell, p. 28.

24 APML, Duveen file.

25 Roth, "Morgan," p. 34; Lawrence, p. 26.

26 Roth, "Morgan," p. 36.

27 Private collection, Paris. See Chavagnac, p. 25, no. 26, pl. vi, and Christie's, New York, 30 October 1993, lot 96.

28 Dell, pp. 32, 33 n. 39.

29 Ibid., p. 27.

30 Roth, "Morgan," pp. 36, 38–39.

31 Memo from Edward Robinson, recounting conversation of 29 November 1912, *The Metropolitan Museum of Art, Archives* (see Roth, "Morgan," pp. 39, 42 n. 69).

32 Roth, "Morgan," p. 39 (APML, *Last Will and Testament of John Pierpont Morgan*, died 31 March 1913, will dated 4 January 1913, codicil dated 6 January 1913).

33 Parke-Bernet Galleries, New York, 6–8 January 1944; 22–25 March 1944; Christie's, London, 22, 23, 29, 30 March 1944. See *Morgan*, Hartford, pp. 196–203.

Saint-Cloud, Chantilly, Villeroy-Mennecy
The Early French Factories

Saint-Cloud originated as a *faïence* manufactory, a royal privilege being granted Claude Révérend in 1664. From Révérend ownership passed to his brother, François (1666); to Pierre Chicaneau and his wife, Barbe Coudret (1674); to a partnership between François Révérend, and Chicaneau's widow and her new husband, Henri Trou (1678); and in 1683 to Henri Trou and Barbe Coudret. Experiments in the manufacture of porcelain were initiated in the 1660s and 1670s by Pierre Chicaneau, whose goal was the discovery of such materials and formulae as would produce a paste that would rival Chinese porcelain. His sons must have carried on after Pierre's death in 1677, as commercial production was not ready until about 1693. Following Trou's death in 1700 his widow and her Chicaneau sons petitioned for a royal privilege that would protect their discoveries; in 1702 Louis XIV granted them letters patent with a ten-year privilege that was renewed in 1713 for another ten years, and in 1722 for twenty more. Henry II Trou became director of the factory in 1710, and was owner from 1722 until his death in 1746. He was succeeded by his son Henry-François who—in the face of mounting debt and competition—closed Saint-Cloud in 1766.

The large Chicaneau-Trou family provided shifting combinations of entrepreneurs, in Paris as well as Saint-Cloud. Jean Chicaneau (1663–1740) managed a branch in the rue de Charonne (before 1715–c. 1723) which was principally a retail outlet, but which was also evidently the source of Saint-Cloud material which he sold for the production of porcelain "dites de Saint-Cloud." A sister factory in the rue de la Ville l'Évêque was established in 1724 under the joint direction of Marie Moreau (d. 1743), wife of Pierre II Chicaneau, and her cousin by marriage, Dominique-François Chicaneau (1686–after 1743).

In 1730 Louis-Henry de Bourbon, prince de Condé (1692–1740), constructed a porcelain manufactory on his Chantilly estate, appointing Ciquaire Cirou as its director. Cirou (1700–55) had presumably learned his craft at Saint-Cloud, where he had been living for several years in 1723. By 1726 he had moved to Paris, being described there two years later as a

faïence painter. It is likely, as Geneviève Le Duc has suggested, that production started up the year following Cirou's appointment, but it was not until 1735 that royal letters patent granted him a twenty-year privilege to manufacture porcelain "pareille à celle qui se faisait antérieurement au Japon." This privilege he gave up in November 1751, and from then until 1792, when the factory was sold to the Englishman Christopher Potter, it experienced a numerous succession of proprietors and directors.

As a young man François Barbin (c. 1689–1765) was apprenticed as a *menuisier*, his father's trade, but in 1729 he delivered several samples of paste and glaze to the chemist Réaumur for testing. By 1734 he was described as a "marchand fayancier porselainier" in Paris, in the rue de Charonne, and within three years had also established a porcelain factory under the protection of Louis-François de Neufville, duc de Villeroy (1695–1766), on the duke's estate. It has been shown that the Paris premises were unlikely to have been a place of manufacture, but were quite certainly one of decoration, and the division of labor between Villeroy and Paris is far from clear. The encroaching monopoly of Vincennes forced Barbin to leave Villeroy late in 1748, but by 1750 he had reestablished himself not far away, at Mennecy. From then until his death—and that of his son which occurred the same year, 1765—the factory was managed by successive combinations of family members. In 1766 Barbin's widow leased it to Joseph Jullien (1725–74) and Charles-Symphorien Jacques (c. 1724–99) who were already lessees of the Sceaux manufactory; they operated Mennecy in absentia, leaving it in the hands of managers. The factory was foreclosed in 1776, but the evidence of inventories makes it clear that it had ceased to function after 1773. It is evident, however, that Mennecy stock continued to be in circulation, as in 1772 Jacques and Jullien, having given up their lease of Sceaux, set up a new factory nearby at Bourg-la-Reine, and the inventory taken after Jullien's death two years later listed a wide assortment of undecorated pieces at Mennecy, of which some were probably completed at Bourg-la-Reine.

Saint-Cloud Vases and Pots-Pourris

1

Pot-pourri

1917.908

Saint-Cloud, 1730–1740

Soft-paste porcelain, H. 4⁷⁄₁₆ × w. 8⅝ × D. 5⅜ in. (11.2 × 21.8 × 13.7 cm)

Provenance: J. Pierpont Morgan

Saint-Cloud was the first French factory to produce pots-pourris in a wide range of models. They were still something of a novelty when Dominique-François Chicaneau advertised them in 1731, the only earlier recorded ones in French porcelain being two examples of a model produced at Rouen before 1696.[1] Hartford's is one of many variant melon and gourd forms, all unpainted and all richly embellished with fully modeled flowering stems.

The practice of mixing and drying flowers to refresh a room gained currency at the end of the seventeenth century. In his *Dictionnaire Universel*, published two years after his death in 1688, Antoine Furetière described "those blends that women make out of various scents mixed together in a pot, to fill a room with a fragrant smell."[2] The inventory taken the next year of the Grand Dauphin's collection included six nearly identical bowl-shaped pots-pourris among the porcelains presented to Monseigneur by the Siamese on their second trade mission in 1686. The first was described as "A large pot-pourri decorated on the body and cover with green leaves and red blossoms. The lid has a flat button finial painted with a green and red rose. The pot without lid is 6½ *pouces*, and 10 *pouces* 2 *lignes* across [and basin-shaped]."[3] Although no attributions are assigned in the inventory the porcelains in the Grand Dauphin's collection were almost all Chinese, and the whiteness and naturalistic form of the Saint-Cloud pot-pourri models might suggest *blanc-de-chine*. But the palette of the Dauphin's pieces corresponds to a style of Japanese porcelains dating c. 1690–1700 in which floral decoration is sometimes painted but more often modeled in high relief or in the round, and enameled in red and green. This type of Japanese porcelain reached Europe early in the eighteenth century: among examples in the Dresden collections at least one, a teapot, was inventoried in 1721.[4] That Saint-Cloud was familiar with the idiom is explicit in Chicaneau's advertisement which mentions table wares "with reliefwork like that of Japan"[5] and is further demonstrated by

a bowl-shaped pot-pourri in the Louvre, its body ornamented with blossoms in high relief like the seventeenth-century Japanese *koro* it was copying.[6] Given the multiplicity of forms and styles exchanged between east and west, however, any model can derive from more than one source, and this one is no exception. What sounds like a cognate model of pot-pourri was described in 1740, in the inventory of the collections of the prince de Condé, as "a large celadon porcelain pot-pourri with relief flowers, in the shape of a melon and garnished with gilt bronze."[7]

The original cover of this pot-pourri was probably like that seen on one of the same model in the Musée des Arts décoratifs, Paris, a flattened seed cluster topped by a bud finial.[8] Like some other examples of the gourd and melon pots-pourris, the base of this one was pierced at the time of manufacture with several circular holes, presumably to accommodate gilt-bronze flowering stems.

The currency of the model in the 1730s is emphasized not just by Chicaneau's advertisement, which he repeated in 1741, but by a very similar Chantilly version formerly in the Halinbourg collection.[9]

Exhibition: *Morgan Loan Exhibition*, New York, 1914, not in catalogue

Literature: Chavagnac, p. 17, no. 12

NOTES

1 One in the MMA, New York, no. 50.211.186; the other sold, Drouot, Paris, 6 December 1983, lot 21.

2 "… ces compositions que les femmes font de plusieurs parfums meslés dans un pot, pour sentir bon dans une chambre." Quoted by Havard, 4, no. 618.

3 See Watson and Whitehead, p. 50, nos. 53–58. "Un grand Pot pourri orné au corps & au couvercle de branches vertes & de fleurs rouges. Le couvercle est terminé par un bouton plat qui a le dessus peint d'une rose verte & rouge, haut sans son couvercle de six pouces & demi, & de diametre dix pouces deux lignes [en forme de jatte]."

4 See Reichel, *Japanese*, no. 70.

5 "… en relief comme celles qui viennent du Jappon." See Chavagnac and Grollier, p. 32.

6 See de Plinval de Guillebon, *Louvre*, p. 50, no. 7. For the Japanese prototype see *Porcelain for Palaces*, p. 208, no. 208.

7 "… un gros pot pouris de porcelaine celadon a fleurs de relief en forme de Melon garnie de Bronze doré d'or moulu." MS. p. 643, inventory of the prince de Condé's collection in 1740 (I am indebted to Christina Nelson for her courtesy in making a copy of the inventory available to me).

8 Lahaussois, *Saint-Cloud*, p. 89, no. 135.

9 Frédéric Halinbourg sale, Drouot, Paris, 22–23 May 1913, lot 128.

1

Saint-Cloud Tea Wares

2

Two cups and saucers

1917.899–900

Saint-Cloud, 1720–1740

Soft-paste porcelain, 1917.899: cup: H. 2^{11}/₁₆ × W. 3¾ × D. 2^{15}/₁₆ in. (6.8 × 9.6 × 7.5 cm); saucer: H. 1^{1}/₁₆ × DIAM. 4¾ in. (2.6 × 12.1 cm); 1917.900: cup: H. 2¾ × W. 3⅝ × D. 2⅞ in. (7 × 9.3 × 7.2 cm), saucer: H. 1^{3}/₁₆ × DIAM. 4^{9}/₁₆ in. (3 × 11.6 cm)

Marks: St C/T on both cups; St C/T/L on saucer 1917.899; St C/T/P on saucer 1917.900, all in underglaze blue

Provenance: J. Pierpont Morgan

The most common of Saint-Cloud productions—clearly the factory's bread-and-butter line—tea wares of this generic model were being made almost from the start. In 1700 the Chicaneau family declared it had been supplying the royal household for several years with "cups, saucers and other porcelain vessels for the service of tea, coffee or chocolate"[1] and a sun-marked teabowl of this type may well have been among them.[2] Corresponding models in silver—the blue painted friezes of the porcelain chased, or possibly even cast, in the silver—can be seen as early as 1702 in drawings of the newest Parisian silver sent to the Swedish court.[3]

This group must date from about 1720 as cups with handles were uncommon before then. Their first securely datable appearance is at Meissen: these curved handles have their parallel in Böttger beaker-cups of 1715/16,[4] although they are characteristic of Saint-Cloud in being designed with a central channel.

The saucer with a simple protective gallery around the well was a Saint-Cloud invention, appearing in the sun-marked period.[5] It is tempting to see this construction as a variation on the Chinese cup stand which could have been known at Saint-Cloud, as Delft versions were made at the Greek A and Metal Pot factories at the beginning of the century.[6]

The factory mark introduced by Henri II Trou[7] frequently appears with an additional letter. L and P have not been recorded, and the significance of these letters is not known. If the letter L on saucer 1917.899 is to be interpreted as a painter's mark it cannot be equated with the incised L on two wine coolers in the Atheneum's collection (catalogue no. 5).

The four pieces do not match up in any combination, although both cups fit saucer 1917.899 as to size, while the other saucer is too large for both cups. The pattern is essentially the same throughout, but has been rendered slightly differently on each piece with variations in drawing, color, and control of the blue. The four marks are also distinctly different.

Exhibition: *Morgan Loan Exhibition*, New York, 1914, not in catalogue

Literature: Chavagnac, p. 5, no. 4

Notes

1 "… tasses, souscoupes et autres vases de porcelaine qui servent a prendre le thé, le caffé, le chocolat." Le Duc and de Plinval de Guillebon, "Saint-Cloud," p. 15.

2 Lahaussois, *Saint-Cloud*, p. 40, no. 34.

3 *Versailles*, p. 58, no. 43.

4 *Böttger*, fig. 1/90.

5 *Porcelaine à Saint-Cloud*, p. 33, no. 16. The body appears to be the transitional one between the very early white and the later creamier one. The word *trembleuse*, referring to this specific design, is thought to date only from the late nineteenth century: both the Oxford English Dictionary and Havard (4, col. 1524) cite 1883, the latter calling it a "terme d'amateur de curiosité." But Savill notes the use of the term at Sèvres as early as 1767 in reference to a cognate model (Savill, 2, p. 674), and the Saint-Cloud version with a continuous ring around the well was imitated at Vincennes (*Vincennes*, p. 106, nos. 281, 282). Is the Saint-Cloud model what is referred to in Henri Trou's inventory as a *porte-gobelet* (Le Duc and de Plinval de Guillebon, "Saint-Cloud," p. 18)?

6 De Jonge, p. 91, ill. 89.

7 It is not certain when this occurred, there being no documentary evidence. The sun mark, plausibly associated with Louis XIV, appears on pieces that could be dated stylistically later than 1715, the year of his death; but Trou became director of the factory in 1710 and could have introduced his mark any time thereafter. He could also have waited until he became owner in 1722, but given the lack of many dated or closely datable pieces the issue must, at least for the time being, be left necessarily vague.

3

Cup and saucer

1934.204

Saint-Cloud, 1720–1740

Soft-paste porcelain, cup: H. 3 1/16 × W. 4 × D. 2 15/16 in. (7.7 × 10.1 × 7.5 cm); saucer: H. 1 1/8 × DIAM. 5 3/16 in. (2.9 × 13.2 cm)

Mark: St C/T on both, in underglaze blue

Provenance: Mrs. Gurdon Trumbull (bequest 1934)

These are of the same basic model as those in the previous entry, differing chiefly in the saucer, which is here fitted with an unbroken *trembleuse* ring. The lambrequin borders are almost identical, and there is a good fit between the pieces, so they are probably original to each other.

3

4

Saucer

1913.598

Saint-Cloud, 1725–1735

Soft-paste porcelain, H. 1¹⁄₁₆ × DIAM. 4⅞ in. (2.6 × 12.4 cm)

Provenance: Reverend Alfred Duane Pell (gift 1913)

Saint-Cloud made frequent use of two imbricated leaf patterns, this one and another with more rounded leaves punctuated by bold mid-ribs. While they seem to have been contemporaneous for a time, this version was perhaps the earlier, as it occurs on simple straight-sided pieces,[1] while the other is more usually found on small pomade pots and *écuelles* with naturalistic finials and handles that point to a later date. The pattern has sometimes been described by modern writers as pineapple or pine cone, but was known in the eighteenth century as artichoke.[1] Among the Meissen porcelains made for the

Parisian merchant Rudolph Lemaire were numerous beakers "a artichaux" or "auf Artischocken arth";[3] by implication, since Lemaire was borrowing Japanese porcelains from Augustus the Strong's collection to be copied at Meissen, they were Japanese, although the pattern is considered rare.[4] Saint-Cloud could have known of it either directly,[5] or through Meissen copies.

The saucer was acquired with a teabowl of modern hard-paste porcelain with unrelated gadrooning around the body.

NOTES

1 Two covered ewers, both with silver rims datemarked 1726–32 (V&A, London, no. C. 460-1909; Lahaussois, *Saint-Cloud*, p. 82, no. 115.

2 Lot 371 in the Randon de Boisset collection, Paris, 27ff. February 1777 comprised "Douze petits pots à crème en feuilles d'artichaut, & un moutardier de même porcelaine" (i.e., Saint-Cloud, as in the preceding lot).

3 Boltz, "Hoym, Lemaire," p. 24, undated list.

4 Assessment by Oliver Impey, in correspondence.

5 The prince de Condé's inventory of 1740 included "deux petites Jattes en forme d'artichaux de Porcelaine ancienne." The term "porcelaine ancienne" generally referred to Japanese porcelain.

4

5

Pair of bottle coolers (*seaux à bouteille*)

1958.238–239

Saint-Cloud, c. 1725–1735

Soft-paste porcelain, 1958.238: H. 7½ × w. 9⅛ × D. 8 in. (19.1 × 23.3 × 20.4 cm); 1958.239: H. 7½ × w. 9¼ × D. 7⅞ in. (19.1 × 23.6 × 20.1 cm)

Mark: incised under glaze on the bottom of each, St C/T/L

Provenance: Philip L. Goodwin (bequest 1958)

The model is a standard one in Saint-Cloud production, having been produced in several sizes,[1] and derives from examples in silver introduced at the end of the seventeenth century. The basic form of these coolers corresponds to a Parisian silver one of 1701–2 with gadrooned rims, lions' head handles, and a frieze of lappets around the lower body.[2] Marked examples of the model bear the factory mark—usually incised rather than painted—associated with the onset of Henri II Trou's tenure in 1710. That it continued in production, or at least use, for some time is apparent from Nicolas Lancret's *Le Déjeuner de Jambon* of 1735, in which two Saint-Cloud *seaux* of this type stand on the table of the revelers.[3] The molded decoration of orientalizing plants is one of several variant compositions in which domestic and exotic flora are combined in a manner reminiscent both of Chinese *blanc-de-chine* and Japanese porcelains of the late seventeenth century. Some of the foliage appears to be based on the outsized plants illustrated in Jan Nieuhof's *Legatio Batavicae* of 1664; on these coolers the central openwork element and the emerging flowering stems are very similar to kakiemon versions of the traditional Chinese ornamental rock and peonies.[4]

The letter L incised in addition to the regular factory mark is not identified. Single letters occur fairly often, both painted and incised, but their significance has not been determined.

NOTES

1 Dominique-François Chicaneau advertised "grands Sceaux à rafraichir du vin & des Liqueurs" in 1731 and again ten years later. The smallest are H. 4¾ in. (12.1 cm); these are the largest size.

2 Hernmarck, 2, p. 108, pl. 290.

3 Munger, *Wickes*, p. 74, no. 15. The plates in the painting, however, are not Saint-Cloud porcelain—no plates are known to have been made by the factory—but are blue and white tin-glazed earthenware, probably of Saint-Cloud manufacture as the factory kept both lines of production going concurrently.

4 Shono, pl. 75 (a dish, c. 1700–10, now in MMA, New York).

5

6

Broth basin and cover (*écuelle*)

1991.11[1]

Saint-Cloud, 1730–1740

Soft-paste porcelain, H. 5⅝ × w. 9⅞ × D. 6½ in. (14.2 × 25 × 16.5 cm)

Provenance: Elizabeth Parke Firestone

The form is borrowed from the *écuelle à oreilles*, as it was known by the fifteenth century,[2] and which had become a regular feature of the French silversmith's repertoire by 1700. The gadrooned rim, berry cluster finial and shaped handles are especially common in Paris silver around 1715 to 1725,[3] and the two former are staple features of Saint-Cloud design.[4] An *écuelle* of essentially the same model is in the Museo Duca di Martina, Naples;[5] another with similar baroque handles (oddly contrasting with a rabbit finial of Japanese origin on its cover) is in the Musée des Arts décoratifs, Paris;[6] and the berry cluster finial occurs regularly throughout the factory's repertoire of bowls and tureens. Four of these *écuelles* are decorated with relief prunus in varying degrees of stylization, this being the most sinuous and leafy.

Écuelles were usually accompanied by underdishes, called either *soucoupes* or *plateaux*, but they must have become separated just as usually, as both silver and porcelain *écuelles* regularly appear alone in eighteenth-century inventories[7] and few survive with their original plates. The Hartford and Paris bowls undoubtedly were made with matching *plateaux*: Chicaneau's 1731 advertisement specifically lists "Écuelles couvertes & leurs soucoupes." Three such ensembles are known, in the Musée des Arts décoratifs, Paris,[8] on the Paris art market in 1968,[9] and in the Metropolitan Museum.[10] The first two, with gadrooned rims and prunus decoration, probably represent the type of *plateau* that originally accompanied this *écuelle*.

NOTES

1 Purchased Christie's, New York, 22 March 1991, lot 26. Museum credit line, J. Pierpont Morgan, by exchange.

2 Havard, I, p. 353.

3 For example, Dennis, p. 27, no. 1, p. 28, no. 3, p. 141, no. 190, p. 147, no. 203.

4 A caster in the V&A with a berry cluster finial (no. C. 440-1909) is helpfully fitted with silver mounts dated 1732–38.

5 Casanova, p. 74, no. 9.

6 Lahaussois, *Saint-Cloud*, p. 85, no. 129.

7 This is especially true of silver (Guiffrey, passim). Lazare Duvaux sold Meissen *écuelles* without underdishes in 1751 and 1752 (LD, 2, p. 74, no. 716, p. 140, no. 1242), and two Chantilly *écuelles* without stands were listed in the Garde-Meuble in 1741 (Le Duc, *Chantilly*, p. 416). But since inventories record an existing, rather than original, condition, some of these absences may be accidental.

8 Lahaussois, *Saint-Cloud*, p. 83, no. 120.

9 Drouot, Paris, 25 June, 1968, lot. 40.

10 No. 24.214.10ab, 11.

6

7

Covered jar

1962.623

Saint-Cloud, 1744–1750

Soft-paste porcelain, silver, H. 5½ × DIAM. 3¹¹⁄₁₆ in. (14 × 9.4 cm)

Mark: (on silver rim) salmon's head, Paris discharge mark for small gold and silver, 1744–1750

Provenance: Forsyth Wickes (gift 1962)

There are a number of jars of this same model and decoration, varying in height from 5⅛ to 7⁷⁄₁₆ in. (13 to 17.9 cm).[1] Most have plain lids fitted with silver rims that, if marked, have rarely been identified. One in the Louvre that has is datemarked 1732–38.[2] The lambrequin borders, allowing for one or two minor variations, are the same on all examples, but they have clearly been painted by different hands at different times. As the mounts on this piece appear to be original these jars would seem to have enjoyed a production span of some twenty years, not surprising for so conservative a factory as Saint-Cloud. They must still have been marketable in the 1750s, as Mennecy found it worthwhile to imitate the format for small toilet jars.[3]

Jars ranging in size from three to seven inches were long, and indiscriminately, called *pots à fard*, or *à pâte*, or *à pommade*, but the height of this one and others like it clearly put it in the category of jars for tea or tobacco.[4] A set of four matching Saint-Cloud jars with silver rims, in their original box fitted with a central slot for a spoon,[5] accords well with a description in the inventory of Procope Ulysse, comte d'Egmont's porcelains taken on 6 July 1743: "a small square box in which there are four porcelain tobacco jars garnished with gilt bronze, and with a small silver-gilt spoon."[6]

NOTES

1 Examples are in the Louvre (de Plinval de Guillebon, *Louvre*, p. 48, no. 5); in the MAD, Paris (no. D. 9530), and in the David Collection, Copenhagen (no. FK 53a–b). Others were sold in Paris: Drouot, 3 June 1960, lot 50; from the Jean Bloch collection; Palais Galliéra, 2 December 1961, lot 73 (two), and Drouot, 23 November 1967, lots 73, 74, from the Gilbert Lévy collection.

2 De Plinval de Guillebon, *Louvre*, p. 48, no. 5.

3 For example, examples in the MMA, New York (no. 55.216.6ab) and the Musée Adrien Dubouché, Limoges (AD 2217).

4 In the 1689 inventory of the collection of the Grand Dauphin, the height of one "petit Pot a paste couvert bleu & blanc" was given as "quatre pouces trois lignes," that of another "trois pouces & demi" (Watson and Whitehead, pp. 28, 43, nos. 120, 298). A *pouce* measured to 3 decimal places 1.066 in. (2.707 cm). Curiously—given the large number of surviving examples—no jars of any kind are mentioned in Chicaneau's 1731 advertisement, which was repeated ten years later.

5 At Mawley Hall, Gloucestershire; this was kindly brought to my notice by Bernard Dragesco.

6 "… une petite cave quaré dans laquelle il y a quatre pots à tabac de porcelaine garny de cuivre doré avec une petite cuillière de vermeil." Le Duc, *Chantilly*, p. 419.

7

8

8

Ewer and basin

1917.921–922

Saint-Cloud, 1722–1726, mounts attributed to Paul Le Riche (1659–c. 1738, master 1686)

Soft-paste porcelain with silver-gilt mounts, ewer (with hinge): H. 7¹¹⁄₁₆ × W. 5⁹⁄₁₆ × D. 4³⁄₁₆ in. (19.5 × 14.1 × 10.6 cm); basin: H. 3⅜ × DIAM. 7³⁄₈ in. (8.6 × 18.7 cm)

Mark: (on silver) the dove of the Holy Ghost (Paris discharge mark for small silver, 1722–1726)

Provenance: J. Pierpont Morgan

Morgan acquired two of these ewers and basins, which differ only in details of the painting. The ground color and decoration are so exceptional that Chavagnac, in publishing the other ensemble,[1] did not recognize it as Saint-Cloud, considering it a rare example of Mennecy. The green ground was identified with Saint-Cloud, however, in the eighteenth century. The posthumous inventory of Madame de Pompadour in 1764 included "A [green] Saint-Cloud porcelain ewer and green basin, with blue lizards garnished in gilt bronze";[2] and in the 1771 sale catalogue of Boucher's collection lot 1067 was "a green

Fig. 8-1 Plate, 1710–25, Chinese, decorated in Holland, 1720–30

8

fish-scale ewer in Saint-Cloud porcelain."[3] This would seem to correspond in type to a monochrome covered ewer in the Victoria and Albert Museum molded, except for a plain midband, with the artichoke pattern.[4] Other green-ground pieces known to survive are a beaker and saucer with prunus decoration[5] and a mustard pot.[6]

The Mennecy origin previously assigned is necessarily precluded by the date of the mounts of all three ewers. Morgan's other ewer bears the same 1722–26 discharge mark, while the London ewer is dated 1726–32. It also bears an incomplete strike of the mark of Paul Le Riche,[7] to whom these mounts can also now be attributed. Received master in the Paris guild in 1686, Le Riche specialized as a *garnisseur*, his mark appearing on the mounts of Chinese, Japanese and Saint-Cloud porcelain and Japanese lacquer dating from 1704–10 to 1732–38.[8] Further linking the green-ground group to Saint-Cloud is the flower painting, which on the mustard pot corresponds closely to the decoration of a number of small covered jars with yellow grounds datable to the same period.[9] The vivid palette is most closely related to Delft wares painted with orientalizing flowers at the turn of the seventeenth century, while the parrot (especially that below the spout, its head turned back) and leggy flora are common features of Dutch-decorated Chinese porcelain that has been dated to about 1725 (fig. 8-1).[10] The underlying scheme of decoration recalls Kangxi vases with luxuriant compositions of birds amid flowering trees painted against yellow or green grounds enameled on the biscuit. These ground colors rarely appear at the Delft factories; they could have been known at Saint-Cloud, however, from Chinese porcelains in contemporary collections, such as the "Four vases or bellied cornet vases in Chinese porcelain decorated with flowers and birds against a dark green ground" acquired in Paris by Count Carl-Heinrich von Hoym in 1722.[11]

The style of painting is so specifically Dutch in character that some explanation is wanted. The list of personnel published by Le Duc and de Guillebon records the presence of some twenty Dutch workers at Saint-Cloud about 1667,[12] but there is no evidence that they established lasting artistic or family ties. J.D. van Dam notes,[13] however, that a depression in the Delft *faïence* industry about 1720 caused factories to close and workers to find employment elsewhere: may we not imagine an émigré painter?

Exhibitions: *Morgan Loan Exhibition*, New York, 1914, not in catalogue; *Discovering the Secrets of Soft-Paste*, New York, 1999, no. 118

Literature: *Discovering the Secrets of Soft-Paste*, p. 193, no. 118

NOTES

1 Chavagnac, p. 25, no. 26, and Christie's, New York, 30 October 1993, lot 96. Honey mentioned it in passing in his discussion of Mennecy (Honey, p. 20), perhaps mindful of the green-ground Mennecy tray, beaker cup and saucer in the MNC, Sèvres (Dupont, p. 60).

2 "Un pot de porcelaine de Saint Cloud et sa jatte verte, avec des lézards bleu garny en bronze doré." Cordey, p. 98, no. 1348.

3 "Un pot verd à ecaille de poisson, en porcelaine de S. Cloud." *Catalogue raisonné Boucher*.

4 No. C. 460-1909.

5 Sotheby's, London, 15 June 1965, lot 92. The beaker possibly the same one, "émaillé jaune verdâtre," sold with an artichoke pattern saucer en suite, Paris, Ferri, 13 March 1991, lots 104, 105.

6 Drouot Richelieu, Paris, 9 December 1994, lot 49.

7 Crowned fleur-de-lis, two *grains de remède*, PLR, device a crescent.

8 *Discovering the Secrets of Soft-Paste*, p. 297.

9 For pieces in a mixture of Chinese, kakiemon and chinoiserie styles see Lahaussois, *Saint-Cloud*, pp. 122–26, nos. 162–65. I believe that a saucer in the Gardiner Museum, Toronto (no. G83.1.1099) and a beaker in the David Collection, Copenhagen (no. FK 36) were painted by the decorator of the Hartford and Christie's ewers and basins.

10 *Europe de la faïence*, p. 63, no. 70; Lahaussois, *Delft*, 1994, p. 90, no. 87. The decoration of the Christie's ewer and basin is somewhat different in character, being smaller in scale and including animals as well as birds.

11 "Quatre vases ou cornets à panse de porcelaine de la Chine, dont le fond est d'un vert foncé à fleurs et oiseaux." Le Duc, *Chantilly*, Paris, 1996, p. 410, no. 438.

12 Le Duc and de Plinval de Guillebon, "Saint-Cloud," pp. 31–52.

13 Verbal communication.

9

Two theatrical figures

1917.897–898

Saint-Cloud or Paris, rue de la Ville l'Évêque, c. 1730–1740

Soft-paste porcelain, 1917.897: H. 7 × w. 3¼ × D. 3⁵⁄₁₆ in. (17.7 × 8.3 × 8.4 cm); 1917.898: H. 7⁹⁄₁₆ × w. 3⅝ × D. 3³⁄₁₆ in. (19.2 × 9.2 × 8.1 cm)

Provenance: J. Pierpont Morgan

These are two of a large group of related figures of pagods attributed to Saint-Cloud. With their animated expressions and theatrical gestures they seem to epitomize European chinoiserie, an impression reinforced by an occasional pigtail, wispy beard, or conical leaf hat: short tufts of hair spring from the otherwise bald heads of Hartford's figures.

The models share distinctive stylistic features with Chinese sculpture in ivory, *blanc-de-chine* and soapstone: the simple block-like modeling, the linear fall of the drapery, and the customary manner in which the hem is draped over the toes of the shoes. Even the theatrical character of these figures may have been derived—albeit unwittingly—from Chinese tradition. Derek Gillman has commented on the spirited gestures of late Ming ivories and their debt to Chinese theater and dance which would have been known to the carvers from woodblock illustrations,[1] and this trait would have carried over naturally into *blanc-de-chine* sculpture which, Gillman convincingly proposes, was developed as a less expensive alternative to ivory.[2] By the eighteenth century the intricacies of trade had resulted in so many exchanges in so many media that there is rarely an identifiable exclusive source, only a complexity of influences; none of the figures in this Saint-Cloud group has been traceable to a specific Chinese model. Somewhat analogous are *blanc-de-chine* robed dancers, of which examples were in Dresden by 1721;[3] but we should perhaps also consider possible familiarity with white Delft figures, such as a lively dancer in the Groninger Museum.[4]

The unidentified modeler of Hartford's figures is the author of several others,[5] his consistent style evident in the strong curves that define the eyebrows and broad nose, the highly stylized flattened ears, and the wide flat hands. All the sculptures in this group are unmarked, leaving open the question whether they were produced at Saint-Cloud or in Paris in the rue de la Ville l'Évêque. From inventories of 1766[6] it is

evident that figures and groups were made at both factories, and the dating of c. 1700–30 proposed for these figures by Bertrand Rondot[7] would allow for production in either place, the Paris factory having been established in 1724. Hartford's pair, and another in the Pflueger collection,[8] may well have been among the "grotesques and tree trunks made for girandoles" advertised by Dominique-François Chicaneau in 1731[9] and again ten years later.[10] If this was indeed their function—and girandoles were generally produced in pairs—they would have been outfitted by a *marchand-mercier* with a gilt-bronze base supporting candle arms. Certainly the Hartford and Pflueger pairs, which stand so abruptly on the surface, call for completion. It is unlikely that they were intended for dessert table decoration, partly for this reason, but also because the custom did not reach Paris until the mid-1740s, and when it did it was not French porcelain that was used but "pantomime pieces, animals, figures and other porcelains from Saxony."[11]

Exhibitions: *Morgan Loan Exhibition*, New York, 1914, not in catalogue; *European Porcelain*, New York, 1949, no. 146; *Discovering the Secrets of Soft-Paste*, New York, 1999, no. 170

Literature: *European Porcelain*, no. 146; *Discovering the Secrets of Soft-Paste*, p. 224, no. 170

NOTES

1 Gillman, p. 48.

2 Ibid., p. 50.

3 Donnelly, p. 340, pl. 103A.

4 No. 1986-421, kindly brought to my attention by C.J.A. Jörg.

5 V&A, London (Honey, pl. 14); MMA, New York (*Linsky Collection*, p. 322, nos. 296, 297); Sotheby's, New York, 21 October 1993, lot 51 (ex-coll. Linsky); Parke-Bernet Galleries Inc., New York, 8 January 1944, lot 481 (a pair, ex-coll. J. Pierpont Morgan); Pflueger collection (Morley-Fletcher, 2, p. 55 [ex-coll. Elizabeth Parke Firestone]).

6 Le Duc, "Saint-Cloud," pp. 76, 80.

7 *Discovering the Secrets of Soft-Paste*, p. 224, no. 170.

8 See note 5.

9 "… grotesques figures & troncs d'arbres pour faire des girandoles." Chavagnac and Grollier, p. 32.

10 Chicaneau again emphasized his production of sculpture in 1743, declaring that he made "lui-même toutes sortes de figures" (de Plinval de Guillebon, *Faïence*, p. 83).

11 "… pieces de pantomime, animaux, figures et autres de porcelaine de saxe." Letter from the Parisian silversmith Claude II Ballin to Philip V of Spain, 12 September 1745; quoted in Bottineau, p. 593. I owe this reference to Lorenz Seelig.

9

10

Covered bowl (*écuelle*) and stand

1917.907

Saint-Cloud and French, c. 1735 and later

Soft-paste porcelain, bowl: H. 4¾ × W. 7¹⁄₁₆ × D. 4¹⁵⁄₁₆ in. (12.1 × 18 × 12.5 cm); stand: H. 1⅛ × DIAM. 6⅞ in. (3.4 × 17.4 cm)

Provenance: comte Xavier de Chavagnac (unconfirmed); Cartier et Fils, Paris, 1905;[1] J. Pierpont Morgan

The ensemble was catalogued by Chavagnac, and again in 1949, as Chantilly, but its composition and decoration are of mixed origin. The body of the bowl is consistent with several models of Saint-Cloud *écuelles*[2] and may be genuine, despite an unusually undulating rim and an awkward placement of flowerheads on the handles. The stand also appears to be Saint-Cloud, but the cover—which does not fit in any rotation—is unidentified, although eighteenth-century. The decoration, too, is assembled: the ground color and painting of the bowl is from one source, that of the cover and stand from another.

About 1730 Meissen began to produce a regular line of tea wares decorated with panels similar to these reserved on a yellow ground and filled with kakiemon-style patterns. Saint-Cloud made considerable use of the yellow ground for toilet jars, small pots-pourris and snuffboxes, but enameled the decoration directly on the yellow, limiting the use of shaped panels as frames or reserves on snuffboxes. Neither the Meissen format nor yellow ground was used at Chantilly during its first, Asian-oriented, period[3] although both appear briefly later, influenced

by Vincennes interpretations;[4] but a Chantilly attribution of this ensemble is readily accounted for by its decoration, especially the manner of painting the leaf finial and the appearance of the quail pattern (not adopted at Saint-Cloud) on the bowl. The decoration, however, is modern. The scale and placement of the reserves is incompatible with design schemes of the 1730s, for which the yellow ground and kakiemon motifs are appropriate, while the rustic model of *écuelle* and the paired reserves are seen at Meissen in the 1740s when the Japanese taste has waned. Neither ground color—the slightly brownish yellow of the bowl, the bright lemon of the cover and stand—is convincing, and the scenes are too symmetrical and cartoonlike when compared to the idiomatic painting of Saint-Cloud and Chantilly.

Exhibitions: *Morgan Loan Exhibition*, New York, 1914, not in catalogue; *European Porcelain*, New York, 1949, no. 102

Literature: Chavagnac, p. 12, no. 11, pl. III; *European Porcelain*, no. 102

NOTES

1 APML, Cartier file, *Composition des Colis*, 16 June 1905, *colis no. 12*: "No. 166 – 1 Bouillon (avec plateau et couvercle) porcelaine Chantilly, fond jaune, cartels blancs, décor japonais."

2 For example, Lahaussois, *Saint-Cloud*, pp. 80–83, nos. 110–20, p. 138, no. 174. That at least the bowl is of Saint-Cloud manufacture was suggested by Bernard Dragesco.

3 The entire decoration of a large yellow-ground bowl with lobed reserves in the V&A, London (no. C. 432-1909), published by Honey as Chantilly, has recently been discovered to be modern (Honey, pl. 18).

4 For example, a yellow-ground cup and saucer c. 1750 with naturalistic flower sprays in shaped reserves (Le Duc, *Chantilly*, p. 156).

11

Saucer

1913.596

Paris, early 18th century

Soft-paste porcelain, H. 1³⁄₁₆ × DIAM. 4⁹⁄₁₆ in. (3 × 11.5 cm)

Mark: M. in underglaze blue

Provenance: Reverend Alfred Duane Pell (gift 1913)

Despite its obvious stylistic affinities with Saint-Cloud porcelain this is certainly of a different manufacture. The body is extremely thick, the glaze dead white in color, and the saucer is exceptionally heavy even for Saint-Cloud, which is notable for that quality. The technique is faulty—the ribbing is haphazard and there is careless painting throughout—and where it is chipped the body appears to be a rough gray-brown.

Several M-marked pieces are known,[1] among them a *trembleuse* saucer almost identical in model and decoration in the British Museum.[2] Similarities notwithstanding, the two saucers are quite different in material, glaze, quality of execution and even form of the mark. The London saucer has been tentatively considered by Aileen Dawson to represent production at the rue de la Ville l'Évêque.[3] This Paris branch of Saint-Cloud was established by 1710 by Pierre Chicaneau and

his wife, Marie Moreau. Following Pierre's death later the same year it was taken over by his cousin, Dominique-François Chicaneau, who continued to direct Saint-Cloud itself. A partnership between Chicaneau and Marie Moreau, undertaken in 1724, ended with Moreau's withdrawal in 1731.[4] This brief episode naturally invites an association between Moreau and the M-marked pieces in Saint-Cloud style, but it is now known that there were other small-scale manufacturers in Paris at the same time, some of them using the Saint-Cloud paste which could be bought from Jean Chicaneau;[5] it is thus not necessary to conclude that the M-marked porcelains must have been made in the rue de la Ville l'Évêque. According to Régine de Guillebon the only mark attributable to productions of La Ville l'Évêque is one with the initials CM and a small cross, and a cup and saucer so marked in the Musée national de Céramique, Sèvres[6] is distinctly more accomplished than Hartford's M-marked example.

NOTES

1 A cylindrical toilet pot, attributed to Saint-Cloud, from the Chavagnac sale (Drouot, Paris, 19–21 June 1911, lot 37); Madame de Guillebon notes there are several M-marked pieces in the MNC, Sèvres that are not remarkable for their quality (correspondence).

2 Dawson, *British Museum*, p. 26, no. 29.

3 Loc. cit.

4 De Plinval de Guillebon, *Faïence*, pp. 81–82.

5 Chicaneau's sales of *matières de porcelaine* are dated 1718, 1721 and 1731; and a stock of *matières propres à faire la porcelaine* was found after his death in the cellar of the house of his niece's husband (ibid., p. 81).

6 De Plinval de Guillebon, "La porcelaine tendre," p. 8 and fig. 1.

11

Chantilly Tea Wares

12

Cup and saucer

1913.600

Chantilly, c. 1735

Tin-glazed soft-paste, cup: H. 1¹⁵⁄₁₆ × W. 3³⁄₁₆ × D. 3³⁄₁₆ in. (4.9 × 8.1 × 8.1 cm), saucer: H. 2 × DIAM. 5⁵⁄₁₆ in. (5 × 13.5 cm)

Marks: on bottom of each, hunting horn in iron red

Provenance: Reverend Alfred Duane Pell (gift 1913)

The so-called "quail" pattern, well established in the Japanese decorative repertoire by the mid-seventeenth century, became one of the most popular of the export patterns to be adopted in Europe.[1] The birds were occasionally shown in their natural colors, sheltering under stalks of millet, but the version that captivated westerners the most was this one in the kakiemon palette, in which blue and red quail bunch together under or near a prunus branch. Like many other kakiemon patterns this one was produced at Meissen as well as Chantilly, and the question inevitably arises as to whether Chantilly pieces of this type derive from Meissen copies of the Japanese rather than the Asian originals. The issue is underscored by the exploits of Rudolph Lemaire. Lemaire, a self-described merchant and citizen of Paris, went to Dresden in 1728, and the following year, on 29 April, negotiated a remarkable contract sanctioned by Augustus II, enabling him to borrow some 220 Asian porcelains, mostly Japanese, from the Japanese Palace to be reproduced at Meissen and to be marketed out of the country, specifically Holland (where blanks were sent to be decorated) and France. At first they were to be unmarked, giving justifiable rise to the suspicion that Lemaire meant to pass this production off as Asian. This adventure, which has been described in detail elsewhere,[2] lasted only two years, ending with Lemaire's deportation in 1731, but it must have contributed to the taste for, and manufacture of, in France, porcelain decorated in the kakiemon style. Not that Lemaire was creating a market: Carolyn Sargentson has shown that the groundwork had already been laid, judging from the large amounts of Japanese porcelain listed in the inventory taken in 1724 of the *marchand-mercier* Thomas-Joachim Hebert.[3] And the prince de Condé's collection was presumably well formed by 1730, comprising porcelains acquired by his grandmother and his two wives,[4] as well as those he would have bought from merchants such as Hebert.[5] But the intense and shared fashion for the kakiemon

13

style at Meissen and Chantilly in the 1730s cannot have been coincidental, and while there seems to be no way of gauging the extent of Lemaire's Parisian trade it must have been influential.

Both cup and saucer are copied from Meissen models of about 1730, of which one example bears a Johanneum number.[6] The missing handle of Hartford's cup will have been slightly squared with lightly scrolled terminals.

NOTES

1 For the history of the pattern in Japan and Europe see *Porcelain for Palaces*, pp. 296–303.

2 Boltz, "Hoym, Lemaire," pp. 3–101. See also *Porcelain for Palaces*, pp. 45–47; Cassidy-Geiger, pp. 4–8; Le Duc, "Lemaire," pp. 54–60.

3 Sargentson, pp. 66–68. Sargentson notes that in 1713, when a first inventory of Hebert's business was taken, there was no porcelain in the stock. It is of course risky to assume that all the Japanese porcelain listed in the 1724 inventory—which Dr. Sargentson very kindly made available to me—was in the kakiemon style, but collecting history suggests that the denser, more robust Imari palette never found much favor in eighteenth-century France.

4 Le Duc, "Condé," pp. 11–13.

5 This is all the more likely as it was Hebert who drew up the inventory of the prince de Condé's collection in 1740.

6 *Anderson Collection*, p. 61, no. 27. An undated list of porcelains made for Lemaire included "12 paar grosse Caffè Schälgen a perdrix," presumably this pattern although not necessarily this model (Boltz, "Hoym, Lemaire," p. 24).

13

Cup and saucer

1962.619

Chantilly, c. 1740

Tin-glazed soft-paste porcelain, cup: H. 2⅜ × W. 3¹¹⁄₁₆ × D. 2¹³⁄₁₆ in. (6.1 × 9.3 × 7.1 cm); saucer: H. 1 × DIAM. 4⅞ in. (2.5 × 12.3 cm)

Provenance: Forsyth Wickes (gift 1962)

The elaborately scrolled handle closely follows a Meissen design current around 1735 to 1740, but the crisply modeled heart-shaped leaves are particular to Chantilly. A similarly-decorated ewer with a handle of variant design is fitted with Paris silver mounts dated 1738 to 1744.[1]

NOTE

1 Gutzwiller sale, Sotheby's, London, 12–13 December 1996, lot 142 (catalogued as Saint-Cloud).

Chantilly Table Wares

14

Bowl

1961.451
Chantilly, c. 1735–1740
Tin-glazed soft-paste porcelain, H. 3¼ × DIAM. 8⅝ in. (8.2 × 22 cm)
Mark: hunting horn in red

Provenance: Mrs. Marion Bayard Benson (gift 1961)

The peony spray occurs with numerous variations in composition and palette at Chantilly, and derives from a kakiemon motif of about 1660–80.[1] As it was also repeated at Meissen there is naturally the possibility that Chantilly was relying on an intermediate Meissen version, but whether such an example was in Condé's collection is uncertain as the only Meissen porcelain in the 1740 inventory with an explicitly identified Japanese pattern was a set of twelve red-dragon plates.[2]

The all over patterning of cherry blossoms inside the bowl is unusual for Chantilly, but not unique. A smaller bowl with a similar peony spray, sold in 1966,[3] was painted with "scattered florettes"—presumably these same flowerheads—inside, and two Meissen-model cups and saucers formerly on the art market[4] were covered with irregularly spaced cherry blossoms. The flowerheads on a lobed saucer sold in 1999[5] were also outlined, as here, entirely in black, instead of the more usual combination of black (for blue and green flowers) and red (for red and yellow ones). Was Chantilly adapting a style borrowed from Saint-Cloud? A Saint-Cloud pot-pourri jar of about 1730–35 is painted with cherry blossoms on a yellow ground,[6] and this all over decoration—but with more European flowerheads—appears on other Saint-Cloud pots-pourris[7] and on a covered jug once in the Dupuy collection,[8] all of about this same date. Japanese porcelain of the early eighteenth century is the ultimate source of this decorative style: Arita bowls with kakiemon decoration painted inside with scattered flowerheads[9] could well have been known at both Saint-Cloud and Chantilly.

NOTES

1 For a version dated 1680–1700 see *Porcelain for Palaces*, p. 151, no. 121.

2 Le Duc, *Chantilly*, p. 399.

3 Sotheby's, London, 22 February 1966, lot 13.

4 Christie's, London, 3 June 1974, lot 7, and 9 April 1979, lot 45, both with horn marks.

5 Alexander sale, Christie's, New York, 30 April 1999, lot 293.

6 De Plinval de Guillebon, *Louvre*, p. 50, no. 7.

7 Musée de Saumur and the Bowes Museum, Barnard Castle (ibid.).

8 Mrs. H. Dupuy sale, Parke-Bernet Galleries Inc., New York, 2–3 April 1948, lot 348.

9 For example, Christie's, New York, 15 September 1999, lots 27, 72.

14

15

Plate

1934.205

Chantilly, c. 1755–1760

Soft-paste porcelain, H. 1⅛ × DIAM. 9½ in. (2.9 × 24.2 cm)

Marks: impressed hunting horn; horn and A in blue enamel; Dᴿ in black enamel

Provenance: Mrs. Gurdon Trumbull (bequest 1934)

There are at least six variants of this pattern. Common to all is the diapered ground, the central wreathed medallion, and shaped reserves on the rim. The latticed field is uniformly a bright blue, the sections on every piece except this one centered by a gold dot: this is the only known example with red centers.

Two principal versions are distinguished by the design of their reserves. In one, represented by the Hartford plate, the frames of the reserves are formed of reverse scrolls not unlike the frames of flower-filled cartouches on Parisian gold boxes dating from the late 1740s to about 1760.[1]

The reserves of the second format are quadrilobed, framed by a plain gold border and festooned inside with wispy vines. Three types of pictorial decoration occur in both formats: flowers in all the reserves, a central scene from Æsop's *Fables* encircled by birds on the rim, or—as seen here—all birds.[2]

There are in addition a few plates with Oudry-like hunting scenes in the center and animals in the reserves,[3] as well as a dish and wine coolers with quite different gilding patterns.[4]

Few of these versions appear to survive in more than a handful of examples, and except for the few bottle coolers they are all plates, oval dishes, or lobed polygonal bowls (*jattes*). Whether any was ever a complete service is not known,[5] but the all-flower pattern with reserves like those seen here exists in the greatest quantity, and an oval dish of that type in the British Museum is dated 1753.[6] As Chantilly (or any other factory except Sèvres) so rarely dated its work this should perhaps be considered significant, and Geneviève Le Duc has proposed an association between that date and the marriage in 1753 of Louis-Joseph, prince de Condé, and Charlotte de Rohan-Soubise.[7] Plates of this pattern have traditionally been said to have been made for Louis-Joseph, and a nineteenth-century label on the back of this one describes it as the *Service Royal du Prince de Condé./Château de Chantilly*. This may have been a dealer's prose, but it may also legitimately reflect a commission on the occasion of the prince's marriage.

A somewhat uneasy balance between oriental and European style reinforces the date of 1753, when Chantilly was moving away from Asian influence to a rococo style inspired by Vincennes. The diapered ground is one of several Chinese border patterns from about 1720 to 1740 adapted by Chantilly in its first period, but the shape of the plates, the style of the gilding, the dentil rims, even the settings of the birds in the landscapes, are all borrowings from Vincennes.

Le Duc suggests that the pattern was current between about 1753 and 1760, noting however, an extended popularity.[8] A lozenge shaped dish in the Museum of Fine Arts, Boston with a different gilded rim border[9] is not, from its shape, likely to date before about 1775, and two wine coolers in the d'Yanville sale of 1907 were said in the catalogue to be dated 1786.[10] The ground pattern appears alone on the rims of plates painted with neat bouquets in the center,[11] and as the sole decoration of tea wares,[12] all datable about 1770–75.

Other more divergent variations have also been noted. Two plates formerly in the Glover collection,[13] with Oudry-like scenes in the center, were painted with architectural landscapes alternating with birds on the rim and were completed with quite different gilded borders. On a plate recently on the Paris art market the basic pattern appeared entirely in light blue, with flowers in all the reserves, the latter edged with still another scrollwork pattern. Departing furthest from the original scheme were a cup and saucer sold in 1985 with a trellis of different design.[14]

Where the marks have been noted, the majority of pieces—including all versions—are painted with the hunting horn and letter R in blue. The letters B and F have also been recorded, and the A on the back of the Hartford plate also appears on one in the Rijksmuseum, Amsterdam.[15]

NOTES

1 For example Somers Cocks, p.177, no. 48 (Jean Moynat, 1748–49); Christie's, London, 26 May 1964, lot 100 (C.B. Lefebvre, 1755).

2 For an extensive list of the pieces in the several versions see Dawson, *British Museum*, p. 42, no. 45. There are in addition an oval platter and two plates in the Philadelphia Museum of Art, the first painted entirely with flowers, the plates with birds.

3 Drouot Richelieu, Paris, 17 May 1995, lot 185 (from the d'Yanville collection); The Bowles Collection (Spero, p 173, no. 181, from the Dupuy and Dunlap collections); Drouot Richelieu, Paris, 17 May 1995, lot 184; and V&A, London, no. C. 329-1905, the two latter with empty and unframed reserves.

4 Munger, *Wickes*, p. 223, no. 177; Fontaine, pl. XXX (Musée Condé).

5 A plate in the Faudel-Phillips collection was said by Rackham to be part of a dessert service (Rackham, p. 26, pl. IIID).

6 Le Duc, *Chantilly*, p. 239.

7 Ibid., p. 238.

8 Ibid., p. 241.

9 Munger, *Wickes*, p. 223, no. 177.

10 Comte d'Yanville sale, Drouot, Paris, 20–22 February 1907, lot 164.

11 Munger, *Wickes*, p. 223, no. 176.

12 Cleveland Museum of Art; Christie's, London, 29 October 1973, lot 98; Le Duc, *Chantilly*, p. 235, covered milk? pot, Musée Condé.

13 Marguerite Glover sale, Parke-Bernet Galleries Inc., New York, 22–23 March 1957, lot 330.

14 Christie's East, New York, 30 January 1985, lot 75.

15 *Bulletin Rijksmuseum*, pp. 90–91, fig. 11.

Chantilly
Private Apartment Wares

16

16

Two covered jars

1917.901–902

Chantilly, c. 1740

Tin-glazed soft-paste porcelain, 1917.901: H. 7⁷⁄₁₆ × DIAM. 4⅛ in. (18.9 × 10.4 cm); 1917.902: H. 7⁵⁄₁₆ × DIAM. 4 in. (18.6 × 10.2 cm)

Marks: hunting horn in iron-red enamel on both

Arms: those of Marquet: argent a fess azure between in chief a crescent reversed gules and in base a lion rampant of the second

Provenance: "collection de M.G.R...," Galerie Georges Petit, Paris, 1905 as from collection of Dupont-Auberville;[1] J. Pierpont Morgan

The jars are among the few armorial porcelains datable to Chantilly's first period, that is, before Cirou's departure in 1751. Two others of the same model are painted with a different coat of arms;[2] and a set of three, and a pair of spice boxes dating about 1745–50, each with a different armorial, have also been recorded.[3]

The Hartford jars are two of four bearing the same arms. A third, lacking its cover, is in the Adrien Dubouché Museum, Limoges,[4] and the fourth, with silver rims, is privately owned.[5] The arms are those of Marquet, originally of Armagnac. By the eighteenth century the family had mostly settled in Paris, several members filling court-appointed functions either there or in the provinces. The owner of these jars may have been Maurice Marquet, who in 1742 obtained letters patent from Louis XV confirming the nobility to which he claimed title.[6] The coronet of a count above the arms, which was used rather freely in French heraldry, would normally consist of nine pearls, but they have been reduced here to seven.

Tobacco jars were sold one at a time or in sets varying in number. Lazare Duvaux sold single ones to M. Pierre La Fresnaye and Madame de Pompadour in 1751,[7] but two in an old lacquer case to the duchess of Mazarin in 1757.[8] The inventory of Procope Ulysse, comte d'Egmont made after his death in 1743, included four Saint-Cloud tobacco jars,[9] and a set of four others fitted—together with a silver-gilt spoon—in a small case.[10] There are differences in the decoration and painting of Hartford's jars, one being embellished with bands of flower sprays on the rims,[11] and the decoration itself being the work of two different painters. They therefore evidently represent two different sets.

The possibility that jars of this approximate size were also used for tea is indicated by an ensemble in the royal palace, Turin, comprising a wood case containing four Saint-Cloud jars, each fitted with an inner pewter lid engraved with the name of a tea.[12]

Exhibitions: *Morgan Loan Exhibition*, New York, 1914, not in catalogue; *European Porcelain*, New York, 1949, no. 118 (erroneously said to be ex coll. Chavagnac)

Literature: Chavagnac, p. 9, no. 5; Buckley, *Antiques*, p. 188, fig. 1

NOTES

1 29–31 May 1905, lot 202.

2 MAD, Paris (no. 33053); Pauline Riggs Noyes collection, Parke-Bernet Galleries Inc., New York, 7–8 February 1947, lot 298.

3 The set of three: Mme Dupuy sale, Parke-Bernet Galleries Inc., New York, 2–3 April 1948, lot 101; Mrs. Mildred Waldheim, Sotheby Parke Bernet, 12 October 1973, lot 156; Dawson, *British Museum*, pp. 38–39, no. 40; the pair: Sotheby & Co., London, 4 July 1967, lot 26.

4 No. ADL. 2921.

5 Le Duc, *Chantilly*, p. 210.

6 Hozier, 1764, registre 5, second part, pp. 1–4.

7 LD, 2, p. 76, no. 734 (16 February), p. 92, no. 883 (11 June).

8 Ibid., p. 342, no. 2973 (28 December).

9 Bernard Dragesco kindly informs me of a set of four Saint-Cloud jars, in their case, at Mawley Hall, Gloucestershire.

10 Le Duc, *Chantilly*, p. 419. Although the porcelain is not identified it could well have been Chantilly: Egmont was associated financially with the factory in 1737, and is recorded as having developed a method of gilding on Chantilly porcelain that he offered to Vincennes in 1741 (Le Duc, "Chantilly, extrême-orient," p. 19).

11 This is the only one of the four so decorated.

12 *Palazzo Reale di Torino*, p. 283, no. 115.

17

Chantilly Figures

17

Budai

1917.903

Chantilly, 1735–1740

Tin-glazed soft-paste porcelain, H. 9⅛ × w. 7¹¹⁄₁₆ × D. 4½ in.
(23.2 × 19.5 × 11.4 cm)

Provenance: J. Pierpont Morgan

The sleek rotundity, grinning face, and bared torso all characterize Budai, the Daoist god of happiness and good fortune. He was well known in Europe through what was probably the single most popular *blanc-de-chine* model exported to the west: a plump seated figure[1] widely copied at the European factories, including Chantilly,[2] where it also served as a springboard for other models, all from the same hand.[3] This figure is one of the group, and was very likely based on a Dehua original. The few Chantilly sculptures that have been matched with their Asian counterparts are seen to have followed the models quite closely in form, if not decoration.[4] No source for this figure has so far been identified, but the most cursory review of *magots* and *pagodes* (the terms being sometimes interchangeable)[5] in eighteenth-century collections[6] hints at a wealth of models that has either not survived or simply been unexplored in modern times.

Four other examples are known. One, with polychrome kakiemon-style enameling of the robe, is in the Musée des Arts décoratifs, Paris.[7] Another, in the Musée national de Céramique, Sèvres, had been long thought to be Chinese, but recent testing—prompted by Bernard Dragesco's recognition—has unequivocally established its Chantilly manufacture.[8] A third is in the Ashmolean Museum;[9] the fourth, in the Palazzo Reale, Turin, has been published as Chinese,[10] but given its exact correspondence to the others is also likely to be Chantilly.

Exhibitions: *Morgan Loan Exhibition*, New York, 1914, not in catalogue; *French and English Art Treasures*, New York, 1942, no. 302

Literature: Chavagnac, pp. 10–11, no. 7; *French and English Art Treasures*, no. 302

NOTES

1 Examples abound, but that at Burghley House, inventoried in 1688, is the earliest documented example (*Burghley Porcelains*, p. 95, no. 13).

2 Incorporated into a *marchand-mercier's* confection including a mantel clock by Julien Le Roy, Vincennes flowers, and gilt-bronze mounts dated 1745–49 (*Linsky Collection*, p. 240, no. 148).

3 For example, the numerous versions of an oriental seated with a covered jar between his knees, the variant models in which globes are substituted for the jars, and a model of Hotei copied from a Japanese original, of which examples are in the MAD, Paris and the Pflueger collection.

4 In addition to Budai mentioned above, the leopard in the Linsky Collection in MMA, New York copies a late seventeenth-century Japanese model of a *shishi*.

5 One definition of pagods in the *Dictionnaire de l'Académie française* (Paris, 1765) is "petites figures ordinairement de porcelaine, & qui souvent ont la tête mobile" [small figures usually of porcelain often with nodding head], while a *magot* is "Une figure grotesque de porcelaine, de pierre, &.c. Magot de la Chine." [A grotesque figure of porcelain, stone, etc. Chinese mandarin.] For Diderot, a *pagod* was a temple idol; *magots* were "figures en terre, en plâtre, en cuivre, en porcelaine, ramassées, contrefaites, bisarres, que nous regardons

comme représentant des Chinois ou des Indiens. Nos appartemens en sont décorés. Ce sont des colifichets précieux dont la nation s'est entêtée; ils ont chassé de nos appartemens des ornemens d'un goût beaucoup meilleur. Ce regne est celui des *magots*." [Earthenware, plaster, bronze or porcelain figures, crouching, spurious, odd, that we look upon as representing the Chinese or the Indians. We adorn our apartments with them. They are precious gew-gaws that have turned the head of the nation; they have ousted from our apartments ornaments of far finer taste. This is the reign of the mandarin.] (Diderot, *Encyclopédie*, 9, Paris, 1765, 861–62, facsimile reprint , 1969, 2, p. 734).

6 Over forty *pagodes*—in white and colored porcelain, *terre des Indes*, stoneware, soapstone, and *carton*—are listed in the inventory of the prince de Condé's collection in 1740.

7 Gauthier, p. 97.

8 Personal communications.

9 Dawson, *Ashmolean*, p. 42, no. 31.

10 *Palazzo Reale di Torino*, p. 390, no. 201.

18

Puppeteers

1917.950–951

Chantilly, 1735–1740

Tin-glazed soft-paste porcelain, 1917.950: H. 7½ × w. 4⅝ × D. 3¹³⁄₁₆ in.
(19.1 × 11.8 × 9.7 cm); 1917.951: H. 7⁹⁄₁₆ × w. 4⅞ × D. 3⅞ in. (19.2 × 12.3 × 9.8 cm)

Provenance: J. Pierpont Morgan

These groups, and another undecorated pair,[1] are the only known examples of Chantilly's most idiosyncratic sculpture. The standing figures represent Japanese Bunraku performers,[2] but as we have come to expect from Chantilly work the models and their decoration are an intricate compound of several Asian sources.

Bunraku emerged as popular entertainment in Osaka at the end of the seventeenth century,[3] differing from Kabuki theater in its use of puppets rather than actors. The puppets were built on wood frames, which were completely hidden by their costumes; their heads were supported by poles with levers which allowed for changes of expression. Women puppets, as seen in these groups, were made without legs or feet, their lower bodies suggested by their kimonos.[4] Up to about 1734 the puppets were manipulated by a single operator who held his puppet aloft while he himself was concealed behind a partition;[5] the limitations of soft-paste porcelain making such a construction impractical, the modeler has adjusted accordingly and the puppets are held in front of the puppeteers.

That Bunraku imagery should have been known at Chantilly bespeaks an unexplored aspect of Condé's collecting. There are no export porcelain figures that could have served as models for these, and the most likely iconographic source will have been Japanese prints, such as those by Masanobu (1686–1764) and Kiyomasu II (1706–63), showing puppeteers in action (fig. 18-1).[6] Evidence of the presence of Japanese prints in European collections before about 1740 is both meager and circumstantial, but some will have reached Dresden by 1708, as Japanese women are depicted on the exterior of the frame that

houses Dinglinger's *Grand Mogul*, completed that year; and Japanese prints were among the more than 1,400 "Chinese and Japanese Paintings" inventoried in the Dresden Kupferstich-Kabinett in 1738.[7] The prince de Condé must also have been familiar with the genre, as several plates in Fraisse's *Livre de desseins chinois* are based on Japanese pictorial sources.[8]

That being said, these groups represent the full maturity of Chantilly's eclecticism, and perfectly demonstrate the ease with which various influences and styles were absorbed and manipulated. In physical type the puppeteers are not Japanese but Chinese, recalling Kangxi standing figures enameled on the biscuit. Even the pose of one figure holding another—although it depicts a Japanese activity—has a Chinese prototype in a remarkably similar group in the Duberly Collection at Winchester College.[9] Also of Chinese origin is the conceit of nodding heads and hands, an idiosyncrasy that pervades Chantilly sculpture. Originally, the head and hands of each figure were movable, being suspended by rods in grooves set inside the necks and wrists. Large standing *blanc-de-chine* figures with detachable heads could be found at Rosenborg, Drottningholm and in Dresden by the early eighteenth century, but closer parallels to the Chantilly models are smaller ones, mentioned both in the Condé inventory of 1740 and in the sale catalogue of François Boucher's collection: "trois Pagodes branlants" [three nodding mandarins] and "une Pagode branlant la tete" [a mandarin nodding his head] are cited in

1740,[10] and while there is no further description it is likely that they were of the same type as the "pagode à tête, langue & mains branlantes," [mandarin with nodding head and moving tongue and hands] about nine inches high, owned by Boucher.[11]

The costumes display an exceptionally free-spirited reworking of diverse influences. The cut of the clothes, their borders and the patterned medallions all derive from Kangxi figures enameled on the biscuit; the palette hovers between a true Chinese *famille verte* and the Japanese kakiemon of the factory's prevailing taste; cherry blossoms, boldly outlined flower heads, random placement—even the phoenixes and dragon which were borrowed from the Chinese—further evoke Japanese style. Added to this mix are the strange panels of bizarre shapes that bring to mind some of the wilder patterns of Indian chintz.[12]

The fluency of this hybrid decoration is surely the work of an experienced designer, and we are teased by our ignorance of the artistic organization of Chantilly. The role of Jean-Antoine Fraisse (c. 1680–1739) has been discussed, somewhat inconclusively.[13] On the one hand his *Livre de desseins chinois* was a *succès d'estime* among collectors[14] and a moderately influential source book for decorators at Chantilly and elsewhere.[15] An assemblage of pictorial and decorative compositions based on Asian textiles, porcelains and lacquers, and even some European prints, it documented—according to Fraisse's preface—the richness of the prince de Condé's collections. But Fraisse was not a printmaker, and even his artistic skill has been called into question.[16]

Fig. 18-1 *The Actors Yamashita Kinsaku I and Hayawaka Hatsuse,* Torri Kiyomasu II, woodblock print, c. 1752

He came to Chantilly in 1729 as a "peintre en toille" [painter on cloth] and from then until 1737 had an atelier in the château—of which he was evidently director—that produced painted cottons. Throughout his career at Chantilly, Fraisse was variously described as "peintre," "peintre en toille," "faiseur de toille peinte," "ouvrier en toille peintes" and "compositeur," designations that have led to the suggestion that he was little if anything more than a technician.[17] But familiar as he was both with Condé's eclectic collection and with textiles in particular, is it not possible that his work is reflected in the costumes of Hartford's groups? Or should we perhaps imagine some collaborative, or supervising hand such as that of Henry-Nicolas Cousinet, whose atelier in the château was adjacent to Fraisse's, and who had been engaged by Condé to "imiter les ouvrages de la Chine" [copy the works of China]?

When acquired by Morgan the groups were mounted as candelabra, with porcelain flowers and gilt-bronze bases. This was very likely their original purpose, corroborated by the white pair fitted with candlearms and white flowers contemporaneous with the groups. The mounts of Hartford's groups, being later in date than the porcelains and of inferior quality, have been removed.

Exhibitions: *Morgan Loan Exhibition*, New York, 1914, not in catalogue; *French and English Art Treasures*, New York, 1942, no. 311; *European Porcelain*, New York, 1949, no. 107

Literature: *French and English Art Treasures*, no. 311; *European Porcelain*, no. 107, pl. XXV; Buckley, *Antiques*, p. 188, fig. 2; Hood, *Bulletin*, p. 134, fig. 7; Roth, "Morgan," p. 201, fig. 4; Le Duc, *Chantilly*, pp. 96–97

NOTES

1 Drouot, Paris, 18 June 1999, lot 43A. I am indebted to Errol Manners for this reference.

2 I thank Susan Miller for this identification.

3 Japanese puppet theater, under the name jōruri, is considerably older; it came to be known as Bunraku only in the 1870s, being named for the puppeteer Uemara Bunraku-ken (1737–1810) (Ortolani, p. 200).

4 Inoura, pp. 149–50.

5 Ibid., p. 152.

6 Gunsaulus, p. 117, no. 2; pp. 75, 87, 88, no. 4.

7 Braütigam, pp.122–28, nos. 145–55 (none related in subject matter to these groups).

8 The plates appear in different order among the several copies of Fraisse. In that owned by the MMA, New York the most obvious Japanese-derived illustrations are plates 13, 35, and 52. I should like to thank Susan Miller for drawing my attention to these.

9 Anthony du Boulay kindly brought this to my notice.

10 Condé inventory pp. 436, 657.

11 *Catalogue raisonné Boucher*, nos. 668, 675. It is not known when Boucher acquired his collection of Chinese figures, but I would suggest it is likely to have been about 1740 when he was exploring Chinese themes that would result in the Beauvais tapestry series, the *Tenture Chinoise*, first woven in 1743.

12 The importation of chintzes into France in the late seventeenth and early eighteenth century was so extensive as to cause numerous trade restrictions designed to protect the domestic textile industry. See Belevitch-Stankevitch, pp. 192ff.

13 Nicole Ballu evaluated his role as that of artistic adviser, the connecting link between the sources of design and Cirou's painters (Ballu, "Chantilly, extrême-orient," p. 106). Geneviève Le Duc considers his position to have been far more mundane (Le Duc, *Chantilly*, p. 115).

14 Le Duc, *Chantilly*, p. 386 n. 54.

15 Ibid., pp. 117–121 for Chantilly decoration copied from Fraisse. A scene of horsemen on one side of a Villeroy bottle cooler in the Cleveland Museum of Art is also take from Fraisse.

16 Ibid., p. 115, and p. 386 n. 58.

17 Ibid., p. 386 n. 58.

19

Seated Chinese

1917.912

Chantilly, c. 1740–1745

Tin-glazed soft-paste porcelain, H. 5¹⁵⁄₁₆ w. 6⅜ × D. 4¹⁵⁄₁₆ in. (15 × 16.3 × 12.5 cm)

Provenance: J. Pierpont Morgan

This figure and the puppeteer groups are by the same modeler, whose style is quite different from that of the author of the sleek rounded Budai-like models. His figures are thinner, more elongated, more expressive; and while derived from Asian exemplars they are more idiomatic. Coloring, too, changes with this group: on most examples the brightly-patterned white robes of the Budai modeler are replaced by those of muted solid-colored grounds with random-patterned reserves. The

Fig. 19-1
Pair of seated figures,
Chinese,
c. 1740–45

19

consistency, and harmony, of these models is such that we may imagine there was what amounts to a partnership between modeler and painter, a rapport that probably existed at one time or another at most of the European factories, but is documented only by the figures themselves.

There are three other examples of the model, differing significantly only in the presence or absence of a rocky base and leafy tree.[1] Also known are four mirror-image figures of a Chinese woman,[2] and within the entire group certain correspondences in painted decoration and base design indicate they were originally conceived as pairs. One "couple," formerly in the Gilbert Lévy collection, still exists as such although set on a modern platform.[3] Flanking a Chantilly pot-pourri raised on stems with Chantilly flowers the figures are clearly related by the manner of their painting. A second pair would be that composed of two figures sold at Christie's in 1960 and 1988, respectively,[4] their costumes again matching exactly in patterning. They, like the Lévy pair, lack a ground and foliage. Possibly complementing Hartford's figure is another sold at Christie's in 1985[5] which, like this one, is set on a mottled rocky base with a leafy tree at the back. The costume is of the same color and pattern type, the only alien element being the head, which is a replacement. There is another example of the Hartford type,[6] the man's robe, gray-violet, for which no corresponding female figure seems to be known; and a single female, her robe patterned with scattered flower sprays, also remains unmatched.[7]

This pairing of the models suggests Chinese influence. Chinese export figures were frequently produced as doubles or mirror images, perhaps in response to the western tradition of symmetrical display; the woman of this Chantilly group closely resembles one of a pair of early Qianlong figures in the Copeland collection, sharing similarities of pose, costume and base (fig. 19-1).[8] Dated not later than 1750 by William Sargent, the model seems to have been fairly common and could have been known at Chantilly where one of the female models was replaced by that of the man.

The figure originally had a nodding head and hand, both of which have since been fixed in place. Figures with movable (and thus replaceable) heads had been produced at Dehua for the export market from the late seventeenth century. Donnelly suggests that the practice of making such figures arose with the use of molds,[9] and production must have been simpler if heads and hands could simply be dropped into place rather than luted and fired. A secondary (and inevitable) result of the technique was the occasional change in identity of a figure: in the 1690s Queen Hedwig Eleanora of Sweden purchased a group of Dehua figures with nodding heads, most apparently depicting Guanyin but some—their heads having been transposed—of clearly secular character.[10] Nodding-head figures of porcelain were recorded at Rosenborg Castle in 1716 and in Dresden in 1721,[11] and several were inventoried in the prince de Condé's collection in 1740.[12]

Chavagnac believed this figure to be Mennecy dating 1766–70, an indication of the unfamiliarity of this repertoire at that time, even to so experienced a scholar.

Exhibitions: *Morgan Loan Exhibition*, New York, 1914, not in catalogue; *European Porcelain*, New York, 1949, no. 112

Literature: Chavagnac, p. 19, no. 16, pl. IV; *European Porcelain*, no. 112; Sargent, p. 124, fig. 57a; Le Duc, *Chantilly*, p. 95

NOTES

1 Formerly in the Gilbert Lévy collection (Alfassa and Guérin, pl. 28); Christie's, London, 1 July 1960, lot 240; Sotheby's, London, 2 March 1982, lot 126 (ill. Le Duc, *Chantilly*, p. 95, priv. coll.)

2 Ex coll. Lévy (as above); Sotheby & Co., London, 25 June 1968, lot 33 (sold again Christie's, London, 25 March 1985, lot 8); Christie's, London, 4 July 1988, lot 3; Paris art market (Kraemer et Cie) 1993.

3 *Elements of Style*, p. 63, no. 14. The platform is the same as it was when the group was illustrated by Alfassa and Guérin.

4 See notes 1, 2 above.

5 See note 2 above.

6 Sotheby's, London, 2 March 1982, lot 126.

7 Kraemer et Cie.

8 Another possible, but on balance less likely, inspiration for the model of the Chantilly woman is an Imari figure of a seated bijin c. 1690 (*Ko-Imari*, p. 202, no. 120.)

9 Donnelly, p. 147.

10 Setterwall, pp. 159, 163. Likewise, the Chantilly *Shou Lao* in the MMA, New York has, with a change of head, become an entirely different character in the model in the Pflueger collection.

11 Donnelly, p. 178, pl. 73B (Rosenborg), p. 338 (Dresden).

12 "Trois Pagodes branlants" [*sic*] and "une Pagode branlant la tête." Nodding-head figures in other materials also reached Europe, but less is known about the history of their importation. A painted clay group of a Chinese mandarin and a boy, the mandarin with nodding head and hands, entered the Danish royal collections in 1732 (Dam-Mikkelsen, p. 174); among François Boucher's extensive collection of Asian objects were a number of *pagodes* in *pâte des Indes* such as "un veillard [*sic*] branlant la tête… en pâte colorée" and "deux jolies pagodes à tête branlante, richement habillées" (*Catalogue raisonné Boucher*, lots 661, 668).

20

Louis XV[1]

1917.1509

Chantilly, c. 1755

Tin-glazed soft-paste porcelain, H. 17¼ W. 9⁹⁄₁₆ × D. 6¹³⁄₁₆ in. (43.9 × 24.3 × 17.3 cm)

Provenance: marquise Turgot, Paris, 1887; comte Raoul Coustant d'Yanville, Paris, 1907; M. Zélikine, Paris, 1908; Jacques Seligmann, London and Paris, 1908;[2] J. Pierpont Morgan

The king is seen at the age of about 50, the informal curling locks of his wig recalling youthful portraits, the rather stolid, frowning expression that of an older man. The bust is one of four related portraits in public collections, of varied historical attribution, but now all attributable to Chantilly.[3] A fifth, sold in Paris in 1912 from the collection of Madame Balletta,[4] is privately owned.

Hartford's example is matched in all essential respects—model, pedestal design, size and construction—by one in the J. Paul Getty Museum.[5] The others—different from these two and somewhat from each other—are in the Minneapolis Institute of Arts[6] and the Museum of Fine Arts, Boston.[7]

Of the four, Boston's is dated, and is also inscribed with the addorsed initials CC, presumably signifying Ciquaire Cirou, Chantilly's proprietor.[8] Its date of 1745, the slightly younger age of the king and its smaller size,[9] combine to make Boston's the earliest of the four portraits. The version in Minneapolis is based on the same model, and must date to the same period. By contrast, the Hartford and Getty portraits show the king at a decidedly later age and originate from a different model.

Several suggestions have been offered as to the sculptural source or sources of the Chantilly busts. Jeffrey Munger has persuasively associated Boston's with the work of Jean-Baptiste Lemoyne, noting the pronounced correspondence between the Chantilly version and extant bronzes by Lemoyne dated 1737 and 1742, further proposing specifically that it may have been based on a (lost) 1745 marble executed for Cardinal Rohan.[10] The currency of Lemoyne's portraits of the king at this time is reaffirmed by two portrait busts in *terre blanche*, both attributed by Geneviève Le Duc to the Paris factory in the rue de Charenton, about 1747;[11] both are even closer to Lemoyne's bronzes in their lightness of expression and sweep of drapery, and one version repeats the design of the socle of Boston's Chantilly example.[12]

Portraits of Louis XV are so plentiful that we need not be surprised to find them in porcelain; but sculpture of this ambition is difficult to achieve in soft-paste porcelain, and in 1745 practically non-existent.[13] That Chantilly should have attempted work of a type entirely different from its previous repertoire is intriguing. Why 1745? Geneviève Le Duc suggests it represents an homage to the king, recognizing his protection of the factory at the moment he was extending exclusive privileges to Vincennes.[14]

Other explanations also come to mind. The previous year the

20

Like the others, Hartford's Louis XV is tin-glazed, a practice occasionally used at Villeroy but not after the move to Mennecy about 1750, and its slightly different composition gives it a cooler and brighter surface appearance than is usual with Chantilly; the obviously different model and treatment of the socle could also be considered factors in separating the portraits into "pairs." Further, at the time Morgan acquired his bust after the Zélikine sale Chantilly was not known to have produced any sculpture of this type, or on such a scale.

A series of details links the four busts. The Boston and Minneapolis ones derive from the same portrait; the Getty and Hartford ones are a different model but share with the others similar treatment of the long tumbling hair. The military trophies connect the Minneapolis bust with the Hartford and Getty ones, and there is a marked stylistic correspondence between the scrolled and foliated cartouche on the face of Boston's pedestal and the shell-filled cartouche on the back of Hartford's.

We are thus considering two portraits of Louis XV produced at Chantilly, either by the same modeler or two different ones. As the factory's records have been lost, the mention on 25 June 1754 of "un buste du Roy"[17] and, on July 17th, of "un buste de porcelaine representant louis quinze"[18] do nothing to assist in authorship, although it may well be relevant to the dating of the Hartford and Getty busts. Despite the absence of factory records Le Duc has been able to provide an extensive list of personnel from other sources, among whom there were several sculptors. The most likely, in several respects, is Louis-Antoine Fournier (c. 1720–74), recorded as a sculptor at Chantilly from September 1753 to July 1758.[19] From 1743–47 he was supplying models to the creamware factory in the rue du Charenton, and from 1746–49 his name appears in the same capacity at Vincennes where he received payment in 1747 for models of naiads and, possibly, for the ambitious figure of a river god.[20] In the course of his peripatetic career Fournier also worked in the Paris branch of Saint-Cloud, in the rue de la Ville l'Évêque, and at some point before arriving at Chantilly, traveled to Sweden, Denmark and Turin.[21] What looks like an intriguing glimpse of Fournier's career is offered in a letter written from Paris 15 August 1757 by the ambassador of Savoy describing his recent visit to Chantilly and the porcelain manufactory.[22] In the course of the visit he was approached by the "principal worker" of the factory who, having fallen out with the new owner (Buquet de Montvallier) wished to work abroad, preferably at Turin where he said he had been before as a sculptor in the studio of Francesco Ladatte.[23] This unnamed worker sought the ambassador's influence with the Turin court in achieving his goal, one that subsequent correspondence shows came to nothing. The ambassador went on to note that Montvallier's wife, although displeased with the worker's behavior, acknowledged his superior talents for the composition of porcelain, sculpture and drawing.

From the evidence at hand the petitioner can only have been Fournier. Still at Chantilly when this letter was written, and briefly recorded at Mennecy the following month,[24] Fournier did shortly leave France, settling in Copenhagen in 1759 as

king had traveled to Alsace to inspect his troops, staying at Metz, Nancy and Lunéville as the guest of his father-in-law, King Stanislas. His time at Metz was prolonged by serious illness, and his recovery and return to Paris were marked by an outpouring of relief. Later that same year, on 11 May, Louis XV took part in the victorious battle of Fontenoy, reinforcing his popularity. Either circumstance (or both, cumulatively) could have been a motivation for Chantilly—owned by the king's cousin—to honor the sovereign. The later portraits, with their military panoplies and Louis' brooding air, perhaps augur the troubling, and absorbing, years of the simultaneous Seven Years' and French American Wars.

The Boston portrait was formerly catalogued by turns as Niderviller porcelain and Ludwigsburg *faïence*,[15] the Getty's as Mennecy;[16] Hartford's was sold in 1887 from the Turgot collection as Saint-Cloud and from the d'Yanville and Zélikine collections as Mennecy; the Balletta bust was sold as Vincennes, and Minneapolis' example was acquired in 1983 as Chantilly. That the four Museum-owned versions can now be accepted as Chantilly—as urged many years ago by Bernard Dragesco— indicates the recentness of scholarship concerning this factory.

director of a porcelain manufactory, remaining until 1766. It must have been Fournier, as Lami tentatively suggested, who exhibited a terracotta self-portrait, of which the model had been executed in Denmark, in Paris in 1774.[25] Given Madame de Montvallier's high appraisal of his talents, and his own statement that he worked with that dramatically rococo designer Ladatte, it is easy to image Fournier's hand in the sweeping shell-form models produced at Chantilly in the early 1750s, but it is a very different style from the relatively modest work attributed to him. This comprises a small, rather plain, portrait bust of Frederick V of Denmark, and several relief portrait medallions, including a self-portrait.[26] If, however, Préaud and d'Albis are correct in attributing the Vincennes river god to Fournier, there is good reason to accept him as the modeler of one or both Chantilly portraits of the king, and possibly even the sculptor of one of them.

Another hand to be considered is that of Henri-Nicolas Cousinet (1706–68),[27] who served both Louis-Henry de Bourbon (1692–1740) and his son, Louis-Joseph (1736–1813). Born in Chantilly, Cousinet was attached to Condé's household between 1733 and 1740, having at first a studio to "imiter les ouvrages de la Chine" and being subsequently described as "dessinateur" (1734) and "Sculpteur des menus plaisirs de S.A.S. Monsieur le Duc" (1736). He was also a silversmith: Cousinet received his mastership in the Paris guild in 1724[28] and was one of those few *orfèvres* to combine silversmithing and sculpture. His work in the former medium consists of a travelling service of 1729–30 for Maria Leczinska;[29] and Louis Réau suggested that the beautifully sculptural set of eight pairs of couples representing different countries, made for the Portuguese court in 1757–58 by Ambroise-Nicolas Cousinet, could have been modeled by his cousin, Henri-Nicolas.[30] Cousinet exhibited sculpture in the Salons of 1751–53 and again in 1756,[31] but the only example of his work known to survive is a terracotta portrait bust hopelessly damaged in World War II.[32] After 1756 Cousinet is recorded both in Paris and at Chantilly, where he died. The suggested dating of Hartford's Louis XV fits into Cousinet's most active period as a sculptor; on the thin evidence at hand it would be unwise to propose an attribution, but it may well be that Cousinet—connected throughout his life with Chantilly—was the artistic instigator of this and possibly both of the Louis XV portraits.

Literature: Buckley, *Antiques*, p. 189, fig. 5; Buckley, *Connoisseur*, p. 47, and fig. 5; Hood, *Connoisseur*, p. 137, fig. 12; McCaughey, pp. 116–17, pl. 40; Le Duc, *Chantilly*, pp. 198–99

NOTES

1 I am deeply indebted to both Geneviève Le Duc and Bernard Dragesco for information and advice most generously given during the preparation of this entry.

2 Marquise Turgot (inherited from her husband), Drouot, Paris, 1–2 April 1887, lot 138, 700 French francs; comte Raoul Coustant d'Yanville sale, Drouot, Paris, 20–22 February, 1907, lot 215, 42,500 French francs; M. Zélikine, Drouot, Paris, 7–9 May 1908, lot 114, 30,000 French francs, to Seligmann; APML, Seligmann file, invoice 8 May 1908, "The bust of Louis XV, on a base adorned with the attributes of royalty in relief, in old white porcelain tender of Mennecy, Ex collection Turgot 1887, Ex Collection d'Yanville 1907," 25,300 French francs.

3 Armin Allen, recognizing the tin glaze, suggested to Linda Roth in the early 1980s that Hartford's bust was attributable to Chantilly.

4 Drouot, Paris, 8–11 May 1912, lot 138.

5 Bremer-David, p. 124, no. 208.

6 Minneapolis, *Acquisitions*, p. 44.

7 Munger, "Louis XV," pp. 29–34.

8 For the proprietor of a patronage factory to sign on behalf of himself rather than his patron is unusual, especially in this instance as Chantilly was already using a hunting horn as its mark. Other interpretations of the addorsed Cs are possible: Dragesco suggests (in correspondence) either Cirou-Chantilly or simply Chantilly, the Cs being doubled as the Ls would later be at Vincennes and Sèvres.

9 Munger, "Louis XV," p. 33. The heights are 12½ in. (31.8 cm) (Boston); 17¹⁵⁄₁₆ in. (45.6 cm) (Minneapolis); 16½ in. (41.9 cm) (Getty); 11¾ in. (28.9 cm) (Balletta, bust only).

10 Munger "Louis XV," p. 31.

11 Le Duc, *Chantilly*, p. 191.

12 Also related, perhaps through the itinerant Dubois brothers, is the Tournai bust of Louis XV, clearly based on a Lemoyne prototype. As both Gilles and Robert Dubois worked at Chantilly and from 1743 to 1745, in the *faïence fine* manufactory in the rue de Charenton; and as Gilles is recorded in 1750 as a modeler at Tournai, their role in the circulation (if not actual production) of the Louis XV portraits may be greater than has been considered. I am grateful to Bernard Dragesco for starting this train of thought.

13 Related to these busts is another sold from the Fitzhenry collection (Paris, Drouot, 13–16 December 1909, lot 190) as a Saint-Cloud bust of a woman. On the same scale as the Hartford model—H. 16¾ in. (42.6 cm)—it would appear from the illustration to be a Chantilly portrait of Maria Leczinska, an attribution suggested to the writer by Bernard Dragesco.

14 Le Duc, *Chantilly*, pp. 200, 203.

15 Munger, "Louis XV," p. 29.

16 Bremer-David, p. 124, no. 208, with a Mennecy attribution dating from 1910. It was again identified as Mennecy when it, and Minneapolis' bust, were both in the collection of Mr. and Mrs. W.B. Meloney in the 1950s.

17 Le Duc, *Chantilly*, p. 404.

18 Kindly communicated by Bernard Dragesco.

19 This biographical account is based principally on Le Duc, "Frédéric V," pp. 62–63.

20 Préaud and d'Albis, p. 143, no. 92.

21 Le Duc, "Charenton," p. 24.

22 Vesme, 2, p. 598. I am indebted to Wolfram Koeppe for this reference.

23 This would place Fournier's stay in Turin between about 1744 and 1746, when he is first mentioned in the rue de Charenton. Marie Moreau died in 1743; Ladatte himself was working in Paris—where Fournier could have met him—off and on between 1720 and 1744 when he returned permanently to Turin. Madame Le Duc, in a letter to the writer, surmises that Fournier was in Turin between 1749 and 1752, that is, between Vincennes and Chantilly.

24 Le Duc, "Charenton," p. 24.

25 Lami, 1, p. 353.

26 Le Duc, "Frédéric V," p. 63, figs. 1, 3.

27 Much of this biographical information has been kindly conveyed by Madame Le Duc.

28 Nocq, *Poinçon*, 1, p. 310.

29 *Louis XV*, p. 347, no. 461.

30 Réau, "L'argenterie," pp. 23–26. Réau's attractive reasoning was that Ambroise-Nicolas was not his own modeler; that the figures bore a stylistic resemblance to Sèvres biscuit sculpture; that Henri-Nicolas as a member of Condé's household would have had opportunity to create models for porcelain; and that it would have been natural for Ambroise-Nicolas to turn to his experienced cousin for such work.

31 Guiffrey, "Académie de Saint-Luc," p. 238; among them was a terracotta sketch of *Generosity* executed for the château of Chantilly.

32 I am grateful to M.C. Jubert, Musée des Beaux-Arts, Reims, for the information concerning the present condition of the bust, which is illustrated in its original state by Gonse, p. 190.

21

Toilet jar

1917.906

The body Chantilly, c. 1735–1740, the decoration modern

Tin-glazed soft-paste porcelain, H. 2⅛ × DIAM. 2¼ in. (5.4 × 5.7 cm)

Mark: hunting horn in red-orange

Provenance: J. Pierpont Morgan

The cylindrical form with recessed foot ring reflects Japanese influence, and as the body is tin-glazed (although exceptionally white and glossy) the fabric appears to be Chantilly. Two covered jars approximately this shape and size were in the Riggs collection[1] and, like this one, were decorated with flowering plum and rocks above a trellis-like border. The decoration here, however, cannot be considered genuine: the colors are too strong and unmodulated—the green in particular being a dark spinach; the individual elements have not been properly articulated, and the suspended-in-air quality that is the definitive charm of Chantilly's kakiemon style is absent. Like all factory marks the horn varies considerably in its appearance, but the rendering here is unusually haphazard.

There is no indication that the jar once had a cover, nor is it possible to tell from the catalogue whether the covers on the Riggs jars were original. When catalogued by Chavagnac it was fitted with a pierced and *repoussé* silver mount.

Exhibition: *Morgan Loan Exhibition*, New York, 1914, not in catalogue

Literature: Chavagnac, p.12, no. 10

NOTE

1 Karrick Riggs collection, Parke Bernet Galleries Inc., New York, 7–8 February 1947, lot 45.

21

22

22

Pair of vases (*vases à oreilles*)

1917.913–914

Mennecy, c. 1760–1765

Soft-paste porcelain, 1917.913: H. 6⅝ × W. 4⅛ × D. 3¾ in. (16.9 × 10.5 × 9.5 cm); 1917.914: H. 6⅝ × W. 4¼ × D. 3¹¹⁄₁₆ in. (16.9 × 10.8 × 9.4 cm)

Marks: D.V. incised on unglazed bottom of each

Provenance: J. Pierpont Morgan

The model is an adaptation of one first produced at Vincennes in 1754,[1] and was given the same designation at Mennecy, a single *vase à oreilles* being listed in the stock of porcelains in the rue de Puits-Massé on 3 October 1765.[2] The original design is attributed to Jean-Claude Duplessis, *père* (see catalogue no. 58) and Vincennes produced it in six sizes.[3] Several Mennecy examples are known, and those whose heights have been noted are between the third and fourth sizes of the Vincennes editions (7⅛–7½ in. or 18–19 cm and 5¹¹⁄₁₆–5¹⁵⁄₁₆ in. or 14.4–15 cm).[4] All are painted like this pair, the garlands more or less ignoring the

panel formed by the lightly molded edges of the leaves just below the neck; and the delicate gilt feathering of the Vincennes leaves has—due to the proscription on the use of gold—been paraphrased here by bold strokes of dark rose pink.

Rosalind Savill has observed that biscuit examples of the Sèvres *vase à oreilles* in the fourth and fifth sizes were included in dessert-table decoration beginning in 1757/58,[5] but these Mennecy versions, being both larger and polychrome, were probably not so used. The factory did produce biscuit vases of other models for the dessert,[6] even though it is not known to have manufactured any complete table services. Such vases, and the sculpture groups of child musicians (catalogue nos. 38 and 39) indicate that Mennecy was supplying a repertoire of independent decorative elements from which the customer could assemble his own table decoration.

Exhibitions: *Morgan Loan Exhibition*, New York, 1914, not in catalogue; *European Porcelain*, New York, 1949, no. 138

Literature: Chavagnac, p. 20, no. 17, pl. IV (one); *European Porcelain*, no. 138

NOTES

1 Savill, 1, p. 135.

2 Duchon, p. 147.

3 Savill, 1, p. 135.

4 Henri Chasles sale, Drouot, Paris, 9–14 December 1907, lot 479 (a pair); Louis

Scheid collection, Drouot, Paris, 21–22, 24–25 March 1933, lot 636 (a pair, H. 6¹¹⁄₁₆ in. or 17 cm); Mrs. H. Dupuy sale, Park Bernet Galleries Inc., New York, 2–3 April 1948, lot 248 (a pair, same height as Hartford's; possibly the pair from the Chasles collection); Gauthier, p. 133 (one); Madame M.L. collection, Drouot, Paris, 15 February 1974, lot 67 (a pair, one with incised DV; H. 6⅞ in. [17.5 cm]; reference kindly supplied by Linda Roth).

5 Savill, 1, p. 135.

6 Grégory, p. 42, figs. 5, 6.

23

Pair of pots-pourris

1917.926–927

Mennecy, c. 1755–1760

Soft-paste porcelain, 1917.926: H. 7¾ in. × w. 7⁷⁄₁₆ × D. 4⅝ in. (19.7 × 18.3 × 11.8 cm); 1917.927: H. 7½ × w. 6⅜ × D. 4⅜ in. (19.1 × 16.3 × 11.2 cm)

Provenance: J. Pierpont Morgan

The generic model was common to Saint-Cloud,[1] Chantilly, and Villeroy in the early 1740s: to the basic composition of a baluster vase—often entwined with a flowering vine—and a leaning tree trunk, Chantilly regularly added oriental figures,[2] while one of two Villeroy examples was densely colored in the turquoise, green and manganese palette of the factory's first period.[3] Pots-pourris were in production at Vincennes in 1746,[4] and among the different models were *pots pourris fleurs de relief*[5] which probably referred to variations on the earlier models with brightly-enameled flowers.

The Hartford pots-pourris represent the last stage of the design and will have followed closely on the heels of the

Vincennes ones, as a few dozen were listed among Mennecy stock in the rue Saint-Honoré in 1754, but not later.[6] Among Mennecy's most ambitious and beautifully executed productions, numerous examples have been recorded, all painted with an exceptional grace and freshness of coloring.[7]

Judging from the daybooks of Lazare Duvaux pots-pourris were sold singly or, less often, in pairs; while not mirror images of each other these two are clearly a pair, the work of the same gifted painter.

Exhibition: *Morgan Loan Exhibition*, New York, 1914, not in catalogue

Literature: Chavagnac, p. 28, no. 30

NOTES

1 Elizabeth Parke Firestone sale, Christie's, New York, 21–22 March 1991, lot 4.

2 Mrs. H. Dupuy sale, Parke-Bernet Galleries Inc., New York, 2–3 April 1948, lot 362; Christie's, London, 28 October 1963, lot 110; *Eighteenth Century French Porcelain*, p. 22, no. 70; Christie's, New York, 18 May 1989, lot 192. A pair of Chantilly pots-pourris of this model but without figures was lot 90 in the sale of the Pinto d'Aguiar collection, Drouot, Paris, 27–28 March 1925.

3 Simon Goldblatt sale, Sotheby's London, 1 May 1956, lot 112; the other, the vase painted with oriental figures in a Chantilly manner, was lot 4 at Christie's, London, 31 March 1980. Both bore the painted D.V. in use up to about 1748.

4 Préaud and d'Albis, p. 136, no. 71.

5 So called in the first inventory of 8 October 1752. (*Vincennes*, p. 92).

6 Duchon, pp. 140–41. Among them were "32 pots-pourris blancs, avec ou sans terrasse, ou blanc à feuillages." The stock inventories published by Duchon are, she acknowledges, incomplete but reflect significant changes in production.

7 A pair in the V&A, London (no. C. 336 and b-1909); single examples in the Duca di Martina Museum, Naples (Casanova, p. 129, no. 59); the MMA, New York (no. 1982.60.263, with the addition of a young girl and her dog); Dallot-Naudin, p. 152; Darblay, p. 88, pl. XXXV (with parrot); Sotheby's, London, 21 November 1978, lot 121.

24

Covered cup and saucer

1917.918

Mennecy, 1765–1770

Soft paste porcelain, cup: H. 4⅝ × W. 4¼ × D. 3¼ in. (11.8 × 10.9 × 8.3 cm); saucer: H. 1¼ × DIAM. 6 in. (3.2 × 15.3 cm)

Marks: incised under glaze: D,V (cup); DV (saucer)

Provenance: J. Pierpont Morgan

This type of landscape painting is well-recorded for Mennecy, occurring on tea sets, *écuelles*, and plates, some with basket-weave rim panels.[1] Some of the landscapes are partially or fully encircled by thin leafy branches, others are unconfined, and occasionally there are additional floral sprays. The scenes have a common, although unidentified, source: in an almost unvarying format one or more figures—isolated, a little pensive—occupy the foreground of an extended pastoral landscape, often perched on a rock or low hill.

The scheme of decoration is surely borrowed from Vincennes: similar landscapes appear on a shell-form dish and a plate with basketweave rim of about 1752–53, each scene being framed by a tree and branches and surrounded by flower sprays.[2] Not surprisingly, several of the Mennecy forms, notably the teapot and *écuelle*, are also based on Vincennes models. This covered cup is related to the *tasse à gobelet à lait* mentioned in the Vincennes inventory of October 1752, but is smaller and more cylindrical.

The tea services, *écuelle* and cup and saucer in the Victoria and Albert Museum appear to have been painted at about the same time. The painting of Hartford's ensemble is heavier, the colors darker, and the rims gilded; all the trademarks of factory decoration are present, but the work would seem to be from a later, and less deft, hand.

A Sceaux plate of c. 1773 painted in the same manner[3] underscores the lingering interconnection between the two factories.

Exhibition: *Morgan Loan Exhibition*, New York, 1914, not in catalogue

Literature: Chavagnac, p. 23, no. 23, pl. V

NOTES

1 Teaset, private collection (Gauthier, pp. 140–41); teaset, MAD, Paris, formerly in the Fitzhenry collection (Drouot, Paris, 13–16 December 1909, lot 139); two *écuelles*, Louvre, no. OA 10300 and Musée des Arts décoratifs, Saumur (de Plinval de Guillebon, *Louvre*, p. 69, nos. 11, 11a); cup and saucer, V&A, London (Honey, pl. 42B); plates (Gauthier, p. 133; Ballu, pl. 16; Duchon, p. 138; Marquereau sale, Drouot, Paris, 27 May 1936, lot 83). Among the many unidentified incised marks recorded are D.V.Q. (Ballu); D/ADV (Louvre); f.D.V., d.V.P., A DV D, and DV D (all MAD, Paris).

2 The dish illustrated in Eriksen and Bellaigue, p. 264, no. 79; the plate in Préaud and d'Albis, p. 66, no. 126.

3 *Nord-Pas-de-Calais*, p. 96, no. 60.

24

Villeroy and Mennecy Table Wares

25

Saucer

1913.599c[1]

Mennecy, 1755–1760

Soft-paste porcelain, H. 1¹⁄₁₆ × DIAM. 4¾ in. (2.7 × 12 cm)

Mark: D,V, incised on bottom

Provenance: Reverend Alfred Duane Pell (gift 1913)

The radial gadrooning is clearly evocative of Saint-Cloud table wares, and there is no doubt that François Barbin was keeping an eye on his closest competitor, as Mennecy produced both blue-and-white and prunus-decorated pieces in the Saint-Cloud manner. These imitations, dating after Barbin's removal from Villeroy to Mennecy 1748–50, also confirm the longevity of Saint-Cloud's conservative style, as it could not have been worth Barbin's while to produce them if they were not still marketable.

NOTE

1 This saucer entered the Atheneum's collection paired with 1913.599a–b.

26

Juice pot (*pot à jus*)

1913.599a–b

Mennecy, 1760–1765

Soft-paste porcelain, H. 3³⁄₁₆ × W. 3 × D. 2⅜ in. (9.1 × 7.6 × 6 cm)

Mark: D, V, incised on the bottom

Provenance: Reverend Alfred Duane Pell (gift 1913)

The shape is based on a Vincennes model in production by 1753 as a component of the first, or main, service of a complete table service, designed to contain meat, fish or vegetable juice.[1] At Mennecy it came in several guises: the inventory of merchandise in the rue Saint-Honoré taken 26, 28 and 29 July 1754 included "white or colored juice pots—apple-, pear-, or artichoke-shaped";[2] Hartford's model appears in the factory's accounts in 1762 as "juice pots with twisted ribbing."[3]

The form survives today, marketed as a *pot de crème* [*sic*]. The term *pot à crème* was originally reserved in the eighteenth century for a footed milk jug belonging to a tea set, and in the

25

Sèvres factory records and the daybook of Lazare Duvaux the two terms clearly defined different objects,[4] but ordinary usage eventually blurred the distinction: in 1782, in the sale of the duc d'Aumont's collection, the catalogue described eight Sèvres "pots à crème couverts, à anses,"[5] which seems to correspond to this form.

The model is a common one; usually painted with *famille rose* flower sprays it was produced at Chantilly, Sceaux and Bourg-la-Reine as well as Mennecy.

The cover is not original to the cup, being slightly too large and having a different scale of ribbing.

Notes

1   *Vincennes*, p. 76.

2   "… pots à jus en blanc ou en couleurs—en forme de pomme ou de poire ou d'artichaut." Duchon, p. 140.

3   "… pots à jus à colonne torses." Ibid., p. 145.

4   On 10 February 1755, Lazare Duvaux supplied two cups and saucers, a teapot and "Le pot à crème à trois pieds" (LD, 2, p. 234, no. 2067).

5   *Duc d'Aumont*, lot 251 (p. 119).

27

Two salt cellars

1917.929–930

Mennecy, c. 1760

Soft-paste porcelain, 1917.929: H. 4¾ × W. 3⅞ × D. 4⅛ in. (12.2 × 9.9 × 10.5 cm); 1917. 930: H. 5⅛ × W. 3¹⁵⁄₁₆ × D. 3⁹⁄₁₆ in. (13 × 10 × 9 cm)

Provenance: J. Pierpont Morgan

A few examples of the model have been recorded, each differing somewhat in the modeling of the shell and in the accessories. Here, the children are a boy and a girl, the latter with a long pigtail down her back; in a D.V.-marked variant formerly in the Firestone collection[1] the child—essentially the same figure as the girl—has become Cupid with a quiver, and Hartford's boy has a near match in another marked salt in the Victoria and Albert Museum.[2] A fifth version, lacking the child, is in the British Museum.[3]

Absent the figure, the model is a tamer version of Juste-Aurèle Meissonnier's designs for salt cellars which could well have been known through Gabriel Huquier's engravings of the 1730s or 1740s.

Salt cellars were normally part of the table service and were thus supplied in varying number. But Mennecy did not produce services, and these two models with their opposing symmetry

26

27

were presumably conceived as an independent pair. These two may not have originated with each other, however, as the painting of the flower work and the general execution of the salt cellar with the girl is more finished than that of the companion piece.[4]

Exhibition: *Morgan Loan Exhibition*, New York, 1914, not in catalogue

Literature: Chavagnac, p. 29, no. 32

NOTES
1 Elizabeth Parke Firestone sale, Christie's, New York, 21–22 March 1991, lot 96.
2 Honey, pl. 47a.
3 Dawson, *British Museum*, p. 56, no. 57 (Miss Dawson suggests the figure was lost in firing).
4 It compares well with that on a snuffbox with silver mounts hallmarked 1756–62 (Firestone sale, 1991, lot 429).

28

Double salt cellar

1917.915
Mennecy, 1760–1765 and later
Soft-paste porcelain, H. 5⅞ × W. 7⁵⁄₁₆ × D. 3³⁄₁₆ in. (14.9 × 18.6 × 8.1 cm)
Provenance: J. Pierpont Morgan

Six other versions of this model are known to exist, one recorded as bearing the Chantilly hunting horn in red, the others attributed either to Chantilly or Mennecy.[1] There is little difference between them, but three are related to the marked Chantilly salt cellar through consistency of painting style,[2] and the remaining three—including Hartford's—are distinguished by the addition of a small flower in the girl's hair.

The model derives from one of a pair of Meissen salt cellars designed by Kändler around 1740 to 1745, a girl and a young man each seated between handled baskets.[3] About 1755–60 Chantilly produced a pleasantly naïve variation of a girl—her

28

posture reversed from the Meissen—seated alongside a vase perched on a rock,[4] before arriving at this more relaxed composition. Only Mennecy, however, seems to have followed Meissen's example and produced a male counterpart, in two quite different models of exceptional grace.[5]

The painting of the salt cellar is pale in color, vague in execution, and the patterning of the skirt unusually dense and small in scale. Nonetheless the palette is compatible with an eighteenth-century date and will have been added before the end of the century.

Exhibition: *Morgan Loan Exhibition*, New York, 1914, not in catalogue

Literature: Chavagnac, pp. 20–21, no. 18

NOTES

1 MAD, Paris (no. 33217, as Chantilly); *Antiques Magazine* 64, July, 1953, p. 19 (advertised as Mennecy by Marion Bayard Benson); Sotheby's, London, 29 March 1955, lot 110 (Mennecy); Sotheby's, London, 1 May 1956, lot 97 (Goldblatt sale; Chantilly); Sotheby's, 4 May 1965, lot 99 (Chantilly, marked); Drouot Richelieu, Paris, 12 March 1997, lot 130 (Mennecy).

2 The MAD, Paris, Goldblatt, and Benson examples.

3 Two similar models by Kändler are recorded: *Meissen*, pl. 5, fig. 7; and Walcha, p. 483, fig. 111. A more rococo version, tentatively attributed to Kändler, is dated c. 1765 (Rückert, p. 184, no. 1002).

4 Sotheby's, 4 July 1967, lot 25, with hunting horn in red. The decoration, which includes some orientalizing flora and fauna, links it with a seated flower vendor in the Linsky Collection at the MMA, New York (no. 1982.60.269).

5 Gauthier, pp. 144–45 (both incised D.V.).

29

29

Covered bowl (*écuelle*) and stand

1917.934

Mennecy, 1750–1755

Soft-paste porcelain, bowl: H. 5⅛ × W. 7¼ × D. 5⅜ in. (12.9 × 18.4 × 13.6 cm); stand, H. 1⁵⁄₁₆ × DIAM. 8 in. (3.3 × 20.3 cm)

Provenance: J. Pierpont Morgan

The all over *Schneeballblüten* or guelder rose pattern originated at Meissen in 1739 in a service designed by J.J. Kändler for Maria Josepha of Saxony and Poland,[1] and is said to have evolved from a Chinese prototype such as a triple gourd vase in the Dresden collections attributed to the Yongzheng period.[2] Produced for about a decade at Meissen it would have been still a relatively current style when it was adapted at Mennecy, where it occurs chiefly on small pots-pourris.[3] As there are examples marked with the painted D.V., in use almost exclusively during Barbin's

first period at Villeroy,[4] these "snowball" pieces must have been among his earliest productions after his move to Mennecy 1748–50. Pots-pourris *en forme de pelotes de neige* [snowball-shaped] were listed in inventories of stock in Mennecy and in the rue Saint-Honoré in 1754.[5] Both at Meissen and Mennecy it was usual to color the tips of the petals: this all white version is less common.

Exhibition: *Morgan Loan Exhibition*, New York, 1914, not in catalogue

Literature: Chavagnac, p. 33, no. 38

NOTES

1 Walcha "Dekor," pp. 48–49, fig. 3.

2 Acquired after 1725 and inventoried in 1779 (Reichel, *Rosa Familie*, p. 30, no. 5).

3 Mrs. H. Dupuy sale, Parke-Bernet Galleries Inc., New York, 2–3 April 1948, lot 261; Gilbert Lévy sale, Drouot, Paris, 23 November 1967, lot 53; Elizabeth Parke Firestone sale, Christie's, New York, 22 March 1991, lot 91.

4 Firestone sale, 1991, lot 91; Christie's, New York, 21 May 1996, lot 122.

5 Duchon, pp. 141, 144.

30

Snuffbox

1917.937

Mennecy, 1750–1756

Soft-paste porcelain, silver gilt, H. 2 × L. 2¹⁵⁄₁₆ × D. 1⅜ in. (5 × 7.6 × 3.5 cm)

Mark: (on insetting rim of cover mount) hen's head (Paris discharge mark for small gold and silver, 1750–1756)

Provenance: J. Pierpont Morgan

There is a surprising number of models of this shoe, differing considerably in the shape of the buckle and in the decoration, which occurs both flat and molded, painted and uncolored.[1] Examples with their original marked silver-rimmed covers are dated 1750–56,[2] just at the time this type of shoe—made of fabric, with a high waisted heel, upturned toe and buckle—was in fashion. Nor would it have been uncommon for such a shoe to have been patterned to match a woman's costume.

Although the silver mounts are appropriately dated the cover is not original to the body. The porcelain is from a different hand, but fits its silver rim neatly; being a little too small for the shoe, it would seem to have been borrowed from another piece of the same date.

30

31

A factory inventory of July 1754 listed 3,934 white and enameled snuffboxes "shaped like a barrel, like fruit, like shoes, like clogs" and 62 "snuffboxes shaped like a shoe, like a shepherd" were cited a month later.[3]

Exhibition: *Morgan Loan Exhibition*, New York, 1914, not in catalogue

Literature: Chavagnac, p. 35, no. 43

NOTES

1 For example, two in MMA, New York (nos. 43.100.29; 1982.60.363); Sotheby's, London, 25 May 1982, lots 152–53; Elizabeth Parke Firestone sale, Christie's, New York, 22 March 1991, lot 436.

2 Sotheby's, London, 25 May 1982, lots 152–53; Firestone sale, 1991, lots 408, 436. A Chantilly snuffbox of the same type is also datemarked 1750–56 (Beaucamp-Markowsky, p. 468, no. 410).

3 "… en baril, en fruits, en souliers, en sabots"; and 62 "tabatières en soulier, en berger." Duchon, pp. 137, 141.

31

Snuffbox

1917.939

Mennecy, 1750–1760

Soft-paste porcelain, silver, H. 1⁹⁄₁₆ × L. 3½ × D. 1¼ in. (4 × 9 × 3.1 cm)

Provenance: J. Pierpont Morgan

Less common than the high-heeled shoe of the previous entry, this model also occurs with variations in the type of buckle and decoration.[1] The cover and unmarked mount are not original, the porcelain being of another, later, manufacture.

This low-heeled form was presumably included among the "tabatières … en souliers, en sabots" inventoried in 1754.[2]

A similar example with silver rims dated 1750–56 was sold from the Firestone collection,[3] and a Saint-Cloud version in the Musée Adrien Dubouché, Limoges also bears marks of the same date.[4]

Exhibition: *Morgan Loan Exhibition*, New York, 1914, not in catalogue

Literature: Chavagnac, p. 36, no. 45

NOTES

1 Sotheby's, London, 11 April 1978, lots 363, 364; Troinitsky, p.67, no. 61.

2 Duchon, p. 137.

3 Elizabeth Parke Firestone sale, Christie's, New York, 22 March 1991, lot 428.

4 Beaucamp-Markowsky, p. 458, no. 396.

32

Snuffbox

1971.52.49

Mennecy, c. 1760

Soft-paste porcelain, silver, H. 1½ × L. 3³⁄₁₆ × D. 1¾ in. (3.8 × 8.2 × 4.5 cm)

Provenance: Henry Schnakenberg (bequest 1971)

The Rijksmuseum, Amsterdam, owns a smaller example of this model, enameled with flower sprays and fitted with silver mounts struck with the Paris discharge mark for 1756–62 and a date letter possibly for 1757–58.[1]

Mennecy was undoubtedly influenced by Meissen snuffboxes with basketweave molding which that factory had been making since about 1740,[2] but there are also parallels with the overall chased or engine-turned (*guilloché*) patterns being used in the decoration of Parisian gold boxes around 1755 to 1765.[3] Among the Mennecy wares waiting to be fired in 1762 were "43 tabatières guillochées de toutes especes."[4] A variant model of this box in which the chrysanthemum is set against a rice-grain ground is in the Musée Adrien Dubouché, Limoges.[5]

The unmarked silver mount does not fit well, lacks the expected thumbpiece, and is a replacement of indeterminate date.

Notes

1 Beaucamp-Markowsky, p. 489, no. 440.
2 Ibid., pp. 186, 200, 207–9, nos. 142, 155, 163–65.
3 For example, Sotheby's, Geneva, 12, 14 November 1985, lot 416 (1753); Christie's, Geneva, 11 November 1986, lot 436 (1759–60).
4 Duchon, p. 145.
5 Fourest, "Boîtes," p. 46, fig. 2.

33

Étui

1917.936

Mennecy, 1760–1765

Soft-paste porcelain, L. 4¼ × DIAM. 1⅛ in. (10.8 × 2.9 cm)

Inscribed: LES BLESSVRES EN SONT DOUCES

Provenance: J. Pierpont Morgan

The dispersal of Mennecy style towards the end of the factory's existence occasionally complicates the attribution of unmarked ordinary pieces. The factory was nominally still in operation in 1775, and had on hand the previous year a considerable stock of material and of fired but undecorated pieces.[1] By this time Mennecy was in the hands of Jullien and Jacques, who in 1772 had established themselves at Bourg-la-Reine, and the unpainted wares were presumably completed there. Even earlier, in 1762, a Mennecy worker, Louis-François Gaignepain, had left to set up for himself at Crépy-en-Valois, evidently specializing in snuffboxes and *étuis* of the sort familiar from marked Mennecy work.[2] The model of the Hartford *étui* was produced at both places: "1 etui forme de carquois uni peint" [1 plain, painted, quiver-shaped *étui*] is listed in Mennecy's Paris stock on 2 August 1762,[3] and *étuis* of the same description were among 94 Crépy models in 1766.[4] The painting on this piece shows enough skill and spirited coloring to suggest it is Mennecy factory work despite its slight sketchiness.

Inscriptions in gold letters on white enameled bands were a feature of English, not French, goldsmiths' work in the eighteenth century, being particularly common to Chelsea "toys". The style of this mount, and the fact that the cover is lined with gold, indicate an English replacement, presumably to offset damage.

Exhibition: *Morgan Loan Exhibition*, New York, 1914, not in catalogue

Literature: Chavagnac, p. 34, no. 40

Notes

1 *Sceaux-Bourg la Reine*, pp. 95, 97.
2 Chavagnac and Grollier, p. 392.
3 Duchon, p. 146.
4 Chavagnac and Grollier, p. 394.

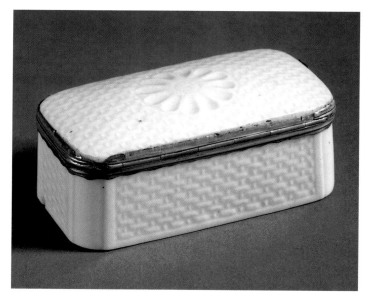

32

33

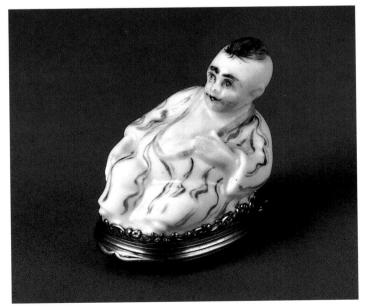

34

34

Snuffbox

1917.938

Mennecy, c. 1760

Soft-paste porcelain, gold, agate, H. 2¹⁄₁₆ × L. 2 × D. 1⁷⁄₁₆ in.
(5.3 × 5.1 × 3.7 cm)

Provenance: J. Pierpont Morgan

The decoration notwithstanding, this is a figure of a recumbent Chinese, a model possibly inspired by similar (reversed) Saint-Cloud and Chantilly ones.[1] Both here and in a second example sold at Christie's,[2] the painter has chosen to ignore the nationality of his character, endowing him with dark bushy eyebrows, eyes conspicuous for a particularly vivid blue encircling a large black pupil, and a slightly blurred rosebud mouth. These distinctive mannerisms are recognizable on other Mennecy boxes, in the Musée Adrien Dubouché, Limoges and a Swiss private collection,[3] and in the small allegorical figure of Winter (catalogue no. 41). The execution of the snuffboxes is at best hasty, and in the case of the Hartford box, slapdash.

The Christie's, Limoges, and Swiss boxes are all fitted with Paris silver mounts dating 1756–62; this box is dated accordingly.

In the other recorded example of this model the figure reclines on a grassy mound, which is here concealed by hinged gold mounts. They and the agate panel serving as cover, appear to be English, of later date.

Exhibition: *Morgan Loan Exhibition*, New York, 1914, not in catalogue

Literature: Chavagnac, pp. 35–36, no. 44

NOTES
1 Beaucamp-Markowsky, pp. 456, 467, nos. 392, 407.
2 Christie's, London, 22 June 1992, lot 12.
3 Beaucamp-Markowsky, p. 486, nos. 434, 435.

35

Dwarf

1917.911

Villeroy, c. 1745–1748

Soft-paste porcelain, H. 6¼ × W. 3⅝ × D. 3½ in. (15.8 × 9.2 × 9 cm)

Provenance: J. Pierpont Morgan

The figure is copied with little variation from an engraving by Martin Engelbrecht (1684–1756), published about 1710 in *Il Callotto resuscitato*, where he is personified as Nicolo Cantabella and, less favorably, as *Savonardischer Wurmschneider* ["Worm-cutter from Savoy"] (fig. 35-1). He carries what is probably meant to be a barrel organ on his back and, in the engraving, a walking stick in his left hand, a detail that has been omitted both from this example and one other, in the Musée des Arts décoratifs, Paris.[1]

Engelbrecht's was the second of several editions of a work

Fig. 35-1 *Savonardischer Wurmschneider*, from *Il Callotto Resuscitato*, Nicolo Cantabella, Augsburg, c. 1710, pl. 1

that differed in the number and authorship of its illustrations, but that remained unchanged in its exclusive and satirical representation of dwarfs.[2] As its title suggests, it followed in the tradition of Callot's *Varie figure gobbi*, originally published about 1622 and reissued throughout the seventeenth century; Villeroy, quite independently of any other French factory, produced a distinctive repertoire of dwarfs drawn from both sources.[3]

Accompanying the engraving is a six-line verse identifying Nicolo Cantabella as one of that band of hangers-on who followed regiments on their campaigns in the eighteenth century. In this case, the campaigner was Prince Eugene of Savoy (1663–1736), and the verse extols his skill in forcing the retreat of the French from the Tyrol in 1701 and again from Turin four years later, during the War of the Spanish Succession.[4]

Its half-finished decoration imparts an unusual ugliness to this figure: the fully painted Villeroy dwarfs, whether their source is French or German, are commonly benign, even

35

slightly humorous, in bearing. The ferocity of Hartford's figure is softened in the Paris version by details of facial features, hair and costume.

Of the eleven known examples of these dwarfs all but four are unmarked; the others—one sold from the Goldblatt collection[5] and three in the Linsky Collection at the Metropolitan Museum[6]—bear the painted D.V. identified with Villeroy. Hartford's model shares with two others the irregular rock-work base of the early period while others are placed on neat square plinths that seem to have been introduced in the early Mennecy years. This repertoire of dwarfs thus seems to straddle the Villeroy-Mennecy periods, their dating complicated by evidence that Barbin had neither sculptors or painters working for him at Villeroy after 1744.[7] There were several *ouvriers* who could conceivably have practiced as sculptors, but the lack of painters is striking, and Geneviève Le Duc has hypothesized that Barbin's Paris premises in the rue de Charonne served as a decorating workshop where Villeroy pieces in the white were brought to be finished.[8]

Exhibition: *Morgan Loan Exhibition*, New York, 1914, not in catalogue

Literature: Chavagnac, pp. 18–19, no. 15; Scott, p. 120, pl. 419; Buckley, *Antiques*, p. 189, fig. 4

NOTES

1 Dallot-Naudin, p. 115.

2 For a detailed discussion and bibliography see Bauer and Verfondern, passim.

3 There are six in the MMA, New York, and two in the Ashmolean Museum in addition to the two examples of this model. Another marked model, formerly in the Goldblatt collection, was sold at Sotheby's, London, 1 May 1956, lot 114. For the Ashmolean figures see Dawson, *Ashmolean*, p. 46, no. 33.

4 I am indebted to Wolfram Koeppe for his translation and interpretation.

5 See note 4.

6 *Linsky Collection*, pp. 312–13, nos. 282–84.

7 Le Duc, "Villeroy," p. 23.

8 Ibid., pp. 9–11.

36

36

Children with a dolphin

1917.909

Mennecy, 1755–1760

Soft paste porcelain, H. 6 × W. 5¼ × D. 3⅜ in. (15.2 × 13.4 × 8.5 cm)

Mark: D.V. incised on unglazed base, the letters glaze-filled

Provenance: J. Pierpont Morgan

The porcelain origin of this group is a Meissen composition in which two children—one lightly draped, the other not—grasp a curvaceous fish improbably emitting a leafy candle socket from its mouth; the group is set on Meissen's standard flower-strewn pad base scarcely seen before 1750, and probably dates from about that year.[1]

Numerous copies and variations of the model in the 1750s attest to its widespread currency. Both Bow (c. 1750–53)[2] and Longton Hall (c. 1756–57)[3] produced variations close to Meissen's, retaining the long thin slippery fish and the function of the model as a candlestand. At Vincennes, thirty *Groupes d'Enfans tenans un Dauphin* in two sizes were listed in 1752:[4] in

Fig. 36-1 *Groupe d'Enfans tenans un Dauphin*, Vincennes, c. 1752

Fig. 36-2 *Groupe d'Enfans tenans un Dauphin* (back), Vincennes, c. 1752

Fig. 36-3 *Boys with Fish*, Chelsea, c. 1755

this version there is no provision for a candle socket and the children, rather than propping up the fish, are grappling with it (figs. 36-1, 2). Pont-aux-Choux produced an almost exact copy of the Vincennes model, substituting a trailing ribbon for the flowers on the base.[5]

Hartford's Mennecy version could have been copied either from Vincennes or Meissen. In favor of the latter are two examples sold from the Gilbert Lévy collection in 1996[6] in which the candle socket was prominent; the presence of flowers strewn on the pad base of Hartford's group also suggests familiarity with the Meissen model which was treated in the same way.

Related to the Vincennes model, but later, judging from a certain staidness of appearance, are two examples in *faïence fine*. One, complete with an elaborate leafy drip-pan and socket in the manner of French gilt bronze, has been published as Pont-aux-Choux (1749–88).[7] The other, in the Victoria and Albert Museum, is called French or Italian.[8] It lacks the drip-pan and socket and differs in a few details, but the children—conspicuous for their curly hair—appear to be identical, and the two groups thus of the same manufacture. A version produced at Chelsea during its red anchor period (1752–58) combines features of both the German and French models with innovations of its own (fig. 36-3).[9] The poses of the children repeat those of Vincennes except for the vigorously out-thrust leg of one copied from Meissen; also copied from Meissen is the flower-decked base. A startling difference is the transformation of the fish into a giant unwieldy carp the children struggle to control, the sinuous tail of the Meissen creature reinvented as a length of drapery. Was this whimsy on the part of the Chelsea modeler or did he, in fact, "read" the Vincennes fish, in accordance with current imagery, as a carp? With its open mouth and bulging eyes it could pass for a dolphin, as it was identified at the time. But it will be recalled that dolphins are almost invariably depicted head down, their tails stretched out behind, or, more usually, waving high in the air. About 1750, however, there was a vogue in Parisian court circles for Asian porcelain figures of carp, often mounted in bronze gilt. These were vertical, their heads up, their tail fins either straight down or slightly curved.

On 16 October 1750 Lazare Duvaux supplied Madame de Pompadour with "Quatre morceaux de porcelaine celadon" of which two were "poissons";[10] the collector Jean-Louis Gaignat (1697–1768) owned both Japanese and Chinese porcelain carp, the latter having been purchased from Duvaux on 2 September 1751.[11] As sketched by Gabriel de Saint-Aubin in the margin of the sale catalogue of Gaignat's collection the next year,[12] these resembled well-recorded models: vertical, with slightly open mouths, their tails slightly curled at the bottom.[13] This was not a collecting taste shared by the English, but the imagery might have been known to the Chelsea modeler, and as the Vincennes model despite its factory designation, is visually more akin to the contemporary representations of carp, he may have so interpreted it.

Meissen may have provided the initial inspiration for this group and its variants but behind it lies an as yet unidentified source, probably a fountain model. The theme of children playing with dolphins or other fauna is endemic to fountain sculpture and was freely borrowed by small-scale sculptors as well, so similarities between this composition and others should be considered as happenstance.[14] In his discussion of French sources of English porcelain sculpture T.H. Clarke offered a small unidentified bronze of this composition as the origin of the porcelain groups:[15] we have only his illustration to go on, but it would seem from its appearance and Clarke's description of pin holes in the surface to be a master mold of the type used in nineteenth-century sand casting.[16] For the time being the sculptural origin of this group remains unidentified.

Exhibition: *Morgan Loan Exhibition*, New York, 1914, not in catalogue

Literature: Chavagnac, pp. 17–18, no. 13

NOTES

1   René Fribourg sale, Sotheby & Co., London, 15 October 1963, lot 490. It is one of two such models, the other—perhaps a little earlier—composed of the same two children in slightly different poses flanking a vertical column of reeds serving as a candlestand; the standing child, his arms around the column, holds a crayfish (Lang, p. 34, no. 57).

2 Charleston, *English Porcelain*, fig. 9 (the fish with a leafy socket issuing from its mouth); Bradshaw, p. 71, no. 28.

3 Sotheby's, London, 13 November 1973, lot 23. Was Longton Hall copying Bow or Meissen? Dr. Watney commented that the number of early Longton Hall figures derived from Meissen was evidently greater even than at Chelsea around 1750 (Watney, "Longton Hall," in Charleston, *English Porcelain*, p. 71).

4 Eriksen and Bellaigue, p. 209, no. 23.

5 In a private collection, this was kindly brought to my attention by Bernard Dragesco.

6 Gilbert Lévy sale, Hôtel George-V, Paris, 10 December 1996, lots 57, 58.

7 Chompret, 3, "Pont-aux-Choux," pl. 11C. This would have been a natural borrowing, as the factory had been founded in part by Vincennes personnel, Claude Imbert Gérin and the Dubois brothers, although by the time this group would have been made the factory was under the proprietorship of another co-founder, Adrien-Pierre Mignon.

8 No. C. 128-1985.

9 The group is not mentioned in Chelsea's 1755 sale.

10 LD, 2, p. 62, no. 621.

11 Ibid., p. 95, no. 896.

12 Dacier, 11, facsimile p. 70.

13 Watson, *Oriental*, p. 88, no. 30; Dauterman, *Wrightsman*, pp. 427–28, no. 197.

14 Bernard Watney suggested that the original model for this group, which is stylistically akin to fountain groups at La Granja by René Frémin (1672–1726) portraying pairs of children playing with fish, may have been the work of Frémin, who returned to France in 1738 (Watney, "Proto-types," p. 351).

15 Clarke, "Chelsea," p. 52 and pl. 24.

16 I am grateful to Clare Vincent for her advice on this point.

37

Amphitrite

1963.463

Mennecy, c. 1750

Soft-paste porcelain, H. 13⅞ × W. 6¼ × D. 5⁵⁄₁₆ in. (35.2 × 15.9 × 12.9 cm)

Provenance: Forsyth Wickes (gift 1963)

A Nereid, and the wife of Poseidon, Amphitrite is shown with a lobster in her left hand, a dolphin at her feet. The model derives from a bronze by Michel Anguier (c. 1612–86), one of a set of six figures of classical deities executed in 1652 (fig. 37-1).[1] Of them all, Amphitrite became the best known, through repetition in a variety of sizes and media beginning in Anguier's lifetime and lasting through the eighteenth century. A marble, now in the Louvre, was from 1680 a familiar site in the gardens of Versailles, and versions in terracotta, marble, and bronze were recorded in numerous eighteenth-century collections.[2]

Anguier's *Amphitrite* was also known through engravings,[3] but Mennecy's version was clearly copied from an example of the sculpture, as the fall of the drapery at the back corresponds exactly to Anguier's treatment (fig. 37-1).[4] Its size, too (surely not coincidentally), falls within the range of heights recorded for bronze casts of Amphitrite.[5] For all its fidelity to the original, however, the Mennecy figure, of which Hartford's is the single known example, differs in telling details. Anguier's *Nereid*—described at the time as "une Amphitrite tranquille"—looks down quietly at the lobster poised on her left wrist, her shoulder a little raised, her body turned, her drapery twisted and flowing.

Here the pose has been constricted and become more frontal, she gazes beyond the lobster, and the simplified drapery tends to hang, ending stiffly rather like a fan in her right hand and like a bath towel over the dolphin's nose.[6]

Amphitrite is one of a small group of serious Mennecy sculptures datable to about 1750 and shortly thereafter. A figure of *Painting* in the Musée des Arts décoratifs, Paris, is marked DV in blue and thus, following Geneviève Le Duc's chronology,[7] represents the period of the factory's transfer from Villeroy to Mennecy 1748–50. A statuette of *Endymion* in the Musée national de Céramique, Sèvres—incised "D.V"—is possibly from the same hand as *Amphitrite*; also at Sèvres is a more muscular figure of *Diana*, also bearing the incised form of the mark. This group is distinctly different in character from

Fig. 37-1
Amphitrite,
Michel Anguier,
bronze, model
1652

the more familiar Mennecy repertoire as exemplified by the Morgan collection, and reveals a little-known ambitious, and effective, sculpture production.

Curiously, given the fame of Anguier's statue, it seems not to have been copied at other Continental factories, although it reappears in reverse in several English pottery versions.[8]

NOTES

1   For a full account of Anguier's sculpture see Charageat, "Amphitrite," pp. 111–23; Fischer, no. 20. Among the many extant versions of the statue are examples in the Louvre, Paris, Dresden, the Toledo Museum of Art, the MMA, New York and the Swedish National Art Museum, Stockholm.

2   Fischer, no. 20.

3   Charageat (Charageat "Amphitrite," p. 117 nn. 1–2) notes engravings by Charpentier and Desplaces.

4   Fischer records several bronzes in French collections between 1710 and 1783, including one sold from the Crozat collection in 1750, and another in 1761.

5   11¼ to 23⅝ in. or 30 to 60 cm (Fischer, no. 20).

6   This detail, although clumsy, is an indication that the Mennecy modeler was copying an early replica of the statue, in which the tip of the dolphin's nose is hidden under Amphitrite's drapery and the square base is vertically rippled to suggest water—approximated here by Mennecy's usual base for the period. In later, i.e., eighteenth-century, versions in bronze, the drapery stops at the top of the dolphin's head, and the base is plain and of varying profile (*Masterpieces from the Louvre*, pp. 17–18, no. 48).

7   Le Duc, "Villeroy," p. 26.

8   Linda Roth has noted the figure as the handle of a creamware centerpiece c. 1790 sold at Sotheby's, New York, 15 April 1996, lot 364. Amphitrite is also seen in two Staffordshire models, one without the dolphin, c. 1775–85, the other—dated 1825—with the dolphin painted brown (Halfpenny, pp. 99, 119).

37 (reverse)

38

Child musicians

1917.949

Mennecy, c. 1760–1765

Soft-paste porcelain, H. 6⅞ × W. 4⅝ × D. 3⅝ in. (17.5 × 11.7 × 9.3 cm)

Provenance: J. Pierpont Morgan

At least three different models of pairs of child musicians were made at Mennecy.[1] This one, known from an unusually large number of examples, exists in glazed white, polychrome and biscuit versions, both marked and unmarked.[2] There are minor variations in details from one to the next, but all are the work of the same modeler, and those that have been painted display a consistency of pattern and coloring. A regular feature of the decoration is the girl's yellow hat striped to simulate straw, seen here in catalogue nos. 39 and 40. Absent from this example is the bow held by the boy in his right hand, the girl's drumstick and the pipe she is blowing which she holds in her left hand, all of which survive in the example in the British Museum.

A lingering influence of the Vincennes and Sèvres *enfants Boucher* is seen here; these are not far from the chubby children of Falconet's models (after Boucher) of *The Lottery* and *The Peep Show* of 1757. But the format is unusual and ingenious, the children facing each other, one seated slightly higher, thus creating a completely circular composition, legible and active from any angle. The groups were undoubtedly intended as table decoration to be seen in the round: a larger *groupe tournant* in the Victoria and Albert Museum of four children, one holding a sheet of music,[3] was perhaps the centerpiece of such a display.

An inventory of the showroom of Charles Hennique in the rue Saint-Honoré on November 14, 1765 listed "3 groupes representant les musiciens" among polychrome groups and "2 groupes de musiciens" among the white glazed ones.[4]

Exhibition: *Morgan Loan Exhibition*, New York, 1914, not in catalogue

38

NOTES

1 In addition to this and the model of the following entry, a third portrays two children jointly playing a tambourine (René Fribourg sale, Sotheby's, New York, 25 June 1963, lot 36; V&A, London, no. C. 321-1909, incised DV).

2 V&A, London, no. C. 320-1909 (polychrome, incised DV); Chavagnac sale, Drouot, Paris, 19–21 June 1911, lot 147 (glazed white, unmarked); Baroness Burdett-Coutts sale, Christie's, London, 9 May 1922, lot 171 (marked but not described); Pauline Riggs Noyes collection, Parke-Bernet Galleries, Inc., New York, 7–8 February 1947, lot 74; Digby collection, Sotheby's, London, 22 June 1951, lot 19 (polychrome, unmarked); Paget collection, Sotheby's, London, 3 May 1946, lot 65 (polychrome, incised DV); Gilbert Lévy collection, Drouot, Paris, 23 November 1957, lot 50 (white glazed, incised DV); Daydi, 2, p. 141, pl. 15 (biscuit, incised DV); Christie's, South Kensington, 6 December 1990, lot 121 (biscuit, incised DV); Scott collection (Scott, pl. 421, white glazed, incised DV); British Museum, London (Dawson, *British Museum*, pp. 60–61, no. 61, glazed white, incised D,V f); collection Château de Groussay, Sotheby's sale at château, 2 June 1999, lot 313. While this list is largely the same as that published by Aileen Dawson it is repeated here for the convenience of the reader.

3 No. C. 322-1909.

4 Duchon, p. 149.

39

Child musicians

1917.940

Mennecy, c. 1760–1765

Soft-paste porcelain, H. 6⁹⁄₁₆ × W. 4¼ × D. 3⁹⁄₁₆ in. (16.6 × 10.9 × 9.1 cm)

Mark: D,V incised

Provenance: J. Pierpont Morgan

This second group of child musicians is by the same modeler as the preceding one and, commonly paired with it, is likewise known from a variety of examples.[1] It was also copied at Chelsea-Derby about 1772 in a version so literal that an example must have been at hand.[2] There is no ready explanation for the appearance of a model from a (then) relatively obscure French factory in England, but the connection between Mennecy and Chelsea-Derby may have been made through Tournai. A variant model of this group in the Cecil Higgins Art Gallery, Bedford, England includes a leafy tree, a favorite device of the Tournai modelers;[3] and a well-known Mennecy *groupe tournant* of three young standing musicians also appears at Chelsea-Derby, the figures again encircling the Tournai tree.[4] This argues not only for the transmission of models from Mennecy to Tournai, but a familiarity with both styles at Chelsea-Derby. This could have been due to the Tournai modeler Pierre Stephan, who signed a contract with William Duesbury in September 1770.

Exhibition: *Morgan Loan Exhibition*, New York, 1914, not in catalogue; *European Porcelain*, New York, 1949, no. 131

Literature: *European Porcelain*, no. 131; Le Corbeiller, "Tournai and Mennecy," p. 56, fig. 3

39

NOTES

1 Paget collection, Sotheby's, London, 3 May 1946, lot 65 (polychrome, incised mark); Pauline Riggs Noyes collection, Parke-Bernet Galleries, Inc., New York, 7–8 February 1947, lot 74 (polychrome); René Fribourg sale, Sotheby's, London, 25 June 1963, lot 36 (polychrome; the same model sold again at Christie's, London, 3 June 1974, lot 5, and illustrated by Williams (*Eighteenth Century French Porcelain*, p. 25); Gilbert Lévy sale, Drouot, Paris, 23 November 1967, lot 50 (polychrome); Mrs. John Christner sale, Christie, Manson and Woods, New York, 9 June 1979, lot 173 (biscuit, incised DV and 3); British Museum, London (Dawson, *British Museum*, pp. 61–62, no. 62; white); Drouot Richelieu, Paris, 12 March 1997, lot 136 (polychrome). A slightly larger group of three children (H. 7½ in. or 19 cm) repeats these two figures and adds a reclining boy holding grapes (Christie's, London, 30 November 1970, lot 9).

2 Le Corbeiller, "Tournai and Mennecy," p. 56, fig. 2.

3 Ibid., p. 54, fig. 1.

4 Ibid., p. 57, figs. 4, 5.

40

40

40

Child musicians

1917.923

Mennecy, c. 1760–1765

Soft-paste porcelain, h. 6¹⁵⁄₁₆ × w. 4½ × d. 3⅛ in. (17.6 × 11.5 × 7.9 cm)

Provenance: J. Pierpont Morgan

Although the composition is essentially the same as that of the previous entry, this group is the work of a different modeler and painter. The faces are more heart-shaped and the features more carefully defined; while the polychrome decoration is closely related to that of the other musical groups—notably in the straw hat and the rosebud-patterned clothing—the faces are uncharacteristically subtly flesh-toned, and the effect is altogether less playful. Another unusual feature is the closed unglazed base instead of the regular open, partially glazed one.

Exhibition: *Morgan Loan Exhibition*, New York, 1914, not in catalogue

Literature: Chavagnac, pp. 29–30, no. 27

41

Winter

1917.947

Mennecy, 1760–1765

Soft-paste porcelain, H. 5¹⁄₁₆ × W. 2³⁄₁₆ × D. 2 in. (12.9 × 5.6 × 5 cm)

Marks: incised D,V

Provenance: J. Pierpont Morgan

This scantily clad young girl, whose brazier is evidently keeping her warm, was presumably represented among the several dozen figures personifying the seasons listed in the stock of Charles Hennique's shop in the rue Saint-Honoré in 1765.[1] Others in this extensive series are all, like this one, stocky

41

young women with flower-sprigged drapery variously holding bunches of flowers or fruit or—in one case—with a basket of flowers at her side.[2] Most, if not all, are the work of the same modeler, but while the painting style is consistent, more than one hand is evident. Given the generic representations the figures could personify gardeners or flower sellers as well as the seasons, but Hartford's—one of two examples known of the model[3]—is unmistakably Winter.

The idea of producing series of allegorical or pastoral figures was fueled by Meissen, where such sets were in production from about 1750 and were known in Paris court circles, Lazare Duvaux having supplied several groups and single figures of the type in 1750 and 1751.[4] These were mostly the work of Friedrich Elias Meyer, whose model of *Taste* from a set of the *Five Senses* (about 1750)[5] is the origin of a Mennecy figure in the Philadelphia Museum of Art.[6] Other Mennecy models, such as *Leda and the Swan*,[7] are less directly comparable but reflect Meyer's themes and style.

The models in the series are simple, and some are repeated, varying only in the accessories and in the work of the *répareur*. The painter of this and other figures in the series is conspicuous for his wide-eyed expression beneath broad dark eyebrows.

Exhibition: *Morgan Loan Exhibition*, New York, 1914, not in catalogue

NOTES

1 There were "48 petites saisons" in color, and 62 biscuit "moyennes saisons de différentes attitudes" (Duchon, p. 149).

2 Sotheby's, London, 21 November 1978, lot 114 (from the collection of the comtesse de la Rochefoucauld, daughter of Aymé Darblay); Parke-Bernet Galleries Inc., New York, 2–3 April 1948, lot 89 (two; Dupuy collection); MAD, Paris (three); Philadelphia Museum of Art (no. 42-59-107); Fritz Katz collection, Sotheby Parke-Bernet Galleries Inc., New York, 8 March 1979, lot 219.

3 Christie's, London, 28 October 1963, lot 123 (incised DV; sold again Drouot, Paris, 25 June 1968, lot 26, identified as a vestal, incised factory mark).

4 LD, 2, p. 43, no. 434, p. 73, no. 702, p. 76, no. 730, p. 83, no. 802.

5 Meister, 1, pp. 434–36.

6 No. 42-59-171, impressed D.V. She lacks the bunch of grapes in her right hand that defines the sense.

7 One example sold Christie's, London, 3 July 1989, lot 43.

42

represents Clio, whose traditional attribute of a book is sometimes augmented by a swan (admittedly remote from the tame parrot-like bird seen here). Mennecy produced another, somewhat similar, model of a young woman with a parrot, whose identity is equally ambiguous.[1]

The modeler is the same as that of *Winter*, but the painting is from a different hand.

Exhibition: *Morgan Loan Exhibition*, New York, 1914, not in catalogue

NOTE
1 Sotheby Parke-Bernet, New York, 8 March 1979, lot 219 (Fritz Katz collection), where it is identified as *Hearing* after the Meissen model by F.E. Meyer. Meyer's figure is, however, quite different from both of these Mennecy ones.

43

Grotesque woman

1917.910

Mennecy and/or Sceaux, 1755–1765

Soft-paste porcelain, H. 7⅞ × W. 4 × D. 4⅛ in. (20 × 10.2 × 10.5 cm)

Inscribed: Nº 135 written in ink inside base rim, and, more faintly, N… 15

Provenance: Cartier et Fils, Paris, 1905;[1] J. Pierpont Morgan

The distinctive facial features—the hooked nose, high cheekbones, the strong lines framing the nose and mouth—are also found on a D.V.-marked figure of a hurdy-gurdy player in the Musée des Arts décoratifs, Paris[2] and on an unmarked figure of a seated woman wearing a turban sold at Christie's in 1968.[3] These three are related in turn to a larger group of grotesque and quasi-oriental models, all but one unmarked. Those that are decorated are sketchily painted with pastel sprigged robes and vehement black eyebrows; they include three theatrical "Chinese" in the Linsky Collection in the Metropolitan Museum of Art,[4] a single figure formerly in the Untermyer collection,[5] another sold at Sotheby's in 1956,[6] and a standing woman wearing a fez in the Musée national de Céramique, Sèvres.[7] Three unpainted models have also been recorded;[8] one—a standing grotesque in the Musée national de Céramique, Sèvres—is particularly close to Hartford's in her dramatic facial features.

Mennecy has been the preferred factory of attribution of the unmarked figures, but Chantilly, Capodimonte and Sceaux have also been proposed. The Christie's model was twice sold as Chantilly,[9] the three white figures have been published as Capodimonte,[10] and the Untermyer model was recently tentatively assigned to Sceaux.[11] Although there are minor differences in modeling there is an overall consistency of style, and all the figures must have been produced at about the same time in the same place. If the first three mentioned above are the work of the same modeler, then the Hartford and Christie's figures could be confirmed as Mennecy, thus carrying the others

42

Clio (?)

1917.945

Mennecy, 1760–1765

Soft-paste porcelain, H. 6 × W. 3½ D. 2¹¹⁄₁₆ in. (15.2 × 8.9 × 6.8 cm)

Mark: incised D.V

Provenance: J. Pierpont Morgan

Of the same genre as the preceding figure of *Winter*, this model belongs to a different set of allegorical and mythological personifications. Her identification is not certain, but she possibly

43

along with them. Certainly the repertoire is compatible with the factory's production of Callot dwarfs in the Villeroy period. The complicating factor is the single marked figure, a richly dressed seated oriental holding a brocade ball and marked with a blue fleur-de-lis, now in the Pflueger collection.[12] Because of the mark and unusual style it has long been attributed to Buen Retiro or Naples,[13] but the modeling is entirely consistent with this group of grotesques, and Bernard Dragesco notes the similarity of the sprigs on the robes of the figure to the flower painting on Sceaux tablewares.[14]

If this group had originated at Sceaux it would not date before Jullien and Jacques began to produce porcelain there in 1763, an odd date for the reintroduction of this subject matter. Could the figures be Mennecy models that, being left white, were acquired by Jullien and Jacques after 1766 when they took up Mennecy's lease, and then decorated at Sceaux? Against a Mennecy attribution is the fact that none of the exotic figures—contrary to normal factory practice—is marked, and all are on a heavier and clumsier scale than is usual for Mennecy sculpture.

Exhibition: *Morgan Loan Exhibition*, New York, 1914, not in catalogue

Literature: Chavagnac, p. 18, no. 14

NOTES

1   APML, Cartier file, *composition des 10 colis*, 9 June 1905, no. 135: "1 Sujet grotesque (vieille femme) en Mennecy."

2   No. 33294. It is based on a Kändler model of about 1740.

3   5 March 1968, lot 160; and again, Christie's, London, 3 December 1979, lot 17. Bernard Dragesco brought this to my attention.

4   *Linsky Collection*, pp. 324–25, nos. 302–4.

5   Christie's, New York, 18 May 1989, lot 198; and again, Sotheby's, London, 13 June 1995, lot 221.

6   Sotheby's, London, 27 November 1956, lot 38.

7   MNC, Sèvres, no. 8789. Probably, but less clearly, associated with this group are two large, vaguely exotic unpainted figures of similar construction. (Sotheby's, New York, 25 October 25 1991, lots 346, 347.)

8   See note 10.

9   See note 3.

10   Mottola Molfino, 2, figs. 172, 173, 176.

11   Sotheby's, London, 13 May 1995, lot 221.

12   Morley-Fletcher, 2, p. 44. I wish to thank Bernard Dragesco for making this connection.

13   Comte R. d'Yanville sale, Drouot, Paris, February 20–22, 1907, lot 287 (Buen Retiro); Christie's, London, 11 October 1976, lot 37 (Naples or Spain, 1756–63); Morley-Fletcher, 2, p. 44, (Buen Retiro).

14   Verbal information.

Fig. 44-1 *The Peep Show*, detail from tapestry *The Charlatan and the Peep Show*, French, Beauvais, 1762

Fig. 44-2 *The Magic Lantern*, French, Sèvres, c. 1760, model by Étienne-Maurice Falconet, 1757

44

The Magic Lantern

1917.924

Mennecy, c. 1760

Soft-paste porcelain, H. 9⁷⁄₁₆ × W. 6½ × D. 5¹¹⁄₁₆ in. (24 × 16.5 × 14.5 cm)

Provenance: J. Pierpont Morgan

The scene is abstracted from a larger composition by François Boucher, his cartoon for one of a set of Beauvais tapestries, the *Fêtes Italiennes*, first woven in 1739 (fig. 44-1).[1] In it the proprietor of the magic lantern, a tall adult, stands in front manipulating the strings that change the scenes; at the right a woman holding a child bends over to peer inside while others look over her shoulder.

Although evidently referring to Boucher, this group corresponds neither to the original composition nor to the Sèvres biscuit version modeled by Falconet in 1757 in which the positions are altered and the personae transformed into *enfants Boucher* (fig. 44-2). The air of lackadaisical adolescence here is unexpected and quite at variance with Boucher's characterizations. And as the only known engraving of the cartoon—by Charles-Nicolas Cochin the Younger (1715–90)—follows the original,[2] Hartford's group must derive from another source.

The elongated curving figures are of a different physical type from that we associate with Mennecy, being closer to those of Tournai's attenuated spiraling *groupes tournants* than to the more upright Mennecy format. But the snub-nosed faces of the girls are consistent with those of Mennecy's musical children, and the palette and dress patterns have their Mennecy counterparts. What is presumably this model was cited by Chavagnac and Grollier, who found mention of a painted group representing *The Magic Lantern*, at 72 *livres*, in archives relating to Charles Hennique, the Parisian merchant who sold Mennecy (and other) porcelains.[3]

One other example of the model, apparently also unmarked, is known. Formerly in the A. Lion collection it was subsequently sold from the collection of Gilbert Lévy.[4]

Exhibitions: *Morgan Loan Exhibition*, New York, 1914; *European Porcelain*, New York, 1949, no. 132

Literature: Chavagnac, pp. 26–27, no. 28, pl. VII; *European Porcelain*, no. 132; Roth, "Morgan," p. 200, fig. 5

NOTES

1 Standen, 12, pp. 112–13.
2 Jean-Richard, pp. 155–56, no. 519.
3 Chavagnac and Grollier, pp. 104.
4 A. Lion sale, Drouot, Paris, 18–19 November 1908, lot 134; Gilbert Lévy sale, Drouot, Paris, 23 November 1967, lot 46.

45

This young girl with her garland is one of a few Mennecy figures of child-adults playing at rusticity. Another plays a psaltery,[1] a third carries a basket of flowers under her arm.[2] All are reminiscent of the *enfants Boucher*, those preadolescent children in country clothing engaged in various pastoral pursuits, modeled by Falconet and others at Vincennes and Sèvres. The Hartford figure evokes a more adult and sophisticated image by Boucher, known through engravings variously entitled *La Bouquetière*, *La Bouquetière galante*, and *La Belle Bouquetière*.[3] The Mennecy figures of this type differ from their Vincennes and Sèvres counterparts in the smartness of their clothes, fashionable about 1760; in this, they may have been inspired by the series of well-dressed mock-pastoral children produced at Meissen after about 1750.

There may have been other models of this group, as Sceaux produced a *faïence* chestnut seller in exactly the same manner and with a very similar base, an indication it might have been copied from a Mennecy original.[4]

The incised letter S also occurs on the psaltery player and on a "figurine de marquise en biscuit",[5] and is one of several letters noted by Chavagnac and Grollier awaiting interpretation.[6] From its prominent size and position it could represent the modeler; Charles Simon (active 1760–75) is the only sculptor recorded by Duchon with this initial working at this date,[7] but there is no real basis on which to make a connection.

Exhibition: *Morgan Loan Exhibition*, New York, 1914, not in catalogue

NOTES

1   *Nord-Pas-de-Calais*, p. 72, no. 37 (in the collection of the Musée et Château, Boulogne-sur-Mer). I am grateful to Laurence Libin for the identification of what he terms a common European folk instrument.

2   Jedding *Europäisches Porzellan*, p. 259, fig. 798 (Museum für Kunst und Gewerbe, Hamburg).

3   Jean-Richard, p. 128, no. 401 (*La Bouquetière*, by Carmontelle), pp. 303–4, no. 1237 (*La Belle Bouquetière*, by François Joullain), p. 389, no. 1612 (*La Bouquetière galante*, by J.B. Tilliard).

4   *Sceaux-Bourg la Reine*, pl. 6, no. 163 (collection Musée de l'Ile-de-France, Sceaux). Apparently en suite, judging from the catalogue description, are two biscuit figures (hts. 6, 6⅜ in. or 15.2, 16.2 cm) sold at Sotheby's, 29 March 1955, lot 118, one a girl playing the hurdy-gurdy, the other a boy playing a drum; both with elaborate coiffures, and ribbons. One was incised J.M.O. which, if intended for Jean-Baptiste Mô, would perhaps date this whole series a little later, as he was working at Mennecy 1768–71.

5   Comte R. d'Yanville sale, Drouot, Paris, 20–22 February 1907, lot 204. This could be the Morgan example, although its height is given as 17 cm (6¹¹⁄₁₆ in.)

6   Chavagnac and Grollier, p. 108. They note the letter S on a biscuit group of *Flora*, *Zephyr and Cupid* in the Grollier collection.

7   Duchon, p. 117.

45

Girl with a garland

1917.948

Mennecy, c. 1760–1765

Soft-paste porcelain (biscuit), H. 6½ × w. 2⅞ × D. 2⅝ in. (16.5 × 7.2 × 6.6 cm)

Mark: (incised inside base) D, V and S

Provenance: J. Pierpont Morgan

46a

46b

46

Girl and putto and two children

1917.919–920

Mennecy, 1755–1760 with later decoration

Soft-paste porcelain, 1917.919: H. 7⅞ × W. 4⅜ × D. 6 in. (20 × 11.2 × 15 cm); 1917.920: H. 6¹¹⁄₁₆ × 5⁵⁄₁₆ × D. 5³⁄₁₆ in. (17 × 13.5 × 13.2 cm)

Mark: DV incised inside base of 1917.919; D,V incised inside base of 1917.920

Provenance: J. Pierpont Morgan

The two groups are consistent in type with Mennecy's pairs of musical children (catalogue nos. 38 and 39), but are set on irregular rockwork bases rather than the more usual striated circular ones. They are further distinguished by the dishabille of the children and their relative inactivity conveyed at its extreme

by a third group, formerly in the Fritz Katz collection, in which two languid children recline end to end on their rocky mound.[1]

Related to these are two other groups in the Musée des Arts décoratifs, Paris.[2] One is a variant of 1917.919: the children are in essentially the same poses, but Hartford's boy is a putto while in the Paris version he is wingless. In the second Paris group the composition is about the same, but the boy clutches a spindle.

Of all the groups only Hartford's are marked. The Katz group was sold as Mennecy, and the Paris ones are justly assigned to Chantilly on the evidence of their tin glaze. More distantly associated is a sixth group, also Chantilly, in which two formally dressed children are seated side by side on rockwork, and are painted in a light coral-based palette normal for the factory.[3] The painting of Hartford's groups must, from its harsh palette and heavy-handed execution, be considered a later addition. Because of this it is difficult to determine whether they are the work of the same modeler as the child musicians, but points in favor are the high rounded forehead and ski-jump nose.

Such groups were undoubtedly intended as dessert-table decoration. Le Duc cites "neuf petites figures pour le dessert" in the Chantilly factory inventory of 1754;[4] and in 1765 Mennecy's

Paris stock included a wide variety of figures and groups some of which from the description—for example, the musicians—seem to have been intended for the purpose.[5]

Exhibitions: *Morgan Loan Exhibition*, New York, 1914, not in catalogue; *Antique Taste*, 1982 (1917.919)

Literature: Chavagnac, pp. 23–24, nos. 24–25; *Antique Taste*, 1982 p. 13 (1917.919)

NOTES

1 Fritz Katz collection, Sotheby Parke-Bernet, New York, 8 March 1979, lot 218. Another example, which seems from an illustration to be painted in a manner similar to Hartford's groups, was lot 89, Drouot, Paris, 3 December 1999.
2 Le Duc, *Chantilly*, p. 181.
3 Ader Tajan, Paris, 29 June 1994, lot 35.
4 Le Duc, *Chantilly*, p. 404.
5 Duchon, p. 149.

47

47

Woman playing a vielle

1917.941

French, modern

Soft-paste porcelain, H. 5⅝ × w. 3³⁄₁₆ × D. 2⁹⁄₁₆ in. (14.3 × 8 × 6.4 cm)

Mark: D,V. incised

Provenance: J. Pierpont Morgan

In type, the figure corresponds to unmarked Mennecy models of seated young women, some playing musical instruments. One, formerly in the Riggs collection, plays a mandolin;[1] a shepherdess from the same collection wears a pert hat brim[2] which, on another mandolin player,[3] is sharply tilted as it is here. Neither modeling nor painting of this figure warrants a Mennecy attribution, however. The chic upswept hairstyle and exaggerated hat brim are in twentieth-century spirit, as are the features of her damaged and restored face. Neither the flat unglazed base nor the form of the mark is consistent with Mennecy practice.

Exhibition: *Morgan Loan Exhibition*, New York, 1914, not in catalogue

Literature: Chavagnac, p. 21, no. 19

NOTES

1 Parke-Bernet Galleries Inc., New York, 7–8 February 1947, lot 278.
2 Ibid., lot 279.
3 Christie's, London, 5 June 1961, lot 63.

48

Snuffbox

1917.935

Mennecy (?), c. 1760 and later

Soft-paste porcelain, silver gilt, H. 1 × L. 2¹¹⁄₁₆ × D. 2 in. (2.5 × 6.8 × 4.9 cm)

Marks: (on silver): crossed laurel branches (Paris charge mark for small silver, 1762–1768); dog's head (Paris discharge mark for small silver, 1762–1768); weevil in rectangle (French mark for work imported from countries with Customs Conventions, 1893 to date)

Provenance: J. Pierpont Morgan

Presumably because of damage, the body of the box was cut down and a new cover supplied:[1] its molded pattern has a different rhythm and direction, and—uncharacteristically of Mennecy—a lobed reserve in the center is filled with a molded flower spray. The two parts have been unified by the application of a dense pink ground color.

The box was probably originally made at Mennecy, the only one of the French factories to produce basketweave snuffboxes in some variety and quantity. Examples with marked Paris mounts are dated between 1750–56 and 1756–62,[2] and nearly four dozen such boxes, some painted with flowers and figures, were listed in the inventory of stock taken in August 1762.[3] In every case the molded surface was left uncolored to emphasize the pattern of basketwork, casting further suspicion on the ground color of this box.[4] The interior of both body and cover are fluently painted with flower sprays consistent with Mennecy work, and being from the same hand, will have been added when the parts were assembled. The silver mounts, which fit badly in the box's present condition, could be the original ones.

Exhibition: *Morgan Loan Exhibition*, New York, 1914, not in catalogue

Literature: Chavagnac, p. 33, no. 39

NOTES

1 For a box of the period of this length, an appropriate height would be about 1½ in. (3.8 cm).

2 For example, Elizabeth Parke Firestone sale, Christie's, New York, 22 March 1991, lots 409, 416, 434, 437, 446, 457.

3 Duchon, pp. 145, 146.

4 For this reason, I would also question the only other Mennecy box I know of with a ground color, one with silver mounts and reserves against a dark blue field, sold at the Hôtel Drouot, Paris, 25 June 1968, lot 15.

48

Bourg-la-Reine Table Wares

49

Triple salt cellar

1917.931

Bourg-la-Reine, c. 1773

Soft-paste porcelain, H. 3¹/₁₆ × w. 4⅛ × D. 3¾ in. (7.8 × 10.5 × 9.5 cm)

Mark: BR incised under glaze on bottom

Provenance: Albert Gérard;[1] J. Pierpont Morgan

The model is borrowed from Sèvres where it was current in the early 1770s, notably in the service of 1771 for Madame du Barry (catalogue no. 138). The inventory of Bourg-la-Reine stock dated 25 May 1774, following the death of Joseph Jullien, recorded "salières à paniers à trois séparations,"[2] and Le Duc notes that the porcelains were classified by decoration, including white pieces with blue fillets and gold, as seen here.[3] Another example of the model in the Ashmolean Museum is painted in the usual Bourg-la-Reine manner with small sketchy sprigs.[4] The puce decoration of cloud-borne putti of Hartford's salt cellar is highly unusual both for the factory and for the period, but seems to have had a parallel—or precedent—at Sceaux in a cabaret in the Chavagnac collection.[5]

Exhibition: *Morgan Loan Exhibition*, New York, 1914, not in catalogue

Literature: Chavagnac and Grollier, p. 113; Chavagnac, pp. 30–31, no. 34

NOTES

1 Albert Gérard sale, Drouot, Paris, 18–23 June 1900, lot 326 (120 French francs).

2 Le Duc, "Bourg-la-Reine," p. 170.

3 Loc. cit.

4 Dawson, *Ashmolean*, pp. 54–55, no. 39.

5 Chavagnac and Grollier, p. 370: "Cabaret de cinq tasses et soucoupes et cafetière, décor amours dans les nuages en camiaeu carmin," with incised factory mark S.X (then in Chavagnac collection, but not in Chavagnac sale).

49

50

Toilet jars (*pots à pommade*)

1917.916–917

Mennecy, c. 1765 and Bourg-la-Reine, c. 1772

Soft-paste porcelain, 1917.916: H. 3⅜ × DIAM. 2⅜ in. (8.6 × 6 cm); 1917.917: H. 3⅜ × DIAM. 2⅜ in. (8.5 × 5.9 cm)

Marks: 1917.916: DV, S incised under glaze on bottom; 1917.917: BR incised under glaze on bottom

Provenance: J. Pierpont Morgan

Modest as they are, these are of interest as guides to the intertwined activities of three factories, Sceaux, Mennecy and Bourg-la-Reine, all at one time or another under the proprietorship of Charles-Symphorien Jacques and Joseph Jullien.[1] In 1763 the two men acquired the lease of the Sceaux *faïence* factory—where Jacques had been employed as a painter since 1754—and began producing soft-paste porcelain. Three years later they acquired Mennecy's lease from the widow of François Barbin, leaving it in the hands of local management while they remained at Sceaux. In 1772, Sceaux having been sold, Jacques and Jullien settled in the neighboring village of Bourg-la-Reine where they had already acquired property, and the next year registered the mark for their new Manufacture Royale de Fayance et de Porcelaine, while still continuing as lessee-proprietors of Mennecy.[2] Jullien died in 1774, and the inventory taken afterwards described a large quantity, at Mennecy, of material and fired but otherwise uncompleted stock including table wares, vases, sculptures and *pots à pommade*.[3] The opportunities for interfactory exchanges of models, decoration and personnel were natural and inevitable,[4] and it is not surprising to find this model produced at all three factories. A distinctive feature of flower painting on BR-marked pieces is the disk-like flower outlined in bright red, seen on one side of 1917.917; the painting on the two jars is so similar in design and sketchiness, although from different hands, that the Mennecy jar would seem to be an example of unfinished stock completed at Bourg-la-Reine. The flower painting of the two covers is again different, both from the jars and from each other, and is indicative of an extensive production that invited an eventual mismatch of parts.

Exhibition: *Morgan Loan Exhibition*, New York, 1914, not in catalogue

Literature: Chavagnac, pp. 22–23, no. 22

NOTES

1 This summary is based on Le Duc, "Bourg-la-Reine," pp. 162–75; and *Sceaux-Bourg La Reine*, pp. 23–24, 95–98.

2 The first historian of Bourg-la-Reine, Dr. Thore, writing in 1868, declared that on 27 July 1774 Jullien and Jacques registered "les marques B.R., pour Bourg-la-Reine, et D.V. pour Villeroi" (quoted by Darblay, p. 80). This has apparently not been verified, but the Mennecy mark was adopted by Jullien and Jacques at least once: a beautiful white figure of a river god in the V&A, London (no. C. 352-1909) is incised DV on the front ledge and painted underneath DV over BR in the same vivid blue. Honey (p. 21) suggested it had been left in the biscuit at Mennecy and glazed at Bourg-la-Reine, and the inventory of 1774 included 48 groups and single figures.

3 *Sceaux-Bourg La Reine*, pp. 95–96.

4 A particularly intriguing example is a Sceaux *faïence* plate painted with a luxuriant tulip and marked DV (*Sceaux-Bourg la Reine*, p. 43, ill. 60).

50

51

Child musicians

1917.932
Crépy-en-Valois, c. 1765
Soft-paste porcelain, H. 7⁹⁄₁₆ × W. 4⅝ × D. 4⅛ in. (19.2 × 11.8 × 10.5 cm)
Mark: DC'O incised

Provenance: J. Pierpont Morgan

Although clearly related to the Mennecy groups of child musicians, like those of catalogue nos. 38 and 39, the group is from the hand of a different modeler working elsewhere. Distinguishing features are the chalky material and matte white surface; the flat pear-shaped face of the boy; the pallid coloring; and the plain circular base with an unusual crescent-shaped depression on the underside.

A number of utilitarian pieces and sculptures marked DCO and DCP have been recorded,[1] and the majority are comparable in material and decorative style to Mennecy work. This was observed by Chavagnac and Grollier who proposed that those marked DCP were possibly made at Crépy-en-Valois, the letters of the mark signifying de Crépy:[2] the similarities of style could be readily accounted for by the fact that Crépy was founded in 1762 by Louis-François Gaignepain who had worked at Mennecy from 1754 until that year. In the same passage, Chavagnac and Grollier noted the existence of several pieces in their collection marked DCO, which they did not describe or attempt to attribute.[3] A link between this mark and Crépy has recently been made through entries in the daybook kept by Gaignepain's Paris partner, the *marchand-mercier* Pierre Bourgeois, from 1764 to 1767.[4] Between October 1765 and February 1766 the factory sold fifteen tobacco jars "en hure de Sanglier et Chien" [boar's head-shaped and dog's head-shaped]: the former would certainly seem to be represented by a pair of jars in the British Museum, marked DCO, their covers modeled as boars' heads.[5] If this connection is valid then the other porcelains so marked must also be thus assigned. In cataloguing this group for Morgan, Chavagnac attributed it unequivocally to

51

Crépy on the grounds of analogies between it and the descriptions of other groups in the daybook. The entries to which he was evidently referring were "two medium sized two-figure groups, flute players" sold on 15 January, 1765, and "a medium-sized two-figure group in white biscuit of a flute player and a hurdy-gurdy player standing on a plinth" sold later that year, on 7 September.[6] Hartford's group, while not corresponding exactly to either of these, nonetheless fits into a documented category of Crépy production. Another entry quoted by Chavagnac includes "les quatre parties du monde" [the Four Continents]:[7] one of these, a young girl representing Africa and marked CREPY, is in the Musée national de Céramique, Sèvres,[8] and Bernard Dragesco has observed that the hairstyle of Africa is identical to that of the girl in Hartford's group.

There is thus no reason not to attribute this group to Crépy, although there is still something inconclusive about this. The considerable variation in material and style among the DCO marked pieces seems strange for this short-lived factory—it closed in 1770—established by (one assumes) an experienced practitioner. The chalky whiteness and clumsiness of this group is matched by another of two seated boys in the Victoria and Albert Museum,[9] and differs markedly from the well-painted smooth glossiness of a Mennecy-like tureen and stand.[10] In turn, none of these is comparable to the creamy silkiness of two small figures marked CREPY in the Metropolitan Museum of Art.[11] Did Gaignepain come away from Mennecy with some of its paste which he subsequently had to replace with other formulas? Changes in paste do not appear to be related to the factory's several known or attributed marks, as the form of the mark on this group is the same as that on the British Museum tobacco jars, which are quite different in material and workmanship. The O, separated from the first two letters by a comma, can be read as the initial of a factory workman.

Exhibition: *Morgan Loan Exhibition*, New York, 1914, not in catalogue

Literature: Chavagnac, p. 31, no. 35

NOTES

1 An extensive list is published by Dawson, *British Museum*, p. 253.

2 Chavagnac and Grollier, p. 395.

3 Ibid. p. 395. None of these appears in the sale catalogue of Chavagnac's collection.

4 Dawson, *British Museum*, p. 253. Extracts from the same source, but without the identification of Bourgeois, were published by Chavagnac and Grollier, pp. 393–94.

5 Dawson, *British Museum*, pp. 251–54, no. 201. A third is in the British American Tobacco Collection (Gage and Marsh, 94–95, no. 13).

6 "… deux moyens groupes de deux figures, flûteurs" and "un moyen groupe de deux figures blanches, en biscuit, de joueur de flute et de vielle, debout sur terrasse." Chavagnac and Grollier, pp. 393–94.

7 Ibid., p. 393.

8 MNC, Sèvres, no. 13418.

9 No. C. 10-1915.

10 Sotheby Parke-Bernet, New York, 4 April 1972, lot 170 (Dr. William P. Harbeson).

11 Nos. 52.70.1, 2.

52

Children with a goat

1917.925

Tournai, 1760–1765

Soft-paste porcelain, H. 6¾ × w. 4⅛ × D. 3¹³⁄₁₆ in. (17.1 × 10.5 × 9.7 cm)

Mark: (incised on base) D.V

Provenance: J. Pierpont Morgan

The composition is based on, but departs from, an unusually peripatetic group by Jacques Sarazin (1592–1660). Executed in 1640, Sarazin's large marble was placed in the gardens of Marly in 1689.[1] In 1749 the sculptor Jean-Joseph Vinache was commissioned to make a copy, also in marble, and the group was transferred to Paris and deposited in the Salle des Antiques of the Louvre where it remained until the Revolution, Vinache's

52

copy (long since lost) having been given by Louis XV to Madame de Pompadour for the garden of her Elysée Hôtel.[2] About 1795 Sarazin's group was again moved, this time to the Jardin des Plantes in Paris, where it remained until acquired by the Louvre in 1925.[3]

Witness to familiarity with the sculpture, and to its popularity, are versions produced by several porcelain factories,[4] presumably as a result of the appearance of the marble in Paris in 1749, which must have caused something of a stir. Even so, Hartford's example is a far cry from the original. Although the modeler retained the two figures and the goat of Sarazin's composition, he considerably altered both character and pose. In the marble the goat stands quietly between two putti, one kneeling, the other standing, his hair rakishly wreathed in vine leaves; in this model, which is one of at least four versions,[5] the goat leaps with his forelegs off the ground as if to escape the teasing of two eighteenth-century scamps.

Chavagnac attributed Hartford's group to Mennecy, no doubt in part due to the mark, and that factory did produce a polychrome model closer to Sarazin's original composition than this one, although the goat has become a dog-like pet of two rather passive boys (fig. 52-1). Dismissing the mark as a false signal, Lucien Delplace correctly attributed Hartford's group to

Tournai in 1970.[6] Characteristic Tournai features are the wide-faced children with slightly sullen expressions and dead-white flesh tones, and the high polygonal base with its flat unglazed bottom. In other well-recognized Tournai versions the children are differently dressed and the figures are set either on a high waisted base with foliage or the more common Tournai base formed of high stepped rocky ledges.[7]

Betrayed by scratchiness and false starts the mark may have been added not so much to falsify an attribution as to enhance the value of what was thought, from its rosy pastel coloring, to be Mennecy work. The Tournai palette as applied to the sculpture is generally rather intense, even when the colors are pastel. The lightness of the tone of this painting suggests familiarity with Mennecy style, a familiarity that could have resulted from marketing practices, as both factories had outlets in Paris, which would have made their productions accessible to each other. An alternate possibility is that of shared workmen, supported by the marked similarity of composition of some of the *groupes tournants* of the two factories, but so far this remains undocumented.[8]

Exhibitions: *Morgan Loan Exhibition*, New York, 1914, not in catalogue; *European Porcelain*, New York, 1949, no. 133

Literature: Chavagnac, p. 27, no. 29; *European Porcelain*, no. 133; Buckley, *Antiques*, fig. 3; Delplace, pp. 86–87.

Notes

1 *Jacques Sarazin*, p. 42.

2 Furcy-Raynaud, "Bâtiments du Roi," p. 367.

3 Digard, "Museum d'histoire naturelle," pp. 160–63.

4 In addition to Tournai and Mennecy, Chelsea turned out a number of highly compressed scent bottles, c. 1765, perhaps—judging from facial characteristics—based on the Tournai model. Even farther removed from the marble, but still recognizable, is a Longton Hall group of two seated putti and a tame grape-eating goat on a scrolled rococo base (Watney, *Longton Hall*, pl. 64A).

5 Polychrome: Soil de Moriamé and Delplace, p. 338, cat. 638, pl. 75; Sir Bernard Eckstein sale, Sotheby's London, 30–31 May 1949, lot 28; white-glazed: Marien-Dugardin, p. 60, fig. 39; biscuit: Comtesse Mimerel sale, Drouot, Paris, 15–16 February 1939, lot 146.

6 Delplace, pp. 86–87.

7 Soil de Moriamé and Delplace, pl. 75; Eckstein sale, 1949, lot 28.

8 Mireille Jottrand wondered whether Nicolas Gauron, recorded at Mennecy in 1753 and active at Tournai 1757–64, might not have had a hand in the appearance of this model at both factories (*Porcelaines de Tournai*, p. 67, no. 69). For a brief consideration of the issue of comparable Mennecy and Tournai work see Le Corbeiller, "Tournai and Mennecy," pp. 54–59.

Fig. 52-1 *Children with goat*, Mennecy, c. 1760–65

Unattributed Figure

53

Harlequina

1917.942
French, the model c. 1760
Soft-paste porcelain, H. 6⅜ × w. 3⅛ × D. 3³⁄₁₆ in. (16.2 × 8 × 8.1 cm)
Provenance: J. Pierpont Morgan

The pose is the conventional one for Harlequina, established by Nicolas Lancret with his painting *Les Comédiens Italiens* of about 1725 to 1728, and widely disseminated through engravings and versions in porcelain.[1] As all the porcelain versions are in reverse of the painted image they will have been copied from any of several engravings, some of which isolated Harlequina from Lancret's composition and presented her as a single figure. Elias Meyer executed a model at Meissen around 1748[2] that could have been influential, but this version is more faithful to Lancret's pose than Meyer's.

The amount of repair and restoration is so extensive that it is all but impossible to determine the original character of this piece, which does not appear to be the work of any of the major French factories.

Exhibition: *Morgan Loan Exhibition*, New York, 1914, not in catalogue

Literature: Chavagnac, pp. 21–22, no. 20

NOTES
1 Hansen, pp. 127–29, figs. 96–103.
2 Meister, p. 327.

53

Vincennes and Sèvres

The Vincennes and Sèvres Factory

The factory[1] was founded at the château de Vincennes in 1740, by Claude-Humbert Gérin, with Roger and Gilles Dubois, formerly of the Chantilly factory. Jean-Louis Orry de Fulvy, *intendant des finances*, and half-brother to Louis XV's Minister of Finance, took charge of the fledgling operation in 1741, obtaining 10,000 *livres* from the Crown to support early research and development.[2] By March 1742 Gérin appears to have created a lovely, white Vincennes paste, at which time he left Vincennes to produce creamware at Pont-aux-Choux,[3] but he returned in 1746, building a new enamel kiln there, which was to remain in use until 1802.

In 1745 Orry de Fulvy, acting through his *valet de chambre* Charles Adam, applied for and was granted a royal privilege for "the manufacture of porcelain in the Saxon manner." Over the next few years Orry de Fulvy capitalized the enterprise by selling shares to various associates, with repeated capital calls to cover the factory's persistent financial needs. Orry de Fulvy died in 1751, at which time the Crown assumed control of the factory through the appointment of Jacques-Dominique Barberie de Courteille as the royal representative for finance and administration. The secrets of porcelain production were placed in the hands of Jean Hellot, director of the Académie des Sciences, who recorded them for posterity. In 1753 the company was reorganized under the name of Eloy Brichard, with one quarter of the shares going to Louis XV. At this time the factory became known as the *manufacture du roi*, and began to mark its wares with the royal cipher (interlaced Ls) and date letters. It was decided that the factory had outgrown its quarters at Vincennes, and plans were made to relocate in a new building at Sèvres, a village located between Paris and Versailles. The factory moved there in 1756, and productions from then on are referred to as Sèvres. In October 1759 Louis XV purchased the factory, and it has remained in the hands of the French State ever since.

The period between 1740 and 1745 appears to have been one of slow progress in the development of a suitable paste and glaze.[4] Between 1745 and 1749, however, enormous gains were made, including the creation of a large palette of colors, growing from sixteen in 1747 to about sixty in 1749.[5] Advances in kiln construction and firing were also made, and the secret of gilding porcelain was acquired in 1748. The chief productions during these years were flowers and sculpture.[6]

The early style at Vincennes was heavily indebted to Meissen porcelain, both for object design and decoration. Around 1750, the factory began to break from the influences of its German predecessor, significantly diversifying its models. The goldsmith Jean-Claude Duplessis provided new models, including service wares and decorative vases and flowerpots (see catalogue no. 54). In 1751 Jean-Jacques Bachelier, working under the direction of Hendrik van Hulst of the Académie des Beaux-Arts, was engaged to supervise the decoration of the porcelain and provide models for the artists. Together this new group of talented artists brought about a complete shift in style from Saxon- and Asian-inspired pieces to entirely original, French productions.

The 1750s were marked by the introduction of numerous forms and decorations. Duplessis was responsible for at least thirty vase designs, many of them reflecting the rococo style, such as the *pot-pourri à jour* (catalogue no. 56) and the *vase à oreilles* (catalogue no. 58). The number of service wares was dramatically increased, thanks partly to the commissioning of a large dinner and dessert service by Louis XV in 1752. Again, Duplessis is known to have created many new models for this service, including *plateaux porte-huiliers* (catalogue no. 82), *compotiers ovales* (catalogue no. 141), and *soucoupes à pieds* (catalogue no. 105). Tea services became a major part of the factory's production, with multiple variations of individual components. Trays designed for the table frequently were used for tea services as well. Various objects for personal use such as jugs and basins and broth basins were designed, including the rare fountain and basin designed by Duplessis in 1754 (catalogue no. 151).

One of the most important innovations of this decade was the introduction of biscuit sculpture in 1752. Duplessis was responsible for sculptural models, and he, in turn, looked to the pastoral work of François Boucher for inspiration. The sculptor Étienne-Maurice Falconet also contributed new models, including *L'Amitié* (catalogue no. 176), *L'Amour*, and *pendant de l'Amour* (catalogue nos. 173 and 174).

Great strides were also made in the factory's decorative repertory. Important ground colors were introduced, including the novel turquoise ground color found on Louis XV's service. Named *bleu céleste*, it became the most sought-after and expensive ground color produced by the factory and remained popular through much of the century. *Bleu lapis*, yellow, green, and pink also made their appearance in this decade. Enameled decoration became more varied, as the factory hired more painters. Flowers continued to be a key part of the decorative repertory, but they were joined by fruit, landscapes, birds, and above all, Boucher cupids and children. In the early part of the decade, elaborate gilding around the painted reserves flourished.[7] Overall gilding patterns also came into being in the 1750s, notably designs called *vermiculé* and *caillouté*.[8]

The 1760s saw a shift in the production of ornamental wares away from the sinuous curves and elaborate shapes and decoration of the rococo to a more restrained, classically influenced style.[9] Falconet was enlisted to design vases as well as sculpture, and may have been responsible for such models as the *vase ferré* (catalogue no. 69). Bachelier also designed vases in the neoclassical style, including the *vase à anses tortillées* (catalogue no. 72), as did Duplessis.[10]

At the same time, table and tea wares witnessed a much less dramatic evolution in style, and the same models that were popular in the previous decade were produced. Painted decoration changed subtly, and the same themes that were popular in the 1750s found an audience in the next decade as well. Ground colors or combinations did go in and out of fashion, the most important change being the introduction of *bleu nouveau* in 1763.[11] Gilding evolved more dramatically, and was characterized in this decade by increasing simplicity and geometry. The practice of mounting plain porcelain with gilt bronze to create vases came into being during this period (catalogue no. 65), as did that of mounting porcelain plaques onto furniture and other interior fittings (catalogue no. 155).

The 1770s were marked by the factory's introduction of hardpaste porcelain. This occasioned the establishment of additional workshops within the factory, and the development of new, high-temperature colors. This new development also had an impact upon the sculpture production, which from 1773 was the charge of Louis-Simon Boizot. In 1774 a special hard paste was developed specifically for sculpture allowing for more ambitious groups to be made, and from this time it seems that sculpture was no longer made in soft paste.[12] Production of soft paste did not cease altogether, however, and wares and vases were made in both pastes until the beginning of the nineteenth century.

Design in the 1770s continued in a firmly classical vein, although vases tended to be more innovative than did table and tea wares. The most notable exception was the extensive dinner and dessert service commissioned by Catherine the Great of Russia, which included a whole new range of decidedly classical models, and a new repertory of classical decorative motifs.[13]

In the next decade, models and decoration were often inspired by the discoveries of "Etruscan" antiquities at Herculaneum and Pompeii. The dessert service for Marie-Antoinette's dairy at Rambouillet, made in hard-paste porcelain and designed by Jean-Jacques Lagrenée, included several new models based on ancient forms, and featured a simplified decorative scheme using a variety of classical motifs.[14] Arabesque decoration became extremely fashionable, and was used for table and tea wares, as well as vases.[15] New ground colors emerged during this decade, for both soft and hard paste.[16] Yellow, which had rarely been used as a ground color since the early 1750s, enjoyed a strong revival.[17] Scientifically accurate botanical and ornithological illustrations became popular models for the decoration of table and tea wares towards the end of the decade, and continued to be used well into the 1790s.[18]

The last decade of the eighteenth century was a difficult one for Sèvres. Despite its royal association, the porcelain factory managed to stay in existence after the Revolution, even though the quantity and quality of its production suffered. Sales dropped dramatically, as its chief clientele, the aristocracy, had been executed or driven into exile. It was only at the beginning of 1800, when the factory came under entirely new management and France's political climate improved, that the once glorious enterprise was placed on the road to recovery serving the new *citoyens*.

NOTES

1 This summary is based on Aileen Dawson's introductions to Vincennes and Sèvres in her catalogue of the British Museum's French porcelain collection. Her account was, in turn, based on the pioneering research by Antoine d'Albis and Tamara Préaud, in such publications as d'Albis, "Premières années," passim; d'Albis, "Early years," passim; d'Albis and Préaud, "Datation," passim; d'Albis, "Gravant," passim, and Préaud and d'Albis, passim.

2 Gérin appears to have financed the factory on his own during the first eighteen months of its existence (d'Albis, "Early years," p. 12, quoting a letter from Gérin to Jean-François de Verdun de Montchiroux, AMNS, TAV. CLXXb).

3 As early as 1742 or 1743 Gérin's formula for porcelain paste had been stolen by François Gravant, who was working under Gérin at Vincennes. He sold the secret to the shareholders of the factory in 1748, taking credit for its discovery.

4 Préaud and d'Albis, p. 81.

5 Dawson, *British Museum*, p. 65.

6 See entries for cat. nos. 168–169, and cat. no. 55.

7 See cat. no. 148.

8 See cat. no. 63.

9 See Eriksen, *Neo-classicism*; Eriksen and Bellaigue, pp. 107–40.

10 He is thought to have designed such models as the *vase en burette* (cat. no. 68), and the *vase chinois* (cat. no. 71).

11 See cat. no. 158.

12 D'Albis, "Hard-paste," p. 47.

13 See cat. no. 144.

14 For more on this service and its models, see cat. no. 119.

15 See cat. nos. 117–19.

16 See cat. no. 122, and cat. no. 97.

17 Morgan's collection includes many soft-paste pieces with yellow grounds dating from the 1780s.

18 Cat. nos. 145–46; cat. no. 116.

54

Pair of vases (probably *urnes Duplessis*)

1917.977–978

Vincennes, 1749–1751

Soft-paste porcelain, 1917.977: H. 9⅛ × W. 5⅛ × D. 4½ in. (23.1 × 13 × 11.4 cm); 1917.978: H. 9 × W. 5⁵⁄₁₆ × D. 4¹¹⁄₁₆ in. (22.9 × 13.4 × 11.9 cm)

White ground with polychrome birds, gilding

Marks: interlaced Ls in blue with dot in center, above, and below on 1917.977; no marks on 1917.978

Provenance: J. Pierpont Morgan

MODEL

Jean-Claude Duplessis (c. 1695–1774) was the artistic director for models at Vincennes and Sèvres possibly from as early as 1745.[1] Among the many designs he created were those for *vases Duplessis* and *urnes Duplessis*. Both these types are often mentioned in the factory sales ledgers, stock lists and kiln records, but unfortunately drawings and plaster models only survive for the *vases Duplessis* and not for the *urnes*.[2] However, evidence in the factory records helps us to differentiate between the two types. While the *vase Duplessis* was available in four sizes and often decorated in a ground color, the *urne Duplessis* came in seven sizes[3] and no reference to ground color was ever given. Descriptions of *urnes Duplessis* in both the sales and painting kiln records show that in almost all instances they were decorated simply with flowers, either in gold or enamel colors.[4]

Most recent literature has muddied these distinctions, and seldom gives any attention to what form the *urne* might be.[5] Matters are exacerbated by the fact that two distinct shapes have both been labeled *vases Duplessis*. In reality only one of these shapes is correctly named. The true *vase Duplessis* has a wide trumpet body, low waist, and s-scrolled handles rising from the stem and belly, and examples are to be found in the Louvre, the Fitzwilliam Museum, Cambridge and the Minneapolis Museum of Art.[6] The other form, while still trumpet-shaped, has a central waist supporting coiled handles and is in all likelihood the *urne*.[7]

Surviving examples of what is here identified as the *urne* range in size from approximately 3⁹⁄₁₆ to 12⅝ inches (9 to 32 cm), which seems to be in line with the seven sizes in the records.[8] Furthermore, most surviving examples of this model are decorated with polychrome or gold flowers, matching the descriptions found in the factory's documents.[9]

Vases like the Atheneum's pair thus seem to have been erroneously labeled *vases Duplessis* when they were probably *urnes Duplessis*.[10]

Yet *urnes Duplessis* vary widely in detail with differences in the proportions of the neck, belly, or base. There can also be differences in the modeling. The neck may have large or small lobes, the latter either underscored by gadroons or left plain. The body may form a graceful curve or else have a marked central shoulder. The foot may be either lobed or plain while the base may be adorned with shells or rocks with flowers. Lastly, the handles may be simple coils or resemble entwined branches, with more or less abundant relief flowers and foliage on the sides.[11]

Urnes Duplessis appear in the sales ledgers as early as February 1753; seventy-five were sold between this date and December 1761. The prices were 24 *livres* for the seventh size, 36 for the sixth size, 36, 42, and 48 *livres* for the fifth size, 60, 72, and 84 *livres* for the fourth size, 72 and 108 *livres* for the third size.[12] Examples of the first and second sizes most often came from the *magasin de rebut* (storeroom for seconds) sold at 30 and 48 *livres*,[13] although in April 1753 Bazin bought one with flowers, of the second size, for 168 *livres*.[14] These urns were sold singly, in pairs,

54

54

and in garnitures of three. Sometimes, like *vases Duplessis*, they were filled with Vincennes flowers, and sold for considerably more.[15]

COMMENTARY

It is not common for *urnes Duplessis* to be decorated with birds, so this makes the Atheneum's pair particularly unusual though not unique, for birds do appear on another pair of *urnes Duplessis* sold in Paris in 1911.[16] There is a group of Vincennes pieces—perhaps the work of the painter Armand *aîné*—featuring fat-bellied birds posed in similar ways to those on the Hartford *urnes*. The small flying birds, most probably by Armand, on a tureen now at the Musée national de Céramique, Sèvres are also much akin.[17] However, the birds on the Hartford vases are less well executed and fall short of Armand's painterly skill: they have not been done with the same care, their feathers are not so regular nor so well articulated, and the palette is muddy with a lack of definition in the juxtaposition of the colors. We may say the same of the birds on the Paris *urnes*.[18]

The poses of the birds are reminiscent of many Vincennes early gilded birds as well. Similar purely fantastic, fat-bellied and long-necked birds may be found flying in the reserves of such pieces as a lapis ground ewer and basin in the Musée national de Céramique, Sèvres.[19] These similarities point to a common design source shared with French "lacquer" furniture and wall panels, namely the remarkable fascination with the style and motifs of Japanese lacquerwork.[20] The exotic bird that flies above the parrot on one of the Museum's pair exemplifies this wonderfully.

TECHNIQUE AND CONDITION

These vases probably were both thrown and molded, the body being thrown and the lobed neck and the foot being molded. The handles were modeled by hand and the relief flowers were made in Madame Gravant's workshop. Taunay's three purples can be found on the tips of the flowers and in the birds.[21] The birds are also colored with the very pale *bleu N° 1* as seen in a working palette belonging to the painter Armand *aîné*.[22] There is no *beau bleu* evident indicating the vases must have been decorated before this color was introduced in 1751.

There is a thin firing crack around the shoulder of 1917.977. In one place the painter has chosen to mask part of the crack with a painted leaf and leaf trail. The foot of 1917.978 has been broken off and repaired. There are corresponding repairs to the leaves around the foot. The entire vase sags, which may have occurred in the kiln.[23]

This pair of vases entered the Museum's collection on a pair of gilt-bronze bases. One of the bases appears to be nineteenth century in date, while the other one is probably from the eighteenth century.[24]

Exhibition: *Morgan Loan Exhibition*, New York, 1914, not in catalogue

Literature: Chavagnac, pp. 57–58, no. 67, pl. XVI

NOTES

1 Savill, 3, p. 977.

2 For details of these drawings and plaster models see cat. no. 59.

3 In the October 1752 and January 1753 inventories *urnes Duplessis* were listed in only five sizes, with molds and models in the sixth and seventh sizes appearing for the first time in the factory's inventory of January 1755 (for 1754). However, they feature among the turned pieces in the biscuit kiln records (IF 5673) from 1753, ranging from the third to seventh sizes (although *urnes Duplessis* are always listed as turned in the kiln records, molds and models of this form probably were made because of the foot). Furthermore, they are listed in the painting kiln records in 1754 and 1755, in the fourth through seventh sizes, all decorated with flowers (IF 5676, fols. 34, 39, 62). This leads us to suppose that all seven sizes were being made by at least 1753 even though molds and models for the smaller sizes were listed among new work for 1754. Curiously, while there are several existing vases of this shape in the first and second sizes, most examples in the kiln and sales records are of the third size and smaller.

4 The only exception to this in the sales records is two sold 24 November 1753, to an unnamed buyer, described as *fleurs camaïeu bleu* (AMNS, Vy 1, fol. 20). *Vases Duplessis* frequently are described as being decorated with *bleu lapis* or *bleu céleste* ground and other more elaborate types of decoration. See cat. no. 59 for more detail.

5 Préaud and d'Albis, p. 131, no. 63, describe this model as *vase Duplessis*, which they say was listed in seven sizes since 1752 (this is true of the *urne* not the *vase*. On p. 130, no. 60, they discuss a *vase Duplessis urne* (the MNC, Sèvres example) but fail to recognize it as the same model. Alexandre Brongniart, in the factory inventory of 1814, mentions a *vase à fleurs balustre rocaille*, which seems to describe the Atheneum's example and which is used in the 1977–78 *Vincennes* exhibition catalogue (pp. 141–42) to differentiate this model from other *vases Duplessis*. Tamara Préaud pointed out to the author that the title *urne* was often used to describe a covered vase, but this may not have always been the case. In the *Dictionnaire universel François et Latin* (*Dictionnaire de Trevoux*), Paris, 1771, p. 87, the Latin word *urna* is defined as "urne, vase, cruche." In this case no distinction between urn and vase is being made.

6 See *Vincennes*, p. 142, no. 426, and Eriksen and Bellaigue, pp. 242–43, no. 61 for the second type. This group is discussed in more detail below and in cat. no. 59. Yet another type of *vase Duplessis*, noted in the biscuit kiln records of 1753 as *vase Duplessis à enfans* or *sans enfans*, is similar in shape to the Louvre and Fitzwilliam models but distinguished by unevenly-sized lobes and, in the case of the vase *à enfans,* the addition of children, ususally in high relief, just at the fullest curve of the body. This type appears to be the only variant clearly distinguishable in the records. See Brunet, *Frick*, pp. 200–2; *Vincennes*, p. 140, no. 418.

7 Earlier attempts were made by scholars to distinguish these two models. Marcelle Brunet, while attributing the Atheneum-type vase to Jean-Claude Duplessis, did not link it to *vases Duplessis* in the documents (Brunet, *Frick*, pp. 206–8). Eriksen in fact suggested that the model may have been that known at the factory as *vase Chantilly*, a name that appears in the early stock lists and sales records (Eriksen and Bellaigue, p. 248). He notes the resemblance of the Vincennes vase to a known Chantilly model (example illustrated Honey, pl. 27), and comments on the relatively large quantity of *vases Chantilly* produced in relation to the large number of Atheneum-type vases to survive; 273 *vases Chantilly* were in stock in 1752. Another Vincennes model of this period, called *vase à fleurs à côtes* in the 19th century, appears even closer in design to the Chantilly model. However, known examples date from 1757 and 1758, and a drawing for this vase, inscribed *demande par Mons. Marmé 1757 2 piesse a anses premier et segonde grandeur* (AMNS, R. 1, L. 3, d. 9, fol. 1) suggests that the model dates only from 1757 and was called *vase Marmet* (see *Vincennes*, p. 137, no. 405). Variants of this vase can be found illustrated in Garnier, plates XII and XXXVI. Two vases similar to plate XXXVI are in MAD, Paris. The type shown in plate XII is the same form as a pair of Chantilly vases sold from the collection of Frédéric Halimbourg, Drouot, Paris, 22–23 May 1913, lot 68 (information on known examples kindly supplied by Tamara Préaud). Yet another Vincennes vase, called *vase Indien E* (this is a 19th-century name, which never appeared in the 18th century) or *vase à oignon*, also resembles a Chantilly *vase à oignon*, and it has been suggested

as a possible candidate for Vincennes' *vase Chantilly* (*Vincennes*, p. 144; for Chantilly onion vases see a pair formerly in the Fitzhenry collection, Drouot, Paris, 13–16 December 1909, lot 20). Eriksen, however, states that this could not be Vincennes' *vase Chantilly* because the latter was thrown and the four-lobed *vase Indien E* could not have been thrown in 1750 (see Eriksen and Bellaigue, p. 220).

8 Eriksen (Eriksen and Bellaigue, p. 247) states that vases of this shape are known in four sizes, $11\frac{7}{16}$, $9\frac{1}{16}$, $7\frac{1}{2}$ and $3\frac{15}{16}$ in. (29, 23, 19, and 10 cm). This author has recorded examples that appear to represent seven sizes: $12\frac{5}{8}$, $11\frac{7}{16}$, $8\frac{7}{8}$–$9\frac{7}{16}$, $7\frac{1}{2}$–$7\frac{13}{16}$, $5\frac{15}{16}$–$6\frac{1}{16}$, $4\frac{3}{4}$–$5\frac{1}{8}$, $3\frac{5}{8}$–$3\frac{15}{16}$ in. (32, 29, 22.5–24, 19–19.8, 15–15.4, 12–13, 9.2–10 cm). Of course, because most of these measurements are taken from published records and may be more or less accurate, trying to determine the variations within a single size is difficult. The covered example at the MNC, Sèvres, no. 8905, appears to be about $12\frac{5}{8}$ in. (32 cm) without its cover (now thought to be a later addition. I would like to thank Tamara Préaud for this information). Some examples are as follows: first size, MNC, Sèvres, no. 8905, H. approximately $12\frac{5}{8}$ in. (32 cm) (without cover—see above); second size, David Collection, Copenhagen, no. 21/1976 (Eriksen and Bellaigue, pp. 247–48, no. 64), H. $11\frac{7}{16}$ in. (29 cm); third size, MNC, Sèvres, no. 6255, H. $9\frac{1}{16}$ in. (23 cm); fourth size, Frick, New York (pair), nos. 34.9.4–5 (Brunet, *Frick*, pp. 206–8), H. $7\frac{1}{2}$ and $7\frac{13}{16}$ in. (19.1 and 19.8 cm); Art Institute of Chicago (pair), nos. 1959.474ab (Chicago, p. 121, no. 151), H. $7\frac{1}{2}$ and $7\frac{5}{8}$ in. (19.1 and 19.4 cm); fifth size, MAD, Paris, no. 28588, H. $5\frac{15}{16}$ in. (15 cm); sixth size, Louvre, Paris, no. OA 6240 (part of garniture of three, illustrated in Préaud and d'Albis, p. 131, no. 63), H. $4\frac{3}{4}$ in. (12 cm); seventh size, Ashmolean Museum, Oxford, no. 1968.275 (Dawson, *Ashmolean*, p. 56, no. 40), H. $3\frac{15}{16}$ in. (10 cm).

9 See examples in the V&A, London (nos. C. 357-359-1909); the Ashmolean Museum, the David Collection, Copenhagen; and the Louvre decorated with gilded flowers; MMA, New York (no. 24.214.4); Art Institute of Chicago; the Walters Art Gallery, Baltimore (no. 48.1794, in *Age of Elegance*, no. 146), for examples decorated with polychrome flowers. There is one pair known with ground color, in the Frick Collection, dated 1755, decorated at the top and bottom with *bleu céleste*. See note 8 above for the Copenhagen, Louvre, Chicago, Oxford, and Frick pieces.

10 A link between these names in the records with our model is suggested (without clarification) in *Vincennes*, p. 141, no. 421.

11 See *Vincennes*, pp. 141–42; Préaud and d'Albis, p. 131.

12 The earliest mention in the sales ledgers is of four *urnes Duplessis 5 gd. fleurs en or*, sold for 48 *livres* each on 3 February 1753 (AMNS, Vy 1, fol. 1v). In January 1753, two of the first size and two of the second size, both in white decorated with relief flowers were in the *magasin de ventes* priced at 60 and 30 *livres* respectively (AMNS, I. 7, 1 January 1753). The example in the MNC, Sèvres (no. 8905), probably corresponds to one of the two first-size urns listed here. In another unusual case, Duvaux paid 108 *livres* each for two imperfect examples of the third size (AMNS, Vy 1, fol. 6v). See also Vy 1, fols. 19, 20, 21, 21v, 35v, 41, 53, 53v, 54v, 77, 77v, 108, 120, 131, 137, Vy 2, fol. 8v, Vy 3, fols. 24, 26, 62.

13 AMNS, Vy 1, fol. 108, 16 December 1755, Bachelier, and Vy 1, fol. 137, 12 September 1756, Parseval.

14 Ibid., fol. 11 (*fournée* 25, late 1749).

15 Ibid., I. 7, 8 October 1752, under mounted vases in the *magasin de Vincennes* and the *magasin de Paris*, where urns of the third and fourth sizes were sold for as much as 380 *livres* and 250 *livres* respectively.

16 For another example decorated with very similar birds, clearly by the same hand, see Galerie Georges Petit, Paris, 22 May 1911, lots 30–31.

17 These works include a tureen in the MNC, Sèvres (nos. 21570 and 21779, illustrated *Vincennes*, p. 131, no. 389), another tureen in the Cleveland Museum of Art (no. 52.3), and a plate in the Musée et Château, Boulogne-sur-Mer, France (Préaud and d'Albis, p. 151, no. 116). Cups and saucers at the MMA, New York (nos. 50.211.172, 173) the Philadelphia Museum of Art (no. 42-59-124), and the British Museum (nos. 1989, 5–6, 4, Dawson, *British Museum*, p. 82, no. 77) may also be by the same artist, although the marks are not drawn with the same characteristic flourish as those on the tureens and on later Armand pieces. Clare Le Corbeiller was the first to point out the similarity between the way the birds are painted, and David Peters echoed this opinion on a visit to the Museum.

18 See note 16 above.

19 MNC, Sèvres, no. 26318.

20 This type of flying bird— appearing frequently in decorative interiors and objects from the last quarter of the 17th century and the first half of the 18th century—ultimately derives from Japanese lacquer. See, for example, a cabinet with Japanese lacquer panels in the Philadelphia Museum of Art, attributed to Weisweiler, c. 1785–90, no. 1963-188-1 (although the cabinet is later than the vases the lacquer is of the type that was popular in the 1750s). Many European pieces reflecting this influence are illustrated in Huth, including a Berlin corner cupboard from 1725, Schloß Charlottenburg (figs. 174–75), and a Dresden cabinet from c. 1715, in the Rijksmuseum (figs. 192–93). For the influence of lacquer on French decorative arts, see Watson, "Lacquer."

21 According to Antoine d'Albis, these colors were expensive and used sparingly.

22 See d'Albis, "Inventaire," p. 369.

23 It may also be the result of the way the vase was reattached to the foot during repair, although this is less likely.

24 The bases were examined by Theodore Dell.

55

Basket of flowers

1917.1234

Meissen and Vincennes, c. 1740s and 1751

Soft- and hard-paste porcelain, gilt bronze, silk, embossed fabric, overall height 24 in. (61 cm)

Basket, white with blue floral centers, polychrome flowers

Marks: none visible

Provenance: Heirs of comte Rouget, Paris (by report); Jacques Seligmann, London and Paris, 1900;[1] J. Pierpont Morgan

Model

The making of porcelain flowers at Vincennes began at least by 1741.[2] It has been plausibly suggested that Henriette Gravant began modeling flowers for Vincennes as early as September of that year, when her husband François was engaged by the factory.[3] In the period 1745 to 1748, flowers were the principal production of the factory. Madame Gravant directed a workshop of women and girls, probably outside the factory, where the porcelain flowers were made by hand after silk and fresh blooms. By 1749 the workshop had grown to a staff of forty-five.[4]

The porcelain flowers were sent in a leather-hard state to the Vincennes factory to be biscuit and glaze fired,[5] and then to be painted by Louis-Jean Thévenet and his wife Françoise Elisabeth.[6] In 1748 the Thévenets were put in charge of a factory workshop devoted to this purpose. In the second half of 1745 alone they decorated more than one thousand flowers. From 1747 to 1752 Claude Le Boitteux was paid to mount flowers on stems of *cannetille* (a fine metal wire wrapped in silk) garnished with silk leaves.[7] Flowers were also mounted on gilded or lacquered (*vernis*) brass, with foliage made of the same material. In both cases the arrangement of the flowers and the forms of the leaves were made to imitate nature.[8]

From 1748, Jean-Claude Duplessis and Le Boitteux were engaged in making the gilt-bronze stands (*terrasses*) for vases of Vincennes flowers.[9] The factory had already given a porcelain bouquet to Madame de Pompadour in 1747, and in 1748 it presented a large vase of flowers on a gilt-bronze stand with three small, sculpted figures to the queen, Marie Leczinska.[10] The best-known example of this type is the bouquet that the Dauphine, Marie-Josèphe of Saxony, presented to her father Augustus III, proprietor of the Meissen porcelain factory. Comprising a large white vase, incrusted with porcelain flowers, it was filled with a huge display of blooms, and sat on a sumptuous gilt-bronze terrace accompanied by two white porcelain groups called *Enfants des arts*. The entire ensemble stood more than three feet high.[11] These bouquets were meant to impress the French and Saxon courts with the quality of porcelain goods being produced by the young Vincennes factory.

FUNCTION

The primary purchasers of Vincennes flowers were the Paris *marchands-merciers*. Between 1745 and 1748 they spent more than 50,000 *livres* to acquire more than 80,000 flowers (or stems). The flowers were used to create bouquets, which were put in Vincennes vases or Meissen baskets. They were also used extensively to decorate clocks, wall lights, and candelabra. In 1749 Lazare Duvaux sold the Dauphine two pairs of wall lights described as having three branches of lacquered metal meant to imitate nature, decorated with the appropriate Vincennes flowers. The flowers are described as well, and on one pair of lights included, on the first branch, lilies, tulips, jonquils, narcissus, and blue hyacinths, on the middle branch, roses, and on the third branch, anemones, violets, and red stock. The junction of the branches was garnished with different flowers and the bottom with primrose and bachelor's buttons. The second pair of lights had double carnations, cornflowers, orange blossoms, tulips, bellflowers, anemones, Dutch hyacinths (*jacinthes d'Hollande à quatre cœurs*), double jonquils, bachelor's buttons, and *grosses jacinthes à cœur de rose*.[12] Each pair cost 1,200 *livres*.

COMMENTARY

The Museum's basket was made at the Meissen porcelain factory in Germany, probably in the 1740s.[13] The flowers are Vincennes soft-paste porcelain. The credit book of Lazare Duvaux describes many objects employing Vincennes flowers, including several bouquets in Meissen baskets. In 1749 Monsieur Genssin paid 1,500 *livres* for a capacious Meissen basket on a large gilt-bronze stand, garnished with many plants in lacquered copper and beautiful Vincennes flowers.[14] He purchased another, smaller basket one year later for 840 *livres*.[15] In 1751 the duchesse de Béjar paid 336 *livres* for what must have been a considerably smaller Meissen basket of Vincennes flowers on a gilt-bronze stand.[16]

It is difficult to determine how near the Museum's basket of flowers is now to the way it was in the eighteenth century.[17] The flowers include anemones, tuberose, lilies, sweet william, hawthorn, lily-of-the-valley, cornflowers, ranunculus, orange blossoms, carnations, china asters, small jonquils, double

jonquils, white narcissus, and French marigolds. There are also some flowers that are difficult to identify, including what the factory listed as hollyhocks, mock-anemones (*façon d'anemone*), *fleurs des champs bleues*, and white flowers with yellow hearts (*fleurs blanches à cœur jaune*). In matching the flowers in the Museum's bouquet to the prices of Vincennes flowers as they were valued in the factory inventory of 1 October 1759, it becomes apparent that the flowers alone must have cost over 200 *livres*.[18] Supplemented by the *cannetille* stems, silk leaves, Meissen basket, and gilt-bronze mounts, the ensemble would have cost considerably more, perhaps in the range of 600 to 800 *livres*.

It is unclear how many of the surviving eighteenth-century bouquets that have appeared in private collections and on the art market are genuine, for some may have been reconstituted, and others made up entirely of flowers from other porcelain factories (and not always of eighteenth-century date).[19] There are only a few others in public collections, notably the flower vase in the Musée national de Céramique, Sèvres,[20] and the ensemble sent to the Saxon court. A similar but smaller basket with simpler gilt-bronze mounts was on the Paris art market in 1992.[21]

TECHNIQUE AND CONDITION

The stems of the Museum's bouquet have been rewrapped and adorned with nineteenth-century fabric leaves. Although some of the bunches probably are as they were in the eighteenth century, there are some stems with two or three types of flowers on them, indicating they were remounted in the nineteenth century. Some silk, probably original, is visible on the upper portion of the lily stem as well as on some of the double jonquil stems. Some of the flowers are painted with *beau bleu*, showing that at least these blossoms were decorated in or after 1751.[22]

Exhibitions: *Morgan Loan Exhibition*, New York, 1914; *Morgan*, Hartford, 1987, no. 58

Literature: *Morgan Loan Exhibition*, facing p. 136; Hutton, "Meissen," pp. 160–61, no. 58; McCaughey, pp. 112–13, pl. 38

NOTES

1 APML, Seligmann file, invoice 14 May 1900: "1 Old Dresden China basket with old Sèvres flowers mounted in guilt [*sic*] bronze. This object comes from the heirs of Comte Rouget of Paris and is guaranteed old but I think that the mount has been reguilt [*sic*]," £500.

2 Préaud and d'Albis, p. 80. For the most extensive account of porcelain flower production at Vincennes, see d'Albis and Préaud, "Bouquets," passim.

3 Préaud and d'Albis, pp. 80–81; d'Albis and Préaud, "Bouquets," p. 71.

4 Préaud and d'Albis, p. 207. Her husband François Gravant furnished the Vincennes factory with its paste and glaze from 1744. Although there is no specific mention of the location of Mme Gravant's workshop, Tamara Préaud believes that the Vincennes factory was far too small to house forty-five women and girls.

5 D'Albis and Préaud, "Bouquets," pp. 75–76.

6 Payments to Thévenet and his wife are documented from 1745. See Préaud and d'Albis, pp. 81–82.

7 Préaud and d'Albis, p. 84. *Cannetille* was used primarily to make embroidery and *passementerie*, especially fringe. Diderot (*Encyclopédie*, IV, p. 600) defined it as gold or silver thread, of varying fineness, which was

55

rolled on the long iron needle of a spinning wheel. *Cannetille* was made and used by the guild of *passementiers-boutonniers*.

8   See LD, 2, p. 28, no. 287, 11 August 1749, Monsieur de Jullienne: "Un très-gros bouquet de différentes plantes en laiton verni imitant la nature, garni de fleurs de porcelaine de Vincennes assorties à chaque plante [a very large bouquet of different naturalistic stems of painted brass, garnished with Vincennes porcelain flowers to match each stem], 1,440 l." See d'Albis and Préaud, "Bouquets," p. 75.

9   Préaud and d'Albis, p. 84.

10 The ensemble is described by the duc de Luynes, quoted in d'Albis and Préaud, "Bouquets," pp. 72–73: "Ce vase est en porcelaine blanche travaillée. Il est accompagné de trois petites figures blanches, le tout est monté sur un pied de bronze doré. Dans le vase, il y a des fleurs naturelles, aussi en porcelaine. Monsieur de Fulvy nous a dit qu'il y avait quatre cent quatre-vingt fleurs. Le pied, le vase et le bouquet peuvent avoir environ trois pieds de haut. La monture seule en bronze doré coûte cent louis. La porcelaine à peu près autant; c'est un ouvrage parfait dans son genre. [The vase is made of white porcelain. It is accompanied by three small white figures, the ensemble mounted on a gilt-bronze pedestal. In the vase there are naturalistic flowers, also in porcelain. Monsieur de Fulvy told us that there were 480 flowers. The pedestal, the vase, and the bouquet may have been about three feet tall. The gilt-bronze mount alone cost 100 *louis*. The porcelain about as much; it is a perfect work of its kind.]"

11 Approximately 43¼ in. (110 cm). It is now in the Porzellan Sammlung of the Zwinger, in Dresden. See Préaud and d'Albis, p. 134, no. 66, illustrated also in color p. 6.

12 LD, 2, p. 22, no. 226, 27 May 1749.

13 See Hutton, "Meissen," p. 160 for a discussion of the Meissen production of baskets.

14 LD, 2, p. 20, no. 205: "Une grande corbeille de Saxe sur une grande terrasse & console de bronze ciselé & doré d'or moulu, garnie de plusieurs plantes en cuivre verni & fleurs de Vincennes très-belles."

15 Ibid., p. 51, no. 521: "Une corbeille de Saxe montée en bronze doré d'or moulu, garnie de fleurs de Vincennes, de 35 louis, 840 l."

16 Ibid., p. 101, no. 941, 5 November 1751: "Une corbeille de Saxe montée en bronze doré d'or moulu, garnie de branchages vernis & fleurs de Vincennes."

17 The bunches may be close to their original state, with the exception of the cornflowers and sweet william—they seem to have been recombined on two different stems (along with an unidentified blue flower on one of the stems).

18 AMNS, I. 7, 1 January 1759, *fleurs non montées*.

19 By the mid-1750s, small workshops in Paris were making flowers in the Vincennes style, and flooding the market with their wares. Antoine d'Albis and Tamara Préaud have suggested that this may be part of the reason why the salability and production of Vincennes flowers seem to wane so suddenly in this period. Even Lazare Duvaux may have been tempted by these imitations, for in 1753, he sold the duc de Villeroy "Une paire de bras à double branche, vernis, garnis en fleurs peintes dans le goût de celles de Vincennes" (LD, 2, pp. 160–61, no. 1437, 7 June 1753). See d'Albis and Préaud, "Bouquets," p. 76.

20 MNC, Sèvres, no. 25058 (Préaud and d'Albis, p. 146, no. 101).

21 H. 15¾ in. (40 cm), illustrated in d'Albis and Préaud, "Bouquets," fig. 3.

22 *Beau bleu* was introduced in 1751. See Préaud and d'Albis, p. 216.

56

Pair of pot-pourri vases (*pots-pourris à jour*)

1917.982–983

Vincennes, 1752–1753

Soft-paste porcelain, 1917.982: H. 10⁵⁄₁₆ × DIAM. 6⅝ in. (26.1 × 16.8 cm); 1917.983: H. 10⅛ × DIAM. 6⁹⁄₁₆ in. (25.7 × 16.6 cm)

White ground with applied flowers, rich polychrome painted flowers and gilding

Marks: elaborate interlaced Ls in blue

Provenance: A.B. Daniell & Sons, London, 1901;[1] J. Pierpont Morgan

MODEL

This form of pot-pourri vase was most likely called *pot-pourri à jour*, after the openwork (*à jour*) of the shoulders and cover.[2] The model was undoubtedly designed by Jean-Claude Duplessis and known at the factory from at least October 1752. The inventory of that year lists four molds, of unspecified size, and examples of the first and third sizes, with or without piercing.[3] With the exception of one entry in 1756, which documents the sale of examples of the second and fourth sizes from the *magasin de rebut*,[4] only the first and third sizes appear in the sales ledgers.[5] Surviving examples are only of the first or third size and thus match the ledgers.[6] Seemingly the factory only produced to completion these two sizes. The Museum's pots-pourris are of the first or largest size. The relief flowers that frame each lobe of the Museum's vases do not appear on all examples of this model.[7]

Three other models of pot-pourri vases were made at Vincennes before 1752, the *pot-pourri Pompadour*, *pot-pourri fleurs en relief*, and an unidentified model simply called *pot-pourri*.[8] While several *pots-pourris à jour* feature in the 1752 inventory of the factory, none can be identified with the Wadsworth Atheneum's pair. One example of the first size was listed as glazed and ready to be sent to the painters' studio in the 1752 inventory. Another example of the first size appears in the next year's inventory, also ready to be painted. At that time, before decoration, both were valued at 60 *livres*.[9] Four others of the first size, glazed and apparently defective, also appear in the inventory of 1753, still valued at 60 *livres*.[10]

COMMENTARY

The sales ledgers show that at least twenty-one pots-pourris of this model were sold in 1753, but only two of them of the first size. One was decorated with monochrome flowers and sold to Lazare Duvaux for 240 *livres*,[11] and the other decorated in *bleu lapis* and gold and sold to Madame de Pompadour for 132 *livres*.[12] The Atheneum's pots-pourris must have cost considerably more than 240 *livres* each. The elaborate polychrome bouquets would have commanded a higher price than the

monochrome floral decoration on the Duvaux piece. Moreover, the flowers are painted in the most lavish Vincennes colors including iron red, the newly introduced *beau bleu*,[13] and all three of the high-quality purples (pink, red and violet) supplied to the factory since 1744 by Salomon Taunay.[14] Taunay's purples were expensive and their generous use on these vases, both in the painted flowers and tipped onto some of the relief flowers, must have added greatly to the cost. The considerable amount of gold that highlights the piercing and relief molding would also have increased their worth.

While in the 1740s Vincennes emulated Meissen's "wood-cut flowers" of the 1730s and early 1740s, the style of Vincennes flower painting in the very early 1750s became more naturalistic in keeping with the style of the "German flowers" which had come into prominence at Meissen around 1745.[15] However, the use of bright, clear colors enhanced by the introduction of a brilliant blue (*beau bleu*) brought about a unique Vincennes style.[16] The floral painting on the Museum's vases reflects this growing naturalism and the assertion of a style no longer drawing on the Meissen model. Thenceforward flowers tended to be in bouquets rather than scattered individually across the porcelain. The dark outlining of the "wood-cut" style disappeared, and one can readily imagine the porcelain painter using bunches of real flowers for his model as well as naturalistic botanical and ornamental prints then available.[17] At the same time, with the broader palette at their disposal, Vincennes painters were now able to look to French and Dutch easel painting for inspiration. The October 1752 inventory of the factory records thirty-one paintings of flowers (by different hands), and seventeen drawings of the flowers from *La bibliothèque du Roy*.[18] Jean-Jacques Bachelier, artistic director, also supplied his own designs for plates decorated with flowers, presumably to be used for models; he probably prepared the same type of painted model for other forms and decorations.[19]

It has not yet been possible to attribute the outstanding flower painting of the Museum's vases to a particular artist, although stylistically we may endeavor to link his work to other Vincennes pieces decorated in this idiom from the early 1750s. The large tureen and stand now at the Musée national de Céramique, Sèvres is almost indubitably by the same anonymous hand, while a water jug at the Museum of Fine Arts in Boston, the first-size *pot-pourri Pompadour* at the Gardiner Museum in Toronto, and an *urne Duplessis* at the Metropolitan Museum of Art are likely to be by this artist.[20] Other slightly earlier pieces (including a punch bowl sold in London in 1985 and now in the Louvre, a broth basin and stand also in the Louvre, another broth basin in a Paris private collection, and a plate in the Musée national Adrien Dubouché, Limoges, France) may also be by this painter.[21] Beside the stylistic similarities of the flower painting shared by these pieces, all of these objects are marked with very ornate interlaced Ls, although, oddly, none of them the same.[22]

We may safely conclude that whoever painted these pieces— not forgetting the Atheneum's vases—must have been among Vincennes' best flower painters, for the quality of draftsmanship is supreme. In the late 1740s and early 1750s, the most highly paid flower painters working at the factory were Louis-Jean Thévenet *père*,[23] Claude-Joseph Cardin,[24] and Pierre-Louis Philippe Armand *jeune* or *cadet*.[25] This last painter earned the most, and may well have decorated the factory's most outstanding early pieces.

Taking the idea farther, we should now examine another tureen and stand painted with birds and flowers at the Musée national de Céramique, Sèvres. The flowers and foliage on both this tureen and stand are remarkably like those on the Atheneum's pots-pourris in style and exquisite quality. So much so that it seems reasonable to suppose that they were also painted by the same hand. We know for sure that birds on the tureen were painted by Armand *aîné*, the bird painter, for it bears his mark. What is interesting to note, though, is that the stand carries another, unidentified ornate mark, not unlike those on the Atheneum's pot-pourri vases, but we do not know whose it is.[26] Might not this mark be that of the best flower painter at the factory, who was in fact the bird painter's brother? In other words, might not Pierre-Louis Philippe Armand have worked alongside his brother in decorating this set? If so, it seems tempting to suggest, albeit cautiously, that Armand *jeune* painted the Museum's vases.[27]

TECHNIQUE AND CONDITION

These pot-pourri vases were molded.[28] After drying they were carved in the leather-hard state to create the piercing and other details prior to firing. The relief flowers on the finials and sides would have been bought from the atelier of Madame Gravant and applied by the factory's *répareurs*.[29] While all the colors are of the highest quality, they are slightly devitrified, probably due to the multiple firings required to produce the vases.[30]

Exhibitions: *Morgan Loan Exhibition*, New York, 1914, not in catalogue; *European Porcelain*, New York, 1949, no. 167; *Morgan*, Hartford, 1987, no. 59

Literature: Chavagnac, pp. 62–63, no. 74, pl. XIX; *European Porcelain*, no. 167; Hood, *Connoisseur*, p. 131, fig. 1; Hood, *Bulletin*, p. 2, fig. 1; Hood, *Apollo*, p. 36; Dauterman, *Wrightsman*, p. 192; Eriksen and Bellaigue, pp. 71, 246, pl. 63; de Bellaigue, "Sèvres," pp. 164–65; McCaughey, pp. 114–15, pl. 39

NOTES

1 APML, Daniell file, invoice 17 July 1901: "A pair of very fine Sèvres-Vincennes porcelain vases and covers, with flowers and foliage in relief on white ground, with flowers painted on the four panels, perforated necks and covers, Highest quality & extremely rare—originally given by Marie Antoinette, & Louis XVI, to the Abbes de Ronceray," £2,200. This provenance is unlikely as these highly rococo pot-pourri vases would have been antithetical to the taste of Marie-Antoinette and thus probably would not have been given as gifts.

2 Eriksen and Bellaigue, p. 246.

3 AMNS, I. 7, 8 October 1752, and 1 January 1753. See *Vincennes*, p. 91, where it states that eighty were sold costing between 60 and 300 *livres*. I have been able to find fifty-one sold from the *magasin de rebut*, and only thirty-seven decorated examples in the sales records through 1757.

4 AMNS, Vy 1, fol. 131, covering a block sale to de la Croix in which individual prices are not given. It is likely that the objects were all in the white. Previous literature including *Vincennes*, p. 91, states that this model was made in three sizes, as suggested by the mention of a first and third size in the inventories. In fact, the second size is never specifically

mentioned in the inventories, and is only mentioned this once in the sales records. De Bellaigue notes the appearance of the fourth size in the 1756 entry cited above ("Sèvres," p. 165 n. 2) and interprets it as a late introduction of an additional size.

5 For decorated examples sold, see AMNS, Vy 1, 1753, first size: fols. 6, 7; third size: fols. 3, 4, 7, 21v, 23, 26v, 27v; 1754, first size: fol. 61v; third size: fols. 48, 54v; 1755, first size: fol. 86; third size: fol. 100v; Vy 2, 1756, third size: fols. 9, 12; unspecified sizes: fol. 14v (probably one of the first and one of the third size).

6 A survey of existing examples suggests that the first size ranges from 10¼ to 10⁷⁄₁₆ in. (26 to 26.5 cm) and the third size from 7 to 7¹¹⁄₁₆ in. (17.8 to 19.5 cm). De Bellaigue suggests ("Sèvres," p. 165) that the Atheneum's pair is of the first or second size. It seems sure, however, that they are of the first size. Extant examples of the first size include: MMA, New York, *bleu céleste*, birds, relief flowers, c. 1753–54; MMA, New York, *bleu céleste*, flowers, c. 1753 (no. 1976.155.157); Sotheby's, Monaco, 25–26 May 1975, *lapis oiseaux or*, c. 1752–53 (perhaps sold to Mme de Pompadour 12 March 1753 for 192 *livres*, AMNS , Vy 1, fol. 7). Extant examples of the third size include: MAD, Paris, pair, *lapis oiseaux colorés* (perhaps sold to Duvaux, 31 December 1753 for 120 *livres* each, Vy 1, fol. 27v); MAD, Paris, in biscuit, with relief flowers; David Collection, Copenhagen, pair, green ground, flowers, c. 1750–52 (Eriksen, *David Collection*, p. 62, no. 27, inv. 5/1975); Christie's, Monaco, 7 December 1987, pair, *enfants camaïeu*, c. 1752 (several appear in the sales records for 1753, ranging from 72 to 120 *livres*); Sotheby's, Monaco, 25–26 May 1975, pair, *lapis oiseaux or* (with one of the first size, listed above, and probably also sold to Mme de Pompadour on the same date); MNC, Sèvres, *enfants camaïeu bleu*; MNC, Sèvres, *enfants camaïeu pourpre*; Drouot-Richelieu, Paris, 6 May 1994, pair, *enfants camaïeu chair colorés*, 1754.

7 Préaud and d'Albis, p. 148.

8 See Eriksen and Bellaigue, p. 71, and AMNS, I. 7, 8 October 1752.

9 AMNS, I. 7, 8 October 1752 and 1 January 1753.

10 Ibid., 1753.

11 AMNS, Vy 1, fol. 6, 20 December 1753. The one sold to Duvaux must have had very lavish monochrome flowers and a lot of gilding to have cost 240 *livres*.

12 Ibid., fol. 7 (17 March 1753 Pompadour).

13 Préaud and d'Albis, p. 216.

14 See d'Albis, "Pourpres," pp. 231–32. These shades of purple were achieved by using ruby glass rather than purple of Cassius. The variations from pink to violet were due to different proportions of gold and variations in the composition of the flux.

15 See Eriksen and Bellaigue, pp. 82–83; Rückert, p. 129.

16 See note 13. See also Préaud, "Sources iconographiques," p. 107.

17 Ibid.

18 AMNS, I. 7, 8 October 1752; the drawings are part of a list of *Desseins Et Estampes de différens maîtres*. The paintings cited must have included many by Bachelier, as well as works by Jan van Huysum (Dutch, 1682–1749). See Eriksen and Bellaigue, p. 85, citing Abbé Le Blanc who states that the painters copied the flowers of van Huysum and Bachelier. See also Préaud, "Sources iconographiques," passim.

19 AMNS, I. 7, 8 October 1752: *Tableaux anciens de M. Bachelier: 15 [forme d'assiettes] a fleurs*. See Savill, 3, pp. 961–64 for Bachelier (active 1748/51–93).

20 MNC, Sèvres, *terrine (ancienne) et plateau*, c. 1751–52, no. 23414, in Préaud and d'Albis, pp. 33, 96, no. 22; *broc ordinaire*, MFA, Boston, c. 1751–53, Forsyth Wickes Collection, no. 65.1871 (Munger, *Wickes*, pp. 163–64, no. 111, also in Préaud and d'Albis, pp. 96–97, no. 23); Gardiner Museum, Toronto, no. G83.1.1095; MMA, New York, no. 24.214.4.

21 Christie's, London, 1 July 1985, lot 43; *écuelle à quatre pans ovale*, c. 1749–53, Louvre, Paris, no. TH. 1225–1226 (in Préaud and d'Albis, p. 147, no. 105); *écuelle à quatre pans*, c. 1751–52, illustrated in Dallot-Naudin, p. 207; *assiette à godrons*, c. 1751–52, Musée national Adrien Dubouché, Limoges, no. ADL. 1331 (in *Vincennes*, p. 28, no. 17). Minor differences in the painting of the leaves leave open the possibility of another hand, however.

22 The mark on the MNC, Sèvres, tureen stand is very similar to that on 1917.982. There is also a resemblance between the shape of the crossed Ls under the Boston water jug and those on the MNC stand. Such similarities, however, are far from conclusive. Tamara Préaud (in Préaud and d'Albis, p. 199) illustrates the central starburst and circle of dots found in the marks on the Atheneum's pot-pourri vases in a table of unattributed marks, viewing these central portions as the painters' marks. I would prefer to see the entire crossed Ls marks as the painters' marks. The starburst does appear inside the mark on the tureen at the MNC, but it does not appear on any other ornate Vincennes mark thus far examined, nor does the circle of dots. Ornate marks were not uncommon in the late 1740s and very early 1750s, and probably were used by more than one painter.

23 Entered the factory in 1741, paid 80 *livres* in 1745, 100 by 1753 (Préaud and d'Albis, p. 214). His mark is known to be an exclamation mark.

24 Entered December 1749, paid 50 *livres*, 100 *livres* by 1753 (ibid., p. 203). His unconfirmed mark is recorded as either a circle containing a dot and a vertical line below (ibid.) or a script G (Peters, *Marks*, p. 21).

25 Entered 1746, paid 40 *livres*, 112 *livres* since January 1753. Peters, *Marks*, pp. 8–9, states that Armand *jeune* entered the factory in 1758, but this does not seem to be the case. He does suggest on the basis of Armand's older brother's mark and the mark of the younger Armand's niece in the 1770s, that Armand *jeune's* mark may be fluidly drawn interlaced Ls with four dots, one at each intersection of the factory mark. The link to the later female Armand's confirmed mark is convincing, but it is not impossible that in his earliest work, Armand *jeune* may have used a slightly different, elaborate mark. See also cat. no. 66.

26 MNC, Sèvres, nos. 21570 and 21779. The bird painter Louis-Denis Armand *aîné* is known to have used ornate marks, for example on a tureen in the Cleveland Museum of Art, c. 1752, no. 52.3 (photograph kindly provided by Henry Hawley) and also an *écuelle* decorated with marine motifs at MAD, Paris (illustrated in Alfassa and Guérin, p. 47, pl. 43). Ornate marks of a somewhat different style than found on Armand's mature works do appear on other objects perhaps by this painter, such as on a cup and saucer in the Philadelphia Museum of Art, no. 42.59.124 (photograph kindly provided by Donna Corbin). For more on this painter see cat. no. 62.

27 This suggestion must be made with caution since much more work needs to be done on these early painters and their marks. Bernard Dragesco has pointed out to the author in conversation that Armand *jeune's* later style, perhaps seen in the flowers on a *vase hollandois* at Waddesdon Manor (1764, Eriksen, *Waddesdon*, pp. 174–75, no. 61) is lighter than that of the Museum's pots-pourris, but this may simply reflect the factory's move from a heavy, somewhat botanical style to a more decorative style as it took place in the 1750s.

28 *Pots-pourris à jour* are listed among molded pieces in the biscuit kiln records. See IF 5673, fol. 6, 28 March 1753.

29 See cat. no. 55 for information on Mme Gravant's atelier.

30 Antoine d'Albis estimates that they were fired six to eight times, once to biscuit, once for glaze, at least three or four enamel firings, and one or two firings for the gold.

57

Pot-pourri vase (*pot-pourri Pompadour*)

1917.962

Vincennes, 1752–1754

Soft-paste porcelain, H. 9½ × DIAM. 5⅝ in. (24.1 × 14.3 cm)

White with blue garlands, birds, and fillets, gold fillets and ribbons

Marks: interlaced Ls in blue[1]

Provenance: possibly Lazare Duvaux; possibly Madame de Pompadour; J. Pierpont Morgan

MODEL

The covered, urn-shaped, pierced vase known as the *pot-pourri Pompadour* was made in four sizes and the Museum's example is of the third.[2] They were produced with variations in the piercing and stem, and when the form appeared without piercing it was called an *urne Pompadour*.[3] Production of this model had begun by 1752 and continued until the 1770s.[4] Based on a drawing in the Sèvres factory's archives inscribed *Vase Pot Pourri Duplessis*, the design of the model is attributed to Jean-Claude Duplessis.[5]

The earliest porcelain pot-pourri vases were made at Rouen before 1700;[6] in the 1740s covered bowls and vases from the Orient and Meissen were being mounted with gilt bronze as pot-pourri vases by Parisian *marchands-merciers*.[7] Vincennes was producing them by 1751, enabling the factory to compete directly with the foreign imports. The two pot-pourri vases, "forme d'urne, en blanc & bleu"[urn shaped, in white and blue] sold by Lazare Duvaux to Madame de Pompadour in August 1752 may be the earliest mention of a sale of vases of this form.[8]

FUNCTION

Pot-pourri—a blend of aromatic spices and flowers—was used to scent the air in bedrooms and other private rooms. It was placed in pierced vases that were displayed, often in groups or garnitures, on furniture or mantelpieces.

COMMENTARY

Pots-pourris Pompadour with *camaïeu* flowers can be found in the sales registers of the factory for 1754. Lazare Duvaux bought two of the third size for 72 *livres* each sometime between July and December.[9] He bought two more costing 108 *livres* each in the same month.[10] He probably sold the first pair to Madame de Pompadour, along with a *pot à pâte, camaïeu bleu*, two more, with flowers, two *pots à pommade*, with flowers, and three more, *camaïeu bleu*, in September 1754.[11] Madame de Pompadour probably bought the second pair in February 1755, along with other objects for the *garde-robe* of her Paris *hôtel*.[12] Two pots-pourris with monochrome blue flowers were listed in the probate inventory of that *garde-robe* after Madame de

Pompadour's death in 1764.[13] Other pots-pourris with blue monochrome flowers appear elsewhere in the same inventory, one pair in an armoire on the first floor of her Paris *hôtel* (both with broken finials) and one pair with other Vincennes and Sèvres brought from Versailles (one with a broken finial).[14] It is possible that the Atheneum's vase was one of these, as its flower finial was broken at some unknown period.

While it is difficult to say with certainty that the Atheneum's pot-pourri was one of the four sold to Duvaux and then to Madame de Pompadour, no other examples of the third size decorated with blue monochrome flowers appear in the sales records for 1753 or 1754. The Fitzwilliam Museum in Cambridge possesses an undamaged pair of the same size with the same decoration, which is likely to be the pair from the *garde-robe* mentioned above.[15]

TECHNIQUE AND CONDITION

The *pot-pourri Pompadour* was thrown, not molded. In the Museum's example the paste is slightly pinkish, and there are tiny bubbles or blisters (the piece was thus described as *grasse cuite*) under the glaze, indicating that it was not fired hot enough during the biscuit firing.[16] The lid has been heavily restored.

Exhibition: *Morgan Loan Exhibition*, New York, 1914, not in catalogue

Literature: Chavagnac, p. 52, no. 58; Savill, 1, pp. 128, 134

NOTES

1　The form of the mark is the same as on the *théière à cuvier à cerceau* discussed in cat. no. 76.

2　Préaud and d'Albis, p. 98; see also Sassoon, pp. 12, 16 n. 1 and Savill, 1, p. 127. It has been suggested that a fifth size may have been made. See Eriksen, *David Collection*, p. 62, no. 28; Sir Geoffrey de Bellaigue, in an unpublished catalogue entry for 1917.962, suggests that known examples measuring 11¹⁄₁₆ and 10¼ in. (28 and 26 cm) indicate two different sizes rather than variations within one size.

3　Savill, 1, p. 127, describes four different versions, the Atheneum's being shape A.

4　Préaud and d'Albis, p. 98 and Savill, 1, p. 128. Dated examples of shape A appear only until 1760 although an undated pair of shape A with *frize colorée* decoration, probably dating from 1761 or 1762, was recently sold in London (Giuseppe Rossi sale, Sotheby's, London, part 4, 10–12 March 1999, lot 389). Savill's shape C, whose main characteristic is the fan-shaped piercing, is known from 1764. A later drawing, dated 1788, suggests that the factory intended to revive the model, which had waned in popularity after the 1760s (AMNS, R. I, L. 3, d. 10, fol. 2). Mme de Pompadour purchased two "pots-pourris de Vincennes, forme d'urne, en blanc & bleu" from Lazare Duvaux on 8 August 1752, for 168 *livres* (See LD, 2, p. 133, no. 1193), which may well have been like the Museum's vase.

5　Savill, 1, p. 127 (AMNS, R. I, L. 3, d. 10, fol. 1). The inscription is in a later hand.

6　See an example at the MMA, New York, no. 50.211.186.

7　See Chilton, pp. 95–96; see also Savill, 1, pp. 24, 29 and 3, pp. 1181–82.

8　See note 4 above.

9　AMNS, Vy 1, 57v, 5 December 1754 (*fournée* 5, September–November 1753).

10　AMNS, Vy 1, 69v, 5–31 December 1754 (*fournée* 10, September 1754–January 1755).

11　LD, 2, p. 215, no. 1883. See Savill, 1, p. 134 nn. 23, 15c (1 and 2). The *pots à pâte* with flowers and three *pots à pommade camaïeu bleu* also appear in

AMNS, Vy 1, fol. 58 (*fournées* 3–4, January–September 1753), for 5 December 1754. Since this list of purchases covers the period from July to December, the sale of these items to Mme de Pompadour in September 1754 does not present a conflict.

12 LD, 2, p. 233, no. 2063. Duvaux sold them for 108 *livres* each, the retail price from the factory. As a preferred dealer, Duvaux was given a 9% discount off the factory's list price. Perhaps these were the two *pots pourry Pompadour 3g. fleurs camay.* that are listed in the painting kiln records for 1755 (*fournée* 10, October 1754–January 1755). See IF 5676, fol.29.

13 Cordey, p. 39, no. 381. See Savill, 1, pp. 128, 134 n. 23.

14 Cordey, p. 41, no. 396 and p. 61, no. 674.

15 No. C13-1947. See Savill, 1, pp. 129, 132 n. 3g. Since three out of the four other blue and white pots-pourris noted in the Pompadour inventory had broken finials, it seems likely that the Fitzwilliam pair, which is not damaged, was from the *garde-robe*.

16 Noted by Antoine d'Albis in an examination of this object. See Glossary.

58

Two vases (*vases à oreilles*)

1917.985–986

Vincennes, 1754–1755

Soft-paste porcelain, 1917.985: H. 4⁷⁄₁₆ × W. 2⅜ × D. 2⅜ in. (11.3 × 6 × 6 cm); 1917.986: H. 4⁷⁄₁₆ × W. 2⅜ × D. 2⁵⁄₁₆ in. (11.2 × 6 × 5.9 cm)

Bleu céleste ground, polychrome flowers, gilding

Marks: 1917.985: interlaced Ls in blue in center of well underneath with date letter B, + for Philippe Xhrouuet *père*;[1] 1917.986: worn factory mark in blue and indistinct other marks in center under foot; later inscription in gold paint N°134[2]

Provenance: possibly Lazare Duvaux, 1756; Cartier et Fils, Paris, 1905;[3] J. Pierpont Morgan

MODEL

These vases were called *vases à oreilles* or "with ears" by the Vincennes factory.[4] They probably were so named because they looked like "reversed ears," as evidenced by an entry in the day-book of Lazare Duvaux where they were described as "deux vases forme d'urne à oreilles renversées"[two urn-shaped vases with inverted ears].[5] They were made in five sizes, the first three sizes introduced in 1754, and the fourth and fifth sizes in 1755.[6]

The Museum's vases are of the fifth size. A single variant of the model exists in the form of a pair in the Kress Collection of the Metropolitan Museum of Art, with additional relief-molded decoration around the reserve.[7]

Two drawings of the model survive at the Sèvres factory, one depicting the outline and interior detail of a single vase and another with two vases, one designated as being of the third size and a smaller one inscribed fifth size.[8] A plaster model also survives.[9]

The design has been attributed to Jean-Claude Duplessis.[10] While it has been suggested that Duplessis may have based his design on Chinese vases or bottles described by Lazare Duvaux as "à oreilles" [with ears], there do not appear to be any Chinese porcelain models in which the handles emerge out of the top rim as in the Vincennes model. It is possible that Duvaux was referring to bottles and vases with "ear-like" or "finger-like" handles attached at the neck as in a celadon example in the Wallace Collection.[11] There are no other obvious sources for this shape of vase, leading us to suppose that it was an entirely original creation by Duplessis. Certainly the foliate nature of the neck is in keeping with his interest in the natural and floral forms of decoration beloved by rococo artists.

Vases à oreilles were sold mostly in pairs or, in the case of the first and second sizes, as parts of garnitures.[12] The first mention of this shape in the sales records was in December 1754, when Lazare Duvaux bought a pair, probably of the second size, decorated with a *bleu céleste* ground and birds.[13] Prices ranged dramatically, from 3 to 840 *livres*.[14] The Atheneum's vases probably sold for 96 *livres*,[15] and may have been two of four sold to Lazare Duvaux in the second half of 1756.[16]

COMMENTARY

When the *bleu céleste* ground color was introduced at Vincennes in 1753, the factory decided to mark this achievement by choosing the new color for the service which Louis XV had ordered in 1751 and which was executed between 1753 and 1755.[17] Like the Atheneum's small vases, the reserves of the royal service were decorated with flowers, but a distinctive gilding pattern distinguished royal service pieces from others with similar decoration, including the Museum's vases. The royal service aside, objects with *bleu céleste* ground were sold by the factory from 1753, and from then on this new color became one of the most sought after and expensive in the factory's repertory.[18]

Philippe Xhrouuet, who was active at the factory from 1750 until 1775, painted the floral bouquets on at least one of the Atheneum's vases.[19] He had been a fan painter before entering the factory, and in his early years at Vincennes he is known to have painted landscapes, flowers, monochrome cherubs on clouds, and birds. On these vases he created four different "floating" bouquets in which roses and tulips figure most prominently. In one reserve the bouquet appears to be hanging upside down, evidence of how by 1754 factory painters learned to use flowers in a purely decorative fashion. This type of floral bouquet became a standard form of decoration at Vincennes from about 1752.

The gilded decoration around the reserves is different on the two vases suggesting they are not a true pair, although if they were two of the four sold to Lazare Duvaux they probably were simply mixed up at a later date. The gilding is relatively ornate, especially for such small vases. The unnamed gilder combined scrolls, diapers, floral sprays, and pebbling to set off the white reserves from the *bleu céleste* ground. Garlands of tiny flowers intrude rather haphazardly into the reserves. Even the foliate openings of the vases are heavily gilded, both inside and out. There probably were at least two firings for the gilding, once when it was placed on the white and again when it was placed on the *bleu céleste*.[20] All of this must have added to the cost of the vases, supporting the hypothesis that they cost 96 *livres* rather than 60 *livres*.[21]

TECHNIQUE AND CONDITION

These baluster-shaped vases were thrown from the foot to the shoulder, and then the top molded. A seam is visible at the shoulder. The ground color is uneven and translucent, typical of the early *bleu céleste* that was made with glass brought from Venice.[22] The elaborate and high-quality gilding is half-polished and half-matte.

Exhibitions: *Morgan Loan Exhibition*, New York, 1914, not in catalogue; *French and English Art Treasures*, New York, 1942, no. 313; *Vincennes and Sèvres Porcelain,* New York, 1980, no. 9

Literature: Chavagnac, p. 65, no. 78; *French and English Art Treasures*, no. 313; Hood, *Bulletin*, p. 10; *Vincennes and Sèvres Porcelain*, no. 9; Savill, 1, pp. 138, 145, 147, and Savill, 3, p. 1078 n. 5

NOTES

1 Active 1750–75. See Savill, 3, pp. 1077–78, Peters, *Marks*, p. 77.

2 This number is an inventory number from Cartier for a *composition des 10 colis* 9 June 1905 (see APML, Cartier file).

3 Ibid.: "N° 134 2 Vases Sèvres Louis XV, fond bleu turquoise, cartels or et fleurs sur fond blanc, année 1754, par Fontaine."

4 For an extensive history of the shape see Savill, 1, pp. 135–38; see also Préaud and d'Albis, p. 183; *Vincennes*, p. 139; Eriksen and Bellaigue, p. 293.

5 LD, 2, p. 278, no. 2450, 4 April 1756.

6 Molds and models in the first and second sizes were mentioned in the 1755 inventory as having been made in 1754 (AMNS, I. 7, 1 January 1755). The third size was documented in the biscuit kiln in November 1754 (IF 5673, fol. 30/32, 29 November) although the inscription on a drawing at Sèvres with two vases of this shape dates the third size to an order of 20 January 1755 (Préaud and d'Albis, p. 183). The fourth and fifth sizes appear in the 1756 inventory as having been made in 1755 (AMNS, I. 7), and the same drawing mentioned above is additionally inscribed *Vase à oreille 5me grandeur 1755* (Savill, 1, p. 135, states that the fifth size may have been introduced in 1754, based on the existence of the Wadsworth Atheneum's vases and the mention of *petits vases à oreilles* in the glaze kiln in July of that year). A sixth size was listed in the sales records for 1760 and again in 1777, but in hard paste (Savill, 1, p. 135, p. 145 n. 8). There is no known example of a sixth size (Savill, 1, p. 135). Savill delineates the sizes as follows: first size: H. 11⅞–12¾ in. (30.1–32.3 cm); second size: 8¼–9 in. (21–22.9 cm); third size: 7⅛–7½ in. (18–19 cm); fourth size: 5¹¹⁄₁₆–5¹⁵⁄₁₆ in. (14.4–15 cm); fifth size: 4⁵⁄₁₆–4⁷⁄₁₆ in. (11–11.3 cm).

7 Savill, 1, pp. 135, 145 n. 3ii; Dauterman, *Kress*, pp. 195–98, 198 n. 33. A vase at the V&A, London, with a similar body but with an undulating rim and loop handles seems at first glance to relate to the *vases à oreilles*, but this piece is not genuine (V&A, London, no. C. 386-1921). Marcelle Brunet (Brunet and Préaud, p. 142 n. 58) suggests that it might be a trial piece, but

Savill notes that the authenticity of the vase has been doubted by Tamara Préaud and Aileen Dawson. This vase is also mentioned as a variant in *Vincennes*, p. 139.

8   AMNS, R. I, L. 3, d. 3, fols. 1 and 2; illustrated in Savill, 1, pp. 136–37. The inscriptions on the drawing with two vases read as such: on the larger vase, *Vases à oreile 3me grandeur suivan La comande du 20 Janvier 1755*; on the smaller vase, *Vase à oreille 5me grandeur 1755*, and on the upper right edge of the drawing, *14 p. Large en dedans/7-9 Large en dedans*.

9   Ibid., 1814 inventory, 1740–80, no. 50, *vase 'à oreille 1re 2me gr'* (see Troude, pl. 91), illustrated in Savill, 1, p. 136.

10 Savill, 1, p. 136. Brunet (*Frick*, p. 234) suggests that the drawings could be by Duplessis. Eriksen attributes the design to Duplessis based on the hand-writing of the inscriptions on the drawing of the third and fifth sizes (Eriksen and Bellaigue, p. 293).

11 The original suggestion was made by Savill, 1, p. 136. The references in Lazare Duvaux were made for 28 December 1752 (p. 148, no. 1313) and 4 February 1754 (p. 191, no. 1694). Chinese examples that may fit this description are illustrated in Scheurleer, p. 330. I would like to thank Clare Le Corbeiller for pointing these models out to me.

12 See Savill, 1, p. 136 for documented and known garnitures including this model.

13 AMNS, Vy 1, fol. 71v, each 144 *livres*.

14 Savill, 1, p. 137. The price of 3 *livres* was for a defective example of the fifth size. The least expensive examples, not defective, were biscuit vases, fifth size, which sold for 8 *livres*. These were often sold as part of table services, to be set on decorated or biscuit pedestals (Savill, 1, p. 135).

15 Ibid., 1, p. 137.

16 AMNS, Vy 2, fol. 13, 20 August 1756–1 January 1757, four *bleu céleste fleurs*, 96 *livres* each. While the entry says two vases, the prices reflect that four were actually sold. There is also an entry in the sales records for a pair of *vases à oreilles bleu céleste fleurs* that sold for 60 *livres* each to Lazare Duvaux and another *bleu céleste fleurs* for 30 *livres* each (AMNS, Vy 2, fol. 14v, 20 August 1756–1 January 1757). The low prices suggests that they were also of the fifth size, and in fact may have had less elaborate gilding than the vases at the Atheneum. No earlier entry in the records corresponds to the Museum's vases, although it is still possible that they were sold shortly after they were produced.

17 For a history of this service see Grégory, pp. 40–46, no. 1, and Savill, "Premier service," pp. 281–84. Many new forms were specially created for this service, which comprised 1,749 pieces. While most pieces were decorated with flowers, on the larger, more important pieces the flowers were combined with fruit.

18 Pieces with *bleu céleste* ground were consistently more expensive than those with other ground colors.

19 For a biography of Xhrouuet see Savill, 3, pp. 1077–78. His mark has often been confused with that of Jacques-François Micaud (active 1757–1801). For a discussion of both painters' marks see cat. no. 91. Since the mark on 1917.986 is indistinct, one cannot prove Xhrouuet was responsible for this vase as well, although there is no appreciable difference in the painting.

20 According to Antoine d'Albis (Préaud and d'Albis, p. 217), gilding on *bleu céleste* had to be fired at a lower temperature than gilding on the white glazed porcelain. He cites Hellot in saying that when the gold is fired on the white it is left unburnished, and only after the gold on the *bleu céleste* is fired does one burnish both golds (see AMNS, Carnet Y.50, p. 65).

21 See note 16 above. Normally, flower painting was one of the least expensive types of painted decoration, but with *bleu céleste* ground and elaborate gilding even small vases with simple bouquets could cost 96 *livres*.

22 See Préaud and d'Albis, p. 217.

59

Vase (*vase Duplessis*)

1917.990

Vincennes, 1755–1756

Soft-paste porcelain, H. 5¹⁵⁄₁₆ × W. 4³⁄₁₆ × D. 4¼ in. (15 × 10.6 × 10.7 cm)

White ground with children in monochrome crimson, gilding

Marks: interlaced Ls in blue with date letter C in center; painter's mark M for Jean-Louis Morin;[1] incised ph[2]

Provenance: perhaps Lazare Duvaux, 1756;[3] J. Pierpont Morgan

MODEL

This form of vase was one of three variants known at the Vincennes factory as *vase Duplessis,* named after the designer of the form, Jean-Claude Duplessis. One model (A), represented by examples in Minneapolis, the Louvre, and the Fitzwilliam Museum, Cambridge, has a low-waisted trumpet body, lobed at the stem and top rim, and elaborate, looped handles rising from the stem and belly. The foot can be either rocky or with shells.[4] A second version (B), which conforms to the Atheneum's vase and may be a rectification of the first model from about 1754, shows a similarly low-waisted trumpet-shaped vase but without lobes at the stem or neck. The handles of this version can be either single or double foliate scrolls but are not formed with an elaborate loop. The base is decorated with relief-molded shells, as is the base on Louvre and Fitzwilliam examples.[5] A third variant of the model (C) with flatter lobes—known as *à enfants* because it is usually decorated with relief-molded children—is the only one clearly distinguishable in the factory records.[6] There are similar vases with a higher waist and narrower trumpet, simply decorated with polychrome or gold flowers, but they were probably called *urnes Duplessis* rather than *vases Duplessis*.[7]

Three drawings of *vases Duplessis* exist in the Sèvres factory archives. The first, probably in Duplessis's hand, clearly relates to the version in Minneapolis, with the scrolled handles and the lobed rim (fig. 59-1).[8] A second shows the same vase without handles, standing on a tall plinth, with both a straight and lobed rim,[9] while a third depicts the same basic shape but without lobes and plinth, inscribed *n° 1 bon* (fig. 59-2).[10]

There are three plaster models that survive.[11] One is specifically for the *vase Duplessis à enfants* (fig. 59-3). Another one has a body with facets of varying proportions extending from the rim to the foot, and double-scrolled handles like the Museum's vase (labeled *vase à fleurs Duplessis orné*) (fig. 59-4).[12] A third model—without a foot and labeled *vase à fleurs Duplessis uni*—combines the circular body of the Museum's example with single scrolled foliate handles (fig. 59-5).[13]

Vases Duplessis are listed in the earliest inventories of the Vincennes factory. They are described as being of the first

59

through fourth sizes, although later factory documents mention a fifth size.[14] No molds or models were listed in the first years, and in 1753 one example was described as turned.[15] Only in 1754 does one encounter mention of molds and models associated with *vases Duplessis*, and these only for the first and second sizes.[16] This may refer to the faceted version for which the plaster model survives.

The sales records at Vincennes and Sèvres list *vases Duplessis* in four sizes from December 1752 to at least December 1762.[17] Prices range from 60 *livres,* for fourth-size vases, *fleurs guirlandes* to 360 *livres* for *bleu céleste* ground with children or birds, probably of the first size.[18] Some first-size examples decorated in *bleu lapis* with flowers or children could cost as little as 108 *livres* while *bleu céleste* vases of the third and fourth sizes could cost considerably more.[19]

Most of the *vases Duplessis* recorded in the sales ledgers had either *bleu lapis* or *bleu céleste* ground colors or, if left white, were decorated with children.[20]

It is difficult to match entries in the sales records with extant vases. Several *bleu lapis* examples fired in 1748 are recorded as having been sold between 1752 and 1754, and could describe the examples in the Louvre or the Fitzwilliam Museum, Cambridge.[21] Jean-François Verdun de Monchiroux bought a fourth-size *bleu céleste* vase decorated with flowers in

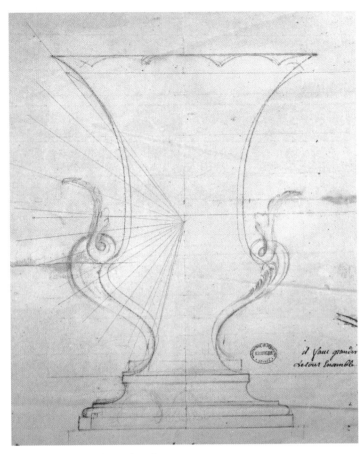

Fig. 59-1 *Vase Duplessis*, drawing

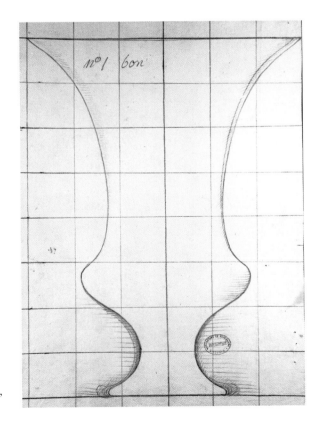

Fig. 59-2 *Vase Duplessis*, drawing

Fig. 59-3 *Vase Duplessis à enfants*, plaster model

Fig. 59-5 Plaster model, labeled *vase à fleurs Duplessis uni*

Fig. 59-4 Plaster model, labeled *vase à fleurs Duplessis orné*

September 1754 which may be one sold by Christie's, London in 1993.[22] In 1756 Lazare Duvaux bought a pair of the second size decorated with blue monochrome and flesh-colored children that could describe a pair dated 1754–55 on the art market in Paris in 1994.[23]

COMMENTARY

It is possible that the Atheneum's vase was one sold to Lazare Duvaux between August and December 1757.[24] It is decorated with crimson monochrome cloud-borne cherubs painted by Jean-Louis Morin, who was active at the factory from 1754 until his death in 1787. During his first four years, Morin specialized in monochrome cherubs on clouds or in landscapes, as well as in trophies.[25] The cherub on one side of the vase reproduces one of four in Bernard Lépicié's *L'Amour oiseleur* after a 1730s composition by François Boucher of the same subject (fig. 59-6).[26] The figure on the other side of the vase is taken from Louis Félix de La Rue's engraving *La Musique*, which was part of a larger series by La Rue again after Boucher, called *Livre des Arts* (fig. 59-7).[27] Morin follows the figure of the cherub rather closely but alters the position of the musical score.[28]

TECHNIQUE AND CONDITION

This vase was both thrown and molded, the body being turned and the handles and foot molded. The painted decoration has been done using Taunay's *pourpre no. 1*, made from crushed ruby glass, mixed with a silver flux (*lune corneé* or *chlorure d'argent*).[29] Crimson (or carmine) had been available at Vincennes since 1748.

Exhibition: *Morgan Loan Exhibition*, New York, 1914, not in catalogue

Literature: Chavagnac, p. 68, no. 81, pl. XXII; Savill, 3, p. 1052 n. 3

NOTES

1 Active 1754–87. See Savill, 3, p. 1051; Peters, *Marks*, p. 54.

2 According to Savill (3, p. 1118), this may be the mark of the *répareur* Philippine (active 1753/54–73/74), who became *chef des répareurs* in 1771. Savill notes the mark on works of 1757, as well as a basin dating from the 1750s.

3 See below for discussion of possible provenance.

4 Type A: Louvre, Paris, no. OA 7610 (see *Vincennes*, p. 142, no. 426); Minneapolis Museum of Art, nos. 82.2.1,2 (see Préaud and d'Albis, p. 159, no. 136); Fitzwilliam Museum, Cambridge, England (see Eriksen and Bellaigue, p. 242, no. 61).

5 Existing examples of type B, which all date from 1754 forward, include: pair decorated with children, 1754–55, Vielliard (Drouot-Richelieu, Paris, 6 May 1994, lot 94); *bleu céleste* with children in landscapes, 1754 (Upton House, Warwickshire, England); *bleu céleste* with crimson children, c. 1755 (Christie's, London, 15 October 1990, lot 34); *bleu céleste* with flowers, c. 1755 (Christie's, London, 11 October 1993, lot 141); *Bleu lapis?* with *caillouté*, birds, c. 1755–60 (Drouot, Paris, 23 November 1967, lot 136); *bleu lapis caillouté* with flowers, 1759 (V&A, London, no. C. 1363-1919); *bleu céleste* with birds, c. 1755–60 (formerly in the Alphonse de Rothschild collection, illustrated in Garnier, pl. LXIX); *rose* ground, blue *œil de perdrix* pattern, landscapes, c. 1760 (Tuck Collection, no. 93, Petit Palais, Paris); *mosaïque* ground and birds in landscapes, c. 1760, (Art Institute of Chicago, no. 1994.378); *bleu céleste* with children in landscapes, 1764, Vielliard (Upton House).

6 For type C, see a pair in the Frick Collection, New York, nos. 18.9.2–18.9.3 (in Brunet, *Frick*, pp. 200–4); pair formerly in the collection of the Earl of Harewood, *bleu céleste* ground with painted rather than relief-molded children (see Tait, "Harewood, Early Sèvres," p. 475, fig. 3).

7 See cat. no. 54 for a complete discussion of this form, often mistakenly called *vase Duplessis* in the literature.

8 AMNS, R. 1, L. 3, d. 6, fol. 1. It is not signed.

9 Ibid., fol. 2.

10 Ibid., fol. 1 bis.

11 AMNS, 1814 inventory, 1740–80, no. 57; ibid., no. 58; ibid., no. 59 (Troude, pl. 100).

Fig. 59-6 *L'Amour oiseleur*, Bernard Lépicié, after François Boucher

Fig. 59-7 *La Musique*, Louis Félix de La Rue after François Boucher

12 These labels date from the early 19th century and do not reflect their 18th-century names.

13 See the example in the Petit Palais, Paris, Tuck Collection, no. 93.

14 In 1756 glaze kiln records list fourth- and fifth-size examples in the firing of 4 May (IF 5674, fol. 56). Two biscuit examples of the fifth size were sold to Hénique in 1759 (AMNS, Vy 3, fol. 5, 2 November 1759). In 1761, twenty-one of the fifth size appear in the factory inventory, fourteen ready to be glazed and seven requiring a second glaze firing (AMNS, I. 7). It is possible that these references to a fifth size are to another vase introduced in 1756, called *vase Duplessis à compartiments*. The inventory of new work for that year lists second- through fifth-size molds of this shape. Furthermore, the entry for the fourteen vases ready to be fired is followed immediately by an entry for *2 idem. forme delancien* suggesting that the previous vases were a new model. One entry for pieces in the Paris sales room lists *vases Duplessis* in seven sizes (AMNS, I. 7, 8 October 1752 and 1 January 1753) and describes works decorated in gilt flowers. In this case the person recording the inventory may have been in error, referring to another vase, called *urne Duplessis,* which was made in seven sizes. See cat. no. 54.

15 IF 5673, fol. 10, 6 August 1753.

16 AMNS, I. 7, new work for 1754 (1 January 1755).

17 Two to Duvaux, 20 December 1752, fourth size, flowers (Vy 1, fol. 6); two to Louis XV, December 1762 (not described).

18 See AMNS, Vy 1, fol. 105v, 9 December 1755, Bailly, and Vy 1, fol. 28v, 31 December 1753, Duvaux, *bleu céleste enfants colorés* and Vy 1, fol. 135, January–August 1756, Duvaux, *bleu céleste oiseaux*. One vase described as first size, *lapis garni de fleurs* sold in January 1753 for 594 *livres*, which probably was actually filled with flowers, accounting for the high cost.

19 For example, see AMNS, Vy 1, fol. 14, 19 September 1753, Remond, first size, *lapis fleurs*, 108 *livres*; Vy 1, fol. 47v, 30 June 1754, third size, Duvaux, *bleu céleste fleurs*, 180 *livres*; Vy 1, fol. 50v, 2 September 1754, Verdun, fourth size, *bleu céleste fleurs*, 180 *livres*; Vy 1, fol. 113, October–December 1755, third size, *bleu céleste enfants colorés*, 216 *livres*.

20 This is the strongest argument for linking the Minneapolis and Atheneum models with *vases Duplessis* while relating the model sometimes called *vase Duplessis à fleurs balustre rocaille* to *urnes Duplessis* (see cat. no. 54).

21 AMNS, Vy 1, fol. 11, 9 April 1753 (*fournée* 3, 1748), first size, Bazin; Vy 1, 52v, 14 October 1754 (*fournée* 7, 1748), first size, Roussel.

22 Ibid., Vy 1 fol. 50v, 2 September 1754; Christie's, London, 11 October 1993, lot 141, 5¹⁵⁄₁₆ in. (15 cm).

23 AMNS, Vy 2, fol. 12v, second size, 240 *livres* each, Duvaux; Drouot-Richelieu, Paris, 6 May 1994, lot 94; it is possible that these vases were the pair taken from enamel kiln in the second half of 1755 (IF 5676, fol. 61, *Enf. cam. Chaires Col. encad.*).

24 AMNS, Vy 2, fol. 14v, 20 August 1756–1 January 1757, *vase Duplessis 4.e gdr. Enfans Camai…96 livres.*

25 For a fuller account of Morin's work at the factory see Savill, 3, pp. 1051–52.

26 See Jean-Richard, pp. 330–31, no. 1377. The engraving was published in 1734. There appear to be two painted versions of Boucher's *L'Amour oiseleur,* one in the Museum of Art, Rhode Island School of Design, Providence, which is in the same sense as the engraving, and another in the reverse sense of the engraving (Ananoff, *Boucher,* 1, pp. 196–97, no. 62). See *Boucher,* pp. 127–29, no. 15 for a discussion of this composition.

27 Jean-Richard, p. 316, no. 1307. See nos. 1294–1311 for others in the series.

28 In at least two other instances, one can see that Morin followed very closely his engraved sources. The figure of a cherub holding grapes above his head found on an orange tub dating from 1755–56 at Waddesdon Manor (Eriksen, *Waddesdon*, pp. 56–57, no. 12) fairly accurately reproduces a figure from Daullé's engraving *La Terre* after Boucher (Jean-Richard, p. 160, no. 540). The same holds true for Morin's cherub holding a floral crown found on a 1755–56 *pot-pourri Pompadour* (Eriksen, *Waddesdon*, pp. 54–55, no. 11). It is based on an engraving by Aveline after Boucher (Jean-Richard, pp. 88–89, no. 245).

29 Information kindly provided by Antoine d'Albis. For more on Taunay's purples see Préaud and d'Albis, pp. 231–32.

60

Pair of vases (*vases à oreilles*)

1917.988–989

Vincennes, 1755–1756

Soft-paste porcelain, 1917.988: H. 7⁷⁄₁₆ × W. 3⁷⁄₈ × D. 3¹⁵⁄₁₆ in. (18.8 × 9.9 × 10 cm); 1917.989: H. 7½ × W. 3¹³⁄₁₆ × D. 3¹³⁄₁₆ in. (19 × 9.7 × 9.7 cm)

White ground, monochrome blue landscapes and children, the latter also with flesh tones, gilding

Marks: interlaced Ls in blue under both; mark for the painter André-Vincent Vielliard *père* above,[1] and dot below, on both; incised scrolling ML on both;[2] incised 2 under 1917.989[3]

Provenance: perhaps Nicolas Bazin;[4] Mademoiselle de Ganay, by tradition; Jacques Seligmann, London and Paris, 1903;[5] J. Pierpont Morgan

MODEL

These vases were called *vase à oreilles*.[6] They are examples of the third size and probably cost 132 *livres* each.[7]

COMMENTARY

The reserves of both vases, painted by André-Vincent Vielliard, are decorated with children in monochrome blue, their faces, arms and legs picked out in flesh tones (described by the factory as *enfants camaïeu chairs colorées*, or children in monochrome with flesh tones). On one side of the vases the children are depicted as musicians, the boy playing a horn and the girl a stringed instrument, probably a *pardessus de viole*.[8] On the other side, the children are "gardening," the boy holding a flower and the girl gathering fruit. The boy with the flower is very close to another figure by Vielliard on a cup of 1758 in the Wallace Collection.[9] In this case he is painted in colors and instead of holding a flower, he is raising a glass into the air. The figure of the boy with the horn is similar to another figure by Vielliard on a 1764 saucer at the British Museum.[10] These similarities imply the use of common models, and indeed in style the figures are reminiscent of François Boucher's painted or sculptural children. However, there are no direct sources to be found in that artist's published works. Perhaps Boucher made drawings specially for the factory that relate to these figures.[11] Whatever their source, it is unlikely that Vielliard copied his models exactly. In fact, he often deviated from his models, adapting them to suit his needs.[12] The awkward poses of the figures not only betray Vielliard's difficulties as a draftsman,[13] but may also stem from adapting figures from one source to another. In many other examples of his painting, Vielliard takes Boucher's cloud-borne, naked putti and transforms them into clothed children inhabiting landscapes.[14] This may help to explain why Vielliard's children, and indeed those on the Atheneum's vases, often sit so uncomfortably in their landscape settings. The

60

60

figures also are painted with Vielliard's typical elongated fore-heads and puffy pink cheeks. Even if they had their genesis in the work of Boucher, Vielliard has clearly put his own stamp on their appearance.

The painting of these vases reflects a genre of decoration that was current at the time, both in interior design and in furnishings. At Madame de Pompadour's château de Crécy, Boucher painted panels with children personifying the arts and sciences,[15] and pairs of children in stucco adorn the cornice of the hôtel de Soubise, Paris.[16] The scenes of children on the Crécy panels are separated by monochrome blue and white landscapes. Furniture decorated in this manner, known as *vernis Martin*, was very fashionable during the early 1750s, and is known to have been sold by Lazare Duvaux.[17] Porcelain with "Boucher children" in monochrome blue fits naturally in these settings.

TECHNIQUE AND CONDITION

These vases are well-potted examples, the base thrown and the upper part molded. The *répareur* would have made the shoulder seam as invisible as he could, but the biscuit firing seems to have brought it out again. The blue used to paint the figures was *beau bleu no. 2*.[18] The beautiful gilding is half-polished, half-matte.

Exhibitions: *Morgan Loan Exhibition*, New York, 1914, not in catalogue; *Continental Table Porcelain*, San Francisco, 1965, no. 231; *Vincennes and Sèvres Porcelain*, New York, 1980, no. 13

Literature: Chavagnac, pp. 67–68, no. 80; *Continental Table Porcelain*, no. 231; Buckley, *Connoisseur*, p. 51; *Vincennes and Sèvres Porcelain*, no. 13; Savill, 1, p. 145 n. 3z

NOTES
1 Active 1752–90. See cat. no. 78.
2 See Savill, 3, p. 1115 for scrolling ML, who suggests that it is the mark of the *répareur* Millot *jeune*, active at the factory in 1751, 1755–71 (or 1755–65, 1767–72). He was a *manœuvre* in 1751 and a soft-paste *répareur* from 1755.

She also notes that the mark is often combined with an incised 2 on other *vases à oreilles*, as on one of the Atheneum vases.

3 Ibid., p. 1125, found on soft paste 1753–88.

4 AMNS, Vy 1, fol. 124, 24 April 1756 (*fournée* 13, January–February 1756), *2 id [vases à oreilles, 3e gr] Enf. cam. ch. col*, 168 *livres* (each). My thanks to Tamara Préaud for this citation. Nicolas Bazin was a dealer approved by the factory. Chavagnac in his catalogue of the Morgan collection, suggests that the Museum's vases were the two sold to Lazare Duvaux in 1755 for 72 *livres* each (Vy 1, fol. 87v, 1 January–1 June 1755, *2 vazes à oreilles Enf. Cam chaires colorées*). I would suggest that this price reflects smaller examples.

5 See APML, Seligmann file, invoice for 22 May 1903: "two Little Old Sèvres vases to match [1917.993–994, cat. no. 151], the same date, they came times passed from Old Mis de Ganay," £4,000 (priced with 1917.993–994).

6 The shape of these vases has been discussed in cat. no. 58.

7 See Savill, 1, p. 135. Marcelle Brunet, in a AMNS file, refers to this pair as of the fourth size and suggests that they were sold by Duvaux to the prince de Soubise (LD, 2, p. 238, no. 2115: "… Deux vases à mettre des fleurs, à cartouches, camayeu bleu, chairs colorées, 300 l." This seems far too expensive, as two vases of the third size sold to Bazin in 1756 cost 132 *livres* each (see note 4 above).

8 This is an 18th-century member of the *viola da gamba* family, frequently used with other "pastoral" instruments such as the *musette*, hurdy-gurdy, and recorder. It was popular with aristocratic amateur musicians of the French court, who were prevented by custom from playing the violin (the violin was played only by professionals for dances and public festivals). It was also used by small children, for whom the bass viol was too large. In 1748 Louis XV engaged the composer Barthélemy de Caix to teach Princess Sophie to play the *pardessus*. See Tina Chancey, introduction to compact disc of Barthélemy de Caix, *Six Sonatas for two Pardessus de Viole*, 1997 (kindly provided by Mr. Daniel Mingledorff).

9 Savill, 2, p. 591, no. C385.

10 Dawson, *British Museum*, pp. 126–27, no. 110.

11 Boucher is known to have supplied the factory with drawings for biscuit sculptures and painted designs. The factory also purchased engravings after his work. In the inventory of 8 October 1752 (AMNS, I. 7) there is a summary list of drawings and prints held by the factory including 23 prints of children by Boucher (*23 Pieces, Estampes, jeux d'Enfans de M. Boucher*). There were also 13 drawings of children by the same artist (*13 Id.[desseins] de M. Boucher, les Enfans*). For more on the relationship between Boucher and the factory see Savill, "Boucher," pp. 162–70.

12 Belfort, "Boucher," pp. 6–35. See also *Boucher*, passim.

13 In 1755 Vielliard was described by the factory as following: "son genre de talens est la peinture qu'il possède fort bien [pour] les fonds de paysages, dessinant mal la figure laissant peu de progres a esperer." The fact that he is noted in 1758 for producing "plus d'ouvrage qu'aucun des peintres de l'attelier," probably explains why his poor draftsmanship was tolerated by the factory. See AMNS, Y.8.

14 Belfort, "Boucher," pp. 9–12, citing Huquier's *La Poésie* and *La Musique* after Boucher (Jean-Richard, pp. 315–16, nos. 1304, 1307) and their use on a pair of *caisses carrées* in the MAD, Paris.

15 These panels are now in the Frick Collection, New York. See Frick, *Paintings*, 2, pp. 8–23.

16 See illustration of the oval salon in Feray, p. 238. This room dates from 1739–40 and was designed by Germain Boffrand.

17 See LD, 2, p. 231, no. 2042, 10 January 1755, to M. d'Azincourt, an "encoignure à jour vernie en blanc & bleu." See for example another *encoignure* as well as the matching *commode* in the Louvre, stamped by Mathieu Criard, supplied to the *marchand-mercier* Hebert in 1743 for the apartment of Mlle de Mailly at Choisy, which was hung with matching blue and white watered silk (Pradère, p. 223, fig. 222).

18 I would like to thank Antoine d'Albis for this information.

61

Pair of vases (*vases cannelés* or *vases à corset*)

1917.995–996

Vincennes, 1755–1756

Soft-paste porcelain, 1917.995: H. 7¹¹⁄₁₆ × W. 5⁵⁄₁₆ × D. 4¹⁄₁₆ in. (19.5 × 13.5 × 10.3 cm); 1917.996: H. 7¹¹⁄₁₆ × W. 5³⁄₈ × D. 4¹⁄₁₆ in. (19.6 × 13.7 × 10.3 cm)

Bleu lapis with *caillouté* gilding, white ground with polychrome floral garlands

Marks: interlaced Ls in blue under both; date letter C and painter's mark for Vincent Taillandier;[1] under 1917.995, one underglaze blue dot and incised j?;[2] under 1917.996, two underglaze blue dots and incised 5[3]

Provenance: J. Pierpont Morgan

MODEL

Duplessis designed this model in 1754.[4] Factory documents refer to it as a *vase cannelé* or occasionally a *vase à côtes* or *à corset*.[5] *Vases cannelés* first appear in the glaze kiln firing of March–June 1754.[6] The factory inventory dated 1 January 1755 (for work of 1754) records three sizes in the list of new molds and models. In the next year's inventory a fourth size is mentioned among glazed pieces ready to be decorated.[7] Fifth and sixth sizes appear in the sales records at the end of 1756, but are not recorded in the inventories.[8] Sometimes the base of the vase includes bracket feet. The Sèvres archives retain a drawing for this model (fig. 61-1).[9] There is also a plaster model, without a knob, which probably represents the second size (fig. 61-2).[10]

Lazare Duvaux sold four *vases cannelés, bleu céleste* for 144 *livres* each to Monsieur de Courgy in 1755, and two *vases cannelés bleu céleste à fleurs*, to the prince de Soubise in 1758, for 864 *livres*.[11] We know of several sales of *vases cannelés* between 1755 and 1758; among them was the sale in 1755 to Duvaux of two vases of the first size with garlands for 300 *livres* each, and two of the second size, *bleu lapis mosaïque* with garlands.[12] Duvaux also bought several pairs in 1756, including, two with garlands for 72 *livres* each; two of the fifth size and two of the sixth size, *bleu céleste*, for 96 and 72 *livres* each, respectively; one of the first size, *lapis caillouté*, for 432 *livres*; and a pair of the fourth size with *lapis mosaïque* for 120 *livres* each.[13] Louis XV's daughter Louise-Elisabeth (Madame Infante), bought a pair of unspecified size decorated with *bleu lapis caillouté* for 192 *livres* in April 1758, and then Duvaux was back again to buy a pair of first-size vases with *bleu céleste guirlandes* in the first half of 1758 for 432 *livres* each.[14]

Vases cannelés feature in a number of public collections ranging in date from 1754 to 1761, the period in which this model appears to have been most popular.[15] A pair of the second size is in the Royal Collection, England, the *bleu lapis* with *caillouté* decoration on the bottom and the fluted areas white

with floral garlands.[16] This same arrangement can be found on a pair of the fifth size at the Musée national de Céramique, Sèvres, only with a green ground instead.[17] White-ground examples with flowers are in the Jones Collection of the Victoria and Albert Museum, London,[18] and Det Danske Kunstindustri-museum, Copenhagen.[19]

COMMENTARY

The Atheneum's vases are probably of the fourth size, and were made between 1755 and 1756. While vases similar to the Atheneum's can be found in the sales records, there are none listed both matching in size and decoration.[20] What makes these vases unusual and stand apart from most extant examples is the application of the ground color to the fluted portion of the body. The effect is to make the fluting less emphatic here than when it is left white. Contrast them with the Copenhagen example where the flutes are white and where the verticality is elegantly enhanced by upright ribbons of lily-of-the-valley blossoms.

The decorator of these vases, Vincent Taillandier, began working at Sèvres in 1753. He specialized in flower painting, including sprays and garlands, and excelled in very small-scale work. He was fond of including large yellow roses in his work, as seen on the lower portion of these *vases cannelés*.[21]

TECHNIQUE AND CONDITION

The upper portion of these vases is decorated under the glaze with *bleu lapis*. The pebbled gilding was known as *caillouté*.[22] The factory mark, in underglaze blue, was painted by the ground color painter while the date letters and painter's marks, in blue enamel, were painted by Taillandier. The presence of underglaze blue dots under the vases is as yet unexplained.[23] The vases originally would have had covers.

Exhibition: *Morgan Loan Exhibition*, New York, 1914, not in catalogue

Literature: Chavagnac, pp. 71–72, no. 84, pl. XXV; *Vincennes*, pp. 140, 148 n. 17; Brunet and Préaud, p. 150; *Royal Collection*, p. 92

NOTES

1 Active 1753–90. See Savill, 3, pp. 1068–69; Peters, *Marks*, p. 69.

2 If j, found on soft paste 1753–73 (Savill, 3, p. 1110).

3 Found on soft paste c. 1747, by 1753–90s (Savill, 3, p. 1127).

4 Eriksen and Bellaigue, p. 91.

5 The designation *à côtes* appears in the inventory of 1755 (I. 7, 1 January 1755, for 1754), when *3 vases Cannelés ou a côt[e]s* were glazed and ready to be decorated. In the kiln records this form was called both *vase cannelés* and *vase à corset*. In the inventory of 1 January 1761 (AMNS, I. 7) one *vaze cannele ou a corset 1re grandr* is listed in the *magasin du blanc*. Gabriel Saint-Aubin's catalogue of the Gaignat sale of 1769 provides confirmation that this describes the same model, for the artist drew this shape beside lot 143, which is described as "Quatre Vases couverts, dits corcets & à ances." See *Royal Collection*, p. 92 and Eriksen and Bellaigue, p. 290 for this reference

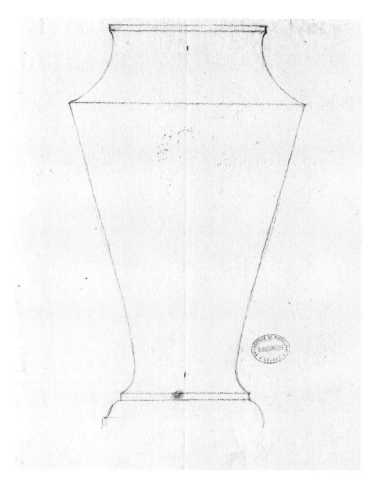

(*Above*) Fig. 61-1 *Vase cannelé*, drawing

(*Above, right*) Fig. 61-2 *Vase cannelé*, plaster model

to St. Aubin. In the 1814 inventory (AMNS, 1814 inventory, 1740–80, no. 80) of the factory the vase was called *vase gobelet à côtes*.

6 Préaud and d'Albis, p. 124 (IF 5674, fol. 20, *fournée de couverte Entre Etat du 5 Mars et certif. du 26 Juin 1754*).

7 AMNS, I. 7, 1 January 1755, *moules en plâtre*; ibid., 1 January 1756, *Pièces en blanc, tant au dépot du blanc, que dans l'attelier de Peinture et Dorure*.

8 AMNS, Vy 2, fol. 13, to Duvaux, last half of 1756, two *bleu céleste,* fifth size, 96 *livres*, two *bleu céleste*, sixth size, 72 *livres*. The sizes work out to be approximately as follows: first size: н. 15¼ (38.5 cm); second size: 13–13⅜ in. (33–34 cm); third size: 9⅛–9¼ in. (23.2–23.5 cm); fourth size: 7⅛ in. (18.1 cm); fifth size: 5¾ in. (14.6 cm); sixth size: 5–5⅛ in. (12.7–13 cm).

4 AMNS, R. 1, L. 3, d. 4, fol. 49.

10 Troude, pl. 101. The plaster model, without its knob, measures 14¼ in. (37.5 cm).

11 LD, 2, p. 265, no. 2331, 22 December 1755 (corresponds to IF 5676, fol. 54, enamel kiln, fired between 10 May and 31 December 1755, and AMNS, Vy 1, fol. 114, 1 October–31 December 1755); LD, 2, p. 357, no. 3083, 24 March 1758.

12 AMNS, Vy 1, fol. 119, last quarter 1755.

13 Ibid., Vy 2, fols. 12, 13, 15v, and 16, 20 August 1756–1 January 1757.

14 Ibid., Vy 2, fol. 58v, April 1758, and fol. 66, 1 January–1 July 1758, probably the pair sold to the prince de Soubise, see note 11 above; see also IF 5676, fol. 60, enamel kiln firing between 10 May and 31 December 1755.

15 *Royal Collection*, p. 92.

16 Ibid., pp. 91–92, no. 96 (c. 1755–57).

17 Brunet and Préaud, p. 150, no. 80 (c. 1755–56).

18 Verlet, *Sèvres*, pl. 42 (1761).

19 Eriksen and Bellaigue, pp. 289–90, no. 102 (1754).

20 A pair of fourth-size vases with *lapis mosaïque* decoration went to Duvaux in 1756, but it seems unlikely that these could refer to the Museum's vases as another pair of the first size decorated with *lapis caillouté* is listed just above this entry, indicating that by this time *mosaïque* was used to describe a different type of decoration (presumably tiny triangles such as appear on a cup and saucer dating 1756, illustrated in *Vincennes*, p. 118, no. 332, and on a tray with three jam pots in the Musée Jacquemart-André, Paris, in Brunet and Préaud, p. 163, no. 116).

21 I would like to thank Bernard Dragesco for making this observation.

22 See cat. no. 63 for more on this pattern.

23 Antoine d'Albis suggested that they either indicate the ground color worker or signify experimental pieces. Eriksen (*Waddesdon*, p. 46, no. 6) reports that they were meant to warn kiln workers to exercise special caution in handling or placing these particular pieces (as per Chavagnac and Grollier, pp. 142–43, purportedly quoting the *Carnet de Gravant*, AMNS, Y42. Not found in the *Carnet de Gravant* by Tamara Préaud or Antoine d'Albis).

62

62

Pair of orange tubs (*caisses* or *caisses carrées*)

1917.997 and 1990.51

Sèvres, 1756–1757

Soft-paste porcelain, 1917.997: H. 5⅝ × W. 4¼ × D. 4¼ in. (14.2 × 10.7 × 10.7 cm); 1990.51: H. 5⅝ × W. 4¼ × D. 4¼ in. (14.2 × 10.7 × 10.8 cm)

Green ground with birds in reserves, gilding

Marks: on both, interlaced Ls in blue with date letter D; crescent above, the mark of Louis-Denis Armand *aîné*;[1] incised 8[2]

Provenance: 1990.51: Lafontaine collection (as per Christie's, 1990);[3] 1917.997: J. Pierpont Morgan

MODEL

The Vincennes and Sèvres factory called orange tubs like these *caisses* or *caisses carrées* (sometimes spelled *quarrées*).[4] They were modeled after the type of wooden container used in the seventeenth and eighteenth centuries to hold orange trees.[5] The Meissen porcelain factory also made a square flowerpot, two of which Lazare Duvaux sold to the président de Lamoignon de Blancmesnil in December, 1749, filled with branches carrying roses.[6]

Orange tubs were first produced in 1753.[7] Molds of the first and third sizes appear for the first time among new work for 1755,[8] although they were being made in three sizes by that year.[9] The first orange tubs made probably were of the second size, such as those dated 1753–54 in the Metropolitan Museum of Art and at Waddesdon Manor, England.[10]

While no model survives at the factory, there are three extant plaster molds, of the first and second sizes.[11]

Caisses first appeared in the sale records on 24 November 1753,[12] but they were not specifically described as *carrées*. They recurred at the end of 1754, when five were sold, all coming from a kiln firing that took place between September 1754 and January 1755.[13] It was only in the last quarter of 1755 that the designation *carrées* or *quarrées* appeared, when Lazare Duvaux bought two of the first size and six of the second size.[14]

Caisses carrées sold for between 36 *livres* for third size, flowers, and 360 *livres* for second size, *bleu céleste oiseaux tres riches*.[15] Decoration encompassed the full range produced by the factory in the 1750s, from flowers on white ground, and monochrome children, to *bleu lapis*, *bleu céleste*, green, and pink grounds with flowers, fruits, birds, children, and trophies.[16] Lazare Duvaux sold two orange tubs with a *bleu lapis* ground and birds to Mademoiselle de Sens in 1754 for 288 *livres*, and two others, perhaps *bleu céleste*, also with birds, to 2nd Viscount Bolingbroke of England in 1756 for 432 *livres*.[17]

FUNCTION

The inventory of October 1752 provides us with the first mention of this form among drawings made for the service of Louis XV. *Caisses* may have originally been intended to embellish the dinner table but they were never in fact made as part of the royal service, nor did they feature in later table services.[18] So we may assume that, in actuality, they were used for more general decoration.[19] Vincennes *caisses* were usually sold in pairs and, like the Meissen version mentioned in Lazare Duvaux, were intended to hold either artificial or occasionally live plants. As a matter of routine, five drainage holes were drilled in the bottom of the leather-hard paste before firing and glazing, even though drip trays were seldom sold with the *caisses*.[20]

COMMENTARY

The Museum's orange tubs were decorated sometime in 1756 or 1757. The reserves are painted with pairs of birds in landscapes or perched on branches. Beautifully tooled gilding with scrolls, flowers, and diapered cartouches surround the reserves—no two are alike. Both *caisses* were painted by Louis-Denis Armand *aîné*, known in earlier literature as "The Crescent Painter."[21] Armand *aîné* entered the factory in 1745 and by 1755 was earning the top rate of 100 *livres* per month. By 1752 he was also receiving yearly bonuses of 300 *livres*, and by 1760, 1,200 *livres* (equal his yearly wages).[22] This made him the highest paid bird painter at Sèvres. In the 1755 Vincennes register of painters Armand is described as possessing a "degree of superiority" in the painting of birds and landscapes such that there was little room for improvement.[23]

Armand's birds are noteworthy for their lively attitudes, expressive "personalities," and careful rendering. In the 1750s he tended to place his birds—often pairs of different species—in the foreground, on or near twisted tree branches, set against pale gray-green landscapes in the distance. The leaves of the trees are small and delicate, and clumps of flowers punctuate the foreground. By the early 1760s his style changed, with the birds and foliage becoming much larger and bolder.[24]

Armand *aîné* appears to have decorated several pairs of *caisses* in the years 1756–57, as four sets, in addition to the Museum's, are known today.[25]

TECHNIQUE AND CONDITION

The green ground color used on these orange tubs was probably *vert Céladon* rather than *vert de Saxe*.[26] *Vert Céladon* was made from copper oxide and was less blue than *vert de Saxe*.[27] The formulae for various greens were known at the Vincennes factory as early as 1747 but no suitable mordant to apply them as ground colors had been developed until 1751.[28] The first mention of green ground is on 28 December 1752 when Lazare Duvaux bought a cup and saucer *fond vert fleurs* for 24 *livres*.[29] Green ground is not mentioned again in sales records until August 1753, once described as *fond verd bleu* and twice as *fond verd*.[30] Green ground then appears once in 1754 and once in 1755, and not until the second half of 1756 is it sold with any regularity.[31] Based on the scarcity of pieces dating from before 1756, it seems likely that the factory had some difficulty producing the green ground and that it only mastered the technique and marketed the new color in the course of 1756. By the second half of 1757 the color was sufficiently popular for Lazare Duvaux to purchase over five hundred pieces in a six-month period.[32]

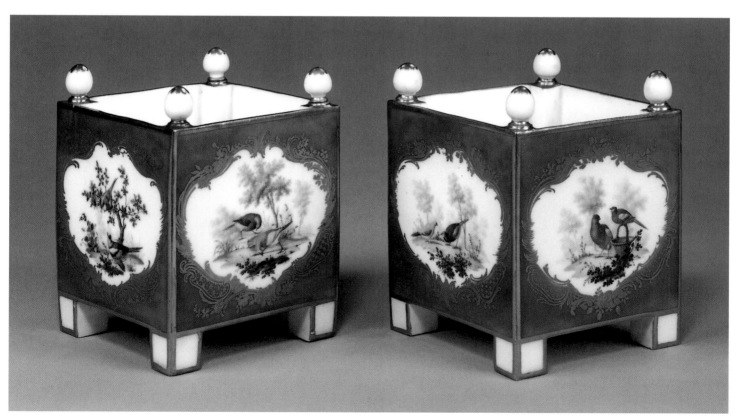

1917.997 has a crack by one of the supporting interior corner columns. This crack, which must have appeared after the biscuit firing, was filled with a mixture of biscuit powder and glaze and the tub refired before glazing.[33] Two of the finials are earthenware (*faïence fine*) replacements. The five holes that traditionally were drilled under the tub were filled in at an unknown date. Some devitrification or crystallization of the glaze has occurred on one of the reserves as well as inside the pot. 1990.51 has not had its holes filled and has its original finials. Again, there is some devitrification on the reserves.

Exhibitions: 1917.997: *Morgan Loan Exhibition*, New York, 1914, not in catalogue; *French and English 18th Century Exhibition*, Montreal, 1950, no. 154; *Vincennes and Sèvres Porcelain*, New York, 1980, no. 14

Literature: 1917.997: Chavagnac, p. 73, no. 85; *French and English 18th Century Exhibition*, no. 154; *Vincennes and Sèvres Porcelain*, no. 14; 1990.51: Dawson, *British Museum*, p. 95, no. 85

NOTES

1 See Peters, *Marks*, p. 8.

2 See Savill, 3, p. 1128 for information on this incised mark. She notes that it is frequently found on *caisses à fleurs* of the 1750s. See also Dauterman, *Wrightsman*, nos. 77a–b; 78a–b; 79a–b.

3 This orange tub was purchased by the Wadsworth Atheneum at Christie's, London, 15 October, 1990, lot 24.

4 The form of these orange tubs was identified by Eriksen (*Waddesdon*, p. 42, no. 4, and Eriksen and Bellaigue, p. 288).

5 Eriksen, *Waddesdon*, p. 42, (whence the English name orange tub) and Brunet and Préaud, p. 144.

6 LD, 2, p. 37, no. 376: "Deux petites caisses de Saxe carrées, avec des branchages portant des roses, 144 l."

7 *Vincennes*, p. 37 mistakenly states that four were in the inventory of January 1754 (for work of 1753) but later correspondence with Tamara Préaud confirms that they do not appear in the factory inventory before January 1756 (for 1755); 3 *caisses carrées* of unknown sizes appear in the biscuit kiln firing between 28 March and 18 June 1753 (IF 5673, fols. 8–9; see Préaud and d'Albis, p. 181).

8 AMNS, I. 7, 1 January 1756 (for 1755).

9 The sizes are approximately as follows: first size H. 6⁵⁄₁₆–7⅛ in. (16–18 cm); second size 5³⁄₁₆–5¹⁵⁄₁₆ in. (13.2–15 cm); third size 3⁹⁄₁₆–4 in. (9–10.1 cm). According to Brunet and Préaud, p. 144, the second size was made in 1753 while the first and third sizes appeared in 1754; Préaud and d'Albis, p. 181, state that the second and third sizes were made in 1755. See I. 7, inventory of 1 January 1756 (for 1755), which lists all three sizes among biscuit and glazed pieces in production. Sizes also appeared in the biscuit and enamel kiln records in 1755. All three sizes first appeared in the sales records in 1755, all coming from *fournée* 12, May–December 1755. No sizes were indicated prior to October of that year. Finally, there was even one mention of a *caisse* in the fourth size from the same *fournée*, sold to Duvaux between 1 October and 31 December 1755 (AMNS, Vy 1, fol. 119, *bleu céleste enfans camayeux*). It is not clear whether this was a clerical error or a unique example.

10 See Préaud and d'Albis, p. 181, no. 197 and Eriksen, *Waddesdon*, p. 42, no. 4. Extant examples suggest that Brunet and Préaud are correct in stating that the second size appeared in 1753–54.

11 AMNS, Casier 0.7.

12 Ibid., Vy 1, fol. 20, unnamed buyer. Although the citation reads *caisses fleurs camayeux bleu*, which does not specifically indicate it was a *caisse carrée*, it may still refer to this shape.

13 Ibid., Vy 1, fol. 66, 23 December, one to Bouderey; fol. 67v, 27 December, two to de Courteille, and fol. 73, 5–31 December, two to Duvaux, all *fournée* 10.

14 Ibid., fol. 118v, 1 October–31 December 1755: two *caisses quarrées 1g. fleurs* (108 *livres* each); two, second size, *fleurs* (72 *livres* each); two, second size, *Enf. Camayeux* (96 *livres* each); two, second size?, *Bleu céleste oiseaux tres riches* (360 *livres* each). Most entries in the sales records do not include the description *carrée*, but it is likely that most citations before and after this time describe the model in question.

15 Ibid. See *Vincennes*, p. 137.

16 Extant examples are numerous, and include: two, second size, *bleu céleste*, flowers, 1753–54, Waddesdon Manor, Buckinghamshire (Eriksen, *Waddesdon*, no. 4); one, third size, *bleu lapis*, flowers, 1754–55, Waddesdon Manor (ibid., no. 6); one, second size, *bleu céleste*, landscapes, 1754–55, Waddesdon Manor (ibid., no. 5); one, second size, *bleu lapis*, children, 1754–55, MNC, Sèvres (*Vincennes*, no. 48); two, third size, *bleu céleste*, children, 1754–55, MAD, Paris (ibid., nos. 49–50); two, second size, crimson monochrome children, 1755–56, Waddesdon Manor (Eriksen, *Waddesdon*, no. 12); two, third size, green ground, flowers, 1756–57, MMA, New York (Dauterman, *Wrightsman*, no. 78); two, third size, *bleu lapis*, landscapes, 1756–57, MAD, Paris (*Vincennes*, nos. 53–54); two, second size, green ground, birds, 1756–57, British Museum, London (Dawson, *British Museum*, no. 85); one, first size, green ground, flowers, 1756–57, British Museum (ibid., no. 83); two, third size, green ground, flowers, c. 1756, MFA, Boston (Munger, *Wickes*, no. 115); two, second size, *bleu céleste*, birds, c. 1756–57, formerly in the Christner collection (Christies, New York, 9 June 1979, lot 237); two, third size, *bleu lapis* and gold diaper ground, cherubs, 1757–58, Philadelphia Museum of Art (nos. 1995-057-022 & 023); two, first size, white ground, birds, 1758–59, Louvre, Paris (*Défi au goût*, p. 81, no. 21); two, second size, pink and green ground, children, c. 1758–63, Waddesdon Manor (Eriksen, *Waddesdon*, no. 44). The model continued to be produced until the 1780s, as seen in a blue ground pair with figures dated 1780 formerly in the Christner collection (Christie's, New York, 9 June 1979, lot 223).

17 LD, 2, p. 227, no. 1994; ibid., p. 295, no. 2590. The latter entry reads: "deux caisses carrées peintes à oiseaux, 432 l." Although a ground color is not specified, this entry closely follows others specifying the *bleu céleste* ground color, and the high price seems appropriate for this color as well.

18 Eriksen and Bellaigue, p. 288.

19 One exception may have been in a dessert service for Lord Bolingbroke, sold by Lazare Duvaux on 20 September 1756, which may have included two *caisses carrées* (LD, 2, p. 295, no. 2590).

20 Trays only appear in the documents in 1757, when molds and models in three sizes are mentioned in new work for 1756. See *Vincennes*, p. 37. A pair dating from 1757–58 in the Philadelphia Museum of Art (see note 16) may be en suite with square trays (*plateaux carrés*) dated 1759, presumably the type sold for use as drip trays. Dawson (*British Museum*, p. 91) notes that none have been discovered but she must not have counted the Philadelphia pair because of the discrepancy of date between the tubs and the trays. She cites Savill as suggesting the *plateau carré* as the appropriate tray for this *caisse*.

21 The mark of the crescent was given by Riocreux to the painter Ledoux but this artist had a short career at the factory and has been disassociated by most authorities from this mark. The attribution to Armand was first tentatively suggested by Zelleke, p. 12, and was subsequently proven by Bernard Dragesco in a lecture to the Société des Amis du Musée national de Céramique, Sèvres, 5 January 1993 ("'Le Peintre au Croissant' identifié: Louis Denis Armand l'aîné à Vincennes et Sèvres de 1745–1788") and has been accepted in all the subsequent literature. Much of the following information is based on Mr. Dragesco's discoveries.

22 See Zelleke, p. 12.

23 AMNS, Y.8, fol. 38.

24 See cat. no. 87 for a discussion of his 1760s style.

25 British Museum (see note 16 above); V&A, London, pink ground, 1757–58, nos. C. 428, 429-1921; Christner collection (see note 16 above); Carnegie Museum, Pittsburgh, *bleu céleste* ground.

26 As per Antoine d'Albis, on examining the objects.

27 See Préaud and d'Albis, p. 233 for technical information on the various green ground colors and these two in particular.

28 Ibid.

29 AMNS, Vy 1, fol. 6. Most of the literature says that green is first sold in 1753, which probably indicates that this earliest reference was missed.

30 Ibid., fol. 11v, 8 August 1753 to M. Le Garde des Sceaux, *beurrier fond verd bleu oiseaux*; fol. 15, same date and buyer, *pot de chambre ovale fond verd oiseaux colorés*; and fol. 15v, unnamed buyer, *moutardiers fond verd oiseaux*.

31 Ibid., fol. 34, 15 January 1754 to Machard, and Vy 2, fol. 1 to Mesdames.

32 Ibid., Vy 2, fols. 48–54v. For more discussion of green ground see Préaud and d'Albis, p. 233; Dawson, *British Museum*, p. 95; and "Le Premier Fond Vert," passim. This last article discusses a bowl marked with the date letter A for 1753–54, which was on the art market in 1988, and which, according to Tamara Préaud, received its enamel decoration July–August 1754.

33 As per technical examination by Antoine d'Albis. Pieces with such flaws appear in the inventories as needing to *repasser en couverte*. Subsequent firings would have then occurred: two for the glaze, two ground color layers, two to three enamel firings, and two gilding firings.

63

Flowerpot (*vase hollandois*)

1917.1003

Sèvres, c. 1755–1757

Soft-paste porcelain, H. 8¹³⁄₁₆ × L. 11⅜ × W. 6¹¹⁄₁₆ in. (overall) (22.3 × 28.8 × 17 cm)

Bleu lapis ground with *caillouté* gilding, polychrome birds in landscapes

Marks: vase: two unidentified incised marks; base: incised 5[1]

Provenance: perhaps Cartier et Fils, Paris, 1901;[2] J. Pierpont Morgan

MODEL

This is a two-part vase, with a fan-shaped upper part pierced with holes at the bottom. At first the factory name for this model was *vase à la hollandoise*, but it was shortened to *hollandoise* and then again to *hollandois*.[3] The name *vase éventail*, frequently found in early writings on Sèvres, is purely a nineteenth-century name.

A drawing exists that shows the outline of the model with two alternate rims, and is inscribed *vazes ou Caisse de chemine pour metre des fleurs par ordre de Mons. de Verdun Le 29 mars 1754* [vases or flower pots for the mantle as per the order of Monsieur de Verdun 29 March 1754].[4] A plaster model of the upper portion also survives, labeled *Vase caisse à fleurs à cartels*, and inscribed *1ere gr*.[5]

The model was introduced in 1754, having been designed by Jean-Claude Duplessis.[6] Models and molds for three sizes appear in the inventory under new work for that year.[7] The third size was not produced until 1758.[8] The proportions of the first size are different from those of the second and third sizes, the first size being proportionally greater in width. In 1758 a new version of the *vase hollandois*, called *hollandois nouveau ovale*, was introduced. This model, taller and more trumpet-shaped, was made in five sizes. The records seldom distinguish it from the earlier *vase hollandois* after the early 1760s.[9]

Vases hollandois were often sold as part of a garniture of three or five vases. Some sets of three comprised one *vase hollandois* of the first size with two smaller ones, while other sets included different vase forms such as *vases à oreilles* or *pots-pourris Pompadour*. Sets of five might combine three *vases hollandois* with vases of other forms.[10] *Vases hollandois* first appeared in the sales records in December 1754, when Lazare Duvaux bought one of the first size and two of the second size, decorated with *bleu céleste* ground, for 1,200 *livres*.[11] They were sold singly, in pairs, and in garnitures as described above, and received a wide variety of decoration, from simple flowers to *bleu céleste* ground with Dutch scenes.[12]

FUNCTION

This vase was meant to hold plants or bulbs in soil. The lower part held water, which would have been drawn through the holes in the upper part. These vases were also used to hold porcelain flowers.[13]

COMMENTARY

It is evident from the sales records that many *vases hollandois* were made with *bleu lapis* ground color and birds in the reserves. Examples of the first size with this decoration ranged in price from 192 *livres*, for one with a break, to 384 *livres*.[14] The registers also record *vases hollandois* with *caillouté* gilding but without further description of the painting in the reserves. One sold for 480 *livres*, and another for 528 *livres*, suggesting that they were decorated with figures, probably like one with children in the Palazzo Pitti, Florence.[15] Another was sold for 336 *livres*, which, based on the cost, may have been painted with birds.[16]

Although the Museum's vase has no painter's mark, the bird decoration may be attributed to the painter Philippe Xhrouuet.[17] A comparison with a number of pieces dating from the 1750s and bearing his mark supports this hypothesis. There is a pot-pourri vase decorated with birds by Xhrouuet in the Victoria and Albert Museum bearing his mark and sharing the same stylization of feathers and foliage and the same use of color.[18] The birds are treated much like the Atheneum's—the tilt of the head, the brushwork of the breast feathers, the broad simplification of form and musculature. In the collection of the Museum Schloss Fasanerie, Germany there are three *bleu lapis vases Hollandois*, marked by Xhrouuet, which share these characteristics as well.[19] Moreover the treatment of the tree foliage is distinguished by the same play of light and shade. Through strong decorative three-dimensional patterns we glimpse branches and twigs but the leaves themselves are scarcely defined.[20]

The pebbled gilding pattern, known at the factory as *caillouté*, was used almost exclusively with *bleu lapis* grounds. Based on surviving dated examples, this type of ornamentation must have been introduced by at least 1755.[21] The pattern was derived from Chinese porcelain where similar gold pebbling can be

63

found sparingly applied on borders, alongside other painted and gilded decoration.[22] *Caillouté* was also used by the Saint-Cloud factory, as evidenced by a spittoon in the Musée des Arts décoratifs, Paris. In this case, however, it is drawn in black on a green ground.[23] An unusual Vincennes flowerpot with a *bleu céleste* ground of about 1755–56 was formerly in the Rosebery collection at Mentmore, and may have been made to assess the effect of *caillouté* gilding with another ground color. From extant Vincennes and Sèvres porcelain it is clear that the factory favored its use on *bleu lapis*.[24]

TECHNIQUE AND CONDITION

The top rim of the vase is very thickly gilded, and shows traces of oval bosses underneath. It is likely that for the first gold firing only these bosses were gilded, but since they did not hold the gold evenly, a further application of gold over the entire rim for the next firing was called for. The gilding has crazed around the edges. The base of the flowerpot is extensively damaged, and the ensuing repairs have severely compromised its appearance.

Exhibition: *Morgan Loan Exhibition*, New York, 1914, not in catalogue

Literature: Chavagnac, p. 76, no. 90; Savill, 1, pp. 72, 75, 88, 90

NOTES

1 See Savill, 3, p. 1127, found c. 1747–90s; used in the 1750s on flower and bulb pots, pot-pourri and ornamental vases, platters, etc. See also Eriksen, *Waddesdon*, p. 114, no. 39.

2 APML, Cartier file, invoice 24 May 1901: "1 Garniture Vincennes, fond bleu de Roy dentelle or, ecusson blanc LXV, paysage oiseaux composée, d'une jardinière avec pied réparé et de 4 vases (en tous 5 pieces)," 60,000 French francs. The Museum's vase entered the collection with two *pots-pourris Pompadour* (cat. no. 64). The description and whereabouts of the other two vases is unknown.

3 For a full accounting of this shape, see Savill, 1, pp. 69–91, from which most of the following information is taken. See also Chavagnac, p. 82, no. 99; Verlet, *Sèvres*, p. 204, pl. 29; Eriksen, *Waddesdon*, pp. 98–101, no. 34; Brunet, *Frick*, pp. 209–13; *Vincennes*, pp. 143–44; Brunet and Préaud, p. 60,

pl. XVIII; Eriksen and Bellaigue, pp. 296–97, no. 107; Préaud and d'Albis, p. 182, no. 201, and Dawson, *British Museum*, pp. 118–19, no. 105.

4 AMNS, R. 1, L. 3, d. 1, fol. 2. The alternate rim describes the *cuvette à tombeau* (see cat. no. 70). See Savill, 1, p. 69.

5 AMNS, 1814 inventory, 1740–80, no. 121. See Savill, 1, pp. 69–70.

6 Eriksen (Eriksen and Bellaigue, p. 296) notes that the inscription on the drawing is in Duplessis's hand.

7 AMNS, I. 7, 1 January 1755 (for 1754).

8 Savill, 1, p. 69. Savill describes the sizes as follows: first size: H. 8½–8¹¹⁄₁₆ × L. 10¼–11⁹⁄₁₆ in. (21.5–22.6 × 25.7–29.3 cm); second size: H. 7¹⁄₁₆–7¾ × L. 7¼–7⅞ in. (18.3–19.7 × 18.4–19.9 cm); third size: H. 6¾–7¹⁄₁₆ × L. 6¹¹⁄₁₆–6⅞ in. (17.2–17.9 × 17–17.4 cm).

9 See Savill, 1, pp. 109–17 for this model.

10 Ibid., pp. 69–71.

11 AMNS, Vy 1, fol. 75v. See Savill, 1, p. 89 n. 14a. Savill lists many of the sales of these vases in note 14a–z.

12 Savill, 1, p. 89 n. 14.

13 Savill, 1, p. 72.

14 AMNS, Vy 1, fol. 135, 1 January–20 August 1756, Duvaux, along with two of the second size, 360 *livres* each; Vy 2, fol. 64, 1 January–1 July 1758, Duvaux, 384 *livres*; Vy 3, fol. 38, July 1760–January 1761, Dulac, 300 *livres*.

15 Ibid., Vy 2, fol. 7v, 23 December 1756, d'Érigny, 480 *livres*; Vy 2, fol. 85, 31 December 1758, one of the first size, 528 *livres* and two of the second size, 360 *livres* each, Louis XV as gift to Maria-Theresa of Austria; first size, perhaps now in Palazzo Pitti, no. A.c.e. 1911, n. 901 (see Eriksen, *Pitti*, p. 54, no. 21, who mistakenly says that the three vases cited above [fol. 85] were sold to Poirier); two smaller vases in the Bearsted collection, Upton House, Warwickshire (see Mallet, p. 7, no. 112; Savill, 1, pp. 71, 88 n. ff).

16 AMNS, Vy 3, fol. 14v, 29 March 1760, de Paulmy, 336 *livres*.

17 For more on Xhrouuet (or Xhrowet, or Secroix, all variants of his name), see Peters, *Marks*, p. 77; Savill, 3, pp. 1077–78. He was active at Vincennes and Sèvres from 1750 to 1775.

18 No. C 421 & A-1921, *bleu céleste*, *pot-pourri Pompadour*, date letter B for 1754–55.

19 Nos. PE858a, b, PE859. Two are dated B (1754–55) and one C (1755–56). I would like to thank Dr. Markus Miller for information and photographs.

20 His work may also be seen on an unmarked *vase hollandois* sold Christie's, New York, 5 May 1999, lot 13, white ground, blue *rocaille* cartouches.

21 See a *vase à oreilles* in the David Collection, Copenhagen, dated 1755–56 (Eriksen, *David Collection*, p. 67, pl. 46, date letter C; this same vase is illustrated in *Vincennes*, p. 139, no. 413, but mistakenly said to be marked with the date letter B). See also cat. no. 61.

22 Eriksen (*Waddesdon*, p. 27, and Eriksen and Bellaigue, p. 98) points out this debt to Chinese porcelain. An example can be seen on a Qing Dynasty "Chinese Imari" bowl from around 1710–30 in the V&A, London (no. C.1498-1910). It does not actually appear on Japanese Imari porcelain. (I would like to thank Oliver Impey and Christian Jörg for advising me on this question.)

23 MAD, Paris, no. 33781, c. 1730. See Rondot, p. 206, no. 137.

24 Sotheby's, London, 24 May 1977, lot 2012.

63

64

64

Pair of pot-pourri vases (*pots-pourris Pompadour*)

1917.1004–1005[1]

Sèvres, 1757–1758

Soft-paste porcelain, 1917.1004: H. 7³⁄₁₆ × DIAM. 5⅝ in. (18.3 × 14.2 cm); 1917.1005: H. 7⅛ × DIAM. 5⁵⁄₁₆ in. (18.1 × 14.1 cm)

Bleu lapis ground with *caillouté* gilding, polychrome birds in landscapes

Marks: interlaced Ls in blue with date letter E, dagger mark underneath for Étienne Evans[2]

Provenance: J. Pierpont Morgan

MODEL

This model of pot-pourri vase was called *pot-pourri Pompadour*. It was designed by Jean-Claude Duplessis and introduced at Vincennes before 1752.[3] The Museum's examples are the third smallest of four sizes.[4]

COMMENTARY

The reserves are by Étienne Evans, who specialized in bird painting at the factory.[5] His work has a sketchy quality, and is marked by a love of exotic, almost comical birds. Evans joined with other Sèvres bird painters to work on a number of dinner and dessert services, including those sold to the Duke of Richmond in 1766,[6] and to the maréchal de Razomousky in 1767.[7]

On the Museum's vases, Evans has created full landscape settings for his birds, which fill the reserves almost entirely. This is an early example of a style more commonly found in the 1760s.[8]

TECHNIQUE AND CONDITION

The vases were molded and the foot applied separately. The paste is grayish in tone suggesting that it was underfired in the biscuit kiln (such objects were labeled *grasses cuites*). It is possible that the reserves may have been more fully painted than usual in order hide this defect. It was difficult to refire such pieces without causing them to bubble.[9] The covers of the vases are missing.

Exhibition: *Morgan Loan Exhibition*, New York, 1914, not in catalogue

Literature: Chavagnac, p. 76, no. 90; Savill, 1, pp. 72, 90 n. 41

NOTES

1 These vases came to the Museum with a *vase hollandois* (cat. no. 63), as a presumed garniture. In fact, they did not form an ensemble, as evidenced by differences in their *caillouté* gilding and painting.

2 Active 1752–86, primarily as a bird painter. See Peters, *Marks*, p. 33.

3 See cat. no. 57 for more on this model.

4 With their covers they probably would measure about 10¼ in. (26 cm).

5 See Le Corbeiller, *Dodge*, p. 183.

6 Now at Goodwood House, West Sussex, England. See Zelleke, pp. 2–33. Evans also contributed to the service now in the Detroit Institute of Arts, formerly in the collection of Count A.D. Chérémèteff (Sheremetev) of Russia. See note 5 above.

7 Now at Waddesdon Manor, Buckinghamshire. See Eriksen, *Waddesdon*, pp. 206–25, no. 75.

8 Before that period, the landscape backgrounds were less developed, and more of the white porcelain was left undecorated. That Evans has already begun to move toward fuller reserves in these vases has led some scholars to doubt their authenticity, but no other factors suggest that they were decorated later.

9 Préaud and d'Albis, pp. 216–17 (*biscuit*).

65

Mounted vase (*vase cloche*, or *gobelet en cloche*[1])

1917.1065

Sèvres, 1763

Soft-paste porcelain, gilt bronze, silver and gold, overall H. (closed) 10⅞ × w. 7³⁄₁₆ × D. 5¹⁵⁄₁₆ in. (27.6 × 18.2 × 15.1 cm); H. (open) 11¹³⁄₁₆ in. (30 cm); H. of statuette and pedestal 3½ in. (8.9 cm)

Green ground

Marks: silver mark of an ear, probably small discharge mark of Tours, 1781–Revolution[2]

Inscriptions: on rim of cover, • *DULAC* • *MᴰD* • *RÜE Sᵀ* • *HONNORÉ* • *JNVENISTE* • Engraved on ends of equestrian pedestal: *Posé Le 20 Juin 1763* and *Louis Le Bien Aimé*

Provenance: Madame de Pompadour, 1763–1764; Marquis de Marigny, 1764–1781; Alexandre Joseph Paillet, 1782;[3] J. & S. Goldschmidt, Frankfurt-am-Main, 1905;[4] J. Pierpont Morgan

MODEL

The Atheneum's vase predates all known records for a vase designed for mounting.[5] The first vase for mounting recorded at the Sèvres factory appears in the glaze kiln records for 1764.[6] *Vases à monter*, seemingly the name for these vases at the outset of production, are also among existing stock in 1764.[7] We know that Horace Walpole purchased three ormolu-mounted blue vases late in 1765 or early in 1766 for John Chute, for 152 *livres* each, one still in the collection at The Vyne, Hampshire, England.[8] The first recorded sale at Sèvres of a vase for mounting, with a green ground, was in 1767.[9] The term *vase à monter* probably refers to more than one model

of vase designed to be mounted such as baluster- and bottle-shaped examples in the Rothschild collection at Waddesdon Manor, England.[10]

Only from 1772 did the sales ledgers refer to *gobelets en cloche* or more frequently *vases cloches*.[11] The qualification *cloche* refers to the vases' reversed bell shape.[12] So had the Museum's mounted vase been made at that time, it would have been named thus.[13] The records tell us that the *cloche* was available in three sizes with a plain *beau bleu*, *bleu lapis*, *verd*, or *bleu céleste* ground. In one instance three *bleu céleste* examples are described as painted with flowers.[14] Without mounts the vases cost between 54 and 120 *livres*, no doubt according to size and ground color.[15]

Vases cloches were fitted with several variations of gilt-bronze mounts. The Hartford vase, for example, sits on a socle decorated with acanthus leaves, resting on a foot of laurel leaves, standing on a plain square base. Laurel leaves cup the bottom of the porcelain body. The rim is decorated with a concave molding with oves, resting between a small rope molding underneath and a larger band with a twist or cable design above. The body of the vase is flanked by two masks in the form of satyrs' heads, from whose horns double laurel swags issue. The cover is decorated with a trophy comprising military symbols, including a flag, cannon, helmet, and laurel leaves.

One finds very similar mounts on other *vases cloches*, varying primarily in the decorative motifs used on the moldings. An example in the Royal Collection, England, has a similar socle of acanthus leaves but the collar is more pronounced, the foot is decorated with crossed ribbons, and the base has chamfered corners and is decorated with a Greek key design. The rim moldings and bands are akin to the Hartford example, but the oves are pierced, distinguishing the vase as a pot-pourri, and the Greek key motif is continued on the band under the rim. The cover is topped by a pine cone finial. The masks and swags are the same.[16] Another version of the satyr-mask type, found on a pair of green vases in the Rothschild collection, Waddesdon Manor, England, rests on a wider, fluted stem, with a ribbon molding cupping the porcelain body, a laurel wreath foot, and a square base with Greek key decoration. The rim moldings are less elaborate than the Hartford and Royal Collection examples, and consist of a guilloche band resting on a rope border. A large acanthus-leaf cap and finial dominate the cover. Again, the masks and the swags are the same.[17] This variant became the standard version of the satyr-mask model.

Yet another close variation of these mounts may be found on a green pair in the Musée des Arts décoratifs, Paris. In these vases—which sit on unembellished square plinths—there is a single swag issuing from the satyrs' heads, and it is bedecked with oak rather than laurel leaves.[18]

A rather different version of the mount features lions' mask ring handles joined by swags of lions' pelts. The stem supporting the vase is similarly proportioned to those on the Waddesdon Manor vases described above, but is decorated with acanthus leaves. The foot boasts an entrelac design on a pounced ground and rests on a square plinth with a Greek-key fretted motif. The rim of the vase consists of a Greek-key collar above

a pierced Vitruvian-scroll frieze and laurel band. The cover is topped by a pine cone finial resting on an acanthus-leaf spray. It is this style of mount that one finds on a vase signed by Dulac in the collection of the Lazienki Palace, Warsaw.[19] Other examples with nearly identical mounts include: a blue-ground pair in the château de Fontainebleau, France;[20] another blue-ground pair known to have belonged to the duchesse d'Orléans and then to her son Louis-Philippe at the château d'Eu;[21] a third blue-ground pair formerly in the collection of the Marquess of Cholmondeley, Houghton Hall, Norfolk, England;[22] and a single vase in Pavlovsk Palace, Russia.[23] The difference between all these vases lies in the decoration of the top rim and the square plinth. The Fontainebleau and château d'Eu examples have a striated design on these elements, while those from the Cholmondeley collection are decorated with Greek-key friezes.[24]

Occasionally these mounted *vases cloches* included interior fittings, primarily candelabra, which were spring-loaded, enabling them to rise up out of the vase when the lid was removed. Such fittings are found in the vases at Fontainebleau, the château d'Eu vases, and those once belonging to the Earl of Swinton.[25]

Fig. 65-1 *Equestrian monument of Louis XV*, model by Edmé Bouchardon, engraved after a drawing by Prévost

Both the lions' head and satyrs' head mounts were used with other materials in the eighteenth and nineteenth centuries. A small pair of red lacquer vases with the satyrs' heads and double swags was formerly in the collection of Mrs. John Jay Whitney, New York.[26] A pair of Chinese powder blue porcelain pot-pourri vases with nineteenth-century lions' head mounts was sold in 1999.[27]

FUNCTION

European goldsmiths began mounting porcelain vases as early as the fourteenth century, when they took rare, oriental porcelain and garnished it with precious metals for display in collectors' cabinets or on sideboards.[28] This practice gathered popularity as more oriental porcelain was imported into Europe. By the middle of the eighteenth century Paris had become the main center of production, but by then the mounts were made of gilt bronze rather than silver gilt or gold. This was a less expensive means of creating decorative objects that would blend well with the gilt-bronze mounted furniture, wall lights, candelabra, and overall decorative schemes of rococo and then neoclassical interiors.

The popularity of mounting oriental porcelain waned after mid-century as pressure was brought to bear on the *marchands-merciers* who commissioned such objects to patronize France's own porcelain factory. Sèvres began producing in the 1760s monochrome wares oriental in character that were intended specifically for mounting.

COMMENTARY

Most *vases cloches* and *gobelets en cloche* were sold to a *marchand-mercier* named Dulac, who had his shop in the rue Saint-Honoré, Paris. Records show that in 1772, and for the next seven years, he bought twenty *vases cloches*.[29] Since he inscribed the lid of the Atheneum's vase, he must have been buying such vases even before that date, perhaps under the rubric of either *vases à monter* or the more generic *pièces d'ornements*.[30] Traditionally scholars have assumed the buyer was the *marchand-mercier* Antoine Dulac, who died in 1765, and whose widow and son (Antoine-Charles) continued the business.[31] However, there were three dealers by the name Dulac in the rue Saint-Honoré at that time, and it has recently been suggested that, in fact, the dealer to whom the Sèvres factory sold its wares was another one of the three: Monsieur Jean Dulac.[32] He was appointed *marchand privilégié du Roi* in 1753, and then *marchand-bijoutier*, having already become a *marchand-gantier-parfumeur* before 1740. He advertised "garniture de cheminées, vases monté[e]s, girandoles," and "pendules de bureaux," all "en or moulu." Some of his bills still exist, and carry the headings "le berceau d'or," or "Dulac marchand-gantier-parfumeur et bijoutier rue Saint Honoré près de l'Oratoire à la tête d'or."[33] The archive at Sèvres retains a list of dealers used by the factory, with their guarantors. It includes Jean Dulac and his wife Marie Anne Garyson, and gives as collateral their house on the rue Saint-Honoré "où pend pour enseigne le berceau d'or" [at the sign of the golden cradle].[34] Dulac's name appears in the Sèvres sales records from 1758 until 1776, although he seems to have retired in 1774. P.A.

Le Baigue succeeded Dulac as *marchand privilégié du Roi* in 1775, buying part of his stock for 66,000 *livres*. Jean Dulac died in 1786.

Instead of the spring-loaded candelabrum that emerges from the vase at Pavlovsk when the cover is removed, the Atheneum's has a silver and gold statuette that rises up. The statuette is a reduction of the equestrian statue of Louis XV by Edmé Bouchardon, *sculpteur du roi*,[35] which was unveiled on 20 June 1763 on the Place Louis XV (now Place de la Concorde) in Paris. The commission for the Bouchardon statue called for a fifteen-foot high bronze figure of the king, mounted on horseback, on a white marble pedestal eighteen feet high and thirteen feet long (fig. 65-1).[36] The corners of the pedestal were marked by four bronze caryatid figures representing the virtues of Force, Justice, Prudence, and Love of Peace. Bas-reliefs decorated the sides of the pedestal. On one side, Louis XV was depicted in a triumphal chariot, being crowned by Victory and preceded by Fame, and receiving homage from the conquered provinces. On the other side the king was depicted procuring Peace for Europe.[37] The front and rear faces bore Latin inscriptions. One translates, "To Louis XV, the best leader, because, as victor at the Scheldt, the Meuse, and the Rhine, he procured peace with arms and with peace he secured the good fortune of his own realm and that of Europe." The rear plaque translates, "The governor [prefect] and magistrates decreed this monument of public piety in 1748 and put it up in 1763."[38]

The City of Paris commissioned Bouchardon to create this monumental sculpture in 1748. Originally it was to commemorate France's victory in the War of Austrian Succession (1740–48), but work on the commission went slowly. The statue had not been cast as of 1758, by which time France was again embroiled in conflict, this time against England and Prussia in the Seven Years' War. Plans had been made to unveil the statue in August, but these were postponed until after the war ended.[39]

The dedication finally took place on 20 June 1763.[40] The peace

Fig. 65-2 *Inauguration of the Statue of Louis XV*, Augustin de Saint-Aubin after Gravelot, 1766

treaty had been signed on 10 February, and by the 17th, the statue left Bouchardon's studio for its three-and-one-half day journey to the Place Louis XV. It was not unveiled until the formal declaration of peace in June.[41]

The ceremonies and festivities surrounding the unveiling lasted three days, and appear to have been inextricably linked to the celebration of the peace.[42] The inauguration of the sculpture was the subject of countless prints, poems, plays, commentaries, medals, reductions and other commemoratives.[43] These included an engraving by Gabriel de Saint-Aubin, dated 1763, depicting allegories of genius (or spirits) unveiling the monument.[44] Augustin de Saint-Aubin recorded the inauguration in an engraving in 1766 (fig. 65-2), and the painter Joseph Vien represented the event on canvas as well.[45] Pigalle made two bronze reductions of the statue for the Hôtel de Ville de Paris, and Bouchardon's pupil, Louis-Claude Vassé, made seven more in 1764. The City of Paris presented them to Louis XV, Madame de Pompadour, and other public figures.[46] It is not surprising, therefore, to find a Sèvres *vase cloche* commemorating this historic occasion.

The gold and silver statuette inside the Museum's vase is a relatively close copy of the original, with adjustments made for the drastic difference in scale. The shape of the pedestal and disposition of the reliefs is the same but the side panels are decorated with trophies rather than multi-figured compositions. The lengthy Latin inscriptions on the original end panels have been replaced with short inscriptions commemorating the king and the date of the unveiling.[47] The gold work is unsophisticated and lacks detail. This must be, in part, due to the softness of the gold, which is near twenty-four carat.

Documents confirm that this *vase cloche* belonged to Madame de Pompadour. In her probate inventory of spring 1764, it is listed among items then at her Paris *hôtel* as "Un vaze de porcelaine verte, garny en bronze doré, contenant la statue équestre de la place Louis quinze."[48] Her reduction of the Bouchardon statue itself also appears in the inventory, where it was in the Grand Salon of her Paris *hôtel*.[49] The particular circumstances under which Madame de Pompadour acquired the Sèvres vase are not known, but we can easily imagine that she commissioned it in 1763 to mark the unveiling of the Bouchardon statue of her king.

Based on its likely date of 1763, the Atheneum's mounted vase and cover appears to have been the first of this type made at Sèvres for Dulac. The inscription on the mounts make it clear that Dulac was responsible in some way for mounting the porcelain. He also inscribed the vase of similar form in the Lazienski Palace, Warsaw.[50] It is highly unusual for a *marchand-mercier* to sign an object in this manner. The inclusion of the words *inveniste* and *invenit* strongly suggests that Dulac wished to take credit for the design itself of the mounts. It is, however, possible that he was presenting himself only as the proprietor of the model even if he had not directly participated in its design. By commissioning such mounts and preserving the lead models used to cast the bronzes, dealers could effectively copyright the design. Dulac probably owned the lead models for the lion masks and satyrs' masks found on this type of mounted vase,

and thus could justify signing the mounts with the word *inveniste*.[51]

Upon Madame de Pompadour's death on 15 April 1764 the vase passed to her brother, the marquis de Marigny, *directeur général des bâtiments du roi*. It is listed in the inventory of his estate, made upon his death in 1781,[52] and was sold with his effects between 18 March and 6 April 1782.[53]

TECHNIQUE AND CONDITION

The lid is cracked and repaired. There has been a repair to one branch of gilt-bronze leaves on the lid. The porcelain body consists of a simple cup and cover.[54]

Exhibitions: *Morgan Loan Exhibition*, New York, 1914, not in catalogue; *Antique Taste*, 1982; *Morgan*, Hartford, 1987, no. 64

Literature: Chavagnac, pp. 112–13, no. 139; Eriksen and Bellaigue, pp. 323–24, no. 136; *Antique Taste*, p. 6, fig. 6, p. 13; de Bellaigue, "Sèvres," pp. 172–73, no. 64; Whitehead, pp. 47–48

NOTES

1 The records sometimes say *vases cloches*.

2 See Carré, p. 166. The reason why the piece carries a discharge mark from Tours is unclear. The date of 1781–92 suggests that it may have been marked after it left Marigny's collection (see below) but there is no evidence to explain why it was marked in Tours rather than Paris. It should, in fact, carry the discharge mark for small works in Paris from 1763 (a dog's head, see cat. no. 199) but perhaps, as it probably was made for Mme de Pompadour (see below), it was exempt from guild rules.

3 Parisian art dealer, c. 1774–1813. See Edwards, passim. I would like to thank Alden Gordon for informing me that Paillet bought this vase (based on an annotated entry in Marigny's sale catalogue) and for providing me with Ms. Edward's dissertation.

4 APML, J. & S. Goldschmidt file, invoice, 29 June 1905: "An old Sèvres-vase, bronze-mounted, of the Louis XVI period," £1,500. "On a bronze socle stands the vase of green Sèvres-porcelain; at the edge of the same are garlands and little heads; on the cover war-emblems of bronze. Raising the cover (which is repaired quite a little) there rises inside a monument, representing a rider on a socle. On this socle one finds the inscription: 'LOUIS LE BIEN AIMÉ,' and the date 1763. On the inside of the cover are the following words: 'Dulac md. Rue St. Honor, Inveniste.'"

5 See below for dating of this vase to between June 1763 and April 1764.

6 IF 5675, fol. 25, 30 December 1764, *vaze à monter* (see Savill, 1, p. 30 n. 41); see also IF 5675, fols. 29, 32, between 31 December 1765 and 1 July 1766, *1 vaze monter* (Eriksen and Bellaigue, p. 323).

7 AMNS, I. 7, 1 January 1765 (for 1764), *Pièces en Biscuit mises au Rebut, vases et Gobelets à monter*. The name for this specific model appears to have changed in the 1770s. For more on *vases à monter* see cat. no. 74.

8 First discussed by Watson, "Walpole," p. 327. See also Eriksen, *Neoclassicism*, pl. 238; Eriksen and Bellaigue, pp. 323–24. The vase now at The Vyne has a new lid made in 1998 by the Sèvres factory. According to a conversation with Bet McLeod, Walpole had a similar garniture in *bleu céleste*.

9 AMNS, Vy 4, fol. 121, unnamed buyer, 13 July 1767: *2 Vases a Monter Verd plein*.

10 Eriksen, *Waddesdon*, pp. 232–35, nos. 79–80. There are other references in the sales ledgers and artists' records to *vases à monter* or *gobelets à monter* but these probably refer to other mounted vases. See cat. no. 74 for other mounted vases that may be candidates for *gobelets à monter*.

11 AMNS, Vy 5, fol. 53v, 1772, Dulac; Vy 5, fol. 110v, second half 1773, Dulac. See Eriksen and Bellaigue, p. 324; de Bellaigue, "Sèvres," p. 172; Verlet, *Bronzes dorés*, p. 206.

12 De Bellaigue, "Sèvres," p. 172.

13 Verlet (*Bronzes dorés*, p. 206) suggests that *vases à monter* and *gobelets à*

monter may also have been used to describe the Atheneum-type mounted vase, but sales ledgers for Dulac show that at least in two cases, *gobelets à monter* appear on the same sheets as a *gobelet en cloche* and a *vase cloche* (see note 11 above).

14 See vases decorated by Bouillat, described in note 15 below. See also enamel kiln firing, 24 April 1779, Bouillat and Boulanger, AMNS, Vl'1, fol. 52.

15 AMNS, Vy 5, fol. 53v, Dulac, 1772; Vy 5, fol. 110v, Dulac, second half 1773. The sales records list *vases cloches* and *gobelets en cloche* for 54, 60, 72, 84, and 120 *livres*, a first-size blue-ground example being 84 *livres* (ibid., Vy 7, fol. 142v, 19 March 1779, Héricourt). Comparing existing examples of mounted vases of this general type, at least two sizes emerge (mounted), one averaging 11¹⁄₁₆ in. (28 cm) in height, the other 16¹⁵⁄₁₆–17⁷⁄₁₆ in. (43–44 cm) in height. In 1774 two of the first size and one of the second size are listed among blue-ground pieces in the *magasin de porcelaine* (ibid., I. 8). An entry in the artists' records for Bouillat *père*, 28 December 1778 (AMNS, Vj'1, fol. 30) describes three *vases cloches 3e Groupes* confirming that in fact three sizes were made. See below for more on the different versions made.

16 No. RCIN 53006 (not in Laking). This vase has a blue ground.

17 Eriksen, *Waddesdon*, pp. 236–37, no. 81. Nearly identical mounts can be found on a green-ground vase sold Christie's, New York, 21 October 1997, lot 277. Another green-ground vase with the same gilt-bronze mounts, differing only in a striated square base, was sold Sotheby's, New York, 10–12 October 1985, lot 109. Still another blue-ground example with a Greek key base (without its cover) sold Sotheby's, New York, 22 and 24 April 1982, lot 46.

18 No. 36216 AB (information kindly provided by Bertrand Rondot). The same style mounts can be found on a green-ground vase sold Palais Galliéra, Paris, 25 November 1976 (illustrated *Connaissance des Arts*, October 1976), later sold Sotheby's, Monaco, 17 June 1988, lot 682; see also Sotheby's, Monaco, 3 March 1990, lot 179.

19 Verlet believes that the porcelain body is not original but is a later replacement.

20 Identified by Christian Baulez as those currently at Fontainebleau. See *L'Estampille / L'Objet d'Art,* June 1992, pp. 34–52. See also Verlet, *Bronzes dorés*, p. 205, fig. 236; Samoyault, "Du Barry," p. 92.

21 Christie's, London, 2 December 1997, lot 40. Patrick Leperlier, who authored the Christie's catalogue entry for these vases, suggests that they could easily have been the ones in Mme du Barry's collection at Louveciennes.

22 Cholmondeley Family and the Late Sir Philip Sassoon, Houghton sale, Christie's, London, 8 December 1994, lot 83.

23 *Pavlovsk*, p. 150, fig. 20.

24 Other examples include a green-ground pair in the Rothschild family collection at Waddesdon Manor, Buckinghamshire, (Greek-key friezes, different than previous pair cited in note 17 above); a blue-ground pair, Sotheby's, New York, 7 May 1983, lot 87A (Greek-key friezes); a lapis blue-ground pair, Palais d'Orsay, Paris, 28 November 1978, lot 110 (Greek-key design, laurel finial); and a blue-ground pair, Palais des Congrès, Versailles, 7 April 1974, lot 120, (Greek key); a green-ground pair from the collection of Lord Ashburton (Christie's, London, 19 March 1964, lot 59); a pair without covers from the collection of the Earl of Swinton (Christie's, London, 4 December 1975, lot 51). It is important to bear in mind that some examples in auctions could be early 19th century or later.

25 See note 24.

26 Sotheby's, New York, 22–25 April 1999, lot 70, last quarter 18th century, H. 12 in. (30.5 cm).

27 Christie's, New York, 27 May 1999, lot 347, catalogued as Louis XVI style, H. 18⅛ in. (46 cm).

28 For information on this general practice see Watson, *Oriental*, passim.

29 AMNS, Vy 5, fol. 53v, 1772, two *gobelets en cloche*, at 54 *livres*, three at 84 *livres*; Vy 5, fol. 110v, second half 1773, four *vases en cloche beau bleu*, at 60 *livres*, one at 84 *livres*; Vy 6, fol. 157, second half 1776, one at 120 *livres*; Vy 6, fol. 223 (misnumbered, actually fol. 225), first half 1777, one at 84 *livres*; Vy 6, fol. 250, second half 1777, one *beau bleu* at 84 *livres*;

Vy 7, fol. 47v, first half 1778, two at 84 *livres*; and Vy 7, fol. 214v, second half 1779, one at 60 *livres*, three together, 432 *livres*, and one at 72 *livres*.

30 An unpublished survey of Dulac's purchases of *pièces d'ornements* made by John Whitehead (kindly shared with the author) reveals that before the second half of 1763 none were priced that correspond to the later prices for *vases* or *gobelets en cloche* (see note 29 above). Dulac did pay 54 *livres* each for two *pièces d'ornements* in the first six months of 1764 (AMNS, Vy 4, fol. 10v). The Hartford vase, being the second size and less expensive than *bleu céleste*, probably cost either 54, 60, or 72 *livres*. Either Dulac paid for the Museum's vase several months after it was delivered to him (it must have been well before Mme de Pompadour's death in April 1764 and probably was sometime near June 1763, the date of the statue commemorated by the Museum's example) or it was not listed as a *pièce d'ornement*. Between 1764 and 1772, when the name *vases* or *gobelets en cloche* appeared in the sales ledgers, Dulac purchased *pièces d'ornements* for various sums, including 54, 60, 72, and 84 *livres*. It is possible that some of these sales included the type of vases for mounting under discussion.

31 Whitehead, pp. 47–49.

32 This new information on Jean Dulac was presented without documentation by Patrick Leperlier in the Christie's, London catalogue (Cholmondeley Family and the Late Sir Philip Sassoon, Houghton, 8 December 1994, lot 83, see note 22 above) for a pair of blue-ground *vases cloches*. The summary that follows is based on Mr. Leperlier's entry. This entry is reprinted with some modification in Christie's, London, 2 December 1997, lot 40, describing the *vases cloches* formerly at château d'Eu (see note 21 above). It has not been possible to obtain further information from Mr. Leperlier.

33 These designations refer to mercantile corporations that controlled and regulated commerce in luxury goods in 18th-century France. They were somewhat akin to artisanal bodies (guilds), each comprised merchants who dealt in more than one type of product. The *marchand-gantier-parfumeur* sold among other items gloves and perfume. The *marchand-bijoutier* sold furniture and porcelain. For an in-depth study of the *marchands-merciers* see Sargentson, passim. Regarding Dulac, it is evident from the Christie's catalogue entries that Mr. Leperlier had access to several extant bills. According to Leperlier, Dulac inherited his signboard *le berceau d'or* from his father Charles Dulac and that it appeared in several of Jean Dulac's bills.

34 AMNS, B 6, l. 4, 1759. This information was kindly provided by Tamara Préaud. Dulac and his wife were financially responsible for themselves and each other.

35 Bouchardon (1698–1762) had been a professor at the Académie Royale de Peinture et de Sculpture since 1745, having won the Prix de Rome in 1722. He executed numerous sculptures at Versailles and in Paris, before being commissioned by the City of Paris to create this equestrian statue. See Duclaux, passim.

36 Engraving by B.L. Prévost, after his own drawing (Cabinet des Estampes de la Bibliothèque Nationale, Collection Hennin, no. 9162 Rés.). For detailed information on this important public sculpture, see Rombouts, passim. See also Duclaux.

37 Duclaux, p. 31, no. 62. The bas-reliefs were actually executed by Jean-Baptiste Pigalle, who completed the caryatids as well upon Bouchardon's death in 1762. See Rombout, p. 257 n. 7; Gaborit, pp. 15–16.

38 On the front: *Ludovico XV / Optimo principi / quod / ad Scaldim Mosam Rhenum / victor / pacem armis / pace / et suorum et Europeae / felicitatem / quaesivit*. On the rear: *Hoc / pietatis publicae / monumentum / praefectus / et / aediles / decreverunt / anno MDCCXLVIII / posuerunt / anno MDCCLXIII*. See *Place Louis XV*, p. 56, no. 57. Translation of Latin inscription kindly provided by James Higgenbotham. The references to the rivers Scheldt, Meuse, and Rhine, correspond to most of the battle zones in the War of Austrian Succession.

39 Rombouts discusses the reasons for the postponement (pp. 261–62). In addition to the political reasons, the statue was in such an incomplete state that the sculptor estimated that eighteen more months were needed to finish it. (See a letter from Bouchardon to Mme de Pompadour in the Bibliothèque Doucet, Paris, Mss. AAP, Carton 36, *Sculpteurs, Edme Bouchardon: Reflexions presentées a Madame de Pompadour au sujet de la*

statee équestre que l'on doit placer dans un mois, le 6 juillet 1758. This letter was kindly brought to my attention by Andrew McClellan, who provided me with a transcription made by Katie Scott.)

40 For a complete accounting of the unveiling see Rombouts, pp. 263–76.

41 The Place Louis XV was as yet unfinished in February.

42 Ibid., p. 265.

43 Duclaux, pp. 35–38, nos. 76–85; Rombouts, pp. 276–82.

44 Duclaux, pp. 35–36, no. 77.

45 Augustin de Saint-Aubin after Gravelot, 1766, Louvre, no. 21168 LR; see ibid., p. 36, no. 78. For the composition by Vien, see a sketch in the Musée Carnavalet, Paris.

46 De Bellaigue, "Sèvres," p. 172 n. 1. See *Place Louis XV*, p. 55, no. 55. See also Granet, passim.

47 Louis XV had been called *Bien-aimé* ("beloved") since his recovery from illness at Metz in 1744.

48 Cordey, p. 207, no. 2518. This reference originally was brought to the attention of Geoffrey de Bellaigue by Rosalind Savill, and published in de Bellaigue, "Sèvres," p. 172 n. 2.

49 Cordey, p. 36, no. 342.

50 *DULAC MD RUE ST HONORÉ A PARIS INVENIT*. See Verlet, *Bronzes dorés*, pp. 72–73, figs. 66–67. See note 19 above.

51 See Sargentson, pp. 50–52. Eventually the Sèvres factory must have obtained the right to sell these vases already mounted, for in 1782 two were sold to Prince Bariatinsky on behalf of the Russian grand duke Paul (travelling as the comte du Nord) for 1,680 *livres* (AMNS, Vy 8, fol. 181, June 1782). See Christie's, London, 2 December 1997, lot 40, p. 74. These are now in the Palace of Pavlovsk, near St. Petersburg (see *Pavlovsk*, 2, p. 150, fig. 20), along with yet another matching *vase cloche*. There is no mention of this third vase in the recorded sale to Prince Bariatinsky.

52 *Inventaire après décès de Marquis de Marigny et de Ménars, 1781*. Minutier Centrale, XCIX 657, no. 961: "Un vase de porcelaine verte garnie de bronze doré, renfermant la statue équestre de Louis XV en or et argent prisé soixante-douze livres."

53 Lot 251: "Une très-petite Statue équestre de Louis XV en or et argent, renfermée dans un vase de 10 pouces de haut, en porcelaine verte, garnie d'ornemens de bronze doré." Annotations on the sale catalogue indicate that it was bought by the dealer Paillet (see note 2 above). Alden Gordon first linked the Atheneum's vase with these items in Marigny's inventory and sale, and allowed Geoffrey de Bellaigue to publish them in *Morgan*, Hartford, p. 172 nn. 3–4.

54 See Eriksen, *Waddesdon*, p. 236, no. 81 for a similar object without its mounts.

66

Flowerpot (*caisse* or *cuvette à fleurs Verdun*)

1989.84[1]

Sèvres, 1765

Soft-paste porcelain, H. 4½ × L. 9½ × W. 4¾ in. (11.4 × 24.1 × 12.1 cm)

White ground, polychrome birds, gilding

Marks: elaborate interlaced Ls in blue, with date letter M; no incised marks

Provenance: Sotheby's, London, 1989; Dragesco-Cramoisan, Paris, 1989[2]

66

66

MODEL

The Sèvres factory called this flowerpot a *caisse* or *cuvette à fleurs Verdun*.[3] A drawing in the archives showing its contours is inscribed *Caise à fleurs unÿe contourne fait Le 7 mars 1754 par ordre de Mo.r de Verdun plus en juillet 1759 fait 2eme et 3eme grandeur* [plain shaped flowerpot made 7 March 1754 as per the instructions of Monsieur de Verdun then in July 1759 made in the second and third sizes].[4] Plaster models in three sizes are recorded in the inventory of January 1755,[5] although as the inscription on the drawing indicates, the second and third sizes were only put into production in 1759.[6] The shape may have evolved from a simpler flowerpot, the *cuvette à fleurs unie*, which was introduced in 1753 and apparently abandoned by 1760.[7] The *cuvette Verdun* may also have been a modification of the *vase à compartiments*, but with alterations to the shape of the back, no central partition, and with simpler scroll handles. The footprints of both vases are indeed very similar, as are the front faces.[8]

According to the records the earliest known sale of the model was in late 1755. *Cuvettes* of the first size were priced between 192 and 600 *livres*. From 1759 (when sizes rarely were specified), prices ranged from 144 to 528 *livres*.[9] Most *cuvettes Verdun* were sold as single flowerpots, although occasionally they formed pairs or parts of garnitures.[10] Examples are known today in all three sizes: some with children or landscapes against a white ground and others with a full range of enameled and gilded decoration against green, pink, turquoise, or blue grounds.[11]

The Museum's flowerpot takes its name from Jean-François Verdun de Monchiroux, who was a *fermier-général* and shareholder of the Vincennes factory from 1745. He was much involved with the operations of the factory, including perhaps the decision to move the facility from Vincennes to Sèvres. He also had some involvement with designs for models,[12] and his name is linked to several other Vincennes and Sèvres shapes, among them a vase, teapot, sugar bowl, cup, salt cellar, salad bowl, juice pot and jam pot.[13] If his many purchases during 1748–49 from Lazare Duvaux are anything to go by, Verdun seems to have been especially interested in flower vases.[14]

COMMENTARY

The Hartford flowerpot is of the third or smallest size. It was painted by Louis-Denis Armand *aîné*, although it is marked only with his characteristically elaborate interlaced Ls and not with his identifying crescent, which he stopped using around 1761. The primary scenes are not confined to small reserves, but encompass the central panels on both sides of the flowerpot. This pictorial approach is enhanced by the use of a white ground so that the entire surface is like a painter's canvas. The large-scale birds and foliage typify Armand's 1760s style.[15] There is a mate to this flowerpot in a private collection in England.[16]

NOTES

1 Museum credit line: Mr. and Mrs. Richard Koopman and Mr. and Mrs. Bernard Schiro, by exchange; Gift of Mrs. James G. Stobridge, by exchange; Gift of James Junius Goodwin.

2 21 February 1989, lot 168.

3 Identified by Verlet, *Sèvres*, p. 201, pl. 18; see also Eriksen, *Waddesdon*,

p. 84; *Vincennes*, p. 40; Brunet, *Frick*, pp. 238–42; Savill, 1, pp. 56–62. The discussion of the form that follows will be based on these earlier sources, especially Savill.

4 AMNS, R. 1, L. 3, d. 2, fol. 3. Brunet (*Frick*, p. 238) and Eriksen (*Waddesdon*, p. 84) also cite a plaster model in the factory archives, which is not found in Troude or in 19th-century inventories (See Savill, 1, p. 61 n. 3).

5 AMNS, I. 7, 1 January 1755, for 1754, *moules en plâtre*. Savill lists the sizes as follows: first size: H. 5¹⁵⁄₁₆–6⁷⁄₁₆ × W. 12½–13⅜ in. (15–16.4 × 31.8–34 cm); second size: H. 4¹⁵⁄₁₆–5⁵⁄₁₆ × W. 10¼–10¹¹⁄₁₆ in. (12.5–13.1 × 26–27.4 cm); third size: H. 3¹⁵⁄₁₆–4⁷⁄₁₆ × W. 9⁵⁄₁₆–9⅝ in. (10–11.3 × 23.7–24.4 cm).

6 Savill, 1, p. 56. Brunet (*Frick*, p. 238) suggests that the addition of smaller editions of vases such as these into the factory's production around 1759–60 was due to a general reorganization of the factory's finances and an effort to produce lower-priced items. Savill also notes other vases that were introduced in smaller sizes in 1759.

7 Savill, 1, pp. 56, 61 n. 8. See also Brunet and Préaud, p. 158, no. 102.

8 See Préaud and d'Albis, p. 182. Although this model only appears in the inventory under new work for 1755, an example at the MNC, Sèvres, can be dated c. 1752–53 (Préaud and d'Albis, p. 150, no. 114).

9 See Savill, 1, pp. 57, 61 n. 10 for many of the sales records.

10 Ibid., pp. 57, 62 nn. 16–17.

11 Ibid., p. 61 n. 2.

12 Ibid., 3, pp. 988–89.

13 Ibid., 1, p. 57.

14 Ibid., 3, p. 989.

15 For Armand, see cat. no. 62. For his 1760s style see cat. no. 87.

16 I wish to thank Bernard Dragesco for this information.

67

Pair of orange tubs (*caisses*)

1917.963–964

Sèvres, c. 1765–1770

Soft-paste porcelain, 1917.963: H. 5¹⁵⁄₁₆ × W. 4⅛ × D. 4⅛ in. (15 × 10.4 × 10.4 cm); 1917.964: H. 5⁵⁄₁₆ × W. 4⅛ × D. 4¼ in. (15.1 × 10.4 × 10.7 cm)

Bleu nouveau ground partly with speckled gilding, polychrome landscapes

Marks: interlaced Ls in blue on both; incised on both, sp[1]

Provenance: A.B. Daniell & Sons, London, 1904;[2] J. Pierpont Morgan

MODEL

The most common model of orange tub at Vincennes and Sèvres, called *caisse carrée*, was designed with square corners.[3] *Caisses* with rounded corners were made at Sèvres from 1765, although not in great numbers.[4] The Wadsworth's tubs, however, are distinguished by their champfered corners and the only other known *caisses* sharing this feature are in the Ephrussi de Rothschild Collection at Cap Ferrat, France.[5] The Museum's

tubs are taller and slimmer than those from Cap Ferrat; the proportions of the traditional *caisse carrée* fall between the two. We do not know why the factory made these few variations or how many of each were produced. The notion of champfered corners may have come from tea caddies made at Vincennes, designed with this same feature.[6]

COMMENTARY

The *bleu nouveau* ground, the rectangular reserves, the myrtle-leaf gilding on the corners, and the incised sp all point to a date sometime in the 1760s, even though the tubs are not marked with date letters.[7]

It is hard to link the landscape painting on the Museum's orange tubs to a specific painter, for there were several painters at Sèvres working in the same "muddy" style. Three of them marked their work, one with a caduceus, one with a mark like a "tree" or "mop head," and one with a monogram that looks like a conjoined AN.[8] The caduceus mark traditionally has been attributed to Edme Gomery, but he was primarily a bird painter and it is unlikely that he was the painter using that mark.[9] Examples of the caduceus painter's work—of a slightly higher quality than the others—may be found in many public collections, such as two rectangular trays at the Victoria and Albert Museum, London,[10] or a *veilleuse* at Waddesdon Manor, England.[11] The "tree" or "mop head" mark has been linked to Jean Bouchet, who was active at the factory from 1757 until 1793, and who appears in overtime records painting landscapes on a variety of pieces.[12] The painter with the AN monogram is responsible for rather sloppy landscapes, such as on a cup and saucer in the Museum's collection and another in the collection at Waddesdon Manor.[13]

There are many known pieces, above all vases, where the front reserve is of a much higher quality than the reserve on the back. Often the inferior painting on the back was executed by one of the "muddy landscape" painters. Unfortunately many such pieces only bear the mark of the painter responsible for the front and we can only guess which of the "muddy landscape" painters might have done the back. Then again, there are other pieces like the Museum's orange tubs that betray a similar muddy style all over and are totally devoid of painters' marks.[14] With current knowledge, the best we can do is attribute the Museum's orange tubs to one of this group.

Exhibitions: *Morgan Loan Exhibition*, New York, 1914, not in catalogue; *French and English 18th Century Exhibition,* Montreal, 1950, no. 149; *Morgan*, Hartford, 1987, no. 66

Literature: Chavagnac, pp. 52–53, no. 59; *French and English 18th Century Exhibition*, no. 149; Brunet and Préaud, p. 139, no. 48; de Bellaigue, "Sèvres," p. 175, no. 66

NOTES

1 Savill, 3, p. 1123, found on soft paste c. 1754–77, 1784.

2 APML, Daniell file, invoice 19 April 1904: "A pair of unusual size Orange Tubs, or square gardenières, with panels of full landscapes, in gros bleu mountings, with rich raised gold decorations, very highly finished, of the finest quality."

3 See cat. no. 62 for this form at Vincennes and Sèvres.

4 De Bellaigue, "Sèvres," p. 175.

5 Nos. 2176–77, Fondation Ephrussi de Rothschild, Villa-Musée "Ile-de-France," Cap Ferrat. H. 5¹⁵⁄₁₆ x w. 4⁵⁄₁₆ x D. 4⁵⁄₁₆ in. (15 x 11 x 11 cm), decorated with trophies by Charles Buteux. De Bellaigue states in "Sèvres," p. 175 that these are dated 1766, but in correspondence with the director of the collection at Cap Ferrat, they are referred to as c. 1770, with no date letter noted.

6 Brunet and Préaud, pp. 50, 127, no. 13.

7 De Bellaigue, "Sèvres," p. 175.

8 This mark is not in Peters, *Marks*.

9 Peters, *Marks*, p. 90.

10 No. C. 1393-1919, white ground with carmine *camaïeu* decoration, dated letter D for 1756–57; no. C. 1377, *bleu céleste plateau tiroir à jour*, date letter F for 1758–59.

11 Eriksen, *Waddesdon*, pp. 108–11, no. 37.

12 Peters, *Marks*, p. 15.

13 See cat. no. 84 and Eriksen, *Waddesdon*, pp. 112–13, no. 38, date letter G for 1759–60.

14 It has been suggested that these landscape painters may be placed in distinctive groups by their method of drawing the factory marks. Having compared many published and unpublished examples of the marks of this group of painters, there do not appear to be enough absolutely distinct ways of drawing the marks to make useful groups. For published examples of some of these marks, see Eriksen, *Waddesdon*, pp. 110–11, no. 37 (caduceus painter); Dawson, *British Museum*, pp. 111–13, no. 99 (no painter's mark); Wadsworth Atheneum, cat. no. 89 (no painter's mark); Hawes and Corsiglia, pp. 197–202 (no painter's mark, two somewhat different styles of factory marks in same set); Wadsworth Atheneum, cat. no. 71 (painter's mark of Dodin, who painted the front reserves and evidently put his mark under that made by the landscape painter); and Casanova, no. 145 (mark of tree or mop head, Jean Bouchet).

68

Pair of ewers (*vases en burette*)

1917.1043–1044

Sèvres, 1767

Soft-paste porcelain, 1917.1043: H. 8⅝ × W. 3½ × D. 3⁹⁄₁₆ (22 × 8.9 × 9 cm); 1917.1044: H. 8⅝ × W. 3⁹⁄₁₆ × D. 3⁹⁄₁₆ in. (22 × 9 × 9 cm)

Bleu nouveau ground, pink and blue floral wreaths, gilding

Marks: both, interlaced Ls in blue with o for 1767

Provenance: probably Jean-Baptiste de Machault d'Arnouville (1701–1794), 1767; Charles-Henri-Louis, son of Machault d'Arnouville (1747–1830); Eugène de Machault (son, 1783–1867); Henriette de Machault (1808–1864); her husband Léonce Melchior, marquis de Vogüé (1805–1877); their grandson, Louis de Vogüé, 1882;[1] A.B. Daniell & Sons, London, 1902;[2] J. Pierpont Morgan

MODEL

There were two variations of this ewer made by the factory, both called *vase en burette*.[3] The Museum's examples conform to one of them, having short necks with a beaded band, ovoid bodies, and gadrooning on the lower portion. The other type—

represented by a pair in the Wallace Collection—has a longer neck with two beaded bands (sometimes with molded zigzags between them), a more bulbous body, and gadroons and flutes on the lower section. A plaster model of the more bulbous version of ewer exists at the factory. Another labeled *pot à eau n° 5* corresponds to the Atheneum's model bar the addition of a dolphin handle.[5] Although *burette* is the French word for cruet it appears to have been used to describe various ewers at Sèvres regardless of their size. The term *buire* [ewer] was also used at Sèvres to describe such forms.

Another style of ewer which is similar in appearance to both styles of *vase en burette*—but has a more elongated body, a shorter neck and a longer spout—was known as a *pot à eau Duplessis uni* or *buire fleurs Duplessis unie*.[4]

It is impossible to tie references in factory documents to either of the two variants of the *vase en burette*. Among new work listed for 1755 there were molds and models for a *burette unie* and a *burette antique*,[6] but these models have not been identified and the date is rather too early for the *vases en burette* under discussion.[7] The next *burette* to feature in the records, introduced in 1765, was the *burette nouvelle*, for which there is no description.[8] Among new work listed for 1766 there are molds and models for *burettes* of the second size, inexplicably valued the same as the *burette nouvelle* molds and models of the previous year.[9] Molds and models for a *buire unie* appeared in 1767.[10] No doubt some of these inventory entries refer to *vases en burette*.[11] That there are surviving examples in two sizes of both the Hartford and Wallace Collection versions does not contradict this notion.[12]

There are few references to *burettes* in the factory's sales ledgers, and descriptions are typically imprecise. In December 1766 Louis XV bought two *bleu nouveau* examples for 300 *livres* each.[13] On 31 December of the same year the secretary of state Bertin bought another *bleu nouveau* pair for 96 *livres* each.[14] On 20 October 1767 a single *burette* was sold to an unnamed buyer for 240 *livres*.[15] Finally, in December 1767 a *bleu nouveau* pair described as *à couronnes* was presented to Machault d'Arnouville, who at that time was Louis XV's comptroller and the minister responsible for the Vincennes factory.[16] They cost 300 *livres* a piece.[17]

The Hartford *vase en burette*, with its simple, ovoid body, reflects the Sèvres factory's commitment in the 1760s to a more classical style. The molded gadroons, beaded collar, and regular, oval reserves painted with restrained floral wreaths all embrace this growing classicism.

COMMENTARY

The Museum's ewers represent the second size. The blue dot or circle inside the factory mark underneath them is probably a sloppy date letter o for 1767.[18]

Links between existing examples of ewers and entries in the sales ledgers are tenuous. The Hartford pair was said by Chavagnac to be that given to Machault, largely, it seems, on the basis of family tradition.[19] This would be entirely convincing were it not for the fact that the pair of vases presented to Machault was priced at 600 *livres*, the amount one would expect

for vases of the first, not second size.[20] It would be more logical for his vases to be either the pair now in the Louvre or the pair now in the Wallace Collection. It is possible that the Hartford ewers were a second pair, listed among *pièces d'ornements* bought by one of the Parisian dealers and then sold to Machault.[21]

The Atheneum's vases should instead be identified with the ewers formerly in the collection of Louis de Vogüé, who had inherited them through his grandfather, Léonce Melchior de Vogüé, from his grandmother, née Henriette de Machault.[22] A nineteenth-century hand-tinted illustration of one of Vogüé's *burettes* shows the same ribbons (although in rose rather than lilac), as well as the same gilded foliate decoration under the spout as on the Hartford ewers.[23] More telling, perhaps, is the distinctive, contoured, double band of gilding around the reserves which is found both on the Museum's and the marquis de Vogüé's *burettes*. Such gilding does not appear on the *burettes* in the Louvre or on a pair at the Musée national de Céramique, Sèvres.

Jean-Baptiste Tandart *aîné*, who specialized in flowers and often painted interlocking floral wreaths, most probably carried out the decoration of these ewers. In 1766 he was paid 72 *livres* in overtime for painting four *burettes* with 6 *couronnes* (3 *livres* per wreath). In the next year he was paid 36 *livres* for decorating six *burettes à 36 cartouches*. Perhaps the painting of the Hartford ewers was included in this payment.[24]

TECHNIQUE AND CONDITION

The ground color of these ewers, called *bleu nouveau*, was derived from the enamel color *beau bleu no. 2*.[25] It appeared in factory production in late 1763.[26] It must have been considered an improvement over *bleu lapis* as it was much more even in tone than the earlier blue. Although there were a few services still made with a *bleu lapis* ground in the 1760s, for the most part *bleu nouveau* superseded it as a ground color from this time.

The lip and foot of one of the ewers has been repaired.[27]

Exhibitions: *Morgan Loan Exhibition*, New York, 1914, not in catalogue; *Antique Taste*, 1982 (1917.1043); *Morgan*, Hartford, 1987, no. 68

Literature: Probably Garnier, pl. VI; Chavagnac, pp. 102–3, no. 126; Eriksen, *Neo-classicism*, p. 372, pl. 280; *Antique Taste*, p. 13 (1917.1043); de Bellaigue, "Sèvres," pp. 178–79, no. 68; Savill, 1, pp. 286–87, 289 n. 11; Munger, *Wickes*, pp. 189, 190 n. 12

NOTES

1 See Garnier, pl. VI (illustrating only one ewer). According to Chavagnac (pp. 102–3), the vases were bought by Machault and descended through another line of family, from son to granddaughter (the marquise de Valanglart) to great-grandson (Charles-Henri, marquis de Valanglart) to his widow (*née* Marie-Louise-Séraphine Le Paige d'Orsenne). See also de Bellaigue, "Sèvres," p. 178, who points out Chavagnac was the nephew by marriage to Mme Le Paige d'Orsenne, and could have had access to documents that confirmed their provenance. However, the reference in Garnier to the marquis de Vogüé makes this line of descent unlikely. A discussion of Chavagnac's suggested provenance will follow.

2 APML, Daniell file, invoice of 12 April 1902: "A pair of finest quality ewers in Sèvres china, in bleu du roi ground, with panels of painted roses, and cornflowers on white ground, fluted gold design on foot," £ 2,350.

3 For a discussion of these models see Savill, 1, pp. 286–90; see also Brunet and Préaud, p. 170, no. 138; de Bellaigue, "Sèvres," p. 178.

4 See Brunet and Préaud, p. 170, no. 137, for an example formerly in the Nicolier collection, Paris. See also Savill, 1, p. 287. This model is taller than the other two.

5 Brunet and Préaud, p. 170, no. 138, cite AMNS, 1814 inventory, 1740–60, no. 5 (now in *casier* 763).

6 AMNS, I. 7. See Savill, 1, p. 286.

7 See *Vincennes*, p. 36.

8 AMNS, I. 7, 1 January 1766, for new work 1765, molds and models for a *burette nouvelle*, 24 *livres*.

9 Ibid., 1 January 1767, for new work for 1766, 24 *livres*. It is unclear from the pricing if the molds and models introduced in the previous year were for the first size.

10 Ibid., molds and models, 48 *livres*; ibid., 1 January 1768 (for 1767), molds and models, 30 *livres*.

11 See Savill, 1, p. 286.

12 For the Atheneum version see a pair of the first size, H. 11⁷⁄₁₆ and 11⅝ in. (29 and 29.5 cm), c. 1766, blue ground with wreaths, Louvre, Paris, no. OA 10.262 (Eriksen, *Neo-classicism*, pl. 280); pair, first size, green ground with wreaths, n.d., MNC, Sèvres, on loan from Salomon de Rothschild collection, nos. 487–88. For the Wallace Collection version see Savill, 1, p. 289, nos. C286–87, first size: H. 10⅞ in. (27.6 cm), c. 1766–67, blue ground with wreaths; a pair in the MFA, Boston (*Wickes*, p. 189, no. 136), second size, H. 8⁵⁄₁₆ in. (21.1 cm), blue ground with wreaths.

13 AMNS, Vy 4, fol. 91v, December 1766.

14 Ibid., fol. 104.

15 Ibid., fol. 122v.

16 He was appointed *contrôleur général des Finances* in December 1745, *Ministre d'État* in 1749, and *Garde des Sceaux* in 1750. He was also *Ministre de la Marine* before being decommissioned and exiled in 1757.

17 AMNS, Vy 4, fol. 139v, 31 December 1767.

18 Chavagnac (p. 103) thought that the dot represented the dot that sometimes appears in the mark of Vincennes pieces before date letters were instituted. De Bellaigue ("Sèvres," p. 178) did not interpret the dot in the center as the date letter o, although he did believe the vases dated from about 1767.

19 See note 1. Chavagnac quotes the Sèvres sales records as reading "deux vases en burettes, bleu nouveau & couronnes de bleuets & roses." Nowhere in the records, in fact, are the *couronnes* described. It is impossible to know why Chavagnac added this bit of detail to his account.

20 Savill (1, p. 289) noted this pricing difference in her discussion of the Wallace Collection ewers in comparison with the pair in the Wickes Collection, MFA, Boston. It would seem that this would also hold true in the case of the Atheneum's vases.

21 The only sales of *pièces d'ornements* costing 96 *livres* in 1767 and 1768 were one item sold in January 1767 to Bailly (Vy 4, fol. 109v), which cannot describe the Museum's pair, and ten items sold during the second half of 1768 to Poirier (ibid., fol. 165v). The latter sale might have included the Museum's pair.

22 Garnier, pl. VI. It is likely that these vases were also in Machault's collection, and Chavagnac confused them with the larger pair given to Machault. For the lineage of Machault's and the Marquis de Vogüé's families, see Jougla de Morenas, 6, p. 493 (Vogüé); 4, p. 495 (Machault). See also Christie's, Monaco, 19 June 1999, lot 80, pp. 94–98, where the same lineage is discussed in relation to a chest of drawers. According to the catalogue, in Léonce Melchior de Vogüé's will it was stated: "Toute cette collection, provenant de sa famille [of his wife, born Machault] et de la mienne et en particulier celles des meubles de Boulle et porcelaines montées, aura d'autant plus d'intérêt qu'elle restera réunie … [the entire collection comes from her family and mine and in particular the Boulle furniture and the mounted porcelains, would be of all the more interest if they remain together]."

23 It is possible that this difference in coloration is the result of the reproduction. It is unclear as to the size of the ewer illustrated in Garnier, and although only a single ewer is reproduced or referred to, it is just as likely that it was one of a pair.

24 See AMNS, F.8, 1766 and 1767. De Bellaigue suggested that the 1766 payment may have been for the Museum's pair but having firmly dated the vases 1767 makes this unlikely.

25 See Préaud and d'Albis, p. 216. Antoine d'Albis believes this same color was later called *beau bleu* and occasionally *bleu du roi*. Savill, 3, p. 1174 differentiates between *bleu nouveau* and *beau bleu* in the factory records but leaves open the possibility that *beau bleu* merely replaced *bleu nouveau* as an appellation.

26 Eriksen states that it was launched in December 1763 (Eriksen and Bellaigue, p. 53). D'Albis states that the first experiments in using *beau bleu* as a ground color occurred in 1757, and that the color made its appearance in Sèvres products between 1760 and 1765 (Préaud and d'Albis, p. 216). Part of the difficulty of pinpointing the appearance of the color precisely is that the sales records become very abbreviated during these years and colors are often not recorded. Even in the list of what was sold to Louis XV at the end of 1763 there are no descriptions of the color or decoration of the pieces although many of his purchases must have been of pieces decorated with the newest ground color. *Bleu nouveau* does appear in December 1763 in items sold to the duc de Choiseul (AMNS, Vy 3, fol. 157v), the duc de Praslin (ibid.), and in the list of end of the year presents from the factory (ibid., fol. 158v).

27 1917.1044. The foot had been off and has been rebonded to the ewer. A treatment report is in the files of the Wadsworth Atheneum.

69

Pair of vases (*vases ferrés*)

1917.1045–1046

Sèvres, 1766

Soft-paste porcelain, H. 17 × DIAM. 7⁷⁄₁₆ in. (43.1 × 18.8 cm)

Green ground with *bleu céleste* oves, white pearls and straps, polychrome landscapes in front, interlocking floral and foliate wreaths in pink, blue, and green on sides and back, gilding

Marks: 1917.1045: interlaced Ls in blue with date letter n, incised square;[1] 1917.1046: traces of interlaced Ls in blue, indistinct incised mark

Provenance: 1917.1046: marquis d'Osmond, 1884;[2] O. du Sartel;[3] E. Sécretan, 1889;[4] both, Charles Wertheimer, London, 1902;[5] J. Pierpont Morgan

MODEL

In the eighteenth century this model was probably called *vase antique* and then *vase ferré*.[6] The reference to *antique* probably relates to the model's classical shape, while *ferré* (chained or fettered in iron) refers to the four pseudo-metal panels bound by ropes suspended from rings. In a late nineteenth-century list of models this vase was entitled *vase antique ferré, dit de Fontenoy*,[7] but the appellation Fontenoy was a nineteenth-century invention.[8] A plaster model survives at the factory.[9]

The design has been attributed to Étienne-Maurice Falconet, who exhibited new models at Versailles in December 1762. An

69

undated pair in the Louvre with pink and blue ground may date from this year, and are noteworthy for the unusual disposition of the ropes suspended from their necks.[10] The surviving plaster model corresponds to this version. The first dated examples of *vases ferrés* are from 1763.[11] The Museum's vases, with their fluted stems and pearl collars, and bay-leaf garlands on the feet, belong to the most common version of the *vase ferré*, which was made in two sizes.[13] A simplified variation appeared in the 1770s, sometimes executed in hard paste.[12]

The sales ledgers do not refer specifically to *vases ferrés* before 1775, and then only a few are described. In the 1760s most vases were listed as *vases d'ornements* making it impossible to identify existing examples in the records. Those recorded from 1775 to 1780 ranged in price from 432 *livres* each for an unspecified pair to 600 *livres* for one with a blue ground and soldiers.[14] Even though the documents do not tell us how many were sold, the model must have been popular for many examples survive today.[15] Blue, green, and *bleu céleste* ground colors were favored, and panels were decorated with pastorals, military scenes, "Teniers" and other rustic scenes, and even cherubs. The side and back panels were painted with wreaths, flowers, or trophies.

FUNCTION

Vases ferrés seem to have been sold both in pairs and as parts of garnitures of three or five. They could be combined with vases of the same model, for instance a garniture of one first-size and two second-size vases, or with vases of different design, such as the *vase à panneaux*, *vase à bâtons rompus*, and *vase à feuille de mirte*.[16]

COMMENTARY

The Atheneum's pair of *vases ferrés* are of the second size. The green ground color is rather daringly combined with turquoise oves and bosses on the rim, a combination that is to be found on three vases in the Louvre, a pair of vases in the Royal Collection, England, and two vases and a clock formerly in the Christner collection, Texas.[17] The primary reserves show two pastoral scenes. The scene with the boy drinking from a cup with a seated girl and goats can be traced to an engraving still at the Sèvres factory (fig. 69-1).[18] While its legend indicates that it was printed for and sold by an English dealer, the original engraving was one of a set of four pastoral landscapes made by Jan de Visscher after the Netherlandish artist Nicolaes Berchem.[19] The Sèvres painter has closely copied the figures from the left foreground section of the engraving. He has even borrowed the landscape background from the print, but eliminated a seated bagpiper and a cow.

The reserve on the second vase is based on an engraving by René Gaillard after François Boucher (fig. 69-2). Entitled *Le Moineau apprivoisé* or *The Tamed Sparrow*, the print was announced in the *Mercure de France* in 1762.[20] It probably was made after a painting now lost of the same title by Boucher dated around 1730.[21] As in the first vase, the Sèvres artist has faithfully copied the figures of the boy and girl, as well as the cows and sheep, and the architectural ruin serving as a backdrop. The two figures, especially the reclining girl, are very close to those in another engraving after Boucher's painting (whereabouts unknown) *Les Enfans du fermier* of around 1720–21.[22] Boucher reused and adapted these figures to a later composition.[23]

There are no painter's marks on the Museum's vases. It is evident, however, that the same painter was responsible for the reserves of several other vases, including: a *vase ferré*, around

Fig. 69-2 *Le Moineau apprivoisé*, René Gaillard after François Boucher

1768, in the Louvre; a pair of *vases "Cyprès Furtado"* [?] in Waddesdon Manor, England; a vase (probably *à ruban* or *à couronne*) at the Wallace Collection; and a *vase à panneaux* at the J. Paul Getty Museum.[24] The figures on all of these reserves are akin to those on a pair of *cuvettes Courteille* from 1760 in the Wallace Collection signed by Antoine Caton.[25] This similarity is especially noticeable when making comparisons: between the figure of the boy drinking on the Museum's vase and the man seated on the ground on the Wallace Collection vase; and between the face of the girl with the basket on the Waddesdon Manor vase and those of the women on the Wallace Collection vases. A later, signed broth basin and stand by Caton in the Wadsworth Atheneum's collection displays a slight change in figure style and a more subdued palette, but the same distinctive style in the painting of the leaves on the trees as on the Louvre and Waddesdon Manor vases.[26]

The side and back panels of the Hartford vases are painted with interlocking foliate and floral wreaths.[27] This manner of decorating the so-called secondary reserves was common from 1765, and was the specialty of Jean-Baptiste Tandart, who in all likelihood was responsible for those on the Museum's vases.[28] On some other *vases ferrés* the back panels are painted with a bouquet of flowers.[29]

There is a first-size green ground *vase ferré* with turquoise oves and bosses in the collection of the Louvre Museum, whose primary reserve depicts a Dutch scene of two muleteers, also derived from a Jan de Visscher engraving after Nicolaes Berchem.[30] The side and back panels are decorated with interlocking wreaths. Traditionally this vase has formed a garniture with another pair of second-size vases decorated with mythological scenes also at the Louvre. Given the unusual combination of decorative genres—Dutch scenes and mythological figures—it was at one time suggested that the central vase of

Fig. 69-1 *Pastoral scene*, Jan de Visscher after Nicolaes Berchem

the garniture belonged with the Atheneum's vases.[31] Upon close examination of the gilding, however, it is clear that the Atheneum's vases do not match the Louvre's. The foot of the Louvre vase is marked by continuous vertical lines in gold, which do not appear on the Hartford vases. Furthermore, the gilding around the central reserves is different: the Hartford gilding is tooled with a wavelike design whereas the Paris vase is tooled with crisscrosses and matte semicircles. Finally, it is unlikely that the factory would have made a garniture of three vases of the same size.

A photograph of the "Louis XVI Room" in Pierpont Morgan's London townhouse at 13, Princes Gate, shows this pair of vases next to a *pot-pourri à vaisseau*.[32]

TECHNIQUE AND CONDITION

The turquoise oves and bosses were enameled with one layer of *bleu céleste*. The lid of 1917.1045 is a replacement, probably of a different manufacture.[33] The finial of 1917.1046 was also broken off and cracked in half. A steel pin was inserted to hold the finial in place.[34] The laurel torus around the foot of 1917.1046 is less crisply modeled than that on 1917.1045. The banding on the torus is centered on the reserves on one vase while on the other vase it flanks the reserves.[35]

Exhibitions: *Rétrospectives des Porcelaines*, Paris, 1884, no. 2; *Morgan Loan Exhibition*, New York, 1914, not in catalogue; *French and English Art Treasures*, New York, 1942, no. 308; *Antique Taste*, 1982 (1917.1045); *Morgan*, Hartford, 1987, no. 67; *Défi au goût*, Paris, 1997, no. 36

Literature: Chavagnac, pp. 103–4, pl. 127; *French and English Art Treasures*, no. 308; *Antique Taste*, p. 9, fig. 10 (1917.1045); de Bellaigue, "Sèvres," p. 178, no. 67; Savill, 1, p. 231 n. 3l; *Défi au goût*, p. 92, no. 36

NOTES

1 See Savill, 3, p. 1134, found on soft paste 1755–87. In the 1760s it is most commonly found on vases. Savill suggests that the square may be a pun on the *répareur's* name, perhaps François Carrette *aîné* (active 1754–70), and then his son François (active 1768/69–87).

2 Drouot, Paris, 9 February 1884, lot 2.

3 Annotated catalogues of the above d'Osmond sale in the Frick Art Reference Library, New York, and the AMNS, note that the vase was bought by M. du Sartel for 1,100 francs.

4 Chevalier, Paris, 4 July 1889, lot 272. Information kindly provided by Pierre Ennès.

5 APML, Wertheimer file, invoice 19 April 1902: "Pair of large fine pâte tendre Louis XVI green Sèvres vases and covers, painted with (Berghem) pastoral subjects and garlands of flowers," £10,000.

6 For a full account of this shape see Savill, 1, pp. 213–33. She discusses various other titles attributed to this model, including *vase à cordes* or *vase à cordons* (de Bellaigue, "Sèvres," p. 178, *Défi au goût*, p. 40). See also Brunet and Préaud, p. 98, pl. XLIII; Eriksen, *Neo-classicism*, pp. 370–71, pl. 274 (for *vase antique*); *Royal Collection*, pp. 54–55, no. 46. The appellation *vase ferré* appears in the factory's records for the first time in the inventory of 1772, although the model was introduced almost ten years earlier (AMNS, I. 8).

7 Troude, pl. 104.

8 Fontenoy alludes to the Battle of Fontenoy, which was successfully waged against the Marshall of Saxony in 1745, too early to have been commemorated in the 1760s. See Chavagnac, p. 104, and Eriksen, *Neo-classicism*, p. 370. The name probably came to be associated with this shape because

the first famous examples with a pink and blue marbled ground, formerly in the Léopold Double collection, were decorated with soldiers in battle thought to represent the Battle of Fontenoy. These are now in the Louvre (no. OA 10592–3, see Brunet and Préaud, p. 98, pl. XLIII. I would like to thank Tamara Préaud for this information).

9 Troude, pl. 104, illustrated Savill, 1, p. 214. See below for variations of this model.

10 Savill, 1, p. 214; *Défi au goût*, p. 41.

11 For example, blue ground vases in the Royal Collection, England (Eriksen, *Neo-classicism*, pl. 274) and the Walters Art Gallery, Baltimore (no. 48 574, see Savill, 1, p. 231 n. 3b).

12 Savill describes the sizes as follows: first size: H. 16⅛–17¾ × W. 6¾–7¹¹⁄₁₆ in. (41–45.1 × 17.1–19.8 cm); second size: H. 12³⁄₁₆–14⅛ × W. 5¼–7⅛ in. (31–35.9 × 13.3–18 cm).

13 De Bellaigue, "Sèvres," p. 178. See Savill, 1, p. 232 n. 3t–v; Eriksen and Bellaigue, pp. 334–35, no. 144, for a garniture of three from 1779.

14 AMNS, Vy 6, fol. 116; ibid., fol. 199v. See Savill, 1, p. 232 n. 17.

15 See Savill, 1, pp. 231–32 n. 3 for a list of many extant vases.

16 See ibid., 1, pp. 214–15, 232 nn. 21–27.

17 Louvre, Paris, no. OA 10253–55; *Royal Collection*, pp. 54–55, no. 46; Christner sale, Christie's, New York, 9 June 1979, lot 251. De Bellaigue ("Sèvres," p. 178) points out that such innovative combinations are to be found on other examples of this model, such as turquoise oves and bosses with blue or pink and blue ground, *bleu lapis* oves and bosses with pale turquoise ground, and green and white oves and bosses with pale turquoise ground.

18 AMNS, drawer C XIII, 18th-century inv. no. P.f. nᵒ 14, nᵒ 186; 19th-century inv. no. P §2 nᵒ18. I would like to thank Pierre Ennès for alerting me to this print and Tamara Préaud for the archival citation.

19 The legend reads "Printed for & Sold by Dubois at ye Golden Head near Cecil Street in ye Strand." See Wessely, no. 93, for the original Netherlandish print, called *The Drinking Boy* by that author. See also Hollstein, 41, no. 63, described as *Herd Playing the Bagpipe*. I would like to thank Kristin Shansky for locating this engraving.

20 See Jean-Richard, p. 262, no. 1033.

21 Ibid.; see also Ananoff, *Boucher*, 1, pp. 192–93, no. 57.

22 Jean-Richard, p. 268, no. 1072, engraved by Louis Michel Halbou; see Ananoff, *Boucher*, 1, pp. 159–60, no. 2.

23 Pierre Ennès originally attributed the composition to *Les Enfans du fermier*, and this association was subsequently accepted by Geoffrey de Bellaigue in "Sèvres," p. 178 (based on the letter by Ennès in the Wadsworth Atheneum files). Ennès and Bellaigue also attributed the large cow and sheep to another engraving after Boucher, *Pastorale*, by Gabriel Huquier *père* (Jean-Richard, pp. 271–72, no. 1089).

24 Louvre, Paris, no. OA 10254 (see *Défi au goût*, p. 91, no. 35); Waddesdon Manor, Buckinghamshire, c. 1775–80 (Eriksen, *Waddesdon*, pp. 280–81, no. 101); Wallace Collection, London, no. C267 (Savill, 1, pp. 235–44); J. Paul Getty Museum, Los Angeles, no. 85.DE.219, c. 1766–70, (Sassoon, pp. 106–11, no. 21).

25 Nos. C208–9 (Savill, 1, pp. 46–55). Savill (1, p. 236) also tentatively attributes the *vase à ruban* (or *à couronne*) to Caton.

26 See cat. no. 164.

27 1917.1045: roses/cornflowers; laurel/pink morning glories with foliage; pink and blue roses/pansies; 1917.1046: roses/cornflowers; bay/oak; laurel/mixed flowers.

28 Eriksen and Bellaigue, p. 132; de Bellaigue, "Sèvres," p. 178. See also cat. no. 68. Other examples of *vases ferrés* with this type of secondary decoration include: pair, blue ground, 1767, Wallace Collection, London, nos. C261–62 (Savill, 1, p. 216); single, green ground, c. 1768, Louvre, Paris, no. OA 10253 (*Défi au goût*, no. 34, formerly in the collection of the Earl of Harewood). A garniture of three blue-ground *vases ferrés* formerly in the collection of Mrs. Henry Walters (Parke-Bernet Galleries, New York, 30 April–3 May 1941, lot 1364) have secondary panels with triple interlocking wreaths.

70

29 See pair with green ground in the Royal Collection, England (*Royal Collection*, p. 54, no. 46).

30 Louvre, Paris, no. OA 10254. See Hollstein, 41, 1992, no. 120, *Farrier Shoeing a Donkey*.

31 This erroneous suggestion originally was put forward by the present author in correspondence with Geoffrey de Bellaigue (see "Sèvres," p. 178 n. 4) and appears again in *Défi au goût*, p. 42. Ennès does not believe that the smaller vases now associated with the Paris vase belong with it.

32 APML, Photo album, "A Souvenir of our happy days in August 1902 at Dover House and 13, Princes Gate," Herbert L. Satterlee, Louise Pierpont Satterlee, Mabel Morgan Satterlee.

33 The inside configuration of the lid differs from the original, and was made to fit the body with porcelain blocks. The pineapple finial, which has been off and reglued, is poorly molded. The green ground also differs from the vase and other lid. It seems to have turned black when the gold was applied and fired, at which time the maker may have tried to polish off the black, leaving traces of black and a matte finish. I am indebted to Antoine d'Albis for many of the above observations.

34 In 1986 both vases were treated. Previous repairs were removed and new brass pins were inserted to hold the finials. Some filling and in-painting and minor regilding took place. See Wadsworth Atheneum files for treatment reports.

35 Savill, 1, p. 215 notes the arbitrary placement of the banding is common on this model.

70

Garniture of three flower vases (*cuvettes à tombeau*)

1917.1047–1049

Sèvres, 1767

Soft-paste porcelain, 1917.1047: H. 7³⁄₁₆ × L. 9½ × w. 6¹⁄₁₆ in. (18.2 × 24.1 × 15.3 cm); 1917.1048: H. 5¹¹⁄₁₆ × L. 7⅝ × w. 5⁵⁄₁₆ in. (14.5 × 19.3 × 13.5 cm); 1917.1049: H. 5¾ × L. 7⅝ × w. 5⅜ in. (14.6 × 19.4 × 13.6 cm)

Bleu céleste ground with polychrome figures in landscapes in front, polychrome floral bouquets in back, gilding

Marks: 1917.1047 and 1917.1049: interlaced Ls in blue with date letter o; ch underneath for Étienne-Jean Chabry;[1] incised coffee bean with stem;[2] 1917.1048: interlaced Ls in blue with o, trace of painter's mark; incised Li[3]

Provenance: Lord Clanricarde (by report); Jacques Seligmann, London and Paris, 1903;[4] J. Pierpont Morgan

70

70

Fig. 70-1 *Le Sommeil interrompu*, Nicolas Dauphin de Beauvais after François Boucher

Fig. 70-2 *Bergère garnissant de fleurs son chapeau et berger dormant*, Gilles Demarteau after François Boucher

MODEL

The shape of these vases has been identified as *cuvette à tombeau*, the name referring to their resemblance to sarcophagus-shaped chests of drawers called *commodes en tombeau*.[5] An example dated 1753–54 is known,[6] but the model only appears in the records in 1754–55.[7] Molds and models for a *vase à tombeau* appear in the factory inventories only in January 1756.[8]

There are two versions of this shape, one with corners in the form of fluted pilasters. This variation only appears on examples of the first size.[9] The vases were made in three sizes, the second and third sizes introduced only in 1759.[10] The design has been attributed to Jean-Claude Duplessis.[11]

The Sèvres factory owns two drawings of flowerpots related to the *cuvette à tombeau*. One, dated 1754, provides an alternate profile for the *vase hollandois*, showing the outline of the *à tombeau* rim on the left side.[12] The second drawing, dated 1759, shows a fully developed profile and section for this shape, and features three different sizes.[13] A surviving plaster model of the version with the curved corners is described in the 1814 factory inventory as *Caisse à fleurs A*,[14] and a second plaster model with the fluted pilasters is listed under the title *Caisse à fleurs A à contreforts cannelés*.[15] These appellations were not used in the eighteenth century.

It is known that first-size *cuvettes à tombeau* were produced by 1754, but the first recorded sale that can be linked to this

Fig. 70-3 *Les Amants surpris*, Gilles Demarteau after François Boucher

model only appears in 1756. Two examples decorated with *bleu céleste* ground and children were sold to Duvaux in that year,[16] while another *bleu céleste* example with birds sold in 1757 for 300 *livres*.[17] Second-size *cuvettes* were not specified in the sales records, and two third-size examples with turquoise ground and "Teniers" scenes were priced at 330 *livres* in 1762.[18] Vases were sold singly, in pairs, or in garnitures with like or different models.[19]

COMMENTARY

The Museum's examples represent the second and third sizes and are among more than a score of *cuvettes à tombeau* known today.[20] Hartford's *cuvettes* are decorated with pastoral scenes by the painter Chabry who began work at the factory in 1764, and who spent the rest of that decade and all the next painting pastoral scenes after François Boucher.[21] The larger of the Atheneum's vases features a composition taken from Boucher's *Le Sommeil interrompu*, engraved by Nicolas Dauphin de Beauvais (fig. 70-1).[22] A copy of the engraving is still at the factory.[23] The composition originally formed part of a larger design, *La Fontaine d'Amour*, created by Boucher for the Beauvais factory as part of a tapestry series called *Noble Pastorale*. The cartoons for the series date from 1748,[24] yet the tapestries were only woven in 1755.[25] Boucher reinterpreted the design in one of two panels executed for Madame de Pompadour's château de Bellevue in 1750, now in the Metropolitan Museum of Art.[26] Chabry utilized this source on at least one other Sèvres flower vase, a *cuvette Verdun* (1766?) sold in New York in 1972.[27]

The scene on 1917.1048 was taken from an engraving by Demarteau after Boucher entitled *Bergère garnissant de fleurs son chapeau et berger dormant* (fig. 70-2).[28] A drawing by Boucher in the opposite sense of the engraving was at one time in the Ephrussi de Rothschild Collection.[29] The engraving was used as a source for several other Sèvres pieces, including a *vase cassolette Bachelier*, probably by Dodin in about 1767, and a 1770 saucer by Chabry, both in the Wallace Collection.[30] Chabry also depicted this pastoral scene on an *écuelle* in the Jones Collection of the Victoria and Albert Museum,[31] and Caton did the same on a *déjeuner à rubans* in 1774.[32] Then in 1777 Dodin painted it on a sugar bowl now in the Calouste Gulbenkian Museum, Lisbon.[33] The scene on 1917.1049 is inspired by yet another engraving after Boucher, this time Demarteau's *Les Amants surpris* (fig. 70-3).[34] There are two drawings that probably relate to the engraving, both in the reverse sense, one in the National Gallery, Washington, and one sold in Paris in 1922.[35] According to the legend on the Demarteau engraving, the print reproduced a painting by Boucher in the collection of Monsieur de la Haye.[36] Another engraving, this one by Gabriel Huquier *père*, called *Berger et bergère assis au pied d'un arbre*,[37] is very close to Demarteau's, differing only in such details as the bagpipe in the foreground, the basket of flowers, and the attendant animals and figures. Chabry's rendition is closer to Demarteau's engraving. Again, the Sèvres factory must have owned a copy of the print, for the scene recurs on a number of pieces between 1767 and 1771.[38]

The gilded decoration on the Museum's flower vases reflects the stylistic restraint typical of Sèvres gilding in the 1760s. Gilding on the front is confined to two geometric borders around the reserves, a band with lozenge-shaped burnishing and a second band of alternating flat beads and dots. The front corners are decorated with foliate interlaces. Gilding on the sides and backs has been reduced to simple fillets. Gilded decoration much like this can be found on a pair of *vases à tombeau* in Waddesdon Manor, England, dated 1766, with one border composed of flat beads alternating with three dots; the decoration of the corners is even more restrained here with a small-scale foliate border following the contours.[39]

TECHNIQUE AND CONDITION

The *bleu céleste* ground on the Atheneum's *cuvettes* is of a later type made after 1755, when Hellot had reformulated the composition.[40] The depth and brilliance of the old Vincennes *bleu céleste* have to our eyes been lost here for the sake of the opacity and evenness of tone afforded by the new formula. Portions of some of the reserves appear matte, denoting devitrification or crystallization of the glaze through overexposure to heat.[41] The color seems to have crawled in places, especially on the shoulders of the vases, an occurrence not uncommon on *bleu céleste*. The interiors of all three vases are filled with dark turquoise or black specks.[42] Three plugged holes under 1917.1047 and 1917.1049 suggest that drainage holes were contemplated but filled before decoration took place. There is a shock in the lower half of the right side panel of 1917.1048.

Exhibitions: *Morgan Loan Exhibition*, New York, 1914, not in catalogue; *French and English 18th Century Exhibition*, Montreal, 1950, no. 160

Literature: Chavagnac, pp. 105–6, no. 129; *French and English 18th Century Exhibition*, no. 160; Eriksen, *Waddesdon*, p. 196, no. 71; Savill, 1, pp. 33, 41 nn. 2t and 3, p. 1018 n. 6

NOTES

1 See Savill, 3, pp. 1017–18 for this artist.

2 Ibid., p. 1136, described as a coffee bean or a coffee bean with a stem. It appears from the 1750s to the 1770s.

3 Ibid., p. 1113, as probably mark of Antoine-Mathieu Liancé (active 1754–77), a *répareur* in soft paste until 1774 and in hard paste after that (see also Eriksen, *Waddesdon*, pp. 330–31). In the 1760s the mark is found on vases, cups, baskets, and tureens.

4 APML, Seligmann files, invoice 22 May 1903: "3 Jardinières in Old Sèvres China, blue turquoise ground with Boucher subjects, dated 1767, decorated by Chabry. They come directly from Lord Clanricarde," £8,800.

5 Geoffrey de Bellaigue first offered this identification in *Royal Collection*, pp. 86–87, no. 90. Savill (1, pp. 32–42) discusses the shape in detail. Much of the following information is taken from this latter source.

6 See a *bleu céleste* vase in the J. Paul Getty Museum, Los Angeles (no. 73.DE.64, in Sassoon, pp. 8–11, no. 2).

7 IF 5676, fol. 34, 4 February 1754–3 February 1755, *caisse en tombeau*. See Savill, 1, p. 41 n. 7; Sassoon, p. 8.

8 AMNS, I. 7, 1 January 1756, new models for 1755. See Sassoon, p. 8. Sassoon also notes that the first factory inventory records a "wide drawing for the shape of a vase with moldings" (*1 Dessein long en forme de Caisse avec architecture*), which may relate to this shape. AMNS, I. 7, 8 October 1752.

9 Savill, 1, p. 32.

10 Ibid. The sizes are defined by Savill as follows: first size: H. 8¾–9¼ × W. 10¾–12 in. (22.2–23.5 × 27.3–30.5 cm); second size: H. 7–7⁷⁄₁₆ × W. 9⁷⁄₁₆–9⅝ in. (17.8–19 × 24–24.5 cm); third size: H. 5⅝–5¾ × W. 7⅛–8½ in. (14.2–14.6 × 18–21.5 cm). See drawing described in note 13 below.

11 Savill, 1, p. 32. See also Eriksen and Bellaigue, p. 91.

12 AMNS, R. 1, L. 3, d. 1, fol. 2 (see cat. no. 63). It is inscribed *vazes ou Caisse de chemine pour metre des fleurs par ordre de Mons. de Verdun Le 29 mars 1754.*

13 AMNS, R. 1, L. 3, d. 1, fol. 7. See Savill, 1, p. 32, illustrated. The inscription reads *cuvette à fleurs fait en juillet 1759 2eme et 3eme grandeur.* Note that the model name does not appear on either drawing.

14 AMNS, 1814 inventory, 1740–80, no. 123; Troude, pl. 130; illustrated in Savill, 1, p. 32.

15 AMNS, 1814 inventory, 1740–80, no. 122. Not in Troude.

16 AMNS, Vy 1, fol. 133v, 1 January–20 August 1756, Duvaux, 840 *livres*; Vy 2, fol. 16, 20 August 1756–1 January 1757, Duvaux, 840 *livres*. See Savill, 1, pp. 33, 41 n. 11a–b.

17 AMNS, Vy 2, fol. 39v, 17 November 1757, Roussel.

18 Ibid., fol. 119, December 1762, presented to de Courteille, with one of the first size (Savill, 1, p. 41 n. 11i).

19 See Savill, 1, pp. 32–34, 41 n. 11.

20 Ibid., p. 40–41 n. 2.

21 See Savill, 3, pp. 1017–18. For another pair of *vases à tombeau* with Chabry reserves after Boucher see Eriksen, *Waddesdon*, pp. 196–97, no. 71. Chabry also painted a Boucher scene on a *plateau tiroir à jour* in the British Museum (no. 1948.12-3,8, Dawson, *British Museum*, pp. 130–31, no. 113).

22 Jean-Richard, p. 96, no. 281.

23 AMNS, *tiroir* D VII, dossier Boucher.

24 Bordeaux, passim.

25 A set of these tapestries is in the collection of the Huntington Library and Art Collections, San Marino, California. See Wark, *Huntington*, pp. 68–69, figs. 7–13. This was the last set of designs provided by Boucher for the Beauvais factory. Of the five recorded commissions for the set, four are known to have been for Louis XV. The figures that comprise *Le Sommeil interrompu* can be found on the far right of *La Fontaine d'Amour*.

26 No. 49.7.47. See Ananoff, *Boucher*, 2, pp. 64–66, no. 363. The painting was also engraved by Huquier (in the same sense as the painting; Jean-Richard, pp. 281–82, no. 1150), Bonnet (same sense as the painting, Ananoff, *Boucher*, 2, p. 65, fig. 1069), and Demarteau (opposite sense to the painting, see Ananoff, *Boucher*, 2, p. 66, no. 363/4, not illustrated).

27 Deane Johnson sale, Sotheby's, New York, 9 December 1972, lot 30. The scene also appears on a *vase cassolette* formerly in the Hodgkins collection (*Hodgkins*, no. 37, Dodin).

28 Jean-Richard, pp. 190–91, no. 687; Ananoff, *Boucher*, 2, p. 253, no. 611/3. Ananoff, *Boucher* also illustrates an oil sketch and a drawing of a similar subject that he relates to this composition. He dates Boucher's work to 1765.

29 See Ananoff, *Drawings*, p. 82, no. 243.

30 Savill, 1, pp. 336–42, no. C303; ibid., pp. 505–26, no. C348.

31 Ibid., p. 525 n. 47 (V&A, London, no. 758 to B-1882, King, pp. 12–13, no. 128). According to Savill, Chabry also painted this scene on a saucer of 1768 in the Mme Dhainaut sale, Sotheby's, 10 December 1936, lot 61, and on an *écuelle* dated 1775 formerly in the collection of Marjorie Merriweather Post, now at the Hillwood Museum and Gardens, Washington, D.C. (see Arend, *Hillwood*, p. 53, fig. 30).

32 Savill, 2, pp. 507, 525 n. 48.

33 Ibid., 1, p. 336.

34 Jean-Richard, p. 180, no. 633. This should not be confused with André Laurent's engraving called *Le Pasteur Galant* (Jean-Richard, p. 316, nos. 1312–13), which shows similar figures in a park.

35 Ibid., p. 180, no. 633. See also Ananoff, *Drawings*, pp. 83–84, nos. 248–49, figs. 49–50. Ananoff entitles these drawings *Tête à tête* and *La conversation galante*, respectively.

36 See Savill, 1, p. 309 n. 21.

37 Jean-Richard, p. 284, no. 1159.

38 Savill, 1, p. 301. See cup and saucer, Dodin, 1767, V&A, London, no. C1411-1919 (with *La Pipée*, also by Demarteau); orange tub, 1771, Dodin, MMA, New York, no. 43.163 4; tea service, 1777, Calouste Gulbenkian Museum, Lisbon (Gulbenkian, p. 100); *vase cassolette Bachelier*, 1767, Dodin, British Museum, London, no. 1948.12–3, 12 (Dawson, *British Museum*, pp. 131–32, no. 114, pl. 8). Neither this engraving nor *Bergère garnissant de fleurs son chapeau et berger dormant* is extant in the collection of the Sèvres factory.

39 See note 21.

40 See Préaud and d'Albis, p. 217.

41 Ibid., p. 220.

42 These must indicate some kind of contamination in the paste.

71

Pair of vases (*vases chinois* or *vases à pied de globe*)

1917.1060–1061

Sèvres, 1769

Soft-paste porcelain, H. (without bronze bases)
12¹³⁄₁₆ × W. 5¹⁄₁₆ × D. 4⁵⁄₁₆ in. (32.5 × 12.9 × 11 cm)

Bleu nouveau ground with polychrome figures in landscapes on front, polychrome landscapes on back, gilding

Marks: interlaced Ls in blue with date letter q, painter's mark K for Charles-Nicolas Dodin;[1] incised scrolling N under 1917.1060;[2] incised R under 1917.1061[3]

Provenance: Earl of Courtown, Gorey, Ireland, by report;[4] Charles Wertheimer, London, 1906;[5] J. Pierpont Morgan

MODEL

This model of vase seems to have had two names in the eighteenth century. It was most often called *vase chinois*, undoubtedly because of the existence of two Chinese heads on the shoulders of the surviving plaster model, but for which no examples are known.[6] In one document it was called *vase à pied de globe*, referring to the molded decoration in the form of a globe stand which supports the body of the vase.[7] Three versions of the model were made. The first—of which the Museum's pair is an example—is known from 1769 and includes the globe-stand bottom, a fluted collar around the stem, a bay-leaf garland around the neck, and a fluted cover. This is the most common type.[8] A drawing in the factory archives shows most elements of this design, with the addition of a beaded band on the shoulder.[9] The second version, introduced around 1774, has a simplified design in which the bay-leaf garland, the pilasters, triglyphs, and guttae of the globe stand, and the fluting around the collar and on the cover have all been eliminated.[10] Two factory drawings appear to relate to this version.[11] The third version is the same as the second, but stands on a square plinth. It probably appeared around 1777.[12]

Fig. 71-1 *Le Berger recompensé*, René Gaillard after François Boucher

Ultimately, the model was made in four sizes, both in soft and hard paste.[13] The factory inventory of 1769 lists the second and third sizes among the plaster models introduced the year before.[14] The first size did not appear until the following year,[15] and it is believed that the fourth size was introduced at nearly the same time.[16]

Sales of *vases chinois* are recorded from 1773 to 1788, although it is possible that in some cases this description refers to other models decorated with chinoiserie subjects.[17] During the early years of their production they must have been among the many *vases d'ornements* listed in the sales ledgers When they were more specifically described it was often as part of a garniture of three, such as that sold to Louis XVI in 1775 for 1,320 *livres*.[18] An example of the first size with a blue ground and marine scene cost 960 *livres*.[19] The Museum's smaller vases would have cost considerably less, perhaps between 320 and 380 *livres*. It is worth bearing in mind that after 1780 the term *vase chinois* more likely referred to a later model.[20]

COMMENTARY

The primary reserves on the Hartford vases are decorated with pastoral scenes after François Boucher by Charles-Nicolas Dodin, whose highly accomplished figural and landscape style lent itself particularly well to the pastoral landscape genre.[21] The left-hand vase shows *Le Berger recompensé*, which was engraved

by René Gaillard after Boucher's painting *Berger accordant sa musette* dated 1748 (fig. 71-1).[22] The right-hand vase shows the pendant to that engraving, also by Gaillard, called *Le Panier misterieux* [*sic*] (fig. 71-2).[23] It is after another painting by Boucher dated 1748, formerly in the collection of the Earl of Rosebery, England.[24] The Sèvres archives possess copies of both engravings.[25] Dodin followed the engravings fairly closely. In *Le Berger recompensé*, he eliminated the attendant animals but retained most of the buildings in the distant landscape. In *Le Panier misterieux* he simplified the landscape considerably, eliminating the ruins and antique vases and modifying the rustic fence. Nevertheless, he accurately copied the figures, as well as details of the drapery.

The scene of *Le Panier misterieux* was taken from the pantomime entitled *Les Vendanges de Tempé*, written by Charles-Siméon Favart (1710–92) and first performed in 1745 at the fair of Saint-Laurent.[26] In this scene, the unnamed little shepherd sets off with Lisette the shepherdess' basket to fill it with grapes and, once it is filled, returns surreptitiously to set it next to her.[27] Boucher, and then Gaillard and Dodin, only deviate from the story by filling Lisette's basket with flowers instead of grapes.

The backs of the Hartford *vases chinois* display the work of an unidentified landscape painter who frequently painted the secondary reserves of ornamental vases as well as other

Fig. 71-2 *Le Panier misterieux*, René Gaillard after François Boucher

decorative objects and tea wares.[28] He seems also to have painted the backs of another pair of fourth-size *vases chinois* in the Bearsted collection at Upton House, Oxfordshire,[29] and a pair of fourth-size *bleu céleste vases chinois* with port scenes on the front in the Huntington Library and Art Collections, California.[30] Seemingly it was this same landscape painter who drew the factory mark on the Atheneum's vases, after which Dodin added his mark of K in a different color of blue enamel.

The gilding on the Hartford vases is similar to that on other examples of this model. The gilded oak-leaf garlands suspended in swags from pins may also be found on a pair of green *vases chinois* at the Art Institute of Chicago.[31] The Wallace Collection boasts a vase of the first size with a more elaborate version of the gilding, where the garlands encompass the entire reserve rather than loop back two-thirds of the way down.[32] The gilded bands around the front reserves of the Atheneum's vases are tooled to create a wave-like pattern alternating with areas of stippling, which is akin to the tooled pattern found on wine glass coolers, lozenge-shaped trays, and ice-cream coolers dating from 1768 and 1769 in the Dodge Collection at Detroit.[33] The bands around the back reserves are tooled in a lozenge-like pattern, also to be found around the secondary reserves of the pair of *vases chinois* in the Bearsted collection, at Upton House.[34]

TECHNIQUE AND CONDITION

The vases sit on gilt-bronze stands dating from the nineteenth century. They are en suite with the stand from a *vase Bachelier à anses tortillées* also in the Morgan collection, with which they have been associated since at least 1906.

Exhibitions: *Morgan Loan Exhibition*, New York, 1914, not in catalogue; *Antique Taste*, 1982 (1917.1060); *Morgan*, Hartford, 1987, no. 69

Literature: Chavagnac, pp. 109–10, no. 134; Hood, *Bulletin*, pp. 8–9, fig. 6; Hood, *Connoisseur*, p. 135, fig. 9; *Royal Collection*, p. 47; *Antique Taste*, p. 13; de Bellaigue, "Sèvres," pp. 180–81, no. 69; Savill, 1, p. 363 n. 3i

NOTES

1 Active 1754–1802, as one of the factory's leading figure painters. See Savill, 3, pp. 1029–32 for a lengthy discussion of his biography. See also Peters, *Marks*, p. 29.

2 See Savill, 3, p. 1116, as found on soft paste 1755–72 and hard paste c. 1779. Savill discusses the possibility that it is the mark of the *répareur* Nantier, who was active from 1767–76, but notes the discrepancy in dates. She also suggests that the mark may in fact be a monogram JV, for Joseph Vernault, active 1748/49–78.

3 Ibid., pp. 1121–22, as possibly the mark of Roger *père*, active 1754–84.

4 As per the dealer's invoice. Courtown House was the principal residence of the Barony and Earldom of the Stopfords. The invoice may be referring to James George Henry Stopford, fifth Baron in 1858 and still living in 1913 (see Gibbs, pp. 468–70). I would like to thank John Gay for this information.

5 APML, Charles Wertheimer file, invoice 7 April 1906: "A pair of Old Sèvres Vases and Covers, gros bleu ground, painted in panels with Boucher subjects in front and landscape on reverse." Sold as a garniture with a *vase Bachelier à anses tortillées* (cat. no.72), £18,500 for all three.

6 AMNS, 1814 inventory, 1740–80, no. 36, *Chinois 1re, 2me, 3me gr.* See Savill, 1, p. 357, illustrated. The Chinese heads appear on a 1780 vase of a different shape, thought by Savill to have been called *vase chinois n[ouvelle] f[orme]*, and later *vase chinois rectifié* (1782), and *chinois de milieu* (1781–82). De Bellaigue ("Sèvres," p. 180) suggests that the model known from 1780 (Royal Collection, England, in *Royal Collection*, no. 40. pl. III) may have appeared as early as 1773, which creates confusion when analyzing the sales records.

7 See Savill, 1, pp. 357–64 for this shape. Eriksen (*Neo-classicism*, p. 373, pl. 282) recognized the model as a *vase à pied de globe* based on overtime payments to Genest in 1769 (AMNS, F.11, see Savill, 1, p. 357). See also de Bellaigue, "Sèvres," p. 180.

8 Savill, 1, p. 363 n. 3a–o.

9 AMNS, R. 1, L. 3, d. 2, fol. 2, illustrated in Savill, 1, p. 358.

10 See a pair in the Walters Art Gallery, Baltimore, no. 46 640 (*Hodgkins*, nos. 48–49). Other known examples are listed in Savill, 1, p. 363 n. 3p–r.

11 AMNS, R. 1, L. 3, d. 2, fols. 3–4, one illustrated in Savill, 1, p. 358. A fourth drawing (R. 1, L. 3, d. 2, fol. 7), attributed to Duplessis based on the inscription in his hand *Vase urne Duplessis* (not to be confused with *vase* or *urne Duplessis* as discussed in cat. nos. 54 and 59), shows the addition of foliage and garlands at the sides (Savill, 1, p. 357).

12 Savill, 1, p. 363 n. 3s–u.

13 Ibid., p. 357. Savill delineates the sizes as follows: first size: H. 24¹¹⁄₁₆–26 × w. 8¾–9½ in. (63–66 × 22.2–24.1 cm); second size: H. 18½–19½ × w. 7⅛–7⁹⁄₁₆ in. (47–49.5 × 18.1–19.2 cm); third size: H. 16⅛ × w. 6¹¹⁄₁₆–6⅞ in. (41 × 17–17.5 cm); fourth size: H. 12½–14⅜ × w. 4⁵⁄₁₆–4¾ in. (31.8–36.5 × 10.9–12 cm).

14 AMNS, I. 7, 1 January 1769 (for 1768), *modèles en plâtre*.

15 Ibid., 1 January 1770.

16 Savill (1, pp. 357, 363 n. 6) notes that the fourth size was recorded in the inventory for new work for 1771 but is known from the Atheneum's vases of 1769. See ibid., n. 3i–o for other examples of this size.

17 Savill, 1, p. 358, specifically where no decoration is described.

18 AMNS, Vy 6, fol. 116v (See Savill, 1, p. 364 n. 14d). The model is usually described in the sales records when sold to the king or a member of court. Otherwise it must have been sold without description.

19 Now in the Wallace Collection, London (no. C309, see Savill, 1, p. 360).

20 See note 6.

21 Savill (3, p. 1030) notes that Dodin's superior draftsmanship, technique, color sense, and command of atmospheric effects placed him on a level above his most talented colleagues, although Genest certainly was at least his equal, as were Pierre-Nicolas and Nicolas Pierre Pithou. Dodin painted many pastoral scenes after Boucher, including *Le Sommeil interrompu* on cat. no. 72 (see note 5 above).

22 Jean-Richard, pp. 259, 262, no. 1032. The engraving is in the opposite sense to the painting. The title of the painting presented here is that given by Ananoff (*Boucher*, 2, pp. 12–13, no. 319) presumably taken from the description from the Salon of 1750, no. 24. The painting was exhibited at the Royal Academy, London, in 1968 as part of the collection of Major John Mills (see Jean-Richard).

23 Jean-Richard, p. 259, nos. 1030–31.

24 See Ananoff, *Boucher*, 2, pp. 14–15, no. 320 (Ananoff, who spells the name Roseberry, says the collection was in London, but the Earl of Rosebery resided at Mentmore, Buckinghamshire and at Dalmeny House, West Lothian, Scotland). He notes that the painting was on the New York art market in 1976. Again, the engraving is in the opposite sense to the painting.

25 De Bellaigue (*Royal Collection*, p. 47) notes that the factory's copies of these engravings are inscribed with 18th-century portfolio numbers, and that these may be two of four engravings described as *Pastorales de Boucher* purchased by Sèvres in 1764 (AMNS, I. 7). Dodin painted *Le Berger recompensé* on a *vase à bandes* of 1771 in the Royal Collection, England (*Royal Collection*, no. 34).

26 The pantomime was recast as a ballet called *La Vallée de Montmorency* that was first performed in 1752. Since the original painting by Boucher was painted in 1748 the original pantomime must have served as inspiration. For more on Boucher and Favart, see Zick, "Montmorency," and Ménager. See cat. nos. 170–72 for more on this topic.

27 Zick, "Montmorency," pp. 28–29.

28 See cat. no. 67 for more on this painter.

29 *Bleu nouveau* ground, the fronts painted with putti, c. 1770, H. c. 12⁷⁄₁₆ in. (31.5 cm) (see Mallet, p. 9, no. 124).

30 Wark, *Huntington*, fig. 111, middle shelf, pp. 112–13.

31 Art Institute of Chicago, nos. 1977 220–221, 1769, Dodin, H. 13⅞ and 14⅛ in. (35.2 and 35.8 cm, published as 32.5 cm or 12¹³⁄₁₆ in Savill, 1, p. 363 n. 3j).

32 Savill, 1, pp. 360–64, no. C. 309.

33 Le Corbeiller, *Dodge*, pp. 192–97. The tooling on the Dodge vases is confined to simple burnished, wave patterns, while on the Hartford vases, the wave pattern is on top of striations, with areas of stippling in between. De Bellaigue ("Sèvres," p. 180) noted this type of tooling on Sèvres dating from 1770–74, but suggested that the Museum's vases may have been the earliest known examples to exhibit this type of tooling. It appears that he had not seen the Dodge Collection pieces.

34 See note 29.

72

Vase (*vase Bachelier à anses tortillées*)

1917.1064

Sèvres, c. 1766–1770

Soft-paste porcelain, H. (without bronze base) 13¹⁵⁄₁₆ × w. 6 × D. 5⅝ in. (35.4 × 15.2 × 14.2 cm)

Bleu nouveau ground with polychrome figures in a landscape on front, polychrome bouquet on the back, gilding

Marks: none

Provenance: Earl of Courtown, Gorey, Ireland, by report; Charles Wertheimer, London, 1906;[1] J. Pierpont Morgan

MODEL

This vase was probably known at the factory by a variety of names. A plaster model, listed in the 1814 inventory as *vase bachelier anse tortillié* [twisted handle] and bearing a label *vase Bachelier anses tortillons* survives at the Sèvres factory.[2] Troude illustrates the model calling it *vase à anses torses* [twisted handles], *modèle de Bachelier*.[3] In 1773 the *répareurs* Censier

72

jeune and Caron *aîné* worked on *vases Bachelier torses ou anses tortillées* and *à tortillons*, respectively, which probably describe this model, and in 1774 the factory listed a blue-ground *vase à anses tortillées* among existing stock.[4] It is also possible that the model was at one time referred to as *vase Bachelier à cartouche de relief* and *vase Bachelier à feuille de sauge*—probably in response to the surviving plaster model, which includes relief-molded sage leaves on the neck and lower body, and stem. Additional molded elements on the plaster model include intertwined foliate handles and a cartouche surrounded by husks hanging from a ribbon which is attached to the shoulder by a pin.[5] Three other porcelain versions of the model are known, one with the cartouche but no sage leaves, one with sage leaves but no cartouche, and most frequently—as in the Hartford vase—one lacking most of the relief decoration.[6] All forms of the model were made in one size.[7]

The design for this model may be attributed to Jean-Jacques Bachelier, as is borne out by the various names assigned to this vase in the documents.[8] Beside being an important canvas painter of flowers, animals, and birds, Bachelier was the artistic director for decoration at the Vincennes and Sèvres factory. He was also responsible for overseeing sculpture there until 1757—when he helped to orchestrate Falconet's appointment as director of sculpture—and later, from 1766 until 1773. From 1765 he supplied plaster models for vases, including the *vase Bachelier à cartouche de relief*, which may describe the model currently under discussion.[9]

We can evince little information about the *vase Bachelier à anses tortillées* from the sales records, as that title never appears in the ledgers. *Vases Bachelier* that might be this model were sold from 1766, and priced between 108 *livres* and 1,800 *livres*.[10]

COMMENTARY

The Museum's vase is an example of the most common version of the model, the one with little or no relief decoration. The main reserve is decorated with a scene of a shepherd and shepherdess, taken from Nicolas Dauphin de Beauvais' engraving *Le Sommeil interrompu* after François Boucher.[11] Although the vase is not marked, the careful details, fresh colors, and distinctive foliage, point to the hand of Charles-Nicolas Dodin.[12] As in his other work, Dodin has remained truthful to the engraving within the space available; thus the primary figural group, the dog and sheep to their right, and the background architecture, are all featured. The only deviations made were to accommodate the reduced height of the composition.

The reserve on the back of the vase is decorated with a large bouquet of flowers by an unidentified artist. Such decoration joined landscapes, wreaths, and trophies as fitting decoration for secondary reserves.

The gilding on the Atheneum's vase is noteworthy for the bands of laurel leaves adorning the neck and cupping the lower body. This is a departure from many other known examples of the *vases chinois*, which don sage leaves on the neck in imitation of the relief-molded version of the model. A floral garland decorates the shoulders of the vase. The band of gilding around the cartouche is alternately burnished and granulated, the latter

highlighted with triple-zigzag tooling, to create a pattern of diagonal ribbons.[13] This same manner of tooling may be found on other Sèvres from the latter half of the 1760s until about 1780.[14] The tops of the handles are decorated with polished gold overlaid with exquisite vermiculated tooling. Other *vases Bachelier à anses tortillées* dating from 1768 and 1769 in the Royal Collection and in the Wallace Collection feature a similar treatment of the handles.[15]

A *bleu nouveau* vase of this model with pastoral decoration was listed as old stock in 1774, priced at 480 *livres*.[16] This perhaps may be identified as the Museum's vase, although it could just as easily be the blue-ground example with pastoral decoration now in the Musée des Arts décoratifs, Paris.[17]

Hartford's *vase Bachelier à anses tortillées* came into the Museum as part of a garniture of three vases, along with a pair of *vases chinois*, but it is unlikely that they had been grouped together at the time of manufacture.[18] The gilt-bronze bases on all three vases date from the nineteenth century, which is probably when the ensemble was created. They have been together since at least 1906, when they were purchased by Morgan.

TECHNIQUE AND CONDITION

The cover of the vase is a later replacement.

Exhibitions: *Morgan Loan Exhibition*, New York, 1914, not in catalogue; *Antique Taste*, 1982; *Makers of the American Renaissance*, Jekyll Island, Georgia, 1988

Literature: Chavagnac, p. 112, no. 138; Buckley, *Connoisseur*, p. 53; *Antique Taste*, p. 13; Savill, 1, pp. 300; 309, n. 3h

NOTES

1 APML, Wertheimer file, invoice 7 April 1906: "An oviform Sèvres two-handled vase, gros bleu ground painted with a Boucher subject in front, and flowers on the reverse. (Forming a set [with cat. no. 71]), £18,500. From the collection of the Earl of Courtown of Courtown House, Gorey, Ireland."

2 AMNS, 1814 inventory, 1740–80, no. 97, H. 14¹⁵⁄₁₆ in. (38 cm) (Savill, 1, p. 299).

3 Troude, pl. 94 (Savill, 1, p. 299).

4 AMNS, Va'1, 10 November 1773, 9 November 1773 (see Savill, 1, pp. 299, 309 n. 5, and de Bellaigue, unpublished catalogue entry for 1917.1064 (in Wadsworth Atheneum file); AMNS, I. 7, 1 January 1774, for 1773, fol. 38 (see Savill, 1, pp. 299, 309 n. 5; *Royal Collection*, pp. 103–4, no. 109; Eriksen and Bellaigue, p. 121). Other names that have been associated with this model but are no longer thought to apply are *vase à col cylindrique* (Eriksen, *Neo-classicism*, p. 373, pl. 283) and *vase à anses tire-bouchon* (Brunet and Préaud, p. 179, no. 165).

5 Savill, 1, pp. 299, 309 n. 6.

6 Ibid. See Savill's note 3 for many existing examples. An example (ibid., 3a) in the MAD, Paris (no. D8829, in Lechevallier-Chevignard, 1, p. 57), comes closest to the plaster model, although the stem is shorter and the molded leaves have been eliminated. An example with the molded cartouche but without the sage leaves (Savill, 1, p. 309 n. 3b) is illustrated in Garnier (pl. XLI). The version with sage leaves and no cartouche (Savill, 1, p. 309 n. 3c) is represented by an example in the Bearsted collection, at Upton House (replaced covers and handles; see Mallet, p. 11, no. 134).

7 Savill, 1, p. 299: H. (with cover) 14⅛ in. (35.9 cm); H. (without cover) 12³⁄₁₆–12⁷⁄₁₆ x W. 5⅞–6⅛ in. (31–31.6 x 14.9–15.6 cm).

8 Active 1748/51–93. See Savill, 3, pp. 961–64 for a biography.

9 Savill, 3, p. 962.

10 Savill, 1, p. 300. This very expensive vase was sold in 1782 to the comte and comtesse du Nord, and was covered in jeweled enameling (AMNS, Vy 8, fol. 181, 25 June 1782, Bariatinsky [their agent]; see Savill, 1, p. 309 n. 10d).

11 Jean-Richard, pp. 96–97, nos. 281–84. See cat. no. 70, fig. 1 for more on this composition.

12 This attribution is reiterated in the unpublished entry for this piece by de Bellaigue. See cat. no. 71 for more on Dodin. Dodin was paid 48 *livres* in overtime in 1766 for decorating the cartouche of a *vase Bachelier* (AMNS, F.8). It is not clear if this was the cost of painting the entire cartouche or simply what he was paid in overtime on the piece. It also may refer to another *vase Bachelier*, notably the smaller *vase cassolette Bachelier*, of which an example in the British Museum is painted by Dodin (dated 1767 and thus not a likely candidate for this overtime record). There is not enough information to link this overtime entry with the Museum's vase.

13 Savill, 3, p. 1140, pattern 15.

14 De Bellaigue, unpublished catalogue entry.

15 Ibid. See *Royal Collection*, pp. 103–4, no. 109 and Savill, 1, pp. 301–4, nos. C292–93.

16 See note 4.

17 See note 6.

18 Cat. no. 71.

73

Pair of vases (*vases urne antique à ornements?*)

1917.1087–1088

Sèvres, c. 1770

Soft-paste porcelain, 1917.1087: H. 15 × W. 8⁵⁄₁₆ × D. 6¼ in. (38.1 × 21.1 × 15.8 cm); 1917.1088: H. 14¹³⁄₁₆ × W. 8³⁄₁₆ × D. 6¹⁄₁₆ in. (37.6 × 20.8 × 15.4 cm)

Bleu nouveau ground, polychrome figures, gilding

Marks: interlaced Ls in blue on both, incised PT on 1917.1088[1]

Provenance: J. Pierpont Morgan

MODEL

The *vase urne antique* was probably designed by Jean-Claude Duplessis,[2] and the earliest version, with a flared, indented neck, matching cover, and pierced, ear-like handles[3] was introduced in 1755.[4] The basic model was made in one size. A few rare versions followed, among them an unusual variation with acanthus leaves and with flowers in relief on the front of the body and neck.[5] In 1771 a mold and model are recorded for a new version of the design.[6] The Museum's vases seem to be a variation of this later *vase urne antique*. Two undated plaster models survive, one conforming to the earlier version of the vase,[7] and the other with acanthus leaves cupping the stem and the body on each side (fig. 73-1).[8] The latter is particularly interesting because it seems to be a prototype of the Museum's vases. Acanthus leaves on the model now cup the stem and the body, while the auricular handles and the four lobes around the neck have disappeared. However, the Museum's vases take the use of the acanthus motif a step further for here the leaves

now emerge from the body to become the handles. Intriguingly enough, no other example of a *vase urne antique* is known from the later period and so for now the Museum's pieces stand alone.

A drawing in the archives shows the outline of another vase of the same shape—without handles, cover, or base—inscribed, *V bouteille* and *vaze à Elefant reduit pour Madame la marquize de pompadour en 1758.*[9] From it we may conclude that the basic design of the *vase urne antique* was reused for the exactly contemporaneous *vase à tête d'éléphant.*[10]

Sales records explicitly referring to the earliest version are limited to the years 1755 through 1758, and demonstrate that the vase cost anywhere from 360 to 960 *livres*.[11] Lazare Duvaux was the main purchaser.[12]

COMMENTARY

The Museum's variations are not marked with date letters or painter's marks but probably date from around 1771.[13] The reserves are skillfully painted with cherubs floating on clouds set against landscape backdrops. This genre of decoration may be found on many other vases dating from this period, and a number of them may be considered to be painted by the same Sèvres artist. Note, for example, the striking similarity of style in the following: a pair of *bleu céleste* vases at the Wallace Collection;[14] a blue-ground *vase chinois* in the collection of Viscount and Viscountess Gage at Firle Place, Sussex;[15] a *vase aux tourterelles* in the Louvre;[16] a pair of *vases Bachelier* in the New Orleans Museum of Art;[17] and a *vase chinois* in the Huntington Library and Art Collections, California.[18] In every case the children are drawn with thin, brown outlines, and then shaded using a stippling technique to create volume. The tree trunks are painted with great detail, using a combination of pale washes and thin brushstrokes to differentiate the textures of the bark. The artist employs brown for the flesh-tones, pale yellow and lilac for the clouds—and what is especially noteworthy—bright yellow, pink, and blue as punctuation. The front reserves of the Hartford vases share all of these elements.

Jean-Baptiste-Étienne Genest, the head of the painter's workshop and one of Sèvres' most talented painters and designers may well have painted the above reserves. This theory rests on stylistic links between the Hartford vases and two plaques—both by the same hand—one in a private collection and the other at Rosenborg Castle, Copenhagen.[19] Although neither is signed, the plaque in Denmark, decorated with soldiers and children, was offered to Christian VII in 1768. In that same year Genest was paid overtime for a plaque representing a military canteen, which perfectly describes the example at Rosenborg Castle.[20] Both plaques reveal the same characteristic thin outlining and stippling of the figures, the same way of painting children's faces, the same distinctive painting of the tree bark and leaves, and the same palette.

Although the figures of the children are very much in the style of François Boucher, a survey of prints after Boucher has failed to reveal any direct sources. It is clear that Genest, who was a canvas painter before coming to Sèvres, had no need of Boucher models and created his figures independently.[21]

The reverse of each vase is decorated with a large trophy, each

73

containing attributes of love (quiver full of arrows, dove, shield with a heart pierced by an arrow, and winged torch) and the pastoral life (bagpipe, basket of flowers, and gardening hat). More than likely they were painted by Charles Buteux *père*,[22] who excelled in such elaborate trophies. Buteux's work may be found paired with the cherubs by Genest on the *bleu céleste* vases in the Wallace Collection.[23]

The gilding around the reserves of the Hartford vases is typical of the late 1760s and 1770s. Tooled bands with geometric patterns border the painted reserves, and surrounding the bands are oak-leaf garlands hanging from rosettes. The front band is tooled differently from the back band.[24] The oak leaves are given dimension by contrasting of matte and burnished gilding, with very sparing use of sharp tooling. The technique is reminiscent of that of early Vincennes as seen on the pair of wine-bottle coolers in the Atheneum's collection (catalogue no. 132).

TECHNIQUE AND CONDITION

These vases were thrown in two parts and then bonded together with wet clay at the shoulder. A seam is visible at the joint. The crack on the front reserve of the vase on the left probably occurred during the enamel firing. The finials of both vases are later replacements, and are attached with screws.[25]

Exhibition: *Morgan Loan Exhibition*, New York, 1914, not in catalogue

Literature: Chavagnac, p. 124, no. 155; Savill, 1, p. 153 n. 3g

Fig. 73-1 *Vase urne antique à ornements*, plaster model

NOTES

1 See Savill, 3, p. 1119, found on vases in the 1770s.

2 Ibid., 1, p. 148.

3 See ibid., pp. 148–53 for a discussion of this model. See also Préaud and d'Albis, pp. 192–93, no. 234.

4 AMNS, I. 7, molds and models for new work, 1756.

5 Savill, 1, pp. 148, 153 n. 3f. See de Costa Andrade, fig. 20.

6 AMNS, I. 8, 1 January 1772 (1771), 1 mold at 150 *livres*, 1 model at 300 *livres*.

7 AMNS, 1814 inventory, 1740–80, no. 114 (also in Troude, pl. 101, called *vase urne antique à oreilles*), illustrated in Savill, 1, p. 148.

8 AMNS, 1814 inventory, 1740–80, no. 115 (in Troude, pl. 109, called *urne antique à ornements*). The plaster model survives at the Sèvres factory.

9 AMNS, R. 1, L. 3, d. 9, fol. 2. See Savill, 1, pp. 148, 153 n. 7, 155.

10 See Savill, 1, pp. 155–62.

11 Savill, 1, p. 148. It is difficult to track later sales as the factory records become unspecific in the 1760s, classifying most vases as *vases d'ornements*.

12 Ibid.

13 This suggestion made by both Rosalind Savill and Geoffrey de Bellaigue.

14 Nos. C314–15. See Savill, 1, pp. 384–88. She dates these to around 1771 and suggests that they might be by Asselin.

15 Dated c. 1769–70 by Sir Francis Watson in an annotated hand list of the collection, 1966, no. 51.

16 No. OA 10591. Illustrated in Brunet and Préaud, pl. XLIV.

17 Formerly in the collection of The Antique Porcelain Company, illustrated in an advertisement in *Apollo Magazine* (November 1983).

18 Wark, *Huntington*, fig. 107. There is also another *vase aux tourterelles* with Dalva Brothers, New York.

19 Rosenborg Castle, Copenhagen (no. 23 1302). Genest worked at the factory from 1752 until his death in 1789 (Savill, 3, pp. 1035–37). He did not mark his pieces, because as head of the painter's workshop he did not have to account for his production in this manner. I would like to thank Bernard Dragesco for pointing out these plaques, and for the suggestion that they are by Genest. In discussions with the author, Dragesco has also expressed the opinion that the body of work under discussion is by Genest.

20 AMNS, Vy 4, fol. 158, *1 Tableau de Soldats*, 960 *livres*. See also F. 10, overtime for Genest, *1 Tableau representant une Cantine*.

21 No direct print sources were found for the Firle Place vase or the pair of vases in New Orleans. Genest was, in fact, responsible for providing models for the other Sèvres painters to copy, and his own paintings were in the possession of the factory (Savill, 3, pp. 1035, 1036 n. 6).

22 Savill, 3, pp. 1007–9. Active at Sèvres 1756–82.

23 See note 14 above.

24 The tooling of the front band is like that illustrated in Savill, 3, p. 1144, no. 78, while the tooling on the back band is in the form of a chevron pattern, similar but not identical to Savill, 3, p. 1140, no. 38.

25 The top of the left acanthus handle of 1917.1087 has been broken off and reglued, and the lower right quadrant of the main reserve has been scratched. The middle of the left acanthus handle of 1917.1088 has been chipped and restored. The trophies on the reverse of both vases are scratched, and small chips on the foliate scroll around the rims of both vases have been restored. Both vases were restored in 1992 by Daedalus, Inc., Cambridge, Massachusetts. Treatment reports are on file at the Wadsworth Atheneum.

74

74

Five mounted vases (*vases et gobelets à monter*)

1917.1096–1100

Sèvres, c. 1770–1775

Soft-paste porcelain, gilt bronze, marble, 1917.1096: H. 13⁷⁄₁₆ (with plinth) and 11⁹⁄₁₆ (without plinth) × W. 8⅜ × D. 4⅝ in. (34.2 [with plinth] and 29.4 [without plinth] × 21.3 × 11.8 cm); 1917.1097–98: H. 11⁹⁄₁₆ (with plinth) and 9¾ (without plinth) × W. 5¾ × D. 4¼ in. (29.3 [with plinth] and 24.7 [without plinth] × 14.6 × 10.7 cm); 1917.1099–1100: H. 9⅝ (with plinth) and 8 (without plinth) × W. 4¹⁵⁄₁₆ × D. 3½ in. (24.5 [with plinth] and 20.3 [without plinth] × 12.5 × 8.8 cm)

Bleu céleste ground with pink roses in roundels surrounded by gilded garlands

Marks: 1917.1096: interlaced Ls with traces of a date letter in blue, T surmounted by a dot for François Binet;[1] conjoined vd in gold for Jean-Baptiste-Emmanuel Vandé *père*;[2] 1917.1097: effaced interlaced Ls in pink, scrolling H in pink for Jacques-François-Louis de Laroche;[3] conjoined vd in gold; incised 6 (or g or 9);[4] two parallel lines in black; 1917.1098: all in gold, interlaced Ls with conjoined vd underneath, scrolling "G."[5]

Provenance: J. Pierpont Morgan

MODEL

The Sèvres factory began making vases and goblets specifically for mounting as early as 1763.[6] The first examples were decorated with plain ground colors, probably in imitation of Chinese porcelain. By 1770 the factory was producing examples decorated with roses in circles on green, dark blue, and turquoise grounds. In September of that year Madame du Barry purchased a garniture of five vases for 942 *livres* from the dealer Poirier described as *bleu céleste à petites Roses et montées en bronze d'oré d'or moulu* [*bleu céleste* with little roses and mounted in gilt bronze].[7]

These unmounted vases were called *vases à monter*, *gobelets à monter*, and occasionally *vases gobelets* in the records. They were made in three basic shapes, undifferentiated in the records, two of which were tapered cylinders and one egg shaped. In the 1774 inventory of old stock fifty vases and goblets in three sizes were recorded in both white and dark blue.[8] They were made specifically to be fitted with gilt-bronze handles, stems, feet, plinths, finials, and handles. The dealers, to whom most of these vases were sold, usually added these mounts. Extant examples of the various models range from about 7⅞ to 11¹³⁄₁₆ inches (20 to 30 cm).[9]

There are no molds, models, or drawings for these forms surviving.[10] Their earliest mention in the factory inventories is in 1764, when ten *gobelets à monter* were listed among pieces of biscuit ready to be glazed.[11] It is not clear to which forms of mounted vases these refer.

The sales records first mention mounted vases in 1767, when two plain green examples were sold to an unnamed buyer for 42 *livres* each.[12] These undoubtedly were a different model, later called *vase cloche*, of kindred form to the Museum's vase mounted with a statuette of Louis XV (catalogue no. 65). The next time mounted vases appear in the sales records is in 1770, when two unspecified examples sold for 48 *livres*.[13] Over the next ten years more than a hundred *vases* or *gobelets à monter* were sold. The principal buyers were the dealers Dulac, Poirier and Daguerre, Madame Lair, and Bazin. Now and then the designer and bronze maker Duplessis *fils* (Jean-Claude's son) bought vases for mounting.[14] Prices ranged from 18 to 120 *livres*.[15] In most cases, there was no mention of the decoration of these vases and goblets, but on occasion the records reveal their appearance. Two vases bought by Duplessis in 1774 were described as *Vases gobelets à Monter 3 Gr beau bleu à petites roses entourées dor* [goblet vases for mounting, third size, blue ground with little roses surrounded in gold],[16] and in March 1775 Madame Héricourt bought several *gobelets à monter* in *beau bleu*.[17] At least once the factory seems to have made mounted vases decorated only with gilded friezes.[18]

COMMENTARY

The presence of five basic styles of mounts used over and over again on various examples suggests that the dealers who bought most of these vases or goblets unmounted each had their own trademark mounts. Taking the mounts on the Museum's garniture as an example, the angular handles with lions' masks on the central vase are also found on a vase formerly in the Fribourg collection, Paris, and three others that sold between 1971 and 1989.[19] The next smallest vases in the Museum's garniture are mounted like several vases sold between 1976 and 1984, including one with a white ground and scattered roses.[20] The egg-shaped vases that finish the Museum's garniture can be found among the garniture formerly in the collection of the Earl of Sefton, Liverpool.[21] The inspiration for these gilt-bronze mounts must have come from some of the many works by classicizing artists such as Stefano della Bella in the seventeenth century,[22] and Louis-Joseph Le Lorrain in the eighteenth.[23]

There are a few mentions of mounted vases in the artists' and kiln firing records during the 1770s.[24] In 1775 Claude Naret put blue ground on twelve first-size *vases gobelets à monter*, while in 1776 Étienne-Jean Grémond *fils*, Edmé-François Bouillat, and François-Antoine Pfeiffer all worked on *vases à monter*.[25] Artists' ledgers from 1777 also record mounted vases, with brief descriptions of their decoration. In 1777, Nicquet, Nicolas Sinnson, and Jacques-François-Louis de Laroche all decorated mounted vases and goblets with *petites roses*, and in 1780 de Laroche decorated the cover of a mounted vase with the same decoration.[26] It is likely that at least one of the Museum's vases was among those decorated by de Laroche during those years.

A number of mounted vases of the types under discussion survive.[27]

TECHNIQUE AND CONDITION

The five vases are in good condition, except for the covers of 1917.1099 and 1917.1100. The former has been broken in half and repaired, and the latter has been broken in several pieces and repaired. The marble plinths are difficult to date, but appear to be somewhat later than the vases, even if still from the eighteenth century.[28]

Exhibition: *Morgan Loan Exhibition*, New York, 1914, not in catalogue

Literature: Chavagnac, p. 134, no. 168, pl. XLVIII; Brunet, *Frick*, pp. 274, 275 n. 10

NOTES

1 Active 1750–75. See Savill, 3, p. 1002; Peters, *Marks*, p. 14.

2 Active 1753–79. See Savill, 3, pp. 1072–73; Peters, *Marks*, p. 72.

3 Active 1758–1802. See Savill, 3, pp. 1039–40; Peters, *Marks*, p. 46.

4 Found on soft paste, 1754–90s. See Savill, 3, pp. 1127–28.

5 "G" tentatively attributed by Peters (*Marks*, p. 75) to Léopold Weydinger *père*, active as a painter and gilder 1757–1806.

6 See cat. no. 65.

7 Archives des Yvelines, E.75. See Eriksen and Bellaigue, p. 132–33, and Savill, 1, pp. 28, 31 n. 67 (citing Wildenstein, pp. 374–75).

8 AMNS, I. 8, 1 January 1774, *Magasin de Porcelaine*, *Bleue de Roy*, and *Magasin de Blanc*. Examples of all three sizes in blue were valued at 24 *livres*, and in white, the first two sizes were 9 *livres* and the third size 8 *livres*.

9 The mounts on known examples vary making it difficult to delineate specific sizes.

10 These would not have been molded but turned on a wheel.

11 AMNS, I. 7, 1 January 1765.

12 Ibid., Vy 4, fol. 121, 4 July 1767.

13 Ibid., fol. 219v, unnamed buyer, 6 November 1770.

14 Ibid.,Vy 5, fol. 176v, 14 November 1774; Vy 7, fol. 93v.

15 Sales include, for example: Vy 5, fol. 180v, first half 1774, Mme Lair, four *gobelets* at 48 *livres*, one at 54, five at 60, four at 42; fol. 185, first half 1774, Dulac, one *gobelet* at 42 *livres*, one at 18; fol. 188v, first half 1774, Poirier and Daguerre, three *gobelets* at 72 *livres*; Vy 6, fol. 104, first half 1776, Poirier and Daguerre, two *gobelets* first size at 48 *livres*, one second size at 36; fol. 217v, first half 1777, Bazin, one *gobelet* at 36 *livres*, one at 42, two at 60, one at 84, two at 96, one vase at 96, and one vase at 120 *livres*.

16 Ibid., fol. 176v. This type of decoration was also used on tea services and other tea wares. See cat. nos. 93, 101.

17 Ibid., Vy 7, fol. 105v, *Ventes à Crédit de L'année 1775, 1776, 1777, et 1778*, items purchased 2 March 1775. Mme Héricourt bought three first-size goblets for 60 *livres* each, six second-size goblets for 48 *livres*, and six third-size goblets for 36 *livres*. In December 1777 a vase already mounted and decorated with a green ground and roses was delivered to the comte d'Artois for his château de Maison (Maison-Lafitte) (ibid., fol. 124v, 5 December 1777). This latter single vase cost 600 *livres*, and thus could not have been the type of vase under discussion here. There are many other entries in the sales records that mention *vases à monter* but their high prices indicate that they were the larger and more elaborate type of vase designed in the 1770s and 1780s (see cat. no. 75).

18 See ibid., Vl'1, fol. 5, enamel kiln firing of 5 May 1778, *3 Vases pour[sic] a monter, frize d'or*, decorated by Vincent. It is possible that there may have been a ground color already on these before the enamel kiln firing, but documents are not specific on this point.

19 See a) three vases, H. 13¹³⁄₁₆ and 9¾ in. (35 and 25 cm), turquoise ground, roses, formerly in the E.M. Hodgkins collection (see *Hodgkins*, p. 89); b) three vases, one tapered H. 11¹³⁄₁₆ in. (30 cm) and two egg H. 8⅝ in. (22 cm), green ground, roses, Drouot, Paris, 19 May 1971, lot 32; c) five vases, tapered H. 11⁷⁄₁₆ in. (29 cm) and egg 8⅛ in. (20.5 cm), green ground, roses, formerly in collection of the Earl of Sefton, Croxteth Hall, Liverpool, exh. London, Partridge Fine Arts, May–July 1985, nos. 69–70; d) tapered vase, H. 11⁷⁄₁₆ in. (29 cm), turquoise ground, roses, Sotheby's, New York, 20 May 1989, lot 172n.

20 See a) two tapered vases, H. 9⁷⁄₁₆ in. (24 cm), blue ground, roses, Ader, Hotel George-V, Paris, 23 June 1976, lot 121; b) one tapered vase, H. 10¹⁄₁₆ in. (25.5 cm), white ground, roses (not encircled with gold), Palais d'Orsay, Paris, 21 February 1978, lot 22; c) two tapered vases, H. 9⁷⁄₁₆ in. (24 cm), blue ground, roses, Drouot, Paris, 26 March 1984, lot 45.

21 See note 19c. The same shape with the same mounts also was sold in Paris in 1971 (note 19b).

22 See di Vesme. Della Bella, in his *Raccolta de Vasi diversi*, c. 1646, created engravings of fantastic vases in the antique style, which seem to have been known to Sèvres designers.

23 Engraved by Claude-Henri Watelet, *Raccolta di Vasi Dedicatat All. Ill.*

Signora Geoffrin Delle Arti Amante riamata, 1752. See Eriksen, *Neo-classicism*, p. 376, pl. 297.

24 The first mention occurs in 1768, when Cuvillier was paid 12 *livres* for putting a blue ground on two *vazes unis à monter* (AMNS, F.10). Records for the early 1770s do not survive.

25 Ibid., F.18.

26 Ibid., Vj'1, fol. 203, 5 May 1777, fol. 151, 12 August 1777, fol. 159, 8 May 1777, and fol. 162, 3 August 1780, respectively.

27 These include: a) one egg vase, H. 10¾ in. (27.3 cm), dated 1775, and two ewers, H. 10 in. (25.4 cm), turquoise ground, roses, in the Huntington Library and Art Collections, San Marino, California, (see Wark, *Huntington*, fig. 111); b) three tapered vases, H. 9 in. (22.9 cm) (smaller pair), turquoise ground, roses, formerly in the Fribourg collection, in Eriksen, *Neo-classicism*, p. 363, pl. 242; c) five vases, green ground, roses, Paris, Petit Palais, Tuck Collection; d) two tapered vases, green ground, roses, H. 10¹¹⁄₁₆ in. (27.5 cm), formerly in Rothschild collection, Paris, Galerie Charpentier, 30 March 1935, lot 115; e) two tapered vases, H. 8½ in. (21.5 cm), plain green ground, Drouot, Paris, 21 February 1975, lot 118; f) two tapered vases, H. 10¼ in. (26 cm), turquoise ground, roses, Drouot, Paris, 23 November 1977, lot 14; g) one tapered vase, H. 9⁷⁄₁₆ in. (24 cm), green ground, roses, Palais d'Orsay, Paris, 30 March 1979, lot 45; h) two tapered vases, H. 8¼ in. (21 cm), plain blue ground, possibly 19th century, Sotheby's, Monaco, 25 June 1979, lot 106. See also notes 19–20 above. Some pairs or sets at auction or in the trade have been doubted by scholars. At least one spurious set with the incised mark of Camille Naudot (late 19th century) has been identified by Bernard Dragesco (as per correspondence with the author).

28 Examination by Theodore Dell revealed nothing to prove that the marble plinths were made in the nineteenth century.

75

Mounted vase (*vase à monter Daguerre*)

1993.29[1]

Sèvres, c. 1783–1786, mounts probably by Pierre-Philippe Thomire (1751–1843)

Hard-paste porcelain, gilt bronze, H. 12⁷⁄₁₆ × W. 7½ × D. 6¹⁄₁₆ in. (31.5 × 19 × 15.3 cm)

Dark blue ground

Marks: none

Provenance: Jacquemar, Inc., New York, 1943; Dragesco-Cramoisan, Paris, 1992

MODEL

In 1782 the *marchand-mercier* Dominique Daguerre commissioned the Sèvres factory to produce an urn-shaped vase that could be mounted in gilt bronze.[2] A drawing dated 29 July of that year shows the outline of the vase, and is inscribed "Vase pour Monsieur D'aguerre comandé ce 29 Juillet 1782. Beau bleu en plein" [vase for Monsieur Daguerre ordered this 29 July 1782. Plain blue ground].[3] The resulting vase, at least sometimes of hard paste,[4] was made in one size.[5] In 1785 the factory considered altering the model and producing it in a larger size, but no examples are known. There are two drawings related to this proposed modification, one inscribed "Monsieur Daguerre's vase requested to look a third bigger than his first model, this 3rd day of August, 1785" and the other, with a modified shoulder and rim, "Vase for Monsieur Daguerre given to make

the same as a wooden model with two bands below previously given, but said wooden model was mislaid and I am having them made after a fired porcelain piece but was told to leave out the bands, this 15th day of April, 1785."[6]

The factory sold these vases and others both mounted and unmounted, although the records fail to specify which model of vase was being sold.[7] It was usually dealers who bought the vases unmounted—among them Daguerre—and they paid between 36 and 192 *livres* a vase.[8]

Mounts for *vases à monter Daguerre* took a variety of forms.[9] One mount transformed the vase into a ewer, the handle fashioned into a female figure standing on a satyr's head.[10] Another type has handles in the shape of elaborate scrolls emerging from a foliate stem with lion-paw feet;[11] a third has trumpeting cherubs at the sides;[12] and a fourth has gryphons between the shoulder and the neck.[13] A fifth type, hitherto unpublished and formerly in the Lagerfeld collection, is marked by handles in the form of double spiral-tailed mermaids with crossed arms.[14]

COMMENTARY

The mounts on the Museum's vase constitute yet another type. The lower part—with alternating arrows and leaves above a stem of four lion's paws, a base with rope molding, and a square plinth—is identical to the lower portion of the Wallace Collection's vases with scrolled handles. The same is true of the collar around the rim.[15] The handles, in the form of female figures with entwined grapevine tails, may be found on a pair of black-ground vases of a different shape in the Royal Collection, England,[16] and on a pair of porphyry vases at the Musée Carnavalet, Paris.[17] They also feature on an alabaster urn in a still-life painting by Gerrit van Spaendonck, signed and dated 1787, formerly in the collection of Louis XVI's brother, the comte d'Artois.[18] Only the Hartford vase has two bands around the upper portion of the body, joined together by Apollo masks.

The mounts on all these vases may confidently be attributed to Pierre-Philippe Thomire, who took over as mount supplier to Sèvres on the death of J.-C.-T. Duplessis *fils* in 1783.[19] Thomire ran a thriving bronze workshop, and was engaged in all aspects of making gilt-bronze mounts, from drawing board to finished article.[20] Thomire supplied the factory on 26 January 1784 with a *Garniture ditte à petite femme en queux de Poissons dorés au matte* [garniture known as the garniture with small mermaids of gilded metal] for 500 *livres*.[21] Scholars have said that these correspond to the Hartford mounts, but it is much more likely that this particular Thomire garniture is the one adorning the *vases Daguerre* from the Lagerfeld collection.[22] The female figures on the Lagerfeld vases are unmistakably mermaids with scaled tails whereas those on the Museum's have no maritime reference. Rather they are more likely to be symbols of fertility with their limbs that rapidly turn into grape vines and with their hands to their breasts.[23]

When mounted, vases could cost staggering sums, from 960 *livres* for a pair or a garniture of three vases to 12,000 *livres* each for two vases with a blue ground and bas-reliefs.[24] There are no examples of mounted blue vases specified in the sales records for

1783 to 1786, suggesting that the Museum's vase may have been one of those sold unmounted to Daguerre. Had it been sold mounted, it would have cost between 700 and 800 *livres*.[25]

TECHNIQUE AND CONDITION

At one time this vase was covered with fake Coteau enamels glued onto the surface, which were removed in 1992. One small spray of gilt-bronze ivy has been resoldered.

NOTES

1 Museum credit line: Gift of Mrs. Edith E. Booth, Gift of Mrs. Benjamin Knower, Bequest of Ruel Crompton Tuttle, Gift of Mrs. Willie O. Burr, Gift of the children of Mrs. Richard M. Bissell, and Purchased for the Hartford Foundation for Public Giving, by exchange.

2 For a full discussion of this vase made for mounting see Savill, 1, pp. 468–80. For this model see also *Royal Collection*, pp. 38–39. For Daguerre, see de Bellaigue, *Waddesdon*, 2, pp. 858–59.

3 AMNS R. 1, L. 1, d. 5, fol. 21 (1). See Savill, 1, pp. 468–69.

4 The Museum's example is hard paste, but Savill (1, p. 472 n. 1) notes that the two in the Wallace Collection have not been tested for type of paste, nor has the example in the Royal Collection, England. Geoffrey de Bellaigue (*Royal Collection*, p. 42) suggests the English pair was made in hard paste. Kiln records in 1785 and 1786 list twenty-two examples of *vases Daguerre* in hard paste (AMNS, Vc'3, 13 September 1785, 30 January, 2 March, 13 May, 5 October, and 3 November 1786). These probably are the same as the *vase à monter Daguerre* under discussion.

5 According to Savill, 1, p. 468, the sizes without mounts are approximately H. 8¹¹⁄₁₆–9⅛ × W. 5¼ in. (22.4–23.1 × 13.3 cm). She rightly points out that measurements of other examples are usually published including the mounts, which makes it difficult to ascertain the exact measurements of the vases themselves.

6 AMNS, R. 1, L. 1, d. 5, fols. 21 (2) and 20. *Vase de M. Daguerre demandé En aparence Dun tierre plus grand que son Pre. model ce 3 aoust 1785*; *Vase pour M. Daguerre donné a faire pareil a un model en bois qui avoit Sy devant donné avec deux bandeaux a dessous mais le dit model en bois a été egarré et je les fait faire d'après une porcelaine cuitte mais l'on m a dit de suprimé les bandeaux ce 15 Avril 1785*. See Savill, 1, p. 468.

7 Savill, 1, p. 470. For more on the Sèvres factory and mounted vases see cat. nos. 65 and 74.

8 Ibid., pp. 470, 475 n. 13, where Savill lists examples ranging from 54 to 144 *livres* sold to Daguerre between 1783 and 1786. See also AMNS, Vy 9, first half 1783, to Daguerre, one *vase à monter* for 192 *livres*. Of the forty-one vases clearly described for mounting that were sold to dealers between 1783 and 1787, Daguerre purchased thirty-nine.

9 Savill, 1, pp. 468–69, describes four sets.

10 Attributed to Jean-Claude-Thomas Chambellan Duplessis *fils*. See Wallace Collection, London, nos. C338–39, Savill, 1, pp. 470–71; Royal Collection, England, nos. L 245, 246, 247, 248, in *Royal Collection*, pp. 38–39, 42–43, nos. 25, 29.

11 Attributed to Pierre-Philippe Thomire. See Wallace Collection, London, nos. C340–41 (Savill, 1, pp. 472–76), similar to mounts on several *vases Daguerre ovale* or *cassolettes à monter*, including Wallace Collection, no. C342 (Savill, 1, pp. 476–80); J. Paul Getty Museum, Los Angeles, no. 73.DI. 77.1-2 (Sassoon, pp. 143–44, no. 28); Royal Collection, England, no. L. 249, 250 (*Royal Collection*, pp. 39–40, no. 26).

12 Harewood sale, Christie's, London, 1 July 1965, lot 37 (Savill, 1, p. 475 n. 2e). See also a pair of polychrome vases dated 1788 in The Rosalinde and Arthur Gilbert collection (no. T.U.141), illustrated in *Connaissance des Arts* 532, October 1996, p. 77. These mounts have also been attributed to Thomire, and include the same alternating arrows and leaves above the stem (I would like to thank Jeanette Hanisee Gabriel for this information).

13 Savill, 1, p. 475 n. 2g, example at Harewood, Yorkshire, England.

14 Lagerfeld sale, Christie's, Monaco, 29 April 2000, lot 305. These mounts include, in addition to the mermaid handles, a rim of the same design as on the Museum's vase; a beaded band around the shoulder; alternating arrows and leaves above the stem; a porcelain foot, that is joined at the base of the vase with a foliate collar; a foot ring of oak leaves; and a square socle resting on small griffon feet. The porcelain ground color is *écaille*.

15 See note 11 above.

16 Previously identified as mermaids (*Carlton House*, p. 191, no. 166). See also Laking, nos. 301–2, Brunet and Préaud, p. 211, no. 262.

17 Bouvier bequest (photograph kindly provided by Christian Baulez). See also *Carlton House*, p. 191.

18 Exhibited in the Salon of 1787. Formerly in the collection of Wendell Cherry, sold Sotheby's, New York, 19 May 1994, lot 129, also illustrated in Segal, p. 246, fig. 70b. See also *Carlton House*, p. 191.

19 AMNS, H.3, letter to Regnier from d'Angiviller 13 August 1783. See *Royal Collection*, pp. 38–39.

20 See Verlet, *Bronzes dorés*, pp. 213–14.

21 AN, OI2061, *dossier* 2. See *Carlton House*, p. 191. Similar mounts, also attributed to Thomire, with handles fashioned like mermaids blowing horns, can be found on a porphyry urn in the Louvre, Paris (no. OA 6620), which was bought by the comtesse du Barry from Daguerre 1 May 1792. See *Louveciennes*, p. 175, no. 23.

22 See note 14. When Geoffrey de Bellaigue first published the Royal Collection vases in the *Carlton House* catalogue, he was unaware of the existence of these vases with their mermaid handles.

23 This suggestion was kindly provided by John Adamson.

24 Savill, 1, pp. 470, 475 n. 13. See AMNS, Vy 9, 3 March 1784, to Monsieur, two *Vases à monteé en Bronze à 480#, 960#*; ibid., Vy 8, fol. 150, 1782, the duc d'Orléans, three *gris agathe*; ibid., fol. 215v, 13 June 1782, Louis XVI to the comte and comtesse du Nord.

25 This is based on comparing the cost of the mounts on the vases in the Wallace Collection decorated with *singeries*, which Savill calculates cost 420 *livres*. Assuming that the plain blue-ground vase was one of the many vases sold to Daguerre unmounted, probably for between 120 and 144 *livres* (as compared to the decorated Wallace Collection vases priced at 480 *livres*), then the Museum's vase, with its more elaborate mounts, should have cost between 700 and 800 *livres*. The only plain-ground mounted vases recorded in the period under discussion were priced as follows: two, *lapis*, 790 *livres* each (AMNS, Vy 9, 27 May 1784, M. le Febure d'Amsterdam); two, ground not described, 480 *livres* each (Vy 9, 3 March 1784, Monsieur); two, *fond rouge*, 960 *livres* each (Vy 9, 22 October 1784, gift to Prince Henry of Prussia); three, *fond pourpre*, 800 *livres* each (Vy 10, fol. 71v, 28 August 1786, gift Louis XVI to the duc de Saxe-Teschen).

76

76

Teapot (*théière à cuvier à cerceaux*)

1917.961

Vincennes, 1751–1752

Soft-paste porcelain, H. 5⅜ × w. 6¹⁵⁄₁₆ × D. 5⅛ in. (13.6 × 17.6 × 13 cm)

White with blue flowers, fillets in blue with gold ribbons

Marks: interlaced Ls in blue;[1] incised cross or x

Provenance: J. Pierpont Morgan

MODEL

Vincennes called their conical teapot with a curved handle, tapered spout, and low waist, a *théière à la Reine*. Teapots like the Museum's example were called *théières à cuvier à cerceaux*.

The form follows the same basic design as the *théière à la reine* but has been embellished with fillets and ribbons—hence the name *cerceau* or hoop—and has an angular handle. The additional epithet *à cuvier* refers to the way it is hooped like a wash tub. Inscriptions on surviving drawings and the sales and inventory records bear out this distinction between *théières à la reine* and *théières à cuvier à cerceaux*.[2] The nomenclature not only applied to teapots but to other wares as well. Hence *gobelets à la Reine* with fillets became *gobelets à cuvier à cerceaux*; *pots à sucre à la Reine* with fillets became *pots à sucre à cuvier à cerceaux*, and so forth. Watering cans were simply called *arrosoirs* even when decorated with hoop-like fillets.[3] It has been suggested that the *théière à la Reine* was larger than *théière à cuvier à cerceaux*,[4] and an example of a teapot *à la Reine* in a private British collection is indeed a fraction of an inch taller than the Museum's teapot.[5] The scarcity of surviving *théières à cuvier à cerceaux* makes it difficult to draw any conclusions from a comparison of size.

There are two drawings of conical teapots in the Sèvres archives (figs. 76-1 and 76-2). The first is inscribed *theÿere à La Reine n°2 Rectifie suivan L'ordre de La comande du 19 fevrÿe*

1753 [teapot *à la Reine* no. 2 modified as per the directive of 19 February 1753] and *fait*; the other, showing two handles, is inscribed: *theÿere a cuvÿe pour Etre à Sersaux et Sans Serceaux Rectifie Suivant L'ordre de La Comande du 19 fevrÿe 1753* [washtub teapot to be with or without hoops modified as per the directive of 19 February 1753] and *fait*. One handle is described as *anse nouveau pour Le cuviers Sans baguettes ou cerceaus* [new handle for wash tubs without piping or hoops], and the other *anse pour Les cuviers avecs Leur serceaus* [handle for wash tubs with their hoops].[6] One of these corresponds to the angular handle found on a teapot of 1754 now in the Museum für Angewandte Kunst, Vienna, in which the curves of the earlier version have been eliminated.[7]

Théières à cuvier à cerceaux first appear in the sales records at the end of 1752.[8] They often were part of ensembles that included cups and saucers and sugar bowls of the same description.[9] Beside the teapot, the Museum für Angewandte Kunst has two cups and saucers, also *à cuvier à cerceaux*, decorated with polychrome flowers, which may have been part of such a set.[10]

COMMENTARY

The Museum's teapot is decorated with two large *camaïeu bleu* bouquets and smaller scattered sprigs and insects; the fillets are also painted blue, and entwined with gold ribbons. The flowers reflect the latest Vincennes style: they are grouped into stylized bouquets, and no longer have a strong, botanical character. The first known use of such bouquets was in 1752; they were simply called *fleurs* in the records.[11] The Hartford teapot may correspond to one that left the enamel kiln on 30 December 1752, along with eighteen cups and saucers and three sugar bowls, all decorated with *fleurs camayeux*.[12]

TECHNIQUE AND CONDITION

The blue used on this teapot is the *beau bleu* created by Jean Hellot and used from July 1751.[13] This new enamel color was immediately favored for fillets and *camaïeu* decoration. The

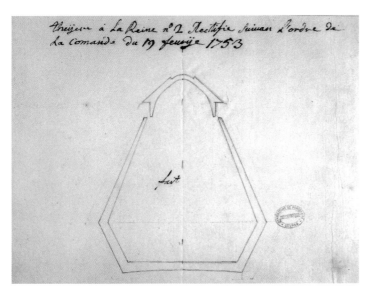

Fig. 76-1 *Théière à la Reine*, drawing

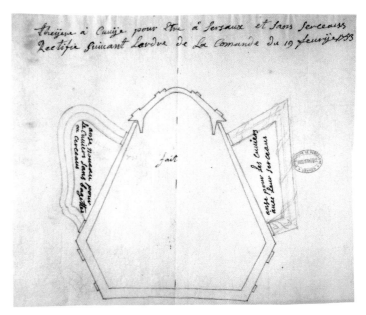

Fig. 76-2 *Théière à cuvier à cerceaux*, drawing

body of the teapot was thrown in two parts and joined at the seam with slip. The spout and handle were modeled by hand. There is no hanging hole under the lid of the Museum's teapot, and thus it was probably biscuit fired before October 1752. Documents tell us that only then were lids hung on metal firing stands in the kiln.[14] The teapot once was fractured at the seam, and the finial was broken and replaced in the nineteenth century by a gilt-bronze finial (for which two holes were drilled in the cover). The current flower knob was made in 1991.

Exhibition: *Morgan Loan Exhibition*, New York, 1914, not in catalogue

Literature: Chavagnac, p. 51, no. 56; Brunet and Préaud, p. 139, no. 47; Préaud and d'Albis, p. 148, no. 106

NOTES

1 The somewhat unusual form of the mark is the same as on a *pot-pourri Pompadour* in the Atheneum's collection, suggesting that the same painter worked on both pieces. See cat. no. 57.

2 AMNS, R. 1., L. 2, d. 4, fol. 3. In most recent publications, *à la Reine* is used to describe the form *unie* while *à cuvier* is coupled with *à cerceaux*. See *Vincennes*, p.133; Brunet and Préaud, p. 139, fig. 47; Préaud and d'Albis, p. 148, no. 106.

3 See Eriksen and Bellaigue, p. 287, no. 100, for an example in the David Collection, Copenhagen.

4 *Vincennes*, p. 133.

5 Brunet and Préaud, p. 139, fig. 47. It should be noted here that the knob on the Museum's teapot is a replacement, but this should not account for such a large differential in height.

6 See note 2 above.

7 Museum für Angewandte Kunst Vienna, inventory nos. Ke 3414–3418 (including cups, saucers, and a sugar bowl—see note 10 below). The Vienna handle is different from the handle on the Atheneum's teapot, which must be the earlier version.

8 AMNS, Vy 1, fol. 6, 20 December 1752, to Lazare Duvaux, *2 théyères à cuvier filet bleu et or*. Préaud and d'Albis, p. 148, states that the earliest teapot *à cuvier* was the one sold to de Mazières on 26 December 1752 (*fournée* 66), which was in fact a few days later than the one sold to Duvaux. According to Eriksen (Eriksen and Bellaigue, p. 269), teapots *à la*

Reine and *à cuvier* were not given these denominations in the stocklists or sales ledgers but just called *théières*; this is proven false by the above entry in the sales registers.

9 See AMNS, Vy 1, fols. 10, 26 December 1752, 28v, 29v, 31 December 1753.

10 See note 7 above. The cups and saucers and teapot are marked with a date letter B for 1754–55. There is also a sugar bowl, marked A for 1753–54. I would like to thank Bernard Dragesco for showing me a photograph of some of these pieces, and Ms. Petroschek and Dr. Neuwirth for providing me with details of the size and marks. A sugar bowl of this same shape, dated B for 1754–55, was on the market in 1984, and perhaps should be paired with the Viennese pieces. See Christie's, London, 2 July 1984, lot 10.

11 I would like to thank Antoine d'Albis for this information. According to Tim Clarke, *bouquets détachés* were invented at Meissen, in use from 1750. See Clarke, "Pack of Hounds" (this reference is given by d'Albis, "Marchands-merciers," pp. 82, 88 n. 10).

12 IF 5676, fol. 2.

13 Préaud and d'Albis, p. 86.

14 Ibid., p. 231, *Supports de cuissons*.

77

77

Cup

1917.980

Vincennes, 1753–1754

Soft-paste porcelain, H. 3³⁄₁₆ × W. 4 × D. 3 in. (8 × 10.2 × 7.6 cm)

Yellow ground with polychrome birds and flowers, gilding

Marks: interlaced Ls in blue with dot in center; modified ∧ underneath (unidentified)

Provenance: J. Pierpont Morgan

MODEL

This cylindrical cup is similar to what was called a *gobelet litron* at Vincennes and Sèvres. While the size is in accord with the first size of a traditional *gobelet litron*,[1] the flared rim is distinctive. Another such cup with flared rim is in the David Collection, Copenhagen,[2] a third is in the Musée des Arts décoratifs in Paris,[3] and two are in a private collection, London.[4] The handle of the Atheneum's cup is also unusual,[5] and appears closest in design to the handle sometimes used on teapots such as: a *théière Verdun* (1753) in the David Collection;[6] a *théière lizonnée* (before 1753) in the Musée des Arts décoratifs, Paris;[7] and a *théière Calabre* (1756) in a Parisian private collection.[8] Both the unusual rim and handle of this cup make us ask if it was an early variant of the *gobelet litron*, that was superseded by the straight-sided cup and delicate handles of the more typical version.[9]

COMMENTARY

The decoration of polychrome birds paired with a polychrome floral border occurs on other yellow-ground pieces from 1753 and 1754. While there is no entry in the sales ledgers for the Museum's cup, other yellow-ground pieces with birds in the sales records include a chamber pot, two wine-glass coolers, one jam pot, and six butter pots with their platters.[10] A mustard pot and platter with polychrome birds and garlands around the reserves (1753) is now in the Metropolitan Museum of Art,[11] and a water jug with the same decoration (1753) is in the Musée des Arts décoratifs, Paris.[12] A platter for a mustard pot (1754–55) is in a Parisian private collection.[13]

The Museum's cup is marked with an unidentified painter's mark that is similar to that of Mutel.[14]

TECHNIQUE AND CONDITION

The yellow ground color is either *jaune jonquille* or *jaune citron*, one of the early yellow ground colors invented by Jean Mathias Caillat and used at the factory. These various tints were made by mixing a lead flux (*fondant*) with Naples yellow.[15] The glaze on this example is somewhat matte, indicating that it devitrified in the kiln.[16] Tiny black dots (*foucasses*) appear on the surface, probably caused by ashes in the kiln that contaminated the glaze.[17]

Exhibition: *Morgan Loan Exhibition*, New York, 1914, not in catalogue

Literature: Chavagnac, pp. 59–60, no. 70, pl. XVII; Brunet and Préaud, p. 32; Savill, 3, pp. 505, 524–25

NOTES

1 Savill (2, p. 501) states that the first size ranged from H. 2⅞–3¹⁄₁₆ in. (7.3–7.7 cm).

2 *Bleu lapis*, birds in gold, no. FK-71, date letter A for 1753–54. See Eriksen and Bellaigue, p. 279, no. 94, and Eriksen, *David Collection*, p. 64, no. 34b (illus. 33b), H. 3³⁄₁₆ × D. 3³⁄₁₆ in. (8.15 × 8.35 cm) (at top) and 3⅛ in. (7.9 cm) (at bottom).

3 White ground, pastoral motifs, landscapes, and birds, no. 28719, with interlaced Ls and dot in center; see *Vincennes*, p. 124, no. 363; H. 2¹⁵⁄₁₆ × DIAM. 2¹⁵⁄₁₆ in. (7.4 × 7.4 cm).

4 H. 3½ in. (8.8 cm). Their diameters at the top are 3½ in. (8.9 cm) while their diameters at the bottom are 3⅛ in. (7.9 cm).

5 See Savill, 2, p. 501, for four handle types typically found on *gobelets litron*.

6 No. 12/1973, in Eriksen, *David Collection*, p. 65, no. 38a.

7 See *Vincennes*, p. 134, no. 397.

8 *Vincennes*, p. 133, no. 394.

9 The straight-sided cup would have been easier to turn and thus less expensive to produce than a cup with a flared rim. It is also possible that there was a special reason for the flared rim that simply is unknown to us today. For *gobelets litron*, see cat. no. 95 .

10 AMNS, Vy 1, fol. 15, 8 August 1753; fol. 21, 18 December 1753; fol. 33v, 14 January 1754; fol. 38, 10 April 1754; fol. 43, 30 June 1754; fol. 54, 27 November 1754; fol. 54v., 27 November 1754.

11 Nos. 54.147.25–26 (*Vincennes*, p. 59, no. 104).

12 No. 25116 (*Vincennes*, p. 74, no. 151).

13 *Vincennes*, p. 60, no. 109.

14 See cat. no. 148. He is known to have painted birds but the birds on the cup do not appear to be by the same hand as those on other marked pieces by Mutel.

15 See Préaud and d'Albis, pp. 224–25, and d'Albis, "Fond jaune," p. 19.

16 See glossary.

17 See glossary.

78

Milk jug (perhaps *pot à lait Bouillard*)

1917.984

Vincennes, 1753–1754

Soft-paste porcelain, H. 3¹¹⁄₁₆ × W. 3¹¹⁄₁₆ × D. 2¹⁵⁄₁₆ in. (9.3 × 9.4 × 7.5 cm)

Yellow ground with children in monochrome blue and flesh tones, gilding

Marks: interlaced Ls in blue with date letter A; painter's mark for André-Vincent Vielliard *père*;[1] incised scrolled V;[2] incised 3[3]

Provenance: perhaps Jean-Jacques-François Machard, 1754;[4] Cartier et Fils, Paris, 1903;[5] J. Pierpont Morgan

MODEL

The fat pear-shaped milk jug with a short waist is usually referred to as a *pot à lait ordinaire*, although there is some evidence that it should, in fact, be called a *pot à lait Bouillard*.[6] Molds for a Bouillard milk jug appeared in the list of new work for 1753, valued at 1.10 *livres*.[7] Three examples emerged from the biscuit kiln on 22 November 1753, and six more on 15 March

78

1754.[8] The first mention of the model in the sales records occurred in December 1753, when Lazare Duvaux bought an example decorated with flowers for 18 *livres*.[9] Many more were sold over the next three years, ranging in price from 18 *livres* for jugs decorated with flowers to 72 *livres* for those with a *bleu céleste* ground and flowers.[10] One example was sold with a basin.[11] Several were sold with other components to form tea sets.[12] *Pots à lait Bouillard* probably had covers attached to the jugs by metal mounts. This model was one of several named for Antoine-Augustin Bouillard, farmer-general, *marchand-mercier*, and shareholder of the Vincennes factory.

There are a number of published examples of this type of milk jug: they include an undated example formerly in the comte de Chavagnac's collection, decorated with a *bleu céleste* ground and cherubs,[13] and a white-ground jug and cover with gilded birds in the Hermitage, St. Petersburg.[14] Another yellow-ground example, this time with plain monochrome children and a cover, once belonged to Morgan along with the milk jug now in the Atheneum.[15]

Turning to the *pot à lait ordinaire*, the first mention of this model in the factory inventory occurred in January 1754, when ten examples with their basins were passed to the painters' workshop.[16] The presence of basins (or *jattes*) characterize the ordinary milk jug in the years that followed. According to the sales records the first jug was sold in June 1754, when Monsieur d'Érigny bought an example decorated in *bleu lapis* and gold.[17] Its form probably can be equated with several small jugs with their basins that resemble miniature versions of the *pot à eau ordinaire* and *jatte*, such as the *bleu lapis* example decorated with gilded birds in the Jones Collection at the Victoria and Albert Museum.[18] Such jugs are distinguished by a longer waist than the Museum's and frequently do not have any spout, although they sometimes included mounted covers. Some also have a marked ridge where the waist meets the bulbous lower half. The shape seems to derive from jugs of the 1740s, which tended to be slightly squatter at the bottom and sometimes had handles that were at ninety degrees to the spout rather than diametrically opposite.[19] Most examples listed in the sales records were sold with basins, and the range in prices suggests that more than one size was produced.[20] An example decorated with flowers cost 36 *livres* while a green-ground set with polychrome children cost an astonishing 600 *livres*.[21]

COMMENTARY

The *pot à lait Bouillard* was clearly differentiated from the *pot à lait ordinaire* in the factory's documents, both denominations sometimes appearing on the same folio of the ledger.[22] While it is difficult to prove unequivocally from the documents that the Hartford shape was a *pot à lait Bouillard*, the sales records do show that Lazare Duvaux purchased a *pot à lait Bouillard jaune enfants camaïeu* along with other components to form a set in December 1754.[23] This may be the *pot à lait Bouillard* listed in the enamel kiln firing of winter or spring, 1754, accompanied by the same tea wares described in the sale to Duvaux.[24] In that same month Bailly purchased another *pot à lait Bouillard jaune enfants camaïeux chaires colorées*, also as part of a set, for 216 *livres*.[25] There are no sales entries during the early 1750s for a *pot à lait ordinaire* with a yellow ground. Still, there is an entry in the enamel kiln records listing a *pot à lait ordinaire jaune enfants camaïeux*, proving that both styles could be decorated in the same manner,[26] and thus allowing for the possibility that the Museum's milk jug is a *pot à lait ordinaire* after all.

The female figure in one of the reserves is reminiscent of François Boucher's sculpture *La Danseuse*, which was designed and produced by the Vincennes factory between 1748 and 1752.[27] A drawing for another *enfant Boucher* called *Le Jeune Suppliant* exists at the factory, and is inscribed "dessein de M. Boucher appartenant à la Manufacture de Vincennes ce 23 aoust 1749" [drawing by Monsieur Boucher belonging to the Vincennes factory this 23 August 1749], indicating that drawings for Boucher children date from this time, if not earlier.[28] *La Danseuse* and the figure on the Museum's jug probably both derive from a common drawing.[29]

Although an exact iconographic source for this model is unknown in Boucher's work, there is some similarity to a painting from about 1754 entitled *La Petite Jardinière*, which, in fact, did directly inspire another Vincennes biscuit figure of the same period, *La Petite Fille à la cage*.[30] Whatever the exact source in Boucher's work, the inspiration could ultimately have been Charles-Simon Favart's *La Vallée de Montmorency*, or *Caprice amoureux*, both plays replete with scenes of dancing shepherdesses.[31]

While the figure of the boy with the drum on the other side of the milk jug also suggests a source in Boucher, no such figure appears among his published works. It is certainly possible that the artist made the drawing of this figure specifically for the factory and that it was among the drawings dating from 1749.

The painting in both reserves shows the painter André-Vincent Vielliard at his best. An uneven painter during his long career at the Vincennes and later Sèvres factory, these early examples of his work display a high level of skill as a draftsman and as a portrayer of charming little figures rarely attained in his later work.[32]

TECHNIQUE AND CONDITION

The yellow ground used on this milk jug was probably called *jaune jonquille* or *jaune citron*.[33] The children in the reserves are painted with *beau bleu no. 2*, called *bleu royal de bohème* by Jean Hellot.[34] The faces are painted with flesh tones, purples and browns. The gilding around the reserves is simple—an early instance of a style that was only to become common in the 1760s.[35] It is somewhat worn around the figure of the dancer as well as on the handle and the rim.[36] The jug is heavily glazed inside.

Exhibition: *Morgan Loan Exhibition*, New York, 1914, not in catalogue

Literature: Chavagnac, p. 64, no. 76

NOTES

1 Active 1752–90. See Savill, 3, pp. 1074–75; Peters, *Marks*, p. 73.

2 See cat. no. 151; also Dauterman, *Marks*, p. 240, as unattributed.

3 Savill, 3, p. 1125. Found on soft paste 1753–90s.

4 Chavagnac, p. 64, states the Museum's milk jug was sold by Lazare-Duvaux 31 December 1753 for 30 *livres*, but this may have been a three-footed milk jug (see AMNS, Vy 1, fol. 29v, *fournée* 1, October–November 1752). There is an entry in the factory sales records for a *pot à laict fond jaune camayeux* sold to Machard on 13 November 1754 for 30 *livres* (AMNS, Vy 1, fol. 53v, *fournée* 6, November 1753–5 January 1754).

5 APML, Cartier file, 14 May 1903: "1 cremier Sèvres fond jaune cartels

enfants camaïeu bleu et rose," 6,000 French francs. Morgan had two yellow-ground milk jugs with monochrome children in his collection, but the other had a cover and the decoration was strictly monochrome blue without flesh tones.

6 This suggestion was first put forth to the author by Bernard Dragesco and the opinion seconded by David Peters.

7 AMNS, I. 7, 1 January 1754 (for 1753).

8 IF 5673, fol. 13; fol. 18.

9 AMNS, Vy 1, fol. 29v, 31 December 1753.

10 Ibid., and Vy 2, fol. 20, Bazin, 5 February 1757.

11 Ibid., fol. 100v, Machard, *bleu céleste fleurs*, 144 *livres*.

12 Ibid., fols. 56v, 57, 63 (probably Bouillard), 72v–73, and 76v.

13 Drouot, Paris, 19–21 June 1911, lot 234.

14 *La porcelaine de Sèvres du XVIIIe siècle*, The Hermitage Museum, Leningrad [now St. Petersburg], postcard booklet, 1976.

15 See note 5. This covered jug was formerly in the Christner collection, Texas (Christie's, New York, 30 November–1 December 1979, lot 211), then in a private collection, England, and now in a private collection in Paris.

16 AMNS, I. 7, 1 January 1754.

17 AMNS, Vy 1, fol. 42v, 25 June 1754.

18 No. 792–1882, King, p. 15, no. 136, pl. 15. An early example with a *bleu lapis* ground and gilded birds and trellises sold at Sotheby's, New York, 15–16 October 1980, lot 350. See cat. no. 159 for the *pot à eau ordinaire*. The *pots à lait ordinaires* tend to have a straighter waist than the water jugs.

19 Préaud and d'Albis, p. 141.

20 There are no molds or models specifically called *pots à lait ordinaires* in the inventories of 1753 and 1754, but there were undesignated *pots à lait* (AMNS, I. 7, 8 October 1752, *moules en plâtre: petits pots au laict a 10s*; *pièces désassorties et défectueuses à repasser en couverte, Pots au laict 3e gre à 6#*). It is difficult to be sure to which models these entries refer. It cannot be the *pot à lait à trois pieds*, for a third size of this milk jug was only introduced in 1756. It seems likely, therefore, that this third-size example refers to the *pot à lait ordinaire*.

21 AMNS, Vy 1, fol. 61, 23 December 1754, Bazin, and Vy 2, fol. 17, 20 August 1756–1 January 1757, Duvaux.

22 Ibid., Vy 2, fol. 101, both to Machard.

23 Ibid., Vy 1, fol. 57, 120 *livres* with other pieces.

24 IF 5676, fol. 18, firing of an unknown date between February and May 1754.

25 AMNS, Vy 1, fol. 63. Although the name *Bouillard* is not written directly next to the words *pot à lait*, it is used to describe the previous item and the symbol for *idem* is used in a way that suggests this was indeed a *pot à lait Bouillard*.

26 See note 24.

27 According to Bourgeois (1913, pl. 4, no. 173) the model was sculpted by Blondeau. The Sèvres factory retains the plaster model and molds. According to Tamara Préaud, the figure was only made in glazed examples until a precise model for new molds was made, allowing for a regular edition in biscuit.

28 Préaud and d'Albis, p. 174. According to Préaud ("Biscuit," p. 31) specialists on Boucher have attributed this drawing to Boucher's workshop.

29 See Ménager, 1, pp. 124–25.

30 See Ananoff, *Boucher*, 2, p. 126, no. 438. Ménager, 1, pp. 124–25 suggests that an engraving by Demarteau after Boucher called *Ninette* shows a figures with the same attitude and hairdo, but the present author does not see a strong resemblance to this figure.

31 Ménager, 1, p. 126. As noted in correspondence with the author, Bernard Dragesco believes that Favart's characters were somewhat older teenagers than the figures represented on the Museum's milk jug and in biscuit as *La Danseuse*. Certainly there is no direct evidence that these individual figures derive from Favart.

32 See for example the *déjeuner Hebert* with *camaïeu bleu* decoration in the Louvre, Paris (illustrated in Préaud and d'Albis, p. 176, no. 186).

33 See Préaud and d'Albis, pp. 224–25 for yellow ground.

34 Ibid., p. 216.

35 I would like to thank Tamara Préaud for this observation.

36 The wear on the handle may have been caused by a loose chain, part of a mount that held the cover to the jug (I am indebted to Didier Cramoisan for this observation).

79

Tray (probably *plateau du roi*)

1961.454

Vincennes, 1754–1755

Soft-paste porcelain, H. ⅞ × L. 9¹⁵⁄₁₆ × W. 6¹⁵⁄₁₆ in. (2.2 × 25.2 × 17.6 cm)

White ground with a monochrome carmine child in a landscape

Marks: interlaced Ls in blue with date letter B, painter's mark of 5 underneath;[1] incised scrolling M[2] and 8[3]

Provenance: Mrs. Marion Bayard Benson (gift, 1961)

MODEL

The Vincennes and Sèvres factory probably called this tray *plateau du roi*.[4] A plaster model survives at the Sèvres factory (fig. 79-1).[5] It was in production by 1753, and was made in two sizes.[6] The first size made an appearance for the first time in the sales records in 1755.[7] That same year trays and tea sets of the second size were also listed in the sales records and factory inventory.[8] A variation with prunus blossom decoration in relief is known from 1755 to 1756.[9]

Fig. 79-1 *Plateau du roi*, plaster model

79

Owing to the lack of size specifications, it is difficult to analyze the prices of tea sets with this tray.[10] Sets with flower motifs ranged from 30 to 108 *livres*.[11] Gold friezes often cost 96 *livres*,[12] and sets with a *bleu lapis* ground were between 144 and 240 *livres*, with many selling at 168 or 192 *livres*.[13] Sets with a green or *bleu céleste* ground ranged from 216 *livres* to an exhorbitant 600 *livres*, with many examples priced at 288 and 300 *livres*.[14]

Surviving examples of *déjeuners du roi* include one with a green ground and children of 1758–59 and another with a *rose marbre* ground of 1761, both in the Wallace Collection.[15] A second-size white ground tray dated 1753–54 accompanied by four small cups (*gobelets Bouret*?) decorated with monochrome children with flesh tones was sold in New York in 1998.[16] It is possible that this was the tray with six *gobelets Bouret 3ᵉg. enfans camayeux chairs colorées* purchased by Lazare Duvaux at the end of 1754 for 108 *livres*.[17] A tray with a monochrome pink landscape dated 1754–55 was in the collection of Elisabeth Parke Firestone.[18] This may have been part of a tea set purchased by Bazin in December 1755 for 84 *livres*.[19]

The Meissen porcelain factory made a tray of this same shape.[20]

FUNCTION

The tray was used either for small tea services or for two jam pots. Those of the first size usually held two cups and saucers and a sugar bowl, or two small cups and saucers, a sugar bowl, and teapot.[21] The second-size tray usually held a cup and saucer and a sugar bowl, although an example is known with four very small components.[22] When used for jam pots, these trays were frequently included in dessert services.[23]

COMMENTARY

The Museum's tray, which is an example of the second size, may have been one of twelve similarly described trays with tea components sold between 1754 and 1755. They all cost between 90 and 96 *livres* for the sets.[24] A second-size tray with similar decoration was sent to Monsieur Caricopo for Mesdames de France on 2 October 1756, priced at 36 *livres*.[25] In the first two years of production, one of the most common decorative schemes on *plateaux* and *déjeuners du roi* was of *enfants camaïeux*.

The decoration of the Museum's tray derives from one of six engravings by Pierre Aveline after François Boucher from a published series called *Premier Livre de Groupes d'Enfans*.[26] The unidentified painter of the tray has taken the left-hand figure from a group of three, and moved him, unchanged, from clouds to a landscape setting. This same painter may have been responsible for a pair of plates with carmine monochrome children in the Ashmolean Museum, Oxford and a saucer in the Museo Duca di Martina, Naples.[27]

NOTES

1 Unidentified painter of flowers and figures, attributed in the 19th century to either A.-J. Carrié and H.-J. Mongenot. David Peters (*Marks*, p. 86) notes that there is no evidence to support either attribution, and that it is unlikely to be Mongenot.

2 Savill, 3, p. 1114, found on soft paste 1754–88. She tentatively attributes it to the *répareur* Pierre Moyé, active 1752/54–65, or perhaps François-Henry Marcou (active 1754–73). The form of the Museum's incised mark differs from that described by Savill, however.

3 Found on soft paste 1754–58, 1767–82, and on hard paste 1780–83. See Savill, 3, p. 1128.

4 The model has been discussed at length by Savill, 2, pp. 590–97. Much of what follows is based on that discussion.

5 AMNS, *casier* 739, L. 11⁷⁄₁₆ × w. 8¼ in. (28.7 × 20.6 cm). See ibid., pp. 590, 596 n. 4, citing *Vincennes*, p. 64.

6 Savill (2, p. 590) lists the sizes as follows: first size: L. 11⅛–11⁷⁄₁₆ × w. 8¼ in. (28.3–29 x 21 cm); second size: L. 9⁷⁄₁₆–10¹⁄₁₆ × w. 6¹¹⁄₁₆–7¹⁄₁₆ in. (24–25.5 × 17–17.9 cm).

7 AMNS, Vy 1, fol. 116v, 1 October–31 December 1755, tea set of the first size with two cups and saucers and a sugar bowl, *lapis enfans camayeux*, 240 *livres*, Duvaux.

8 Ibid., I. 7, 1 January 1756, *Pieces en couverte prêtes à passer au feu*, twenty-eight trays, second size, each 5 *livres* 10 *sols*; ibid., *magasin du blanc*, twenty-three trays, second size, each 6 *livres*. Thirty-seven other trays were ready to be decorated, and valued at 7 *livres* each (their higher value suggests that they were of the first size).

9 Louvre, Paris, no. TH 1246 (see Savill, 2, p. 596 n. 3s and *Vincennes*, p. 63, no. 118).

10 It cannot be assumed that if there is no designation this means the tray is of the first size, especially before late 1755, when sizes start to appear in the sales records. This, in fact, is the only time that a first-size set is listed with its components in the sales ledgers. One can reasonably assume that many pieces with two or three components were of the second size, while those with more components were of the first size. It can also be reasonably assumed that within examples decorated the same way, the more expensive sets probably were larger.

11 AMNS, Vy 2, fol. 41v, 5 December 1757, Boudry, second size, *30 livres*; fol. 38, 15 October 1757, unnamed buyer, second size, 72 *livres*; fol. 43v, 15 December 1757, unnamed buyer, second size, 96 *livres*; fol. 29v, 2 July 1757, unnamed buyer, no size, 102 *livres*; fol. 49, 1 July 1757–1 January 1758, Duvaux, no size, 108 *livres*.

12 Ibid., Vy 1, fol. 52, 7 October 1754, D'Azincourt, cup and saucer, sugar bowl; Vy 2, fol. 49, 1 July 1757–1 January 1758, Duvaux.

13 Ibid., Vy 2, fol. 64v, 1 January–1 July 1758, Duvaux, 144 *livres* (*lapis*); fols. 101, 103v, 9 December 1755, Machard and Bazin, *lapis et or* (first size?, included two cups and saucers, sugar bowl, and teapot) and *lapis enfans camayeux*, 168 *livres*; fol. 114v, 1 October–31 December 1755, Duvaux, *lapis enfans camayeux*, two *gobelets Bouret et soucoupes*, third size, sugar bowl and teapot, 192 *livres*; Vy 2, fol. 78, 30 December 1758, Mme de Pompadour, *lapis rubans*, 196 *livres*; Vy 1, fol. 116v, 1 October–31 December 1755, Duvaux, first size, *lapis enfans camayeux*, 240 *livres*.

14 Ibid., Vy 1, fol. 91, 28 July 1755, Gaudin, *bleu céleste fleurs*, 216 *livres*; fol. 103, 9 December 1755, Bazin, *bleu céleste fleurs*, 240 *livres*; fol. 77, 5–31 December 1754, Duvaux, *bleu céleste fleurs* (cup and saucer, sugar bowl, and teapot) 288 *livres*; Vy 2, fol. 49, 1 July 1757–1 January 1758, Duvaux, *verd guirlandes* and *verd rubans*, 288 *livres*; Vy 1, fol. 56, 5 December 1754, unnamed buyer, *bleu céleste guirlandes*, 300 *livres*; Vy 2, fol. 75,

21 December 1758, Bouret, *rubans verd*, 384 *livres*; Vy 3, fol. 1v, October–December 1758, Mme Duvaux, second size, *verd mosaïque*, 480 *livres*; Vy 2, fol. 49, 1 July 1757–1 January 1758, Duvaux, *verd mosaïque*, 600 *livres*.

15 Nos. C.384–86, C.387–89, in Savill, 2, pp. 590–97.

16 Sotheby's, New York, 25 April 1998, lot 102.

17 AMNS, Vy 1, fol. 74v, 5–31 December 1754 (*fournée* 10, September 1754–January 1755).

18 Christie's, New York, 21 March 1991, lot 203, second size, Mutel.

19 AMNS, Vy 1, fol. 102, 9 December 1755, *paisage camayeux*, with a cup and saucer, sugar bowl. It could also have been part of a set sold to an unnamed buyer on 29 March 1756 for 72 *livres* (ibid., fol. 122, second size).

20 Vienna Art Auctions, Vienna, 2 December 1998, lot 214.

21 Because the sales records rarely designate size, it is difficult to be sure which size is being described. It is likely, however, that in most cases it would take the larger tray to hold more than two or three pieces (cup and saucer being counted as one in this instance). See AMNS, Vy 1, fol. 116v, 1 October–31 December 1755, Duvaux, two cups and saucers, one sugar bowl, *lapis enfans camayeux*, 240 *livres*; fol. 101, Machard, 9 December 1755, *lapis et or*, 168 *livres*, two *gobelets Bouret et soucoupes 3e g.*, sugar bowl and teapot.

22 Ibid., fol. 122, unnamed buyer, 29 March 1756, *paysage camayeux*, 72 *livres*; probably the one sold at Christie's, London, 15 December 1990, lot 16. The set included two cups and saucers, a teapot, and sugar bowl, described as "miniature." They must have been third- and fourth-size pieces (measurements not given). Savill (2, pp. 592, 597 n. 27) also notes overtime records for Thévenet, 1762 (AMNS, F 6) describing a second-size set including two third-size *gobelets litron et soucoupe*, a fourth-size sugar bowl, and a fifth-size teapot.

23 Savill, 2, p. 593.

24 AMNS, Vy 1, fol. 62v, 23 December 1754, Bailly, with covered cup and saucer, sugar bowl, 90 *livres*; fol. 66, 23 December 1754, Gaudin, cup and saucer and sugar bowl *Bouillard*, 90 *livres*; fols. 71, 74v, 75, 76, 5–31 December 1754, Duvaux, cup and saucer and sugar bowl *Hebert*, 90 *livres*; cup and saucer and sugar bowl *Hebert*, 96 *livres*; third-size cup and saucer *litron*, third-size sugar bowl, 90 *livres*; and cup and saucer *Hebert*, sugar bowl, 90 *livres*, respectively; fol. 84, 14 May 1756, Bazin, cup and saucer, sugar bowl, 96 *livres*; fol. 88v, 1 January–1 June 1755, Duvaux, cup and saucer, sugar bowl, 96 *livres*; fol. 99v, 9 December 1755, Machard, three with cup and saucer, sugar bowl, each 96 *livres*; fol. 106, 9 December 1756, Bailly, cup and saucer, sugar bowl, 96 *livres*.

25 Ibid., Vy 2, fol. 1.

26 Jean-Richard, pp. 87–88, no. 239.

27 Nos. 1971-331-32 (see Dawson, *Ashmolean*, pp. 61, no. 43) and Casanova, p. 159, no. 86.

80

80

Cup and saucer (*gobelet Hebert* and *soucoupe unie*)

1917.998

Sèvres, 1757–1758 (cup) and 1761–1762 (saucer)

Soft-paste porcelain, cup: H. 2½ × W. 3⅞ × D. 2¹⁵⁄₁₆ in. (6.4 × 9.8 × 7.5 cm); saucer: H. 1¼ × DIAM. 5⁵⁄₁₆ in. (3.1 × 13.5 cm)

White ground, pink trellis pattern, polychrome flowers, reserves with polychrome children in landscapes

Marks: cup: interlaced Ls with date letter E; incised cm;[1] 274 in old enamel (probably old inventory number); saucer: rubbed interlaced Ls with date letter I (rubbed); possible painter's mark for André-Vincent Vielliard *père* above (rubbed);[2] incised reverse S;[3] 274 in old enamel (inventory number)

Provenance: probably Edouard Chappey, Paris, 1906;[4] J. Pierpont Morgan

MODEL

This type of pear-shaped cup has been identified as a *gobelet Hebert* based on drawings for a sugar bowl and teapot of essentially the same shape, called *Hebert* in the Sèvres archives.[5] The model was in production by October 1752 when *gobelets pour M. Hebert* are mentioned as being ready for glazing.[6]

The cups were made in three sizes, the first and second documented in 1753 and the third size appearing at the end of 1754.[7]

Gobelets Hebert could be sold with one of three styles of saucer: one with lobes and a recessed center for the cup; one with lobes and no recess; and a third with no lobes or recess. The plain saucer does not appear to have been paired with this cup until 1755, but appears more frequently in the 1760s. *Gobelets Hebert* are mostly found in the sales records associated with tea services, above all *déjeuners Hebert*, but likewise with other types.[8] Cups and saucers of this shape cost between 15 *livres* for first size, with flowers to 144 *livres* for third size, *bleu céleste enfants colorés*.[9]

COMMENTARY

The Museum's cup and saucer were probably paired in the nineteenth century. Close scrutiny of the trellis patterns reveal a difference in the shape of the stylized pink flowers where the trellises intersect: on the cup they are square while on the saucer they form a quatrefoil. Furthermore, the date letters on the cup and saucer do not coincide; the cup is marked E for 1757–58, the saucer I for 1761. What seems more likely is that the Museum's cup belongs with a cup and saucer in the Marcus collection at the Museum of Fine Arts, Boston, and with a cup and saucer formerly in the Firestone collection.[10] The scrolled pink band around the reserve matches exactly, as do the trellis decoration and the style of the children in the reserves. Even the formation of the mark under the cup seems to be by the same hand. The saucer, in contrast, is very close to a teapot, sugar bowl, milk jug

169

and two cups and saucers dated 1761 in the Victoria and Albert Museum.[11] Again, the band around the reserve as well as the trellis pattern, with its quatrefoil intersections, match the London pieces very well. There is every likelihood that the set in London originally included more cups and saucers.[12]

The reserve on the Hartford cup depicts a milkmaid with what looks like a butter churn. Although she is akin to Boucher's children-farmers, a direct source in this artist's work has not been found. There is no painter's mark on the cup, but the style of the painting points to the prolific Vielliard.[13] Like many of Vielliard's children, the milkmaid's pose suggests that she might originally have been floating on clouds in true Boucher fashion and has only been brought down to earth by the Sèvres painter.[14] Vielliard probably painted the reserve on the saucer too for traces of a mark like his are visible above the interlaced Ls. Again, while the figure bespeaks Boucher, it does not match anything in the artist's published works.[15] The rather awkward physiognomy of the boy, with his very pronounced forehead and puffy cheeks, is more commonly found from the 1760s in Vielliard's figures after the Dutch artist David Teniers than in his Boucher-like children.[16]

The Museum's cup was made just at the time that the pink ground color was being introduced at Sèvres.[17] This color was only in favor for a relatively short time, from 1757 to 1762, and with a revival from 1772 to 1775. It could be used alone, combined with green, covered with blue patterning to resemble marble or lace, or else used with the white ground to create various trellis patterns.[18] A tray dated 1757–58 in the Wallace Collection is decorated with the same trellis ground as the Atheneum's cup and the cup and saucer in Boston, differing only in the shape of the cartouche surrounding the reserve.[19] The factory described these trellis patterns on pink ground as *rose mosaïque*.[20]

Several tea services decorated with pink trellis patterns were sold in 1758, all appearing in the sales records in December.[21] Individual cups and saucers and sugar bowls were also sold with this decoration.[22] The cups and saucers at Boston, those from the Firestone collection, and the cup at the Atheneum might have been included among any of these transactions.[23]

As for the Museum's saucer it is impossible to know for sure when it was sold. In the sales records for 1761 decoration is seldom described and no *rose mosaïque* appears; in 1762 pieces with *rose mosaïque* decoration were noted only twice.[24] Extant examples with this decoration include: a *déjeuner tiroir* in the Musée des Arts décoratifs, Paris;[25] a *déjeuner corbeille quaré*, 1757–58, sold in 1972;[26] a *gobelet litron* and saucer dated 1761, sold in 1960;[27] and a pair of *seaux à verre* formerly in the McIlhenny collection, Philadelphia.[28]

Exhibition: *Morgan Loan Exhibition*, New York, 1914, not in catalogue

Literature: Chavagnac, pp. 73–74, no. 86; Brunet and Préaud, p. 32; Hawes and Corsiglia, pp. 192–93; Savill, 2, p. 500

NOTES

1 Savill, 3, p. 1095, found on soft paste, 1755–75, perhaps the mark of Claude Marsillon, *répareur*, 1756–58.

2 Active 1752–90, see Savill, 3, pp. 1074–75; Peters, *Marks*, p. 73.

3 Found by 1753–66. See Savill, 3, p. 1122, who comments that it may also have been used later as well. It can also look like a scrolling 2.

4 APML, Chappey file, invoice 30 April, "1 Tasse à café fd blanc quadrillé rose Du Barry à [semis] de fleurs à décor de fillette et garçon dans paysage (1757) coutant 8500."

5 AMNS, R. 1, L. 2, d. 8, fol. 2, and R. 1, L. 2, d. 4, fol. 6. First identified by Eriksen in *Waddesdon*, p. 38. See also *Vincennes*, p. 122. *Gobelets Hebert* are discussed more fully in Savill, 2, pp. 496–97, from which most of the information on the shape is taken.

6 AMNS, I. 7, 8 October 1752, *Pièces en biscuit prêtes à passer en couverte*.

7 Savill, 2, p. 496. According to Savill, the sizes are as follows: first-size cup, H. 2⅞–3⅜ in. (7.2–8.5 cm), saucer, DIAM. 5¹⁵⁄₁₆ (15 cm); second-size cup, H. 2⁵⁄₁₆–2⅝ in. (5.8–6.7 cm), saucer, diam. 5⅛–5⅝ in. (13–14.2 cm); third-size cup, H. 2–2³⁄₁₆ in. (5.1–5.6 cm), saucer, DIAM. 4⅝–4¹⁵⁄₁₆ in. (11.8–12.5 cm).

8 Ibid.

9 Ibid., 2, pp. 496, 500 nn. 17–18.

10 Elisabeth Parke Firestone sale, Christie's, New York, 22 March 1991, lot 222, marks effaced.

11 Nos. 791-791d-1882 (King, pl. 4, p. 10, no. 120).

12 One of the two cups and saucers (no. C. 1402-1919) did not enter the V&A with the Jones Collection group but may in fact belong with it. Tea sets tended to get broken up with the many cups and saucers likely candidates to be sold separately.

13 The cup in Boston, while not marked by Vielliard, also seems to have been painted by him.

14 See cat. no. 60 for a discussion of Boucher and Vielliard.

15 Boucher did create at least two compositions with bagpipe players. One was engraved twice, once by Aveline under the title of *Innocence* (Jean-Richard, p. 77, no. 196) and again by Demarteau as *L'Enfant berger* (Jean-Richard, p. 207, no. 780). Another design is represented by a drawing in the British Museum, London, illustrated in Ananaoff, *Boucher*, 2, no. 337/5. The figure on the saucer, however, assumes a different pose than either of these figures.

16 According to Savill, Vielliard painted "Teniers" scenes from 1758/59 until the mid-1760s. See for example the *cuvette Verdun* in the Wallace Collection (Savill, 1, pp. 101–5).

17 See Eriksen and Bellaigue, pp. 52–53 for pink ground color. The first time pink appears in the sales records is on 28 December 1758 (AMNS, Vy 2, fol. 75v, unnamed buyer).

18 A second type of trellis pattern in pink and white can be found on the Museum's *déjeuner Courteille* (cat. no. 83). See Savill, 2, p. 601 for descriptions of other trellis patterns.

19 Savill, 2, pp. 598–602, no. C390. Hawes and Corsiglia, p. 192, felt that the difference in the cartouche was enough to prove that this tray was not from the same tea set as the Boston cup and saucer. This opinion is shared by the present author.

20 Savill, 2, p. 601.

21 AMNS, Vy 2, fol. 77, 30 December 1758, the king, *déjeuner tiroir* (first size, 600 *livres*); fol. 78, 30 December 1758, Mme de Pompadour, *déjeuner quaré* (second size, 240 *livres*); fol. 79v, 1 December 1758–1 January 1759, Duvaux, *déjeuner corbeille triangle* (432 *livres*), *tiroir* (second size, 300 *livres*), *quaré* (second size, 240 *livres*); fol. 82, December 1758, Dulac, *déjeuner quaré à jour* (second size, 240 *livres*), *tiroir* (second size, 300 *livres*), *corbeille quarée* (432 *livres*); fol. 89, December 1758, Poirier, *déjeuner quaré* (240 *livres*).

22 Ibid., fol. 80v, 1 December 1758–1 January 1759, Duvaux, two cups and saucers and one sugar bowl of undetermined shape, 132 *livres* and 144 *livres* respectively; fol. 81v, December 1758, Bachelier, cup and saucer Hebert, 120 *livres*.

23 *Gobelets Hebert* could accompany many different styles of trays in addition to the *plateau Hebert*. See Savill, 2, pp. 496 and 500 n. 13.

24 AMNS, Vy 2, fol. 115v, Mme de Pompadour, 12 June 1762, *déjeuner quaré* (second size, 96 *livres*, perhaps the partial tea set in the V&A, London including the Atheneum's saucer); fol. 117, 25 June 1762, Mme de Pompadour, *déjeuner quaré mosaïque Chinois* (third size, 120 *livres*).

25 No. GR 202A-D. It is undated.

26 Sotheby's, New York, 9 December 1972, lot 29, with a sugar bowl of a different trellis than the other pieces.

27 Sotheby's, London, 6 December 1960, lot 81.

28 Christie's, New York, 20–21 May 1987, lot 640, no date given.

81

Rectangular tray (*plateau tiroir*)

1917.1001

Sèvres, 1757–1758

Soft-paste porcelain, H. 1⅜ × L. 9⁵⁄₁₆ × w. 6⅝ in. (3.5 × 23.7 × 16.8 cm)

White ground with monochrome blue landscape and children, the latter with flesh tones, gilding

Marks: interlaced Ls in blue with date letter E, painter's mark for André-Vincent Vielliard *père* above,[1] dot below; incised bc[2]

Provenance: possibly Cartier et Fils, Paris, 1900;[3] J. Pierpont Morgan

MODEL

It is thanks to its resemblance to a drawer [*tiroir*] of a desk that the Sèvres factory called this tray a *plateau tiroir*. Usually there is a molded edge to the tray but it may be masked somewhat by the use of ground color. Oftentimes such trays stood on four small feet, which were either round, cone- or baluster-shaped.[4] The Museum's tray has baluster-shaped feet.

Two eighteenth-century molds for this tray survive at the Sèvres factory, although plaster models do not.[5] *Plateaux tiroir* seem to have been produced first in 1756, in two sizes;[6] in the inventory of January 1757—covering production of 1756—four of the second size in biscuit were listed, ready to be glazed.[7] Among molded pieces mentioned in the records for biscuit firings for April–May 1756 are *plateaux tiroir*, some with feet and some without.[8] The first recorded sale of a *déjeuner tiroir* was in December 1756, when one decorated with flowers was sold to the dealer Machard for 48 *livres*.[9]

The inventory of January 1759—for work of 1758—records molds and models for a version of the *plateau tiroir* distinguished by a pierced, Vitruvian-scroll side (akin to another tray, the *plateau carré à jour*).[10] Examples of this version exist with the date letter E.[11]

The *plateau tiroir* was sold almost exclusively as a part of a tea set.[12] The price of *déjeuners tiroir* varied widely, from as little as 30 *livres* for an all-white set to 600 *livres* for a *rose mosaïque* example of the first size sold to Louis XV in December 1758.[13]

COMMENTARY

The Atheneum's tray is of the first size. The painting on it by André-Vincent Vielliard depicts a scene of two children playing a game called *le Tourniquet* or *la Loterie*. This game was also portrayed in a Sèvres biscuit sculpture of 1757 designed by Étienne-Maurice Falconet.[14] Vielliard's composition is similar to an engraving by Jean-Baptiste Le Prince after François Boucher entitled *La Chasse*, although the engraving shows two children trapping birds instead of playing a game, and the positions of the children's hands have been modified accordingly. The scene on the Museum's tray is in the opposite sense of the engraving.[15]

The unusual gilding along the edge of the tray, which includes alternating large and small dentils and a unifying scallop underneath, is similar to the gilding on the service given by Louis XV to Maria-Theresa of Austria in 1758.[16] It is also akin to the border of a cheese-drainer (*fromager*) dating from 1755–56.[17]

A *déjeuner tiroir* decorated with children sold to an unnamed buyer for 144 *livres* on 30 September 1758.[18] Another with children sold to the dealer Dulac for 132 *livres* in 1759,[19] while a third sold to Madame Lair for the same price in 1760.[20] It is possible that the Museum's tray was included among these sales.

TECHNIQUE AND CONDITION

There must have been some problem in at least one of the firings of this tray.[21] The underside is dotted with both bubbles and black specks. The bubbles appear to be in or under the glaze, while the black specks rise above the glaze. Scratches on the exterior of all four sides have been reglazed. There is one hole at the bottom edge where a kiln support must have lodged, and two equally spaced black accretions where other supports must have touched. Most of the glaze flaws occur on the underside of the tray, although there are a few bubbles and black specks on the interior wall. Some minor warping has occurred as well.

There are at least two possible explanations for the technical problems found on this tray.[22] Perhaps there was some kind of contamination during the first firing leading to the formation of either bubbles or of a residue on the exterior of the tray. In an attempt to salvage the tray someone may have tried to scrape away the blemishes from the outside wall and then refired it. At that point either refiring did not get rid of the original glaze flaws or further contamination left the black specks. Examination of the glaze-kiln records show that in May 1757, seven *plateaux tiroir* were glazed, six emerging in good state, and one needing to be reglazed.[23] In August of that year, thirty-eight examples were glazed, thirty-one with good result, five needing to be reglazed, with two breaking. A note in the margin indicates that there were problems with black specks or *taches*.[24] Finally, in 1758 twenty-one examples were glazed, sixteen well, three needing a second glazing, while two were broken. Again, *taches* are noted.[25] This lends credence to the theory that the refiring might have been done in the factory early in the life of the tray.

The other possible explanation is that the tray was refired at a later date, perhaps if it was regilded. Although this theory would not resolve the issue of the scraped and reglazed walls, nevertheless it would account for the speckling as well as the existence of the two rough kiln-stand marks underneath which were not typical of eighteenth-century firings. The fact that the

existing gilding shows little wear compared to the rest of the tray adds some support to this theory. There is nothing to rule out the concurrent validity of both theories. Maybe some firing flaws occurred at the factory that someone tried to scrape away, and then in the nineteenth century the tray was regilded. This would satisfactorily explain why there are extra kiln-support marks and why the speckling is so bad.

Exhibition: *Morgan Loan Exhibition*, New York, 1914, not in catalogue

Literature: Chavagnac, p. 75, no. 88

NOTES

1 Active 1752–90. See Savill, 3, pp. 1074–75; Peters, *Marks*, p. 73.

2 See Eriksen, *Waddesdon*, p. 102, no. 35, who notes that this mark often appears on trays dating 1757–59 as well as on dishes in the Bedford service of 1763 and the Starhemberg service of 1766.

3 APML, Cartier file, invoice for 11 May 1900: "1 plateau Sèvres camaïeu bleu sur fond blanc," with other items, 28,000 French francs.

4 See *Vincennes*, pp. 67, 69 n. 5; and Préaud and d'Albis, p. 194, no. 238, where this shape is discussed. In current literature the name *à pieds* is used to refer the version with feet, but this title does not appear in the inventories or sales records of the factory, although it does appear in the biscuit kiln records (IF 5673, fol. 56, 12 April 1756).

5 *Vincennes*, p. 67; Préaud and d'Albis, p. 194, no. 238.

6 Trays of the first size are approximately 9⁷⁄₁₆ in. (24 cm) in length, and second size trays are between 6¹¹⁄₁₆ and 7¹⁄₁₆ in. (17 and 18 cm). A tea set designated third size was sold to Mme de Pompadour on 28 June 1763 (AMNS, Vy 3, fol. 157) for 24 *livres*. No extant trays that could be third size are known to this author.

7 AMNS, I. 7, 1 January 1757, *Pieces en Biscuit pretes a estre mises en Couverte*.

8 IF 5673, fols. 56–57, 12 April 1756.

9 AMNS, Vy 2, fol. 6v, 21 December 1756.

10 AMNS, I. 7, 1 January 1759 (for 1758), *moules* and *modèles en plâtre*. See Dawson, *British Museum*, pp. 101–2, no. 91.

11 See an example with pink ground (part of a tea set) in the V&A, London, first size, decoration by Méreaud (no. 2020-E-1855, information kindly provided by Terry Bloxham); one with *bleu lapis* and *écaille* gilding, birds in landscape, Christie's, Monaco, 7 December 1987, lot 174.

12 Exceptionally, some individual *plateaux tiroir* rather than *déjeuners tiroir* were sold to Lazare Duvaux during the first half of 1758 (AMNS, Vy 2, fol. 64).

13 Ibid., fol. 77, 30 December 1758. Price ranges for tea sets of this shape are extremely wide. The following price ranges pertain to 1757–62 and encompass both the first and second sizes: flowers, 30–144 *livres*; landscapes, 60–144 *livres*; gold fillets or friezes, 60–120 *livres*; monochrome children, 84–144 *livres*; birds, 54–192 *livres*; *bleu lapis*, 96–360 *livres*; pink ground, 190–600 *livres*; green ground, 96–432 *livres*; and *bleu céleste* ground, 192–288 *livres*.

14 Bourgeois, 1913, no. 403, pl. 6, called *Marchands de plaisirs ou Tourniquet*.

15 See Jean-Richard, p. 332, no. 1384. Vincennes-Sèvres used Boucher's composition frequently but usually in the same sense as the engraving. There is a preparatory drawing for a related painting in the V&A, London, and there is a painting showing the same two figures before a fire in a landscape, published as *Hiver*, recorded in a Paris private collection (See Ananoff, *Boucher*, 2, p. 73, no. 373). Painters transferred engraved designs to porcelain by pouncing, that is tracing the engraving on a sheet of paper and then poking tiny holes in the paper following its main outlines. Then black powder was brushed through the holes to transfer the design to the porcelain. Vielliard may have transferred the main elements of the composition in the opposite sense to the original engraving, and then modified the details according to his own ideas. For more on pouncing see Préaud and d'Albis, p. 228 (*poncif*). For another example of Vincennes using this engraving see cat. no. 151.

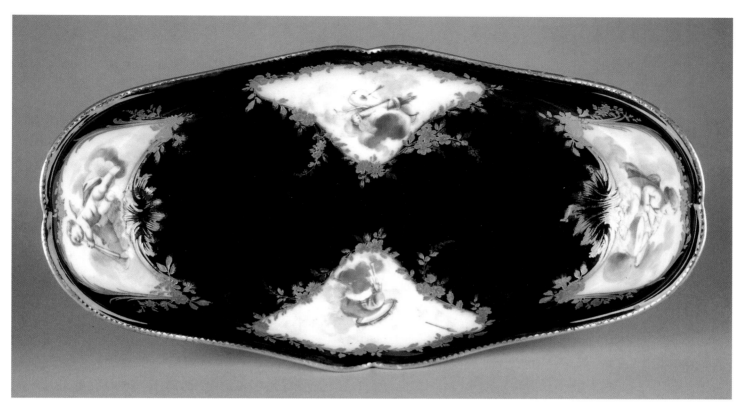

82

16   Illustrated in *Tables royales*, p. 335, and in Winkler, p. 231, fig. 186.

17   See Préaud and d'Albis, p. 192, no. 231, now at MNC, Sèvres.

18   AMNS, Vy 2, fol. 69v.

19   Ibid., Vy 3, fol. 3v, October–December 1759.

20   Ibid., fol. 19v, April–July 1760.

21   Most of the following observations were made by Antoine d'Albis upon examination of the tray.

22   It has been suggested that the entire tray has been redecorated but the enamel decoration and marks seem perfectly genuine.

23   IF 5674, fol. 73, 13 May 1757.

24   Ibid., fol. 91, 24 August 1757.

25   Ibid., fol. 95, 30 December 1758.

82

Tray (*plateau en porte-huilier*)

1917.1002

Sèvres, 1757–1758

Soft-paste porcelain, H. 2¹/₁₆ × L. 10⅝ × W. 5½ in. (5.2 × 27.1 × 14 cm)

Bleu lapis ground with carmine putti and trophies in reserves

Marks: interlaced Ls with date letter E, in gold; underglaze blue dot at foot rim; bc incised[1]

Provenance: possibly Cartier et Fils, Paris, 1901;[2] J. Pierpont Morgan

MODEL

Trays of this shape were called *porte-huiliers*, so named because the tray was originally designed to hold two crystal bottles for oil and vinegar.[3] The first known mention of this tray at Vincennes was of a terracotta model with wax ewers, listed in the inventory of October 1752.[4] It is possible that it was one of several shapes designed by Duplessis for the *bleu céleste* service made for Louis XV and delivered beginning in 1753, for the first mention of a *porte-huilier* in the Vincennes sales records is of the four sold with this service.[5] Molds and models for this tray first appear in the January 1755 inventory for the work of 1754,[6] and at least twenty-eight examples were in production at the time of the inventory. A second size was mentioned in the inventory in 1758, although existing examples seem all to be of one size.[7] In 1763 a new version of the *porte-huilier* appeared, called *porte-huilier à carcasses*, with two openwork circular galleries attached to the tray to house the oil and vinegar bottles.[8]

   Porte-huiliers cost from as little as 18 *livres* (*fleurs*) to as much as 108 *livres* (*roze attributs et fleurs*).[9] Most of the single trays sold into the early 1760s were simply decorated with flowers, and cost 24 or 27 *livres*. The *bleu céleste* tray which was part of the Louis XV service cost 96 *livres*.

FUNCTION

Porte-huiliers held the oil and vinegar that was required as a dressing for the many salads accompanying a meal. Like today, salad might have comprised a variety of ingredients, including vegetables in combination with meat, fish, or fowl.[10] Before the advent of porcelain, *porte-huiliers* were made in silver, or else in lesser metals, pottery, or wood,[11] and in the case of grand silver

Fig. 82-1 *Les Éléments: la Terre*, Louis Félix de La Rue after François Boucher

services, were often incorporated into the centerpiece.[12] Porcelain *porte-huiliers* were also made by the Meissen porcelain factory, one of which was sold by Lazare Duvaux in 1748.[13]

Porte-huiliers were not always included in formal services sold by the Sèvres factory. While four were in Louis XV's first porcelain service, none were recorded in the services made for Maria-Theresa of Austria (1758), the Elector of Palatine (1760), the Duke of Bedford (1763), Christian VII of Denmark (1768), Madame du Barry (1770–71), Gustav III of Sweden (1771), or Joseph II, Emperor of Austria, travelling under the name of comte de Falkenstein (1777).[14] *Porte-huiliers* may be found, however, in other French royal services, including one bought for the château de Fontainebleau (crimson floral garlands, 1757), as well as a small green service from 1758, a pink service from 1759 (*roze attributs de Chasse*), and a blue mosaic-ground service with polychrome cherubs and trophies from the 1760s.[15] They may also be found in two services delivered to the duc d'Aiguillon for the ministry of foreign affairs in 1773.[16] In these later services the *porte-huiliers* were of the *à carcasses* variety and were included in the second part of the service, along with juice pots, sauceboats, salad bowls, and lemon trays (*bateaux*).[17] Four *porte-huiliers à carcasses*, priced at a remarkable 360 *livres* each, were supposed to be included in the great service ordered by Louis XVI in 1783 but they had not been delivered by 1793 when the king was executed and the factory ceased work on the service.[18]

When porcelain *porte-huiliers sans carcasses* were sold as cruet stands, they could be mounted with holders for the oil and vinegar bottles. The *porte-huilier* from the Fontainebleau service has a set of holes in the porcelain, no doubt to secure some type of silver-gilt receptacles.[19] In November 1758 Lazare Duvaux sold to Louis XV a "huilier de porcelaine de France, vert, garni de ses carcasses et porte-bouchons des caraffes en or ciselé, & les caraffes en cristal, 1,140 l. [Green Sèvres porcelain cruet set garnished with tooled gold carafe holders and stoppers and crystal carafes, 1,140 *livres*]."[20] Once garnished in this way a cruet tray became a very costly part of a dinner service.

Upon their introduction, *porte-huiliers* were also used as trays

for small tea sets, usually comprising a cup and sugar bowl. In December 1754 Lazare Duvaux bought a *plateau en porte-huilier* decorated in monochrome with children, accompanied by a matching *gobelet à la reine* and a sugar bowl of the same shape for 168 *livres*.[21] Cups and sugar bowls of other shapes were also paired with this type of tray. Saucers were rarely sold with the cups, owing to the limited amount of space provided by the narrow tray.[22] From 1754 through 1761 *porte-huiliers* were sold as tea trays more than three times as often as they were sold as cruet stands.[23]

Tea sets with *porte-huilier* trays ranged in price from about 48 *livres* for flowers to 360 *livres* for *bleu céleste enfants colorés*.[24] If the Museum's tray were part of a set, it would probably have cost 144 *livres*.[25]

COMMENTARY

The Hartford *porte-huilier* is decorated with cherub musicians in the end reserves and trophies in the side reserves. This combination of cherubs and trophies may be found on other oblong shapes, including a basin for a water jug in the Wallace Collection, dated 1757–58.[26] The cherub playing the kettle-drums on the Museum's tray derives from an engraving by Louis Félix de La Rue after François Boucher—one of a series of *The Elements* (fig. 82-1).[27] The source for the horn-blowing cherub is unknown. While the style of the figures is in the manner of Jean-Louis Morin, the quality of the draftsmanship, especially noticeable in the drum-playing cherub, reveals the hand of a less-skilled painter. It is possible that the Hartford tray was one purchased by Lazare Duvaux during the first half of 1757, or perhaps was part of a tea set he sold to Monsieur le Président Ogier to be given as a gift on 11 April 1758.[28]

The presence of the factory mark in gold is unusual but not unique in the 1750s. There are several other examples, all with the date letter E, among them: a cylindrical pot with green ground and birds at Waddesdon Manor; a pink *pot à lait couvert* formerly on the art market; a green *cuvette Courteille* at the Walter's Art Gallery, Baltimore; a *plateau carré* with green ribbons in a private collection; a pink trellis *déjeuner carré à jour*; and a green *vase à oreilles* with children.[29] It is likely that they were the work of a particular gilder active during the years 1757–58, who happened to mark his pieces while he had gold on his brush, and whenever the painter had failed to do so earlier.

TECHNIQUE AND CONDITION

Several minor problems must have occurred in the biscuit and glaze firings of this tray. In the reserve with the horn-blowing cherub and in the well of the tray there are small firing cracks or scratches that occurred before glazing. The black speckles (*végétations salines*) on both the top and the underside of the tray must have appeared at the time of glazing. Other signs of contamination in the glaze firing include pitting and two small specks of foreign matter on the underside of the tray. Moreover, the glaze has crawled or pulled away from the body just below the horn-blowing cherub. The piece was decorated, nevertheless, and evidently much used, since it is heavily scratched and the gilding around the reserves and the rim is worn.

Exhibition: *Morgan Loan Exhibition*, New York, 1914, not in catalogue

Literature: Chavagnac, p. 75, no. 89

NOTES

1 Eriksen, *Waddesdon*, p. 102, no. 35.

2 APML, Cartier file, invoice 24 May 1901: "1 Ravier, Vincennes, fond gros bleu, cartels amours camaïeu roses," 2,000 French francs.

3 Trays of this shape have sometimes been confused with another more geometric tray called a *bateau*. The Sèvres records clearly distinguish the two shapes while at the same time pricing them the same and often listing them in the same entry.

4 AMNS, I. 7, 8 October 1752, and again listed in the January 1753 inventory: *1 modèle de porte-huile en terre cuite et ses burettes en cire*.

5 AMNS, Vy 1, fol. 69 (*fournée* 10, October 1754–January 1755), 96 *livres*, second installment of the service.

6 AMNS, I. 7, 1 January 1755 (for 1754), *moules* and *modèles en plâtre*.

7 Ibid., 1 January 1759 (for 1758), *moules* and *modèles en plâtre*. Examples range in length from 10⅝–11¹⁄₁₆ in. (27–28 cm).

8 Ibid., 1 January 1764 (for 1763), *moules* and *modèles en plâtre*: *de la carcasse à jour du porte huillier*. This model does not appear to have been distinguished from the earlier plain *porte-huilier* tray in the inventories or sales records in the years immediately following its introduction. There is one ambiguous entry in the sales record of 1758 for a *porte huillier Verd a porte Caraffes 168 livres*, sold to Mme Victoire, 11 April. This is a much higher price than other examples without tea wares, and could indicate some sort of structure for the cruets. However, the early date, significantly before mention of the *à carcasses* version in the inventory, suggests that the factory provided some kind of metal holders for the cruet bottles. Yet another inconsistency occurs in the biscuit kiln records for 8 November 1756, when two *porte-huiliers garnis* appear. This, in fact, suggests porcelain holders, although Tamara Préaud postulates that they could simply be two wells, like in a saucer.

9 AMNS, Vy 3, fol. 2, to Mme Lair, October–December 1759.

10 See Savill, "Starhemberg," p. 28.

11 Havard, 4, pp. 510–11.

12 Gruber, pp. 179–90.

13 LD, 2, p. 10, no. 92, to M. de Saint-Martin: "un huilier de Saxe avec ses caraffes de cristal, 78 l."

14 Perhaps this is due to the fact that cruet sets were still being incorporated into centerpieces and were not always needed as separate components. See Gruber, pp. 171–87. For listings of many of the major services with their components and archival references see *Grands services*.

15 For discussion of these royal services see Peters, "Louis XV et XVI," pp. 110–23.

16 AMNS, Vy 5, fol. 89v, 26 August; fols. 93v–94, 28 September 1773. Of course, services were often put together by dealers like Mme Lair from their stock, making it difficult to have an accurate accounting of 18th-century services and their components.

17 In the service sold in September 1773 the "second" and "third" services were combined.

18 See de Bellaigue, *Louis XVI*, p. 257.

19 Peters, "Louis XV et XVI," p. 112; see also *Vincennes*, p. 67, no. 31 for the *porte-huilier* now at the MNC, Sèvres.

20 LD, 2, p. 380, no. 3278.

21 AMNS, Vy 1, fol. 73v, 31 December 1754. Duvaux also sold a *déjeuner sur porte-huilier* to Mme de la Reynière on 28 December 1754 (p. 229, no. 2014).

22 There exists a similarly-shaped tray but with a flatter bottom, that seems to have been inspired by the *porte-huilier*, and may indeed have been a variant with the same name. This tray could have held both a cup and saucer and sugar bowl. An example was with John Whitehead in 1990, dated G for 1759 and decorated with a polychrome landscape by the caduceus painter. I would like to thank David Peters for pointing out this variant, and John Whitehead for providing a photograph. Another example was formerly in the Hodgkins collection (*Hodgkins*, no. 12).

23 By 1761 the sales records at the factory had stopped differentiating shapes in their descriptions of tea sets sold to dealers, so that tracking *déjeuners en porte-huilier* becomes nearly impossible. Most of the information on pricing that follows pertains to the years 1754 to 1761.

24 AMNS, Vy 1, fol. 116v, 1 October–31 December 1755, Duvaux.

25 In the sales records, tea sets decorated with *bleu lapis* ground and children in monochrome ranged from 144 to 168 *livres*, but considering the problems in firing evident in this piece I would expect the price to have been on the lower side of the range. It is also possible that the Museum's tray may even have been sold as a *rebut* although this would be difficult to prove.

26 Savill, 2, pp. 705–8, nos. C452–53.

27 Jean-Richard, p. 313, no. 1284.

28 AMNS, Vy 2, fol. 28, 144 *livres*; LD, 2, p. 359, no. 3102, "Envoyé a M. le baron Korff: un déjeuner en porte-huilier de porcelaine de France gros-bleu, peint à enfans, 216 livres."

29 Eriksen, *Waddesdon*, p. 82, no. 26; formerly with Dragesco-Cramoisan, Paris; formerly in the Hodgkins collection (*Hodgkins*, no. 15); Deane Johnson sale, Sotheby's, New York, 9 December 1972, lot 29, now on the art market, London; Sir Charles Clore sale, Christie's, Monaco, 6 December 1985, lot 4 (Savill, 3, p. 1180 n. 52). I would like to thank Bernard Dragesco for pointing out most of these examples to me.

83

Tea service with three cups and saucers (*plateau Courteille, gobelets Hebert et soucoupes unies*)

1917.1006–1009

Sèvres, 1757–1758

Soft-paste porcelain, tray: H. 1⅞ × L. 12⅞ × W. 9⅛ in. (4.7 × 32.7 × 23.2 cm); 1917.1007: cup: H. 2⅜ × W. 3¹¹⁄₁₆ × D. 2⅞ in. (6 × 9.4 × 7.3 cm); saucer: H. 1⅛ × DIAM. 4¾ in (2.8 × 12 cm); 1917.1008: cup: H. 2⅜ × W. 3¹¹⁄₁₆ × D. 2⅞ in. (6 × 9.4 × 7.3 cm); saucer: H. 1³⁄₁₆ × DIAM. 4⅝ in. (3 × 11.8 cm); 1917.1009: cup: H. 2⅜ × W. 3¹³⁄₁₆ × D. 2⅞ in. (6 × 9.5 × 7.3 cm); saucer: H. 1⅛ × DIAM. 4¾ in. (2.8 × 12 cm)

Rose ground with intersecting ribbons, polychrome children in landscapes, gilding

Marks: tray: incised BP[1] and D;[2] 1917.1007, cup: interlaced Ls with date letter E, incised BR;[3] saucer: interlaced Ls with date letter E, mark for André-Vincent Vielliard *père*, above,[4] dot below; incised I or H;[5] 1917.1008: cup: traces of interlaced Ls, incised LL; saucer: interlaced Ls with date letter E, mark for Vielliard *père*; incised scrolling M; 1917.1009: cup: worn interlaced Ls with date letter E, incised LL; saucer: interlaced Ls with date letter E, mark for Vielliard *père*, incised I or H.

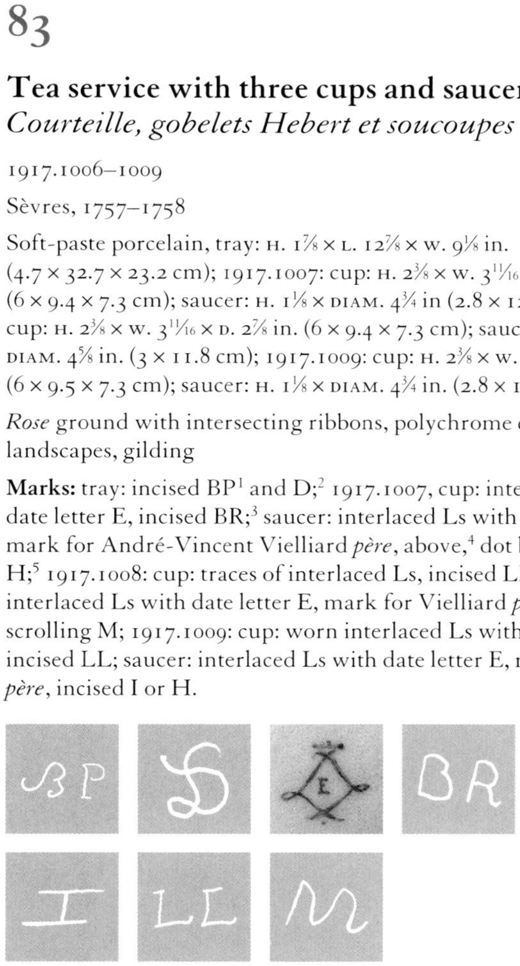

Provenance: A.B. Daniell & Sons, London, 1901;[6] J. Pierpont Morgan

83

MODEL

The factory name for this tray was *plateau Courteille*, named for the marquis de Courteille (1696–1767), Louis XV's *intendant des finances* from 1748 and royal representative to the factory from 1751.[7] There are five variations of the tray, with either acanthus or scrolling handles, indented or rounded corners, or no handles at all.[8] Those without handles were for mounting in small tables, often two-tiered, and were called *plateaux de chiffonnière*. Of these, trays with rounded corners were used on the top tier whereas those for the lower tier had indented corners to accommodate the table legs.[9] Examples with handles were used as tea trays, in combination with various cups and saucers, teapots, sugar bowls, milk jugs, tea caddies, and coffee pots. The Atheneum's tray has scrolling handles and indented corners.[10]

The *plateau Courteille* was produced in two sizes, as recorded in the inventory of January 1759 for new work of 1758.[11] The sizes are not specified in the sales records, and appear to vary according to each version of the tray.[12] The first-size tray could hold a service of up to eight pieces.[13]

Louis XV and Madame de Pompadour bought the first *déjeuners Courteille* listed in the sales ledgers in December 1758. Both services were decorated with a pink ground, and cost 720 *livres* each. The records tell us that Madame de Pompadour's had flowers in the reserves.[14] Other *déjeuners Courteille* ranged in price from 156 *livres* for flower decoration to 840 *livres* for pink, green, blue, and yellow ground with miniatures.[15] There are several surviving examples dating from 1757–58, including some that do not appear in the sales records.[16]

COMMENTARY

It appears that the Atheneum's service, which is of the smaller or second size, is unrecorded.[17] It is likely that it originally included a teapot, sugar bowl, and milk jug. The surviving cups are *gobelets Hebert*, and are paired with plain saucers, in typical 1760s fashion.[18] They are of the second size.

The pattern of interlaced ribbons was in fashion primarily in 1757 and 1758, just as the pink ground was being introduced, and may have been called *à rubans* in the sales records. The pattern of white ribbons on a pink ground featured on the Museum's tray also occurs on a *vase Hollandois* dated 1757–58 in the Wallace Collection, and on a pair of *vases Hollandois* of the same date at Harewood House, Yorkshire.[19] Sometimes the ribbons themselves were done in pink ground against the white. An oval basin at the Musée national de Céramique, Sèvres,[20] and on a water jug (perhaps its mate) in the Palazzo Pitti, Florence are fine examples of this reversed color scheme.[21]

The reserves of the tray and cups and saucers show children in landscapes, engaged in various adult occupations. The boys and girls on the cups and saucers are gardening, playing music, fishing, and catching birds. The scene on the tray shows a boy at an easel painting a seated girl, and probably signifies the allegory of painting. While only the saucers are marked as such, it is likely that André-Vincent Vielliard painted the entire tea service.

The depiction of allegories using children became enormously popular in the middle of the eighteenth century, and such motifs were soon found alike on porcelain, furniture, and tapestries.[22] François Boucher and Carle Vanloo both painted important decorative cycles that included allegories of the arts for Madame de Pompadour. The Boucher series depicted allegories of the arts and sciences, the latter including horticulture, as well as fishing and fowling, and is said to have been part of the decoration of her château de Crécy.[23] The Vanloo cycle, depicting *Painting, Sculpture, Architecture,* and

Music, was painted for her château de Bellevue.[24] None of the porcelain reserves in the Museum's service are based directly on the Vanloo or Boucher compositions, but they were certainly done in kindred spirit. The identical scene of children painting that appears on the tray may also be found on a 1757–58 pink-ground *plateau Courteille* without handles at the Huntington Library and Art Collections in California.[25] That tray was marked by Vielliard.

TECHNIQUE AND CONDITION

When the tray was molded the modeler made a hole in the back from which to hang it on a metal support in the kiln. However, it was never used, for the very long support needed would have bent during firing, so a *pupitre* was used instead.[26] The tray has a crack running from the top through part of the reserve. A chip at the top edge indicates where the impact occurred. One of the cups was broken into five pieces and repaired. The use of purple around the gilding is typical on *rose*-ground Sèvres, and may have been inspired by the outlined gilding around the reserves on Meissen porcelain.[27]

Exhibition: *Morgan Loan Exhibition*, New York, 1914, not in catalogue

Literature: Chavagnac, pp. 77–78, no. 92; Savill, 1, pp. 72, 90 n. 51, 616, 620 n. 3r, 621 n. 28

NOTES

1 Savill, 3, p. 1092, found on soft paste 1754–72, possibly for Baptiste Paris, active as a *répareur* 1754–64. Savill notes that his mark is most commonly found on *plateaux Courteille*.

2 Dauterman, *Marks*, pp. 187–88 illustrates several incised D marks, but gives no proposed attribution for those closest to those on the Museum's tray.

3 According to Dauterman, *Marks*, (p. 182) BR may be Nicolas Brachard *père*, active as a soft-paste *répareur* 1756–72.

4 Active 1752–90. See Savill, 3, pp. 1974–75; Peters, *Marks*, p. 73.

5 Savill, 3, pp. 1107–8, found on soft paste 1753–90s.

6 APML, Daniell file, invoice for 17 July 1901: "A very fine Sèvres porcelain tray or Plateau, Rose du Bari ground with white trellis bands, also, 3 cups and saucers to match, painted with Boucher subjects, in panels, also in centre of plateau, also from Marie Antoinette, & Louis XVI, as above [said to be given by them to the 'Abbes de Ronceray' along with two pot-pourri vases, cat. no. 56]," £2,145.

7 See Savill, 3, pp. 974–75 for a more complete biography of de Courteille. The factory name for this tray was first identified by Eriksen (*Neoclassicism*, p. 134). See Savill, 2, pp. 615–21 and 805–14 for a detailed account of this shape.

8 Savill, 2, p. 615.

9 Ibid., p. 805.

10 The Museum's tray is the only example with handles and indented corners listed in Savill, which underscores the rarity of this variation. It appears that the other extant trays with indented corners are table trays, not tea trays.

11 AMNS, I. 7, 1 January 1759 (for 1758), molds only.

12 Savill, 2, p. 615 gives ranges for each version but acknowledges that it is difficult to determine the factory sizes. The first-size trays seem to have been approximately 13⅞ and 14⅛ in. (35–36 cm) in length, while the second-size trays probably were approximately 12¹³⁄₁₆ in. (32.5 cm) long. Extant trays listed in Savill include examples 11¹³⁄₁₆, 12¹³⁄₁₆, 13, 13½, 13⅞, 14, and 14¼ in. (30, 32.5, 33, 34.3, 35, 35.5, and 36.2 cm) long, making it impossible to know where the line between the two sizes should be drawn.

13 Ibid., p. 616, citing a 1757–58 example from the Alfred de Rothschild collection with four cups and saucers, a milk jug, teapot, sugar bowl, and tea caddy.

14 AMNS, Vy 2, fols. 77, 78.

15 Savill, 2, pp. 616 and 620 n. 12. See also cat. no. 103.

16 They include one (first size) with a green ground and children, another (second size) with green ground with flowers, and a third (second size) with green ground and trophies. See Savill, 2, p. 620 n. 3a, 3f, 3n. Another green ground service dated 1761 was sold Christie's, New York, 5 May 1999, lot 47, decorated with trophies.

17 It is unlikely that the pink ground service sold to Louis XV for 720 *livres* would have been of the second size, even if it had been decorated with children in polychrome. Of course, it is difficult to be absolutely sure since most of the sales records give no size indication and the difference in the size of this model is so uncertain.

18 See cat. no. 80 for more on this shape.

19 Savill, 1, pp. 72–75, 88–91.

20 MNC, Sèvres, no. 19.377, dated 1757–58, also decorated with children by Vielliard. The slight difference in the trellis pattern appears in the intersection of the ribbons.

21 Also dated 1757–58 (no. A.c.e.1911, no. 3); see Eriksen, *Pitti*, p. 56.

22 Savill, 1, pp. 305–6. See also Standen, "Country Children," pp. 111–33. While some of the figures on the cups and saucers recall the work of Boucher, there is no exact correlation with this artist's published prints. For Vielliard and his adaptation of Boucher children, see cat. no. 60.

23 The panels are now in the Frick Collection, New York, and were by tradition designed for an octagonal boudoir. They probably were painted between 1750 and 1753. See Frick, *Paintings*, 2, pp. 8–23.

24 The paintings are likely to be the versions in the collection of the Fine Arts Museums of San Francisco. The cycle was commissioned in 1752. See Rosenberg and Stewart, pp. 292–306.

25 Wark, *Huntington*, pp. 116–17, fig. 113, middle shelf.

26 See glossary.

27 The outlining around Meissen gilding appeared because the gold was applied on iron red, which fluxed the gold on hard paste. This iron red is probably what Sèvres was copying.

84

Cup and saucer (probably *gobelet Bouillard et soucoupe*)

1917.1014

Sèvres, 1758–1759

Soft-paste porcelain, cup: H. 1¹¹⁄₁₆ × W. 2¹³⁄₁₆ × D. 2³⁄₁₆ in. (4.3 × 7.1 × 5.5 cm); saucer: H. ¹³⁄₁₆ × DIAM. 3⅝ in. (2 × 9.2 cm)

Dark blue and green ground, polychrome landscapes, gilding

Marks: cup: effaced interlaced Ls in blue with traces of a date letter; unidentifiable painter's mark; incised ch? and H or I;[1] saucer: interlaced Ls in blue with date letter F, painter's mark in the form of a monogrammed AN or AV[2]

Provenance: perhaps Cartier et Fils, Paris, 1901;[3] J. Pierpont Morgan

MODEL

This cup probably is a *gobelet Bouillard*.[4] It is the same shape as a cup depicted in a factory drawing inscribed *goblet pour le dejeune boillard fait suivan La Comande du 19 fevrÿe 1753* [cup for the Bouillard tea set as per order of 19 February 1753] and *fait* [made].[5] *Boillard* refers to Antoine-Auguste Bouillard, who was a *fermier-général*, a *marchand-mercier*, and a shareholder in the Vincennes factory from 1745.[6] In addition to the cup and saucer, a milk jug, sugar bowl, teapot, vase, *jatte* [basin], and tea set were named for Bouillard.[7]

Gobelets Bouillard et soucoupes were made in three sizes. At least the first and third sizes were in production in 1753.[8] The first known appearance in the factory records of the model is in the list of turned pieces that were placed in the biscuit kiln on 22 November 1753.[9] The *gobelet Bouillard*'s first mention in the sales records is in February 1754, when two decorated with flowers were sold to an unnamed buyer, along with a sugar bowl and milk jug of the same form, for 48 *livres*.[10] *Gobelets Bouillard* sold for between 6 and 102 *livres*.[11] They were included in tea sets, with or without saucers, and could be included in tea services sold without trays.[12]

COMMENTARY

The Museum's cup and saucer match the third-size *gobelet Bouillard et soucoupe*. The blue and green decoration is just as pleasing when the cup is placed upside down in the saucer. François Boucher depicted cups and saucers in this fashion in his painting *Le Déjeuner* of 1739.[13]

The combination of dark blue and green grounds only came truly into vogue at Sèvres in 1759. The factory may have made at least one attempt to combine dark blue and green as early as 1752, for eight pomade pots decorated with landscapes are listed in the October inventory as being *fond bleu et verd*.[14] Furthermore, a water jug and basin dated 1753–54 are known with blue and green ground decoration.[15] Still, this color combination appears chiefly in the period from 1758 until 1762.

In 1758 there were only six pieces with blue and green ground decoration recorded in the sales ledgers, all described as *lapis et verd*.[16] There followed a gap of some eighteen months, until December 1759, before the combination of blue and green appeared again in the sales records but it was now described as *saffre et verd* [zaffer and green]. It was customary for the latest innovation from the factory to be presented to the king during the end of year sales at Versailles: when in 1759 Louis XV bought several pieces with *saffre et verd* decoration, was he purchasing items with a newly discovered blue ground color?[17] In the very same year Madame de Pompadour bought three tea sets and a *pot-pourri vaisseau* all of which were described as *saffre et verd*.[18] In 1760 the factory sales records listed pieces decorated with *lapis et verd* as well as others with *saffre et verd*.[19] All this points to a distinction between two different blue ground colors, but as explained below the issue is rather more complex.

The painter of the landscape scenes on the Hartford cup and saucer is unidentified. His mark appears on a cup and saucer in the collection of Waddesdon Manor, England, also decorated with landscapes and dated 1759, as well as on a *vase à comparti-ments* of 1757 with landscapes, at one time on the art market in Paris.[20]

The Museum's cup may have belonged to a tea set, and may perhaps be coupled with a sugar bowl of the third size in the Jones Collection of the Victoria and Albert Museum.[21]

TECHNIQUE AND CONDITION

The deep blue ground color on the Hartford cup and saucer was either *bleu lapis* or *saffre*, and was applied under the glaze. There is still much confusion about the use of these terms by the Sèvres factory. We do not know if *saffre* and *lapis* were used synonymously or if *saffre* was employed to describe the use of a different compound. Without chemical analysis, it is impossible to tell, for the blue on pieces labeled with either epithet is identical to the naked eye. However, of *saffre*, the *Académicien chimiste*, Pierre-Joseph Macquer, wrote that it could be fired at high temperatures without change.[22] This assertion supports the theory that Sèvres was experimenting with a new blue ground color of greater stability. It is clear that for some time the factory was experimenting with various ingredients to achieve the effect of the blue used by the Japanese. Attempts to recreate this blue, labeled *bleu lapis, bleu ancien*, or *bleu antique*, employed various ingredients including cobalt.[23] In 1754 Charles-Antoine Cuvillier was taken on by the *atelier des couleurs* specifically to work with zaffer.[24] *Saffre* appears in the enamel kiln records at the end of 1755 in the description of twelve pieces while *bleu lapis* is used to describe others on the same page.[25] Lazare

Duvaux sold a covered cup that he described as "safre camayeu" to Madame de Pompadour on 24 December 1755.[26] Perhaps the concentration of the use of the term *saffre* in 1759 marks a technical milestone along the road to perfecting a dark blue.[27] The dearth of references to *saffre* after 1760 leads us to ask if the term *lapis* was used loosely thenceforward to embrace any items with a dark blue ground.[28]

The green used on the Atheneum's cup and saucer was *vert céladon*, and it covers the underside of the saucer completely.[29] This may have been done in order to hide the black speckling (*végétations salines*) that is still visible through the transparent green. The gilding appears to have been applied quickly, and is not of the highest quality. The outside of the saucer is not gilded, suggesting that there was only one low-temperature firing. This may account for the uneven wear of the dentil rim around the cup, which has worn away where it intersects the green.[30]

Exhibition: *Morgan Loan Exhibition*, New York, 1914, not in catalogue

Literature: Chavagnac, pp. 81–82, no. 97; Munger, *Wickes,* p. 172 n. 12

NOTES

1 Dauterman (*Marks,* p. 185) illustrates one incised ch mark but it does not resemble the mark underneath this cup. For H or I see Savill, 3, pp. 1108–9.

2 See below for discussion of this mark.

3 APML, Cartier file, invoice for 24 May 1901: "1 Tasse et Soucoupe, Sèvres, mignonette fond bleu, cartels vert et or, paysage fond bleu," 2,000 French francs.

4 This model was always paired with a plain, shallow saucer. Savill, 2, p. 527 notes that it is difficult to distinguish this form from a *gobelet Bouret,* leaving open the possibility that the Museum's cup is actually a *gobelet Bouret. Gobelets Bouret* were recorded in three sizes. Molds and models for this form appear among new work for 1753 (I. 7, 1 January 1754). See *Vincennes,* pp. 115, 129. Préaud and d'Albis (p. 96, no. 26) identify a small cup with a more elaborate handle (called a *tasse à toilette* in *Vincennes,* p. 115, no. 318) as the *gobelet Bouret,* stating that it is shorter and stockier than a *gobelet Bouillard.* However, the example illustrated is 1¾ in. (4.4 cm), the largest measurement of the third size as given by Savill (see below, note 8). Savill, on the other hand, states that the third size of the *gobelet Bouillard* sometimes was made with an elaborate handle and in these cases called *tasse à toilette* (p. 527). Clearly there are no definitive answers here as to distinguishing the two forms. In correspondence with the author, Tamara Préaud suggests that perhaps the denominations Bouret and Bouillard relate specifically to size, the smaller cups of this shape being Bouret. She knows of no surviving examples of a large *gobelet Bouret.* However, in 1774 Morin decorated 18 first-size *gobelets Bourets* (AMNS, F.17).

5 AMNS, R. 1, L. 3, d. 2, fol. 6. See Savill, 2, pp. 527–32 for a complete account of this form. See also Eriksen, *Waddesdon,* p. 94; Brunet, *Frick,* pp. 268–71; *Vincennes,* pp. 115–19; Préaud and d'Albis, p. 122, no. 44; Sassoon, pp. 102–5; and Dawson, *British Museum,* p. 105.

6 For more on Bouillard see Savill, 3, pp. 970–71.

7 Ibid., 2, p. 528.

8 Ibid., pp. 527, 532 n. 7, based on existing examples. She notes that the second size is not documented and the earliest dated example known is from 1757, but this does not preclude all three sizes being introduced in 1753. According to Savill, the sizes are as follows: first size: cup: H. 2⁵⁄₁₆–2¾ in. (5.8–6.9 cm), saucer: DIAM. 5⅛–5⅝ in. (13–14.3 cm); second size: cup: H. 2–2¹⁄₁₆ in. (5–5.6 cm), saucer: DIAM. 4⅝–4¾ in. (11.8–12.1 cm); third size: cup: H. 1⁹⁄₁₆–1¾ in. (3.9–4.4 cm), saucer: DIAM. 3⁹⁄₁₆–3¹¹⁄₁₆ in. (9–9.6 cm).

9 IF 5673, fol. 13.

10 AMNS, Vy 1, fol. 35v. See Savill, 2, p. 527. These were part of *fournée* 7, 4–23 February 1754.

11 Savill, 2, p. 527.

12 Ibid. See note 10 above for a small tea set without tray. Those sold without saucers were often the third size. See Dawson, *British Museum,* p. 105; Savill, 2, p. 527.

13 Louvre, Paris, illustrated in *Boucher,* p. 180. Cups are also shown upside down in Boucher's *Woman Fastening Her Garter, with Her Maid,* 1742, in the Thyssen-Bornemisza Museum, Madrid, Spain (ibid., p. 196). The porcelain in these paintings looks to be Chantilly (see Le Duc, *Chantilly,* pp. 111–12, 361). Perhaps the practice developed because it was easier to carry cups and saucers on a tray when the cups were upside down.

14 AMNS, I. 7, *Pièces tournées au magasin de ventes.* Savill, 1, p. 112 believes that only the blue was a ground color, and suggests that the records may simply be referring to some green pots and some blue pots. It is also possible that the green in this case is not a ground color but an enamel color. There are records of greens *pour fonds* from 1747 (AMNS, Carnet Y 43, *Cahier Nº 1 des Procédés de Caillat pour les couleurs à Porcelaine de la Manufacture de Vincennes 1753* [*sic*], giving recipes for a green ground), which could explain the use of green as a ground color on the rim of a *vase Parseval* (c. 1749–51, MAD, Paris) illustrated in Préaud and d'Albis, p. 128, no. 58.

15 Savill, 2, pp. 112, 117 n. 27. See *Vincennes,* p. 71, no. 138.

16 AMNS, Vy 3, fols. 66–66v, 1 January–1 July 1758, two cups and saucers, two teapots, Duvaux; fol. 68, 28 August 1758, two cups and saucers, Mme Lair. Eriksen (Eriksen and Bellaigue, p. 52) characterizes these pieces as experimental.

17 AMNS, Vy 3, fol. 7, 28 December 1759, to Louis XV, *1 Grand Déjeuner quaré Saffree Et verd Enfans,* 1,080 *livres; 1 Déjeuner quaré 2e gdr. Saffre et Verd Enfans,* 168 *livres; 1 idem. fleurs,* 120 *livres; 1 Déjeuner Tiroir 2e gdre. Saffre et Verd fleurs,* 216 *livres; 1 Gobelet a Lait et Soucoupe, Saffre et Verd,* 288 *livres.*

18 Ibid., fol. 7v: *1 Déjeuner Courteille,* 720 *livres; 1 Déjeuner quaré, 2e. gdr.,* 240 *livres; 1 Déjeuner Duvaux,* 168 *livres; 1 Gobelet Bouret 3e gdr.,* 36 *livres; 1 Pot poury Vaisseau Saffre et Verd Tesniers,* 960 *livres.* See also Eriksen and Bellaigue, pp. 101–4 regarding the end of the year sales at Versailles.

19 See for example AMNS, Vy 3, fol. 8v, 1 January–1 April, 1760, *1 Gobelet Bouillard et Soucoupe Lapis et Verd,* to Poirier, 78 *livres,* and fol. 9v, same date, *1 Déjeuner Quaré 3e Saffre et Verd,* 96 *livres,* to Dulac.

20 See Eriksen, *Waddesdon,* pp. 112–13.

21 No. 790B-1882. See King, p. 22, no. 158, mistakenly paired with a similar cup and saucer (as per Mr. Robin Hildyard).

22 Eriksen and Bellaigue, p. 52.

23 Préaud and d'Albis, pp. 217–18.

24 Ibid., p. 204. In the factory inventory of 1 January 1754 (AMNS, I. 7), *saffre* is listed among *Matieres a composer les couleurs.*

25 IF 5676, fol. 42, 31 December 1755.

26 LD, 2, p. 266, no. 2336. It seems unlikely that these should be specifically called *saffre* if it were the same color as *lapis.* These seem to be among the rare occasions when *saffre* appears in the records without being used with green.

27 Antoine d'Albis believes that *saffre* and *lapis* were used to describe the same color (see Préaud and d'Albis, pp. 218, 230). Savill (3, p. 1174) leaves open the question.

28 In the late part of the century, the term *bleu lapis* was once again employed by the factory, but in this case to describe a brilliant blue streaked with gold to imitate lapis lazuli. See *Royal Collection,* pp. 36–37, no. 21.

29 See cat. no. 62 for a discussion of the green grounds. Another blue and green saucer in the Jones Collection of the V&A, London is covered on the underside with green (see King, p. 22, no. 158).

30 Technical information kindly provided by Antoine d'Albis. Similar uneven wear of the gilding appears on the sugar bowl in the V&A, London, that may have been en suite with this cup (see note 21).

85

Tea service with tray, teapot, sugar bowl, and two cups and saucers (*plateau Hebert, théière Calabre, pot à sucre Hebert, gobelets Hebert et soucoupes*)

1917.1017–1021

Sèvres, 1759

Soft-paste porcelain, tray: H. 1⁷⁄₁₆ × L. 11¼ × W. 9⅛ in. (3.6 × 28.6 × 23.1 cm); teapot: H. 4⅛ × W. 5½ × D. 3¹⁄₁₆ in. (10.4 × 14 × 7.7 cm); sugar bowl: H. 3⁷⁄₁₆ × DIAM. 2⅞ in. (8.7 × 7.2 cm); 1917.1020: cup: H. 2³⁄₁₆ × W. 3³⁄₁₆ × D. 2¹¹⁄₁₆ in. (5.5 × 8.4 × 6.8 cm); saucer: H. 1⅛ × DIAM. 4⅝ in. (2.9 × 11.8 cm); 1917.1021: cup: H. 2³⁄₁₆ × W. 3¼ × D. 2⅝ in. (5.6 × 8.3 × 6.7 cm); saucer: H. 1⅛ × DIAM. 4⅝ in. (2.8 × 11.8 cm)

White ground with polychrome garlands of flowers, blue bows, and gilding

Marks: tray, teapot, cups and saucers: interlaced Ls in blue with date letter G and painter's mark of fleur-de-lis for Vincent Taillandier;[1] tray: incised mark in the form of a treble clef,[2] and possibly a J;[3] teapot: incised 3 or scrolling E (?) and 4;[4] sugar bowl: interlaced Ls in blue and fleur-de-lis (no date letter); 1917.1020: cup: incised FR;[5] saucer: incised I or H;[6] 1917.1021: cup: incised FR and I?; saucer: incised I or H

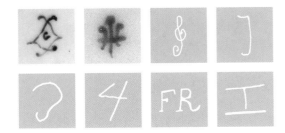

Provenance: A.B. Daniell & Co., London, n.d.;[7] J. Pierpont Morgan

MODEL

This tea service comprises a *plateau Hebert*, a *théière Calabre*, a *pot à sucre Hebert*, and two *gobelets Hebert* with *soucoupes unies*. The *plateau Hebert* probably was introduced in the second half of 1752. Two molds and countermolds (working molds) for *plats de M. Hebert* appear in the inventories of October 1752 and January 1753, which probably refer to a tray of the first size.[8] The inventory of January 1754 for new work of 1753 lists molds and models for *plateaux Hebert* in two sizes, although an example of undesignated size already appears in the biscuit kiln in November or December 1752.[9] The tray was made with or without handles, and a version was made with relief decoration.[10] The Museum's tray is of the second size.

The first recorded sale of a tray of this shape was to Monsieur Hebert himself, in August 1753.[11] It was decorated with children and garlands of flowers in monochrome, and accompanied by two cups and saucers. The tray cost 600 *livres*.[12] Only three more were sold in 1753, all to Lazare Duvaux in December.[13]

The *plateau Hebert* soon became a popular tray for tea services, and during the next two years over eighty were recorded in the sales ledgers. They ranged in decoration from simple flowers or gold fillets to very elaborate colored grounds with figures, landscapes, birds, and flowers.[14] Usually they were accompanied by a cup and saucer, sugar bowl, and milk jug, most frequently of the *Hebert* shape. Occasionally these trays were sold with just cups and saucers,[15] or with jam pots.[16] Two trays were even included in the dinner service given by Louis XV to the Elector of Palatine in April 1760, to be used for ice-cream cups.[17] Still, after 1755, as additional trays were introduced into the factory's repertory, sales of the *plateau Hebert* decreased, so that by 1759, the year the Museum's tea set was made, only one *plateau Hebert* appears in the records.[18]

The teapot *Calabre* was produced by late 1752, and listed in two sizes in 1753. Eventually it was made in six or more sizes, the Museum's being one of the smaller examples, perhaps of the fifth or sixth size.[19] The name of the form is known from a plaster model at the Sèvres factory, which is labeled *théière Calabre* (fig. 85-1).[20] There are two drawings still in existence, one inscribed *theÿere Verdun du 19 fevrÿe 1753, 2e grandeur, Rectifie suivan La Comande ordoné La ditte est adapte aux goblet Calabre [a]insÿ quau goble Verdun, fait* [Verdun teapot of 19 February 1753, second size, modified as per the order given; said piece matching the Calabre cup as well as the Verdun cup. Made],[21] and the other *petitte theÿere bouret 1760* (fig. 85–2).[22] While this inscription seems to confuse the form with two other teapots, the *théière Verdun* and the *théière Bouret*, it has been postulated that the *théière Verdun* refers to a similar but rounder teapot with a flatter lid and short spout.[23] The *théière Bouret* is close in profile to the *Calabre* but with two bands on the spout.[24] The *théière Calabre* was the most common form of teapot made by the factory and after 1756 usually was listed in the registers as just *théière*.[25] Examples of the latter ranged in price from 12 to 120 *livres*.[26]

Like the tray, the sugar bowl was also named *Hebert*.[27] A drawing at the Sèvres archives of this form is inscribed *sucrÿe hebert n°2 faite suivan Lordre de la Comande du fevrÿe 1753* [Hebert sugar bowl, no. 2 made as per the February 1753 order],

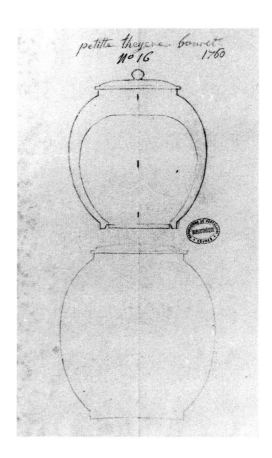

and *fait* [made].[28] A model is preserved at the Sèvres factory,[29] and molds and models are listed among the new works for 1753.[30] The *pot à sucre Hebert* was made in three sizes. Lazare Duvaux bought examples of the second and third sizes in December 1753, although in general sizes were not specified in the sales records.[31] The Museum's represents the third size.[32] The factory probably priced it at 12 *livres*.[33] The *gobelets Hebert* are of the third size, and if sold individually probably would have been priced at 10 or 12 *livres*.[34]

COMMENTARY

The garlands and ribbons were painted by Vincent Taillandier, who was especially skilled at painting flowers, notably on a small scale, and frequently decorated tea and other wares with garlands of flowers suspended from ribbon bows.[35] Among the flowers included in this set are roses, lilacs, morning glories, cornflowers, and tulips.

Tea sets decorated with flowers are difficult to identify in the sales records, especially in the later 1750s and 1760s.[36] It is possible that the Museum's tea service was the one sold to Madame Adélaïde in December 1760 for 144 *livres*.[37] Alternatively, Madame Adélaïde's tea set could be a *déjeuner Hebert* decorated with garlands, dated 1759, at the Musée national de Céramique, Sèvres.[38]

Exhibition: *Morgan Loan Exhibition*, New York, 1914, not in catalogue

Literature: Chavagnac, p. 86, no. 103; Brunet and Préaud, p. 32, pl. 3; Savill, 2, p. 4 n. 3y

Fig. 85-1 *Théière Calabre*, plaster model

NOTES

1 Active 1753–90. See Savill, 3, pp. 1068–69 for more on this painter.

2 Ibid., p. 1134. Found on works 1757–64.

3 Ibid., p. 1110 for a more pronounced j.

4 Ibid., pp. 1126–27. Savill says that 4 can be found with 3 or scrolling E on a teapot dated 1756.

5 Ibid., p. 1102, identified as possibly François-Firmin Fresne or Dufresne (*répareur* active 1756–67) or François-Denis Roger (*répareur* active 1755/56–83/84).

6 Ibid., p. 1108.

7 Dealer label with object, no date of purchase available.

8 AMNS, I. 7, 8 October 1752, *moules en plâtre* and 1 January 1753, *moules en plâtre et soufre*. They were valued at 8 *livres* each, the same value placed on the molds for the first-size *plateau Hebert* (see below). It has been suggested that *plats Hebert* were trays without handles, while *plateaux Hebert* referred to the version with handles (*Vincennes*, p. 64). It is more likely that the factory used the name *plats* when first recording the tray, which probably was without handles at first, but quickly changed to calling them *plateaux*, whether or not they had handles.

9 Ibid., 1 January 1754 (for 1753); IF 5673, fol. 3, between 4 November and 28 December 1752. For more on this shape see *Vincennes*, p. 67; Eriksen and Bellaigue, pp. 270–71; and Préaud and d'Albis, pp. 176–77. There is also a *modèle en soufre* (see glossary) of a *déjeuner Hebert 2e grandr.* listed in the inventory of 1 January 1754 (for 1753), valued at 4 *livres*. There is no reason to believe that in this case *déjeuner* was meant to include the components of a tea set, for these were thrown on a wheel and did not require molds.

10 Occasionally the sales records mention the trays as having handles, as in December 1753, when one *à anses* was sold to Duvaux (AMNS, Vy 1, fol. 30, 31 December 1753). The first recorded sale of a *déjeuner Hebert* with relief decoration was in December 1754 (ibid., fol. 74, 5–31 December 1754, Duvaux).

11 Thomas-Joachim Hebert was both a *marchand-mercier* and *secrétaire du roi*. See Sargentson, p. 154. Formerly it was thought that there might be two Heberts, one the dealer and the other *secrétaire du roi*. See Savill, 3, pp. 982–83.

12 AMNS, Vy 1, fol. 15, 7 August 1753 (*fournée* 4, 16 July–September 1753). The cups and saucers were priced separately at 72 *livres* each. Savill (2, p. 496) states that the high price points to a *bleu céleste* ground for this set although it is not described as such.

13 AMNS, Vy 1, fol. 30, 31 December 1753. Two were without handles, and one with handles, and all were decorated with flowers and were accompanied by tea wares. They must have been among the new models featured at the end of the year sale by the factory.

14 In 1754 Duvaux bought one set with *bleu céleste* ground and children for 840 *livres* and two with *bleu céleste* ground (one *pointillé*) and landscapes for 600 *livres* (AMNS, Vy 1, fol. 72, 5–31 December 1754). Simple sets decorated with flowers generally cost between 96 and 120 *livres* (ibid., fol. 46, 30 June 1754, Duvaux, and fol. 53, 29 October 1754, Berryer).

15 Ibid., fol. 80, 26 March 1755, with ten *gobelets Bouret, 3e g.*, Aulagnier, 240 *livres*.

16 Ibid., fol. 93, 1 June–1 October 1755, with two *pots à confitures*, Duvaux, 192 *livres*.

17 Ibid., Vy 3, fol. 29.

18 Ibid., fol. 92v, 1 *déjeuner Hebert fleurs*, unnamed buyer, 120 *livres*. The form was still considered useful, and was bought by dealers as well as private patrons well after 1760. It was even made in hard-paste porcelain (AMNS, Vy 5, fol. 133, 17 November 1773, *Dejeuner hebert de 4 pieces paysage fleurs et guirlandes en or porcelaine dure*, Louis XV, 204 *livres*.) For more examples of *déjeuners Hebert* in these later years see cat. no. 86.

19 For a full discussion of the *théière Calabre* see Savill, 2, pp. 577–79. While stating that it is impossible to know precisely how the factory sized these teapots, Savill (2, p. 577) divides known examples into six groups according to height: A: 6½ in. (16.5 cm); B: 5³⁄₁₆–5¹³⁄₁₆ in. (13.2–14.7 cm); C: 4⅝–5 in. (11.8–12.7 cm); D: 4⁵⁄₁₆–4⁹⁄₁₆ in. (11–11.6 cm); E: 3½–4⅛ in. (8.9–10.5 cm) (more than one size?); F: 2¾ in. (7 cm).

20 Ibid. See also *Vincennes*, p. 133, and AMNS, 1814 inventory, 1740–60, no. 7, today in *casier* 763. It was named for Pierre Calabre, *conseiller secrétaire du roi, et de ses finances*, shareholder in the Vincennes factory from 1750. See Savill, 3, p. 972.

21 AMNS, R. 1, L. 2, d. 4, fol. 5, see Savill, 2, p. 577.

22 Savill, 2, p. 577.

23 Ibid., based on Eriksen, *David Collection*, p. 65, no. 38a. *Verdun* is not simply another name for this shape, as both *Verdun* and *Calabre* teapots appear in the same archival records (Savill, 2, p. 577).

24 *Vincennes*, p. 135. Savill (2, p. 577) suggests that in the early years the smallest size *théière Calabre* was called a *théière Bouret*. This parallels the theory that the smallest size *gobelet Bouillard* was called a *gobelet Bouret* (see cat. no. 84).

25 Savill, 2, p. 577.

26 Ibid., p. 578.

27 First identified by Eriksen in *Waddesdon*, pp. 80–81.

28 AMNS, R. 1, L. 2, d. 8, fol. 2, illustrated in Savill, 2, p. 575.

29 See *Vincennes*, p. 84. Even though models and molds were made, *pots à sucre Hebert* were turned. They appear in the biscuit kiln records with other turned pieces (IF, 5673, fol. 181, 8 March 1754), and in the enamel kiln records, again with other turned pieces (IF 5676, fol. 9, 5 January 1754). It is not clear why a mold would have been necessary for a turned sugar bowl.

30 AMNS, I. 7, listed without ditto marks but in succession with molds and models for cups and saucers *Hebert* and a teapot (as explained to the author by Rosalind Savill). No sizes are indicated, implying they are for the first size.

31 Ibid., Vy 1, fol. 30. This would indicate that all three sizes appeared in 1753. However, as Savill (2, p. 575) states, two sizes were presumably introduced in 1753 (the first size, by omission, appearing in the list of molds and models in the inventory, the second size indicated on the drawing for the model), while the third appeared as new work for 1755 (although an example dated 1754 exists; see AMNS, I. 7, January 1756, molds and models). This implies that the third size was not made earlier, an inconsistency that is at present inexplicable.

32 Savill, 2, p. 575: first size 4½–4¾ in. (11.4–12 cm); second size 3¹¹⁄₁₆–4¼ in. (9.3–10.7 cm); third size about 2¹⁵⁄₁₆–3⁹⁄₁₆ in. (7.5–9 cm). See pp. 575–76 for a full discussion of the shape.

33 Ibid., p. 575 (see AMNS, Vy 2, fol. 84, Sayde, first quarter of 1758).

34 See cat. no. 80. For sizes, see Savill, 2, p. 496. The sales records rarely specify the sizes being sold, and often in the 1760s fail to define the shape.

35 For examples, see *plateau du roi* of 1759 (Dauterman, *Wrightsman*, p. 219, no. 87); *déjeuner Hebert* of 1761 (MNC, Sèvres, no. 7751, illustrated in *Porcelaine de France*, 1987, p. 37, no. 10); and *théière Calabre* (Savill, 2, pp. 581–82).

36 At this period dealers bought tea items in large quantities at which time they were listed in the sales records by objects (trays, teapots, etc.) rather than by sets. Furthermore, after early 1757, when tea services were listed in the sales records, their components were not specified, making it impossible to know for certain which of many *déjeuners Hebert* is being sold.

37 AMNS, Vy 3, fol. 45, *déjeuner Hebert guirlandes*. I wish to thank Geoffrey de Bellaigue for initially pointing out this sale.

38 See note 35 above.

86

Tray (*plateau Hebert à anses*)

1917.1022

Sèvres, 1759

Soft-paste porcelain, H. 2⅜ × L. 18⅛ × w. 13¾ in. (6 × 45.9 × 34.7 cm)

Pink ground with green wave-like scrolls and diapers, polychrome birds in a landscape, and gilding

Marks: interlaced Ls in blue with date letter G[1]

Provenance: J. Pierpont Morgan

MODEL

The tray is one of two versions of the *plateau Hebert* with handles.[2] This type has eight lobes of nearly the same dimension. The other version of the model has the same number of lobes, but they are alternately large and small. There are plaster models of both types at the Sèvres factory (figs. 86-1 and 86-2).[3] While some surviving examples have simple handles with leaf scrolls at their points of attachment, the Museum's tray has more elaborate foliate-scrolled handles. This is indeed in keeping with its grand scale, for it is one of the rare extant examples of this shape in the first size.[4]

COMMENTARY

The Atheneum's tray entered the Museum with a teapot, sugar bowl, milk jug, and cup and saucer, none of which were part of the original tea set.[5] The true matching pieces are a *théière Calabre* (or *Verdun*), a *pot à sucre Hebert*, a *pot à lait à trois pieds*, and four *gobelets Hebert*. Of these the teapot, sugar bowl, and one cup and saucer are in the collection of the Museum of Fine

Arts, Boston (fig. 86-3). Another cup and saucer are in an American private collection, and a third sold at auction in New York in 1999.[6] The milk jug was formerly in the René Fribourg collection.[7] Its whereabouts as well as that of a fourth cup and saucer are not known.

The original tea set including the Hartford tray may have been the pink and green *déjeuner Hebert* with four cups, a sugar bowl, and teapot that was sold to Louis XV at Versailles in December 1760. However, there is no milk jug listed. One can either surmise that there was another pink and green set very much like this one, which is absent from the sales records, or that the milk jug was overlooked when the sale was recorded and that this is indeed Louis XV's set. The sales ledger tells us that the tray in the king's set cost 960 *livres*, while the accompanying pieces cost 348 *livres*.[8] The overall price was extremely high, as compared to several other tea sets purchased by Louis XV at the same time ranging in price from 108 to 336 *livres*. While the sheer size of the set must have accounted for some of the price, the expense also suggests a very elaborate decoration, like that found on the Museum's tray and its companion pieces.[9] The king bought several other pink and green pieces in December 1760, including at least two garnitures and three flower vases.[10]

The Museum's tray is decorated with a pink ground, green scrolls and diapered waves, and a large reserve with four birds in a landscape. The style of painting is unmistakably that of Armand *aîné*, the factory's foremost bird painter.[11] Traces of the original factory mark under the tray suggest the elaborate interlaced mark and crescent that was Armand's trademark. The extant date letter on the tray and accompanying pieces in Boston shows that the ensemble was made in 1759. During this period Armand's style is delicate and small in scale, and he paints small-leafed trees and distant landscapes framed by curving trees in the foreground. It is very similar to the decoration of the *grand plateau Corbeille* in the Nelson-Atkins Museum of Art, Kansas City, which also depicts birds framed with curving trees

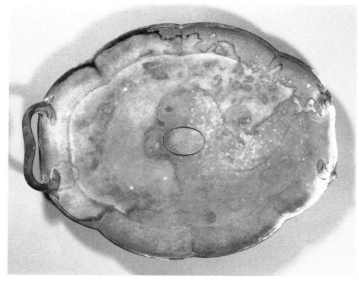

Fig. 86-1 *Plateau Hebert*, plaster model

Fig. 86-2 *Plateau Hebert*, plaster model

Fig. 86-3 Partial teaset, Sèvres, 1760

in the foreground, and a small, straight tree in the distance, and is marked with Armand's crescent.[12]

TECHNIQUE AND CONDITION

Owing to its size, the tray had to be supported in the kiln by a *pupitre*. There are groups of small dots outside the foot rim showing where it held up the tray.[13]

Exhibition: *French and English Art Treasures*, New York, 1942, no. 305

Literature: Chavagnac, p. 92, no. 110, pl. XXXIV; *French and English Art Treasures*, no. 305

NOTES

1 The painted mark is in matte, dark blue enamel and is extremely sloppy. Under and to the side of the mark are traces of another mark in blue enamel. Seemingly the original mark, the form of which will be discussed below, almost disappeared in the first firing and a replacement was made. David Peters believes that the replacement mark was made at a later date but this opinion is not shared by other scholars. Antoine d'Albis attributes the mark to the gilder Capelle, and suggests that the original painter's mark did not fire properly and that Capelle remarked and fired it with the gilding (which was at a lower temperature than enamels are fired and accounts for the matteness of the blue). This author believes that, although it may not be attributable to a specific gilder, the mark could well have been added at the time of the gilding.

2 For *plateau Hebert*, see cat. no. 85.

3 AMNS, 1814 inventory, 1740–60, no. 4, L. 11¹⁄₁₆ in. (28 cm); ibid., no. 3, L. 12¹⁄₈ in. (31 cm). They both have handles with leaf scrolls at the points of attachment to the tray. An example of the second type of tray is in the MNC, Sèvres, 1759, no. 7751, second size. (Tamara Préaud kindly provided me with photocopies of the models.)

4 According to Bernard Dragesco (letter in file), only one other *plateau Hebert* of the first size is known, the example in the MAD, Paris (*Vincennes*, 1756 or before, no. 31888, illustrated in Louvre, *Nouvelles acquisitions*, 1995, p. 182, no. 71a). It also has the more elaborate leaf-scroll handles. Other known examples of *plateaux Hebert* with handles include: MNC, Sèvres, no. 23178, c. 1753, yellow ground with monochrome children, second size (*Vincennes*, p. 67, no. 132); Louvre, Paris, 1753–54,

white ground with monochrome children, second size (Préaud and d'Albis, p. 176, no. 186); MAD, Paris, white ground with garlands, monochrome purple, 1755 (*Vincennes*, p. 46, no. 74); Palais Galliéra, Paris, 2–3 June 1970, lot 222, 1768, roses and garlands, second size; Sotheby's, New York, 9–10 October 1990, lot 391, c. 1753–60, white with flowers, second size; ibid., lot 410, 1785–90, white with cornflowers, second size.

5 See cat. nos. 87–88 for the other pieces that were accessioned with this tray.

6 MFA, Boston, nos. 1983.111–113; Christie's, New York, 5 May 1999, lot 37. This set was formerly in the American private collection just mentioned. I would like to thank Bernard Dragesco for bringing the Boston pieces to my attention.

7 René Fribourg sale, Sotheby's, New York, 15 October 1963, lots 448–49. The Fribourg collection also included a cup and saucer that are now one of the two from the American private collection. I would like to thank Bernard Dragesco for bringing these pieces to my attention.

8 AMNS, Vy 3, fol. 43v. The tray is listed as one item, and described as a *grand déjeuner Hebert*, and the other pieces are listed on the line below as: *1 cabaret de 4 Gobelets a 54". 1 pot a sucre a 60" Et theyere 72" montant ensemble.*

9 A comparable tea set, but with a *plateau corbeille* decorated with a *bleu céleste* mosaic pattern, was sold to Louis XV in 1758 as part of a diplomatic gift to be delivered to Maria-Theresa of Austria (see AMNS, Vy 2, fol. 85, December 1758). It is now in the collection of the Nelson-Atkins Museum of Art, Kansas City, Missouri. The tray to this set is also large (equally described as a *grand déjeuner*) and was accompanied by a teapot, sugar bowl, and four cups and saucers. It cost 1,440 *livres*, the additional cost probably due to the raised and pierced edge of the tray.

10 Ibid., fol. 43v, December 1760. Of these, there were four *vases Hollandois* and *à bobèches* (listed together, priced at 360 *livres* each) costing 1,440 *livres*, only 132 *livres* more expensive than the grand tea set.

11 The matching pieces of this set are clearly marked Armand. See cat. nos. 62 and 66 for this artist.

12 See note 9 above.

13 Information kindly supplied by Antoine d'Albis upon examination of the tray. For information on *pupitres* see glossary. The number of dot groups shows that the tray was fired at least three times, although we know that with two ground colors, enameling, and elaborate gilding the tray must have been fired no fewer than five or six times.

87

87

Partial tea service with teapot, sugar bowl, and milk jug (*théière Calabre, pot à sucre Calabre, et pot à lait à trois pieds*)

1917.1023–1025

Sèvres, 1760

Soft-paste porcelain, teapot: H. 5⅜ × W. 7⅛₆ × D. 4¼ in. (13.6 × 18.9 × 10.7 cm); sugar bowl: H. 4¾ × DIAM. 4 in. (12 × 10.1 cm); milk jug: H. 4¾ × W. 4¹⁵⁄₁₆ × D. 3⅝ in. (12 × 12.5 × 9.2 cm)

Pink and green ground, polychrome birds in landscapes, gilding

Marks: teapot and sugar bowl: elaborate interlaced Ls in blue with date letter H; milk jug: indecipherable incised mark on foot

Provenance: J. Pierpont Morgan

MODEL

The teapot, of the *Calabre* form, is probably of the first size as recorded in the documents of the factory. One larger example is in the collection at Goodwood, Sussex, but may have been a special order of inordinate size.[1] Other examples of the first size can be found at Goodwood, the Fitzwilliam Museum, Cambridge, and the Frick Collection, New York.[2] A pink and green teapot of this size would probably have cost 96 *livres*.[3]

The sugar bowl is also of the *Calabre* shape. One is recorded in the enamel kiln firing of 30 December 1752, and Lazare Duvaux purchased one in May 1753 that had been fired in the fall of 1752.[4] The model appears to have been made in three sizes.[5] A drawing of this shape in the archives is inscribed *Sucrÿe*

Calabre n° 2eme grandeur Rectifie suivan l'ordre de la comande du 19 fevrÿe 1753 [Calabre sugar bowl of second size modified as per order of 19 February 1753] (fig. 87-1).[6] At least two different covers were used with this model, one simply rounded and another with a domed center and slightly flanged rim.[7] A plaster model still remains at the factory.[8] Examples may be found in many collections, including Waddesdon Manor, England, the Frick Collection, and the Victoria and Albert Museum.[9] The Hartford sugar bowl is of the first size, and may have cost as much as 78 *livres*.[10]

The milk jug on three feet is also of the first size. The form, called *pot à lait à trois pieds* (or sometimes *à pieds*) was introduced in 1752.[11] The first and second sizes were recorded by 1753, and a third size in 1756.[12] Molds and models survive at the factory.[13] Most examples have relief-molded flowers and foliage near the feet and handles.[14] The handle is of the crabstock type, and ultimately derives from Chinese porcelain. The three-footed

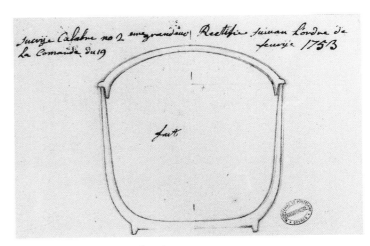

Fig. 87-1 *Sucrier Calabre*, drawing

form can also be found in silver cream jugs from the first half of the eighteenth century as well as Meissen milk jugs of the 1740s.[15] Milk jugs of the second size were most often associated with tea sets while jugs of the first and third sizes were more often sold individually.[16] Pink and green milk jugs of unspecified form were sold in 1760 and 1761 from 12 to 78 *livres*.[17] In the 1750s milk jugs of the first size cost from 18 *livres* decorated with flowers to 144 *livres* decorated in *bleu céleste* with birds.[18] The Museum's example probably cost at least 78 *livres*.

Commentary

It is difficult to determine precisely how many other pieces would have accompanied the Hartford teapot, sugar bowl, and milk jug, but it is likely that several cups and saucers would have been needed to complete this set. If the set included a Sèvres tray, it probably would have been one of the factory's larger models, such as the *grand plateau carré* or the *plateau Courteille*.[19] There are no entries in the sales records of the factory for 1760 and 1761 that can be linked to the Museum's pieces. The only pink and green tea services mentioned therein were the *grand déjeuner Hebert* purchased by Louis XV in December 1760[20] and a *déjeuner*, without distinction, bought by the dealer Dulac in the spring of 1761.[21] The latter tea set cost 528 *livres*, which was less expensive than other examples with a large tray. Furthermore, there are no recorded sales to a single individual of a matching pink and green teapot, milk jug, and sugar bowl.

The central reserves of the teapot, sugar bowl, and milk jug are painted with birds sitting in trees by Armand *aîné*. The teapot and sugar bowl bear his trademark of elaborate interlaced Ls but without his identifying crescent. By the 1760s Armand frequently omitted his crescent but his painting style remains identifiable nevertheless. In this case, one can see a change in scale of both the birds and the landscape that typifies Armand's work from 1760 on. Branches and leaves are fuller, almost plumper. The birds and trees are pushed to the foreground, and the trees are cropped by the gilded frame, so that the scenes begin to break out of the reserves.[22] This new approach to scale and space is evident in many other works by Armand from this period.[23]

Technique and Condition

The cover of the teapot has been broken in two, and the knob has been off and reglued. The cover of the sugar bowl is green only and does not belong with it. One foot of the milk jug has been off and reglued.

Exhibitions: *French and English Art Treasures*, New York, 1942, no. 305; *Vincennes and Sèvres Porcelain,* New York, 1980, no. 30 (milk jug)

Literature: Chavagnac, pp. 91–92, no. 110; *French and English Art Treasures*, no. 305; *Vincennes and Sèvres Porcelain*, no. 30 (milk jug); Savill, 2, p. 583 n. 3f

Notes

1 Savill, 2, p. 577; see cat. no. 85 for listing of sizes and more on this shape. Savill believes that size C corresponds to the second factory size, and thus size B would be first size.

2 Ibid., 2, p. 583 n. 3.

3 Pink and green teapots appear in the sales records for 1760 and 1761, priced at 72, 78 and 96 *livres*: AMNS, Vy 3, fol. 44v, December 1760, to members of court, 96 *livres*; Vy 3, fol. 49v, 1 April–1 July 1761, to Poirier, 78 *livres*. The teapot included in the *grand déjeuner Hebert* sold to Louis XV in December 1760 appears to have been the second size (probably the one now in the MFA, Boston, H. $4\frac{13}{16}$ in. (12.2 cm, size C of Savill) and cost 72 *livres* (Vy 3, fol. 43 v). See cat. no. 86 for this latter teapot.

4 IF 5676, fol. 2; AMNS, Vy 1, fol. 8v, *fournée* 70. See Préaud and d'Albis, p. 122, no. 45, and *Vincennes*, p. 83, for more on this shape.

5 *Vincennes*, p. 83 suggests that it was made in two sizes, but comparing existing examples three or four basic sizes emerge according to height: first size: $4\frac{5}{16}$–$4\frac{15}{16}$ in. (11–12.5 cm); second size: $3\frac{9}{16}$–$4\frac{1}{8}$ in. (9–10.5 cm); third and possibly fourth size: $2\frac{3}{16}$–$2\frac{15}{16}$ in. (5.5–7.5 cm).

6 AMNS, R. 1, L. 2, d. 8, fol. 1.

7 See Sotheby's, New York, 5 November 1998, lot 160, and Christie's, New York, 23 May 1995, lot 32.

8 AMNS, 1814 inventory, 1760–80, no. 3. This model has a very round cover, indicating that it may date from the nineteenth century. I would like to thank Tamara Préaud for this information.

9 Eriksen, *Waddesdon*, p. 48, no. 8, 1754, H. $2\frac{3}{4}$ in. (7 cm); Brunet, *Frick*, pp. 214–17, 1756, H. $2\frac{5}{8}$ in. (6.7 cm); V&A, London, no. C.387-1921, 1753, H. $3\frac{3}{8}$ in. (8.6 cm) (*Vincennes*, p. 84).

10 An unspecified *pot à sucre Roze Et verd* is recorded as having been sold to a member of court at Versailles in December 1760 for this price (AMNS, Vy 3, fol. 44v). Other probably smaller pink and green sugar bowls sold from 39 *livres* (Vy 3, fol. 43v, December 1760, Louis XV) to 66 *livres* (Vy 3, fol. 49v, 1 April–1 July 1761, Poirier). The sugar bowl included in the *grand déjeuner Hebert* cited above (note 3) was a *pot à sucre Hebert*, first size, and cost 60 *livres*.

11 The factory inventory of 8 October 1752 lists *1 petit pot au lait nouveau à 3 pieds* as ready to be glazed (AMNS, I. 7).

12 Savill, 2, pp. 564–69 discusses this form of milk jug in detail. She lists the sizes as follows: first size: H. $4\frac{7}{16}$–$5\frac{1}{16}$ in. (11.3–12.9 cm); second size: $3\frac{5}{8}$–$4\frac{1}{8}$ in. (9.2–10.4 cm); third size: $2\frac{15}{16}$–$3\frac{1}{4}$ in. (7.5–8.3 cm).

13 Brunet, *Frick*, p. 266, as wrongly dated 1760–80 in the 1814 inventory of factory models; Savill, 2, p. 568 n. 4; AMNS, *tiroir* 0.287. There is a mold inscribed *pot à lait intermediaire* without handles, feet, or spout. It may be eighteenth century. There are three plaster models, which Tamara Préaud believes to be nineteenth century.

14 Savill, 2, pp. 564, 568 n. 1, states that a version was made with relief decoration, and cites an example in an English private collection. This decoration must have been more elaborate than the small leaves and flowers traditionally found near the feet and handles of most examples.

15 Ibid., 2, p. 564. See for example a cream jug by Guillaume Henry c. 1730 at the Sterling and Francine Clark Art Institute, Williamstown, Massachusetts (Wees, pp. 366–67, no. 254).

16 Savill, 2, p. 564. These other sizes could occasionally be part of matching ensembles as well, as evidenced by the Museum's example.

17 AMNS, Vy 3, fol. 44v, December 1760, to a member of court, one for 78 and another for 12 *livres*, and Vy 3, fol. 49v, 1 April–1 July 1761, Poirier, 66 *livres*.

18 Savill, 2, pp. 564, 569 n. 13.

19 It is known that many tea services were sold without matching Sèvres trays, but were supplied with lacquer or *tôle* trays by the *marchands-merciers*. For discussions of tea services and their make-up see Savill, 2, pp. 489–95.

20 See cat. no. 86.

21 AMNS, Vy 3, fol. 50v, April–July 1761.

22 The way the central reserve is cropped by the pink and green ground has led some scholars to doubt the ground color decoration on the Atheneum's

88

pieces. There is no other evidence, however, to suggest that redecoration has occurred, and this manner of cropping, in fact, does occur on other pieces by Armand from 1760. There was a general stylistic trend in the 1760s to move away from decoration contained within the reserves to a more pictorial decoration that filled the reserves. One sees it especially in landscapes and "Teniers" scenes. See Eriksen and Bellaigue, p. 97.

23 Other published examples include the *pot-pourri Hebert* (c. 1760) in the Wallace Collection, London (no. C254, Savill, 1, pp. 184–87); cup, 1760, Wallace Collection (no. C368, ibid., 3, pp. 547–48); pair of *vases à oreilles*, 1761, Waddesdon Manor, Buckinghamshire (Eriksen, *Waddesdon*, pp. 130–31, no. 45); and pair of pot-pourri vases, 1763, Waddesdon Manor (ibid., pp. 170–71, no. 59).

88

Cup and saucer (*gobelet Bouillard* and *soucoupe*)

1917.1026

Sèvres, 1760

Soft-paste porcelain, cup: H. 2⅜ × W. 3¹¹⁄₁₆ × D. 2¹³⁄₁₆ in. (6 × 9.4 × 7.1 cm); saucer: H. 1³⁄₁₆ × DIAM. 5⅜ in. (3 × 13.7 cm)

Pink and green ground, polychrome birds, gilding

Marks: cup: interlaced Ls in blue with date letter H; partially effaced painter's mark, probably for François-Joseph Aloncle;[1] incised dt[2] and a 3 or B; saucer: interlaced Ls in blue with date letter H; painter's mark of a dagger, for Étienne Evans;[3] incised 3[4]

Provenance: J. Pierpont Morgan

MODEL

The cup is of the *Bouillard* form.[5] It is of the first size, and may have cost as much as 66 *livres*.[6]

COMMENTARY

François-Joseph Aloncle, one of the factory's chief bird painters, painted the reserve of the Hartford cup. Its gilding and the shape of the pink scrolls seem to match closely those on a cup in the collection of the Art Institute of Chicago, also painted by Aloncle in 1760,[7] those on a cup sold in London in 1994,[8] as well as those on a cup in the collection of Earl Spencer at Althorp.[9] It is possible that these cups, with their saucers, were all part of a large tea service, perhaps that sold to the dealer Dulac in 1761 for 528 *livres*.[10] It is also possible, although less likely, that Aloncle decorated several cups and saucers in the same manner, which were sold separately. It is not uncommon to find entries for cups and saucers sold singly or in pairs.[11]

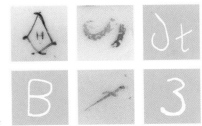

Marks

The saucer was painted by Étienne Evans, another of the factory's bird painters. It appears to match a saucer and cup by Evans, dated 1760, which were sold in Paris in 1960.[12] The pink scroll and the gilding pattern also match the saucers that are paired with the cups painted by Aloncle cited earlier. One can speculate that a ground color painter prepared numerous cups and saucers in the same manner before turning them over to the enamel painters Evans and Aloncle.

Since different artists painted this cup and saucer, it is likely that they were brought together at a later date. They entered the Museum's collection with the *plateau Hebert*, teapot, sugar bowl, and milk jug discussed in catalogue nos. 86 and 87. The similarity of the ground color decoration allows for the possibility that they were originally part of the same service, although their authorship—assuming that they were reunited with their appropriate mates—suggests that they were not. It is possible, however, that in an especially large service, perhaps with eight or ten cups and saucers, the cups and saucers may have been painted by more than one artist.[13]

Exhibition: *French and English Art Treasures*, New York, 1942, no. 305

Literature: Chavagnac, p. 93, no. 110; *French and English Art Treasures*, no. 305

NOTES

1 Active 1758–81, specializing in birds. See Savill, 3, pp. 995–96.

2 Attributed by Dauterman (*Marks*, pp. 68, 190–91) to a *répareur* named Delatre *cadet, aîné* (active c. 1752–c. 1776).

3 Active 1752–1800, Evans specialized in painting birds. See Eriksen, *Waddesdon*, p. 325; Préaud and d'Albis, p. 206.

4 Savill, 3, p. 1125.

5 See cat. no. 84 for this shape.

6 Sizes were seldom specified in the sales records but one example with a pink and green ground was sold to the king in 1760 for 39 *livres* (AMNS, Vy 3, fol. 43v, December 1760) while another was sold to Bachelier for 66 *livres* in the same year (ibid., fol. 41v, second half 1760). Presumably the more expensive one was of the first size.

7 No. 1965.1209, information kindly provided by Ghenete Zelleke.

8 Christies, London, 28 February 1994, lot 144.

9 See Charleston, "Althorp," p. 81. Another cup and saucer (lacking painter's marks) with similar decoration is in the MAD, Paris (no. 28585), but the pink appears to occupy a greater proportion of the ground. This may just be a minor variation.

10 AMNS, Vy 1, fol. 50v, April–July 1761. There were other tea sets with pink and green ground sold in 1760, but it is impossible to know which, if any, were decorated with birds. Furthermore, two of them were small sets with a square tray and unlikely to have included four cups and saucers. See AMNS, Vy 3, fol. 45, December 1760, *1 Déjeuner Quare 3e. gd. Roze Et verd*, 78 *livres* to the Dauphine; ibid., fol. 46, December 1760, to Mme and Mlle de Courteilles, *1 Déjeuner Quaré 3e. gd. Rozes Et Verds*, 120 *livres*.

11 See note 6 above: the king bought a pair, while Bachelier bought a single.

12 Galerie Charpentier, Paris, 24 June 1960, lot 187.

13 For the various sizes of tea sets see Savill, 2, p. 492.

89

Tray (*plateau losange*)

1917.1031

Sèvres, 1763 (possibly with some redecoration)

Soft-paste porcelain, H. 2³⁄₁₆ × L. 14¾ × W. 10¹³⁄₁₆ in. (5.5 × 37.4 × 27.4 cm)

Green ground with polychrome landscape, gilding

Marks: interlaced Ls in blue with date letter K; incised J?[1]

Provenance: Cartier et Fils, Paris, 1901;[2] J. Pierpont Morgan

MODEL

This tray is a *plateau losange*.[3] Dated 1763, it is the earliest known example of this version of the shape.[4]

COMMENTARY

The large, central reserve of the Museum's tray is painted with a sketchy landscape, in a style typical of a large group of landscapes found on tea wares as well as on the backs of many Sèvres vases. They appear to be the work of two or three different painters. The Museum's *plateau losange* is probably painted by the same hand as a tea set now in the Museum of Fine Arts, Boston.[5]

TECHNIQUE AND CONDITION

The green ground is matte with an orange-peel like texture. Its somewhat dirty tone suggests the ground color contained too much copper. There are some reglazed scratches and the foot rim is covered with black specks suggesting a refiring with turpentine oil. The gold has been applied with a heavy hand, lacking the lightness of touch expected on an entirely eighteenth-century piece. It is thus possible that the reserve is original but that the green ground and gilding were added later.

Exhibition: *Morgan Loan Exhibition*, New York, 1914, not in catalogue

Literature: Chavagnac, p. 99, no. 121; Savill, 2, pp. 604, 612 nn. 3b, 9

NOTES

1 See Savill, 3, p. 1110, found on soft paste 1753–73.

2 APML, Cartier file, invoice 24 May 1901: "Plateau Vieux Sèvres, forme lozange fond gros vert, cartel et paysage," 4,500 French francs.

3 See cat. no. 92 for a full discussion of this shape.

4 Savill, 2, p. 604.

5 Hawes and Corsiglia, pp. 197–202, no. 69. For more on these landscapes see cat. no. 67.

90

Tea service with tray, teapot, sugar bowl, and two cups and saucers (*plateau forme de corbeille ovale* or *corbeille ovale contournée, théière Calabre, pot à sucre Hebert, gobelets Hebert et soucoupes*)

1917.1181–1185

Sèvres, 1764

Soft-paste porcelain, tray: H. 2⅛ × L. 11⅞ × W. 9⅝ in. (5.3 × 30.1 × 24.5 cm); teapot: H. 4¼ × W. 5⁵⁄₁₆ × D. 3³⁄₁₆ in. (10.7 × 13.4 × 8.1 cm); sugar bowl: H. 3½ × DIAM. 2¹³⁄₁₆ in. (8.9 × 7.1 cm); 1917.1184: cup: H. 2⅝ × W. 3¹⁵⁄₁₆ × D. 3³⁄₁₆ in. (6.7 × 9.9 × 7.8 cm); saucer: H. 1¼ × DIAM. 5¼ in. (3.1 × 13.3 cm); 1917.1185: cup: H. 2⅝ × W. 3¹⁵⁄₁₆ × D. 3⅛ in. (6.6 × 10 × 7.9 cm); saucer: H. 1³⁄₁₆ × DIAM. 5¼ in. (3 × 13.3 cm)

White ground with polychrome *frizes colorées*, carmine, green, and yellow pierced border, gilding

Marks: on all pieces: interlaced Ls in blue with dot in center, L underneath, either the mark of Denis Levé[1] or perhaps the date letter for 1764; + above for Philippe Xhrouuet *père*;[2] tray: incised coffee bean with stem;[3] sugar bowl: incised T or I;[4] both cups: incised O;[5] saucer (1917.1185): incised reversed S;[6] inscribed inside lid of sugar bowl in black: n° 127

Provenance: Séguier,[7] comte de Loisne, and Foucher de Brandoy, by report;[8] Edouard Chappey, Paris, 1906;[9] J. Pierpont Morgan

MODEL

This tea service is made up of a tray called *plateau forme de corbeille ovale* or *corbeille ovale contournée*, a fourth- or fifth-size *théière Calabre*,[10] a third-size *pot à sucre Hebert*,[11] and two *gobelets Hebert* of the second size.[12] The tray appears in the inventory of new works for 1755, where one mold and one model of a *corbeille ovale de 11 pouces* are listed.[13] The model is one of eight basket trays put into production that year, the others being round (in two sizes), square, lozenge-shaped, octagonal, and triangular, and one *15 pouces de long*.[14] These must have been designed for Louis XV's *bleu céleste* service, which was made and delivered to the king over the course of three years, from 1753 to 1755. In the 1755 delivery, there were thirty-one basket trays listed, directly corresponding to those listed in the inventory of new work.[15]

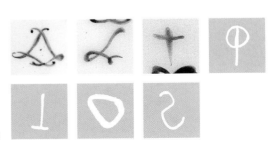

Marks

Documentary references to oval basket trays after 1755 are scarce, for from this date on the shape of the tray is rarely designated.[16] They do not seem to have been included in many of the subsequent services that are identifiable in the records. In fact, the first time one finds *corbeilles* in a known service is in 1766, when Louis-César-Renaud, vicomte de Choiseul, later second duc de Praslin, purchased a dessert service decorated with *frizes colorées*, which included two oval basket trays.[17] Two *grandes corbeilles* of unspecified shape were also included in a *bleu céleste* service purchased by the baron de Breteuil in April 1768,[18] and four *corbeilles lozanges* were part of Madame du Barry's 1770–71 service decorated with garlands and blue vases.[19]

Déjeuners corbeille ranged in price from 144 *livres* (*lapis oiseaux*) to 1,440 *livres* (*grand déjeuner bleu céleste mosaïque*).[20] Prices ranged widely according to the richness of the decoration as well as to the size of the tea set.[21] Between 1757 and 1766, only one *déjeuner corbeille ovale* is specifically listed, decorated with a *bleu céleste* ground and priced at 480 *livres*.[22]

FUNCTION

The first documented use of a basket tray as part of a tea service was in 1756, when Lazare Duvaux purchased a *corbeille triangle fleurs* along with two cups and saucers and a sugar bowl for 168 *livres*.[23] From this date these trays were used more for tea sets than for dessert services.

COMMENTARY

The decoration on the Museum's tea set is similar to that on the tray in the vicomte de Choiseul's service, and thus would have been described as *frizes colorées*.[24] It probably cost between 360 and 480 *livres*.[25]

Exhibitions: *Morgan Loan Exhibition*, New York, 1914, not in catalogue; *French and English Art Treasures*, New York, 1942, no. 317

Literature: Masson, p. 9; *French and English Art Treasures*, no. 317

NOTES

1 Active 1754–93, 1795–1805. See Peters, *Marks*, p. 49. David Peters suggested that in this case the L may be the date letter. The significance of the dot in the center of the factory mark is unknown.

2 Active 1750–75 (ibid., p. 77). See also Savill, 3, pp. 1077–78.

3 See Savill, 3, p. 1136, found on a range of objects 1750s–70s.

4 Ibid., pp. 1108–9, found on soft paste 1753–90s. The mark is very small and near the rim, making it look like ⊥.

5 Ibid., p. 1117, found on soft paste 1754–82.

6 Ibid., p. 1122, found on soft paste c. 1753–66.

7 There was a Séguier sale at Christie's, London, 6 June 1842, but nothing fitting the description of the Museum's tea service appears. The provenance of Séguier is mentioned only in the Museum's early record cards, with no references.

8 These names were also mentioned in the Museum's early records, also without reference. I have been unable to find any sales records corresponding to these names.

9 APML, Chappey file, invoice 30 April 1906: "1 Cabaret Sèvres guirlandes de fleurs fond oeil de perdrix violet bord du plateau ajouré, 2 tasses et soucoupes Sucrier & Théière," 40,000 French francs (with another tea service, cat. no. 104).

10 Savill, 2, p. 577.

11 Ibid., p. 575.

12 Ibid., p. 496.

13 AMNS, I. 7, 1 January 1756, *moules en plâtre* and *modeles en plâtre*. Eleven *pouces* translates to 11¹¹⁄₁₆ in. (29.7 cm), which corresponds within less than half an inch to the Museum's tray (for *pouce* see glossary).

14 It is unclear to what shape this last object refers. Also in the inventory of new models there are molds and models *d'après la Corbeille de 15. Pouces*, as well as after the other baskets noted above. These probably were additional molds to allow several *mouleurs* to work at the same time on

these basket trays (as per Tamara Préaud). In the inventory of 1 October 1759 (AMNS, I. 7), when Charles Adams's earlier inventories are restated, these same molds and models after the baskets are listed, but this time the list reads *moule pour le Déjeuner d'après la Corbeille de 15 pouces*, etc. This probably should be interpreted as *moule pour le plateau de déjeuner …*, and would have been made from the model of the basket tray.

15 One *grande corbeille de 15 pouces de long*; two *ronde de 11 pouces*; two *id. de 9 pouces*; two *quarées de 7 pouces ½*; two *ovales contournées de 11 pouces ½*; four *lozanges de 11 p.*; fourteen *octogones de 8 p.*; and four *triangles de 8 p.* See AMNS, Vy 1, fols. 119v–20, 31 December 1755, *Service en Bleu Céleste Livré au Roy*. See also Grégory, p. 46; Peters, "Louis XV," p. 64.

16 References in the biscuit kiln records (IF 5673) include: fol. 60 (April/May 1756), *1 Platteau forme de corbeille ronde*; fol. 62 (20 July 1756), *1 Platteau forme de Corbeille 1ere gr.*; fol. 113, (August/September 1758), *4 plateaux forme de Corbeilles*; and fol. 115 (August/September 1758), *2 plateaux ovales forme de Corbeilles*. Basket trays are also in the glaze kiln records (IF 5674, fols. 58, 77, 91, and 95).

17 AMNS, Vy 4, fol. 85v. See Christie's, New York, 21 May 1997, lot 90; again Christie's, London, 17 April 2000, lot 89.

18 AMNS, Vy 4, fols. 142v–43, 16 April 1768, 288 *livres*.

19 Ibid., Vy 5, fol. 17, 29 August 1771, 216 *livres*.

20 AMNS, Vy 3, fol. 14v, first quarter 1760, Machard; ibid., Vy 2, fol. 85, December 1758, for Maria-Theresa of Austria, now at the Nelson-Atkins Museum of Art, Kansas City, Missouri (no. F89-27/1, L. 17⅜ in. [44.1 cm]).

21 The model for the *plateau corbeille triangle* measures 8¼ in. (21 cm) (see Préaud and d'Albis, p. 197, no. 248) while the tray at Kansas City measures 17⅜ in. (44.1 cm). To see how much decoration must have influenced the pricing (as in all Sèvres models), one can trace the *plateau corbeille lozange* from 1757 to 1766. It measures 11¹¹⁄₁₆ in. (29.7 cm), and sold for 720 *livres* in March 1759 (AMNS, Vy 2, fol. 89, unnamed buyer, green with birds); 360 *livres* in December 1759 (ibid., Vy 3, fol. 6v, birds); 528 *livres* in October 1760 (ibid., fol. 26v, Sprot, green ribbons); 240 *livres* (ibid., 35v, Mme Lair, second half 1760, birds); and 600 *livres* in August 1762 (ibid., fol. 117, Mme de Pompadour, green trellis). The other designated shapes also varied greatly in price, and as one would expect, a moderately decorated large tray could be less expensive than an elaborately decorated smaller tray (*ovales frizes colorées*, 192 *livres*, Vy 4, fol. 85v, 1 October 1766, to vicomte de Choiseul; *triangle, roze mozaïque*; 432 *livres*, Vy 2, fol. 79v, December 1758, Duvaux). It is also important to note that the factory lowered its prices in 1760.

22 AMNS, Vy 3, fol. 1, last quarter 1759, to Mme Duvaux.

23 Ibid., Vy 2, fol. 12, 20 August 1756–1 January 1757. As Eriksen has pointed out (Eriksen and Bellaigue, p. 92), the factory discovered early on that trays used for dinner and dessert services could effectively be used for tea sets. Examples of such mixed use include the *plateau porte-huilier*, the lozenge-shaped stand for sauceboats, the radish dishes, and the tray for ice cups (*plateau Bouret*).

24 See note 17 above.

25 An unspecified tea set with *frizes colorées* was sold to Étienne-François, duc de Choiseul for 480 *livres* in December 1765 (Vy 4, fol. 57), while a tea set *Courteille frizes colorées*, which is larger than the *corbeille ovale*, sold to Delorme on 22 May 1765 for 528 *livres* (fol. 38). If one tries to price the component parts, using the tray from the vicomte de Choiseul service as a starting point (192 *livres*), then one may suggest that the teapot cost 54 *livres*, and the sugar bowl and cups and saucers 48 *livres* each, for a total of 390 *livres*. (See fol. 57 for sale of these components decorated with *frizes* sold to Mme Sophie 12 April 1765.) Among the various *déjeuners corbeille* sold from 1757 to 1766, none were priced at 390 *livres*, but examples were sold for 360 *livres* (Vy 3, fol. 6v, *lozange oiseaux*, 28 December 1758, Mme Louise), and 432 *livres* (*triangle roze mozaïque* and *quarré roze mozaïque*, Vy 2, fols. 79v, 82, December 1758, Duvaux and Dulac).

91

Tea service with tray, teapot, sugar bowl, milk jug, and cup and saucer (*plateau octogone, théière Calabre, pot à sucre Calabre, pot à lait à trois pieds, gobelet Hebert et soucoupe*)

1917.1032–1036

Sèvres, 1764

Soft-paste porcelain, tray: H. 1⅛ × DIAM. 9³⁄₁₆ in. (2.9 × 23.4 cm); teapot: H. 3⅝ × W. 4¹³⁄₁₆ × D. 2¾ in. (9.2 × 12.2 × 7 cm); sugar bowl: H. 2¹⁄₁₆ × DIAM. 2⅜ in. (5.3 × 6 cm); milk jug: H. 3⅛ × W. 3⅜ × D. 2¹¹⁄₁₆ in. (8 × 8.6 × 6.8 cm); cup: H. 2⅛ × W. 3⁵⁄₁₆ × D. 2¹¹⁄₁₆ in. (5.5 × 8.4 × 6.8 cm); saucer: H. 1¹⁄₁₆ × DIAM. 4⅝ in. (2.7 × 11.7 cm)

White ground with *frizes colorées* in blue, purple, carmine, and gold, polychrome floral garlands

Marks: interlaced Ls in blue on all pieces with date letter L for 1764; painter's mark of x for Jacques-François Micaud *père* under factory mark on all except teapot;[1] incised fj on tray;[2] incised reverse S on teapot and saucer;[3] incised I on sugar bowl;[4] incised IC on foot of milk jug;[5] incised FR on cup[6]

Provenance: J. Pierpont Morgan

MODEL

The Sèvres factory called this tray *plateau octogone*. It first appeared in the inventories as part of the production of 1757, when twenty-two white glazed examples were in stock.[7] There were no models or molds listed.[8] The documents did not specify sizes. Based on known examples and the uniform pricing in the inventories during the 1760s, it is likely that the tray was made in only one size during this period, although there is evidence that a second size was made at a later date.[9] Three versions of the tray exist, one with eight double-lobed projections (present example), one with a uniformly scalloped rim,[10] and a third without lobes but with two handles.[11]

The first time a *plateau octogone* appeared in the sales records was in 1757 when two decorated with gilded friezes were sold to the dealer Machard.[12] On the other hand, the first mention of a *déjeuner octogone* in the sales records was in December 1760.[13] While only two were specified during the next five years, there must have been others among the many tea sets sold without description in the 1760s.[14]

The teapot is probably a *théière Calabre*.[15] The sugar bowl is also the *Calabre* shape, and represents the smallest size. The milk jug was called *pot à lait à trois pieds* and is of the third size.[16] The cup and saucer is the *Hebert* form and is of the third size.[17]

91

COMMENTARY

The decoration consists of small cartouches with diaper patterns, carmine and purple laurel garlands, and polychrome floral swags. The palette of *beau bleu*, red, purple, and gold, used with diapers or trellises, and often shells, can be found on much Sèvres in the first half of the 1760s. In the factory records this type of decoration was called *frize colorée*, and made its appearance at court in December 1761.[18] Tea services, broth basins, flower vases, and cups and saucers were similarly decorated and sold during the next few years. In 1766 the vicomte de Choiseul bought a large dessert service in the same style.[19] Another octagonal tray with *frize colorée* decoration by Thévenet was made in 1763.[20]

Jacques-François Micaud *père*, who was active at the factory from 1757 until 1801, executed the *frizes colorées* on the Hartford tea set.[21] In the 1760s overtime records tell us that he was paid for *frizes colorées*, *frizes riches*, *étoffes riches*, and other decorative work. He also excelled at painting flowers, combining them with other decorative motifs such as trellises, mosaics, foliage, and ribbons. His mark was either a plain or serif x, and always appeared under the factory mark. In the past it has often been confused with the mark of Xhrouuet, which was a plain or serif + and always appeared above the factory mark.[22] According to the overtime records for 1764, Micaud was paid 27 *livres* for decorating a *plateau 8gne avec 1 gobelet et soucoupe 2e g.: 1 pot à sucre 3e g.: 1 theyere 3e g: un pot à lait 3e g.* [octagonal tray with 1 cup and saucer of 2nd size; 1 sugar bowl of the 3rd size; 1 teapot of the 3rd size; 1 milk jug of the 3rd size].[23] Since there is so much uncertainty surrounding the sizes of the teapots and sugar bowls it is difficult to know if this is the Atheneum's tea set. Besides, the Museum's cup and saucer are of the third size, not the second size as described in the overtime payment. Still, the factory records are often mistaken leaving open the possibility that this payment refers to the Hartford set.

Another *déjeuner octogone* with *frize colorée* decoration is in the collection of Firle Place, Sussex. It is the same size as the Atheneum's tea set, and is dated 1761. The decoration is by Louis-Jean Thévenet. An octagonal tea set with two cups and saucers (*litron et soucoupe*), a milk jug, and sugar bowl, decorated with classical scrolls and floral garlands, was sold in Paris in 1983.[24]

TECHNIQUE AND CONDITION

The cup has been damaged and repaired.[25] The purple shows signs of crawling indicating that too much gum arabic was mixed with the pigment causing some of it to lift off.[26] The *beau bleu* is rather thinly applied, especially in the *vermiculé* border, almost creating the appearance of *bleu Fallot*.[27]

Exhibitions: *Morgan Loan Exhibition*, New York, 1914, not in catalogue; *Design in the Service of Tea*, New York, 1984; *Morgan*, Hartford, 1987, no. 65

Literature: Chavagnac, pp. 96–97, no. 117; de Bellaigue, "Sèvres," p. 174, no. 65

NOTES

1 See Savill, 3, pp. 1049–51 for a biography of this painter. See also Peters, *Marks*, p. 53 to distinguish this painter's mark from that of Philippe Xhrouuet.

2 Savill, 3, p. 1101, found on soft-paste 1759–76.

3 Ibid., p. 1122, found on soft-paste 1753–66.

4 Ibid., pp. 1108–9.

5 Dauterman, *Marks*, p. 202.

6 Savill, 3, p. 1102, found on soft-paste 1757–68 and on hard-paste 1774–81.

7 AMNS, I. 7, 1 January 1758 (for 1757). Much of this information was published by Sir Geoffrey de Bellaigue in "Sèvres," p. 174.

8 A plaster model of a different octagonal tray appears in the 1814 inventory of models at the factory (AMNS, 1814 inventory, 1780–1800, no. 1).

9 De Bellaigue states that two sizes were made, and in correspondence with the author cites an entry in the artists' records for 3 June 1788, under the painter Bouillat: *1 Dejeuner Octogone 2 beau bleu fleurs sur terasse 36* [*livres*] *Vu*. See AMNS, Vy 4, fol. 42v. Perhaps this describes the later model of tray as evidenced by the plaster model cited in note 8 above.

10 See Firestone sale, Christie's, New York, 21–22 March 1991, lot 204; René Fribourg sale, Sotheby's, London, 25 June, 1963, lot 43.

11 See cat. no. 106.

12 AMNS, Vy 2, fol. 46v, 31 December 1757.

13 Ibid., Vy 3, fol. 28v, unnamed buyer, decorated with garlands, *72 livres*. See de Bellaigue, "Sèvres," p. 174.

14 Only two octagonal tea sets are specifically listed in the sales records during the next few years: AMNS, Vy 4, fol. 13v, 4 July 1764, unnamed buyer, no decoration specified, *192 livres*; Vy 4, fol. 56, December 1765, two unspecified, Louis XV, *240 livres* each.

15 For a discussion of this shape and the problems of identification see cat. no. 85. This example is size E according to the groups defined by Savill (2, p. 577).

16 See cat. no. 87 for these shapes.

17 See cat. no. 80.

18 See AMNS, Vy 3, fols. 83–85.

19 See Wilkie, pp. 64–65; Christie's, New York, 21 May 1997, lot 90; same service, Christie's, London, 17 April 2000, lot 89.

20 See Paris, Maître Delorme et Fraysse, 20 May 1995, lot 260, DIAM. 9¹⁄₁₆ in. (23 cm). I would like to thank Tamara Préaud for this reference.

21 See Savill, 3, pp. 1049–51 for the biographical information that follows.

22 See David Peters, entry for the Choiseul dessert service, Christie's, New York, 21 May 1997, lot 90.

23 AMNS, F.7.

24 Drouot, Paris, 2 June 1983, lot 100, unspecified date, tray DIAM. 9¹⁄₁₆ in. (23 cm).

25 Repaired in 1986, treatment report on file at Wadsworth Atheneum.

26 See Préaud and d'Albis, p. 224 for gum arabic. D'Albis states that Hellot was aware of this potential problem with gum arabic.

27 For this color see cat. no. 94.

92

Tray (*plateau losange*)

1917.1041

Sèvres, 1765

Soft-paste porcelain, H. 2⅜ × L. 14⅞ × w. 10¹⁵⁄₁₆ in. (6 × 37.6 × 27.7 cm)

White ground with *bleu nouveau* and gilded diapered panels, red and gold roundels and borders, foliate garlands, blue and green enamel on pierced sides, gilding

Marks: interlaced Ls in blue with date letter M inside, mark of Louis-Jean Thévenet *père* to the left;[1] incised L[2]

Provenance: possibly Cartier et Fils, Paris, 1901;[3] J. Pierpont Morgan

MODEL

Five variations of lozenge-shaped trays were made at Sèvres. One had plain, undulating sides with scrolled handles; another had plain sides without handles; a third had pierced sides and no handles; a fourth had pierced sides with zigzag batons and no handles; and the fifth had pierced sides with zigzag batons that extended to form handles.[4] The Museum's tray corresponds to this last version, which was made in one size.[5] A drawing inscribed *plateau de la saussiere seul 18* is in the Cooper-Hewitt Museum, New York.[6] Two plaster models remain·at the Sèvres factory, one labeled *plateau de déjeuner losange à reliefs*. This model shows two options, one with zigzag moldings (*bâtons rompus*), like the Hartford example, and one with scrolled handles.[7]

The earliest mention of a *plateau losange* in the factory records was in 1756 when two were taken from the glaze kiln.[8] The Museum's version is known from 1763, and probably was variously referred to as *plateau losange à jour*, *plateau losange à jour à anses*, and *plateau losange à anses bâtons rompus*.[9]

The sales records usually do not specify version or size, making it impossible to know exactly how much such trays cost. A tray could cost as little as *30 livres* (probably one of the small, simple versions with flowers), while a *bleu céleste* tea set with this tray cost *336 livres*. An unspecified *déjeuner losange* was sold to the king in 1763 for *528 livres*.[10] Without tea components, the Atheneum's tray might have cost *72 livres*.[11]

The Frankenthal factory copied Sèvres' *plateau losange*. An example dated 1778 was sold by Sotheby's in 1980, and an example from 1768–70 was exhibited at the Kurpfälzisches Museum in Heidelberg in 1993.[12]

FUNCTION

The *plateau losange* could either be sold as part of a tea service or else separately.[13] However, the version with plain sides and no handles usually functioned as a stand for a two-handled sauce-boat.[14]

COMMENTARY

Louis-Jean Thévenet decorated the Hartford tray in *frizes colorées*.[15] He was one of the earliest documented painters at the factory, coming to Vincennes either in 1741 or 1745. He specialized in flower painting, and even made paintings of flowers from nature to serve as models for the other painters.[16] By 1760 he spent an increasing part of his time painting friezes such as on the Museum's tray. A partial tea set, marked Thévenet, dated 1763 and 1764, and displaying decoration very close to this tray (with floral rather than oak-leaf garlands) was on the art market in 1969 and again in 1972.[17] In 1765 he was paid 43 *livres* in overtime for *1 platteau losange à jour avec 2 gobelets et soucoupes 1e g: 1 pot a sucres 3e g: et 1 theyere 2e g* [1 pierced lozenge tray with 2 cups and saucers of the 1st size; 1 sugar bowl of the 3rd size; and 1 teapot of the 2nd size].[18] Is it the Hartford tray that is listed here?

TECHNIQUE AND CONDITION

The surface of the tray as well as the gilded rim are quite worn, with losses to blue diapered panels and to the oak leaf garlands. The *bleu nouveau* is thinly applied, and in places has crawled away from the glaze. This may have been because the layer was too thickly applied or because it was not dry enough when the color was powdered on.[19]

Exhibition: *Morgan Loan Exhibition*, New York, 1914, not in catalogue

Literature: Chavagnac, p. 99, no. 121; Brunet, *Frick*, pp. 274–75

NOTES

1 Active 1741/45–77. See Savill, 3, pp. 1071–72 for an extensive biography of this painter.

2 Ibid., p. 1111, found on soft paste 1755–75, 1787, possibly the mark for the *répareurs* Lauvergnat *aîné* (active 1749/52/54–72/73) and Lauvergnat *jeune* (active 1754–74/75).

3 APML, Cartier file, invoice 24 May 1901: "1 Plateau vieux Sèvres, forme lozange fond blanc guirlandes à jour, vertes et bleues," 7,200 French francs.

4 See Savill, 2, pp. 602–13 for a full account of this shape. The following information is largely based on this account.

5 Ibid., p. 602. In the records two sizes of *plateaux losange* appear but they probably only refer to the model with plain, undulating sides and scrolling handles. The Museum's version ranges from L. 14⅝ to 14¹¹⁄₁₆ × w. 10⅝ to 10¹⁵⁄₁₆ in. (36.9–37.3 × 27–27.8 cm).

92

93

6 New York, Cooper-Hewitt, National Design Museum, Smithsonian Institution, no. 1938 88 8315 C3438. See Savill, 2, pp. 602, 613 n. 5.

7 AMNS, 1814 inventory, 1740–60, nos. 1 and 2. See Savill, 2, pp. 602, 613 n. 4.

8 IF 5674, June 1756. See Brunet, *Frick*, pp. 272, 275 n. 2, and Savill, 2, p. 603.

9 See Savill, 2, p. 603. These names appear respectively in 1764, 1778, and 1783.

10 AMNS, Vy 4, fol. 156, December 1763, Louis XV; see also Vy 4, fol. 53, 17 October 1765, Delorme; Vy 4, fol. 87v, 18 October 1766, unnamed buyer.

11 A tray described as *plateau losange frises colorées* was sold to Mme de Pompadour on 7 February 1762 (ibid., fol. 115).

12 Sotheby's, New York, 15 October 1980, lot 2; *Solitaires Frankenthal*, p. 51, no. 27. See also Sotheby's, New York, 13–14 June 1979, lot 147, c. 1775–80 (reference kindly provided by Tamara Préaud).

13 Savill, 2, pp. 604, 612 n. 3, for examples of tea sets. See also Eriksen, *Waddesdon*, p. 244.

14 Savill, 2, p. 604. Eriksen (*Waddesdon*, p. 244) notes that *plateaux losange* originally were made for sauceboats.

15 See cat. no. 91 for more on this type of decoration.

16 Savill, 3, p. 1071.

17 Sotheby's, London, 25 March 1969, lot 33 and Christie's, London, 8 July 1972, lots 176–80.

18 AMNS, F.8, 1765.

19 I should like to thank Antoine d'Albis for this information.

93

Tea service with tray, teapot, sugar bowl, milk jug, and two cups and saucers (probably *plateau Duplessis, théière Calabre, pot à sucre Hebert, pot à lait à trois pieds, gobelets Hebert et soucoupes*)

1917.1051–1056

Sèvres, 1768

Soft-paste porcelain, tray: H. 1½ × L. 12⅝ × D. 9⅛ in. (3.8 × 32.1 × 23.1 cm); teapot: H. 4³⁄₁₆ × W. 5¼ × D. 3³⁄₁₆ in. (10.6 × 13.3 × 8 cm); sugar bowl: H. 3½ × DIAM. 2⅞ in. (8.9 × 7.3 cm); milk jug: H. 3³⁄₁₆ × W. 3³⁄₁₆ × D. 2½ in. (8.1 × 8.4 × 6.4 cm); cups: H. 2³⁄₁₆ × W. 3³⁄₁₆ × D. 2⅝ in. (5.5 × 8.4 × 6.6 cm); saucers: H. 1¼ × DIAM. 4¾ in. (3.1 × 12.1 cm)

Blue *pointillé* ground with roundels of pink roses, carmine stripes, foliate and gilded garlands

Marks: on all pieces: interlaced Ls in blue with date letter P and x underneath for Jacques-François Micaud *père*;[1] incised marks: tray: Fi in script,[2] and FR;[3] teapot: jc;[4] sugar bowl: scrolling sp;[5] 1917.1055: cup: E or reversed 3;[6] saucer: 8;[7] 1917.1056: cup: script LX;[8] saucer: 8

Provenance: J. Pierpont Morgan

MODEL

These trapezoidal trays were made in two sizes, the first size ranging from 13¾ to 14 inches (35 to 35.6 cm), and the second size from 11⅞ to 12⅝ inches (30.1 to 32.1 cm).[9] A drawing of this tray without handles is in the Sèvres factory archives, but bears no inscription (fig. 93-1).[10] When decorated with landscapes or figural reserves, the tray could be oriented either with the long or short side up.[11]

Since 1968 this tray has been classified as a *plateau Duvaux*.[12] More recently, it has been suggested that, in fact, the model for this tray was the *plateau Duplessis*, named after the factory's designer Jean-Claude Duplessis. There is much to be said in favor of this argument, as set out below.[13]

The name *déjeuner Duvaux* (that is a tea set with a *plateau Duvaux*) first appeared in the sales records of the factory in 1758, when an example with garlands was sold for 72 *livres* to the dealer Machard.[14] Six molds and one model for the tray were listed among new work of 1758 in the inventory of 1 January 1759, each valued at a very low 1 *livre*.[15] The tray again appeared in the list of undecorated white porcelain in the inventory of 1 October 1759, where it was valued at only 4 *livres*.[16] A survey of the sales records from 1758 to 1768 shows that the average *déjeuner Duvaux* cost less than 100 *livres*. The most expensive one, decorated with a pink ground and flowers, sold for 216 *livres* to Machard in 1758.[17] Next in cost were *déjeuners* which sold for 126 *livres*, such as a green one to the dealer Dulac in 1760 and a *bleu céleste* one to Madame de Pompadour in the same year.[18]

The very low values assigned to the molds, models, undecorated, and decorated examples of *plateaux Duvaux*, as compared to other trays, indicate that they were quite small. In 1759, the plaster model for a second-size *porte-huilier* was valued at 1 *livre*, the same as the model for a *plateau Duvaux*.[19] Undecorated plain-sided square trays (about 5⅞ in. or 15 cm) were listed at 5 *livres*, and second-size *plateaux tiroir* (about 6¹¹⁄₁₆ in. or 17 cm) at 6 *livres*, compared to 4 *livres* for an undecorated *plateau Duvaux*.[20] One finds further evidence that the *plateau Duvaux* was small by examining the painters' overtime records. From

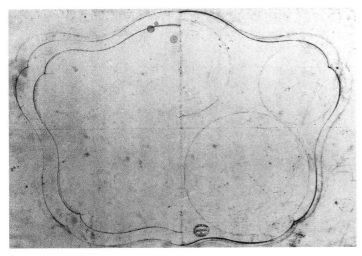

Fig. 93-1 *Plateau Duplessis*, drawing

1762 through 1769, ten tea sets with this tray appeared, and all but one including only two pieces in addition to the tray. When the accompanying pieces were described, they were usually a cup and saucer and a sugar bowl.[21] In comparison, most tea services with the trapezoidal tray under discussion included five or six pieces.[22]

The *plateau Duplessis* was introduced slightly later than the *plateau Duvaux*. It was first recorded in 1760, when two were listed among *pièces extraordinaires* in the factory's inventory.[23] A second size appeared in 1761, when molds and models were listed at 8 *livres* each.[24] Two examples ready for glazing in that same year were valued at 15 *livres* each, and undecorated examples were valued at 21 *livres*.[25] When comparing values for other trays in 1762, only the *plateaux Courteille* and *Hebert* come close, the *plateau Courteille* valued the same at 21 *livres* and the *Hebert* at 18 *livres*.[26] This indicates that the *plateau Duplessis* must have been of a comparable size.[27]

Overtime records from 1761 to 1768 included *déjeuners Duplessis* of the first and second sizes.[28] A first-size example, for which the painter Xhrouuet was paid 24 *livres* in 1761, included six pieces: a teapot, sugar bowl, milk jug, tea caddy, and two cups and saucers.[29] He was paid 60 *livres* the following year for a *déjeuner Duplessis* with the same components.[30] Second-size *déjeuners Duplessis* usually included five pieces, such as the one decorated by the painter Thévenet in 1762, which contained a teapot, sugar bowl, milk jug, and two cups and saucers.[31]

The sales ledgers mentioned very few *déjeuners Duplessis* by name during the 1760s, when probably most of them were produced, and many of those were not described. The least expensive example, sold to an unnamed buyer in 1764, cost 144 *livres*, its decoration not specified.[32] The most expensive one, painted with green ground and flowers and sold to Monsieur de Laborde in 1761, was 720 *livres*.[33] It is clear from these prices that the tray must have been considerably larger than the *plateau Duvaux*.

It is difficult to match with any certainty specific documentary references with surviving trays or tea services. Still, it is possible that the *déjeuner Duplessis* decorated with *mosaïque* and sold to the duc d'Orléans in 1760 is the same one that appeared on the Paris art market in 1994, dated 1760. This is decorated with flowers and triangular patterns, the latter called *mosaïque* by the factory.[34] It is also possible that the tea set with a green ground and flowers dated 1761, formerly in the Christner collection, Texas, and now in a private collection, London, was the one sold to Monsieur de Laborde in July 1761 for 720 *livres*.[35] In 1762 Méreaud *jeune* was paid 47 *livres* for decorating a second-size *plateau Duplessis*, with accompanying components, which might correspond to a tray now in New Orleans, Louisiana.[36] A *plateau Duplessis* and two cups and saucers dated 1761 and decorated with *frizes colorées* by Xhrouuet was on the London art market in 2000 and may be part of the set for which Xhrouuet was paid 24 *livres* in 1761.[37]

It is not difficult to imagine that this undulating tray with its delicate branch handles would be named after the man who must have been responsible for its design. As with other Sèvres models more securely attributed to Duplessis, the tray is marked by a restrained rococo style, and betrays an understanding of sculptural form while at the same time providing a simple surface for the factory's painters to decorate.[38]

The accompanying pieces to the Museum's tray are a *théière Calabre*, of one of the smaller sizes,[39] a third-size *pot à sucre Hebert*,[40] a third-size *pot à lait à trois pieds*,[41] and two cups and saucers *Hebert*, also third size.[42]

The Vienna Porcelain Factory produced a tray based on this model in the 1770s,[43] as did the Minton factory in England in the nineteenth century.[44] A photograph of a Sèvres *déjeuner Duplessis* with *frizes colorées* from the Samson factory, Paris— the original Sèvres tray and two cups and saucers recently on the London art market—proves that it was copied there as well.[45]

COMMENTARY

The decoration of the Museum's tea service is of a type that was first employed about 1767 and continued into the 1780s.[46] With minor variations, this consisted of individual roses in white roundels surrounded by either gilt laurel leaves or a plain gold band (called *roses encadrées d'or*). The ground colors most frequently used were *bleu céleste* or green. Sometimes, as on the Hartford tea set, a white ground decorated with tiny dots of enamel was employed. In many cases, also as on the Museum's set, the roses were arranged in bands divided by purple lines and undulating laurel leaves and berries. The pattern covered the entire surface of the porcelain, eliminating the reserve and creating an overall effect similar to a textile pattern.[47] This approach to decoration became more and more frequent in the later 1760s and 1770s. Other textile patterns featured multi-colored stripes punctuated by white bands with entwined laurel trails, such as found on a *pot de chambre ovale* of 1770 in the Musée des Arts décoratifs, Paris.[48]

Exhibition: *Morgan Loan Exhibition*, New York, 1914, not in catalogue

Literature: Chavagnac, p. 108, no. 132; Brunet, *Frick*, p. 270 n. 9; Hawes and Corsiglia, p. 203 n. 8, no. 69; Savill, 2, pp. 564, 568 n. 10; Savill, 3, p. 979 n. 21

NOTES

1 Active 1757–1810. For more on this artist see cat. no. 91.

2 Savill, 3, p. 1101, found on soft paste, 1759–76.

3 Savill, 3, p. 1102, as possibly for François-Firmin Fresne or Dufresne, active 1756–67 as soft-paste *répareur*. Savill alternatively suggests that FR was used by François-Denis Roger, active 1755/56–83/84.

4 Ibid., p. 1111, found 1756–74 on soft paste.

5 Ibid., p. 1123, found on soft paste c. 1754–77, 1784.

6 Ibid., pp. 1100, 1126, found on soft paste, 1754–73.

7 Ibid., p. 1128, found on soft paste 1754–58, 1767–82.

8 Unidentified, not noted in Savill or Dauterman.

9 Known examples include: first size: 1759/60, MMA, New York, no. 37.20.9, green with flowers, 13¹¹⁄₁₆ in. (34.7 cm); 1760, Jones Collection, V&A, London, no. 768-768F-1882, pink with trophies, 14 in. (35.6 cm) (King, p. 9, no. 119); 1761, private collection, London, green with flowers, 13¹³⁄₁₆ in. (35 cm) (Christner sale, Christie's, New York, 9 June 1979, lot 250); 1761, Ader, Picard, Tajan, Paris, 18 November 1992, lot 66, *frize colorée*; 1763, Christie's, New York, 6 October 1980, lot 26, pink trellis with landscape, 14 in. (35.5 cm); second size: 1760, private collection, California, *petit vert*, fruit; 1760, Adar, Picard, Tajan, Paris, 29 June 1994,

lot 71, *mosaïque et fleurs*, 12 in. (30.5 cm); 1761, Markus collection, MFA, Boston, pink trellis with landscape, 11⅞ in. (30.1 cm) (Hawes and Corsiglia, no. 69); 1762, private collection, New Orleans, Louisiana, *frizes colorées*; 1763, Waddesdon Manor, Buckinghamshire, blue with "Teniers" scene, 12⅜ in. (31.5 cm) (Eriksen, *Waddesdon*, pp. 166–67, no. 58); 1765, Sotheby's, New York, 4 May 1985, lot 103, *bleu lapis vermiculé*, birds, 12¼ in. (31.1 cm); 1767, MMA, New York, no. 64.101.361-368, grey-blue scale pattern, birds, 12⅝ in. (32.1 cm); 1769, Det danske kunst-industrimuseum (Danish Museum of Decorative Art), Copenhagen, *bleu céleste pointillé*, landscapes, 12⅝ in. (32 cm) (Christie's, London, 28 May 1977, lot 141); 1780s, Christie's East, New York, 4 March 1981, lot 114, 13 in. (33 cm).

10 AMNS, R. 1, L. 2, d. 7, fol. 1. The pencil style of the drawing looks like others attributed to Duplessis. See below for more on his role.

11 For example, a tray in the MMA, New York (no. 37.20.9) is meant to have the short side on top while one at Waddesdon Manor, Buckinghamshire, is oriented the other way. See note 9 above.

12 First identified by Eriksen in *Waddesdon*, p. 166, no. 58.

13 For Duplessis, see Savill, 3, pp. 977–79. It is Savill who first made the suggestion that the tray was not named Duvaux but rather Duplessis (ibid., p. 979 n. 21). Her initial observations and comparisons of the two trays in the records form the basis of the argument to follow.

14 AMNS, Vy 2, fol. 83. See Eriksen, *Waddesdon*, p. 166.

15 AMNS, I. 7, 1 January 1759 (for 1758), *moules* and *modèles en plâtre*.

16 Ibid., 1 October 1759 (for 1758), *magasin du blanc*. See Savill, 3, p. 979 n. 21.

17 AMNS, Vy 2, fol. 83, 27 December 1758.

18 Ibid., Vy 3, fol. 37, 1 July 1760–1 January 1761; fol. 84v, 24 December 1761.

19 Ibid., I. 7, 1 January 1759 (for 1758).

20 Ibid., 1 October 1759, *magasin du blanc*.

21 See ibid., F.6–F.11.

22 For example, the set in the Markus collection, MFA, Boston, has five pieces, while the set sold in Paris in 1994 (*mosaïque et fleurs*) included six pieces. See tea sets described in note 9 above.

23 AMNS, I. 7, 1 January 1761, for 1760. See Savill, 3, p. 979.

24 AMNS, I. 7, 1 January 1762, for 1761. See Savill, 3, p. 979.

25 AMNS, I. 7, *Pieces en couverte prête a passer au Feu*; ibid., *magasin du blanc*.

26 Ibid., *magasin du blanc*. In this entry, *plateaux Duplessis* were listed together with *plateaux Courteille*. It must refer to second-size *plateaux Courteille*, for in the *magasin du blanc* of the previous year, *plateaux Courteille* specified as second size were 21 *livres* (AMNS, I. 7, 1 January 1761, for 1760).

27 A second-size *plateau Courteille* measures approximately 12¹³⁄₁₆ in. (32.5 cm) (see cat. no. 83), the same size as our trapezoidal tray.

28 AMNS, F.6–F.10.

29 Ibid., F.6, 1761.

30 Ibid., 1762.

31 Ibid. Thévenet was paid 40 *livres*.

32 Ibid., Vy 4, fol. 13, 4 July 1764.

33 Ibid., Vy 3, fol. 58v, 10 July 1761. Other entries in the sales records include: Vy 3, fol. 44, December 1760, *mosaïque*, 336 *livres*, duc d'Orléans; Vy 3, fol. 82v, 24 December 1761, probably *petit verd et frize*, 432 *livres*, to Louis XV (it not described but follows two other objects described as *petit verd et frize*); Vy 3, fol. 156, December 1763, two unspecified sets, 548 and 600 *livres*, Louis XV; Vy 4, fol. 194, 9 December 1769, unspecified, 432 *livres*, Mme Du Barry; Vy 5, fol. 121, *frize riche 5 pièces*, 384 *livres*, marquis de Houchin. In the inventory of old stock dated 1 January 1774, a *déjeuner Duplessis frise Coloriée riche* was valued at 360 *livres* (AMNS, I. 8).

34 This set was sold Sotheby's, London, 9 February 1960, lot 112, again Christie's, London, 4 February 1980, lot 33, and again Christie's, London, 4 December 1985, lot 31. See note 9 above.

35 See notes 9 and 34 above. Savill (3, p. 979) suggests that the Atheneum's tea set may have been the one described as *déjeuner Duplessis à 5. Pièces* decorated by Xhrouet in 1768 (AMNS, F. 10). We now know that the x mark under the factory mark is that of Micaud and not Xhrouuet. See cat. no. 91.

36 See note 9.

37 With John Whitehead, June 2000. The fact that Xhrouuet was paid only
    24 *livres* for the decoration as compared to the 40 *livres* paid to Thévenet
    for another *frize colorée* example does leave open the possibility that this is
    not the same set.

38 See Eriksen and Bellaigue, pp. 81–82 for Duplessis's style.

39 See cat. no. 85.

40 Ibid.

41 See cat no. 87.

42 See cat. no. 80.

43 See Sotheby's, New York, 22 and 24 April, 1982, lot 115; also Palazzo Pitti,
    Florence, no, A.c.e. 1911, nos. 1508–11 (c. 1770–75, information kindly
    provided by Sheila Tabakoff).

44 See Christie's, New York, 11 March 1998, lot 85, dated 1879, L. 12⅝ in.
    (32 cm).

45 See note 37. The photograph is now in the AMNS. I would like to thank
    Tamara Préaud for this information.

46 See Eriksen and Bellaigue, p. 132.

47 Another 1768 tea set, decorated by Xhrouuet (according to the auction
    catalogue) with a *plateau Hebert*, was once in the Vigier collection, Paris
    (sold Palais Galliéra, Paris, 2–3 June 1970, lot 222, and again at Drouot,
    Paris, 19 February 1980, lot 164). See also a cup and saucer, 1769, by
    Micaud, in the Louvre, Paris (Thiers collection, saucer in Verlet, *Sèvres*,
    p. 224, pl. 99e).

48 Verlet, *Sèvres*, p. 214, pl. 70.

94

Teapot (*théière Calabre*)

1917.1058

Sèvres, 1768

Soft-paste porcelain, H. 4¼ × W. 5⅜ × D. 3³⁄₁₆ in. (10.8 × 13.6 × 8 cm)

Bleu Fallot ground with *œil de perdrix* gilding, polychrome *incrusté* flowers

Marks: interlaced Ls in blue with date letter P, script b for Bertrand;[1] incised JC[2]

Provenance: J. Pierpont Morgan

MODEL

This teapot is the *Calabre* form. It is probably of the fourth or fifth size.[3]

COMMENTARY

The Museum's teapot may be related to a milk jug and sugar bowl in the Musée des Arts décoratifs, Paris;[4] a cup and saucer on the art market in 1998;[5] another cup and saucer in an American private collection; and possibly an *écuelle*, also decorated by Bertrand in 1768, once in the collection of William Randolph Hearst.[6] They all have the *œil de perdrix* gilding, inlaid flowers, and bellflower borders.

This teapot and the cup and saucer described in catalogue no. 95 came into the Atheneum's collection as part of a set with a redecorated tray (catalogue no. 185). Those pieces will be discussed separately.

TECHNIQUE AND CONDITION

The ground color used for this teapot was known as *bleu Fallot*, a deep purplish blue developed by the Sèvres worker Jean-Armand Fallot in 1765, the year of his arrival at the factory.[7] This unique color was usually covered with either circles of dots, or *œil de perdrix* [partridge eye] gilding, or even with a tiny gilded pattern of four dots grouped together to create a shimmering surface.[8] Moreover, it usually was combined with sprays of flowers after areas of the ground color were scraped away to receive them. The resulting decoration known as *fleurs incrustées* [inlaid flowers] was used on both decorative pieces and wares from 1766 to at least 1771.[9] This includes an important group of fifteen vases with *grisaille* reserves that may have been sold to Versailles in 1769.[10]

Bertrand, the painter of the Museum's teapot, specialized in this type of decoration. In the overtime records for 1768 and 1769 he was paid for painting *fleurs incrustées*.[11]

Exhibitions: *Morgan Loan Exhibition*, New York, 1914, not in catalogue; *Design in the Service of Tea*, New York, 1984[12]

Literature: Chavagnac, pp. 108–9, no. 133

NOTES

1 Active 1757–75. See Savill, 3, p. 1001, Peters, *Marks*, p. 13.

2 See Savill, 3, p. 1111, found on soft paste 1756–74.

3 See cat. no. 85 for this shape.

4 Savill, 1, p. 55 n. 52 (sugar bowl, no. GR169, milk jug, no. GR270).

5 Sotheby's, London, 21 April 1998, lot 43, formerly sold Sotheby's, London, 9 November 1993, lot 456, *gobelet litron*, H. 2⅜ in. (6 cm). Another *gobelet litron* with the same decoration, dated 1768 and painted by either Méreaud or Bertrand (Sotheby's, New York, 15–16 October 1980, lot 362, attributed to Méreaud) probably was not part of the same group as it is 2¹¹⁄₁₆ in. (6.8 cm) tall.

6 See Forrest, fig. 6.

7 Savill, 3, pp. 1032–33. Tamara Préaud has recently found Fallot's full name in the Saint-Cloud parish register for 1765 (kindly provided in correspondence with the author).

8 See cat. no. 95; as in this teapot; see the *vases œufs* (?) at the J. Paul Getty Museum, Los Angeles (Sassoon, pp. 94–101, no. 19).

9 See Eriksen and Bellaigue, p. 132; Sassoon, p. 96.

10 See Savill, 1, pp. 377–79.

11 AMNS, F.10, 1768 and F.11, 1769. See cat. no. 95.

12 Exhibited with tray and cup and saucer, nos. 1917.1057, 1917.1059 (cat. nos. 95 and 185).

95

Cup and saucer (*gobelet litron et soucoupe*)

1917.1059

Sèvres, 1769

Soft-paste porcelain, cup: H. 2⁷⁄₁₆ × W. 3⅛ × D. 2¼ in. (6.2 × 7.9 × 5.7 cm); saucer: H. 1¼ × DIAM. 5 in. (3.1 × 12.6 cm)

Bleu Fallot ground with *pointillé* gilding, polychrome *incrusté* flowers

Marks: interlaced Ls in blue with date letter q on both; script b for Bertrand;[1] incised sp on cup;[2] incised reversed scrolling S under saucer[3]

Provenance: J. Pierpont Morgan

MODEL

This cup was known as a *gobelet litron*, and was the most frequently produced model of cup at the Sèvres factory. The name *litron* refers to a traditional cylindrical measure, most often made of wood, which was used for grain, flour, salt, and peas. In 1670, an ordinance was passed that standardized the Parisian *litron* at the equivalent of 3¹¹⁄₁₆ inches (9.4 cm) high and 4¹⁄₁₆ inches (10.3 cm) in diameter.[4] Sèvres followed the form of the *litron* but not the standard measure.

Gobelets litron were already being made by October 1752, at the time of the factory's first inventory.[5] They are known with at least seven different styles of handles, ranging from a simple scroll to ear-shaped scroll, from a question-mark to a dolphin.[6] It seems that the style of handle was chosen according to the size of the cup.[7] These cups were paired with simple saucers with deep sloping sides.

There are no early drawings known for the *gobelet litron*, but there are several dating from 1782 to 1801.[8] It was made in five sizes, both in soft and hard paste.[9] When first listed in the factory inventory, the *gobelet litron* was specified in the first and *moyen* sizes.[10] By 1753 the first three sizes had appeared in the documents, while the fourth and fifth sizes did not appear until 1757.[11] *Gobelets litron* were included in tea sets, most often of the third size, but also were sold independently.[12] Sales of this model were numerous and sizes often were not specified. Before 1760 the more expensive examples cost in the range of 168 *livres*. Some later examples, which should be viewed as special "cabinet pieces," cost considerably more, such as the *bleu céleste* cup and saucer with views of the château de Bellevue sold to Madame Adélaïde in 1783 for 504 *livres*.[13]

FUNCTION

Cups of this shape were used for tea, and less frequently for coffee and chocolate. The smallest sizes probably were made for display.[14]

95

Commentary

The Museum's cup and saucer probably are of the third size.[15] They were decorated by the painter Bertrand with *bleu Fallot* ground color incrusted with polychrome flowers.[16] In 1769 he was paid two *livres* each for decorating three *gobelets et soucoupes litron en fleurs incrustés sur fond Bleu* [*litron* cups and saucers with inlaid flowers against a blue ground].[17] In that same year he was paid overtime for decorating thirteen *gobelets litron et soucoupes* of the second size, as well as a sugar bowl, teapot, milk jug, and two small vases, all with the same decoration.[18] There is a *gobelet Calabre* of the same date with the same decoration in the collection of the Sterling and Francine Clark Art Institute, also marked Bertrand.[19]

Exhibitions: *Morgan Loan Exhibition*, New York, 1914, not in catalogue; *Design in the Service of Tea*, New York, 1984[20]

Literature: Chavagnac, pp. 108–9, no. 133; Savill, 2, pp. 505; 524 n. 18

Notes

1 Active 1757–75. See Savill, 3, p. 1001, Peters, *Marks*, p. 13.

2 Savill, 3, p. 1123, found c. 1754–77, and 1784 on soft paste.

3 Ibid., p. 1122, found 1753–66 on soft paste. This saucer extends the dates for this *répareur* by at least three years.

4 Savill, 2, pp. 501, 524 n. 16, citing Eriksen, *Waddesdon*, p. 132, and Diderot, *Encyclopédie*, IX, p. 594.

5 AMNS, I. 7. For a complete discussion of this form see Savill, 2, pp. 501–26. Most of the following information comes from this source.

6 Savill illustrates four of the known handles and describes the rest (2, p. 501). She notes that occasionally the cup is known with a cover or two handles.

7 Ibid.

8 Ibid., pp. 501, 524 n. 4. See AMNS, R. 1, L. 2, d. 2, fols. 6 bis, 13 (no. 18), 14, 26, 26b, 27.

9 Ibid. Savill describes the sizes as follows: first size: cup: H. 2⅞–3 1/16 in. (7.3–7.7 cm), saucer: DIAM. 5⅝–6⅛ in. (14.3–15.5 cm); second size: cup: H. 2 9/16–2¾ in. (6.5–7 cm), saucer: DIAM. 5⅛–5⅝ in. (13–14.2 cm); third size: cup: H. 2¼–2⅜ in. (5.7–6 cm), saucer: DIAM. 4 11/16–5 1/16 in. (11.9–12.9 cm); fourth size: cup: H. 1¾–1⅞ in. (4.5–4.8 cm), saucer: DIAM. 4⅛–4 5/16 in. (10.5–11 cm); fifth size: cup: H. 1¼–1⅜ in. (3.2–3.5 cm), saucer: DIAM. 3 1/16–3⅛ in. (7.8–7.9 cm). The Museum's cup measures 2 7/16 in. (6.2 cm), which does not fall within the categories set forth by Savill.

10 See note 5.

11 IF 5673, fol. 5, 28 March 1753 (first and third sizes); fol. 10, 6 August 1753 (second size); fol. 69, 17 February 1757 (fourth size); fol. 90, 15 November 1757 (fifth size). See Savill, 2, pp. 501, 524 n. 6.

12 Savill, 2, pp. 501–2.

13 Ibid., p. 502 (AMNS, Vy 1, fol. 67, 24 December 1754, first size, *bleu céleste*, children; Vy 9, illegible folio number, 21 November 1783).

14 Savill, 2, p. 502.

15 See note 8 above. The cup is slightly taller than Savill's third-size cups but the diameter of the saucer falls within her category for third size.

16 See cat. no. 94 for more on this type of decoration.

17 AMNS, F.11, 1769.

18 Ibid.

19 Williamstown, Massachusetts, no. 1068. I would like to thank Beth Carver Wees for providing this information.

20 Exhibited with tray and teapot, nos. 1917.1057–1058. See separate entries for these objects (cat. nos. 94, 185).

96

Tray (*plateau à baguettes*)

1917.1063

Sèvres, 1769

Soft-paste porcelain, H. 2⅜ × L. 15⅛ × W. 10⅜ in. (6 × 38.4 × 26.4 cm)

White ground with green, yellow, blue, red, and puce trellis pattern, polychrome landscape, gilding

Marks: interlaced Ls in blue with date letter Q for 1769; incised j[1] and 3?;[2] embossed paper label, EX MUSEO DOUBLE; 2394 scratched into glaze

Provenance: Léopold Double collection, Paris, 1881;[3] probably Cartier et Fils, Paris, 1901;[4] J. Pierpont Morgan

MODEL

There has been some uncertainty as to the eighteenth-century name for this model of tray. Recent literature has called it both a *plateau ovale polylobé*[5] and a variation of a *plateau à rubans*.[6] The first designation seems to have been adopted as a convenient, descriptive name without precedence in the eighteenth century while the latter is, in fact, an eighteenth-century name. It probably refers to a similar tray with ribbons that is more lozenge shaped.[7]

The primary clue to the eighteenth-century name of this tray may be found in the factory's sales ledgers. In October 1773, Monsieur Gantier, perhaps on behalf of Paul Petrovich, Grand Duke of Russia, son of Catherine the Great, purchased a *dejeuner a baguette fond d'or emaillé avec attributs, armes et guirlandes cy 840 [livres]* [tea set *à baguettes* gold ground enameled with attributes, weapons and garlands here 840 (*livres*)].[8] This probably included a tray—of the same model as Hartford's—decorated with the grand duke's coat-of-arms, now in the Musée national de Céramique, Sèvres.[9] The word *baguette* means piped or molded and probably refers to the rim around the tray that resembles piping on upholstery.

There is no mention of this shape in the factory's inventories, which from the 1760s often grouped pieces together in categories such as *plateaux à ornements*. It is possible that the Museum's tray could have been just so described, like one of the 120 *plateaux à ornements et à jour* [ornamented and pierced trays] valued at 24 *livres* and ready for glazing in 1768.[10] No plaster model of the tray survives. It was made in one size.

Déjeuners à baguettes are mentioned in both the overtime and piecework records, and the sales records. The first mention in the overtime records was in 1769 when Méreaud *jeune* was paid 102 *livres* for decorating two [*déjeuners*] *grands à 4* [*pièces*] *Baguettes, en rozes détachées*.[11] Another entry in the overtime records describes the tray as *a baguettes et Rubans*,[12] which even more accurately describes the model. The sales records, notoriously lacking in detail from the middle of the 1760s on, show a few *déjeuners à baguettes* being sold from 1773. Several are listed in that year, ranging from 324 *livres* to 840 *livres*, the latter being the gold ground set for Paul Petrovich. The other examples cited in the sales records are not described.[13] Later references are sparse. There was, for example, only one identifiable sale in 1776 and one in 1777.[14]

There are a number of known examples of this shape, besides the one made for Paul Petrovich. Among these are a tray of 1768 decorated with roses, ribbons, and wreaths of gilt foliage, at Waddesdon Manor, England;[15] a tea set dating between 1765 and 1770 with *frizes colorées* and garlands in the J. Paul Getty Museum;[16] a tea set dated 1772 with a green ground and flowers, sold at Sotheby's, New York, in 1995;[17] a set dated 1774 with a *bleu céleste* ground and flowers, sold at Christie's, New York, in 1999;[18] a set dated 1775 with a blue ground and harbor scenes in the Metropolitan Museum of Art;[19] and a hard-paste set dated 1773 in the Sterling and Francine Clark Art Institute, Williamstown.[20] None of these, however, can be linked with specific mentions in the painters' or sales records.
The Meissen porcelain factory copied this tray from Sèvres.[21]

COMMENTARY

The decoration of the Museum's tray includes a large oval landscape scene that may have been painted by Jean Bouchet.[22] The pattern that covers the ground is very unusual, both in the trellis work design and in the startling combination of green, yellow, red, blue and puce. A cup and saucer (*gobelet Bouillard?*) apparently with the same decoration was in the collection of Edouard Chappey, Paris, in 1905.[23] A broth basin and stand, also with the same ground pattern but with reserves in monochrome carmine, is in the Walters Art Gallery, Baltimore.[24] A small oval tray with a landscape by Vielliard, formerly in the Van Slyck collection, Baltimore, and a small lobed tray on the art market in 2000, both undated but with landscapes by Vielliard, also bear the same ground pattern.[25]

Exhibition: *Morgan Loan Exhibition*, New York, 1914, not in catalogue

Literature: Chavagnac, p. 111, no. 137

NOTES

1 See Savill, 3, p. 1110, found 1753–73 on soft paste.

2 Ibid., p. 1125, found on soft paste, 1753–90s.

3 Sold Charles Mannheim, Paris, 30 May–4 June 1881, lot 43: "Grand Plateau oblong à lobes, à anses simulées par des nœuds de rubans, en ancienne porcelaine de Sèvres, pâte tendre, décoré d'un large médaillon de paysage de forme ovale avec figures. Le fond à quadrillages rouges et jaunes sur fond vert est rehaussée d'œils de perdrix bleus et rouges. Le bord blanc et or est enrichi de petites côtes à hachures d'or. Époque Louis XV. (Lettre Q., 1768 [*sic*])" [Large lobed tray with handles in imitation ribbon knots, in old, soft-paste Sèvres porcelain, decorated with a wide landscape scene with figures within an oval-shaped reserve. The red and yellow check pattern against a green background is highlighted with blue and red partridge eyes. The white and gold border is enhanced with little ribs hatched with gold. Louis XV period. Letter Q., 1768].

4 APML Cartier file, invoice 24 May 1901: "1 Plateau vieux Sèvres quadrilles rubans, nœud à jour, décor quadrille, cartel paysage," 7,000 French francs.

5 Brunet and Préaud, p. 176, no. 156.

6 Dawson, *British Museum*, p. 141 n. 1.

7 Ibid.

8 AMNS, Vy 5, fol. 115, 1 October 1773.

9 MNC, Sèvres, no. 5273. This tray is mentioned in the entry in Brunet and Préaud (note 5 above), and is linked to the sales entry by Pierre Ennès in "Comte du Nord," p. 221 n. 28. For an illustration of this tray see *La France et la Russie*, no. 477. I would like to thank Tamara Préaud for acquainting me with this tray and its documentation.

10 AMNS, I. 7, 1 January 1769, for 1768.

11 AMNS, F.10, 1768.

12 AMNS, F.16, 1774, Schrade, 60 *livres*. Other entries in the overtime records include: F.11, 1769, Xhrouuet, *frizes riches*, 48 *livres*; F.16, 1774, Vincent, 60 *livres*.

13 See AMNS, Vy 5, fol. 127v, 24 December, Versailles, one for 324, one for 396 *livres*; fol. 132, 27 December, Mme Sophie, 384 *livres*; fol. 134v, December, comte de Provence, 384 *livres*; and fol. 135, December, Mme Sophie, 384 *livres*.

14 AMNS, Vy 6, fol. 133, 21 October 1776, comte de Brionne, *1 Déjeuner Baguette*, 300 *livres*; fol. 205v, 31 July 1777, Parent de Lion, *1 Plateau Baguette et Rubans*, 12 *livres*. The latter obviously was undecorated or a factory second (although not indicated).

15 Eriksen, *Waddesdon*, pp. 242–43, no. 84.

16 No. 89.DE.25, no date, gilded by Le Guay. See Bremer-David, pp. 139–40, no. 232.

17 11 October 1995, lot 305, Xhrouuet.

18 5 May 1999, lot 52, painted by Tandart *aîné* and gilded by Vandé *père*.

19 Dauterman, *Kress*, pp. 236–39, no. 57a–h, Morin.

20 No. 1955.1342. Others include Garnier, pl. XXVIII, floral decoration; Lord Hillingdon sale, Christie's, London, 21 June 1976, lot 78, *bleu céleste*, 1774; Sotheby's, London, 12 June 1984, lot 180, green ground, 1775; ibid., lot 176, white ground with roses and forget-me-nots, Méreaud *jeune*, 1775; Wadsworth Atheneum, no. 1917.1090–1094 (cat. no. 104), Nöel, 1776; Christie's, London, 26 March 1984, lot 172, *bleu céleste*, flowers, date unknown; white with roses, c. 1780, illustrated in *Gazette de l'Hotel Drouot*, 15 July 1994.

21 See an example with a blue ground sold Sotheby's, New York, 19–20 October 1994, lot 281.

22 Active at Sèvres 1757–93. See Peters, *Marks*, p. 15; Casanova, p. 218, no. 145. He also painted a cup and saucer dated 1773 in an American private collection, and probably was responsible for painting a tea set in the MFA, Boston (no. 58.1354). His style is similar to one or two other Sèvres painters, including the caduceus painter, who decorated many tea wares as well as the backs of many vases. See cat. no. 67 for more on these painters.

23 Masson, p. 5, lower shelf. The illustration is in black and white and therefore the colors cannot be confirmed, but the trellis pattern looks to be the same and the landscape is in the same style.

24 No. 48.721. It is marked 1769 with the name "Panic" (?) underneath, perhaps the mark of a painter named Panicet (1768–69, see Peters, *Marks*, p. 58). I would like to thank Bernard Dragesco for acquainting me with this object and William R. Johnston for sending me detailed information on its mark.

25 Sotheby's, New York, 26 September 1989, lot 301; with Michelle Beiny, June 2000.

97

Tea kettle (*bouillotte* or *bouillotte chine*)

1917.1156

Sèvres, c. 1778–1785

Hard paste porcelain, gilt-bronze, wood, H. (without handle) 5⁵⁄₁₆ in. (13.1 cm); H. (with handle) 6¹⁵⁄₁₆ in. (17.6 cm) × W. 7⁷⁄₁₆ in. (18.8 × 14.1 cm) × D. 5⁹⁄₁₆ in. (14.1 cm)

White ground with pink roses, gilding

Marks: shadow of interlaced Ls; shadow of mark attributed to Weydinger family of gilders;[1] incised gn;[2] in unfired enamel, x 36 L C.K.

Provenance: J. Pierpont Morgan

MODEL

This model was called *bouillotte* and probably also *bouillotte chine*. While sales records simply call them *bouillottes*, the term *bouillotte chine* appears in other factory documents by 1780.[3] The term *bouillotte chinoise* may occasionally have been used to describe the model, independent of the decoration. In May 1780 the painter Gremond decorated a yellow *bouillotte chinoise* with *guirlandes, oiseaux, et petites fleurs* [garlands, birds and small flowers].[4] *Bouillottes* were made exclusively in hard-paste porcelain.[5]

Factory records as well as surviving examples reveal that the *bouillotte* or *bouillotte chine* was made in two sizes.[6] A survey of kiln registers from 1778 through 1785 show that 123 were fired, and sales ledgers from 1776 to 1784 list sixty-nine *bouillottes*.[7] Prices ranged from 36 to 360 *livres*, clearly depending on the size and decoration.[8] They were sold with silver-gilt and wood handles, of at least two different designs.[9]

A drawing for a related *bouillotte* with a fluted body and

fluted handle is in the Sèvres archives.[10] A fluted example in white was on the art market in 1987.[11] Both the fluted and unfluted models appear to have drawn inspiration from silver designs of the period. This is not surprising given that before the advent of hard-paste porcelain in France, *bouillottes* were often made in this metal. A silver kettle by Jean-Louis Dieudonné marked Paris, 1785 shows a resemblance to the Sèvres model.[12]

Decoration varied widely, and included many of the new hard-paste ground colors developed by the factory. Kiln records and painters' records mention *fond brun*, *noir*, *laque*, *pourpre*, *violet*, *maron*, *agathe*, *brun étrusque*, *or*, *rouge*, *couleur de Bellevue*, *jaune*, *beau bleu*, *lapis*, and *chatoyant* [brown, black, lacquer (dark red?), purple (porphyry?), violet, chestnut, agate, Etruscan brown, gold, red, "Bellevue," yellow, blue, lapis, and iridescent].[13] Many types of decoration were used, including simple gilding, gold dots (*pois d'or*), friezes, cornflowers, roses, garlands, bouquets, stripes (*zebre*), arabesques, landscapes, birds, figures, "Etruscan figures," and Chinese scenes. Chinese scenes were particularly favored in the period between 1778 and 1781, and were a specialty of the painters Jean-Jacques Dieu and Louis-François L'Écot.[14] Kettles with Chinese scenes must have been among the most expensive sold, fetching prices of over 300 *livres*.[15] Parisian lacquered-metal kettles from the 1750s may have been the source of inspiration for the faux-lacquer kettles produced by the Sèvres factory.[16]

COMMENTARY

There are at least ten known Sèvres *bouillottes*, including Hartford's.[17] Most are decorated lavishly, which probably contributed to their survival. The Atheneum's *bouillotte* is more simply decorated, and may have been one of four decorated with *petites roses* listed in the kiln records of 1780, gilded by Weydinger and painted by Nicolas Sinnson.[18] Other *bouillottes* with *petites roses* decoration appear in records dating from 1778 to 1782, as painted by Jean-Nicolas Le Bel and François-Pascal Pfeiffer, and gilded by Henry-François Vincent and L'Écot.[19] This type of decoration was commonly found on soft-paste objects in the 1770s and 1780s, including two wine glass coolers (*seaux crennélés*) from 1776 and 1777 on the New York art market in 1997.[20]

TECHNIQUE AND CONDITION

Hard-paste porcelain was produced at Sèvres from 1769, although experimentation with a new kiln and several different formulas for pastes and glazes continued through much of the 1770s.[21] It had many advantages over soft paste, including hardness and resistance to scratching and thermal shock, lower preparation costs for paste, shorter firing times, and more economical use of gold. Tea kettles, previously made of metal, could now be made of porcelain, as they could withstand very hot water and perhaps even direct contact with a flame.[22]

The lid of the Museum's tea kettle may be a replacement, as the pink of the roses and the color of the leaves differ from those on the body.[23] The handle has twisted and loosened at the junctures with the kettle. The mark must have originally been painted in gold.

Exhibition: *Morgan Loan Exhibition*, New York, 1914, not in catalogue

Literature: Munger, "Bouillotte," pp. 103–4 n. 2h

NOTES

1 See Peters, *Marks*, p. 75. The mark may refer to the zodiac sign for Leo, referring to the senior member of the Weydinger family, Léopold *père* (active 1757–1806).

2 Mark of Charles Godin, active 1769/70–1800/16/17. He was a *répareur* of soft paste until 1774, and then of hard paste. See *Royal Collection*, pp. 36–37, no. 21, and then Savill, 3, p. 1105.

3 See AMNS, Vj'1, fol. 46v, 30 April 1780, Buteux *jeune*, *1 Bouillotte forme chine fond jaune guirlande groupes et rubans vu*; fol. 357, 3 May 1780, L'Écot, *1 Bouillotte forme chine fond rouge frize chinois et graté vu*. The term is used again in subsequent workers' and kiln records, including biscuit kiln records for 2 September 1785 when six of the second size were fired (ibid., Vc'3) and on 3 October 1785 when twenty-seven of the second size were fired (ibid.). There was also mention of a *bouillotte nouvelle* in the piece-work records for 1780 (ibid., F.22, April, Schrade), but to what this referred there is no evidence. Perhaps it was the gadrooned version described below (see note 11).

4 AMNS, Vj'1, fol. 332, 3 May 1780. The adjective *chinoise* is here used to describe the model and not the decoration. In many other instances, however, *chinois* clearly describes the decoration, as in an entry against L'Écot on 14 January 1780: *1 Bouillotte fond noir chinois et dore vu* (Vj'1, fol. 356v).

5 See Sotheby's, London, 21 April 1998, lot 42, entry compiled with the assistance of David Peters. See also Dawson, *British Museum*, pp. 144–45, no. 122.

6 Sizes are approximately: first size: H. 11¼ in. (28.5 cm); second size: H. 7⅛–7⅞ in. (18–20 cm) (with handle), H. 5⅛ in. (13 cm) (without handle). See below for extant examples. For records, see AMNS, V'l, fol. 182v, 6 November 1781, enamel kiln: *2 Bouillottes chine 1e et 2e Lapis Dieu*; Vl'2, fol. 3, 28 January 1782, *1 Bouillotte chine 2e Barbeaux Lebel Prevost*; fol. 3v, 28 January 1782, *1 Bouillotte chine 1e Petites roses LeBel L'Écot*.

7 *Bouillottes* continued to be made after 1785. There are also *bouillottes anglaises* listed in the kiln records, which probably were a different shape. The sales records do not distinguish the various models.

8 Sales records list *bouillottes* priced at 36, 60, 72, 96, 120, 144, 192, 216, 240, 288, 312, and 360 *livres*. None are described enabling a breakdown of price per type of decoration or size.

9 One, such as on the Museum's kettle, was made with the sides in the form of a lyre with a rosette at the top, while the other had sides decorated with bellflowers and acanthus-leaf pivots and terminals. For the former, see the example in the MFA, Boston, and the latter, see Sotheby's, London, 21 April 1998, lot 42. Records indicate that the factory sold the kettles with their mounts in almost every instance. On 21 January 1783 (AMNS, Vy 8, fol. 269), a *beau bleu* example without mounts was sold to Bertrand, consul to Trieste, for 42 *livres*.

10 Inscribed *Bouillotte* on front and *Porcelaine De Sèvres/ P. F. N13 / N.38* on reverse. See AMNS, R. 2, dossier Duplessis.

11 Photograph at the AMNS. Another, with gilding, is in a Paris private collection (Munger, "Bouillotte," p. 103 n. 2g).

12 MMA, New York, formerly in the Puiforcat collection (Dennis, 1, no. 268, cited in Munger, "Bouillotte," p. 104 n. 9). See also Brault-Lerch, pl. XIX, or Nocq, *Orfèvrerie*, pl. LVIII, or Réau, *Louis XVI*, fig. 213 (Dawson, *British Museum*, p. 145 n. 14).

13 See AMNS, Vl'1, fols. 32 (16 November 1778), 90v (24 January 1780), 148 (4 February 1781), Vl'2, fol. 5v (26 February 1782), 6 (26 February 1782), 8 (25 March 1782), 37v (21 November 1782), 77 (10 November 1783); F.27 (August 1785), overtime record for Le Guay, and Vj'1, fol. 225 (12 July 1780), 119v, 9 November 1778, 169v (21 October 1780), 279v (13 October 1787), Vl'1, fol. 182v (6 November 1781), and Vj'2, fol. 15 (30 August 1787). Twice something called *fond nouveau* appears, once in the kiln records (Vl'1, fol. 162, 28 May 1781), and once in the painters' records (Vj'1, fol. 356, 20 April 1779, L'Écot). This color may be what was later called *chatoyant* (see Préaud, "Vocabulaire," pp. 122–23).

14 See AMNS, Vj'1, fol. 119 (25 May 1778), Dieu, *2 Bouillottes chinois 72/ 144*; fol. 356v (14 January 1780), L'Écot, *1 Bouillotte fond noir Chinois et dore*. See Peters, *Marks*, pp. 29, 47.

15 In December 1778 three were sold to Versailles (Vy 7, fol. 65, 24 December 1778; fol. 67, 25 December 1778 and fol. 69v, 26 December 1778) each for 360 *livres*. These probably correspond to two of four decorated by Dieu in that year (Vj'1, fol. 119, 25 May 1778, *2 Bouillottes Chinois vu 72 144*, and fol. 119v, 9 November 1778, *2 Bouillottes, une brune l'autre couleur de Bellevue chinois 1 vu 42 1 vu 60*). See also Vl'1, fol. 32, 16 November 1778, *1 Bouillotte fond brun Chinois Dieu*. Those on gold, black, or lacquer grounds probably cost the full 360 *livres* while others on white ground may have cost slightly less, between 240 and 312 *livres*.

16 See Huth, no. 336, in the collection of Colonial Williamsburg.

17 White ground, chinoiserie decoration, 1778, Dieu, H. 11¼ (28.5 cm), David Collection, Copenhagen (Eriksen, *David Collection*, p. 73, no. 62, formerly sold Drouot, Paris, 24 April 1972, lot 82); *café au lait* ground, chinoiserie decoration, 1778, Dieu, H. 5⅛ in. (13 cm) (without handle), MNC, Sèvres, no. 23260 (Brunet and Préaud, pl. XLIX); aventurine ground, chinoiserie decoration, 1778, Dieu, H. 7 3/16 in. (18.3 cm), British Museum, no. Franks 385 (Dawson, *British Museum*, pp. 144–45, no. 122); white ground, chinoiserie decoration, no date, H. (without handle) 5⅛ in. (13 cm), sold Drouot, Paris, 24 April 1972, lot 82; salmon ground, chinoiserie decoration, 1779, no painter's mark but probably Dieu or L'Écot, H. (with handle) 7⅛ in. (18 cm), H. (without handle) 5⅛ in. (13 cm), private collection, USA (see advertisement for N. Ikodinovic & Co., S.C., in *International Ceramics Fair and Seminar Ltd., London, Handbook*, June 1990, p. 65); white ground, birds in landscapes, 1779, Castel and Vincent, H. 7⅛ in. (18 cm), MFA, Boston, no. 1975.658; gold ground, *groupes* [flowers], 1779, Parpette, H. 7⅛ in. (18 cm), Dalva Brothers, New York, formerly in the Hector Binney collection (Sotheby's, London, 5 December 1989, lot 146); "wine red" ground (*lacqué*?), flowers, 1782, Bulidon, no dimensions (Sotheby's, Geneva, 14 November 1989, lot 3, not illustrated); brown ground, Etruscan figures, c. 1784, probably Asselin, H. 7⅞ in. (20 cm) (Sotheby's, London, 21 April 1998, lot 42, today at the Art Institute of Chicago).

18 AMNS, Vl'1, fols. 136v (10 December 1780), Sinneson [Sinnson] and Vindiger [Weydinger]; 140v (20 December 1780), Sinneson and Vindiger. See Peters, *Marks*, p. 67, and note 1 above.

19 AMNS, Vl'1, fol. 35 (8 December 1778), LeBel and Vincent; and Vl'2, fol. 3v (28 January 1782), Le Bel and L'Écot. See Peters, *Marks*, pp. 46, 59.

20 Sotheby's, New York, 1 November 1997, lot 224. These were painted by Jean-Jacques Pierre *jeune*, who also excelled in this type of decoration. David Peters believes that he may have been responsible for the painting on the Museum's kettle.

21 For the newest and most thorough discussion of the advent of hard paste at Sèvres see d'Albis, "Hard-paste," passim. Munger ("Bouillotte," p. 105) notes there is uncertainty regarding how the water was heated or kept warm.

22 D'Albis, "Hard-paste," pp. 42–43, 45.

23 The leaves on the kettle itself are painted in two different greens, one a blue-green and the other a more yellow-green.

98

Tea service with tray, sugar bowl, milk jug, and cup and saucer (*plateau tiroir à jour, pot à sucre Bouret, pot à lait à trois pieds, gobelet Bouillard et soucoupe*)

1917.1066–1069

Sèvres, 1770

Soft-paste porcelain, tray: H. 1⅛ × L. 9¾ × W. 6 13/16 in. (2.8 × 24.7 × 17.3 cm); sugar bowl: H. 3⅞ × DIAM. 3 3/16 in. (9.8 × 8 cm); milk jug: H. 4 × W. 4 3/16 × D. 2 15/16 in. (10.1 × 10.6 × 7.4 cm); cup: H. 2 7/16 × W. 3⅝ × D. 2¾ in. (6.1 × 9.2 × 7 cm); saucer: H. 1⅜ × DIAM. 5 5/16 in. (3.4 × 13.4 cm)

Bleu céleste ground with *pointillé* pattern, cherubs in *grisaille*, green laurel trails, gilding

Marks: on tray, sugar bowl, cup and saucer: interlaced Ls in blue with date letter R, painter's mark of five dots for Jacques Fontaine;[1] interlaced Ls in blue on foot of milk jug; incised scrolling J.f on tray;[2] I or T on sugar bowl;[3] illegible incised mark on cup; rectangle containing a cross on saucer[4]

Provenance: J. Pierpont Morgan

Model

The tray is a version of the *plateau tiroir* that had been introduced at the factory in 1756.[5] In January 1759 molds and models for a variation with pierced sides were listed in the factory inventory.[6] Known examples date from 1757.[7] Like the version with plain sides, the *plateau tiroir à jour* was made in two sizes.[8] The Museum's tray is of the first size.

The rim of the tray takes the form of a Vitruvian scroll—an ancient decorative form of continuous wave-like scrolls based on architectural motifs found in the work of the Roman architect Vitruvius. This scroll was one of many classical motifs revived in the eighteenth century, and its appearance on this model of tray in 1757 has been noted as the earliest sign of the classical revival at Sèvres.[9] It is believed that when Étienne-Maurice Falconet was made head of the factory's sculpture studio in that year, he introduced such classical motifs to the decorative repertory.[10]

The sugar bowl, known as a *pot à sucre Bouret*, was made in three sizes and dates from 1753.[11] The example in the Atheneum's tea service is of the second size. A plaster model was listed in the 1814 factory inventory,[12] and a drawing of the bowl and cover, without a knob, still survives at Sèvres.[13] This type of sugar bowl was used in a variety of tea sets, and was still being made in the 1780s.[14]

The three-footed milk jug was called *pot à lait à trois pieds*,[15] and the cup and saucer probably a *gobelet Bouillard et soucoupe*.[16] It is unusual for this tea set to have been supplied with a milk jug instead of a teapot.[17]

98

COMMENTARY

The decorative scheme on this tea set was in vogue for both table and tea wares in the early 1770s. By 1769 *pointillé* grounds had come into general use in a variety of hues: pale blue or turquoise, green, rose, mauve, or yellow.[18] Artists such as Taillandier and Fontaine combined them with small reserves of trophies,[19] flower baskets,[20] and often—as here—putti in *grisaille*. Not only did Fontaine decorate the Atheneum's tea set in this manner, he also repeated the scheme on a *déjeuner Hebert* now in the Musée national de Céramique, Sèvres,[21] as well as on a *gobelet Bouillard* now in the J. Paul Getty Museum.[22]

The decoration of this tea set clearly reflects the Sèvres factory's full adoption of the neoclassical style by 1770. Note especially the featured monochrome putti in imitation of marble reliefs, and the oak garlands with berries and simple gilded borders that surround the reserves.

By 1770 the factory sales records seldom qualify tea sets by name, so that this *déjeuner à tiroir* could have been among many unnamed *déjeuners* sold at the time. We do know, however, that in 1772 Louis XV bought a *déjeuner à tiroir* described as first size, *fond Taillandier* for 240 *livres*.[23] This may refer either to the Hartford set or to one very similar. Perhaps a cup and saucer in the collection of Dalva Brothers, New York, were originally part of the Museum's set.[24]

TECHNIQUE AND CONDITION

The *pointillé* ground pattern on the Hartford tea service is distinguished by small white circles outlined with darker dots, applied on a pale ground. This design is often confused with another ground pattern, *fond Taillandier*, which consists of an overglaze ground covered with small circles of gilded dots, punctuated with white circles containing colored dots and edged with gilding.[25] This confusion is not limited to later scholarship, but also occurred during the eighteenth century at the Sèvres factory.

In this tea set the *bleu céleste* is slightly uneven, with a certain amount of bubbling, suggesting that the color had been thinly sieved on in powder form. The pattern of white circles on the *bleu céleste* ground may have been created by a resist method. This involved systematically placing dots of wax or some other sticky substance where the white circles were to be and then powdering the rest with the turquoise pigment. After firing, the blue enamel dots that surround the circles were added.[26]

Part of the pierced edge of the tray has been damaged and restored with plaster of Paris.[27]

Exhibitions: *Morgan Loan Exhibition*, New York, 1914, not in catalogue; *Morgan*, Hartford, 1987, no. 72

Literature: Chavagnac, pp. 113–14, no. 140; Buckley, *Connoisseur*, pp. 52–53; Hood, *Connoisseur*, pp. 7–8 (not illustrated); de Bellaigue, "Sèvres," p. 185, no. 72

NOTES

1 Active at Sèvres 1752–1800 (see Savill, 3, pp. 1033–34). In the later 1760s Fontaine specialized in painting putti, trophies, and classical heads in *grisaille*, often in small reserves surrounded by laurel garlands on *pointillé* grounds. Fontaine also worked as a gilder and burnisher.

2 Unidentified. This mark does not appear in Savill. Dauterman, *Marks* (p. 207) includes several J.f marks but none drawn in the same manner as on the Museum's tray.

3 Savill, 3, p. 1108, sometimes read as I, H, or T.

4 Savill, 3, p. 1136, found on soft paste 1756–76.

5 See cat. no. 81 for the simple version of this model.

6 AMNS, I. 7, 1 January 1759 (for 1758), *moules* and *modèles en plâtre*.

7 See Dawson, *British Museum*, pp. 101–2, no. 91.

8 Extant examples indicate that the first size ranged from 9⁹⁄₁₆ to 9¾ in. (24.2–25 cm) long, while the second size ranged from 7 to 7½ in. (17.8–19 cm).

9 Eriksen, *Neo-classicism*, p. 368, pl. 268.

10 Ibid.

11 For this shape see Savill, 2, pp. 570–74. She suggests the sizes were: first size: H. 4¼–4¹³⁄₁₆ in. (10.8–12.2 cm); second size: H. 3⁹⁄₁₆–3¹⁵⁄₁₆ in. (9–10 cm); third size: H. 3³⁄₁₆–3½ in. (8–8.8 cm).

12 Ibid, p. 570. See also Brunet, *Frick*, pp. 214, 217 n. 2.

13 AMNS, R. 1, L. 2, d. 8, fol. 2. It is inscribed *boete à sucre Bouret no 1 fait suivan L'ordre de La Comande de 19 fevrÿe 1753* and *fait*. See Savill, 2, p. 570; Eriksen (*Waddesdon*, p. 62, no. 14) identified this shape based on the drawing. Another drawing from 1753 shows a very similar sugar bowl, with slightly more curved sides, and is inscribed *Sucrÿe pour La theÿere Verdun 2me grandeur suivan La Comande ordone Le 19 fevrÿe 1753* (AMNS, R. 1, L. 2, d. 8, fol. 2, illustrated in Savill, 2, p. 570).

14 Savill, 2, p. 570.

15 See cat. no. 87.

16 See cat. no. 84. It could also have been called a *gobelet Bouret*.

17 De Bellaigue, "Sèvres," p. 185, no. 72.

18 Savill, 2, pp. 612, 1176.

19 See a covered cup and saucer, MFA, Boston (Munger, *Wickes*, p. 198, no. 145).

20 See a *déjeuner losange* in the Wallace Collection, London, nos. C396–400, in Savill, 2, p. 611.

21 MNC, Sèvres, nos. 23.263,1,2,3.

22 Sassoon, pp. 102–5, no. 20.

23 AMNS, Vy 5, fol. 42, December 1772. See de Bellaigue, "Sèvres," p. 185, no. 72.

24 Same date and painter, information kindly shared by Leon Dalva.

25 See Savill, 3, pp. 1175–76.

26 For an example in an unfinished state, with the ground color applied and the white circles undecorated, see a *théière Calabre* at MNC, Sèvres, 1765, no. 26296, illustrated in MNC, *Nouvelles acquisitions 1979–1989*, p. 159, no. 223.

27 Detailed treatment report from 1987 in Museum file.

99

Partial, compiled tea set with tray, sugar bowl, milk jug, and cup and saucer (*plateau losange, pot à sucre Bouret, pot à lait à trois pieds*, and *gobelet Bouillard* and *soucoupe*)

1917.1078–1081

Sèvres, 1773, 1775, 1779

Soft-paste porcelain, tray: H. 2½ × L. 14⁹⁄₁₆ × W. 10¹³⁄₁₆ in. (6.4 × 37 × 27.4 cm); sugar bowl: H. 3¹⁵⁄₁₆ × DIAM. 3¼ in. (10 × 8.3 cm); milk jug: H. 4 × W. 4⅛ × D. 2¹⁵⁄₁₆ in. (10.2 × 10.5 × 7.4 cm); cup: H. 2⁷⁄₁₆ × W. 3⅝ × D. 2¹³⁄₁₆ in. (6.2 × 9.2 × 7.1 cm); saucer: H. 1³⁄₁₆ × DIAM. 5¹⁄₁₆ in. (3 × 12.8 cm)

White ground with purple and gold diaper pattern over a pale blue enamel field, polychrome roses and garlands, pink and blue enamel on pierced sides, gilding

Marks: tray: interlaced Ls in blue with date letter u, comma above for Charles-Louis Méreaud *jeune*;[1] dot in blue; incised IP,[2] scrolling j;[3] sugar bowl: interlaced Ls in blue with date letter u, comma above; S in rose for Pierre-Antoine Méreaud *aîné, père*;[4] milk jug: interlaced Ls in blue with date letter u, dot in blue; cup: interlaced Ls in blue with date letters bb, comma above; incised 36d (or possibly 36a),[5] and 17;[6] saucer: interlaced Ls in blue with date letter x, comma above, script B for Jean-Pierre Boulanger *père* in rose below;[7] incised script ml[8]

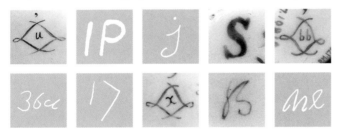

Provenance: Cartier et Fils, Paris, 1903;[9] J. Pierpont Morgan

MODEL

The tray, called *plateau losange* by the factory, first appeared in 1756.[10] The sugar bowl was called *pot à sucre Bouret*, and probably is of the second size.[11] The milk jug is a *pot à lait à trois pieds*, also of the second size.[12] The cup and saucer are probably a *gobelet Bouillard* and *soucoupe* of the first size.[13]

COMMENTARY

As indicated by their varying dates, the components of this tea set were assembled sometime after their manufacture, probably in the nineteenth century. Differences in date and in the gilded foliate design tell us that even the cup and saucer do not match each other.

The decoration of these pieces was probably described as *mosaïque et fleurs*. Other examples decorated with this pattern are a *gobelet litron* sold at Christie's, London, in 1986, and a cup and saucer in the Musée des Arts décoratifs, Paris.[14] The design is reminiscent of French textiles of the 1760s and 1770s, particularly silks, which were characterized by floral motifs encased in meandering ribbons set against plain or patterned backgrounds.[15]

The Museum's cup probably is en suite with the cup in the Musée des Arts décoratifs, Paris, also dated 1779. In the records of the painting kiln for that year, it is noted that Méreaud *jeune* decorated two *gobelets Bouillard mozaïque et fleurs*.[16] Perhaps this refers to the Hartford and Paris examples.

TECHNIQUE AND CONDITION

The sugar bowl has some pitting in the glaze on the lower portion of the bowl. The cover, which has a different gilded foliate border, either is a later replacement from the factory, a married piece from a later sugar bowl, or else was decorated to match in the nineteenth century.[17] The ground color that underlies the diaper pattern throughout the set was not sieved on as were many Sèvres ground colors, but rather was applied as a thin wash of color.[18] The roses have been heightened with white (*blanc à rehausser*). The set should have a teapot as well.

Exhibition: *Morgan Loan Exhibition*, New York, 1914, not in catalogue

Literature: Chavagnac, pp. 119–20, no. 149; Savill, 2, pp. 567; 572

NOTES

1 Active 1756–80. See Peters, *Marks*, p. 52; Savill, 3, pp. 1047–48.

2 See Savill, 3, p. 1110, for soft-paste worker, known 1757–78.

3 Ibid., for soft-paste worker known 1753–73.

4 Active 1754–91. See Peters, *Marks*, p. 52. See also Préaud and d'Albis, p. 211.

5 See Savill, 3, p. 1130 for the mark 36, which is found on soft paste 1758, 1770–90s. While Savill notes the combination of the number 36 with the letters a and c, she does not document it with the letter d.

6 Not in Savill or Dauterman. See the *seau à verre* from a service for Marie-Antoinette now in the Ashmolean Museum, Oxford, in Dawson, *Ashmolean*, pp. 70–71. This service is dated 1784.

7 Active 1754–85 as both a gilder and painter. See Peters, *Marks*, p. 16; Savill, 3, pp. 1004–5.

8 Savill, 3, p. 1115, found on soft paste 1755–63, c. 1775–82. She states that the mark possibly is that of Millot *jeune* (active 1751, 1755–71, or 1755–65, 1767–72), and then Montlouis Lauvergnat (active 1772–78/79).

9 APML, Cartier file, invoice for 3 June, 1903: "1 Plateau Vieux Sèvres ajouré forme losange, décor quadrillé boutons de roses sur fond blanc; 1 sucrier, 1 cremier, 1 tasse avec sa soucoupe assortis au plateau losange ci-dessus," 13,000 French francs.

10 See cat. no. 92 for this shape.

11 See cat. no. 98 for this shape.

12 See cat. no. 87 for this shape.

13 See cat. no. 84 for this shape.

14 Christie's, London, 30 June 1986, lot 206 (as possibly by Thévenet, but, in fact, the same cup and saucer sold by Sotheby's, London, 17 June 1969, lot 248, as by Méreaud, 1773); MAD, Paris, no. D10716, Méreaud, dated bb for 1779, incised 36a.

15 See for example, Devoti, no. 175 (Paris, MAD); and Tuchscherer and Sano, 1, nos. 197, 171.

16 AMNS, Vl'1, fol. 75v, 25 October 1779.

17 Antoine d'Albis suggests the lid might be a genuine factory replacement or marriage from a different sugar bowl, but Bernard Dragesco believes it to be a redecorated lid. The gold foliate border is thinner (in design) than the other pieces but the gilding itself is more thickly built up and has pitted. The floral painting and ground appear genuine to this author.

18 As per Bernard Dragesco.

99

100

Cup and saucer (*gobelet litron et soucoupe*)

1917.1157

Sèvres, 1767

Soft-paste porcelain, cup: H. 2¾ × W. 3⅝ × D. 2¾ in. (6.9 × 9.2 × 6.9 cm); saucer: H. 1⅜ × DIAM. 5⅝ in. (3.5 × 14.2 cm)

White ground with bands of stippled blue enamel, polychrome garlands and flowers, gilding

Marks: cup: interlaced Ls in blue with date letter o, x underneath for Jacques-François Micaud *père*;[1] saucer: same factory and date mark, incised 8[2]

Provenance: J. Pierpont Morgan

MODEL

This is the second largest size of *gobelet litron et soucoupe*.[3] The cup has an ear-shaped scroll handle commonly found on cups of the first through fourth sizes. Second-size cups could also have an indented scroll handle.[4] It is unlikely that this cup and saucer would have been part of a tea set for usually *déjeuners* included third-size cups and saucers.[5] Instead, they probably would have been sold separately.

COMMENTARY

The decoration of this cup and saucer, with its emphasis on linear and floral patterns, bears a strong resemblance to textile designs in vogue in the 1760s. In many cases, the roses that overlaid the vertical stripes were encircled with gilded or painted foliage, such as on a tea set also in the Atheneum's collection.[6] In the present example the roses float freely. The white porcelain is also allowed to become an integral part of the design, as will occur more and more in the next decade.[7] The artist has cleverly masked a firing flaw inside the saucer with a wispy foliate spray.

This type of decorative pattern can be found on many other pieces of Sèvres from the same period, including a small cup and saucer, also by Micaud, in the Sterling and Francine Clark Art Institute in Williamstown.[8]

TECHNIQUE AND CONDITION

No ground color has been applied to this cup and saucer. The pale blue bands that serve as background for the roses were created by stippling blue enamel on the white ground. The roses have been heightened with white made from tin oxide (*blanc à rehausser*), to create variations in the tones.

Exhibition: *Morgan Loan Exhibition*, New York, 1914, not in catalogue

Literature: Chavagnac, p. 105, no. 128[9]

NOTES

1 Active 1757–1810. See Peters, *Marks*, p. 53; Savill, 3, pp. 1049–50. See cat. no. 91 for more on this artist and the distinction between his mark and that of Xhrouuet.

101

2 Savill, 3, p. 1128, found on soft paste 1754–58, 1767–82.

3 See cat. no. 95 for more on this shape. See also Savill, 2, pp. 501–26.

4 Ibid., p. 501 for handles. The Museum's cup has Savill's handle B.

5 Ibid.

6 See cat. no. 93. The relationship between Sèvres decoration and textiles is discussed further in this entry, although much work needs to be done on the subject.

7 See cat. no. 137.

8 Dated 1767, no. 1083. I should like to thank Beth Carver Wees for supplying me with a photograph of this piece.

9 As by Xhrouuet.

101

Cup and saucer (*gobelet litron et soucoupe*)

1917.1062

Sèvres, 1769, with possible later decoration

Soft-paste porcelain, cup: H. 3 1/16 × W. 3 15/16 × D. 2 15/16 in. (7.7 × 9.9 × 7.4 cm); saucer: H. 1 7/16 × DIAM. 5 15/16 in. (3.7 × 15.1 cm)

Yellow ground with roundels of pink roses, gilded garlands

Marks: both: interlaced Ls in blue with date letter q, ... for Jean-Baptiste Tandart *aîné*;[1] cup: incised Jp; inscribed in brown paint f[e?]mos 8946/ [e?]f[e?]ai; saucer: incised +

Provenance: perhaps Edouard Chappey, Paris, 1905;[2] J. Pierpont Morgan

MODEL

The cup was called a *gobelet litron*.[3] It is the largest or first size of this type. The saucer with its deep sloping sides is also the largest size. The scroll handle with molding is frequently found on this form.[4]

COMMENTARY

The decoration of this cup and saucer was described in various ways at the factory, such as *roses encadrées d'or* [roses encircled with gold] or *roses détachées* [free-floating roses]. In overtime payments for 1769, Tandart was paid four *livres* each for decorating five *gobelets litron et soucoupes* of the first size with *roses détachées*.[5] While the reference is not specific enough to link with the Museum's cup and saucer, it probably refers to this type of object and decoration.[6]

TECHNIQUE AND CONDITION

Significant bubbling and black spotting underneath the saucer may indicate refiring. The enamels of both the cup and saucer are well painted and genuine. It is possible although not certain that the saucer was regilt.[7] The inside of the saucer is rather worn. The yellow is of an egg-yolk tone.

Exhibition: *Morgan Loan Exhibition*, New York, 1914, not in catalogue

Literature: Chavagnac, p. 111, no. 136

102

NOTES

1 Active 1754–1800, primarily as a flower painter. See Savill, 3, pp. 1070–71, and Peters, *Marks*, p. 69.

2 APML, Chappey file, invoice 26 June 1905: "1 Tasse en ancienne porcelaine de Sèvres pâte tendre à fond jaune décorée de roses dans médaillons blanc entourés de feuillages or Année 1770," 9,900 French francs.

3 See cat. no. 95 for this shape. The handle conforms to Savill's shape C (2, p. 501).

4 Savill, 2, p. 501.

5 AMNS, F.11, 1769; at the same time, he was paid 3 *livres* each for painting the same decoration on two *gobelets litron* of the second size.

6 For more on this type of decoration see cat. no. 93.

7 As per comments by Antoine d'Albis and David Peters.

102

Two cups and saucers (*gobelets litron et soucoupes*)

1917.1167–1168

Sèvres, 1769

Soft-paste porcelain, 1917.1167: cup: H. 2¾ × W. 3⅝ × D. 2¾ in. (7 × 9.2 × 7 cm); saucer: H. 1⁹⁄₁₆ × DIAM. 5½ in. (3.9 × 14 cm); 1917.1168: cup: H. 2¾ × W. 3⁹⁄₁₆ × D. 2¹¹⁄₁₆ in. (6.9 × 9.1 × 6.8 cm); saucer: H. 1⁷⁄₁₆ × DIAM. 5¾ in. (3.7 × 14.6 cm)

Bleu céleste pointillé ground, brown roundels with white cameos, *grisaille* trophies, pink ribbons, gilding

Marks: 1917.1167: cup: no painted marks; incised qi;[1] saucer: small blue interlaced Ls; incised qi; 1917.1168: cup: in blue, interlaced Ls with date letter q, m above for Jean-Louis Morin;[2] incised 3; saucer: same painted marks; incised qi

Provenance: J. Pierpont Morgan[3]

MODEL

These two cups are of the *litron* shape, corresponding to the second size.[4] The saucer for one of the cups (1917.1167) is of the first size.[5]

COMMENTARY

The marked cup and saucer were painted by Jean-Louis Morin, who in the overtime records for 1769 was paid 1 *livre* 10 *sols* each for painting 181 medallions on different pieces.[6] These medallions probably contained just the type of *grisaille* head on a brown background that Morin used here. This motif was meant to look like an antique cameo, and was combined with *pointillé* grounds and gilded laurel garlands, especially in 1769.[7]

The second cup and saucer, without any painter's marks, are also painted with cameos and garlands suspended from pink bows on *pointillé* ground, but differ from the Morin examples in details. The cameos are larger, especially on the cup, changing the proportion of decoration to ground. The gilding pattern of oak-leaf garlands is the same, but the tooling is not. On the Morin cup and saucer the bands around the reserves are all tooled in the same manner, that is, with three invected lines interrupted at quarter turns with crisscrossed ribbons. The unmarked cup and saucer, on the other hand, are more elaborately tooled, with the bands around each reserve receiving different treatment. These include alternating crescents, beading, ribbons, lozenges, and wavy lines.

Other examples of this combination of *pointillé* ground with cameo medallions and *grisaille* trophies may be found in the Wallace Collection,[8] the Victoria and Albert Museum,[9] and the Walters Art Gallery, Baltimore.[10] A two-handled cup and saucer attributed to Morin was sold in New York in 1997.[11]

Exhibition: *Morgan Loan Exhibition*, New York, 1914, not in catalogue

NOTES

1 See Dauterman, *Marks*, p. 230, citing two saucers from 1769, one in the V&A, London, and one in the Sterling and Francine Clark Art Institute, Williamstown, Massachusetts.

2 Active 1754–87. See Savill, 3, pp. 1051–52; Peters, *Marks*, p. 54. For more on this artist see cat. no. 160.

3 Since these cups and saucers are not in Chavagnac, we may suppose that they were purchased after 1910, the date of that publication. An invoice of 24 April 1902 from Cartier et Fils, Paris (APML, Cartier file) lists "1 Ecrin Contenant 2 Tasses & Soucoupes en Sèvres 1768 décor œil de perdrix & medaillons camées fond bleu Swednoise," 3,500 French francs, which seems to describe the Museum's cups and saucers. They are said to date from 1768, a year earlier, however, and, based on the invoice date, one would expect them to appear in Chavagnac. Thus it is unclear to which objects the Cartier entry refers.

4 See cat. no. 95 for this shape, and Savill, 2, pp. 501–26. These examples have Savill's handle B.

5 For examples of mismatched sizes, see Savill, 2, p. 501.

6 AMNS, F.30. See also Savill, 3, p. 1051.

7 Savill, 3, p. 1051.

8 *Gobelet Bouillard*, 1769, no. C359 (Savill, 2, pp. 529–31); *théière Calabre*, 1769, no. C381 (ibid., pp. 581–83).

9 *Gobelet Calabre*, 1769, no. 1981-1855.

10 *Gobelet litron*, 1769, no. 48 686.

11 Christie's, New York, 21 October 1997, lot 224.

103

Cup and saucer (*tasse à thé et soucoupe*)

1917.1160

Sèvres, perhaps 1775 or 18th-century paste with 19th-century decoration

Soft-paste porcelain, cup: H. 1¹⁵⁄₁₆ × W. 3¾ × D. 3⅛ in. (4.9 × 9.5 × 7.9 cm); saucer: H. 1³⁄₁₆ × DIAM. 4¹¹⁄₁₆ in. (3 × 11.9 cm)

Yellow ground, polychrome reserves, gilded scrolls and ciphers

Marks: on both, interlaced Ls in blue and date letter x; scrolling B for Jean-Pierre Boulanger;[1] four dots below on cup; five dots below on saucer, meant to be Jacques Fontaine;[2] incised o on saucer[3]

Provenance: J. Pierpont Morgan

MODEL

This cup and saucer was called a *tasse à thé* at the Sèvres factory, and as the name implies, was specifically meant for drinking tea. These teacups appear to have been made in only one size, and were first mentioned in the factory records in 1773.[4]

COMMENTARY

The Museum's cup and saucer are difficult to date. They are meant to be part of a tea set sold to the prince de Deux Ponts along with a *plateau Courteille*, *théière Calabre*, *pot à sucre Bouret*,

pot à lait à trois pieds, two other teacups, and a *boîte à thé* in June 1775.[5] It was in fact one of four identically composed tea services that he bought at the same time, each one a different color.[6] The pink ground set is now at the Victoria and Albert Museum.[7] The yellow ground set, without any cups and saucers, was sold in 1979.[8] Both the pink and yellow sets are decorated with the cipher PN.

There are several problems with the Museum's cup and saucer, suggesting that some or all of the set may have been decorated later to match the tea service. The cup is painted with reserves of putti in landscapes, as are most other pieces in the service, but the mark underneath seems to be a misinterpretation of Fontaine's mark and the painting is crude for this artist. The gilding is worn, but there is no obvious evidence of redecoration or refiring.

The saucer is decorated with landscapes, as is the saucer at the Victoria and Albert Museum, but bears the mark used by Fontaine rather than that of a landscape painter.[9] The surface is extremely matte and the gilding crude and worn. In the center of the saucer there are traces of a *patera* or wreath design. This design can be found gilded on the London saucer but in different proportion to the rest of the gilding. Moreover, the tooling of the gilding on the Hartford saucer seems to be trying to match that on the cup but falls short in the feathering.

The cup and saucer present something of a challenge for there is not enough evidence to dismiss them entirely. Their inconsistencies lead one to ask whether the saucer is a replacement for a broken original, or whether both pieces are replacements. If so, then the quandary for scholars is attempting to decide if the replacement piece(s) had been made deliberately to deceive. The quality of workmanship leaves much to be desired and yet both cup and saucer were marked in such a way that they might be passed off as being the work of Fontaine. We do know that when Morgan bought them he believed them to be genuine.

Exhibition: *Morgan Loan Exhibition*, New York, 1914, not in catalogue

Literature: Chavagnac, p. 131, no. 164

NOTES

1 Active as gilder 1754–85. See Peters, *Marks*, p. 16.

2 Active as painter of figures and flowers, 1752–1800. See ibid., p. 34.

3 Found on soft paste 1754–82. See Savill, 3, p. 1117.

4 AMNS, Vy 5, fol. 71, 27 May 1773, to the prince de Conti. See Dawson, *British Museum*, p. 157.

5 AMNS, Vy 5, fol. 249, 14 June 1775. I would like to thank Rosalind Savill for this information.

6 Ibid., fol. 248v, in green, blue, and pink.

7 No. C.440-446-1921. See Dawson, *British Museum*, p. 157.

8 Christie's, London, 2 October 1979, lot 27. Both Geoffrey de Bellaigue and Rosalind Savill kindly pointed out this sale.

9 The saucer in the V&A, London has the mop-head mark attributed to Bouchet. See cat. no. 67.

104

Tea service with teapot, sugar bowl, two cups and saucers (*plateau à baguettes, théière Calabre, pot à sucre Bouret, gobelets litron et soucoupes*)

1917.1090–1094

Sèvres, 1776

Soft-paste porcelain, tray: H. 2⅜ × L. 15³⁄₁₆ × W. 10½ in. (6 × 38.6 × 26.7 cm); teapot: H. 4¼ × W. 5⅝ × D. 3⅛ in. (10.7 × 14.3 × 7.9 cm); sugar bowl: H. 3¹⁵⁄₁₆ × DIAM. 3⅛ in. (9.9 × 7.9 cm); 1917.1093: cup: H. 2⅜ × W. 3 × D. 2³⁄₁₆ in. (6 × 7.6 × 5.6 cm); saucer: H. 1¼ × DIAM. 4⅞ in. (3.1 × 12.4 cm); 1917.1094: cup: H. 2⁵⁄₁₆ × W. 2¹⁵⁄₁₆ × D. 2³⁄₁₆ in. (5.8 × 7.5 × 5.6 cm); saucer: H. 1⅜ × DIAM. 4¾ in. (3.4 × 12.1 cm)

White ground with polychrome floral garlands, gilded diaper, *patera*, scrolls, scallops, and border, light blue ribbons

Marks: tray: interlaced Ls in black with date letter y for 1776; zodiacal sign for Libra, also in black, for Guillaume Noël;[1] incised Tb or Th;[2] scrolling M;[3] BZ;[4] teapot: same factory, date, and painter's marks but in pink; sugar bowl: traces of mark in pink; 1917.1093: cup: same painted marks as teapot, incised pn,[5] incised cross potent;[6] saucer: interlaced Ls with date letter y in pink; 1917.1094: cup: same painted marks as teapot, incised c;[7] saucer: same painted marks as saucer 1917.1093

Provenance: Edouard Chappey, Paris, 1906;[8] J. Pierpont Morgan

MODEL

The tray was called *plateau à baguettes* in the eighteenth century.[9] The teapot is one of the smallest sizes of the *théière Calabre*, a shape introduced by 1752.[10] The sugar bowl or *pot à sucre Bouret* is also an early shape produced from 1753. It is of the second size.[11] The cups and saucers are third-size *gobelets litron et soucoupes*.[12]

COMMENTARY

The most striking aspect of this tea service's decoration is the primacy of gilding over enamel decoration or ground color. The painted flower garlands play a secondary role to the elaborate gilded diaper pattern, decorative scrolls, and feathered-scallop design. All of these elements play off against the white porcelain. Another *déjeuner à baguettes* decorated with a striped gilded pattern was on the art market in Geneva in 1989. It was catalogued as being hard paste and dating from about 1770.[13]

Exhibition: *Morgan Loan Exhibition*, New York, 1914, not in catalogue

Literature: Masson, pp. 2, 9; Chavagnac, p. 128, no. 161; Savill, 2, p. 524 n. 18; p. 584 n. 16

104

NOTES

1 Active 1755–1800, painter of flowers and patterns, gilder and burnisher. See Savill, 3, pp. 1053–54; Peters, *Marks*, p. 55.

2 Savill, 3, p. 1110 (Jb).

3 Ibid., p. 1114, found on soft paste 1754–88.

4 Dauterman, *Marks*, pp. 42, 183, identified as possibly the mark of Bizard, who was a *répareur* in soft paste 1771–97.

5 Savill, 3, p. 1118, found on soft paste c. 1750–53, 1761–62, 1784–86.

6 Ibid., p. 1135, found on soft paste 1759, 1770–78, 1788–89.

7 Ibid., p. 1092, found on soft paste 1748, by 1753–79.

8 Masson, pp. 2, 9; bought from Edouard Chappey, Paris, 30 April, 1906: "1 Tête à tête fond blanc décor guirlandes de fleurs quadrillés et rinceaux or, nœuds de rubans bleus décor de Guillaume Noel 1775 offert par le Roi à Mme Sophie," (perhaps together with 1917.1181–85, cat. no. 90) 40,000 French francs.

9 See cat. no. 96 for this shape.

10 See cat. no. 85 for this shape.

11 See cat. no. 98 for this shape.

12 See cat. no. 95 for this shape.

13 Sotheby's, Geneva, 14 November 1989, lot 1.

105

Tea service with tray, teapot, sugar bowl, milk jug, and cup and saucer (*soucoupe à pieds, théière Calabre, pot à sucre Bouret, pot à lait à trois pieds, gobelet litron et soucoupe*)

1917.1101–1105

Sèvres, 1780

Soft-paste porcelain, tray: H. 1⁷⁄₁₆ × DIAM. 8¹⁵⁄₁₆ in. (3.7 × 22.7 cm); teapot: H. 4¼ × W. 5⁵⁄₁₆ × D. 3¹⁄₁₆ in. (10.8 × 13.5 × 7.8 cm); sugar bowl: H. 4 × DIAM. 3¼ in. (10.2 × 8.2 cm); milk jug: H. 4 × W. 4⅛ × D. 2¹⁵⁄₁₆ in. (10.1 × 10.5 × 7.4 cm); cup: H. 2⁷⁄₁₆ × W. 3 × D. 2³⁄₁₆ in. (6.1 × 7.6 × 5.6 cm); saucer: H. 1¼ × DIAM. 4⅞ in. (3.1 × 12.4 cm)

White and yellow ground with polychrome flowers and garlands, puce diapers, gilding

Marks: on tray, teapot, milk jug (effaced) and cup and saucer: interlaced Ls in blue with date letters cc and painter's mark of script B.n. for Nicolas Bulidon;[1] on sugar bowl: 112/ 30/ 92 in mauve; incised 19 on tray;[2] incised 27 and 43a on teapot;[3] incised B and 4 on feet of milk jug;[4] incised 34a and 3 on cup;[5] incised 36a on saucer;[6] inside cover of sugar bowl: in brown enamel, afur, 8166, and |]laf[7]

Provenance: J. Pierpont Morgan

MODEL

This tea service is composed of a footed tray with twelve lobes called a *soucoupe à pieds*, a *théière Calabre* of the fourth size,[8] a *pot à sucre Bouret* of the second size,[9] a *pot à lait à trois pieds* of the second size,[10] and a third-size *gobelet litron et soucoupe*.[11]

The *soucoupe à pieds* was introduced in 1755, probably as part of Louis XV's *bleu céleste* service.[12] Initially it was called an *assiette à confitures*.[13] Four molds and one model for *assiettes à confitures avec un pied* are listed among new work for 1755 in the factory's inventory.[14] These early trays had molded gadrooned decoration culminating in interlaced acanthus bands at the interstices of each scallop. Of note is the fact that their rims flared out rather than turned upward as happened in slightly later examples. The David Collection, Copenhagen boasts a tray dated 1757–58 with flared out rim, perhaps from the service given to Maria-Theresa of Austria by Louis XV in 1758.[15]

It is likely that within the first year of production, the form was modified and the name changed to *soucoupe à pieds*, although at first both names may have been used to describe the original version of the model.[16] The factory's inventory for 1756 lists both *assiettes à confitures* and *soucoupes à pieds*, the former among pieces in the process of being glazed and fired, and the latter among pieces in the *magasin du blanc* and *magasin de ventes*.[17] Seven *assiettes à pieds* are also listed, among pieces needing to be glazed a second time.[18] We cannot tell if these two names were used interchangeably for the same model at this date or if the revised footed tray had already been introduced with the names reflecting the two different forms.

The only mention in the sales records for *assiettes à confitures* is under the entry for the Louis XV service in December 1755.[19] The first time *soucoupe à pieds* is mentioned is in December 1756, when the dealer Bazin bought a tray of this type decorated with flowers for 33 *livres*.[20] During that month sales of nine more trays were recorded, often paired with groups of six or seven ice-cream cups (*tasses à glace*).[21] There are also two entries that show the tray being used as the basis for tea sets. In the last half of 1756 Lazare Duvaux bought a *déjeuner à soucoupe* decorated with gold friezes for 132 *livres*, and a *soucoupe à pieds* with a cup and saucer, sugar bowl, and milk jug, all decorated with a *bleu céleste* ground and flowers.[22] Thirty-seven more trays were sold in 1757, thirteen in 1758, and nineteen in 1759. They usually were accompanied by ice-cream cups. No more tea sets with this tray appeared in those years.

Prices for *soucoupes à pieds* during the years 1756 to 1760 ranged from 27 to 120 *livres*. Trays with gold fillets usually cost 27 *livres*, those with flowers 33 *livres*, with garlands 48 *livres*, with mosaic decoration 60 *livres*, and with green or turquoise ground 120 *livres*.[23]

There are two versions of *soucoupes à pieds*. The first has a sharply scalloped shape, and the second a more undulating rim. It seems that the wavier version appeared later, probably replacing the earlier version.[24]

There are a number of extant examples of *soucoupes à pieds*, some with accompanying ice-cream cups and some with tea wares. Examples from several dessert services survive, such as

105

105

two with mosaic decoration from 1766 delivered to the vicomte de Choiseul;[25] four with *œil de perdrix* ground from about 1766 belonging to Prince Starhemberg's service;[26] four with *bleu céleste* ground and birds, 1766–67, from a service for Alexis or Cyril Razoumovski;[27] four *bleu céleste* examples with birds, 1772, from the prince de Rohan's service;[28] and three *beau bleu* examples with figures, 1791, from the Louis XVI service.[29]

COMMENTARY

The Museum's tea set was decorated by Nicolas Bulidon, and may have been the one listed under his name in work records for July 1780.[30] In November a tea set of the same description with decoration by Bulidon and Buteux was fired in the enamel kiln, and may also refer to the Museum's set.[31]

TECHNIQUE AND CONDITION

There is a fine pitting on the sugar bowl, teapot, and cup, but this does not seem to be the result of a later firing. The roses on the sugar bowl are somewhat orange, indicating that they were underfired, perhaps due to their placement in the kiln.

Exhibition: *Morgan Loan Exhibition*, New York, 1914, not in catalogue

Literature: Chavagnac, pp. 134–35, no. 169

NOTES

1 Active 1763–92. See Peters, *Marks*, p. 18. Savill, 3, pp. 1006–7 gives his dates as c. 1750–after 1817.

2 Not in Savill.

3 27 not in Savill, 43a found on soft paste 1765–69, 1779–90s (Savill, 3, p. 1132).

4 B found on soft paste 1754–88, perhaps 1790s, and on hard paste c. 1780–83, attributed tentatively to Nicolas Brachard *père*, active 1754–1800/9 (ibid., p. 1088–89); 4 found on soft paste 1753–87 (ibid., pp. 1126–27).

5 3 found on soft paste 1753–90s (ibid., pp. 1125–26); 34a not in Savill, although 34 is noted on soft paste, primarily plates, 1781–92 (ibid., p. 1129).

6 Found on soft paste 1758, 1770–90s (ibid., p. 1130).

7 Presumably these are the marks of a later collector.

8 See cat. no. 85 for this shape and for a discussion of the sizes, which are only tentatively designated.

9 See cat. no. 98 for this shape.

10 See cat. no. 87 for this shape.

11 See cat. no. 95 for this shape.

12 Savill, "Premier service," p. 283, no. 77, ill. p. 134.

13 Ibid. See AMNS, Vy 1, fols. 119v–20, 21 *assiettes à confitures* priced at 120 *livres* each.

14 AMNS, I. 7, 1 January 1756. The molds were valued at 2 *livres*, and the model at 3 *livres*.

15 Eriksen, *David Collection*, p. 68, no. 49. A profile photograph shows the rim clearly.

16 The entry in the sales ledger for the Maria-Theresa service lists *soucoupes à pieds* and not *assiettes à confitures* (see AMNS, Vy 2, fol. 85).

17 AMNS, I. 7, 1 January 1757, *Pièces en Biscuit pretes a estre mises en Couverte*, and *Pièces en couvertes prêtes à passer au feu*.

18 Ibid., *Pièces en Blanc qui doivan passer en Couverte*.

19 See note 13 above.

20 AMNS, Vy 2, fol. 5v, 21 December 1756.

21 Ibid., fols. 7, 8, 16, 16v, and 17.

22 Ibid., fol. 16v. The total cost of these components was 396 *livres*.

23 See for example, ibid., fol. 17, 20 August 1756–1 January 1757, Duvaux; fol. 29v, 1 January–1 July 1757, Duvaux; fol. 52v, 1 July 1757–1 January 1758, Duvaux; Vy 3, fol. 29v, April 1760, Elector of Palatine; and Vy 2, fol. 52v, 1 July 1757–1 January 1758, Duvaux.

24 See extant examples listed below, those dated after 1780 with undulating lobes. This opinion is seconded by David Peters.

25 See Christie's, New York, 21 May 1997, lot 90; again Christie's, London, 17 April 2000, lot 89.

26 Waddesdon Manor, Buckinghamshire. See Savill, "Starhemberg," p. 29; AMNS, Vy 4, fol. 86v, 6 October 1766.

27 Waddesdon Manor, Buckinghamshire. See Eriksen, *Waddesdon*, pp. 206–17, no. 75.

28 MMA, New York, in Dauterman, *Wrightsman*, pp. 265, 267.

29 Royal Collection, England. See de Bellaigue, *Louis XVI*, pp. 15–17, fig. 12. Other surviving trays include: three from the Sartine Service, 1768–87 (date of pieces not specified), formerly in the Nelson A. Rockefeller collection, Sotheby's, New York, 11 April 1980, lot 251; tray, blue with flowers, 1769, Sotheby's, New York, 9–10 October 1990, lot 363; two trays, green ground with flowers, 1776, Sotheby's, New York, 23 April 1977, lot 60; tea set, 1781, Christie's, London, 2 November 1978, lot 252; tray, 1786, yellow ground with flowers, Christie's, London, 3 March 1986, lot 239; tea set, 1788, blue with birds, Sotheby's, New York, 11 April 1980, lot 258.

30 AMNS, Vj'1, fol. 326, Bulidon, 1 July 1780: *1 Dejeuner a soucoupe a pied de 4 pieces bordure jaune et petites roses 36 #.*

31 Ibid., Vl'1, fol. 129, 13 November 1780: *1 Dejeuner à soucoupe à pied frize jaune et roses Bulidon, Buteux.* None of the Museum's pieces are marked Buteux. It is impossible to say to which member of this family the kiln record refers, or if it indeed refers to the Museum's set. Charles Buteux *père* decorated two such tea sets in 1780, one on 13 June with borders and flowers and one on 14 July with garlands and ribbons (AMNS, Vj'1, fol. 38v). Charles-Nicolas Buteux *fils*, decorated a set on 29 May 1780 with *frize riche, fond jaunes, et roses* (ibid., fol. 43), and Mlle Buteux, a gilder and painter, decorated one with garlands on 22 September 1780 (ibid., fol. 47). It is possible that the Museum's set was one of these.

106

Tea service with tray, sugar bowl, milk jug, and cup and saucer (*plateau octogone, pot à sucre Calabre, pot à lait à trois pieds, gobelet litron et soucoupe*)

1917.1108–1111

Sèvres, 1783

Soft-paste porcelain, tray: H. 1³⁄₁₆ × W. 9⁹⁄₁₆ × D. 8⁷⁄₁₆ in. (3 × 24.2 × 21.4 cm); sugar bowl: H. 2⁷⁄₈ × DIAM. 2½ in. (7.3 × 6.3 cm); milk jug: H. 3³⁄₁₆ × W. 3⁵⁄₁₆ × D. 2⁷⁄₁₆ in. (8 × 8.4 × 6.2 cm); cup: H. 1¹³⁄₁₆ × W. 2¹¹⁄₁₆ × D. 1¹⁵⁄₁₆ in. (4.6 × 6.8 × 4.9 cm); saucer: H. 1 × DIAM. 4⅛ in. (2.5 × 10.4 cm)

White ground, blue *pointillé* border and feathering, polychrome garlands, gilding

Marks: all pieces: interlaced Ls in blue with date letters FF underneath, stippled crown above for Jean-Charles Sioux *aîné*;[1] GI for Étienne-Gabriel Girard;[2] incised 8 on tray;[3] incised 29 on sugar bowl;[4] incised 36 and 27 on cup;[5] 41 on saucer[6]

Provenance: J. Pierpont Morgan

MODEL

The tray is a version of the *plateau octogone*, which may have been introduced in the 1770s or early 1780s.[7] It differs from the earlier models of octagonal tray made at Sèvres in having a

106

uniformly scalloped rim and foliate handles.[8] The sugar bowl is of the *Calabre* shape, and of the third, or smallest size.[9] The milk jug is an example of the third or smallest size *pot à lait à trois pieds*.[10] The cup and saucer represent the fourth-size *gobelet litron et soucoupe*.[11] The set is probably missing a teapot.

A few surviving examples of this form of octagonal tea set are known. One dated 1783–84, decorated with a blue ground and military scenes by Morin, was in the collection of the vicomtesse Vigier.[12] Another dated 1786–87, decorated with a yellow ground, floral garlands, and blue flowers sprigs, is in the Musée national de Céramique, Sèvres.[13] Two others are in the George R. Gardiner Museum of Ceramic Arts, Toronto, one from 1786, with yellow ground and arabesque decoration by Denis Levé, and the other with yellow ground and blue dots, from about 1785.[14]

Marks

COMMENTARY

This tea service was decorated by Jean-Charles Sioux *aîné*. He specialized in monochrome garlands of tiny flowers, which he painted in both blue and carmine enamels on hundreds of pieces of Vincennes and Sèvres.[15] Before entering the factory in 1752, Sioux was a fan painter specializing in borders. In January 1755 the factory wrote of Sioux that "son genre de talens est la Peinture, qu'il possède assès mediocrement, mais assidu et laisse peu de progrès à esperer" [His kind of talent is Painting, which he possesses in quite mediocre quantity, but he is hard-working and leaves little hope of progress].[16] In January 1758 management took a slightly more charitable view of this painter, decribing him as "faisant fort Joliment ces Petites Guirlandes camayeux qui plaisent au Public, et produisant de L'ouvrage honnetement …" [doing little monochrome garlands very prettily which appeal to the Public, and producing work honestly …].[17] His mark was thought to be a dotted circle but recent research has proven that it was a stippled crown.[18]

It is impossible to assess sales of *déjeuners octogones* in the 1780s, for models are seldom specified in the records. Artists' records do reveal that in April 1783 Sioux decorated a small octagonal service of four pieces with feathering, garlands and roses.[19] The kiln firing of 30 June 1783 included an octagonal tea service decorated with garlands by Sioux and Girard.[20] Both of these references must pertain to the Museum's tea service. In that same year Sioux also painted a *déjeuner Hebert* and a broth basin with similar decoration, both pieces now at Osterley Park, Isleworth, Middlesex, England.[21]

Exhibition: *Morgan Loan Exhibition*, New York, 1914, not in catalogue

Literature: Chavagnac, p. 138, no. 174

NOTES

1 See Peters, *Marks*, p. 68. Active 1752–92.

2 Active 1762–1800, as gilder and flower painter. See Peters, *Marks*, p. 38.

3 Savill, 3, p. 1128, found on soft paste 1754–58, 1767–82, and on hard paste 1780–83. This tray extends the years in which the mark was found on soft paste by one or two.

4 Ibid., p. 1129, found on soft paste 1782–90s.

5 Ibid., p. 1130. 36 found on soft paste 1758, 1770–90s. Savill, suggests that its early appearance on a cup of 1758 perhaps means the piece was a later replacement. 27 does not appear in Savill.

6 Ibid., p. 1131, found on soft paste, 1780–90s, primarily on cups and saucers.

7 Surviving examples all date from the mid-1780s.

8 See cat. no. 91.

9 See cat. no. 87 for this shape.

10 Ibid.

11 See cat. no. 95 for this shape.

12 Sold Drouot, Paris, 5–6 May 1970, lot 200, DIAM. of tray 9⁵⁄₁₆ in. (23 cm); later sold Drouot (M. Ferri), Paris, 28 June 1996, lot 61.

13 MNC, Sèvres, no. 9081-1-4.

14 No. G83.1.1077, with other tea components (see Christner sale, Christie's, New York, 30 November 1979, lot 212); No. G83.1.1076.

15 Numerous pieces with this type of decoration and the stippled crown mark of Sioux may be found in the collections of the MAD, Paris, MNC, Sèvres, the V&A, London, and the Wadsworth Atheneum (see cat. nos. 159, 165, and 154).

16 AMNS, Y.8, fol. 51.

17 Ibid. See Eriksen, *Waddesdon*, p. 335.

18 See biography in Eriksen, *Waddesdon*, pp. 335–36; Eriksen and Bellaigue, pp. 154, 170, no. 160. Reattribution of this mark is based on recent work by David Peters, Rosalind Savill, and this author. See note 1.

19 AMNS, Vj'2, fol. 242, 1 April 1783: *1 petite déjeuner octogone de 4 pieces, hachure et Guirle et Rozes*.

20 Ibid., Vl'2, fol. 62.

21 Nos. 31 and 32 in display case, both dated FF and marked with Sioux's stippled crown. See ibid., Vj'2, fol. 242, 29 July 1783, for a *déjeuner Hebert et 4 pieces*, garlands and *pointillé* border; 11 August, for a broth basin, *ancienne forme*, second size, same decoration.

107

Cup and saucer (*gobelet litron et soucoupe*)

1917.1119

Sèvres, 1783

Soft-paste porcelain, cup: H. 2⁷⁄₁₆ × W. 2¹⁵⁄₁₆ × D. 2³⁄₁₆ in. (6.1 × 7.5 × 5.6 cm); saucer: H. 1³⁄₁₆ × DIAM. 4¾ in. (3 × 12 cm)

White ground with blue and pink flowers, green wreath, yellow borders with blue and pink friezes, gilding

Marks: cup: interlaced Ls in blue with date letter ff; painter's mark of the heraldic sign for ermine, for Cyprien-Julien Hirel de Choisy;[1] incised 48a;[2] saucer: same painted marks; gilt vd for Pierre-Jean-Baptiste Vandé *fils* or *aîné*;[3] traces of another gilded mark above factory mark; incised 36[4]

Provenance: J. Pierpont Morgan

MODEL

The cup is an example of a third-size *gobelet litron*.[5] The ear-shaped handle is typical of this model. The saucer is also of the third size.

COMMENTARY

The extremely regular pattern of abstract flowers and gilded dots is reminiscent of small, repeat-pattern textile designs. The top and bottom friezes of interlocking zigzags on a yellow band looks mechanical, as if created with a draftsman's compass.

The register of painters for 1783 records that Choisy decorated six third-size cups and saucers with small friezes and tiny flowers.[6] The Museum's cup and saucer may have been among these, as the description could well apply. Choisy is also recorded as decorating cups and saucers with the gilder Vandé, although this collaboration is documented in 1784, when eight *gobelets litron 3e g. frize riche Choisy Vandé* were fired.[7] It is also possible that the Hartford cup and saucer were among these, decorated at the end of 1783 and fired early in 1784. However, the quantity of similar cups and saucers produced during these years make it impossible to match with certainty individual examples with specific documentary references.

A similarly-decorated cup and saucer of about 1786 was once in the Hector Binney collection.[8]

TECHNIQUE AND CONDITION

The pinkish hue of the paste on the bottom of this cup suggests that it was exposed to a lower temperature during firing, probably through being placed on a saggar. When an item was placed on a saggar for firing in the kiln, the temperature at the point of contact was lowered.[9]

Exhibition: *Morgan Loan Exhibition*, New York, 1914, not in catalogue

Literature: Chavagnac, p. 146, no. 185

107

NOTES

1 Active 1770–1812 as painter of flowers and patterns. See Peters, *Marks*, p. 24.

2 See Savill, 3, p. 1133. Found on soft paste 1761?, 1777–92, including cups and saucers in the 1780s.

3 Active 1779–1824 as gilder and painter of flowers and patterns. See Peters, *Marks*, p. 72.

4 Savill, 3, p. 1130, found on soft paste 1758, 1770–90s.

5 See cat. no. 95 for this form.

6 AMNS, Vj'2, fol. 94v, 30 September 1783, *6 Gobelets et Sce 3e g. petite frize et fleurette*.

7 Ibid., Vl'2, fols. 89v, 90v, 19 February 1784.

8 Sotheby's, London, 5 December 1989, lot 130.

9 As per comments by Antoine d'Albis.

108

Cup and saucer (*gobelet litron et soucoupe*)

1917.1116

Sèvres, 1786

Soft-paste porcelain, cup: H. 2⅜ × W. 2¹⁵⁄₁₆ × D. 2¼ in. (6 × 7.5 × 5.7 cm); saucer: H. 1¼ × DIAM. 4¾ in. (3.1 × 12 cm)

Yellow ground with monochrome brown landscapes, polychrome arabesques on white border, gilding

Marks: both: interlaced Ls in blue with date letters ii, mark in the form of a branch for Jean-Baptiste-Étienne-Nicolas Noualhier *fils*;[1] shadow of 2000 on cup and 2000 in gold on saucer, for Henry-François Vincent *jeune, père*;[2] incised 48a on cup;[3] incised 46 on saucer[4]

Provenance: possibly Edouard Chappey, Paris, 1904;[5] J. Pierpont Morgan

MODEL

This cup and saucer represent the third-size *gobelet litron et soucoupe*.[6]

COMMENTARY

The Hartford cup and saucer were painted by Noualhier *fils*, who probably took the mark of a branch from his father, who had been a flower painter from 1753 to 1766.[7] In October 1786 the younger Noualhier was credited with decorating six cups and saucers of the third size, yellow ground, with arabesques, figures, and landscapes, directly on the ground color (*sur le fond*).[8] In the kiln firing for 11 December of that year, there were six cups and saucers, third size, with landscapes on a yellow ground by Noualhier and Vincent.[9] It is likely that the Museum's cup and saucer were among these pieces.

Another cup and saucer with continuous monochrome landscapes on a yellow ground are illustrated in an exhibition catalogue of 1993 from the Musée Carnavalet, Paris.[10] The painting appears to be by the same hand as the Museum's cup and saucer, suggesting that they may also have been part of the group decorated by Noualhier in October.[11]

The continuous landscape friezes must have been copied from engravings. The closest parallel is with two prints by Israel Silvestre, from a series called *Petite suite de vues d'Italie* of 1643. The landscape on the cup seems to be based on a *Vue du temple*

du soleil while that on the saucer *Vue du Pont Sainte Marie à Rome*.[12]

Exhibition: *Morgan Loan Exhibition*, New York, 1914, not in catalogue

Literature: Chavagnac, p. 144, no. 182;[13] Burollet, p. 210[14]

NOTES

1 Active 1779–82, 1786–91. See Peters, *Marks*, p. 55. This mark is newly identified by Peters.

2 Active 1753–1800. See Savill, 3, pp. 1076–77; Peters, *Marks*, p. 74.

3 Found on soft paste 1777–92. See Savill, 3, p. 1133.

4 Not in Savill.

5 APML, Chappey file, invoice 25 April 1904: "1 Tasse et sa soucoupe ancienne pâte tendre de Sèvres à décor de grisailles fond jaune."

6 See cat. no. 95 for this form.

7 Peters, *Marks*, p. 55.

8 AMNS, Vj'4, fol 277, Noailhier [*sic*] *fils*.

9 Ibid., Vl'3, fol. 36: *6 gobelets et S. 3g Paysage sur fond jaune Noaillhier Vincent.*

10 *Tables d'Égoïstes*, p. 61. There is no information in the catalogue as to the date, marks, or whereabouts of this set.

11 This is, of course, speculation as the date of the cup and saucer from the Paris exhibition is unpublished.

12 For the cup, see Faucheux, suite 10, no. 6 or suite 13, no. 2; for the saucer, suite 10, no. 4. This information was very kindly provided by Maxime Préaud.

13 As by Sinsson.

14 Mistakenly assumed to be at the MMA, New York.

109

Sugar bowl (*pot à sucre Calabre*)

1917.1118

Sèvres, 1786

Soft-paste porcelain, H. 3⅞ × DIAM. 3³⁄₁₆ in. (9.8 × 8 cm)

Yellow ground with blue sprigs, brown scrolls, white border with blue flowers, gilding

Marks: interlaced Ls in blue, date letters jj (below left of factory mark), mark of a fleur-de-lis underneath, probably for Madame Taillandier;[1] 9· in gold for Charles-Nicolas Buteux *fils aîné* or *aîné*;[2] incised 40[3]

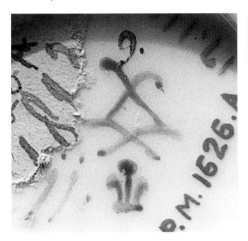

109

Provenance: J. Pierpont Morgan

MODEL

The Sèvres factory called this sugar bowl a *pot à sucre Calabre*.[4]

COMMENTARY

This sugar bowl may have been one of several teapots and sugar bowls decorated with forget-me-nots (*souvenirs*) by Madame Taillandier in October 1786.[5] A teapot with very similar decoration, including the toothed gilding and the brown wave frieze, is at the George R. Gardiner Museum of Ceramic Arts, Toronto,[6] and a matching cup and saucer were on the art market in 2000.[7] They may originally have been part of the same service.

Exhibition: *Morgan Loan Exhibition*, New York, 1914, not in catalogue

Literature: Chavagnac, p. 145, no. 184; Savill, 3, p. 1069 n. 1b

NOTES

1 Geneviève Taillandier, *née* Le Roy, active 1774–98. Savill, 3, p. 1068, Peters, *Marks*, p. 69.

2 Active as gilder and painter 1763–1801. See Peters, *Marks*, p. 19.

3 Found on soft paste 1776–90s. See Savill, 3, p. 1131.

4 See cat. no. 87 for this shape.

5 AMNS, F.28, piecemeal records, Mme Taillandier, *12 Theyeres, et Pot à Sucre, Souvenirs 1# 5s 15 #* and *6 [idem] 1# 6#*.

6 No. G.83.1.1078.

7 Christie's, New York, 24 May 2000, lot 167.

110

Cup and saucer (*gobelet litron et soucoupe*)

1917.1114

Sèvres, 1786

Soft-paste porcelain, cup: H. 2⅜ × W. 3 × D. 2³⁄₁₆ in. (6 × 7.6 × 5.6 cm); saucer: H. 1³⁄₁₆ × DIAM. 4¹³⁄₁₆ in. (3 × 12.2 cm)

Yellow ground with brown flower sprigs, blue and gilded bands, green, blue, and yellow morning glories

Marks: cup: interlaced Ls in blue with date letters ii; painter's mark phj for Jean-François-Henry (Francisque) Philippine *cadet*;[1] incised 47 and 41;[2] saucer: same painted marks; incised 43[3]

Provenance: possibly Cartier et Fils, Paris, 1903;[4] J. Pierpont Morgan

MODEL

This cup and saucer are a *gobelet litron et soucoupe* of the third size.[5] The handle is ear shaped, one of four handle styles found with this type of cup.[6]

110

COMMENTARY

The decoration of tiny brown flower sprigs scattered over the yellow ground typifies the simple patterns found on everyday Sèvres in the 1780s. The border is decorated with a band of unopened morning glories (*volubilis* in French, as it appears in the factory records). Morning glories were another popular decorative motif of this period.

Exhibition: *Morgan Loan Exhibition*, New York, 1914, not in catalogue

Literature: Chavagnac, p. 143, no. 180

NOTES

1 Active 1783–91, painting flowers, birds, and patterns. See Peters, *Marks*, p. 60.

2 41 is usually found on cups and saucers in the 1780s (Savill, 3, p. 1131); 47 is not found in Savill.

3 Savill, 3, p. 1132, found on cups and saucers in the 1780s.

4 APML, Cartier file, invoice 30 May 1903: one of two "tasses et soucoupes Sèvres, fond jaune décors semis et bordure fleurs," 6,000 French francs. Also see record of shipment of objects to Morgan at Princes Gate, London, 3 June 1903: "1 Tasse et soucoupe Sèvres fond jaune avec semi de fleurs et bordure fleurs sur fond blanc – par Pithou." The identification by Cartier of the painter as Pithou may indicate that this refers to a different cup and saucer although perhaps the dealer simply misidentified the mark.

5 See cat. no. 95 for this form.

6 Savill, 2, p. 501, shape B.

III

Cup and saucer (*gobelet litron et soucoupe*)

1917.1115

Sèvres, 1786

Soft-paste porcelain, cup: H. 2½ × w. 3¹⁄₁₆ × D. 2⁵⁄₁₆ in. (6.3 × 7.8 × 5.8 cm); saucer: H. 1³⁄₁₆ × DIAM. 4¾ in. (3 × 12.1 cm)

Yellow ground with blue and brown flower sprigs, blue, yellow, and green morning glories, brown and gilded borders

Marks: cup: interlaced Ls in manganese with date letters ii, painter's mark script P. B. in manganese for Jean-Joseph-Philippe Boucot *fils*, *cadet*;[1] incised 48, 11;[2] saucer: same painted marks; incised 48; paper label inscribed SEVRES/1785./par Barrat[3]

Provenance: probably Cartier et Fils, Paris, 1903;[4] J. Pierpont Morgan

MODEL

The yellow ground cup is slightly larger than the third-size *gobelet litron*,[5] while the saucer is of the third-size.[6] The handle of the cup conforms to the ear-shaped version often found on the *gobelet litron*.[7]

COMMENTARY

The decoration of small blue flower sprigs on a yellow ground can be found on other tea wares in the 1780s. The vertical arrangement of the flowers on the cup is somewhat unusual in its regularity, and contrasts rather strikingly with the naturalistic border of open morning glories.

Exhibition: *Morgan Loan Exhibition*, New York, 1914, not in catalogue

Literature: Chavagnac, p. 144, no. 181

NOTES

1 Active painting flowers, patterns, and birds, 1785–91. See Peters, *Marks*, p. 15.

2 Savill, 3, p. 1133, found on soft paste 1761?, 1777–92; and ibid., p. 1129, found on soft-paste 1753, 1769–88, and on hard paste, 1780–86.

3 François-Marie Barrat (uncle) used the mark FB while his nephew used JB.

4 APML, Cartier file, invoice 30 May 1903, one of "2 Tasses et soucoupe Sèvres, fond jaune décors semis et bordure fleurs," 6,000 French francs; see also record of shipment to Morgan at Princes Gate, London, 3 June 1903: "1 Tasse et soucoupe Sèvres fond jaune avec semi de fleurs et bordure fleurs sur fond blanc – année 1795 [*sic*] par Barrat."

5 See cat. no. 95 for this form. The third size according to Savill (2, p. 501) ranges from H. 2¼ to 2³⁄₈ in. (5.7 to 6 cm), while the second size ranges from H. 2⁹⁄₁₆ to 2¾ in. (6.5 to 7 cm).

6 The third size saucer (Savill, 2, p. 501) ranges from DIAM. 4¹¹⁄₁₆ to 5¹⁄₁₆ in. (11.9 to 12.9 cm).

7 Ibid., shape B.

111

112

Cup (*gobelet litron*)

1917.1158

Sèvres, 1786

Soft-paste porcelain, H. 2⅜ × W. 3 × D. 2³⁄₁₆ in. (6 × 7.6 × 5.6 cm)

Yellow ground with blue flowers, white border with polychrome decoration

Marks: interlaced Ls in blue with ii or jj below left, fleur-de-lis for Madame Geneviève Taillandier;[1] gilded vd for Pierre-Jean-Baptiste Vandé *fils* or *aîné*;[2] incised L and 29[3]

112

Provenance: J. Pierpont Morgan

MODEL

The cup is the third size *gobelet litron* with an ear-shaped scrolled handle.[4]

113

COMMENTARY

The scattered cornflowers and ribbon and rose border are very nicely painted. It is possible but by no means certain that this cup was part of a tea set that was taken out of the kiln on 11 December 1786 and described as yellow ground and frieze.[5]

Exhibition: *Morgan Loan Exhibition*, New York, 1914, not in catalogue

NOTES

1 *Née* Le Roy, active 1774–98, painter of flowers, ground patterns, and decorative patterns. See Peters, *Marks*, p. 69.

2 Ibid., p. 72. Vandé was active as a gilder and painter from 1779–1824.

3 See Savill, 3, p. 1111 for incised L, perhaps Dorvilliers Lauvergnat, active 1773/75–1798/99/1800. See Savill, 3, p. 1129 for incised 29, found 1782–90s on soft paste.

4 See cat. no. 95 for this form. See Savill, 2, pp. 501–26, for sizes and handle shapes (this shape B).

5 AMNS, Vl'3, fol. 36v, 11 December 1786: *1 Cabaret complet en litron 3g et assortiment 1 g. fond jaune frize Taillandier Vandé*. Presumably this should be interpreted as a tea set without a tray composed of several third-size cups and saucers and a first-size teapot, sugar bowl, and milk jug. A fuller description would have mentioned cornflowers, so this kiln record entry may refer to another set.

113

Cup and saucer (*gobelet litron et soucoupe*)

1917.1127

Sèvres, 1787

Soft-paste porcelain, cup: H. 2⅜ × W. 2¹⁵⁄₁₆ × D. 2³⁄₁₆ in. (6 × 7.5 × 5.6 cm); saucer: H. 1³⁄₁₆ × DIAM. 4¹³⁄₁₆ in. (3 × 12.2 cm)

Yellow ground with polychrome landscapes, purple and blue friezes, purple monochrome landscapes directly on the yellow ground

Marks: cup: interlaced Ls in blue with mark below of either Pierre-Joseph-André Vielliard *fils* or André-Vincent Vielliard *père*,[1] date letters KK; incised 21 and 46;[2] saucer: same painted marks as cup; incised 40[3]

Provenance: Edouard Chappey, Paris, 1904;[4] J. Pierpont Morgan

MODEL

This *gobelet litron* and saucer are third-size examples.[5] The ear-shaped scroll handle is found on most examples during the 1780s.[6]

COMMENTARY

There is a matching cup and saucer to the Hartford set in the Fitzwilliam Museum, Cambridge.[7] The combined decoration of landscapes and geometric friezes was one of the many specialties of the painter André-Vincent Vielliard, notably in the 1770s and 1780s. This style was adopted by his son, Pierre-Joseph-André, who entered the Sèvres factory in 1783.

The factory's artist records for 1787 describe many third-size cups and saucers being sent to Vielliard *père*, some specifying yellow ground and landscape, some landscapes and friezes. None describe yellow ground with landscapes and friezes.[8] On the other hand, on 30 June 1787 Vielliard *fils* is recorded as having received for decoration two cups and saucers, third size, yellow ground, landscapes, and friezes. He was paid 9 *livres* each for the sets.[9] It is likely that this refers to the cups and saucers in the Atheneum and Fitzwilliam Museum. This seems to have been the only instance where Vielliard's son is recorded painting landscapes and friezes.

One of the more pronounced decorative elements on the Hartford cup and saucer is the continuous landscape with buildings painted in monochrome purple that rings the bottom of the cup and the inside of the saucer. There are also a rake and watering can as well as a rake and basket on the cup that are reminiscent of the elder Vielliard's designs of the 1760s and 1770s, when garden implements were among his favored motifs.[10]

Exhibitions: *Morgan Loan Exhibition*, New York, 1914, not in catalogue; *Morgan*, Hartford, 1987, no. 77

Literature: Chavagnac, p. 150, no. 192; de Bellaigue, "Sèvres," p. 192, no. 77; Savill, 2, p. 567

NOTES

1 Pierre-Joseph-André Vieillard was active 1783–93. See Peters, *Marks*, p. 73. André-Vincent Vieillard was active 1752–90. See ibid.; Savill, 3, pp. 1074–75. Some have speculated that Vielliard's son, who used the same mark as his father, always put it under the factory mark. This is not universally true. See cat. no. 163 for an example of a piece marked under the factory mark but painted by the father three years before the son began working at the factory.

2 Neither 21 nor 46 are listed in Savill.

3 See Savill, 3, p. 1131, found 1776–90s on soft paste.

4 APML, Chappey file, invoice 25 April 1904: "1 Tasse et Soucoupe ancienne pâte tendre de Sèvres à décor camaïeu violet sur fond jaune & reserves de paysages sur médaillons fond blanc," 10,000 French francs.

5 See cat. no. 95 for this shape.

6 Handle B in Savill, 2, p. 501.

7 No. C61-1961. See de Bellaigue, "Sèvres," p. 192 n. 2. A water jug and basin with the same decorative scheme is in the Rosebery collection at Dalmeny House, West Lothian, Scotland.

8 AMNS, Vj'4, fol. 255v, *Vieillard père, paysage et frize*. He received two for decoration on 5 January, and four for decoration on 11 January, and was paid 6 *livres* for each ensemble. De Bellaigue ("Sèvres," p. 192, no. 77) dates this cup and saucer 1788, according to the then current interpretation of

Sèvres date letters. Therefore he suggests that this cup and saucer was one of six decorated by the elder Vielliard in 1788, four in January and two in March. It is also recorded that a cup and saucer, third size, were fired on 9 July 1787, decorated with a yellow ground and landscapes, by Vielliard (AMNS, Vl'3, fol. 60). As the Hartford cup and saucer are part of a set of at least two, it is unlikely that they were the ones described in this kiln firing.

9 AMNS, Vj'4, fol. 261, *2 Gobelets et S 3e fond jaune paysage et frize 9 18*.

10 De Bellaigue, "Sèvres," p. 192. See, for example, the cup and saucer in the Wallace Collection, London, dated 1766 (Savill, 2, pp. 548–54). In mentioning this motif of the continuous landscape in relation to the elder Vielliard, Savill (3, p. 1074) says that de Bellaigue (*Royal Collection*, p. 112, no. 117) attributes it to his early training as a fan painter. It certainly is logical for the younger Vielliard to have decided to mimic his father in this manner on the rare occasion that he engaged in landscape painting.

114

Cup and saucer (*gobelet litron et soucoupe*)

1917.1128

Sèvres, 1787

Soft-paste porcelain, cup: H. 2⁷⁄₁₆ × W. 3 × D. 2³⁄₁₆ in. (6.1 × 7.6 × 5.6 cm); saucer: H. 1¼ × DIAM. 4¾ in. (3.1 × 12.1 cm)

Yellow ground with blue sprigs, polychrome roses, polychrome and gilded cipher

Marks: cup: interlaced Ls in blue with date letters KK, painter's mark m:x for Marie-Claude-Sophie Xhrouuet (or Secroix);[1] incised L or possibly 7[2] and 41;[3] saucer: same painted marks; incised 46[4]

Provenance: J. Pierpont Morgan

MODEL

The cup and saucer are of the third-size *gobelet litron et soucoupe*.[5] The ear-shaped handle is one of four used on this form of cup, and is the one most frequently found in the 1780s.[6]

114

COMMENTARY

The yellow ground is scattered with small forget-me-nots (*souvenirs*). The reserve of the cup is in the shape of a double convex, and contains the cipher DB crowned. The D and the crown are in gold. The circular reserve of the saucer contains a small bouquet of roses. The cipher probably belonged to a couple, the man with the initial D and the woman with the initial B. It should not be confused with the cipher of Madame du Barry, Louis XV's last mistress.[7]

The marks on the cup and saucer belong to Mademoiselle Xhrouuet, daughter of Philippe Xhrouuet. Her mark can also be found on two round fruit dishes in the Frick Collection, New York.[8] She painted bouquets on plates and service wares from 1781 to 1783, and decorated a small *gobelet litron* of 1783 with blue and carmine flower buds.[9] She also worked on service wares in 1785 and 1786.[10] The Musée national de Céramique, Sèvres has an octagonal tray decorated by Mademoiselle Xhrouuet, also with a yellow ground and forget-me-nots.[11]

Exhibition: *Morgan Loan Exhibition*, New York, 1914, not in catalogue

Literature: Chavagnac, p.151, no. 193

NOTES

1 Active 1775–88 as a gilder and painter of flowers and patterns. See Peters, *Marks*, p. 77.

2 For L, see Savill, 3, p. 1111. She notes that this mark is found from 1755 to 1775, and possibly is the mark for both Lauvergnat *aîné* (active 1749/52/54–1772/73), and Lauvergnat *jeune* (active 1754–74/75). The mark also is known on a saucer from 1787, and Savill postulates that it may have been a piece left undecorated until that year or perhaps made by another soft-paste *répareur* Dorvilliers Lauvergnat (active 1773/75–1798/99/1800). The presence of the Atheneum's saucer, also dated 1787, reinforces the argument for Dorvilliers Lauvergnat.

3 Ibid., p. 1131, found on soft paste c. 1779, 1780–90s.

4 Not in Savill.

5 See cat. no. 95 for this shape.

6 Savill, 2, p. 501, shape B.

7 Her initials would not have had a gilded crown above.

8 Brunet, *Frick*, pp. 298–305, nos. 18.9.35, 18.9.41.

9 Ibid., p. 304, as in the C. Le Tallec collection, Paris.

10 See Peters, *Marks*, p. 77, notation. Peters refers to Artists' Lists and Service Lists, in Peters, *Plates and Services*.

11 MNC, Sèvres, no. 9081-1.

115

Cup and saucer (*gobelet litron et soucoupe*)

1917.1129

Sèvres, 1787

Soft-paste porcelain, cup: H. 2⁷/₁₆ × W. 3⅛ × D. 2⁵/₁₆ in. (6.1 × 7.9 × 5.8 cm); saucer: H. 1¼ × DIAM. 4¾ in. (3.1 × 12 cm)

Yellow ground with white border, polychrome arabesques, brown fillets, gilding

Marks: cup: interlaced Ls in blue with date letters KK, scrolling L for Denis Levé underneath;[1] incised 11 and 48;[2] saucer, same painted marks; incised 48

Provenance: probably Cartier et Fils, Paris, 1903;[3] J. Pierpont Morgan

MODEL

The cup and saucer are a third-size *gobelet litron et soucoupe*. The cup has an ear-shaped scroll handle typical of the period.[4]

COMMENTARY

The arabesque decoration of the cup and saucer was one of Denis Levé's specialties. It is possible that the Museum's example was one of six decorated by Levé in May 1787, for which he was paid four *livres* each.[5] The rather summary handling of the decoration of the Atheneum's cup and saucer bespeaks hasty execution by the artist.

Levé was also responsible for a *déjeuner octogone* of 1786 with kindred decoration that was formerly in the Christner collection.[6] There is also a very similar *gobelet litron et soucoupe* in the Thiers collection at the Louvre.[7]

Exhibition: *Morgan Loan Exhibition*, New York, 1914, not in catalogue

Literature: Chavagnac, p. 151, no. 194

115

Inscriptions: cup: Bananier Du Congo; arbre appellé condé de Congo

Provenance: J. Pierpont Morgan

MODEL

The cup and saucer are examples of a second-size *gobelet litron* and *soucoupe*.[4]

COMMENTARY

The cup and saucer were not originally paired, as evidenced by the different borders found on each. The primary decoration consists of a series of word puzzles or rebuses that speak of love and desire. The cup reads: "Je vaincrai la Raison d'Iris" and "J'aime très fort," which may be interpreted as "I will overcome Iris's reason" and "I love [you] very much."[5] The central rebus of the saucer reads: "Elle a l'amitié d'un chacun" meaning "She has everyone's love." The three other roundels read: "J'ai mille tourments," "Je lui dois tout," and "Elle réjouit," meaning: "I have a thousand torments," "I owe her everything," and "She delights."

The vogue for cups and saucers with rebuses only lasted from 1787 until 1789. In some examples, the rebus was painted on a white ground without being separated into reserves.[6] In many other examples, these pictographs were isolated in reserves,

NOTES

1 Active as painter of flowers, patterns, and birds, 1754–93, 1795–1805. See Peters, *Marks*, p. 49.

2 See Savill, 3, pp. 1129, 1133.

3 APML, Cartier file, invoice 30 May 1903: "1 Tasse Sèvres fond jaune décor fleurs et oiseaux," 2,500 French francs. See also notice of shipping to Morgan at Princes Gate, London, 3 June 1903: "1 Tasse et soucoupe fond jaune et blanc fleurs et oiseaux – année 1786 – par Levé père."

4 See cat. no. 95 for this shape. See also Savill, 2, pp. 501–26.

5 AMNS, Vj'4, fol. 166, 26 May 1787: *6 Gobelets et soucoupes 3 fond Jaune arabesque 4 24 Vu*. I would like to thank Sir Geoffrey de Bellaigue for making this reference known to me.

6 Christie's, New York, 30 November and 1 December 1979, lot 212.

7 No. Th.1317, dated 1787.

116

Cup and saucer (*gobelet litron* and *soucoupe*)

1917.1174

Sèvres, 1787

Soft-paste porcelain, cup: H. 2¾ × W. 3½ × D. 2⅝ in. (6.9 × 8.9 × 6.6 cm); saucer: H. 1⅜ × DIAM. 5⁵⁄₁₆ in. (3.4 × 13.4 cm)

Yellow ground with polychrome rebuses, borders with landscapes

Marks: cup: all in blue, interlaced Ls with date letters KK (flanking factory mark), painter's mark D for Decambos;[1] incised 41 and 11(?);[2] saucer: in carmine, interlaced Ls flanked by KK, D underneath; incised 31[3]

so that they formed only one part of the decorative scheme, albeit the most important one. Yellow seems to have been the preferred ground color for this type. Other examples include a *gobelet litron et soucoupe* in the Thiers collection of the Louvre, dated 1787, and one at Woburn Abbey, Bedfordshire, England.[7] Further examples were on the art market in 1976, and 1980 and 1999.[8]

In a departure from the arabesques and decorative borders of standard secondary decoration, exotic flora and trees are arrayed in friezes around the Museum's cup and saucer. The trees (a banana tree native to the Congo and a fruit-bearing tree called a *Condé de Congo*) are identified by the inscriptions underneath the cup, echoing the French Enlightenment's more scientific approach to nature. From the middle of the 1760s naturalistic decoration at Sèvres shifted away from the fanciful approach to nature toward a greater exactitude in its representation, especially in the painting of birds.[9] A similar shift in the painting of exotic flora also took place at Sèvres, although it occurred later, mostly from the 1790s.[10] While we know that the painters had reference books at their disposal to provide ornithological models, we have not yet been able to establish what books they turned to for botanical sources. At Sèvres in the late 1780s and early 1790s there are documentary references to pieces decorated with *fleurs étrangères* but this term is thought to have been more generic than specific.[11]

Exhibition: *Morgan Loan Exhibition*, New York, 1914, not in catalogue

NOTES

1 Peters, *Marks*, p. 27. His given name is not known. He was active at Sèvres 1776–88 both as a gilder and painter.

2 For 41 see Savill, 3, p. 1131, found on soft paste c. 1779–90s, usually on cups and saucers. It is not certain the second incised mark is an eleven. This mark was found on soft paste primarily from 1769–88. See ibid., p. 1129.

3 Not in Savill.

4 See cat. no. 95 for more on this shape, as well as Savill, 2, pp. 501–26.

5 I would like to thank Sir Geoffrey de Bellaigue for assistance with the rebuses.

6 See cat. no. 124 for more on this type of decoration.

7 Louvre, Paris, no. TH 1316, 1787, third size; probably 1787 (see de Bellaigue, "Woburn," pp. 422–23).

8 Christie's, London, 2 February 1976, lot 82; Christie's, London, 4 February 1980, lot 51, sold again Christie's, New York, 5 May 1999, lot 74.

9 See cat. nos. 145–46 for more on this topic.

10 See Eriksen and Bellaigue, p. 133.

11 Ibid.

116

117

117

Covered cup and socketed saucer (*gobelet et soucoupe enfoncée*)

1917.1123

Sèvres, 1787

Soft-paste porcelain, cup: H. 4⅝ × W. 4¼ × D. 3⁷⁄₁₆ in. (11.8 × 10.8 × 8.7 cm); saucer: H. 1⁷⁄₁₆ × DIAM. 5¹⁵⁄₁₆ in. (3.7 × 15.1 cm)

Yellow ground with polychrome arabesques

Marks: cup: interlaced Ls in blue with date letters KK, script L. for Denis Levé;[1] incised 6 (or 9 or g)[2] and 37a;[3] saucer: same painted marks; incised 37[4]

Provenance: perhaps S. Lion, Paris, 1903;[5] J. Pierpont Morgan

MODEL

This type of cup and saucer was known at the Sèvres factory as *gobelet et soucoupe enfoncée*.[6] They were made in two sizes, both in soft and hard paste.[7] The tapered cup is based on an earlier Vincennes model called *gobelet à la Reine*, a form known from at least 1752. The handle is the same as on the *gobelet à la Reine* and on the *gobelet Hebert*. Sometimes this same shaped cup was given two handles and called a *gobelet à lait*.[8] Some examples were made with covers, usually topped with a fruit knob.

The *gobelet enfoncé* was introduced in one size in 1759, when it was described in the factory stock list as a *gobelet antique*. The entry for the saucer read: *la soucoupe le milieu est enfoncé*.[9] The cup may have been described as antique because its straight shape evoked antique silver vessels.[10] The second size probably was introduced around 1772.[11] The model should not be confused with another cup and saucer set known as a *trembleuse*, which, while commonly made at the Saint-Cloud porcelain factory, seldom appears in Vincennes and Sèvres porcelain. This cup sits on a saucer with a raised central rim rather than a deep

233

center well. *Trembleuses* often were included in traveling sets.[12] The first recorded purchaser of a *gobelet et soucoupe enfoncée* was Madame de Pompadour, who bought three in 1762.[13] Factory sales records indicate that most of the buyers of this form in the 1760s and 1770s were members of the royal family or members of the court.[14] While it has long been thought that these cups and socketed saucers were meant for the elderly, to help them keep their drinks steady, it is known that they were, in fact, purchased by one as young as a seventeen-year-old Marie-Antoinette.[15] It is more likely that this type of cup and saucer was used in the sick room, and may in fact have been designed for Madame de Pompadour, the only known purchaser of the model until she died in 1764.[16]

COMMENTARY

The Museum's cup and saucer are of the first size, and were decorated by Denis Levé with arabesques composed of birds, trophies, fountains, floral sprigs, and vases of flowers. It is possible that this example was one of two decorated by Levé and Baudouin, fired on 17 June 1787.[17]

Exhibition: *Morgan Loan Exhibition*, New York, 1914, not in catalogue

Literature: Chavagnac, p. 148, no. 189; Savill, 2, pp. 675, 685 n. 6

NOTES

1 Active 1754–93, 1795–1805. See Peters, *Marks*, p. 49.

2 Savill, 3, p. 1127. Found on soft paste 1754–90s.

3 Found on soft paste c. 1773–88. See Savill, 3, p. 1130.

4 Ibid.

5 APML, L miscellaneous file, invoice S. Lion, Paris, 29 June 1903: "Grande tasse trembleuse vieux Sèvres pâte tendre fond jaune décorée d'oiseaux et rinceaux époque Louis XVI," 9,000 French francs. This could also refer to 1917.1124 (cat. no. 118).

6 Savill, 2, pp. 674–87 discusses this shape in great detail. The following information on this form is based on her discussion. See also Sassoon, pp. 78–80; Munger, *Wickes*, pp. 193–95.

7 Savill (2, p. 674) states the sizes to be as follows: first size: cup: H. 3⅛–3⁹⁄₁₆ in. (8.5–9 cm) (without cover) or 4⁹⁄₁₆–4¾ in. (11.5–12 cm) (with cover); saucer: H. 1¼–1¾ in. (3.2–4.5 cm) × DIAM. 5¹¹⁄₁₆–6⅜ in. (15–16 cm); second size: cup: H. 2⅞–2¹⁵⁄₁₆ in. (7.2–7.4 cm) (without cover) or 3¾–4⅛ in. (9.5–10.5 cm) (with cover); saucer: H. 1⅛–1½ in. (2.8–3.8 cm) × DIAM. 4¾–5³⁄₁₆ in. (12–13.2 cm).

8 Sassoon, p. 78.

9 Savill, 2, p. 674. See AMNS, I. 7, 8 October 1759 (first nine months of 1759), *moules en plâtre*.

10 As suggested by Tamara Préaud.

11 Savill, 2, p. 674. See AMNS, Vy 5, fol. 72.

12 Savill, 2, p. 674. The term *trembleuse* was used in the late nineteenth century and through much of the twentieth to describe cups and saucers of the *enfoncé* style. See also cat. no. 2, n. 5.

13 Savill, 2, p. 675. See AMNS, Vy 3, fol. 117, 10 August 1762.

14 Savill, 2, p. 675.

15 Ibid. Eriksen (*Waddesdon*, p. 180, no. 63) notes that in an engraving after J.-B. Huet called *La Jarretière,* by L.-M. Bonnet, a young woman is pictured using a *gobelet et soucoupe enfoncée*.

16 Savill, 2, p. 675.

17 AMNS, Vl'3, fol. 57, 17 June 1787: 2 *Gobelets enfoncé* 1[gr.] *fond jaune arabesque Levé Baudouin*.

118

Cup and saucer (*gobelet et soucoupe enfoncée*)

1917.1124

Sèvres, 1787

Soft-paste porcelain, cup: H. 4¾ × W. 4³⁄₁₆ × D. 3½ in. (12.1 × 10.6 × 8.9 cm); saucer: H. 1⅜ × DIAM. 5¹⁵⁄₁₆ in. (3.4 × 15 cm)

Yellow ground with polychrome arabesques, white border with green and pink garlands, blue ribbons, gilding

Marks: cup: interlaced Ls in carmine with date letters KK, and heraldic sign for ermine for Cyprien-Julien Hirel de Choisy;[1] GI in gold for Étienne-Gabriel Girard;[2] incised 34 and 3;[3] large yellow dot;[4] saucer: same painted and gilded marks; incised 34

Provenance: perhaps S. Lion, Paris, 1903;[5] J. Pierpont Morgan

MODEL

This form of cup and saucer was called a *gobelet et soucoupe enfoncée*.[6]

COMMENTARY

The decoration of the Hartford cup and saucer, including the motif of the vase of flowers emerging from the delicate scrolls, can be found on many others of this period. Painters' records indicate that Choisy decorated two yellow-ground cups and socketed saucers with arabesques in September 1787, for which he received 18 *livres* each.[7] The gilder Girard does not appear in the painters' and gilders' register for this year. It is very likely that this cup and saucer set is one of two fired on 10 December 1787.[8]

119

Exhibition: *Morgan Loan Exhibition*, New York, 1914, not in catalogue

Literature: Chavagnac, p. 149, no. 190; Savill, 2, pp. 675, 686 n. 6

NOTES

1 Active 1770–1812, as painter of flowers and patterns. See Peters, *Marks*, p. 24.

2 Gilder, active 1762–1800. See ibid., p. 38.

3 34 appears on soft paste from 1781–92 (see Savill, 3, p. 1129); 3 appears on soft paste 1753–90s (ibid., pp. 1125–26).

4 Significance unknown but it also appears on the bottom of 1917.1125 (cat. no. 119).

5 APML, L miscellaneous file, invoice S. Lion, Paris, 29 June 1903: "Grande tasse trembleuse vieux Sèvres pâte tendre fond jaune décorée d'oiseaux et rinceaux epoque Louis XVI," 9,000 French francs. This could also refer to 1917.1123 (cat. no. 117).

6 See cat. no. 117 for this form.

7 AMNS, Vj'4, fol. 97, 1 September 1787: *2 Gobelets enfoncé 1e fond jaune arabesque 18# 36#* (Choisy). I should like to thank Sir Geoffrey de Bellaigue for pointing out this reference.

8 Ibid., Vl'3, fol. 78v: *2 Gobelets enfoncé 1\grandeur\ fond jaune arabesque Choisy*.

119

Cup and saucer (*gobelet à anses étrusques et soucoupe*)

1917.1125

Sèvres, 1787

Soft-paste porcelain, cup: H. 3⅛ × W. 4½ × D. 3⁵⁄₁₆ in. (7.9 × 11.4 × 8.4 cm); saucer: H. 1⁹⁄₁₆ × DIAM. 6¾ in. (3.9 × 17.1 cm)

Yellow ground with white border, polychrome arabesques, gilding

Marks: both: interlaced Ls in blue with date letters KK; script L. underneath for Denis Levé;[1] incised 48;[2] yellow dot[3]

Provenance: J. Pierpont Morgan

MODEL

This two-handled cup (with its saucer) was known by three names at the Sèvres factory. While its most common was *gobelet à anses étrusques*, it was also called *gobelet à anses botte*,[4] and *gobelet à anses étrusques allongées*.[5] The model was one of many forms designed for a service intended for Marie-Antoinette's fantasy dairy on the grounds of the hunting lodge Rambouillet.[6]

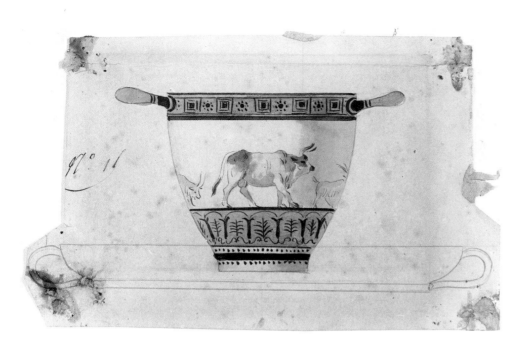

(*Left*)
Fig. 119-1 Drawing of a cup, attributed to Jean-Jacques Lagrenée *jeune*

(*Opposite*)
Fig. 119-3 *Gobelet de la laiterie et soucoupe*, drawing

(*Below*)
Fig. 119-2 *Gobelet à anses étrusques*, plaster model

This small, neoclassical pavilion, begun by 1784, was ready for visitors by spring 1787. It was meant to be the final stop on the tour of Rambouillet's picturesque garden, where within a cool interior, one could partake of fruit and dairy refreshments. These included ice creams, sorbets, fruits, and cheese (like *crème fraîche*), as well as milk and cream.

The furnishings of the dairy reflected the latest taste for neoclassical design, drawing inspiration from the archeological excavations of domestic sites at Herculaneum and Pompeii. The designs for the porcelain shapes were based in large part on collections of antique pottery either known through books of engravings or, in the case of the collection formed by Dominique Vivant-Denon, physically in the possession of the Sèvres factory.[7] The decoration of the Rambouillet service was also inspired by the excavations at Herculaneum and Pompeii, as well as by ancient Roman wall paintings and Raphael's decoration for the Vatican *Loggia*. In an attempt to emulate antiquity, the Rambouillet porcelain was designed to be without gilding.

The *gobelet à anses étrusques* was designed by Louis-Simon Boizot, *sculpteur du roi*, director of sculpture at the Sèvres factory from 1773 until 1809.[8] A watercolor in the factory archives attributed to Jean-Jacques Lagrenée *jeune* shows a drinking cup near in shape to the *gobelet à anses étrusques*, but closer to a classical drinking vessel called a *skyphos* (fig. 119-1). The latter is characterized by horizontal looped handles attached at the rim, and a tapered foot. In all probability the original idea for the Sèvres cup and saucer was proposed by Lagrenée and refined by Boizot.[9]

A plaster model without handles still survives at the Sèvres factory (fig. 119-2).[10] A drawing showing the cup and the saucer with coiled feet is inscribed *Gobelet de la laiterie et Sa Soucoup avec le pied Grandie pour la reusite ce Mois de juin 1787* [cup like from the *laiterie* and its saucer with the foot successfully enlarged this month of June 1787] (fig. 119-3).[11] Another

drawing showing the various components of the Rambouillet service includes the *gobelet à anses étrusques*.[12]

Many of the forms designed for Rambouillet were integrated into everyday production at Sèvres. During the course of 1786 and 1787, for example, many more cups and small bowls were produced than were needed for the dairy. They were decorated and sold to the general public. Some were made of hard paste, and some of soft paste. Four different cup shapes were made for the dairy, and then put into general production. In the documents they were usually described generically as *gobelets de la Laiterie* making it difficult to distinguish between them.

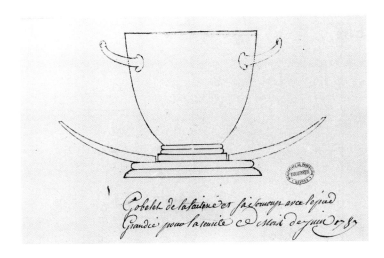

Gobelet de la faïence et faïencier avec le pied
Grandie pour la réunite et était de juin 1783

COMMENTARY

The Museum's cup and saucer are soft paste.[13] They are decorated with arabesques and gilding on a yellow ground with white bands, in the same manner as a host of other cups and saucers of the 1787–89 period.[14] This is in marked contrast to the more severe decoration on the pieces made for the dairy, betraying a less intellectual, less archeological approach common to Sèvres' more commercial production. It is possible that this set was one of four cups and saucers decorated by Denis Levé and Weydinger and fired on 10 December 1787.[15] Piecework and overtime records indicate that Levé was paid 42 *livres* in November 1787 for decorating four cups with arabesques, their form not specified.[16]

Exhibition: *Morgan Loan Exhibition*, New York, 1914, not in catalogue

Literature: Chavagnac, pp. 149–50, no. 191

NOTES

1 Active 1754–93, 1795–1805, as painter of flowers, patterns, birds, and arabesques. See Peters, *Marks*, p. 49.

2 Savill, 3, p. 1133, found on soft paste primarily 1777–92.

3 Significance unknown. See 1917.1124 (cat. no. 118) for same marking.

4 *Botte* (in the eighteenth century) referred to the stirrup-like step—held by leather straps from the side of a carriage—that resembled the handles on this Sèvres cup. The term was used interchangeably with *anses étrusques* (Schwartz, p. 14).

5 The most current information on this shape may be found in Selma Schwartz's article cited above. She states that the name *gobelet à anses botte* can be found primarily in the hard-paste records of the factory (see for example AMNS, Va'10, 1786, Remy). Tamara Préaud suggests (in correspondence with the author) that there is a minor difference between the *gobelet à anses étrusques* and the *gobelet à anses botte* [*de la Laiterie*] in the area of the foot: the examples for the *laiterie* have three round moldings that make up the foot, which differs from the Museum's cup. Schwartz uses the names interchangeably, simply noting that later examples of this shape at Sèvres did not have coiled feet. The painting kiln registers call them all *gobelets étrusques*. Préaud also notes that the term *anses botte* could be used with the *gobelet à bandeau* (see Schwartz, figure 2b, "H"). A *gobelet Étrusque* is known from 1781 (AMNS, Va'7, 1781, Broquet, Marcou).

6 Again, see Schwartz for an account of the dairy, its place in French garden and architectural history, and the commission for the porcelain service. The information that follows is taken from this article.

7 Vivant-Denon sold his important collection of 525 "Etruscan" pottery vessels to the French crown (through the comte d'Angiviller) in 1785. Originally meant to be housed in the soon-to-be established Louvre Museum, the collection was transferred to the Sèvres factory in 1786 for storage. It was used throughout the rest of the century and well into the 19th as inspiration for Sèvres porcelain. The collection is at the Musée nationale de Céramique, Sèvres.

8 For information on Boizot, see Savill, 3, pp. 967–69. Schwartz points out that in the hard-paste record for Marcou (AMNS, Va, 1789) this form was called *gobelet Boizot de la laiterie a botte*, indicating that Boizot was the designer of the shape. See Schwartz, p. 17.

9 Schwartz, pp. 17, 30 n. 55. For the drawing, see AMNS, R. 2, D. 4. Previous literature on this form of cup and saucer attributed the design solely to Lagrenée. See Brunet and Préaud, p. 220; Eriksen and Bellaigue, p. 350.

10 AMNS, labeled: *1780–1800, no. 6, Gobelet à anses étrusques, Laiterie, 1786*. See Schwartz, pp. 16, 33 n. 98.

11 AMNS, R. 1, L. 2, d. 2, fol. 19.

12 Ibid., R. 2, *dossier Laiteries*, D§6, 1788, no. 1, illustrated in Schwartz, fig. 2a,b.

13 Schwartz says that soft-paste examples only were made in 1788 but the Museum's cup and saucer date from 1787. This discrepancy undoubtedly is due to the revised interpretation of the date letters that has occurred since her article was published (see Peters, *Marks*, pp. 4–5).

14 See cat. nos. 117–118 for example.

15 AMNS, Vl'3, fol. 76, *4 Gobelets de la laiterie fond Jaune arabesque Levé Weydinger*.

16 AMNS, F.29. He also decorated six cups with arabesques in February for 12 *livres*, six in March for 12 *livres*, two in April for 24 *livres*, and two in May for 30 *livres*.

120

Cup and saucer (*gobelet litron et soucoupe*)

1917.1120

Sèvres, 1787

Soft-paste porcelain, cup: H. 2⁷⁄₁₆ × W. 3 × D. 2³⁄₁₆ in. (6.1 × 7.6 × 5.6 cm); saucer: H. 1³⁄₁₆ × DIAM. 4¾ in. (3 × 12.1 cm)

Yellow ground with blue and green flowers

Marks: cup: interlaced Ls in blue with dated letters KK to the right of the mark; pb for Jean-Joseph-Philippe Boucot *fils, cadet*;[1] incised 21 and 48;[2] saucer: same painted marks; incised 46[3]

Provenance: J. Pierpont Morgan

MODEL

This is a third-size *gobelet litron*, with an ear-shaped handle.[4]

COMMENTARY

The vine decorating the yellow ground cup and saucer is laden with stylized bellflowers.

120

Exhibition: *Morgan Loan Exhibition*, New York, 1914, not in catalogue

Literature: Chavagnac, p. 146, no. 186

NOTES
1 Active 1785–91. See Peters, *Marks*, p. 15.
2 Savill, 3, p. 1133.
3 Not in Savill.
4 See cat. no. 95 for this form.

121

Saucer (*soucoupe*)

1917.1159

Sèvres, 1787

Soft-paste porcelain, H. 1³⁄₁₆ × DIAM. 4¹³⁄₁₆ in. (3 × 12.2 cm)

Yellow ground with blue flowers, purple bands, polychrome bouquet, gilding

Marks: interlaced Ls in blue with KK underneath; painter's mark cm for Michel-Gabriel Commelin;[1] incised 44[2]

Provenance: J. Pierpont Morgan

121

Marks

MODEL

This saucer would have accompanied a *gobelet litron* of the third size.[3]

COMMENTARY

There is no gilding on the rim, although strangely, a dentil design seems to have been molded into its exterior.

Exhibition: *Morgan Loan Exhibition*, New York, 1914, not in catalogue

NOTES

1 Active 1768–1802, specializing particularly in floral border patterns. See Savill, 3, pp. 1024–25; Peters, *Marks*, p. 25.

2 Savill, 3, p. 1132, found 1769, 1778–90s.

3 See cat. no. 95.

122

Cup and saucer and sugar bowl (*gobelet litron et soucoupe, pot à sucre Bouret*)

1917.1130–1131

Sèvres, 1788

Soft-paste porcelain, cup: H. 2¾ × W. 3⁹⁄₁₆ × D. 2⅝ in. (7 × 9.1 × 6.6 cm); saucer: H. 1⅜ × DIAM. 5⁵⁄₁₆ in. (3.5 × 13.4 cm); sugar bowl: H. 4⁹⁄₁₆ × DIAM. 3⁹⁄₁₆ in. (11.6 × 9.1 cm)

Bleu azur ground with gilding, polychrome ciphers and emblematic landscape, white border with polychrome arabesques

Marks: cup: interlaced Ls in blue with date letters LL to the right, painter's mark p underneath for Guillaume Buteux;[1] gilded LG for Étienne-Henry Le Guay *aîné, père*;[2] incised 11 (with traces of blue), 43;[3] saucer: interlaced Ls in blue with date letters LL; DT in blue underneath for Gilbert Drouet;[4] LG in gold; sugar bowl: interlaced Ls in carmine with date letters LL; B.n. in script above (in carmine) for Nicolas Bulidon;[5] incised 41[6] and 29

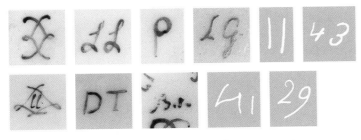

Provenance: probably Cartier et Fils, Paris;[7] J. Pierpont Morgan

MODEL

The cup and saucer are a second-size *gobelet litron et soucoupe*.[8] The sugar bowl is of the Bouret shape,[9] and may be of the second size.[10]

COMMENTARY

The cup and sugar bowl are decorated with a floral cipher DS crowned. The identity of the lady with those initials is unknown. The saucer does not bear the cipher, but instead

reveals an emblematic scene in the central well. A winged, lighted torch and an unlit torch sit atop an altar, with a garland of roses, a quiver of arrows, and more roses at its base. These attributes are set against a landscape backdrop. It is clear that the ensemble is some kind of allegory of love. The lighted torch symbolizes the fire of love, and the unwonted addition of wings evinces a link with Cupid or Venus. The quiver of arrows certainly belongs to Cupid. Is the crown of roses is being offered as a gift on the altar of love?

According the documents, the blue used on this cup and saucer was called *fond azur*. It is close to *bleu Fallot* but perhaps has a slightly more purple tone.[11]

The painters' and gilders' registers for 1788 record that on 4 January Bulidon was given a sugar bowl of the second size with an azure ground to decorate with arabesques and a *chiffre*.[12] On the same date Drouet was given a cup and saucer to decorate in the same manner,[13] and Guillaume Buteux a cup and saucer *fond azur* to paint with arabesques and *chiffre*.[14] The entries for Bulidon and Buteux must refer to the Museum's cup and sugar bowl; that for Drouet the Museum's saucer. One wonders, therefore, whether a cup by Drouet and a saucer by Buteux still survive.

Although floral ciphers had been used to decorate Sèvres porcelain in the 1770s, notably on services designed for Madame Du Barry and Maria Carolina Luisa of Naples, it was only in the 1780s that initials were in widespread use.[15] The comte d'Angiviller, the government minister in charge of the factory, had seen this type of decoration in use at a rival Parisian factory in the rue de Clignancourt and requested that Sèvres adopt it as well.[16] Jean-Jacques Bachelier, the artistic director of the factory, is known to have designed initials, as did the painter Pithou *jeune*.[17] Cups and saucers with floral ciphers must have made charming tokens of love. As we see from the Museum's collection, this type of decoration was also used on service pieces and tea sets of the period (see catalogue nos. 114, 137, and 139).

The Atheneum's cup and saucer and sugar bowl display remarkably rich decoration. The arabesque borders are beautifully executed in the style of ornamentalists such as Henri Salembier.[18] It is likely that Bulidon, Buteux, and Drouet were using a common source for the border. The gilded decoration is quite elaborate, especially for the 1780s, and shows Étienne-Henry Le Guay's consummate skill in this arena. His mark is found frequently on pieces that have been richly gilded.[19] On the Museum's cup, saucer, and sugar bowl, he borders the reserves on one side with gilded oak leaves and on the other side laurel leaves. The painted border is enhanced by a second, gilded border of elegant foliate scrolls. These are punctuated by a baldachin hanging from two strings, with a third string with tassel passing through its center. Variations of this last motif are found in late eighteenth-century engravings of arabesque designs by artists such as Jean Démosthène Dugourc.[20]

TECHNIQUE AND CONDITION

Bleu azur seems first to have come into use in 1786, when piece-work records for the painter Dieu mention a saucer *fond bleu azur chinois*.[21] The kiln records first mention *bleu azur* in

describing an octagonal tea set with arabesques among the contents of the firing on 16 April 1787.[22] Until that date, the blues mentioned were *beau bleu*, *lapis*, and *petit bleu*. Given that *bleu azur* and *beau bleu* appear on the same page in the kiln records, it is clear that the two colors were not the same.[23] *Bleu azur* features in the kiln records into the nineteenth century.[24]

Exhibition: *Morgan Loan Exhibition*, New York, 1914, not in catalogue

Literature: Chavagnac, p. 152, no. 195

NOTES

1 Active 1782–94, painter of flowers, patterns, and ground colors. See Peters, *Marks*, p. 20.

2 Active 1748–49, 1751–96, painter and gilder. See ibid., p. 48; Savill, 3, pp. 1045–47. Savill also records him at the factory 1742–43.

3 For incised 11 see Savill, 3, p. 1129, found on soft paste primarily 1769–88. For 43, see ibid., p. 1132, found primarily 1779–90s.

4 Active 1785–1825, painting flowers, birds, and patterns. See Peters, *Marks*, p. 30. This mark should be distinguished from that of Nicolas Dutanda, who placed periods after the D and T.

5 Active 1763–92 as a painter of flowers and patterns. See Peters, *Marks*, p. 18; Savill, 3, pp. 1006–7.

6 Savill, 3, p. 1131, found c. 1779–90s on soft paste.

7 Paper label inside cup.

8 See cat. no. 95 for this shape. See also Savill, 2, pp. 501–26.

9 See cat. no. 98 for this shape. See also Savill, 2, pp. 570–74.

10 Savill appears uncertain of the sizes, but suggests that the first size ranged from H. 4¼ to 4¹³⁄₁₆ in. (10.8–12.2 cm). As will be demonstrated in notes 12

and 13 below, documents suggest that this may in fact be a second-size example.

11 For *bleu Fallot* see cat. no. 94.

12 AMNS, Vj'4, fol. 55: *1 Pot à sucre 2 g fond azure Arabesques et chiffre Vu*. I would like to thank Sir Geoffrey de Bellaigue for this and the following reference.

13 Ibid., fol. 123, 4 January 1788: *1 Gobelet. et S 2 fond azure Arabesques et chiffres Vu*.

14 Ibid., fol. 65v, 4 January 1788: *1 Gobelet et S 2 fond azure Arabesque et Chiffre Vu*.

15 See cat. nos. 137, 139, and 140.

16 De Bellaigue, "Paintings and drawings," p. 668. See AMNS, H.3. See also Eriksen and Bellaigue, p. 133. The comte d'Angiviller succeeded the marquis de Marigny as *surintendant des bâtiments, arts et manufactures* in 1774.

17 De Bellaigue, "Paintings and drawings," p. 668. There are two sheets in the AMNS by Pithou *jeune* (Petit casier BVIII, dossier Pithou). I would like to thank Tamara Préaud for this information.

18 De Bellaigue, "Paintings and drawings," pp. 752, 757 fig. 67.

19 Savill, 3, p. 1046.

20 See Berliner and Egger, 1, p. 116, no. 1472 (illustration vol. 3, pl. 1472).

21 AMNS, F.28, March 1786 (I wish to thank Tamara Préaud for this reference).

22 Ibid., Vl'3, fol. 51.

23 Ibid., fol. 57v, 17 June 1787. Also appearing on this page were *petit bleu* and *bleu céleste*.

24 Until *an 6* (1797–98) and then from 1814 on.

123

Cup and saucer (*gobelet litron et soucoupe*)

1917.1122

Sèvres, 1788

Soft-paste porcelain, cup: H. 3¹⁄₁₆ × W. 3¹⁵⁄₁₆ × D. 2¹⁵⁄₁₆ in.
(7.7 × 9.9 × 7.4 cm); saucer: H. 1⁷⁄₁₆ × DIAM. 6¹⁄₁₆ in. (3.7 × 15.4 cm)

Yellow ground with brown arabesques, polychrome still lifes against
a pale blue background, gilding

Marks: cup: interlaced Ls flanked by date letters KK, gilder's mark of
2000 for Henry-François Vincent *jeune, père*[1] above, all in gold;
incised 41; incised 7;[2] saucer: interlaced Ls with KK for 1788, vd for
Pierre-Jean-Baptiste Vandé *fils* or *aîné*, all in gold;[3] incised A38[4]

Provenance: probably Edouard Chappey, Paris, 1904;[5]
J. Pierpont Morgan

MODEL

This cup and saucer represent the first size *gobelet litron et
soucoupe* made at Sèvres.[6] The ear-shaped scrolled handle was
one of four used with this model.[7]

COMMENTARY

The decoration of the cup and saucer is dominated by floral still
lifes in the manner of Gerrit van Spaendonck and his younger
brother Cornelis. These Dutch-born artists worked in France
during the second half of the eighteenth century. Gerrit was a
painter and printmaker, who specialized in flower painting in
both small and large scale. His compositions often included a
vase of flowers sitting on a marble shelf, with fruit beside it.[8]
Cornelis often repeated the motifs of his brother, but also
frequently painted baskets of flowers and fruit.[9] The work of
both brothers was probably known to the Sèvres factory
through engravings long before Cornelis's appointment in 1795
as the factory's *artiste en chef*. Cornelis was to remain active there
throughout the first decade of the nineteenth century providing
pictorial models for the porcelain painters.[10]

Although the cup and saucer are marked only with gilders'
marks, we have reason to believe that the reserves were in fact
painted by Philippe Parpette. Among other motifs this painter,
gilder and enameler specialized in painting baskets of flowers
and fruit.[11] A kiln entry records the firing in November 1787 of
a first-size *gobelet litron* decorated with a basket of flowers

against a yellow ground by Parpette and with gilding by Vincent.[12] No saucer is mentioned as being fired on that occasion. Now, the Hartford cup was gilded by Vincent and is anonymously but masterfully decorated with a basket of flowers. May we not suppose that the cup in the November kiln record is indeed the Atheneum's? That Hartford's matching saucer was gilded by Vandé and not by Vincent strengthens further this hypothesis.

A second-size *gobelet litron et soucoupe* with Vincent's mark and the letters PP was on the market in Monaco in 1987.[13] The catalogue of the auction considered PP the date letters for 1793. It is just as likely, however, that these letters denote the mark for Parpette instead.[14] Comparing the still lifes, especially the bunch of grapes on the Monaco saucer and on the Hartford cup, both objects look as though they were painted by the same hand.

Besides the basket and vase of flowers, the Museum's cup and saucer are decorated with two brown enamel neoclassical friezes, the narrower of the two being a foliate band. The larger frieze is made up of foliate scrolls intersected vertically by arrows and horizontally by a bar with floral finials. Between the scrolls are alternating baskets of flowers and a generic vessel, probably meant to convey a classical urn. Eighteenth-century borders like this hark back to Renaissance ornament and to the Renaissance interpretation of Antiquity. The borders are thus reminiscent of the kind of decoration found for example on Italian sixteenth-century earthenware.

The gilded border around the reserves is tooled with imbricated disks and ribbons. This pattern is the principal gilded decoration on the service made for Louis XVI in the 1780s and 1790s, and is thought to have had its roots in the gilding of the *bleu céleste* Louis XV service of 1753–54, composed of gold pastilles. The more formalized disks found on the Hartford cup and saucer appear at Sèvres around 1779, and were much favored in the 1780s.[15]

Exhibition: *Morgan Loan Exhibition*, New York, 1914, not in catalogue

Literature: Chavagnac, pp. 147–48, no. 188

NOTES

1 Active 1753–1800 as gilder. See Savill, 3, pp. 1076–77, who notes that Vincent worked at Saint-Cloud before coming to Vincennes. He worked primarily on useful wares but occasionally gilded vases as well.

2 For 41, see ibid., p. 1131, found on soft paste c. 1779, 1780–90s; 7 not in Savill.

3 Active 1779–1824 as gilder and painter of flowers and patterns. See Peters, *Marks*, p. 72.

4 Found on soft paste 1779–90s. See Savill, 3, p. 1131.

5 APML, Chappey file, invoice 25 April 1904: "1 Tasse & Soucoupe anc[ien] pâte tendre Sèvres fond jaune décor arabesques & Vase de fleurs," 20,000 French francs (together with two other cups and saucers).

6 See cat. no. 95 for this shape.

7 Shape B in Savill, 2, p. 501.

8 See *Flowers in an Alabaster Vase with Fruit on a Marble Plinth*, oil on canvas, 1781, Noordbrabants Museum, 's-Hertogenbosch, illustrated in Mitchell, *Flower Painters*, p. 256. The Sèvres factory decorated many cups and saucers of the 1770s through 1790s with baskets and vases of flowers on marble ledges. See for example two dated 1776 sold in London in 1986 (Sotheby's, 30 June, lots 202–3).

9 See *Basket of Flowers*, oil on panel, Broughton collection, England (in Grant, p. 78, no. 121, pl. 42). For more on Cornelis and Gerrit see Mitchell, "Van Spaendonck," and Mitchell, *Flower Painters*, pp. 241–42.

10 Van Spaendonck was employed by the factory from 1795 to 1800, and then worked on a freelance basis in 1802 and 1803, and in 1808 through 1809. See Peters, *Marks*, p. 72 for dates.

11 Parpette was active 1755–57 and again 1773–1806. See Peters, *Marks*, p. 58. See also Savill, 3, pp. 1055–57. Savill notes that Parpette was paid piece-work for much of his time at Sèvres, as was the case in 1787.

12 AMNS, Vl'3, fol. 72v, 20 November 1787: *1 Gobl.lit. 1ère.g. fond jonquille Corbeille Parpette Vincent*. I would like to thank Sir Geoffrey de Bellaigue for pointing out this reference to me.

13 Christie's, Monaco, 7 December 1987, lot 237 (now in a private collection, France).

14 The marks are all in gold, with 2000 above for the gilder Vincent and .P.P. below. There is no date letter inside the factory marks (I would like to thank the owner of the cup and saucer for transcribing the marks).

15 De Bellaigue, *Louis XVI*, pp. 25–26.

124

Cup and saucer (*gobelet litron et soucoupe*)

1917.1134

Sèvres, 1788

Soft-paste porcelain, cup: H. 2 7/16 × W. 2 15/16 × D. 2 3/16 in. (6.1 × 7.5 × 5.6 cm); saucer: H. 1 1/8 × DIAM. 4 13/16 in. (2.9 × 12.2 cm)

White ground with blue border, polychrome decoration with rebuses, gilding

Marks: cup and saucer: interlaced Ls in blue with date letters LL; painter's mark of y underneath, for either Edmé-François Bouillat *père* or Madame Geneviève-Louise Bouillat (*née* Thévenet);[1] another y (?) above, perhaps for one of the Bouillats; incised 46[2]

Provenance: Cartier et Fils, Paris, 1901;[3] J. Pierpont Morgan

MODEL

The cup and saucer are a third-size *gobelet litron et soucoupe*.[4]

COMMENTARY

The floral rims of the cup and saucer are composed of chains of pink forget-me-nots. The rest of the decoration consists of rebuses, or verbal and pictorial puzzles employing images, musical notes, and parts of words or individual syllables to convey meaning. In France, rebuses enjoyed great popularity in the seventeenth century and must have seen a revival in the latter part of the eighteenth century.[5] According to Denis Diderot's *Encyclopédie*, they originated in Picardy among the ecclesiastics who, at carnival, created satires about the adventures and intrigues in the village, making use of equivocal allusions to mask otherwise libelous and scandalous remarks.[6]

The rebus on the Atheneum's cup translates "Show yourself as nature has made you without artifice/ and you will be adored

124

by every mortal." That on the saucer translates: "To captivate forever the swain who loves you/ you need no finer apparel than yourself unadorned."[7] Sentiment of this nature proved to be the common theme of rebuses at Sèvres: they were mostly painted on cups and saucers, undoubtedly to be given as romantic gifts by hopeful gallants. But their use in decoration only enjoyed a brief popularity from 1787 to 1789.

The first use of a rebus as decoration appears in the kiln records in December 1787 when two *gobelets litron* of the second size painted and gilded by Chulot and Girard were fired. These had yellow grounds and probably resembled the Museum's cup and saucer with rebuses and exotic plants.[8] Four more were recorded that year.[9] Rebus decoration reached a peak in 1788 when the kiln records show forty-three cups and saucers of this genre.[10] Two were decorated by Noualhier and Boileau, and forty-one by one or more members of the Weydinger family. Production seems to have dropped off in 1789, with only six recorded, none after March of that year.[11] Rebuses also occur in the painters' records, but only in 1788. Six cups and saucers were given to Bouillat *père* to decorate on 22 December,[12] and were possibly among the eleven gilded by Weydinger and fired before the end of the year.[13] Three more were given to Guillaume Buteux on that date, and also may have been gilded by Weydinger.[14] Finally, in November 1788, Taillandier painted rebuses on six cups and saucers. These may well have been gilded by Weydinger and fired on 9 December.[15]

The marks on the Museum's cup and saucer create some confusion as to their authorship. The "y" that is under the factory mark might belong to either Monsieur or Madame Bouillat, as might the incomplete "y" above the interlaced Ls. While it is possible that the two Bouillats could have collaborated on the decoration of the cup and saucer, it seems unlikely. Madame Bouillat was paid three *livres* each for painting twelve sets of cups and saucers in November and twelve more in December 1788.[16] It is not likely that she would have been paid so much for only partially decorating these pieces, so we may assume that she must have worked on twenty-four cups and saucers and her husband on another six. They probably were among those gilded by one of the Weydingers. The second "y" appearing on the Atheneum's cup and saucer is thus unexplained, but cannot be seen as Weydinger's mark.[18]

Exhibitions: *Morgan Loan Exhibition*, New York, 1914, not in catalogue; *Morgan*, Hartford, 1987, no. 78

Literature: Chavagnac, pp. 154–55, no. 198; Wendell, pp. 1–8; de Bellaigue, "Sèvres," p. 193, no. 78

NOTES

1 Bouillat *père* was active 1758–1810; Mme Bouillat 1776–98. This husband and wife team seems to have used the same basic form of Y for their mark, making it difficult to distinguish their work barring other documentary evidence. See Peters, *Marks*, p. 16; Savill, 3, pp. 1002–4 for Bouillat. See below for further discussion.

2 Not in Savill.

3 APML, Cartier file, invoice 24 May 1901: "2 Tasses et Soucoupes, Vieux Sèvres fond blanc décor myosotes et Rebus," 2,400 French francs. See cat. no. 125 for second cup and saucer.

4 See cat. no. 95 for this shape. See also Savill, 2, pp, 501–26. The handle is Savill's shape B.

5 See Wendell, p. 1, and de Bellaigue, "Sèvres," p. 193 n. 1.

6 Diderot, *L'Encyclopédie,* XV, pp. 842–43.

7 Cup: *De vos seuls agréments/ montrez vous décorée/ et de tous les mortels/ vous serez adorée*. Saucer: *Pour fixer sans retour le pâtre qui vous aime/ vous êtes à vous même votre plus bel atour [sic]*. I wish to thank Sir Geoffrey and Lady de Bellaigue for their translations of these rebuses.

8 AMNS, Vl'3, fol. 75v. See cat. no. 116.

9 Ibid., fol. 77v, 10 December 1787, two, second size, *litron*, Weydinger; ibid., fol. 80, 28 December 1787, two, second size, *litron*, Weydinger.

10 Ibid., fols. 83v, 88v, 119, 119v, and 122.

11 Ibid., fols. 128, 130, and 136.

12 Ibid, Vj'4, fol. 43.

13 Ibid., Vl'3, fol. 122. De Bellaigue ("Sèvres," p. 193) suggested that this cup and saucer may have been decorated in 1788 but fired in 1789, based on his reading of the date letters LL for 1789 and his attempt to reconcile that with the 1788 entry for Bouillat. The revised dating system used in this catalogue makes this suggestion unnecessary.

14 Ibid., Vj'4, fol. 66, and Vl'3, fol. 122.

15 Ibid., Vj'4, fol. 242v, and Vl'3, fol. 119.

16 AMNS, F.30, November and December 1788. I would like to thank David Peters for pointing out this reference to me and helping me to analyze the marks on this cup and saucer.

17 In 1788 the Weydingers are listed as having gilded forty-one cups and saucers with rebuses. If thirty of them were decorated by the two Bouillats, six by Taillandier, and three by Buteux, then in theory all of them could have been gilded by the Weydingers and fired in December 1788.

18 See Peters, *Marks,* p. 75, where the mark (unconfirmed) believed to have been used by members of the Weydinger family is illustrated. Ten members of that family worked in the factory at one time or another, five of them active in 1788.

125

Cup and saucer (*gobelet litron et soucoupe*)

1917.1135

Sèvres, 1788

Soft-paste porcelain, cup: H. 2⁷⁄₁₆ × w. 2¹⁵⁄₁₆ × D. 2³⁄₁₆ in. (6.1 × 7.5 × 5.6 cm); saucer: H. 1³⁄₁₆ × DIAM. 4¹¹⁄₁₆ in. (3 × 11.9 cm)

White ground with polychrome decoration with rebuses, gilding

Marks: cup: interlaced Ls in blue with date letters LL, Y underneath for either Edmé-François-Bouillat *père* or Madame Bouillat;[1] | | above;[2] incised 40 and 50;[3] saucer: same painted marks; incised 46[4]

Provenance: Cartier et Fils, Paris, 1901;[5] J. Pierpont Morgan

MODEL

This *gobelet litron et soucoupe* is of the third size.[6]

COMMENTARY

This ensemble is decorated with rebuses expressing sentiments of love.[7] The cup translates: "Oh nymph, of coral and alabaster/ I love you more than Anthony ever loved/ beautiful Cleopatra." The saucer may be translated as: "When you surrender your hand/ to my burning kisses/ I cannot resist/ venturing further on this enchanted path."[8]

The mark underneath the interlaced Ls is that of either Monsieur or Madame Bouillat, and undoubtedly was one of thirty decorated by these two painters during 1788.[9] The two lines above the factory mark may be an unidentified painter's mark. However, it has not been previously cited in the literature on Sèvres marks and is unfamiliar to scholars working in this area.[10]

The border comprises a garland of blue forget-me-nots. Simple gilded bands surround the rims and the well of the saucer.

Exhibition: *Morgan Loan Exhibition*, New York, 1914, not in catalogue

Literature: Chavagnac, pp. 154–55, no. 198; Wendell, pp. 1–8

NOTES

1 See cat. no. 124 for these painters.

2 Unidentified mark. See more discussion below.

3 40 found on soft paste 1776–90s. See Savill, 3, p. 1131. 50 is not in Savill.

4 Not in Savill.

5 APML, Cartier file, invoice 24 May 1901: "2 Tasses et Soucoupes, Vieux Sèvres fond blanc décor myosotes et Rébus," 2,400 French francs (together with 1917.1134, cat. no. 124).

6 See cat. no. 95 for this shape. See Savill, 2, pp. 501–26 for *gobelets litron*. The handle conforms to Savill's shape B.

7 See cat. no. 124 for more on rebuses.

8 *Je t'aime, nymphe au teint de corail et d'albâtre/ plus qu'Antoine n'aima la belle Cléopâtre; A mes baisers de feu/ quand tu livres ta main/ je ne puis m'arrêter/ dans un si beau chemin.* I would like to thank Sir Geoffrey and Lady de Bellaigue for translating these rebuses.

9 See cat. no. 124 for these entries in the Sèvres documents.

10 David Peters has remarked in correspondence with the author that he has never encountered this mark and therefore is hesitant to treat it as a painter's mark. Further research may shed more light on this issue.

126

Cup and saucer (*gobelet litron et soucoupe*)

1917.1132

Sèvres, 1788[1]

Soft-paste porcelain, cup: H. 2$\frac{7}{16}$ × W. 2$\frac{15}{16}$ × D. 2$\frac{1}{4}$ in. (6.1 × 7.5 × 5.7 cm); saucer: H. 1$\frac{1}{8}$ × DIAM. 4$\frac{3}{4}$ in. (2.9 × 12.1 cm)

Yellow ground with blue and brown scrolls, gray marbled border and central medallion with polychrome rosette and arabesques, gilding

Marks: cup: interlaced Ls with date letters LL (outside of factory mark), Sc underneath for Sophie Binet, all in blue;[2] incised 43 and 47;[3] saucer: same painted marks; incised 46[4]

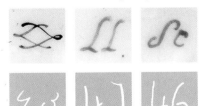

Provenance: probably Cartier et Fils, Paris, 1903;[5] J. Pierpont Morgan

MODEL

This is a third-size *gobelet litron et soucoupe* with an ear-shaped scroll handle.[6]

126

COMMENTARY

The primary decorative borders on this cup and saucer consist of acanthus-leaf scrolls punctuated with small trumpets filled with flowers, which would have been described as arabesques by the factory. The border ornament is set against an underlying marble-like pattern in pale gray. The origin of the design is taken from antiquity, as is the modified Vitruvian scroll at the bottom of the cup and around the saucer's central reserve. That reserve is filled with a foliate *patera* that also echoes antiquity.

It is possible that this cup and saucer were one of six sets decorated by the then Mademoiselle Chanou in August 1788.[7] A matching example was with a London dealer in 1996.[8]

Exhibition: *Morgan Loan Exhibition*, New York, 1914, not in catalogue

Literature: Chavagnac, p. 153, no. 196

NOTES

1 Chavagnac believed that while LL might refer to the date of the cup and saucer, it was more likely that it referred to the painter Louis-François L'Écot, active 1761–64, 1772–1800. He painted arabesques, among other types of decoration. He seems, however, to have formed his Ls differently than those that are on the Museum's cup and saucer. See Peters, *Marks*, p. 47.

2 *Née* Sophie Chanou, active 1779–98 as painter of flowers and patterns. See Peters, *Marks*, p. 14.

3 For 43 see Savill, 3, p. 1132, found on soft paste 1765–69, 1779–90s.

4 Not in Savill.

5 APML, Cartier file, invoice 30 May 1903: "1 Tasse Sèvres fond jaune rinceaux cornets de fleurs," 3,500 French francs. See also shipping document, 3 June 1903: "1 Tasse et soucoupe Sèvres fond jaune et blanc rinceaux et cornets de fleurs – année 1787 – par Madame Binet."

6 See cat. no. 95 for this shape. See Savill, 2, pp. 501–26 for *gobelets litron*. The handle conforms to Savill's shape B.

7 AMNS, Vj'4, fol. 273v, 23 August 1788: *6 Gobl et sce 3e. g fond Jaune frize et arabesque 2# 10s 15# Vu.* Sir Geoffrey de Bellaigue kindly pointed out this reference.

8 John Whitehead, with same markings. I should like to thank Mr. Whitehead for providing the Museum with photographs and information. See also Ader, Tajan, Paris, 29 June 1994, lot 96.

127

127

Cup and saucer (*gobelet* or *tasse à anse Boizot et soucoupe*)

1917.1136

Sèvres, 1790

Soft-paste porcelain, cup: H. 2¾ × W. 3½ × D. 2⅞ in. (7 × 8.9 × 7.2 cm); saucer: H. 1³⁄₁₆ × DIAM. 5³⁄₁₆ in. (3 × 13.1 cm)

Yellow ground and carmine borders, polychrome arabesques, gilding

Marks: cup: interlaced Ls in carmine with date letters NN; heraldic sign of ermine, for Cyprien-Julien Hirel de Choisy;[1] incised 41;[2] saucer: same painted marks; incised 40[3]

Provenance: J. Pierpont Morgan

Model

This model of cup was called a *gobelet* or *tasse à anse Boizot*. The identification is based on a drawing in the Sèvres archives showing the profiles of three cups and saucers (fig. 127-1). The third profile, numbered 76, is inscribed *Gobelet et soucoup Boizot a anse a canelure*.[4] The unusual handle, with its characteristic volute, can also be found on one of the large tureens of the service made for Marie-Antoinette's dairy at Rambouillet.[5] This service was designed by Jean-Jacques Lagrenée *jeune*, with modifications and additions probably made by Louis-Simon Boizot. The handles of both the cup and the tureen link Boizot to the designs of each. *Canelure* may be a misspelling of *cannelure* or grooving, which could well characterize this handle. Surviving examples indicate that the cup and saucer were made in only one size.[6]

The *gobelet Boizot* must have been introduced around 1786, when the *façonneur* Le Comte *fils aîné* was paid for working on four *gobelets Boizot anse canelé*.[7] The style of *gobelet* does not appear in the kiln records until September 1789, when five were fired, variously decorated with chinoiseries and arabesques.[8] Six

more were fired in December decorated with *fleurs étrangères*.[9] Kiln records show that over fifty more were produced during the course of 1790.[10]

Commentary

The decoration of the Atheneum's cup and saucer is very rich and striking in its contrast of the yellow and carmine bands. The scheme is composed of an arabesque design, overlain with swags of roses spilling out of dark blue vases. Dark blue medallions with gilded flowers punctuate the décor. It is possible that the Hartford cup and saucer set was one of six *tasses Boizot et Sc^p Blanches arabesques et fond* decorated by Hirel de Choisy on 19 September 1790, for 18 *livres* each.[11]

Exhibition: *Morgan Loan Exhibition*, New York, 1914, not in catalogue

Literature: Chavagnac, p. 155, no. 199

Notes

1 Active 1770–1812. See Peters, *Marks*, p. 24.

2 See Savill, 3, p. 1131.

3 Found on soft paste 1776–90s. See Savill, 3, p. 1131.

4 AMNS, R. 1, L. 2, d. 2, fol. 23. Although he does not discuss the shape in detail, Christian Béalu (Béalu, p. 14, fig. 5) identifies it as a *gobelet Boizot*.

5 See cat. no. 119 for this service, and illustration in Schwartz, p. 14, fig. 2a.

6 There are few published examples of this form. See Verlet, *Sèvres*, pl. 94b (MNC, Sèvres, H. 2¾ in. or 7 cm); Casanova, no. 181, brown with dots and gold with white band decorated with arabesques and medallions with revolutionary symbols; Béalu, no. 5 (Musée Carnavalet, H. 2¾ in. or 7 cm); *Nord-Pas-de-Calais*, p. 130, no. 104 (Musée et Château, Boulogne-sur-Mer, no. L. 462, H. 2¹¹⁄₁₆ in. or 6.8 cm); Drouot, Paris, 22 November 1996, lot 193, red ground, central white band with arabesques. An unpublished example at the MAD, Paris, 1788, measures H. 2¹¹⁄₁₆ in. or 6.8 cm. The saucer is slightly larger than the Hartford example, measuring H. 1⅜ × 5⅜ in. (3.5 × 13.6 cm) (I wish to thank Bertrand Rondot for this information). It probably does not indicate another size. There is a photograph at AMNS of one from a tea service, Hermitage, St. Petersburg, 1790, black ground and chinoiserie decoration in gold. In one instance kiln records are ambiguous as to sizes. In AMNS, VI'3, fol. 164 (actually a second folio numbered 164), dated 21 March 1790, cups and saucers are listed consecutively as follows: *2 Gobelets fe [form] Boizot arabesque Trager Mirey/ 2 id. 3e gre Verd et Noir id. Levé Girard/ 1 id. 2e gre. Frize riche Tardy Girard.* It may

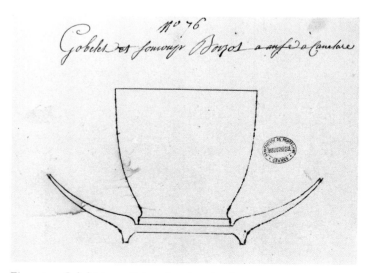

Fig. 127-1 *Gobelet à anse Boizot*, drawing, detail

be that *idem* just refers to *gobelet* and not the shape, as this is the only time this author has found more than one size listed for this shape.

7 Ibid., Va'10 (4), January 1786.

8 Ibid., Vl'3, fols. 152, 154v, 28 September 1787.

9 Ibid., fol. 159, 20 December 1789.

10 Ibid., Vl'3, fols. 161–72.

11 Ibid., Vj'5, fol. 59. Kiln registers for 1790 also record a three-piece tea set decorated with arabesques by Choisy fired on 31 May (ibid., Vl'3, fol. 168: *3 Pièces d'un cabaret arabesques Choisy*). While this is not specific enough to allow identification, it is certainly possible that the Museum's cup and saucer could have been included in such a cabaret.

128

Two cups and saucers (*gobelets* or *tasses à anse Boizot et soucoupes*)

1917.1137–1138

Sèvres, 1792 and 1793

Soft-paste porcelain, 1917.1137: cup: H. 2¹¹⁄₁₆ × W. 3½ × D. 2¹³⁄₁₆ in. (6.8 × 8.9 × 7.1 cm); saucer: H. 1³⁄₁₆ × DIAM. 5³⁄₁₆ in. (3 × 13.2 cm); 1917.1138: cup: H. 2¾ × W. 3½ × D. 2¹³⁄₁₆ in. (6.9 × 8.9 × 7.1 cm); saucer: H. 1⅛ × DIAM. 5⅛ in. (2.9 × 13 cm)

Blue ground with polychrome birds and garlands on white, gilding

Marks: 1917.1137: cup: interlaced Ls in blue with date letters PP, mark of a sword underneath for Étienne Evans;[1] IN for Jean Chauvaux *jeune* or *cadet*;[2] incised 18 and 46;[3] saucer: same painted marks; incised 46; 1917.1138: cup: interlaced Ls in blue with date letters qq, same painter's and gilder's marks; incised 18 and 46; saucer: *Sevres* and IN in blue;[4] incised 46

Provenance: A.B. Daniell & Co., London, n.d.;[5] J. Pierpont Morgan

MODEL

This model of cup and saucer was called *gobelet* or *tasse à anse Boizot et soucoupe*.[6]

COMMENTARY

The decoration of these two sets—not a true pair as seen by their different borders and gilded patterns—includes oval reserves of birds, some taken from Georges-Louis Leclerc, comte de Buffon's *Histoire naturelle des oiseaux*, published in Paris from 1770 to 1786.[7] The parrot on one cup (1917.1137) may be from Buffon, his *Petite Perruche verte, de Cayenne* (fig. 128-1). The blue-necked bird on saucer 1917.1137 is Buffon's *La Gorge-bleue* (fig. 128-2). This same bird is on one side of cup 1917.1138 as well. The penguin on saucer 1917.1137 is *Le Manchot, du Cap de Bonne-Espérance*, and the third bird on the saucer is a *Grèbe de Cayenne* (figs. 128-3 and 128-4).[8] The remaining birds have yet to be identified, but do not appear to be from Buffon.[9]

Factory records tell us that the bird painter Evans was given six *tasses Boizot et Sc. Beau bleu* on 22 November 1791.[10] A note adjacent to this entry says that they were not produced until 1793. In the work records for 4 February 1793 there is an entry for six *tasses Boizot Beau bleu de 1791 frize et oiseaux*, for which

Marks

Fig. 128-1 *Petite Perruche verte, de Cayenne*, Buffon

Fig. 128-2 *La Gorge-bleue*, Buffon

Fig. 128-3 *Le Manchot, du Cap de Bonne-Espérance*, Buffon

Fig. 128-4 *Grebe de Cayenne*, Buffon

Evans was paid 24 *livres* each.[11] These must be the six mentioned in 1791 but not yet decorated. Kiln records show that twelve *tasses Boizot beau bleu oiseaux* decorated by Evans and gilded by Chauvaux the younger, were fired on 1 October 1793.[12] Hartford's cups and saucers may well have been part of this group.

The painting of the birds on the Museum's pieces is sloppy, and may be attributed to the minimal skill of Evans, even though he was one of the factory's more experienced bird painters. He was described in the factory staff register in 1755 as being a mediocre bird painter, with little hope for improvement.[13]

TECHNIQUE AND CONDITION

The paste of both cups and saucers was badly prepared, as evidenced by widespread inclusions and black speckling (*végétations salines*). On one saucer a gilded spot on the exterior indicates that it touched a gilded object while in the kiln. A mass of black specks inside one cup suggests that ash or some other contaminant dropped inside during firing. The overall quality of the paste, glaze, painting, and gilding reflects the diminishing standards in use at the factory during the French Revolution, and especially during the period known as The Terror.

Exhibition: *Morgan Loan Exhibition*, New York, 1914, not in catalogue

Literature: Chavagnac, pp. 155–56, no. 200

NOTES

1 Peters states he was active 1752–86, especially as a painter of birds (Peters, *Marks*, p. 33). However, he was active until 1800.

2 Gilder and painter, active 1764–1800. See ibid., p. 24. See also Savill, 3, pp. 1021–22.

3 Not in Savill.

4 *Sevres* mark found from 1793, when date letters officially ceased to be used. See Brunet and Préaud, p. 341.

5 Paper labels for this firm were found on three of the four pieces.

6 See cat. no. 127.

7 A copy of this set still exists in the factory archives, which was borrowed by the factory in 1781 and purchased later in the 1780s. For more on the use of Buffon's publication and ornithologically accurate birds see cat. nos. 145–46.

8 Buffon, 6, pl. 359; 6, pl. 361; 10, pl. 382; 9, pl. 404.

9 A survey of published ornithological engravings by the English naturalist George Edwards did not produce any matches with the birds on the Museum's cups and saucers.

10 AMNS, Vj'5, fol. 97v.

11 Ibid., fol. 98. Even though he marked the Museum's cup and saucer, there are no ordinary work records for Chauvaux during this time to document this work.

12 AMNS, Vl'3, fols. 228v and 229v. These were recorded in two six-cup batches.

13 Ibid., Y.8, fol. 53: "… avant d'entrer à la manufacture il peignoit des evantails: son genre de travail est la peinture en oiseaux, travaillant fort mediocrement et laissant peu de progrès à esperer…" His monthly wage never increased beyond 66 *livres*, as compared with another bird painter Aloncle, who already in 1774 was paid 78 *livres* per month.

129

129

Cup and saucer (*gobelet litron et soucoupe*)

1917.1153

Sèvres, c. 1794–1800

Soft-paste porcelain, cup: H. 2⁷⁄₁₆ × W. 2¹⁵⁄₁₆ × D. 2¼ in. (6.1 × 7.5 × 5.7 cm); saucer: H. 1⅛ × DIAM. 4¹¹⁄₁₆ in. (2.9 × 11.9 cm)

Yellow ground with white borders, polychrome flowers, gilding

Marks: in blue, *Sevres* and painter's mark LP for Mademoiselle Louise-Thérèse (?) Parpette;[1] GI for Étienne-Gabriel Girard[2]

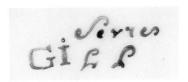

Provenance: J. Pierpont Morgan

MODEL

The cup and saucer are third-size examples of the *litron* form, with the typical ear-shaped handle.[3]

COMMENTARY

The design of roses and blue flowers on bands of yellow and white creates a decorative, if not sophisticated effect.

TECHNIQUE AND CONDITION

The paste is badly prepared, evidenced by the saucer's pocked surface. The green enamel of the leaves has been applied very thinly, on top of which outlines and shadows have been painter in an oily black. The gilding is thin and rather sloppy, and has a distinctly brassy tone. This lapse in quality was not unusual during the Revolutionary period, when factory resources were severely diminished.

Exhibition: *Morgan Loan Exhibition*, New York, 1914, not in catalogue

Literature: Chavagnac, p. 160, no. 206[4]

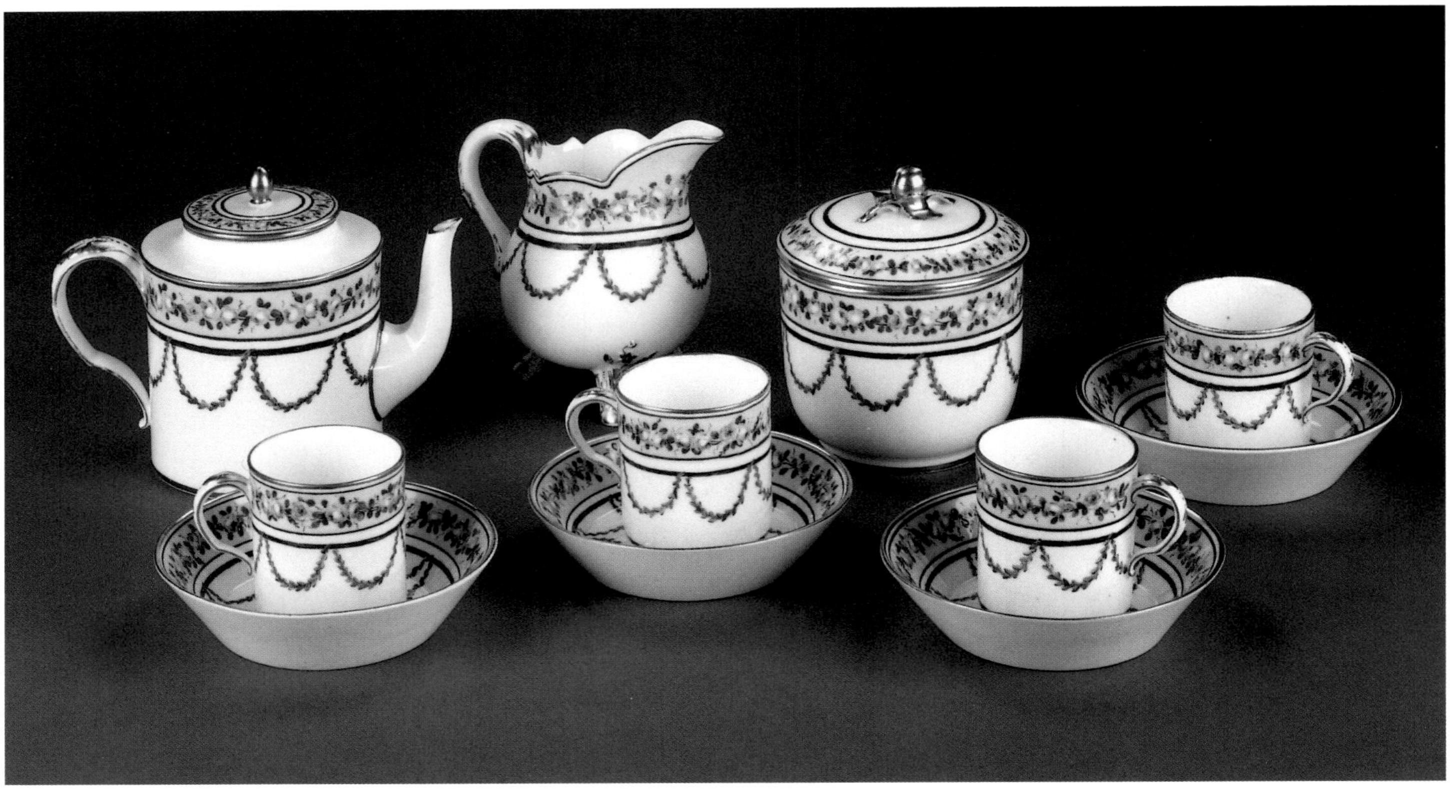

130

Notes

1 This is Mlle Parpette *aînée*, who was active 1787–88, and 1794–1825 (?). See Peters, *Marks*, p. 58.

2 Active 1762–1800. Girard was a gilder and also painted flowers. See ibid., p. 38.

3 See cat. no. 95 for this form. See Savill, 2, pp. 501–26, handle shape B.

4 As by L'Écot and perhaps Genest (GI).

130

Tea service with teapot, sugar bowl, milk jug, and four cups and saucers (*théière litron, pot à sucre Calabre, pot à lait à trois pieds, gobelets litron et soucoupes*)

1917.1139–1145

Sèvres, c. 1795–1796[1]

White ground with yellow border, polychrome garlands and flowers, gilding

Soft-paste porcelain, teapot: H. $4\frac{13}{16}$ × W. $6\frac{1}{4}$ × D. $3\frac{3}{4}$ in. (12.2 × 15.9 × 9.5 cm); sugar bowl: H. $4\frac{9}{16}$ × DIAM. $3\frac{15}{16}$ in. (11.5 × 9.9 cm); milk jug: H. $4\frac{9}{16}$ × W. $4\frac{7}{16}$ × D. $3\frac{3}{8}$ in. (11.6 × 11.2 × 8.5 cm); 1917.1142: cup: H. $2\frac{7}{16}$ × W. 3 × D. $2\frac{1}{4}$ in. (6.1 × 7.6 × 5.7 cm); saucer: H. $1\frac{1}{4}$ × DIAM. $4\frac{11}{16}$ in. (3.1 × 11.9 cm); 1917.1143: cup: H. $2\frac{3}{8}$ × W. 3 × D. $2\frac{3}{16}$ in. (6 × 7.6 × 5.5 cm); saucer: H. $1\frac{1}{4}$ × DIAM. $4\frac{7}{8}$ in. (3.2 × 12.3 cm); 1917.1144: cup: H. $2\frac{3}{8}$ × W. $2\frac{15}{16}$ × D. $2\frac{1}{8}$ in. (6 × 7.4 × 5.4 cm); saucer: H. $1\frac{1}{8}$ × DIAM. $4\frac{5}{8}$ in. (2.8 × 11.7 cm); 1917.1145: cup: H. $2\frac{3}{8}$ × W. $3\frac{1}{16}$ × D. $2\frac{1}{4}$ in. (6 × 7.7 × 5.7 cm); saucer: H. $1\frac{1}{8}$ × DIAM. $4\frac{5}{8}$ in. (2.8 × 11.7 cm)

Marks: on all pieces: in black, *Sevres*, monogrammed RF; script A D for Mademoiselle Durosey *aînée*;[2] teapot: incised 28, 41;[3] sugar bowl: incised 41; 1917.1142: cup: 34, 28;[4] saucer: 29;[5] 1917.1143: cup: 44, 51;[6] 1917.1144: cup: 44; saucer: 48;[7] 1917.1145: cup: 47, 29; saucer: 48

Provenance: Cartier et Fils, Paris, 1902;[8] J. Pierpont Morgan

Model

This large tea service may have been accompanied either by a porcelain or painted tin tray.[9] The teapot is a shape called *théière litron* by the Sèvres factory, and was probably introduced in the 1780s.[10] A drawing in the factory archives from 1788 shows the outline of the body but no handle or spout (fig. 130-1).[11] Four earlier drawings in the factory are inscribed *teyere pour Les Litrons* but these appear to relate to a different shape, a teapot with angled walls and a double-curved handle.[12] A plaster model $6\frac{11}{16}$ inches (17 cm) high is still in the factory archives.[13]

Litron teapots were listed in four sizes in the 1788 inventories.[14] The earliest known example with secure decoration dates from 1786.[15] There were two variations of the form, one with an angular spout and one with a curved spout.[16] The Museum's teapot has the latter shape.[17]

The sugar bowl in this tea service is the model known as *pot à sucre Calabre*.[18] The present example corresponds to the first size. The milk jug is also an example of the first-size *pot à lait à trois pieds*, and the cups and saucers are third-size *gobelets litron et soucoupes*.[19]

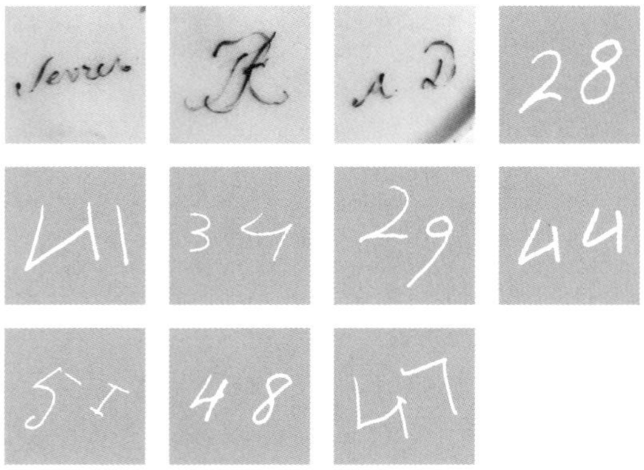

Marks

COMMENTARY

The decoration by Mademoiselle Durosey is typical of the simple and somewhat uninspired decoration that was common on everyday wares made at Sèvres during the Revolutionary period.

Exhibition: *Morgan Loan Exhibition*, New York, 1914, not in catalogue

Literature: Chavagnac, pp. 156–57, no. 202

NOTES

1 See dating proposed by Béalu, p. 39.

2 Active 1793–1803. See Peters, *Marks*, p. 31.

3 Savill, 3, p. 1131, lists 41 as found on pieces 1780–90s.

4 Ibid., p. 1129; 34 is found 1781–92. The Museum's cup thus extends the period in which this mark is found.

5 Ibid., found 1781–90s.

6 44 found 1778–90s (ibid., p. 1132).

7 Ibid., p. 1133, found 1777–92. Again, this saucer extends the period in which this mark is found.

8 APML, invoice, Cartier et Fils, 24 April 1902: "1 Service à thé Sèvres 1793 composé de 11 pièces bordure jaune & fleurs avec guirlandes sur fond blanc," 4,000 French francs.

9 See Savill, 2, pp. 491–92.

10 AMNS, Vy 1, fol. 28, 31 December 1753. See Sassoon, pp. 158–61 for this shape.

11 AMNS, R. 1, L. 4, d. 2, fol. 11. It is inscribed *theyere Litron grandie de plus que La 1er. Gr. D'un 10e. et demandé par M. Basin Le 8 avril 1788*. See Sassoon, p. 158.

12 AMNS, R. 1, L. 2, d. 4, fol. 2. See Sassoon, p. 158. The exact inscriptions are: *teÿere pour les litron janvijer 1753 le bas servira de boete à sucre; fait bon lanse bon ausÿ la constituer au goblet des dit litrons*, and *boete à sucre*; and *...pour les litrons (n° 1) faite le 19 fevrije suivan l'ordre de la comande du dit jour*, and *fait*. These most probably relate to a number of *théières à litron* sold from 1753.

13 AMNS, 1814 inventory, 1760–80, no. 1, *Théière Litron Ancienne* (Sassoon, pp. 158, 160 n. 1). For a discussion of several examples of this shape with earlier date letters, see Sassoon, p. 158. He convincingly argues that these are redecorated examples.

14 AMNS, I. 8, 1788, *magasin du blanc* (Sassoon, p. 158). The sizes may be: first size: H. 5½ in. (14 cm); second size: H. 4¼–4¹⁵⁄₁₆ in. (12–12.5 cm); third size: H. 3¾–3¹⁵⁄₁₆ in. (9.5–10 cm); fourth size: H. 3½–3⁹⁄₁₆ in. (8.8–9 cm).

15 For a list of other examples see Sassoon, p. 158. In addition to those listed see also: one without a cover (with a matching sugar bowl), Sotheby's, New York, 26 June 1982, lot 74 (dated 1787, yellow ground and arabesques); one hard paste, with cornflowers, 1790, Christie's, London, 3 October 1988, lot 89; another soft paste, pink *œil de perdrix* ground, fruit (en suite with helmet milk jug), 1782, Christie's East, New York, 27 October 1988, lot 249 (not examined by author for authenticity).

16 For the angular spout see the example in the J. Paul Getty Museum, Los Angeles (Sassoon, p. 158).

17 See also the teapot formerly in the Rockefeller collection, Sotheby's, New York, 11 April 1980, lot 245.

18 See cat. no. 87 for this shape.

19 For the milk jug, see cat. no. 87 and for the cups and saucers, see cat. no. 95.

Fig. 130-1 *Théière litron*, drawing

131

Helmet milk jug (*pot à lait aiguière*)

1917.1146

Sèvres, 1793

Soft-paste porcelain, H. 5¹⁵⁄₁₆ × w. 5¹³⁄₁₆ × D. 3¼ in. (15.1 × 14.8 × 8.3 cm)

Yellow ground with polychrome floral garlands, gilding

Marks: *Sèvres* and *R.F.* with date letters qq in blue; ... for Jean-Baptiste Tandart *aîné*;[1] v..D. in gold for Pierre-Jean-Baptiste Vandé *fils* or *aîné*;[2] incised 6 or 9[3]

Provenance: J. Pierpont Morgan

MODEL

There is little known about this model of milk jug. It probably was called *pot à lait aiguière*, but this name is rarely seen in the factory documents. In 1788 *pots à lait forme Eguere* in three sizes were fired in the glaze kiln.[4] In June 1805 three *pots à lait aiguière* were also glaze fired.[5] The model is probably the *pot à lait buire* that appears in the register of *tourneurs* and *mouleurs* in 1788.[6] This is the name used to describe a plaster model of the appropriate shape (fig. 131-1). It is one of two surviving at

(Below)
Fig. 131-1 *Pot à lait buire*,
plaster model

131

the Sèvres factory.[7] A drawing without inscription of this form
also survives at the Sèvres factory (fig. 131-2).[8]

This model seems to date from the late 1780s.[9] Other period
helmet jugs include a yellow-ground example, about 1793, in
the Victoria and Albert Museum, a blue-ground jug, 1790, in the
Louvre, and a white-ground jug with arabesques, 1789, in
the Musée national de Céramique, Sèvres.[10]

COMMENTARY

The Museum's milk jug was made in 1793 and decorated by
Tandart and Vandé. It may correspond to one of two *pots à lait
guirland sur fond jaune* decorated by Tandart 5 *frimaire* 1793
[25 November].[11] On 22 *frimaire an* II [17 December 1793], three
pieces of a tea set decorated by Tandart and Vandé with yellow
ground and garlands were fired in the enamel kiln and may
have included the Museum's milk jug.[12]

Exhibition: *Morgan Loan Exhibition*, New York, 1914, not in
catalogue

Literature: Chavagnac, p. 157, no. 202, Dawson, *British Museum*,
p. 165, no. 136

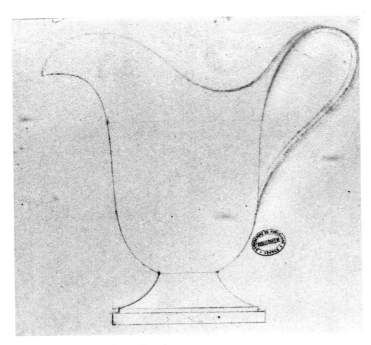

Fig. 131-2 *Pot à lait buire*, drawing

NOTES

1 Active 1754–1800. See Savill, 3, pp. 1070–71; Peters, *Marks*, p. 69.

2 Active as gilder and painter 1779–1824. See Peters, *Marks*, p. 72.

3 Found on soft paste c. 1754–90s. See Savill, 3, p. 1127–28.

4 AMNS, Vc'2, 10 and 24 March 1788. Extant examples support there being three sizes, although it is difficult to know when one size ends and the next begins. The third size seems to have ranged from 4¼ to 4½ in. (10.8–11.4 cm), the second size from 5⁷⁄₁₆ to 5¹⁵⁄₁₆ in. (13.8–14.8 cm), and the first size from 5¹⁵⁄₁₆ to 6⁵⁄₁₆ in. (15.1–16 cm). These measurements were taken largely from auction catalogues, and include obviously redecorated pieces, whose paste nevertheless is probably legitimate.

5 Ibid., Vc'5, 19 *messidor an* XIII [7 July 1805].

6 Ibid, Va'11, 1788, Le Riche, Berthault, Le Pin, Bougon *aîné*, Chanou *jeune*. Three sizes are mentioned (I am indebted to Tamara Préaud for this reference).

7 Ibid., 1814 inventory, 1780–1800, no. 4 (*casier* 776). The one inscribed underneath in early-19th-century writing, *pot lait Buire*, measures 6⁵⁄₁₆ in. (16 cm), and is lacking a handle (broken). The other model, with a handle, is 6⅞ in. (17.5 cm). The body measurements of both models are the same.

8 AMNS, R. 1, L. 2, d. 9, fol. 16.

9 A jug decorated with pink *œil de perdrix* ground and fruit by Pierre and Vincent (Christie's East, New York, 27 October 1988, lot 250, not examined by author to confirm decoration) is dated 1782, is possibly legitimate, which would put the introduction of the model in the early part of the decade. Tamara Préaud thinks it unlikely that this example has period decoration. There are many examples known with date letters in the 1750s and 1760s that appear to have been decorated in the nineteenth century. Among them are: Christie's, London, 13 December 1954, lot 148, yellow ground and birds, "1756, Aloncle;" Christie's, London, 29 June 1987, lot 158, birds and mosaic (matching Palatine service), "1759, Aloncle;" Van Slyke sale, Sotheby's, New York, 26 September 1989, lot 321, blue ground, putto, n.d. (style of 1750s); Christie's, London, 2 October 1979, lot 24, pink ground, flowers, "1770;" British Museum, London, no. 1948,12-3,45, pink ground, flowers and fruit, "1770," (see Dawson, *British Museum*, pp. 165–66, no. 136). Dawson lists other dubious examples as well.

10 V&A, London, no. C.381-1909, yellow ground, arabesques, Vincent, 5⁷⁄₁₆ in. (13.8 cm); Louvre, Paris, no. Th. 1242, blue ground, basket of flowers, Cornailles, 1790, 5¹⁵⁄₁₆ in. (14.7 cm) (Brunet and Préaud, p. 219, no. 285); MNC, Sèvres, no. 13.195, white ground, arabesques, Bouillat and Lafrance, 1789 (Dauget and Guillemé-Brulon, p. 41). This last example may have been part of two tea sets fired 2 March 1789, decorated by Bouillat and Lafrance, *fond, arabesques* (AMNS, Ve'2, fol. 128v). See Dawson, *British Museum*, pp. 165–66 for other examples. A white ground example with blue borders and arabesques, 1788, was on the art market in New York in 1999 (Christie's, New York, 16–18 November 1999, lot 229).

11 AMNS, Vj'5, fol. 207, Tandart.

12 Ibid., Vl'3, fol. 232v (mid-December 1793): *3 pièces de cabaret fond jau[ne] Guirland Tandart Vandé*.

132

Two wine bottle coolers (*seaux à bouteille ordinaires*)

1991.9–10[1]

Vincennes, c. 1751–1753

Soft-paste porcelain, 1991.9: H. 7¾ × w. 10⅜ × D. 8⅜ in. (19.7 × 26.4 × 21.3 cm); 1991.10: H. 7¹⁵⁄₁₆ × w. 10⅝ × D. 8⁵⁄₁₆ in. (20.2 × 27 × 21.1 cm)

White with gilded floral decoration

Marks: interlaced Ls under both; 1991.10, incised S[2]

Provenance: probably Guillaume-Joseph Dupleix de Bacquencourt, 1753;[3] Elizabeth Parke Firestone[4]

MODEL

Vincennes began making wine bottle coolers in about 1745.[5] By 1749, the form had evolved to the *seau à bouteille ordinaire*, represented by the Museum's examples.[6] In that short span of time the factory had experimented with proportions, moldings, and handles, the latter developing from entwined branches or foliage to more stylized leaf scrolls. The experimenting continued after 1749, culminating in a March 1753 revision of the model,[7] probably part of a factory-wide directive to reappraise and rectify as necessary models for all Vincennes porcelain. The Hartford coolers appear to have been made before that revision. We may assume this because their top rims share the same profile as a cooler at Waddesdon Manor, England, marked 1753–54, but have a different profile than the rim of another cooler in the same collection dated 1754–55.[8]

In the inventories of 8 October 1752 and 1 January 1753 there were two drawings of *seaux à bouteille* for Louis XV's early service.[9] One is described as being in pastel ornamented with painting and gilding, and the other, described specifically as *uni*, in white and black crayon.[10] They may have been by Duplessis, but they do not appear to survive. Another drawing still in the factory's archives relates to the rectification of the model, probably undertaken by Duplessis at the insistence of the director Boileau and the shareholders of the company (fig. 132-1). It is inscribed: "Drawing of wine bottle coolers shortened by 8 *lignes* [about ¾ inch or 18 mm] by order of Monsieur Boileau, 27 March 1753. On the 30 of said month it was decided by Messrs Verdun and company (of shareholders) to shorten it by 4 *lignes* [about ¹¹⁄₃₂ inch or 9 mm] only and to narrow it by two *lignes* [about ⁷⁄₃₂ inch or 5 mm]."[11] The drawing shows the general shape of the cooler, but depicts it standing on two feet rather than on a circular base. Another drawing showing the outline of the cooler in ten sizes is undated but is inscribed on the reverse *seau à verre ordinaire du Roy*.[12] A plaster model for the shape remains in the factory archives.[13]

In the October 1752 inventory there were four plaster molds of *grands Seaux à Bouteilles unis* valued at 1 *livre* each.[14] Three coolers, described as turned, were biscuit fired and ready to be glazed. At least twenty-one others were in the process of production.[15]

COMMENTARY

The earliest known sale recorded of *seaux* decorated with flowers and baskets like the Hartford coolers was made to the duc de Richelieu on 2 September 1751 (not recorded until October 1752) for 144 *livres* each. They had been fired in 1750.[16] It is likely that the Museum's coolers were two of four sold to a Monsieur Duplex on 10 January 1753, described as *blanc et or*. They had been fired sometime in the summer or fall of the previous year, and sold for 144 *livres* each.[17] There must have been two similar pairs, with different gilded borders, and the Museum has one cooler from each pair.

Monsieur Duplex was Guillaume-Joseph Dupleix de Bacquencourt, who was named *conseiller au Grand Conseil* on 23 October 1752. Born in Bordeaux in 1727, he was one of several tax farmers in the circle of Madame de Pompadour, along with the Bourets and the Parsevals, early financial backers of the Vincennes factory.[18] The coolers seem to have formed an ensemble with sixty plates *à godrons*, eight *compotiers ovales gravés*, and eight *compotiers à ozier* bought by Dupleix on 16 December 1752.[19] All were white decorated with gold. Monsieur Dupleix also bought fourteen *vases Chantilly* decorated with gold, two of the first size, and six each of the second and fourth sizes, when he bought his coolers in January. It is likely that an *assiette à godrons* illustrated in Garnier with gold bouquets in the center and on the rim is one of the sixty bought by Dupleix.[20]

The decoration of these wine bottle coolers bespeaks the factory's rapid mastery of gilding on soft-paste porcelain. In 1748 the marquis de Fulvy purchased the secret for gilding from a Benedictine monk Hippolyte Lefaure (Frère Hippolyte), and afforded the monk a yearly pension and the right to supply the factory with most of its requirement of prepared gold.[21] The earliest gold decoration, aside from simple bands, was highly dependent on Meissen decorative schemes, as exemplified by a two-handled cup and saucer with chinoiserie motifs in the British Museum.[22] Such tiny landscapes with chinoiserie figures frequently appeared on Augsburg- and Dresden-decorated Meissen in the 1730s.[23] Vincennes quickly forsook this imitative style and began ornamenting vases and wares with delicate floral sprays and fantastic birds.[24] In 1752 and 1753 Vincennes gilding was at its zenith, its pieces often richly adorned with birds in landscapes painted in gold and set in reserves framed by elaborate rococo gilding.[25]

The Atheneum's *seaux à bouteille* were made during this very fertile period. Small gold flowers have given way to extravagant floral sprays and entwined garlands, and the gilder has used an originally German technique of burnishing (without chiseling) to create naturalistic renderings without even a touch of color.[26] These decorations may have been inspired by Japanese lacquer, which was eagerly

132

132

collected in eighteenth-century France, notably by Madame de Pompadour.[27]

TECHNIQUE AND CONDITION

At Vincennes, gold leaf was mixed with gum arabic and ground into a fine powder, and then washed and strained according to different weights to produce what the factory called fine or heavy gold (*or fin* and *or gros*).[28] It then was mixed with a binding agent, called a mordant, and applied to the glazed porcelain with a brush. There were two mordants used at Vincennes. One, likely to have been used on these coolers, was made of garlic, onions and vinegar, and was mixed with powdered gold and painted onto the glaze. The other was made with gum arabic.[29] Each application required a separate firing, at a low temperature. After firing, the gilding appeared uniformly matte. Decorative details were attained by tooling and polishing the gold.

The gold on both of the Museum's coolers appears to be slightly thicker at the edges, suggesting that it may have shrunk during the firing. The delicate foliate swags, on the other hand, have a liquid quality to them. The cooler with the herringbone border (1991.10) has a large period firing crack underneath. It has been filled with bisque and glaze and then refired. Both coolers show some wear to the gilding, and on one side of 1991.10 horizontal abrasions suggest an overzealous cleaning at some stage.

Literature: Préaud and d'Albis, p. 132 (illustration of detail)

132

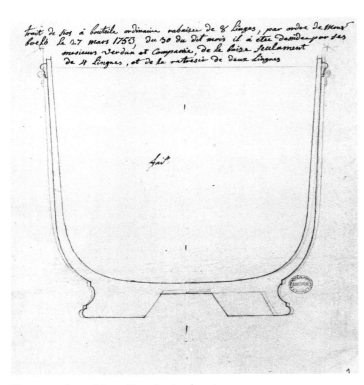

Fig. 132-1 *Seaux à bouteille ordinaire*, drawing

NOTES

1 Credit line, Gift of J. Pierpont Morgan, by exchange.

2 Savill, 3, p. 1122, found on soft paste by 1753–75, with a note that it was possibly used earlier.

3 See text below for discussion of factory sales records and identity of purchaser.

4 Christie's, New York, 21 March 1991, lot 163.

5 See Eriksen and Bellaigue, p. 214, no. 29 for an early example.

6 For the evolution of this form see Eriksen, *Waddesdon*, p. 36, no. 1, p. 51, no. 9, p. 77, no. 23; *Vincennes*, pp. 98–100; Eriksen and Bellaigue, pp. 228–29, no. 47, p. 265, no. 80, pp. 267–68, no. 82; Préaud and d'Albis, p. 154.

7 According to a drawing in the factory archives, discussed in detail below (text and note 11). The rim profile is also different than the one depicted on another drawing of this model, also discussed below (text and note 12). See also their probable sales history, which places them in a kiln firing of October 1752 (text and note 17 below).

8 Eriksen, *Waddesdon*, pp. 36–37, no. 1, and pp. 50–51, no. 9. They also have the same rim profile as a cooler with the date letter A from the Louis XV service in the Wrightsman Collection, MMA, New York, Dauterman, *Wrightsman*, pp. 226–27, no. 93B (marks described by Dauterman reversed, according to Clare Le Corbeiller).

9 1753–54. See cat. no. 58.

10 AMNS, I. 7, *1 Dessein de Seaux a Bouteilles en pastel orné de Peinture et Dorure/ 1 idem uni, en Crayon blanc et noir*, together 11 *livres*.

11 AMNS, R. 1, L. 1, d. 5, fol. 1: *Trait de sios [seaux] à bouteille ordinaire rabaisee de 8 Lignes, par ordre de Mons boeló Le 27 Mars 1753, du 30 du dit mois il a etee dessidee par ses mesieurs Verdun et Companie de Le baize seulament de 4 Lingnes, et de Le ratresir de deux Lingnes.* See Eriksen, *Waddesdon*, p. 36, no. 1; see Eriksen and Bellaigue, p. 267, no. 82 for interpretation of the directive. See also Sassoon, p. 146.

12 Sassoon, pp. 146, 151. See AMNS, R. 1, L. 1, d. 5, fol. 5a.

13 Sassoon, p. 146. See AMNS, 1814 inventory, 1760–80, no. 5.

14 AMNS, I. 7. Here is one of many instances that molds were made for pieces that were in fact turned. In view of the low price, it may be that the molds were for the handles only.

15 Ibid.

16 AMNS, Vy 1, fol. 13v, *fournée* 36 (1750).

17 Ibid., fol. 5, *fournée* 66. The link between these coolers and Dupleix was first pointed out in the Christie's sale catalogue for the Firestone Collection. Tamara Préaud has dated *fournée* 66 to between summer and October 1752 (Préaud and d'Albis, p. 92 n. 1). This precludes their being the four that left the kiln 30 December 1752 (IF 5676, fol. 2) cited by Christie's in its catalogue.

18 It is unlikely that Duplex could have been the Marquis de Dupleix as stated in the Christie's catalogue of the Firestone Collection as he was still in India in 1753, and the records say Monsieur Duplex and not the Marquis de Duplex. This and the following information were kindly provided by Bernard Dragesco. For Dupleix de Bacquencourt, see Antoine, p. 93 and Gallet, p. 176. For the Bouret brothers, Étienne-Michel and François Bouret d'Érigny, see Savill, 3, pp. 971–72. For Parseval, see Préaud and d'Albis, p. 128.

19 AMNS, Vy 1, fol. 4v. For *assiettes à godrons* see Préaud and d'Albis, p. 124, no. 48; for *compotier gravé*, see ibid., p. 70, no. 6, and for *compotier mosaïque* p. 70, no. 7.

20 See Garnier, pl. VIII. I would like to thank David Peters for pointing this plate out to me.

21 See Eriksen and Bellaigue, p. 54; Préaud and d'Albis, p. 30.

22 Eriksen and Bellaigue, p. 212, no. 26.

23 Meissen seems to have limited its gold decoration to chinoiserie or hunting subjects, with the exception of gilded decoration on black lacquered Böttger stoneware around 1720, which included birds and occasionally flowers. (I would like to thank Sheila Tabakoff and Meredith Chilton for advice regarding Meissen gilding.)

24 See, for example, the many *urnes Duplessis* (like cat. no. 54) decorated with gilded birds and flowers, such as in the David Collection, Copenhagen (Eriksen and Bellaigue, p. 247, no. 64). See also a pedestal in a private collection, Paris (Préaud and d'Albis, p. 157, no. 133) and the *tasse à toilette* at the Fitzwilliam Museum, Cambridge (ibid., no. 131). This type of gilding can be found on pieces that date from about 1749 through 1752. By this time Meissen was no longer using gold as primary decoration.

25 See the *bleu lapis* wine bottle cooler in the collection of Waddesdon Manor, Buckinghamshire (Eriksen, *Waddesdon*, p. 36, no. 1).

26 The impression of three dimensionality, especially evident on the flower petals, was achieved by contrasting polished and unpolished areas. The tradition of burnishing gold for naturalistic effects seems to have originated at the Meissen factory (or on Meissen pieces decorated by outside gilders). However, by the late 1740s and early 1750s gold as the primary decoration and chinoiseries of all types were out of fashion at Meissen. When the technique of gilding was taken over by Vincennes it was applied to a different idiom, that of naturalistic flowers. Burnishing was then combined with tooling to achieve the richest of effects.

27 See Watson, "Lacquer," passim. Figure 3, p. 108 of Watson's article shows a pot-pourri fashioned from a Japanese lacquer vase of c. 1720, decorated with large gold floral sprays reminiscent of the Vincennes coolers under discussion.

28 The description of gilding at Vincennes is taken from several sources. See d'Albis, "Hellot," pp. 265–66; Savill, 3, p. 1173; Eriksen and Bellaigue, pp. 54–56; Préaud and d'Albis, pp. 120, 225–27.

29 For extensive discussions of the mordants used at the factory see Préaud and d'Albis, pp. 225–26.

133

Pair of salt cellars (*salières à gondole*)

1917.999–1000

Sèvres, 1757–1758

Soft-paste porcelain, both: H. 1⁹⁄₁₆ × L. 4 × D. 2⁷⁄₁₆ in. (4 × 10.2 × 6.2 cm)

White ground with carmine garlands

Marks: 1917.999: interlaced Ls in blue with date letter E, painter's mark of three dots forming a triangle;[1] 1917.1000: no painted marks, incised cn[2]

Provenance: probably M.L. Fould Collection, Paris, 1884;[3] J. Pierpont Morgan

MODEL

The Sèvres factory called this form of salt cellar a *salière à gondole*. Molds and models appear in the inventory of 1758 under new work for 1757.[4] A plaster model labeled *salière Duplessis* is still in the factory archives (fig. 133-1).[5] The first mention of the shape in the sales records occurs on 11 October 1757, when six, possibly decorated with flowers, were sold to an unnamed buyer.[6] A pair decorated with a green ground and flowers was once in the collection of the comte Henry Costa de Beauregard, Paris.[7]

COMMENTARY

The Museum's salt cellars relate to another pair that appeared on the art market in Paris in 1993.[8] They may be comparable to the ten salt cellars that were included in a service sold through Lazare Duvaux on 5 September 1757 to Louis XV for his palace at Fontainebleau.[9] This service is decorated with floral garlands in monochrome carmine as well, but those garlands are in swags, suspended by ribbons, while on the Museum's salt cellars there are interlaced floral trails.

TECHNIQUE AND CONDITION

There is some evidence that the Museum's salt cellar with the mark of three dots was refired at a later date. It has heavy blackening on its base, as well as on the exterior and inside. The interior is also scraped and abraded. The gilded dentil inside the rim is cruder than its companion salt cellar. Two small gilded chips give further weight to this theory. It is possible that the original gilding became too worn, and that it was regilded, perhaps even at Sèvres in the eighteenth century. This would explain the appearance of the interior of the salt cellar. Contamination by its contents through use would have caused discoloring during a later firing.

Exhibitions: *Rétrospectives des Porcelaines*, Paris, 1884; *Morgan Loan Exhibition*, New York, 1914, not in catalogue

Literature: *Rétrospectives des Porcelaines*, p. 176, no. 705; Chavagnac, no. 87, p. 74, pl. XXVI; Brunet and Préaud, p. 153, no. 89

133

Fig. 133-1 *Salière à gondole*, plaster model

NOTES

1 The mark of an unidentified flower painter active c. 1756–57, specializing in monochrome flowers. See Peters, *Marks*, p. 88. See also a water jug and basin, dated 1757, with *camaïeu rose* decoration sold Christie's, New York, 5 May 1999, lot 23 (now thought to be decorated later after an example in Garnier, pl. IX).

2 Savill, 3, p. 1096, found on soft paste 1757–67, 1771–86?, usually on vases. Dauterman (*Marks*, pp. 186, 57) attributes it to a member of the Chanou family.

3 See 1884 exhibition below.

4 AMNS, I. 7, 1 January 1758.

5 Ibid., tiroir 269-241, L. 4¹¹⁄₁₆ x D. 2¹³⁄₁₆ in. (11.9 x 7.1 cm), 1814 inventory 1760–90. In Brunet and Préaud it was said that no plaster model survived.

6 Ibid., Vy 2, fol. 37v, 9 *livres* each.

7 Paris, Drouot, 2 April 1924, lot 34.

8 Ader, Tajan, Paris, 25 October 1993, lot 120 (bought in and offered again at Christie's, Monaco, 20 June 1994, lot 24). Although the catalogue states they were decorated by Sioux and Fontaine, this is a misreading of the marks. One was marked with a circle, the mark of an unidentified flower painter from c. 1752, c. 1753–57 (Peters, *Marks*, p. 88). The other mark is three dots, the same as on one of the Hartford salt cellars.

9 LD, 2, pp. 329–30, no. 2866. See also AMNS, Vy 2, fols. 48v–52v, second half 1757. Ten *salières* of an unspecified shape, with garlands, were included in this sale (see fol. 52v), costing 18 *livres* each. Supplements to the service were sold to both Louis XV and Louis XVI throughout the second half of the 18th century, some of which were later sold in Monaco in 1987 (Christie's, Monaco, 7 December 1987, lot 253). For more on this service see Peters, "Louis XV et Louis XVI," pp. 112, 123.

134

134

Pair of chestnut baskets (*marronnières à ozier* or *marronnières tenant au plateau*)

1917.1010–1011

Sèvres, c. 1759–1760

Soft-paste porcelain, 1917.1010: H. 5⁵⁄₁₆ × L. 10⁵⁄₈ × w. 8⁵⁄₁₆ in. (13.4 × 26.9 × 21.1 cm); 1917.1011: H. 12³⁄₈ × L. 10¹⁄₂ × w. 8³⁄₈ in. (31.4 × 26.6 × 21.2 cm)

Pink and green ground, gilding

Marks: both: interlaced Ls in blue; incised coffee bean with stem[1]

Provenance: J. Pierpont Morgan

MODEL

Chestnut baskets were made at Sèvres from 1757.[2] The following forms of *marronnières* are described in the factory stock lists and sales records: *unie*, *à compartimens*, *contourné*, *forme Pompadour*, *ovale*, *à jour*, *à ozier* and *tenant au plateau*. In fact, only two forms of chestnut baskets are known today, which must mean that more than one of the above titles was used to describe the same form.[3] For example, the basket model (such as the Museum's *marronnières*) was probably recorded in two or even three ways: as *à ozier* [basketweave],[4] *tenant au plateau* [attached to the stand], or perhaps *à jour* [pierced]. It is conceivable that the other model, the bowl-shaped *marronnière*, might have been recorded as *à jour* also, or *ovale*. *Marronnières à ozier*

were among the models introduced in 1758, while *marronnières tenant au plateau* featured in the glaze and sales records of 1759.[5] *Marronnières à ozier* were made in only one size.

Given that the sales records are so imprecise, it is difficult to know which form of *marronnière* was sold for what price. The range of prices was from 48 *livres* to 360 *livres*, although the average price varied from 108 to 240 *livres*.[6] Baskets described as *tenant au plateau* sold for 144 *livres* and 168 *livres* in 1759 (decoration not described) and for 240 *livres* in 1760 (listed with service pieces decorated with *mosaïque oiseaux*, although probably white with blue fillets).[7] Owing to the intensive labor and skill required to create the pierced walls, objects with very little painted decoration commanded very high prices. The number of examples spoiled in firing because of the inherent weakness of the pierced walls also had a bearing on the price. Chestnut baskets were sold singly, in pairs, occasionally in fours, and sometimes as part of dessert services.[8]

While the Museum's chestnut basket is the most common form of *marronnière à ozier*, there seem to have been two other versions made. The first of these—where the cover lacks the top row of piercing—is represented by an example at the J. Paul Getty Museum. The other model—where the basket-work piercing is more elaborate—is exemplified by a basket formerly in the Chappey Collection, Paris.[9] At least seventeen *marronnières à ozier* are known today.[10]

FUNCTION

Edible chestnuts are the fruit of the sweet chestnut tree and occur in two types, the *châtaigne* and the *marron*, the former consisting of three small nuts within one husk and the latter containing a single, large nut. In the seventeenth and eighteenth centuries *marrons* were served in several ways: they could be roasted and peeled, and then either served with syrup as a compote, covered with sugar (perhaps with a bit of lemon), or poached in syrup and then glazed with sugar (*marrons glacés*).[11] Pierced baskets must have allowed the air to circulate around the chestnuts so that they did not become too soft, and allowed excess syrup to drain into the stand.[12] Chestnuts were primarily autumn and winter fare. Recommended menus for the fall published in *Les Soupers de la cour* of 1755 list chestnuts as part of the dessert service, to be served both in compotes and on plates (or perhaps in baskets). The author of that book tells the cook to place the chestnuts in cinders and cook them until their skin can be removed, then simmer them for fifteen minutes in clarified sugar, then off the fire put them in the juice of bitter oranges, place in the compote dish, and dress with a little more sugar.[13] Chestnuts could also be skinned and cooked, covered with *nonpareille* (tiny sugar pellets, lightly heated as chestnuts are rolled in them) and then caramel, and afterward dried.[14] For a party of twenty-five to thirty guests, for which there were thirty compotes or plates of desserts, there were two compotes and two plates of chestnuts suggested.[15] Chestnuts could also be cooked and mashed and served as a vegetable course. In this case they would not have been served in a *marronnière*.

COMMENTARY

The Atheneum's chestnut baskets were made about 1759 or 1760. In these years the factory produced both ornamental and useful wares with the pink and green ground colors combined.[16] In fact, the vogue for this combination seems to have been confined primarily to these years.

There are no entries in the factory sales records during 1759 or 1760 that describe the Museum's pair of chestnut baskets, and there is no evidence of any dinner or dessert services being sold with pink and green decoration. However, in 1773 there were four pink and green *marronnières* in the sales room at Sèvres, selling for 168 *livres*.[17] These were probably old stock, whose decoration was by then out of favor (accounting for the low price). Two of these may be the Hartford baskets.[18]

TECHNIQUE AND CONDITION

Both basket and stand were molded separately. When first molded both elements would have been made with solid walls, their design of chevrons and ribbons molded in slight relief. Before firing but after the paste was leather-hard, a *répareur* created the openwork by cutting around the chevrons and ribbons, and joined the basket to the stand. In the bottom well of the stand, which was not pierced, it is possible to see the design in relief with the background not cut away. The ground color painter then applied the green to the ribbons and the pink to the chevrons before sending the basket to the gilder, who then outlined and enhanced the relief design.[19]

Exhibitions: *Morgan Loan Exhibition*, New York, 1914, not in catalogue; *Morgan*, Hartford, 1987, no. 63 (no. 1917.1010)

Literature: Chavagnac, pp. 78–79, no. 93; Hood, *Bulletin*, p. 10; Brunet and Préaud, p. 157, no. 101; Wilson, "Getty," p. 50, fig. 68; de Bellaigue, "Sèvres," p. 171, no. 63 (no. 1917.1010); Savill, 2, pp. 759, 761 n. 4d, 762 n. 28; Sassoon, p. 67

NOTES

1 Savill, 3, p. 1136, found from the 1750s. This incised mark is frequently found on objects from the 1760s and early 1770s such as flowerpots, tureens and their stands, baskets, and wine glass coolers (Eriksen, *Waddesdon*, p. 196, no. 71). It can also be found on three flowerpots (*cuvettes à tombeau*) in the Wadsworth Atheneum's collection (see cat. no. 70).

2 Sèvres chestnut baskets have been discussed by de Bellaigue, "Sèvres," p. 171; Savill, 2, pp. 758–62 and Sassoon, pp. 64–68. The following summary of the form is taken from these sources.

3 The other surviving model is a covered and pierced bowl with a separate stand. Examples can be found in the David Collection, Copenhagen (Eriksen, *David Collection*, p. 70, no. 54a, dated 1758), and in the MNC, Sèvres, no. 8847 (see Verlet, *Sèvres*, formerly in the Morgan collection).

4 *Ozier* is an old spelling for the French word *osier*, meaning water willow, and is used to describe wickerwork. Meissen extended the meaning of the term in 1735 to cover relief-molded basketwork.

5 AMNS, I. 7, 1 January 1758; IF 5674, fols. 97, 101, glaze kiln, 2 April 1759 and AMNS, Vy 2, fol. 8v, December 1759.

6 Prices of 300 and 360 *livres* probably applied to the bowl-shaped *marronnière* rather than the basket type (Savill, 2, p. 758).

7 AMNS, Vy 3, fol. 8, to the court, last quarter 1759; Vy 3, fol. 29, sold to Louis XV for the Elector of Palatine, April, 1760.

8 Although the literature on chestnut baskets refers to their inclusion in dessert services as frequent, in fact they were more often sold separately than with services. Between 1758 and 1762 thirty-seven *marronnières* were listed in the sales records, only eight of which were included in services. Out of the thirteen 18th-century services described in *Grands services*, only three list *marronnières*: the service for Maria-Theresa of Austria, the Palatine Service, and the Louis XVI Service. Of twenty services or ensembles that appear to have been services sold between 1760 and 1763, only four included *marronnières*. Of course, they may have been included in less grand "services" that may not have been described as such in the records, such as two with flowers sold to Louis XV in 1759 along with 50 plates (two different sizes), four *compotiers*, two *saussières*, and one *seau à glace*. While this does not seem to describe a full service it does describe some sort of ensemble. (See AMNS, Vy 3, fol. 7, last quarter 1759.) See Sassoon, pp. 66, 68 nn. 18–46 for recorded sales of chestnut baskets.

9 See Savill, 2, p. 758; Sassoon, pp. 64–68.

10 Listed in Sassoon. See also a pair in green and white at the Quirinale, Rome (Ghidoli, p. 124).

11 De Bellaigue, "Sèvres," p. 171 (La Varenne and Gilliers); Savill, 2, p. 760 (Diderot, *Encyclopédie*, III, 1772, p. 240). The *Larousse Gastronomique* states that *marrons glacés* are poached in vanilla-flavored syrup for forty-eight hours, during which time they are basted constantly with the sugar syrup while the heat is gradually increased. Then they are cooled and coated with liquid sugar to create a shiny, glazed coating.

12 Savill, 2, p. 760.

13 *Soupers de la cour*, 2, pp. 228–29.

14 Ibid., pp. 333, 335.

15 Ibid., 1, pp. 34–35.

16 While the first mention of this combination of ground colors appears in the sales records in December 1760 (AMNS, Vy 3, fol. 41v, second half 1760, *Gobelet & sou.pe Verd Et Roze*, Bachelier), many examples exist which are dated 1759. See Savill, 1, pp. 98–99, no. C226 (*vase à compartiments*, 1759); nos. C234–38, pp. 119–26 (*cuvette à tombeau, vase hollandois nouveau ovale, piédestal en gaine*, 1759). See also below no. 1917.1022–26, 1759 and 1760 (cat. nos. 86 and 87).

17 AMNS, I. 8, 1774 (for 1773), fol. 20.

18 See de Bellaigue, "Sèvres," p. 171, no. 63; Savill, 2, pp. 759, 762 n. 28; Sassoon, p. 66.

19 The handle of 1917.1011 has been broken off and reglued, with some filled repair under the handle.

135

135

Chestnut basket (*marronnière à ozier* or *marronnière tenant au plateau*)

1917.1016

Sèvres, 1759–1760

Soft-paste porcelain, H. 5⁵⁄₁₆ × L. 10¹¹⁄₁₆ × D. 8⅜ in. (13.5 × 27.1 × 21.3 cm)

White ground with blue fillets and gilding

Marks: interlaced Ls in blue with date letter G; unidentified painter's mark of a crown above; incised square[1]

Provenance: probably Cartier et Fils, Paris, 1902;[2] J. Pierpont Morgan

MODEL

This model of chestnut basket was made at Sèvres from 1757.[3] It is likely that an example decorated in this way would have cost either 120 or 192 *livres*. In 1760 one for 192 *livres* was sold to the dealer Sayde (*marronnière filets bleux*) while in 1761 two were sold as part of a service decorated with *ornemens bleux* to the comte de Durfort for 120 *livres* each.[4] It is possible that the Museum's basket was one of these.

COMMENTARY

This basket is formed of ribbons and chevrons, which have been left white, creating a more continuous interlaced effect.[5] It is possible to see the relief-molded details of these elements that in other examples would have been picked out in color or gold. On the Hartford basket only the rims, rope moldings, and top of cover with handle, have been highlighted in blue and gold.[6]

Another chestnut basket with blue fillets and gilding, which may be the mate to the Museum's example, recently sold from an American private collection, although there is no painter's mark and the interlaced Ls are ornate and do not match those on the Hartford basket.[7] The recently sold basket was formerly in the collection of Major-General Sir George Burns, the son of J. Pierpont Morgan's sister Mrs. Walter Burns. It is possible that either the two chestnut baskets were once together in Morgan's collection or that the brother and sister bought them at the same time, splitting the pair.[8] Another pair of white baskets with blue fillets is in the Residenzmuseum, Munich, and was included in a dinner and dessert service given by Louis XV to the Elector of Palatine in April 1760.[9]

The mark of a crown that appears underneath the Museum's chestnut basket is unusual. While the painter Sioux *aîné* uses a crown as his mark, the form of that crown is significantly different from that on the Atheneum's *marronnière*, the latter being much neater and more elaborate.[10] The factory mark and date letter are also much neater than those usually drawn by Sioux. They are, in fact, surprisingly similar to the mark that appears on the bottom of another chestnut basket, now in the Wallace Collection.[11] In this case, the interlaced Ls are surmounted with an unidentified mark of a candlestick with a smoking candle. The significance of this mark is unclear, as is its relationship to the mark on the Hartford basket.

Exhibition: *Morgan Loan Exhibition*, New York, 1914, not in catalogue

Literature: Hood, *Bulletin*, p. 10; Wilson, "Getty," p. 50; Savill, 2, pp. 759, 761 n. 4b, p. 1037 n. 2; de Bellaigue, "Sèvres," p. 85, no. 102; Sassoon, pp. 67–68

Notes

1 For the incised mark see Savill, 3, p. 1134. Savill speculates that it might be a pun on a name, perhaps François Carrette *aîné* (active 1754–70), and his son François (active 1768/9–87).

2 APML, Cartier file 2, invoice 24 April, 1902: "1 Marronniere Sèvres 1760 ajourée, decors filets bleus & or sur fond blanc avec couvercle," 1,500 French francs.

3 See cat. no. 134 for this model.

4 AMNS, Vy 3, fol. 13, 1 January–1 April 1760; Vy 3, fol. 86v, 31 December 1761. These two sales may have been for the two different models of chestnut baskets, the basket shaped and the bowl shaped. It is difficult to know, with similarly simple decoration, which would have cost more, a single bowl-shaped example or two basket-shaped examples.

5 See the pink and green examples discussed in the entry for cat. no. 134.

6 A large firing crack exists in the basketwork of the stand. There are also three large unexplained areas of bubbling glaze underneath. Normally this might be a sign of the use of turpentine in redecoration, but had the piece been redecorated it would have been made more elaborate. There are no other signs of redecoration.

7 Christie's, New York, 5 May 1999, lot 24.

8 The information on this second chestnut basket was published by Wilson, "Getty," p. 50. The invoice from Cartier et Fils pertaining to the Museum's basket shows that, at least in this purchase, there was only one basket included. Furthermore, in 1902 photographs of Morgan's house one white chestnut basket is visible on top of a piece of furniture. It does not appear that there were two, at least in the photograph. Unless Morgan bought the mate to the basket later, after the photograph was taken, it cannot be said that both the basket in Hartford and the basket in the Christie's sale were in Morgan's collection. I would like to thank Mr. Robert E. Parks at the Pierpont Morgan Library for sending me photocopies of the photographs of Morgan's house.

9 Residenzmuseum, Munich, nos. Res. Mü. K II.Sev./11–12. They are marked with the date letter G for 1759 (I would like to thank Dr. Sabine Glaser for this information). See also AMNS, Register Vy 3, fol. 29.

10 For a discussion of this painter's mark see cat. no. 106.

11 See Savill, 2, p. 760 (no. C473).

136

Punch Bowl (*jatte à punch*)

1917.1050

Sèvres, 1768

Soft-paste porcelain, H. 5¹⁵⁄₁₆ × DIAM. 13³⁄₁₆ in. (15.1 × 33.5 cm)

Bleu céleste ground with polychrome floral bouquets, gilding

Marks: interlaced Ls in blue with date letter P; painter's mark of P ', for Jean-Jacques Pierre *jeune*;[1] incised OO[2]

Provenance: Duveen Brothers, London, 1906;[3] J. Pierpont Morgan

Model

This bowl was known simply as a *jatte à punch*. Two molds for the model were listed in the earliest inventory of the factory, from October 1752, priced at 6 *livres*.[4] Punch bowls must have been made even before this, for one decorated with flowers that had left the kiln in 1749 was sold in 1753.[5] Punch bowls normally were accompanied by a mortar and spoon, which were not priced separately.

Function

Punch was usually a mixture of tea, lemon, sugar and alcohol. In France it was first called *bolle-ponche* [punch bowl] and was recorded there in the middle of the seventeenth century. The name punch is said to derive from the Sanskrit word *panch*, meaning five, which in turn is the number of ingredients used in a classic punch recipe (water being the fifth ingredient).[6] The mortar, or small, deep bowl, was for mixing fruit and spices to be used in the punch.

Punch bowls were included in most dessert services, and were one of the most expensive components. Three were in the Vincennes *bleu céleste* service for Louis XV, one priced at 1,000 *livres* (without a spoon) and delivered in 1753, and two more, priced at 1,200 *livres* and 1,500 *livres*, delivered in 1754.[7] Of the thirteen eighteenth-century services described in the exhibition *Les Grands Services de Sèvres*, ten included a punch bowl.[8]

Commentary

The Museum's punch bowl originally was paired with a mortar now at Waddesdon Manor, England.[9] The sales records do not allow us to identify the buyer of the set or the price set by the factory, as the several punch bowls and mortars sold from 1768 through 1770 are rarely described, and none is specifically noted as being *bleu céleste*. Prices of punch bowl sets sold from these years were 168, 192, 240, 480, and 528 *livres*. Only one entry, for 240 *livres*, is described as decorated with flowers.[10] In 1771 a *bleu céleste* punch bowl was sold to the baron de Breteuil for 480 *livres*.[11] Also in 1771 Louis XV offered a service to the future king of Sweden, Gustav III, on the occasion of his visit to Paris

136

in that year. It too was *bleu céleste* decorated with birds, and the punch bowl cost 600 *livres*. One would therefore expect the Hartford punch bowl to have cost between 480 and 600 *livres*.

The reserves with large bunches of fruits and flowers were painted by Pierre *jeune*, who specialized in flower painting during his career at the factory. According to the surviving documents and examples, he most often painted borders combining various flowers, foliage, and ribbons and pearls, but also painted bouquets and sprays of flowers. The factory must have appreciated his talents for he progressed from a monthly wage of 12 *livres* in 1763 to 78 *livres* by 1774. In 1768, when this punch bowl and mortar were decorated, Pierre was earning 45 *livres* a month.[12]

A watercolor painted by Claire de Chavagnac, daughter of the comte de Chavagnac who advised Morgan on his Sèvres collection, shows Morgan's "Louis XVI" drawing room at his London home with the Museum's punch bowl upon a table.[13]

TECHNIQUE AND CONDITION

The *bleu céleste* ground has a slightly mottled appearance, indicating that the color was sieved on, probably in two layers. Traces of powdered pigment appear in the interior, where it must have fallen in the course of application. The gold is thick and was applied in two layers, each fired separately. This is typical of gilding on *bleu céleste*, for the color contained large amounts of copper causing it to absorb the gilding during firing.[14] A hole was drilled under the foot of the bowl, initially to be used for a kiln support but never used. Given the weight of the piece, it must have been decided to support the bowl with a *pupitre*, as evidenced by the two indentations underneath the gilding on the exterior of the foot rim.[15]

Exhibition: *Morgan Loan Exhibition*, New York, 1914, not in catalogue

Literature: Chavagnac, pp. 106–7, no. 130

NOTES

1 Active 1763–1800. See Savill, 3, pp. 1059–60 for more on this artist. Chavagnac (p. 107) thought the P underneath the mark was a repetition of the date letter, and subsequently identified the mark (the comma) as belonging to Thévenet *père*.

2 See Dauterman, *Marks*, pp. 239–40, unattributed, found 1760s–70s.

3 APML, Duveen file, invoice 19 July 1906, "1 Fine Old Turquoise Sèvres Bowl painted with flowers and fruit in panels by Pierre Sr. (damaged)," £1,200.

4 AMNS, I. 7, 8 October 1752.

5 Préaud and d'Albis, p. 74, no. 14. See AMNS, Vy 1, fol. 2, 17 March 1753, *fournée* 19.

6 Toussaint-Samat, p. 603.

7 See Savill, "Premier service," p. 284, no. 81. See also Grégory, pp. 45–46. The 1,200 *livres* bowl was described as *moins parfait*.

8 *Grands services*.

9 See Eriksen, *Waddesdon*, pp. 240–41, no. 83. Geoffrey de Bellaigue, in correspondence with the author, was the first to link the two pieces.

10 See AMNS, Vy 4, fols. 150, 151, 153, 180, 182v, 193, 194v (flowers), 198, 206, 213, 225v, 232v.

11 AMNS, Vy 5, fol. 1v, 16 February 1771. This seems to have been an addition to a service bought by Breteuil in 1768 (Vy 4, fols. 142v–43),

which, based on surviving service pieces from this period, David Peters believes was either decorated with birds and palm/garland gilding, or possibly flowers with hatched/panel gilding. At the price of 480 *livres*, one would think that it was decorated with flowers. Perhaps price differences also reflect whether a spoon was included in the set.

12 Savill, 3, pp. 1059–60.

13 See fig. 2 in introduction. This drawing is in the collection of Yveline de Chavagnac, Paris, who very kindly brought it to my attention.

14 See Sassoon, p. 8. See also Préaud and d'Albis, p. 217.

15 As observed by Antoine d'Albis.

137

Wine glass cooler (probably *seau à verre échancré*)

1917.1070

Sèvres, 1771

Soft-paste porcelain, H. 4⅛ × W. 6³⁄₁₆ × D. 4⅞ in. (10.5 × 15.7 × 12.4 cm)

White ground with polychrome and gilded ciphers, polychrome garlands, pale blue and gilded urns

Marks: interlaced Ls in blue with date letter S, SS (crossed) for Nicolas Catrice;[1] incised LF,[2] and GR;[3] painted inscription n° in black

Provenance: Madame du Barry, 1771; Edouard Chappey, Paris, 1905;[4] J. Pierpont Morgan

MODEL

This wine glass cooler probably was called a *seau à verre échancré* by the factory, although the appellation was infrequently used. *Échancré* means indented or cut into and refers to the undulating top border of the cooler. The indentations helped support the glass as it was placed with the stem up in the cooler filled with iced water or crushed ice. The term first appeared in the inventory for 1758 but in this case must have described a larger, multi-glass cooler, later called a *seau crennelé*.[5] The first time *échancré* was used to describe an individual wine glass cooler seems to have been in 1773. Madame du Barry purchased two *seaux à verre échancrés* with *figures chinoises* for 192 *livres* each in August of that year.[6] Louis XV bought a *seau à verre échancré* decorated with garlands for Fontainebleau in September.[7] Six were included in a service (painted with a blue border, children, and baskets) delivered to the duc d'Aiguillon, minister of foreign affairs, to be sent as a diplomatic gift for Maria Carolina Luisa, queen of Naples. They were priced at 96 *livres* each.[8]

The few surviving examples of this form of *seau* indicate that it was being made from at least 1757 to 1758.[9] In the Victoria and Albert Museum there is one decorated with pink ribbons in scroll form and flowers on a white ground, dated 1757–58,[10] as well as a white and green example.[11] There is a pair decorated with flowers in the Art Institute of Chicago, dated 1758–59, one painted by Méreaud *père* and the other by Cornailles.[12]

137

Another set of four, decorated with carmine garlands tied with ribbons and dated 1763, is in the Jones Collection at the Victoria and Albert Museum. These were part of a service belonging to Louis XV.[13] Most of the other examples of this shape that are known relate to the same service as the Atheneum's example.

FUNCTION

Wine glass coolers, called *seaux à verre* in French, are small versions of wine bottle coolers.[14] They came into limited use in the early part of the eighteenth century, as Louis XV relaxed some of the rules of court etiquette and began hosting more intimate suppers, usually after the hunt.[15] The coolers were designed to keep glasses chilled, as they were now often placed on the table rather than the sideboard. According to one historian, coolers were also meant to prevent the glasses from touching the tablecloth.[16] A painting of 1735 by Jean-François de Troy, entitled *Le Déjeuner d'huîtres*, shows this more informal arrangement, with glasses placed in Chinese or Japanese porcelain bowls at each setting.[17] In 1738 the duc de Luynes wrote: "Everybody, even the king, is waited upon by blue-liveried stewards, or castle stewards; but the waiting is easy for every guest has his glass in a cooler before him, and the water and wine are on the table. Seigneur Lazure, who looks after the private rooms here [Compiègne] serves at table as he does at Versailles."[18]

As the century progressed, the practice of having more intimate dinners with fewer servants spread and individual wine glass coolers became more common components of dinner services. While Louis XV's *bleu céleste* service of 1753 and 1754 included twenty-four coolers,[19] most identifiable services of the 1750s and 1760s included *seaux crennelés*, which were larger, usually oval-shaped glass coolers that held twelve glasses at a time. These were most often placed on the sideboard rather than on the table.[20] Individual coolers featured more in services from the 1770s,[21] although they did not make *seaux crennelés* obsolete.[22] Many services contained both varieties of coolers.[23]

Wine glass and wine bottle coolers often served as flowerpots in the nineteenth and twentieth centuries and were thus frequently but erroneously referred to as *cache-pots* in the literature and in the trade.

COMMENTARY

The *seaux à verre échancrés* under discussion here belonged to a large service ordered by Madame du Barry, Louis XV's last mistress, in 1770 and delivered in August 1771.[24] This well-known service comprised 322 pieces, valued at 21,438 *livres*. It was decorated with small pale-blue vases and garlands of flowers, and Madame du Barry's cipher of DB, the D in gold and the B in flowers. The scheme was designed by Augustin de Saint-Aubin (1736–1807), a designer and draftsman who exhibited at the annual Salon from 1771 to 1793.[25] His drawing showing two proposals for the decoration of a plate, one corresponding to this service as executed, is in the collection of the Bibliothèque de l'Institut, Paris. It is inscribed *Projet d'un service pour être exécuté à Sevres pour Madame du Barry, 1770.*[26] The use of antique *cassolettes* and simple garlands of flowers reflects the period's return to classical design, albeit in a highly decorative way. The absence of a ground color allows the white body of the porcelain to become an important part of the design.[27]

Madame du Barry's service included four *seaux à liqueur ronds*, two *seaux à liqueur ovales*, four *seaux à demi-bouteille*, eight *seaux à bouteille*, four *seaux crennelés*, and thirty-six *seaux à verre*.[28] The last-mentioned cost 60 *livres* each. The model of wine glass cooler is not specified in the documents, but it is likely that they were all of this *échancré* shape.[29] Other examples have come on the art market over the years.[30]

Exhibitions: *Morgan Loan Exhibition*, New York, 1914, not in catalogue; *Continental Table Porcelain*, San Francisco, 1965, no. 249

Literature: Masson, pp. 1, 8; Chavagnac, p. 114, no. 141;[31] *Continental Table Porcelain*, no. 249

NOTES

1 Active as a flower painter 1757–74. Mark possibly the musical sign for repeat. See Peters, *Marks*, p. 22.

2 Savill, 3, p. 1112, as found on soft paste 1758–73. Probably for Louis Lefief, active 1758–74/75, who is recorded as having turned various *seaux* in 1773 (see AMNS, Va'1).

3 Dauterman, *Marks*, pp. 199–200, attributed to Claude-Jean-Baptiste Grémont *père*, active 1746–48, 1754–75, or Marguerite Grémont, active c. 1752–c. 1780.

4 APML, Chappey file, invoice 30 June 1905: "2 Cachepots ancienne porcelaine tendre de Sèvres à fond blanc décor de fleurs au centre chiffre de la du Barry," 16,500 French francs. 1917.1070 is one of these *seaux*. Morgan also bought two *seaux à verre* in this same pattern from A.B. Daniell & Sons, London, in 1900 (APML, Daniell file, invoice 25 May 1900: "A pair of small shaped Seaux in finest Sèvres porcelain pâte tendre, with festoons of flowers, & initials 'DB' in flowers and gold (part of service originally made for Madame Du Barri) A.D. 1771 £245." It seems likely that another glass cooler in the Museum's collection (cat. no. 194, a 19th-century fake, to be discussed later) came from Daniell. This means that one from Chappey and one from Daniell were kept by J.P. Morgan, Jr. after his father's death and sold at his death (Parke-Bernet Galleries, New York, 8 January 1944, lot 474). The catalogue states that they were dated 1770 but this must be incorrect. They were sold again at Parke-Bernet on 21 November 1952, lot 338, also dated 1770.

5 AMNS, I. 7, 1 January 1759 (work of 1758), molds and models, with consecutive entries: *2 [moules] du seau ovale Echancre a 12 verres,* 8 *livres/ [moules] du meme seau rond,* 8 *livres/ [moules] du meme seau a 6 verres,* 4 *livres.*

6 AMNS, Vy 5, fol. 135v, 31 August 1773, along with ten plates and other items for a small dessert service for Louveciennes.

7 Ibid., fol. 133, 48 *livres.*

8 Ibid., fol. 123, 4 December 1773. A *seau crennelé* was also included in this service, priced at 256 *livres.*

9 Because the term *échancré* only appears in the factory records in 1773, and then only rarely, it is likely that coolers of this shape were often lumped together with their simpler, plain-rim counterparts in the documents.

Perhaps this form may be recognized in the few wine glass coolers listed among molded pieces that one occasionally finds in the biscuit kiln records (for example, IF 5673, fol. 108, 2 July 1758 and fol. 110, 24 July 1758).

10 No. C.426-1921.

11 No. C.427-1921. It is decorated with green geometric interlaces which overlay a floral background.

12 Nos. 1987.236.1.2. I would like to thank Ghenete Zelleke for this information.

13 Nos. 760-61a-1882, decorated by Catrice. They were part of a credit sale purchase in December 1763 by Louis XV as a supplement for the Fontainebleau service, namely 24 *seaux à verre* at 48 *livres*. See note 7 for another supplement to the Fontainebleau service. I would like to thank David Peters for pointing out the relationship of these coolers to this Louis XV service. Another pair formerly in an American private collection is decorated in the same manner as the service with children and a blue border sent to Maria-Carolina-Luisa, queen of Naples, in 1774 (Christie's, New York, 5 May 1999, lot 54, see note 8 above). There is some doubt as to their authenticity, however.

14 See cat. no. 132 for this type of object.

15 See Saule, p. 58. Instead of being served by the *Bouche*, or officers assigned to serve the king his meals, Louis XV, at his unofficial suppers, was served by his personal staff, supervised by his *premier valet de chambre*. See note 18 below.

16 Havard, 3, p. 925.

17 Chantilly, Musée Condé. See Saule, p. 58.

18 Luynes, 2, p. 195 (quoted in Saule, p. 67 n. 128) "Tout le monde, le Roi même est servi par des garçons bleus ou garçons du château; mais le service est facile, car chacun a son verre dans un seau devant soi, et l'eau et le vin sont sur la table. Le Sr Lazure, qui a soin ici [Compiègne] des cabinets, sert sur table comme il fait à Versailles."

19 AMNS, Vy 1, fols. 45v, 68v. Another eleven *seaux à verre* were sold to Louis XV in 1760, probably as part of a simple service with flowers. See Vy 3, fol. 43v, December 1760.

20 See cat. no. 146 for more on this shape and its use.

21 At least six services from the 1770s included individual wine glass coolers: Mme du Barry, 1771 (see text); Gustav III, Sweden, 1 October 1771 (AMNS, Vy 5, fol. 11); comtesse d'Artois, November 1773, Vy 5, fol. 119v, 2 coolers; the duc d'Aiguillon for the ministry of foreign affairs, 4 December 1773, Vy 5, fols. 122v–23, six coolers (see note 8 above); Mme du Barry, August 1773, Vy 5, fol. 135v, two coolers (see note 6 above); Joseph II of Austria (under the name comte de Falkenstein), 1777, Vy 5, fol. 206v, twelve coolers.

22 At least thirteen services from the 1770s and 1780s included *seaux crennelés*. In 1758, coolers for six glasses were also listed in the inventory of new models and molds.

23 For example, a service sent to Gustav III of Sweden contained 72 individual coolers and eight *seaux crennelés* (see note 21 above).

24 AMNS, Vy 5, fol. 17. Pieces from the service are in many public collections, and have been published frequently. See *Grands services* pp. 30–31; Verlet, *Sèvres*, pp. 215–16, pl. 73; *Louis XV*, no. 535; Brunet and Préaud, p. 186, no. 187; Louvre, *Nouvelles acquisitions*, 1985, pp. 148–49, no. 84; Munger, *Wickes*, p. 200, no. 148.

25 See Cayeux.

26 Identified by Grandjean and Brunet in *Grands services*, p. 31. The alternate design consists of a continuous frieze of fruit-bearing grapevines with a cluster of grapes on a vine in the center. Mme du Barry's cipher is not part of Saint-Aubin's original drawing.

27 See Louvre, *Nouvelles acquisitions*, 1985, p. 149, and Munger, *Wickes*, p. 200.

28 AMNS, Vy 5, fol 17.

29 A pair of *seaux à liqueur ronds* in the collection of Waddesdon Manor, Buckinghamshire (Eriksen, *Waddesdon*, p. 262, no. 92, called *seaux à verre*) apparently is not authentic. I would like to thank David Peters for this information. For more on fake pieces from this service see cat. no. 194. A Christie's sale of 30 October 1947, lot 52, describes several *seaux*, two of

138

which were 5¾ in. (14.6 cm) wide, that were probably of this simple shape. It is impossible to know, however, if they were genuine.

30 Six were in the sale of Mme C. Lelong, Paris, Galerie Georges Petit, 28 April 1903, lot 151. Two were sold Baudoin/Ader, Paris, 17–18 December 1936, from the collection of François Coty. Seven are described in a Christie's, London, sale, 30 October 1947, lot 52. Two pairs were sold at Christie's, London, 28 October 1963, lots 133 and 134, and a single one at Christie's, London, 5 October 1981, lot 2. This same cooler was resold at Phillips, London, along with a second, probably fake example, on 4 December 1991, lot 205. See also one sold Ader, Picard, Tajan, Paris, 1 December 1997, lot 74. It will become evident from cat. no. 194 that some of these may not be authentic. (I would like to thank Letitia Roberts for helping me track some of these sales.) It is also possible that some of these sales include coolers from previous sales. This is difficult to determine from catalogues.

31 Chavagnac illustrates 1917.1071, which will be discussed in cat. no. 194.

138

Triple salt cellar (*salière à trois compartiments*)

1917.1072

Sèvres, 1771

Soft-paste porcelain, h. 3⅜ × w. 4⅛ in. (8.5 × 10.4 cm)

White ground with pale blue vases, polychrome flowers and garlands, gilding

Marks: abraded interlaced Ls in blue

Provenance: Madame du Barry, 1771; Cartier et Fils, Paris, 1902;[1] J. Pierpont Morgan

MODEL

The Vincennes factory probably made some form of triple salt cellar from at least 1752, for the October 1752 inventory lists two salts *à 3 marons* valued at 24 *livres* each.[2] The biscuit kiln records list two *salières à trois compartiments* between November 1753 and February 1754.[3] It is not clear whether these describe the same form. The inventory describing new work for 1757 lists molds and models for a *salière en 3 parties*.[4] A plaster model without handles and with traces of an old label still remains at the Sèvres manufactory.[5]

Many different descriptions of salt cellars appear in the factory sales records, the first dating from 9 November 1752.[6] Described simply as *salières fleurs*, they were probably rectangular in shape.[7] Eight were included in Louis XV's *bleu céleste* dinner service in 1754.

On the whole, few salt cellars were sold until 1756, at which time several other forms of salt cellar were listed in the sales records.[8] Among those mentioned between 1756 and 1760 are *feuille de vignes*,[9] *à ozier*,[10] *à pans coupé*,[11] *pour mesdames*,[12] *couverte*,[13] *à marons*,[14] *en trois parties*,[15] *gondoles*,[16] *doubles*,[17] *à ances* [*sic*],[18] and *à panier*.[19] Clearly those described as having three parts must refer to the Atheneum's model. *Salières à ances* [*sic*] [with handles] probably describe the same model.

FUNCTION

Salt cellars have long been an indispensable household object. In thirteenth-century France salt became expensive when it was subjected to taxation.[20] From then on and into the Renaissance the wealthy had salt cellars made of precious metal, which were often highly complex and decorative. They usually were placed in the center of the table or next to the master of the house.[21] Many were equipped with locks to prevent anyone from mixing in powdered arsenic, which looked very much like salt. The lower classes, on the other hand, would make salt cellars out of little hollowed-out cubes of bread.[22]

As the centuries progressed, the decorative and symbolic importance of salt on the table decreased. By the second half of the eighteenth century salt cellars were generally small, often made in sets with one placed in front of each diner. This was true of both metal salt cellars and the porcelain versions that came into fashion with the advent of this new material.[23] It was not uncommon to vary the ingredients used in these salt cellars, to include celery or garlic salt, or other powdered spices.[24]

From the first dinner service created for Louis XV in 1753–54 salt cellars became a standard component of most services sold by the Sèvres factory. Among those with *salières à trois compartiments* that are documented are: the service given by Louis XV to the Duchess of Bedford in 1763; the Starhemberg service of about 1766; Madame du Barry's service of garlands and antique vases (including the example under discussion); the service given to the future Gustav III of Sweden in 1771; two services bought by the foreign ministry in 1773 as diplomatic gifts; a service given to the Duchess of Manchester in 1783; and a second service given to Gustav III in 1784.[25] Sometimes single or double salt cellars, or both, were also present in these services.

COMMENTARY

The service made for Madame du Barry in 1771 contained 12 three-part salt cellars, but no single or double salt cellars.[26] Another triple salt cellar from this service was sold from the Coty collection in Paris in 1936.[27] There are other examples in the Musée national de Céramique, Sèvres, and in the Musée et Château, Boulogne-sur-Mer.[28]

Exhibition: *Morgan Loan Exhibition*, New York, 1914, not in catalogue

Literature: Chavagnac, p. 115, no. 142

NOTES

1 APML Cartier file, invoice 23 April 1902: "1 salière triple en Sèvres (du Barry service) décor vases et guirlandes de fleurs," 1,200 French francs.

2 AMNS, I. 7, 8 October 1752, *pièces en couverte, cuite*. See Dawson, *Ashmolean*, p. 54, no. 39. *Marrons* are chestnuts, and may have been used figuratively to describe the three compartments. See cat. no. 134 for *marrons*.

3 IF 5673, fol. 15. See *Vincennes*, p. 96; Dawson, *Ashmolean*, p. 54.

4 AMNS, I. 7, 1 January 1758.

5 AMNS, *casier* 787. Tamara Préaud believes that this plaster model is a re-edition, dating from the 19th or 20th century.

6 AMNS, Vy 1, fol. 5, Mme de Pompadour, 9 November 1752.

7 Préaud and d'Albis, p. 162, no. 145.

8 From the earliest sales registers until 1756, salt cellars appear six times, thirty-three sold in total. See AMNS, Vy 1, fols. 5, 6v, 26v, 45, and 87.

9 Ibid., fol. 127v, unnamed buyer, 3 June 1756, *6 livres*. Thought to be a footed salt cellar with vines now in the MNC, Sèvres, no. 5837 (see *Vincennes*, p. 95, no. 235).

10 AMNS, I. 7, 1 January 1758, molds and models 1757.

11 Ibid.

12 Ibid.

13 AMNS, Vy 2, fol. 30v, unnamed buyer, 1 July 1757, *fleurs, 12 livres*.

14 Ibid., fol. 37v, unnamed buyer, 8 October 1757, not described, *108 livres*.

15 Ibid., 11 October 1757, not described, *15 livres*.

16 Ibid., *9 livres*. See cat. no. 133 for this form.

17 Ibid., fol. 52v, Duvaux, 1 July 1757–1 January 1758, *verd fleurs, 72 livres*. See example in the Starhemberg service, c. 1766, at Waddesdon Manor, Buckinghamshire (Savill, "Starhemberg," pp. 25, 28).

18 AMNS, Vy 2, fol. 78v, Mme de Pompadour, 30 December 1758, not described, *24 livres*.

19 Ibid., Vy 3, fol. 7v, Mme de Pompadour, December 1759, *fleurs, 24 livres*. The same shape might be described by several names.

20 Toussaint-Samat, p. 465. The salt tax or *gabelle* was created by Philippe le Bel at the end of the thirteenth century. This tax was levied arbitrarily on the lower classes of France, who not only had to pay the tax but were required to buy salt in fixed quantities. The nobility, clergy, and prominent citizens were exempt from paying this onerous tax. The *gabelle* continued to be levied in France until the French Revolution.

21 Ibid., p. 824, and Gruber, p. 161.

22 See Havard, 4, pp. 823–31.

23 Gruber, p. 165; Havard, 4, p. 831.

24 See Dawson, *Ashmolean*, p. 54; Gruber, p. 165.

25 See AMNS, Vy 3, fol. 125; Savill, "Starhemberg," p. 28; Vy 5, fol. 17; Vy 5, fol. 11; Vy 5, fols. 89v, 93v; de Bellaigue, "Diplomatic Gift," passim; Vy 5, fols. 113, 136v (see *Grands services*, pp. 33–34). This is not meant to be a complete listing of all documented services that include a three-part salt cellar.

26 AMNS, Vy 5, fol. 17. For more on this service see cat. no. 137.

27 Drouot, Paris, 17–18 December 1936, lot 39.

28 No. 16489 (see Brunet and Préaud, p. 186, no. 187); *Nord-Pas-de-Calais*, pp. 126–27, no. 99. There was a pair in the Chappey Collection, Paris, as well. See Masson, p. 21.

139

Mustard tray (*plateau de moutardier ordinaire*)

1917.1074

Sèvres, 1773

Soft-paste porcelain, H. 1⅜ × L. 7⅛ × w. 5½ in. (3.5 × 18 × 13.9 cm)

White ground with polychrome baskets, wreaths, and putti, gilding

Marks: interlaced Ls in blue with date letter u; five dots in diamond form for Jacques Fontaine;[1] # in gold for Michel-Barnabé Chauvaux aîné, *père*;[2] monogrammed vd in gold for Jean-Baptiste-Emmanuel Vandé *père*;[3] incised 74

Provenance: Maria Carolina Luisa, queen of Naples, 1773; probably Edouard Chappey, Paris, 1905;[4] J. Pierpont Morgan

MODEL

This stand was made to accompany a mustard pot (*moutardier ordinaire*). Mustard pots with trays were made from at least 1752. Several forms were mentioned in the inventory of October

1752, including *moutardiers à cerceaux*, *moutardiers unis*, *moutardiers façon de Barils*, *moutardiers de differentes grandeurs ovales*, *moutardiers à ornemens de M. Duplessis*, and *barils à moutarde*.[5] Trays are listed with the glazed *moutardiers unis* as well as with unspecified mustard pots in biscuit and in white ready for decoration.[6]

At first the mustard tray at Vincennes had pointed sides and ends, closely copying a Meissen model.[7] Then the design must have been rectified in 1753, for a drawing of the mustard pot, with a cross-section and full view of the tray in its revised form bears an inscription noting that this was a redesign (fig. 139-1).[8] This new shape with indented sides and ends conforms to the Hartford tray. Three wax models for *plateaux de moutardiers* appear in the list of new work for 1753 and probably are of the modified shape.[9] *Moutardiers nouveaux* are listed among plaster models for which there were as yet no molds.[10] Molds for both must still have been forthcoming.[11]

The earliest recorded sale of a *moutardier* with its stand was to Lazare Duvaux in December 1752.[12] Mustard pot sets ranged in price from 18 *livres* for a simple example with flowers to 120 *livres* for *bleu céleste* with flowers or birds.[13] Louis XV's first service with a *bleu céleste* ground included six sets.[14] Many mustard sets were made in yellow, which may have a direct correlation to the color of mustard itself.[15] Examples of trays in the newer form may be found in the Musée des Arts décoratifs, Paris, and in the collection at Firle Place, Sussex.[16]

FUNCTION

Mustard has been used as a condiment since antiquity. Seeds of the *Sinapis* plant were crushed into a fine powder, and from there could be mixed with vinegar, grape must (from whence came the name mustard or *moutarde* in French), or honey.[17] If it were used in powder form it would have been sprinkled from a caster resembling that used for sugar.[18] When served as a paste or sauce it was placed on the table in a container accompanied by a spoon. Although many mustard pots were made of silver or silver-gilt, these materials were not well suited for serving mustard, which contained corrosive vinegar. Porcelain mustard pots provided a better alternative.

In the Middle Ages mustard was kept in small wooden or stone barrels on dressers. This custom continued into the eighteenth century, when mustard pots often were shaped like barrels.[19] Most Vincennes and Sèvres mustard pots conformed to this tradition.

Mustard usually was served as an accompaniment to roasted meats. In the eighteenth century other ingredients were mixed with it, such as capers, anchovies, and champagne (for women).[20]

COMMENTARY

Mustard pots and their stands were sold separately as well as with most savory services.[21] The Sèvres sales registers record that a service for six persons, decorated with blue borders, children, and baskets, was delivered to the duc d'Aiguillon, foreign minister, on 4 December 1773.[22] The ministry of foreign affairs listed this service among gifts made in January 1774 by Louis XV to Maria Carolina Luisa (Marie-Caroline-Louise), queen of Naples, daughter of Maria-Theresa of Austria and sister of Marie-Antoinette, who was married to Ferdinand IV of Naples and III of Sicily. It was given on the occasion of the birth of Maria Carolina Luisa's daughter Louise, goddaughter of the French king.[23] The service included 114 pieces and 39 biscuit figures, and was valued at 12,424 *livres*. The Museum's tray (with its pot, now lost) was one of two *moutardiers* included in that service. The floral cipher of a crowned CL probably

refers to Charlotte-Louise, as the queen of Naples was known in France in the 1770s.[24]

The decoration reflects the same taste for a somewhat sweetened classical decoration on a white ground found on Madame du Barry's service. It also presages the decoration of the dinner set known as *service des Asturies* that was presented in 1774–75 to Louis XV's granddaughter Marie-Louise of Parma, wife of the prince of Asturia, the future Charles IV of Spain.[25] This service also is adorned with a cipher CL, which has been the cause of some confusion in the past. However here the C, for Carlos, is in gold and the L, for Luisa, is in flowers, and the cipher is not crowned.[26]

It is not known when the Maria Carolina Luisa service was dispersed, but in 1971 approximately forty pieces came on the art market.[27] Clearly many pieces of the service had been sold before then for the Museum's mustard tray was in J. Pierpont Morgan's collection before it was catalogued in 1910. Many examples from this service are in public collections today.[28]

TECHNIQUE AND CONDITION

There are scattered firing flaws on the exterior of the mustard tray, two of which appear to have been caused by contact with a kiln support.

Exhibition: *Morgan Loan Exhibition*, New York, 1914, not in catalogue

Literature: Chavagnac, pp. 116–17, no. 145

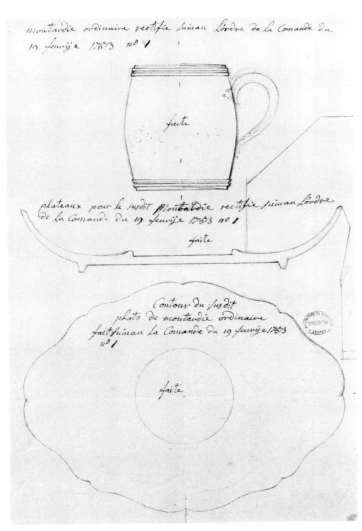

Fig. 139-1 *Moutardier et plateau*, drawing

NOTES

1 Active 1752–1800. He painted flowers, cherubs, *grisaille* heads or trophies in imitation of classical cameos, and patterned grounds (*pointillé*). He also worked as a gilder. For more on Fontaine see Savill, 3, pp. 1033–35; Peters, *Marks*, p. 34.

2 Active 1752–88. Chauvaux worked primarily as a gilder, although he was also known to have been a painter. For more see Savill, 3, pp. 1020–21; Peters, *Marks*, p. 24.

3 Active 1753–79. Vandé was a gilder, burnisher, and a painter. See Savill, 3, pp. 1072–73; Peters, *Marks*, p. 72.

4 See Masson, p. 21, second shelf.

5 AMNS, I. 7, 8 October 1752.

6 Ibid., *pièces en Biscuit prêtes à etre mises en couverte*; *pièces en Blanc entre les mains des peintres*.

7 See Jedding, *Meissener Porzellan*, pp. 97–98, no. 79, for an example dated c. 1730–35, L. 6¹¹⁄₁₆ in. (17.3 cm). See also Wark, *Meissen*, p. 254, no. 626. This slightly late example measures 7⅛ in. (18 cm), indicating that the Sèvres model was close in size to the Meissen original.

8 AMNS, R. 1, L. 1, d. 8, fol. 1, inscribed *moutardie ordinaire rectifie suivan l'ordre de la comande du 19 fevrÿe 1753 n°1, faite* and *Plateaux pour le susdit moutardie rectifie suivan l'ordre de la comande du 19 fevrÿe 1753 n°1, faite, contour du susdit plato de moutardie ordinaire fait suivan la comande du 19 fevrÿe 1753 n°1, faite.*

9 AMNS, I. 7, 1 January 1754 (for 1753).

10 Ibid., *Modeles en Plâtre dont il ny a point encore de moules.*

11 See Brunet and Préaud, p. 204, no. 239. They were not listed in the inventory of the following year but the list probably included only new work for 1754, which technically might not have included a design from 1753.

12 AMNS, Vy 1, fol. 6, 28 December 1752 (*fournée* 66, 1752), one decorated with flowers, for 30 *livres* and one with flowers and birds for 36 *livres*. See Préaud and d'Albis, p. 122, no. 43.

13 The average set with flowers cost 30 *livres* (AMNS, Vy 1, fol. 18,

15 October 1753, unnamed buyer). A yellow ground example with garlands cost 48 *livres* (ibid., fol. 22, 18 December 1753, Bailly), as did a white ground set (ibid., fol. 61v, 23 December 1754, Bazin). A *bleu lapis* set with colored birds was sold to Bazin for 60 *livres* on 23 December 1754 (ibid.) and the *bleu céleste* sets for Louis XV's service were priced at 96 *livres* (ibid., fol. 45, 30 June 1754). The more expensive *bleu céleste* set with flowers was sold to Bailly on 23 December 1754 (ibid., fol. 62).

14 See note 13 above.

15 *Vincennes*, p. 58.

16 See *Vincennes*, p. 60, no. 107, dated 1753–54, *bleu lapis* ground; *bleu Fallot fond Taillandier* and flowers, c. 1766–67; see also a *bleu céleste* example with flowers, dated 1766, in the Elisabeth Parke Firestone sale (Christie's, New York, 21 March 1991, lot 291) and another with *mosaïque* decoration, 1760, sold Christie's, Monaco, 7 December 1987, lot 203.

17 For information on mustard, see Gruber, pp. 173–75; Toussaint-Samat, pp. 526–29.

18 It would have been smaller. See Gruber, p. 174.

19 Ibid. Savill, "Starhemberg," p. 28, suggests that the barrel shape, usually associated with alcohol, may refer to the white wine that was mixed with ground mustard to make Dijon mustard (*blanc de Dijon*).

20 Toussaint-Samat, p. 528.

21 See *Grands services*.

22 AMNS, Vy 5, fols. 122v–23.

23 See Verlet, "Reply," p. 43 (Paris, *Archives des Affaires étrangères, Journal des présents du roi*, 2095, fol. 26).

24 Eriksen and Bellaigue, p. 155, referring to the *Almanach Royal*.

25 See Brulon, "Asturies,", p. 339. Pierre Ennès suggests that the Maria Carolina Louisa service may be related in some way to another service begun for Mme du Barry but abandoned in favor of the service with garlands and vases (in *Tables royales*, p. 338, nos. 293–95). In private correspondence, David Peters mentions a service for Mme du Barry with *chiffre*, *corbeilles*, and *enfants*, which seems to be that service. Its history is unclear.

26 Pierre Verlet was able to separate this service from the Maria Carolina Louisa service in his 1956 article for *Cahiers de l'art céramique*. See note 23.

27 Sotheby's, London, 30 March 1971, lot 176 (see Eriksen and Bellaigue, p. 155).

28 See a *seau à demi bouteille* in the Louvre, Paris (no. OA 10879), a plate in the Musée et Château, Boulogne-sur-Mer (L. 449), another plate in the MMA, New York (no. 1972.23), and a plate in the MNC, Sèvres (no. 23423).

140

Pair of salt cellars (*salières simples*)

1917.1075–1076

Sèvres, 1773

Soft-paste porcelain, 1917.1075: H. 1⁹⁄₁₆ × L. 3⅜ × W. 2⁹⁄₁₆ in. (3.9 × 8.5 × 6.5 cm); 1917.1076: H. 1⁹⁄₁₆ × L. 3⅜ × W. 2⁹⁄₁₆ in. (3.9 × 8.6 × 6.5 cm)

White and *bleu nouveau* ground, polychrome baskets, wreaths, and trophies, gilding

Marks: 1917.1075: interlaced Ls in blue with date letter U, five dots in diamond form for Jacques Fontaine;[1] incised script L;[2] 1917.1076: effaced interlaced Ls in blue; incised j[3]

Provenance: Maria Carolina Luisa, queen of Naples, 1773; J. Pierpont Morgan

140

MODEL

This model is called *salière simple* in the Vincennes-Sèvres factory's sales records. Many different models of salt cellars are recorded in the factory documents.[4] The earliest mention of salt cellars in the factory inventory is in the list of plaster molds for 8 October 1752, when twelve *moules de Salieres de 3 différentes grandeurs à 5 sols* are described.[5] Among glazed and fired pieces in the same inventory there were seventeen unspecified salt cellars valued at 40 *sols* and two *à 3 marons* valued at 24 *livres*.[6] The unspecified salt cellars probably were of a simple, trencher shape, such as one in the Musée des Arts décoratifs, Saumur, France.[7] Like most of the early models this form may have been modified in the course of 1753, for the biscuit kiln records list two *salières simples forme nouvelle* among pieces coming out of the kiln on 28 September 1754.[8] In the January 1755 inventory three different models of salt cellars appear among glazed pieces ready to be painted: eight *salières ordinaires*, four *salières nouvelle forme double*, and two *salières nouvelle forme simple*. This is the first mention of a *salière simple*. It is possible that the *salières ordinaires* or standard salt cellars refer to the trencher-shaped model mentioned above, while the new, simple salt cellars conform to the Museum's pair. By 1757 molds for six different models of salt cellar were in stock.[9]

There is a plaster model in the archives of the Sèvres factory that conforms to the Museum's example, although its dimensions differ slightly.[10] The 1814 factory inventory of models listed it as a *salière carrée*.[11]

Early sales registers do not designate particular models of salt cellars. The first recorded sale was of nine *salières fleurs* sold to Madame de Pompadour on 9 November 1752.[12] Like most simple or unspecified models decorated with flowers they cost 12 *livres* each. The first mention of another model of salt cellar in the sales records occurs with the sale of *sallieres couvertes fleurs* and *sallieres non couvertes* in 1757.[13] Relatively few sales of any type of salt cellar were recorded between 1753 and 1757, but there was a noticeable increase in their sales beginning in 1758. Different models are now described, such as *salières à trois parties*, *gondoles*, and *doubles*. Only with the service given by Louis XV to Maria-Theresa, Empress of Austria, in December 1758, does one find specific mention of *salières simples*.[14]

COMMENTARY

The Atheneum's salt cellars were two of four delivered to the duc d'Aiguillon, minister of foreign affairs, as part of a service presented by Louis XV to Maria Carolina Luisa, queen of Naples.[15] The service also included two double salt cellars. While the larger pieces of the service were marked by a cipher of CL, the salt cellars were not. However, it is clear from the rest of their decoration—trophies, baskets of flowers, laurel wreaths, and a blue border with gilded oak leaves—that these salt cellars were from the same service.[16]

Exhibition: *Morgan Loan Exhibition*, New York, 1914, not in catalogue

Literature: Chavagnac, p. 117, no. 146

NOTES

1 See cat. no. 139.

2 Found on soft-paste 1755–75, 1787. See Savill, 3, p. 1111. Possibly for Lauvergnat *aîné* (active 1749/52/54–72/73), and Lauvergnat *jeune* (active 1754–74/75).

3 Found on soft paste 1753–73. See Savill, 3, p. 1110.

4 See cat. no. 138.

5 AMNS, I. 7, 8 October 1752, *moules en plâtre*. No model is listed. In this same inventory there is an unfinished *esquisse en cire* of salt cellars in the form of a small basket (*petit panier*).

6 Ibid. See cat. no. 138.

7 See Préaud and d'Albis, p. 162, no. 145.

8 IF 5673, fol. 27. Tamara Préaud has suggested that these could correspond to four *salières Verdun* cited in the biscuit kiln records for 28 February 1754 (IF 5673, fol. 15).

9 AMNS, I. 7, 1 January 1758 (for 1757): *à ozier* (two sizes); *à pans coupé*; *à gondole*; *quarré unie*; *en 3 parties*; and *pour Mesdames* (two sizes). The biscuit kiln records also list nine *sallieres a tombeaux* among pieces emerging from the kiln on 6 September 1757 (IF 5673, fol. 85). This model is unidentified.

10 AMNS, *casier* 790, L. 3⁹⁄₁₆ × D. 2¾ in. (9 × 6.9 cm), incised Leroy.

11 Ibid., 1814 inventory, 1740–60, no. 4, *salière simple carrée 1r et 2e gr*; nos. 1–2, *carrée 1r et 2e g*.

12 Ibid., Vy 1, fol. 5.

13 Ibid., Vy 2, fol. 30v, unnamed buyer, 1 July 1757.

14 Ibid., fol. 85, December 1758, valued at 36 *livres* each.

15 See cat. no. 139 for this service.

16 The larger pieces also have cherubs in panels rather than trophies, as the latter may have been deemed more appropriate to the less monumental elements of the service and in any case would fit more easily in the smaller panels.

141

Pair of oval fruit dishes (*compotiers ovales*)

1917.1082–1083

Sèvres, probably 1774

Soft-paste porcelain, 1917.1082: H. 1¹¹⁄₁₆ × L. 10¹¹⁄₁₆ × W. 7⅝ in. (4.2 × 27.2 × 19.3 cm); 1917.1083: H. 1¹¹⁄₁₆ × L. 10⁹⁄₁₆ × W. 7¹³⁄₁₆ in. (4.3 × 26.8 × 19.8 cm)

Pink ground, polychrome flowers, gilding

Marks: 1917.1082: interlaced Ls in brown with effaced mark of Jacques-François-Louis de Laroche;[1] LG in blue for Étienne-Henry Le Guay *aîné*, *père*;[2] BD in blue for François Baudouin *père*;[3] incised pg;[4] 1917.1083: interlaced Ls in brown, marks for Le Guay and Baudouin in blue; incised script j[5]

Provenance: probably Jacques Dumoulin, 1774;[6] John Julius Angerstein (1735–1823), 1860;[7] Willoughby J.G. Loudon, 1902;[8] Duveen Brothers, London, 1902;[9] J. Pierpont Morgan

273

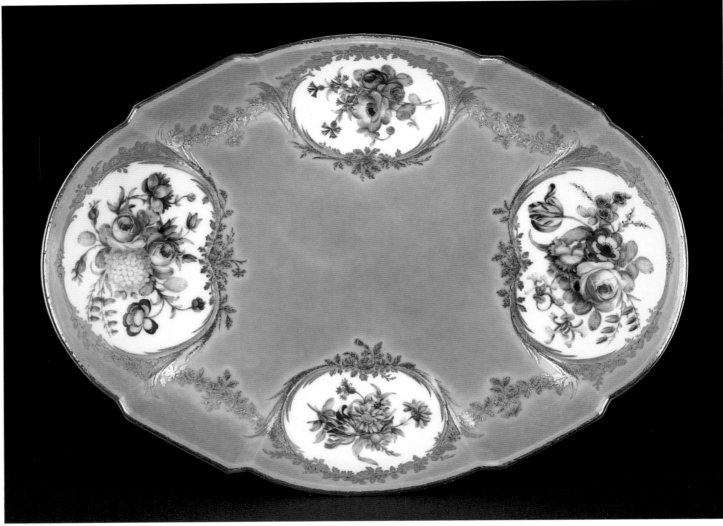

141

MODEL

It is believed that the *compotier ovale* was created in 1754,[10] for in that year four plaster models and molds in two sizes were listed in the factory inventory.[11] Moreover records show that six *compotiers* of unspecified size emerged from the biscuit kiln on 8 May, and that one of the second size was taken from the kiln on 21 June.[12] There are no surviving models, molds, or drawings.

Compotiers ovales do not appear in the sales records until the second half of 1756, when Lazare Duvaux bought fourteen, ranging in price from 27 to 36 *livres*.[13] Until that time one finds various other models of *compotiers* mentioned, including *quarré, à feuille de choux, gauffré, à côtes, Berryer, Lizonné, Courteille, rond gravé, ovale gravé, tourné, mosaïque,* and *rond*.[14] It was also in 1756 that one finds *compotiers* mentioned frequently without specification, so that some examples of the oval model may escape detection in the sales records. Since six molds and models appear under new work for 1761 in the factory inventory, we can suppose that a third size was introduced in that year.[15]

FUNCTION

Compotiers, including *ovales*, featured in many dessert services.[16] They were used to serve cold, sweet dishes, chiefly fruit compotes made with fresh or dried fruit that had been cooked in some type of spiced syrup.[17] Such compotes would have accompanied ice creams, fruit pastes, various cookies and pastries, marzipan, and cheese.[18] In 1761 the comte d'Argental purchased a service including two *compotiers ovales guirlandes bleux* for 30 *livres*.[19] Four decorated with flowers were sold to the comte de Bachy in August of that year, along with plates, sugar bowls, cups and saucers, stands, and tureens.[20] We know that the service ordered in 1766 by the vicomte de Choiseul, later duc de Praslin, had at least four *compotiers ovales*, three of them of the second size, and one of the first.[21] Around that same year Prince Starhemberg, Austrian ambassador to France, received a large dinner and dessert service that included oval fruit dishes as well.[22] Furthermore, four *compotiers ovales* were part of a *bleu céleste* service probably purchased by Cyril Razoumovski in 1767.[23] These cost 72 *livres* each. In what appears to be a dinner and dessert service sold to Monsieur de Beaujon in 1775, four *compotiers ovales* accompanied four each of *compotiers quarrés,*

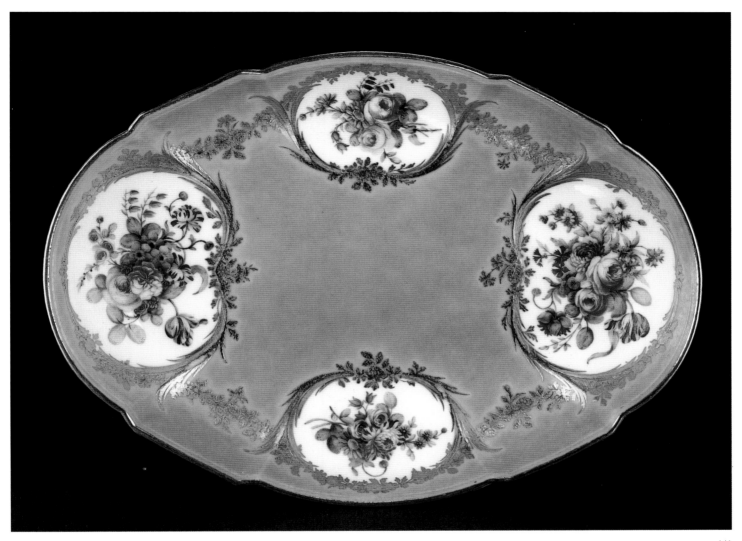

141

compotiers ronds, and *compotiers coquilles*, and cost 48 *livres* apiece.[24] Their decoration was not described but surviving elements have a *bleu céleste* ribbon entwined with garlands of flowers.[25] Four *compotiers ovales* featured in the service given to the Duke of Manchester in 1783,[26] and four were part of the Eden service of 1787.[27]

COMMENTARY

The Museum's fruit dishes may have been part of a service delivered to the Paris *marchand-mercier* Jacques Dumoulin.[28] By 1860 they were in the collection of John Julius Angerstein (1735–1823),[29] reported to be the natural son of the Empress Anne of Russia, and a founder of the Lloyd's group of insurers in London. Angerstein was also a notable art collector who formed a small but distinguished collection of paintings following the advice of Sir Thomas Lawrence.[30]

Pieces from this dessert service may be found in public and private collections in the United States and abroad. Three ice-cream cups are in a private collection in England, six more are in the collection of the Hillwood Museum and Gardens, Washington, D.C., and four recently were sold in New York.[31]

There are four plates at the Huntington Library and Art Collections, California,[32] another plate with Dalva Brothers, New York,[33] and a shell-shaped *compotier* in the Musée national de Céramique, Sèvres.[34] The collection was split up sometime in the middle of the nineteenth century, and some pieces, including the Hartford *compotiers ovales*, were purchased by the art dealer Duveen in 1902 from the Willoughby J.G. Loudon sale.[35]

TECHNIQUE AND CONDITION

The pink ground color of these pieces is very opaque and somewhat violet in tone. It differs significantly from the pink ground introduced at Sèvres in the late 1750s, which was more translucent and purer in tone. It seems likely that a different formula was being used in these later pink grounds, although there is no written record for either recipe.[36] Common to both pink grounds is the tendency for yellowing around the gilding, which seems to be the result of an adverse reaction between the gold and the pink ground.[37]

Exhibition: *Morgan Loan Exhibition*, New York, 1914, not in catalogue

Literature: Chavagnac, p. 122, no. 152

NOTES

1 Active 1758–1802, painter of flowers, ground colors, and patterns. See Peters, *Marks*, p. 46.

2 Active 1748–49, 1751–96, as painter and then gilder. See Peters, *Marks*, p. 48; Savill, 3, pp. 1045–47 (as also working 1742–43).

3 Active as gilder 1750–1800.

4 Unattributed. See Dauterman, *Marks*, p. 228, for examples in the Philadelphia Museum of Art and in the Carnegie Museum, Pittsburgh.

5 Savill, 3, p. 1110, as found on soft paste 1753–73. The appearance of this incised mark on a piece that probably was decorated in 1774 may only indicate that the fruit dish was fashioned sometime before it was decorated. It may also indicate that the *répareur* worked beyond the previously recorded 1773.

6 See note 28 below.

7 Placed for sale at Christie's, London, 10 May 1860, lot 122, as part of a dessert service comprising ninety-seven other pieces. This service remained unsold. See cat. no. 142 for two more pieces from this service.

8 Christie's, London, 4 February 1902, lot 238.

9 Annotations in above sale catalogue (1902), kindly provided by Mr. Richard Wenger. See also APML, invoice, 11 April 1902: "2 Old Rose du Barry Sèvres Oval dishes," £1,325.

10 See Dawson, *British Museum*, pp. 138–39, no. 119; Préaud and d'Albis, p. 187, no. 218 (calling it a *compotier Courteille gravé*, which was made in both round and oval forms. Préaud suggests that *Courteille* was the original name, which was not used consistently).

11 AMNS, I. 7, 1 January 1755, new molds and models for 1754, molds valued at 2 *livres* (first size) and 1 *livre*, 10 *sols* (second size), and models at 3 and 2 *livres* respectively. Two of the first size and one of the second size were in the *magasin du blanc*, valued at 8 and 6 *livres* respectively. From surviving examples we may suppose that the sizes are as follows: first size: L. 10⅝–11½ in. (27–29.2 cm); second size: c. 9⁷⁄₁₆–10⁵⁄₁₆ in. (24–25.8 cm), and third size: c. 8¼ in. (21 cm) (see below for third size).

12 IF 5673, fols. 22, 23.

13 AMNS, Vy 2, fol 13, 20 August 1756–1 January 1757.

14 See *Vincennes*, pp. 40–43 for these and other early *compotiers*.

15 AMNS, I. 7, 1 January 1762. Based on this reference in the inventory, Dawson (*British Museum*, p. 139 n. 2) writes that the model may have been revised. She gives the date of 1766, but this is clearly a typographical error. The present writer has found no evidence to suggest a revision.

16 While occasionally the shape is specified, in many cases fruit dishes are listed as *compotiers differens* or just *compotiers*. Extant services provide us with more evidence than do factory records.

17 Savill, "Starhemberg," p. 28. In *Soupers de la cour* (4, p. 225) there are a number of recipes for fruit compotes. To make a peach compote, one peeled and cut the peaches, cooked them in a little water and sugar, then dressed them in the *compotier* with fine sugar and light syrup, and perhaps some *eau de vie*. Such compotes served as a means of preserving fruit for use out of season.

18 Savill, "Starhemberg," p. 33 n. 17, citing Noël-Waldteufel, in *Tables royales*, p. 83, no. 90.

19 AMNS, Vy 3, fol. 58, 1 July 1761. Part of this service is in a private collection, Paris. I would like to thank David Peters for this information.

20 Ibid., fol. 61v, 17 August 1761. The items sold could have been used for either the dessert or savory service (for example the tureens, which would have been part of the savory service). Together, however, these items would not have been enough to make up a traditional service of either type.

21 Christie's, New York, 21 May 1997, lot 90; Christie's, London, 17 April 2000, lot 89. The larger dish measured 11⅜ in. (28.9 cm) and the smaller dishes 9½ in. (24.1 cm). These are among the few examples of second size *compotiers ovales* that have been published.

22 Savill, "Starhemberg," p. 28, pl. IV. This service is now at Waddesdon Manor, Buckinghamshire, England.

23 Eriksen, *Waddesdon*, p. 210, no. 75B.

24 AMNS, Vy 5, fol. 235, 19 May 1775.

25 See Sotheby's, Zurich, 5 December 1991, lot 287; Sotheby's, New York, 1 November 1997, lots 226, 227. I would like to thank David Peters for this information.

26 De Bellaigue, "Diplomatic Gift," pp. 92–99.

27 Dawson, "Eden Service," pp. 288–97.

28 AMNS, Vy 5, fol. 185v, first half 1774; supplement Vy 6, fol. 13v, second half 1775. The service consisted of thirty-six plates at 33 *livres*, four *compotiers* at 39 *livres* (probably round), eight *compotiers* at 42 *livres* (probably four *carré* and four *coquilles*), four *compotiers* at 45 *livres* (probably *ovale*), two *sucriers* at 120 *livres* (see cat. no. 142), twenty-four *tasses à glace* at 18 *livres*, four *plateaux* at 42 *livres* (probably *plateaux Bouret*), two *plateaux* at 120 *livres* (probably *plateaux à 2 pots*), and two *seaux à glace* at 240 *livres*. In the 1775 supplement there were two *corbeilles fond rose* at 144 *livres* (probably *plateaux losanges corbeille à jour*), one at 144 *livres* (probably *1 plateaux ovale corbeille à jour*) and two at 96 *livres* (*2 plateaux carrés corbeille à jour*). The identification of these items in the sales register with specific shapes has been made by David Peters.

29 Christie's, London, 10 May 1860, lot 122 (see note 7 above). The identification of this service with the pieces bought by Dumoulin and subsequently in the collection of John Julius Angerstein is taken, with permission of David Peters, from Service List 74-6 of Part 5 (iii) of Peters, *Plates and Services*.

30 Tuohy, passim. His paintings formed the nucleus of the collection of the National Gallery of Art in London.

31 Nos. 24.101.1–.6. See Arend, *Hillwood*, p. 42, fig. 21; Christie's, New York, 5 May 1999, lot 36 (two marked 1775, marks for Buteux *fils aîné*, Thévenet, and Chauvaux *aîné* on three, Thévenet and Chauvaux on one).

32 Wark, *Huntington*, pp. 117, 119, figs. 113–14. The catalogue states that these plates are dated Y for 1776. In fact, three are dated X for 1775, and the fourth Y for 1776 (information taken from labels written by Jeffrey Weaver, kindly furnished by Elizabeth Pergam).

33 Marked with date letter X, painted by Méreaud *jeune* and gilded by Baudouin.

34 MNC, Sèvres, no. 23241.

35 See note 8 above. Two *plateaux losange corbeille à jour* sold at Sotheby's, London, 30 May 1949, lot 20, appear to have been part of this service, as were two *compotiers coquilles* and two *seaux à glace* sold from Baroness Burton's collection in 1950 (Christie's, London, 22 November 1950, lots 131, 137). A pair of square fruit dishes sold at Christie's, London, 3 December 1984, lot 38, was also part of the service. This information taken with permission of David Peters from his manuscript on Sèvres services cited above (note 29). Peters traces the sales histories of most of the components in this service.

36 Antoine d'Albis, in correspondence with the author, notes that although the painter Xhrouuet was paid a bonus in 1758 for providing a pink ground color, Hellot never mentions the composition of the new color or the details of its invention. D'Albis suggests that the 1758 pink may have been based on Taunay's carmine, mixed with a yellow flux containing silver.

37 See Savill, 3, pp. 1175, 1179 n. 34. She alludes to the traditional theory that the gold chloride in the *rose* ground discolored when placed next to gilding. Antoine d'Albis (in written correspondence) believes that when the gilding was added, the area around it probably became superheated, because gold as a metal acts as a conductor of heat. According to d'Albis, such superheating caused the tiny particles of gold in the pink ground to dissolve, leaving only the yellow flux (see note above). Thus, in d'Albis's theory, the yellowing is not due to the gold chloride in the pigment but to the silver in the flux, since the flux used to produce any pink color always contains a certain amount of silver.

142

142

Pair of sugar bowls and attached stands
(*sucriers de Monsieur le Premier*)

1917.1084–1085

Sèvres, 1774

Soft-paste porcelain, 1917.1084: H. 4¹¹⁄₁₆ × L. 9⁵⁄₁₆ × W. 6¹⁄₁₆ in. (11.9 × 23.6 × 15.4 cm); 1917.1085: H. 4¾ × L. 9¼ × W. 6¹⁄₁₆ in. (12.1 × 23.5 × 15.3 cm)

Pink ground with polychrome flowers, gilding

Marks: on both: interlaced Ls in blue with date letter v, FB underneath for François-Marie Barrat *oncle*;[1] LG for Étienne-Henry Le Guay *aîné*, *père*;[2] BD for François Baudouin *père*;[3] 1917.1084: incised script L / D; 1917.1085: incised script LD[4]

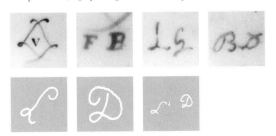

Provenance: probably Jacques Dumoulin, 1775;[5] John Julius Angerstein (1735–1823), 1860;[6] J. Pierpont Morgan

MODEL

This form of sugar bowl and stand was introduced in 1758. Called *sucrier de Monsieur le Premier*, it was named for the *premier écuyer*, Henri-Camille, marquis de Béringhen (1693–1770) who served as one of the most important officers in the king's household—in charge of the *petite écurie*, the *premier écuyer* had the particular honor of helping the king into his carriage or onto his horse.[7] Molds and models for the new sugar bowl with this name were listed in the factory inventory of 1759, describing the new models of 1758. Both the stand and cover were molded separately.[8] A notch was sometimes cut out of the latter to accommodate a spoon.[9] A drawing of this model inscribed *sucrier tenant au plateau dit de Mr le Premier* is at the Cooper-Hewitt Museum in New York.[10] Two *sucriers* and three *plateaux* were fired in biscuit form sometime between 8 August and 16 September 1758.[11]

The first mention of the *sucrier de Monsieur le Premier* in the factory sales records occurs at the end of 1758, when Madame de Pompadour bought an example decorated with *verd palmes* [green with palm-leaf gilding] for 240 *livres*, corresponding to the price of the most expensive examples.[12] Lazare Duvaux also bought two decorated with a pink ground (also for 240 *livres*) and two decorated with flowers.[13] The model then appears with some regularity from 1759, and often was included in dessert services. The least expensive examples, decorated either with

277

gold friezes or flowers, cost 60 *livres*.[14] An example decorated with *lapis caillouté* cost 168 *livres* in 1761,[15] as did the *bleu Fallot* examples in the comte de Starhemberg's service in 1766.[16] An example with green ribbons was sold to an unnamed buyer in 1759 for 216 *livres*, possibly accompanied by a matching porcelain spoon for 72 *livres*.[17]

FUNCTION

By the time the *sucrier de Monsieur le Premier* was introduced in 1758, several other designs of sugar bowls were already in production. Among them were *sucriers feuille de choux, sucriers gauffrés, sucriers rond unis, sucriers ovales, sucriers à compartiments*,[18] and *sucriers Gondoles*.[19] All were conceived as table rather than tea ware, and were meant to hold finely powdered or granulated sugar to be sprinkled on fresh fruit, particularly melon.[20] Sugar was also served at table in casters of silver, gold, or ceramics. Curiously enough, Sèvres was not one of the manufacturers of casters.[21]

COMMENTARY

The two *sucriers* in the Museum's collection may have been part of the service bought by the dealer Dumoulin in 1774[22] and owned by John Julius Angerstein. They cost 120 *livres* each, half of what similarly decorated examples sold for in 1758.[23] Although the pink ground color had gone out of production in the later 1760s, it was revived briefly in the years 1772–75, during which period this service was made.[24]

The floral decoration on the sugar bowls and stands was by François-Marie Barrat, and the gilding by both Étienne-Henry Le Guay and François Baudouin. Baudouin probably was responsible for the gilded edges; the overtime records of 1774 note that he was paid 1 *livre* each for *filets d'or* on two *sucriers de Monsieur le Premier*.[25] On the other hand, the oval compote dishes from this service were painted by J.-F.-L. Laroche but with gilding still by Baudouin and Le Guay.[26]

TECHNIQUE AND CONDITION

For a discussion of the pink ground color and yellowing around the gilding, see catalogue no. 141. The *sucrier* 1917.1085 has been broken across one quarter of the stand and repaired with rivets.

Exhibitions: *Morgan Loan Exhibition*, New York, 1914, not in catalogue; *French and English Art Treasures*, New York, 1942, no. 303

Literature: Chavagnac, p. 123, no. 153; *French and English Art Treasures*, no. 303

NOTES

1   Active 1769–91, 1795–96. See Peters, *Marks*, p. 11. See also Savill, 3, pp. 1000–1. Barrat was noted as a flower painter.

2   Active as painter and gilder 1748–49, 1751–96. See Peters, *Marks*, p. 48; Savill, 3, pp. 1045–47.

3   Active as gilder 1750–1800 (Peters, *Marks*, p. 12).

4   Unpublished.

5   AMNS, Vy 5, fol. 185v, first half 1774. See cat. no. 141 for a complete list of this sale.

6   Christie's, London, 10 May 1860, lot 122, as part of a dessert service comprising ninety-seven other pieces. These sugar dishes were not

included in the sale of Mr. Willoughby J.G. Loudon in 1902 (see cat. no. 141). All of the information on this service is taken with permission of David Peters from Service List 74–6 of Part 5 (iii) of Peters, *Plates and Services*.

7   *Grand Larousse Universel*, 5, p. 3555. A wine glass cooler, as yet unidentified, was also named after *Monsieur le Premier*. It seems to have been introduced in the same year as the sugar bowl. See AMNS, I. 7, 1 January 1759, for 1758. There are also documentary references to a *seau à bouteille* (ibid., Vy 3, fol. 30, 16 December 1760), an *assiette de Monsieur le Premier* (*Vincennes*, p. 33), an *écuelle de Monsieur le Premier* (ibid., p. 51 and Préaud and d'Albis, pp. 166–67, no. 158, I. 7, 1 January 1754, *modèles en soufre, moules en plâtre*), and a *saladier de Monsieur le Premier* (see Préaud and d'Albis, p. 186, no. 214; AMNS, R. 1, L. 1, d. 1, [c], inscribed in ink: *saladie ou compotie pour Monsieur Premie fait le 27 mars 1754 fait suivan les mezure demande*).

8   AMNS, I. 7, 1 January 1759 (for 1758). Four molds and one model for the *platteau du sucrier de Mr le Premier* as well as the *sucrier* were made.

9   Brunet and Préaud, p. 188, no. 191.

10 Ibid. The inventory number of the drawing is 1938.88.8314.

11 IF 5673, fol. 113.

12 AMNS, Vy 2, fol. 78, 30 December 1758.

13 Ibid., fol. 80, 1 December 1758–1 January 1759. The examples with flowers cost 60 *livres* each.

14 For example, ibid., fol. 88, 1 February 1759, Boudry (*frize d'or*) and 23 April 1759 (*fleurs*), unnamed buyer.

15 Ibid., Vy 3, fol. 80v, 28 November 1761, Bonnet (as part of a service).

16 Savill, "Starhemberg," pp. 28–29.

17 AMNS, Vy 2, fol. 92v, 1 July 1759. The sale also included a *pot à sucre*, which could account for the spoon.

18 See *Vincennes*, pp. 84–87.

19 AMNS, Vy 2, fol. 77v, sold to Louis XV, 30 December 1758.

20 This is the suggestion of Barbara Ketcham Wheaton in private correspondence.

21 See Bonifas, p. 119, no. 83.

22 AMNS, Vy 5, fol. 185v.

23 See note 13 above for the pink ground examples sold to Duvaux for 240 *livres* each.

24 Eriksen and Bellaigue, p. 53.

25 AMNS, F.16.

26 The shell-shaped compote dish at the MNC, Sèvres is marked by Baudouin, Michel-Barnabé Chauvaux and François Drand. All three were gilders, but Drand is also recorded as a painter. The four plates at the Huntington Library and Art Collections were decorated by (1) François Barré (?), (2) Chappuis, Barré (?), and perhaps Bouillat; (3) Barré (?) and Baudouin *père* and (4) Taillandier and Drand. This information was kindly provided by Elizabeth Pergam of the Huntington Library and Art Collections, taken from gallery labels written by Jeffrey Weaver.

143

143

Butter dish with attached stand
(*beurrier tenant au plateau*)

1917.1106

Sèvres, 1780

Soft-paste porcelain, H. 3⅛ × DIAM. 7¹⁵⁄₁₆ in. (7.9 × 20.1 cm)

Green ground with polychrome flowers, gilding

Marks: interlaced Ls in blue with date letters cc; nq underneath for Nicquet;[1] LG in gray for Étienne-Henry Le Guay *aîné*, *père*;[2] incised 38a[3]

Provenance: Cartier et Fils, Paris, 1899;[4] J. Pierpont Morgan

MODEL

Butter dishes of this form were called *beurrier* or *beurrier tenant au plateau* in factory records and were made either with a separate or attached stand.[5] The dish was made with or without handles,[6] and two sizes were noted in the records.[7] Butter dishes were uncommon in France until the middle of the eighteenth century;[8] their form was based on Delftware butter tubs, perhaps via Meissen.

Drawings of this form in the Sèvres factory archives show how the model lent itself to being either a butter or cheese dish (fig. 143-1).[9] As a cheese dish, it would have feet, be pierced, and have different handles.[10] There is another drawing showing a butter dish with a slightly rounded cover, and a separate stand with feet.[11] A biscuit model with a more rounded cover and no knob also survives at the factory.[12]

The model was in production at least by 1752, when forty-nine *beurriers* and fifty-four *plateaux* in biscuit were ready for glazing.[13] In July of that year, Monsieur de Courteille, the *intendant des finances* and royal representative for the Vincennes factory, purchased two examples decorated with flowers for 36 *livres* each.[14] Prices for butter dishes thus decorated ranged from 42 to 48 *livres* for the first size and 30, 36, and 42 *livres* for second size.[15] A yellow-ground example of the second size with birds sold for 42 *livres*, as did a butter dish with a monochrome landscape.[16] A first-size dish with floral garlands cost 60 *livres*, one with *fond verd bleu* and birds cost 120 *livres*, *lapis* and gold cost 144 *livres*, and *lapis* with colored birds cost 156 *livres*.[17] Second-size dishes with *lapis* ground and polychrome birds sold for 130 *livres*, and with gold decoration for 120 *livres*.[18] Butter dishes were almost always included in savory dinner services, and could be much more costly, depending on the decoration. Two *bleu céleste beurriers* of the first size were in the Louis XV service of 1753–54, and cost 240 *livres* each.[19]

COMMENTARY

The Museum's butter dish carries the mark of the painter Nicquet, who in July 1780 decorated four green-ground *beurriers* with groups of flowers. Later that month he decorated another dish, without a cover, implying that one of the four

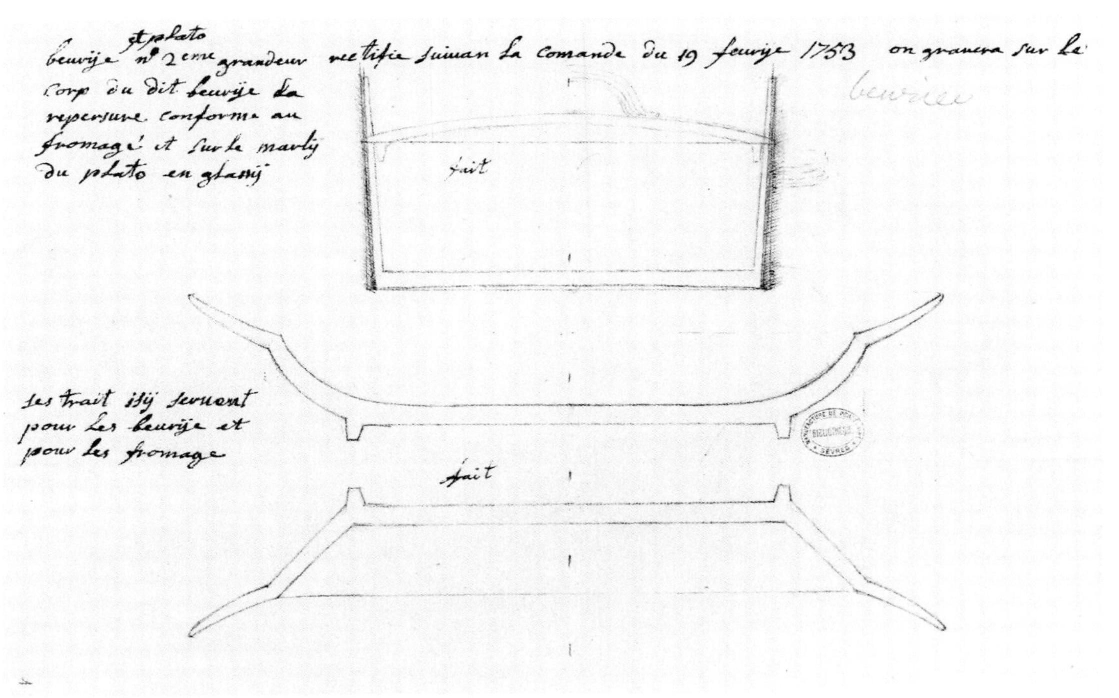

Fig. 143-1 *Beurrier*, drawing

dishes had been broken.[20] In August three *beurriers* of the same description decorated by Nicquet and Le Guay were fired in the enamel kiln.[21] There is no mention of what happened to the fourth butter dish.

On an unknown date in 1780 the dealer Bazin bought what appears to have been a service—or perhaps a supplement to a service—that may have been decorated with a green ground and flowers. Within this group were three *beurriers*, priced at 96 *livres* each.[22] It is believed that the Museum's butter dish and stand was one of these. However, the sales register records this sale of the butter dishes as taking place in the first half of 1780, negating the notion that they were the same as those painted in July and fired in August. Yet all is not straightforward for the entry for Bazin's purchase appears in the ledger alongside sales from the third quarter of that year, leaving open the possibility that the list included pieces bought even as late as August.[23]

Another butter dish with the same decoration was sold in Paris in 1976, and may also be one of the three decorated by Nicquet and sold by Bazin.[24]

The pieces bought by Bazin could have been a supplement to one of many green-ground services with groups of flowers produced at Sèvres from the 1760s. These services included pieces sold to the *contrôleur-général* Monsieur Bertin in 1763 and 1764 and to the comte du Châtelet in 1767.[25] Another service with green-ground decoration and groups of flowers was delivered to the comtesse d'Artois in 1773, but this probably was too small a set to have needed the large supplement sold to Bazin in 1780.[26]

As early as 1753 ground-color services with floral decoration were made at the factory, beginning with the *bleu céleste* service of Louis XV. Production continued with only minor alterations through the 1780s. The gilding pattern on the Museum's butter dish and stand, with its palm branches and floral garlands, dates

from the early 1760s, and recurred continually over the next twenty-five years. By standardizing the gilding patterns clients could easily build up or expand their services.[27]

TECHNIQUE AND CONDITION

The green ground color is slightly matte and lacks the translucency found in greens from the 1750s and early 1760s.[28]

Exhibition: *Morgan Loan Exhibition*, New York, 1914, not in catalogue

Literature: Chavagnac, p. 135, no. 170

NOTES

1 Active as flower painter 1764–92. See Peters, *Marks*, p. 55.

2 Active as painter and gilder 1748–49, 1751–96. See Savill, 3, pp. 1045–47; Peters, *Marks*, p. 48.

3 See Savill, 3, p. 1131. The mark is found on soft paste 1779–90s.

4 APML, Cartier file 2, invoice 20 May 1899: "1 Beurrier Sèvres fond vert et or cartels blancs fleurs variées," 5,000 French francs.

5 Préaud and d'Albis, p. 122, no. 41.

6 See an example in MNC, Sèvres (no. 25182), 1760, in MNC, *Nouvelles acquisitions 1979–1989*, p. 155, no. 216.

7 The diameters of the stands are approximately 9¹/₁₆–9³/₁₆ in. (23–23.7 cm) for the first size and 7¹¹/₁₆–8¹/₁₆ in. (19.5–20.5 cm) for the second size.

8 See Havard, 1, pp. 305–6.

9 AMNS, R. 1, L. 7, d. 1, fols. 1–2. The caption for fol. 2, in Duplessis's hand, reads: *beurÿe et plato n° 2eme grandeur rectifie suivan la comande du 19 fevrije 1753 on gravera sur le corp du dit beurÿe la repersure conforme au fromagé et sur le marlÿ du plato en glassÿ/ fait/ ses trait isÿ servent pour les beurÿe et pour les fromage/ fait.*

10 See Eriksen and Bellaigue, p. 266, no. 81; *Vincennes*, p. 34; Préaud and d'Albis, p. 122.

11 AMNS, R. 1, L. 1, d. 7, fol. 5.

12 Ibid., 1814 inventory 1740–60, no. 1, *casier* 781.

13 AMNS, I. 7, 8 October 1752.

14 AMNS, Vy 1, fol. 10v (*fournée* 58, 1752), 14 July 1752. See Préaud and d'Albis, p. 122, no. 41; Tamara Préaud, in MNC, *Nouvelles acquisitions 1979–1989*, p. 155 n. 3.

15 See for example AMNS, Vy 1, fol. 29v, 31 December 1753, Duvaux, 42 *livres*; fol. 74, 5–31 December 1754, Duvaux, 48 *livres*; fol. 15, 8 August 1753, M. Le Garde des Sceaux, 30 *livres*; fol. 29v, 31 December 1753, Duvaux, 36 *livres*; fol. 30v, 31 December 1753, Duvaux, 42 *livres*.

16 Ibid., fol. 38, 20 April 1754, Bailly; fol. 12v, 4 December 1753, de La Boexières.

17 Ibid., fol. 23v, 22 December 1753, de Duras; fol. 11v, 8 August 1753, M. Le Garde des Sceaux; and fol. 29, 31 December 1753, Duvaux. The ground color referred to as *verd bleu* in the sale to de Duras is unidentified.

18 Ibid., fol. 29v, 31 December 1753, Duvaux.

19 Ibid., fol. 45, 30 June 1754 (second delivery). Some other services that included butter tubs were the Maria-Theresa service, 1758, green ribbons and flowers, 240 *livres* (Vy 2, fol. 85); Palatine service, 1760, *mosaïque*, birds, and flowers, 60 *livres* (Vy 3, fol. 29); Bedford service, 1763, *lapis vermiculé*, 120 *livres* (Vy 3, fol. 125); Christian VII, king of Denmark service, 1768, *lapis caillouté*, 120 *livres* (Vy 4, fol. 180).

20 AMNS, Vj'1, fol. 206, 16 and 31 July 1780.

21 Ibid., Vl'1, fol. 120v, 21 August 1780.

22 This information was generously provided by David Peters in correspondence with the author. See ibid., Vy 7, fol. 257v, first six months 1780. The butter dishes, as well as the plates, and ice-cream cups, were the same price as comparable green-ground pieces with groups of flowers included in a small service delivered to the comtesse d'Artois in 1773, lending weight to the argument that the pieces bought by Bazin were decorated in the same manner.

23 These pieces appear at the very end of the list of items sent to Bazin, making it likely that they were purchased as a group at the end of the recording period.

24 Palais Galliéra, Paris, 29–30 November 1976, lot 99, with another similar butter dish dated 1772 that may correspond to one of two sold to Mme Lair that same year (AMNS, Vy 5, fol. 51). The latter is not pictured, and no artists' marks are given for either example.

25 See AMNS, Vy 3, fol. 158, 1 May 1763; Vy 4, fol. 32v, 6 September 1764 (including two *beurriers* at 96 *livres*); fol. 124v, 31 December 1767 (dessert service). I would like to thank David Peters for this information.

26 Ibid., Vy 5, fol. 114v, 15 November 1773, including only twenty-four plates and one butter dish. This is the opinion of David Peters.

27 Evidence of such standardization can be seen in existing colored-ground plates and service wares such as two *bleu céleste* plates sold at Christie's, London, 15 October 1990, lot 45. While appearing to have very similar although not identical gilding, one is dated 1772 and the other 1782. Similar palm branch and floral gilding, with the addition of a bow at the bottom of the reserves, appears on a pair of green *seaux à bouteille* from 1764 (Christie's, Monaco, 6 December 1985, lot 9), and on a pair of green *seaux crennelés* dated 1774, without the bows, sold at the same auction (lot 10). The decoration of this latter pair is akin to the Museum's butter dish, as is the decoration on a pair of green plates sold in Paris (Ader, Tajan, 29 June 1994, lot 67) dated 1786. Other green-ground pieces with palm and floral gilding were sold in Paris in 1976 from the collection of Philippe de Rothschild (Palais Galliéra, 29–30 November 1976, lots 100–2). These included two butter dishes mentioned in note 24 above, as well as compote dishes and plates. Not all pieces are illustrated, however, and their dates are not given, making it impossible to determine whether they match the Museum's butter dish in date or decoration.

28 For more on early green grounds see cat. no. 62.

144

Plate (*assiette unie*)

1917.1095

Sèvres, 1785

Soft-paste porcelain, H. 1⅛ × DIAM. 9⅜ in. (2.8 × 23.8 cm)

Bleu céleste ground with *grisaille* cameos on brown, cipher, polychrome floral and foliate decoration, gilding

Marks: interlaced Ls in blue with hh inside, script B.n. above, for Nicolas Bulidon;[1] LG in gold for Étienne-Henry Le Guay *aîné*, *père*;[2] incised 24

Provenance: perhaps Léopold Double, Paris, 1881;[3] A.B. Daniell & Sons, London, 1902;[4] J. Pierpont Morgan

COMMENTARY

This plate is a factory replica of plates from a very large service commissioned by Catherine the Great of Russia in 1776, and delivered in 1779.[5] It differs, though, in outline, date and size, since the original plates were round-rimmed and measured approximately 10⁷⁄₁₆ inches (26.5 cm), whereas the Hartford plate, dated 1785, has a slightly wavy border and measures 9⅜ inches (23.8 cm).[6] In all other respects the Museum's plate is identical, even down to the empress's cipher.

The original dinner and dessert service for sixty people, consisting of 797 pieces, was in the newest, neoclassical style. The decoration comprised a *bleu céleste* ground (meant to imitate turquoise stone), painted cameo heads and bas-relief scenes from mythology and Greek and Roman history, and a central medallion with the crowned floral monogram of Catherine the Great with laurel and myrtle branches tied together with ribbon.[7] It took three years to manufacture, and required new shapes, new colors and new decorative designs. The plates sold for 242 *livres*.[8]

The Museum's plate was one of a handful of pieces made by the factory in imitation of the service and sold to dealers and individuals. Madame du Barry purchased a teapot in this style in July 1779, and another one in 1788.[9] There is no record of a souvenir plate in the sales ledgers, although in 1786 an *assiette du Service de Russie* was listed in the inventory of available stock.[10] Another souvenir plate of the same shape as the Museum's example, dated 1782, was sold in London in 1981.[11]

Kiln and painters' records suggest that the Museum's plate was part of the enamel kiln firing for 1 August 1785.[12] It is possible that François-Pascal Philippine was responsible for the cameo scenes, and that Nicolas Bulidon painted the flower garlands.[13]

The cameo scenes on the Atheneum's plate were taken from Roman history. The cameo on the top depicts Hannibal vowing to destroy Rome, that on the right, the Roman army passing under the Candine yoke, and the one on the left, Numa Pompilius establishing the laws of the city.[14] In a portfolio of

144

drawings for the Russian service now in the print department of the Bibliothèque nationale, Paris[15] there are designs for all three scenes, perhaps the work of Jean-Baptiste-Étienne Genest.[16] The Hannibal scene was illustrated partially on a drawing of a *pot à crème* and fully on a drawing for a *compotier quarré*.[17] It was depicted on one plate from the original service, besides appearing on another plate dated 1782,[18] and one dated 1784 decorated by Charles-Nicolas Dodin for a service made for Louis XVI between 1783 and 1793.[19] The Roman army under the Candine yoke appeared in another drawing for the Russian service, and later on was also used for a plate in the Louis XVI service.[20] Numa Pompilius was illustrated in the drawing of a saucer for the Catherine the Great service, and afterwards on a plate of 1784 attributed to the painter Asselin in the Louis XVI service.[21]

Exhibitions: *Morgan Loan Exhibition*, New York, 1914, not in catalogue; *Morgan*, Hartford, 1987, no. 76

Literature: Chavagnac, pp. 132–33, no. 166;[22] de Bellaigue, "Sèvres," pp. 190–91, no. 76; de Bellaigue, *Louis XVI*, pp. 84, 86, 90

NOTES

1 Active 1763–92, as painter of flowers, friezes, attributes, monograms. See Savill, 3, pp. 1006–7; Peters, *Marks*, p. 18.

2 Active as painter and more often as gilder, 1748–49, 1751–96. See Savill, 3, pp. 1045–47; Peters, *Marks*, p. 48.

3 Mannheim Galleries, Paris, 30 May–4 June 1881, lot 74 (not illustrated). There is no indication of a date letter for the plate making it impossible to know if this was one of the original plates of the Catherine the Great service (see below) or Hartford's later replica. Morgan did buy other Sèvres from the Léopold Double Collection (see cat. no. 96). The history of the original service is well documented, including the period in the 19th century when about 160 pieces were looted from the Winter Palace, Saint Petersburg and sold in London. Most of these pieces were repurchased by Tsar Alexander II in 1857, although several original plates must not have been returned. Two were sold at Christie's, London, 11 April 1877, lots 160–61 and subsequently at Christie's, London, 21 May 1886 (Earl of Dudley sale), lots 96–97 (see Christie's, Monaco, 8 December 1990, lot 25). Other plates are in the British Museum, London, the Fitzwilliam Museum, Cambridge, and the MNC, Sèvres. See Dawson, *British Museum*, p. 141.

4 APML, Daniell file, invoice 17 April 1902: "A Sèvres China Dessert Plate of the celebrated Service executed for the Empress Catherine of Russia, in turquoise blue ground, with letter "E" and crown, and Roman numerals II with panels of paintings by Bulidon, and gilding by Le Guay," £418.

5 Much has been written on this service. The discussion that follows is largely based on the work of Butler, "Sèvres Imperial court," passim; Savill, "Cameo fever," passim; de Bellaigue, "Sèvres," pp. 190–91, no. 76; Dawson, *British Museum*, pp. 141–44, no. 121.

6 The Hartford plate was called *assiette unie*, and was in production by 1752. See Préaud and d'Albis, p. 168, no. 162.

7 The cipher was on all pieces of the service save the ice-cream cups, tea and coffee cups, and teapot. See Butler, "Sèvres Imperial court," p. 455.

8 See AMNS, Vy 7, fols. 202v–3v, June 1779, reproduced in *Grands services*, pp. 36–37, no. 11.

9 AMNS, Vy 7, fol. 152, 14 July, 216 *livres*; Vy 10, fol. 243, 29 April, 144 *livres* (see de Bellaigue, "Sèvres," p. 191 n. 4).

10 AMNS, I. 8, 30 March 1786, 150 *livres* (see de Bellaigue, "Sèvres," p. 191 n. 5).

11 Christie's, London, 5 October 1981, lot 6 (as part of the original service). The scene of Hannibal vowing he would destroy Rome also appears on this plate.

12 AMNS, Vl'2, fol. 145, gilded by Le Guay (de Bellaigue, "Sèvres," p. 191 n. 5).

13 AMNS, Vj'3, fol. 220, 30 April 1785, *1 Assiette bleu celeste Service de Russie*, and ibid., fol. 58v, 14 May 1785 (see de Bellaigue, "Sèvres," p. 191 n. 5).

14 De Bellaigue, "Sèvres," p. 191.

15 Manuscript memoranda in the Bibliothèque nationale, Département des Estampes (Lf.8 *pet. fol.*), entitled "Service de Porcelaine de la Manufacture Royale de Seves, Pour L'Impératrice de Russie 1778" and "Dessins et Devis du Service de Porcelaine Pour L'Impératrice de Russie 1778." See de Bellaigue, *Louis XVI*, pp. 84, 86, 90.

16 Eriksen, *Waddesdon*, p. 326. See cat. no. 73 for more on this artist.

17 De Bellaigue, *Louis XVI*, p. 84.

18 Ibid. See Christie's, London, 5 October 1981, lot 6.

19 De Bellaigue, *Louis XVI*, pp. 83–84.

20 1784, Dodin, see ibid., pp. 85–86.

21 Ibid., pp. 89–90.

22 Chavagnac believed that the date letters should be read as bb for 1779, thus making the plate compatible with the original service after which this plate was made.

145

Four plates (*assiettes unies*)

1917.1147–1150

Sèvres, 1793

Soft-paste porcelain, 1917.1147: DIAM. 9¹¹⁄₁₆ in. (24.6 cm); 1917.1148: DIAM. 9½ in. (24.1 cm); 1917.1149: DIAM. 9⁵⁄₁₆ in. (23.7 cm); 1917.1150: DIAM. 9⅜ in. (23.9 cm)

Yellow ground with black friezes, polychrome birds, gilding

Marks: on all: interlaced Ls in blue, date letters qq; 1917.1147: painter's mark y for Edmé-François Bouillat[1] and Sc in black for Sophie Binet;[2] incised JB;[3] 1917.1148: painter's mark of a dagger for Étienne Evans,[4] Sc in black; incised JB; 1917.1149: Sc in black, incised 34;[5] 1917.1150: painter's mark of hatchet for Pierre-Joseph Rosset aîné,[6] incised 24[7]

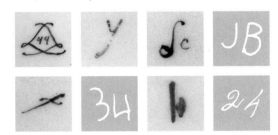

Inscriptions: 1917.1147: *La grande Linotte des vignes*; 1917.1148: *oiseau-Mouche à larges tuyaux de Cayenne*; 1917.1149: *Moineau, du brésil.*; 1917.1150: *Couroucou, a queue rousse, de Cayenne.*

Provenance: Jacques Seligmann, London and Paris, 1903;[8] J. Pierpont Morgan

MODEL

Plates known as *assiettes unies* were made at Vincennes from at least 1752.[9] Two biscuit models with this name still survive at the factory, one with a plain, circular edge and the other with alternating large and small lobes.[10] The plain one was made

145

145

Fig. 145-1 *La Grande Linotte des vignes,* Buffon

Fig. 145-2 *Oiseau-mouche à larges tuyaux de Cayenne*, Buffon

Fig. 145-3 *Moineau, du brésil,* Buffon

Fig. 145-4 *Couroucou, a queue rousse, de Cayenne,* Buffon

from about 1790, and reflects the factory's move toward simpler, more severe forms under the influence of classical antiquity.[11]

COMMENTARY

The Museum's plates are decorated with identifiable birds, their names inscribed on the reverse of each plate. They are based on François-Nicolas Martinet's illustrations for the comte de Buffon's ornithological treatise *Histoire naturelle des oiseaux*, published in ten volumes between 1770 and 1786. The Sèvres factory owned a copy of the treatise, and began producing wares based on these illustrations around 1781.[12] The first plate shows *La Grande Linotte des vignes* (a song bird called a linnet) (fig. 145-1),[13] the second, *Oiseau-mouche à larges tuyaux de Cayenne* (a hummingbird) (fig. 145-2),[14] the third, *Moineau, du brésil* (a sparrow) (fig. 145-3),[15] and the last, *Couroucou, a queue rousse, de Cayenne* (a tropical bird called a trogon) (fig. 145-4).[16]

Decorator records may be linked to at least two of the four Atheneum plates. In February 1793, Bouillat *père* was paid six *livres* each for painting eighteen yellow-ground plates with Buffon birds.[17] Also in February of that year, Evans decorated seven plates of the same description, as well as two more in December.[18] The Museum's two plates must have been among these. Rosset decorated twelve yellow plates with Buffon birds in January 1794, but this is too late to refer to the third Hartford plate.[19] The fourth plate does not bear a painter's mark, however, and appears to be by a different hand.

The black frieze decoration on three of the four plates was carried out by Sophie Binet, born Sophie Chanou.[20] Still recorded under the name Mademoiselle Chanou, she was given six plates with yellow ground and birds to decorate with black friezes in January 1793, for which she was paid 3 *livres* each.[21] In March of that year she decorated eighteen more yellow-ground plates with friezes, but there is no mention of birds or of the color of the friezes.[22] She also decorated thirteen more yellow plates with black friezes in July.[23] Any one of these entries could have included the Museum's plates.

The kiln records list a number of plates that may correspond to Hartford's as well. In May 1793 twenty-four were fired, with the gilder Weydinger as the only decorator listed.[24] These could have included some of the plates decorated in February by Evans and Bouillat. On 9 August 1793, seven plates with a yellow ground and birds by Evans and Weydinger were fired, and on 18 April 1794 nine more, with Buffon birds by Evans and gilding by Weydinger were listed.[25] These also could have included the Museum's plates, although the April firing does not specify that the birds were after Buffon. The plate by Rosset might have been included in any of these groups.

These plates are among a large number of yellow-ground service pieces with the same "Etruscan" border and birds after Buffon's history. It is uncertain to which service the Museum's plates belonged.[26]

Exhibitions: *Morgan Loan Exhibition*, New York, 1914, not in catalogue; *Morgan*, Hartford, 1987, no. 79 (1917.1148)

Literature: Chavagnac, pp. 158–59, no. 203; de Bellaigue, "Sèvres," pp. 194–95, no. 79

NOTES

1 Active 1758–1810. See Savill, 3, pp. 1002–4; Peters, *Marks*, p. 16. Bouillat worked on Buffon birds from 1784 (Savill, 3, p. 1003).

2 Active 1779–98. See Peters, *Marks*, p. 14.

3 Found on soft paste 1757–85. See Savill, 3, p. 1110.

4 Active 1752–1800. See Préaud and d'Albis, p. 206. Peters, *Marks*, p. 33, gives end date of 1786, which is incompatible with the production of this plate and earlier literature on Sèvres artists.

5 Found on soft paste 1781–93. See Savill, 3, p. 1129 (as last found 1792).

6 Active 1753–99. See Savill, 3, pp. 1064–66; Peters, *Marks*, p. 66.

7 Not in Savill.

8 APML, Seligmann file, invoice 29 May 1903: "4 plates of the Service of Buffon, with yellow ground, at frs. 7,000 a piece 28,000 francs [£1,120]."

9 AMNS, I. 7, 8 October 1752, molds and models, *assiette unie*.

10 Ibid., 1814 inventory, 1740–60, no. 1 (see Préaud and d'Albis, p. 168, no. 162); 1760–80, no. 2 (*assiette de dessert unie*). The first of these plaster models bears no relation to the Museum's plate. The second one seems to predate the model for the Hartford plate, which is only known from 1790.

11 An earlier exception seems to have been the plates from the Catherine II service, executed in 1778–79. There was a discussion of plate shapes in a manuscript of designs and instructions written for this service, which included dessert plates with a plain edge. The author of the manuscript states: "L'Assiette est parfaitement ronde sans aucun chantournement, sa forme est celle d'une Patère antique, tant soit relevée sur ses bords, destinées d'abord aux Sacrifices, les Étrusques avaient établi l'usage des Patères dans toute l'Italie. On ne servait que dans les Temples, comme on les voit sur les médailles et sur les bas reliefs antiques, ou le Sacrificateur est représenté la Patère à la main, ayant la forme du Disque ou d'une assiette; c'est de là que la forme de notre assiette est tirée." Bibliothèque nationale, Lf. 8 *pet. fol.*, quoted in Dawson, *British Museum*, p. 143. I should like to thank David Peters for providing information concerning plate design at the factory.

12 De Bellaigue, "Sèvres," p. 194.

13 Buffon, 4, pl. 485.

14 Ibid., 7, pl. 672.

15 Ibid., 4, pl. 291.

16 Ibid., 6, pl. 736.

17 AMNS, Vj'5, fol. 28v, six on 4 February and twelve on 14 February.

18 Ibid., fol. 98, 4 February; 26 February; and fol. 98v, 9 *nivôse* (29 December) 1793.

19 Ibid., fol. 191v, 3 *pluviôse* 1794 (21 January). In the records this entry looks as if it is listed under 1793, although it was actually 1794 (the scribe failed to record the change to a (pre-Republican) new year.

20 See note 2 above.

21 AMNS, Vj'5, fol. 76v, 18 January 1793.

22 Ibid., 15 March 1793. Some yellow-ground pieces with Buffon birds are decorated with identical friezes but in dark violet (see cat. no. 146).

23 Ibid., fol. 77, 24 July 1793. There is no mention of birds, but the friezes are specified as black.

24 Ibid., Vl'3, fol. 226. Weydinger could refer either to Léopold *père*, active 1757–1806, or Joseph-Léopold *fils* or *jeune*, later *aîné*, active 1775–1804, 1807–8, 1811, 1816–29. See Peters, *Marks*, pp. 75–76.

25 AMNS, Vl'3, fol. 228, 9 August 1793, birds, but not identified as Buffon birds; fol. 238, 29 *germinal an* II (18 April 1794).

26 There were four services with the same decoration listed in the sales records between 1791 and 1795 (see Arend, "Birds," pp. 6, 8 n. 3). David Peters has worked to unravel the different services, but is hesitant to assign the Museum's plates to a particular service. (see Peters, *Plates and Services*).

146

146

Two wine glass coolers (*seaux crennelés*)

1917.1151–1152

Sèvres, 1794

Soft-paste porcelain, 1917.1151: H. 4¹¹⁄₁₆ × L. 12¹⁄₁₆ × W. 7¹³⁄₁₆ in. (11.9 × 30.6 × 19.8 cm); 1917.1152: H. 4¾ × L. 12⅛ × W. 7¹¹⁄₁₆ in. (12.1 × 30.8 × 19.5 cm)

Yellow ground with dark violet friezes, polychrome birds, gilding

Marks: on both: *Sevres, R F*, date letters rr, painter's mark cm for Michel-Gabriel Commelin,[1] fx in black for Françoise-Philippine (*née* Le Grand) Descoins,[2] gilder's mark of 2000 for Henry-François Vincent *jeune, père*[3]

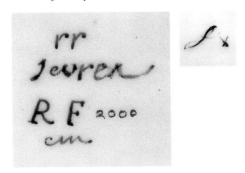

Inscriptions: 1917.1151: *Saracou de Cayenne* and *Gros Bec de Virginie appelle Cardinal hupe*; 1917.1152: *Rollier des Indes.* and *perroquet de la Nouvelle Guinée*

Provenance: comtesse de Gramont, by report; Jacques Seligmann, London and Paris, 1903;[4] J. Pierpont Morgan

MODEL

This oval wine glass cooler was called a *seau crennelé, seau à verres crennelé*, or sometimes *verrière*. It was introduced in 1758, and initially called a *seau ovale Échancré à 12 verres*.[5] By October of that year it was called *seau à verres crennelé*.[6] Molds for these wine glass coolers were priced at 8 *livres*, and undecorated examples were valued at 30 *livres*. The factory seems to have experimented with other wine glass coolers with scalloped edges as well, for in the January 1759 inventory of new models there also appear *seau échancré rond à 12 verres* and *seau échancré rond à 6 verres*.[7] It is not known if either of these models was produced.[8]

A plaster model survives at the Sèvres factory (fig. 146-1).[9] A drawing from about 1760 to 1775 is in the collection of the Cooper-Hewitt Museum, New York, and shows a *seau crennelé* decorated with flowers as well as a side view of the foliate handle. It is inscribed *No. 10. Seau Crenelé pour contenir verres et Liqueurs 120˝* [No. 10. crenellated cooler for holding glasses and liqueur (bottles?) 120 *livres*] and *Anse du d. Seau* [handle for said cooler].[10]

Sales records reveal that examples with flower decoration usually cost 144 *livres*, but occasionally were priced at 96 or 120 *livres*.[11] Prices for examples with *bleu lapis* ground ranged from 168 to 204 *livres* with *caillouté* gilding and flowers,[12] and 240 *livres* for *vermiculé* gilding and flowers.[13] *Bleu céleste* examples cost 192, 204, and 240 *livres*, decorated with flowers, birds, and flowers, respectively.[14] Among the more expensive examples were those in the Maria-Theresa service of 1758, decorated with green ribbons and garlands of flowers, which cost 480 *livres* each, and those made for the elaborate Louis XVI service of 1783–93 for 720 *livres* each.[15]

The Sèvres factory made at least three other forms of *seau crennelé*. One form tapers more toward the foot and has strap handles.[16] Another version, made for the Catherine the Great

146

service, has a pure oval shape, more vertical crenellations, and mask handles.[17] The third style, made for the *Service arabesque* that was intended for Louis XVI, has nearly straight sides, claw feet, and crenellations with straight tops and semi-circular dips.[18] In the factory records no distinction was made between the various forms of *seau crennelé*.

FUNCTION

These coolers were used to chill wine glasses. They were sometimes sold individually or in pairs.[19] Elaborately decorated examples usually were sold as part of a dessert service. In December 1758 two appear in the description of the service given to Maria-Theresa of Austria by Louis XV.[20] They were listed as *seaux crennelés à liqueur*. Like the inscription on the Cooper-Hewitt drawing, this suggests that the coolers could be

Fig. 146-1 *Seau crennelé* plaster model

used for both wine glasses as well as for small liqueur decanters.[21] However, there were other coolers specifically made for holding liqueur bottles, which were oval with a porcelain divider in the middle. These were also included in dessert services, and usually along with the *seaux crennelés*. It is unclear why the latter should have been required for liqueur decanters when there were already coolers available for such a purpose. *Seaux crennelés* were included in most of the major services sold or presented as gifts over the next thirty-six years.[22]

Wine glass coolers with crenellated rims originated in England, where they were called monteiths. According to an account of 1683, the name derived from a Scotsman named Monteigh who wore a cloak with the bottom in the form of u-shaped notches. Notched silver wine glass coolers called monteiths were documented as early as 1689.[23] They were also made on the continent by the early eighteenth century, both in silver and then in *faïence* and porcelain.[24] In France they were often called *verrières*, and were usually oval, shallower than English monteiths, with handles on the sides. Like other wine bottle or glass coolers, they would be filled with either cold water or crushed ice, and glasses would be placed bowl down for cooling.[25] They would have been put on the buffet or on small side tables during the meal.

COMMENTARY

The Museum's coolers are decorated with birds after François-Nicolas Martinet's illustrations for the comte de Buffon's treatise *Histoire naturelle des oiseaux*, published in ten volumes between 1770 and 1786.[26] The first cooler illustrates the *Saracou de Cayenne* and the *Gros-Bec de Virginie appellé Cardinal hupé* (figs. 146-2 and 146-3). The second cooler shows the *Perroquet, de la Nouvelle Guinée* and the *Rollier des Indes* (figs. 146-4 and 146-5).[27] The birds were painted by Michel-Gabriel Commelin while the dark violet friezes were painted by Madame Descoins.

Fig. 146-2 *Saracou de Cayenne*, Buffon

Fig. 146-3 *Gros-Bec de Virginie appellé Cardinal hupé*, Buffon

Fig. 146-4 *Perroquet, de la Nouvelle Guinée*, Buffon

Fig. 146-5 *Rollier des Indes*, Buffon

The work of both Commelin and Madame Descoins is recorded in the painters' work records.[28] Henry-François Vincent was the gilder.

A small service decorated with a yellow ground and Buffon birds was delivered on 21 or 22 February 1794 to Citizen Duriau for Citizen Auguste Jullien. It included four *verrières* priced at 170 *livres* each, two of which may correspond to the Museum's coolers.[29]

TECHNIQUE AND CONDITION

The yellow ground color appears uneven, perhaps due to the mordant not being applied well. The friezes are dark violet although in most lights they appear black.

Exhibition: *Morgan Loan Exhibition*, New York, 1914, not in catalogue

Literature: Chavagnac, p. 159, no. 204, pl. L

NOTES

1 Active 1768–1802. See Savill, 3, pp. 1024–25; Peters, *Marks*, p. 25.

2 Active 1780(?)–99(?). See Peters, *Marks*, p. 28 (previously attributed to Fumez).

3 Active 1753–1800. See Savill, 3, pp. 1076–77; Peters, *Marks*, p. 74.

4 APML, Seligmann file, invoice 28 May 1903, 44,000 French francs [£1,760], as coming from the "countess" de Grammont [*sic*]. A letter dated 27 May 1903 in the same file reads: "I am sending you with the present two Verrières in yellow Sèvres. You see they are coming from the service called 'de Buffon.' They are decorated by Vincent and are dated 1794. As you asked me this morning, I am sending them to you on view; they are the biggest pieces I have ever seen, and I will call to-morrow for the answer. I have not bought them, as I consider the price too high for me, and as I cannot make anything out of them."

5 AMNS, I. 7, 1 January 1759, molds and models for new work 1758. For the term *échancré* see cat. no. 137.

6 Ibid., 1 October 1759, *magasin du blanc*.

7 Ibid., 1 January 1759, molds and models.

8 There is no further mention of these models in the documents.

9 AMNS, 1814 inventory, 1740–60, no. 2.

10 No. C.H.M. 1938-88-8316, illustrated in an exhibition catalogue *Cooper-Hewitt Collection*, no. 146.

11 See for example, AMNS, Vy 2, fol. 89, unnamed buyer, 31 March 1759, two at 144 *livres*; ibid., 90v, unnamed buyer, 23 April 1759, one at 120 *livres*; Vy 3, fol. 39v, Machard, second half 1760, two at 96 *livres*.

12 Ibid., Vy 3, fol. 60, comte du Châtelet, August 1761 and fol. 80v, Bonnet, 28 November 1761; Vy 4, fols. 158, 180, November 1768/ 1 July 1769, gift to Christian VII of Denmark.

13 Ibid., Vy 3, fol. 125, Duchess of Bedford (through the duc de Praslin), 1 June 1763. This is the same price as the coolers with a *bleu Fallot* ground given to Count Starhemberg in 1766 (ibid., Vy 4, fols. 86–86v, October 1766).

14 Ibid., Vy 4, fols. 142v–43, baron de Breteuil, April 1768; Vy 5, fol. 11, Gustav III of Sweden, 1 October 1771; Vy 5, fol. 33v, prince de Rohan, 7 September 1772.

15 Ibid., Vy 2, fol. 85, December 1758 (in Hofburg, Vienna, no. 180529, illustrated with glasses inside in Winkler, p. 230), and de Bellaigue, *Louis XVI*, pp. 15, 230, no. 164. It should be noted that the prices for Vincennes and Sèvres were higher in the 1750s than in the next decades. This must account for some of the difference in cost between the Maria-Theresa service and later services. The Louis XVI service was one of exceptional cost due to its elaborate decoration. Among many other surviving examples are: *bleu lapis caillouté*, flowers, 1760, Waddesdon Manor, Buckinghamshire (Eriksen, *Waddesdon*, pp. 114–15, no. 39); blue ground,

birds, 1764, Mrs. Henry Walters sale Parke-Bernet, New York, 2–3 May 1941, lot 1365; *bleu céleste*, birds, 1766–67 (Razoumovski service), Waddesdon Manor (Eriksen, *Waddesdon*, pp. 222–23, no. 75N); *bleu céleste*, birds, 1767, Waddesdon Manor (ibid., pp. 226–27, no. 76); white, *camaïeu carmine* children, 1768/69, René Fribourg sale, Sotheby's, London, 25 June 1963, lot 66; white, roses, *mosaïque* border (Sartine service), 1768–87, Sotheby's, New York, 11 April 1980, lot 251; *bleu lapis caillouté*, flowers, 1769, Palais Galliéra, Paris, 7 December 1971, lot 21; white, flowers, 1769, Pitti Palace, Florence (Eriksen, *Pitti*, p. 79, no. 39); *bleu céleste pointillé*, children, c. 1770, Georges Petit, Paris (Chevallier-Mannheim), 5–10 May 1890, lot 379; *bleu céleste*, birds, 1774, Christie's, London, 15 October 1990, lot 36; green, flowers, 1774, Christie's, Monaco, 6 December 1985, lot 10; white, landscapes, garlands, ciphers (princesse des Asturies service), 1775, hard paste, Palacio Real, Madrid (illustrated de Bellaigue, *Louis XVI*, p. 21, fig. 16); green, fruits and flowers (Joseph II service), 1777, Hofburg, Vienna (Verlet, *Sèvres*, p. 217, pl. 80); white, flowers, 1782, Sotheby's, Monaco, 26 May 1980, lot 301 (formerly Wrightsman Collection, MMA, mistakenly said to measure 7½ in. or 19cm); white, claret border, pearls and flowers (Marie-Antoinette service), 1784, hard paste, Ashmolean Museum, Oxford (Dawson, *Ashmolean*, pp. 70–73, no. 49); white, *verd pointillé* border, birds, c. 1784/86, Nissim de Camondo, Paris (Brunet and Préaud, p. 217, no. 279); white, pale blue border with arabesques, 1790, Sotheby's, New York, 9–10 October 1990, lot 415.

16 See Christie's, Monaco, 4 December 1988, lot 47, 1780, part of a service decorated with roses and cornflowers, probably delivered to a dealer named Manoel (16 October 1780). According to David Peters, who helped catalogue this object, the cooler is more round than oval and may relate to the *seau échancré rond à 12 verres* in the 1759 factory inventory (see note 7 above).

17 See *Tables royales*, p. 327, no. 247.

18 Dated 1784, hard-paste porcelain, Museo Duca de Martina, Naples, illustrated in de Bellaigue, *Louis XVI*, pl. III; see also Peters, "Louis XV et Louis XVI," p. 121.

19 From 1758 to 1761 over twenty-five were sold, either singly or in pairs, but not in obvious services. All of them were decorated with flowers.

20 See note 15 above.

21 Liqueur decanters were small, with relatively long necks.

22 These included the Elector of Palatine (1761), the Duchess of Bedford (1763), Count Starhemberg (1766), Christian VII of Denmark (1768), Mme du Barry (1771), Gustav III of Sweden (1771), the prince de Rohan (1772), Joseph II of Austria (1777), the Duchess of Manchester (1783), Louis XVI (1783–93) and William Eden (1787). For many of these services see *Grands services* and *Tables royales*.

23 For a lengthy discussion of the origins and history of the monteith see McNab, *passim*.

24 A *faïence* example was sold Christie's, Monaco, 4 December 1988, lot 9, Marseille *faïence*, Veuve Perrin, c. 1765.

25 See cat. nos. 132 and 137 for other coolers.

26 See cat. no. 145 for more on this source.

27 Buffon, 8, pl. 38; 4, pl. 37; 7, pl. 713; 3, pl. 619.

28 AMNS, Vj'5, fol. 68, 3 *pluviôse an* II (21 January 1794), Commelin, *2 Seaux Crenneles jonquille Oiseaux Buffon 1" Vu* and fol. 236, 27 *pluviôse an* II (15 February 1794), Descoins, *2 Seaux Crennelés Petite frize en voiolet* [*sic*]. There were two *seaux crennelés* fired on 24 *pluviôse an* II (12 February 1794) decorated with birds by Commelin, but they apparently were gilded by Vandé, not Vincent and preceded the decoration of the friezes by Mme Descoins (AMNS, Vl'3, fol. 234v). Moreover, they were not described as *oiseaux Buffon*, which normally was the way they were listed in the kiln records. I should like to thank David Peters for help with these and the following references.

29 Ibid., Vy 11, fol. 214v, 3 *ventôse an* II (21 February 1794). Two coolers with the same decoration were also included in a service delivered to Citizen Speelman in October 1795 for 7,200 *livres* (devalued paper *assignots*, but price still calculated in *livres* (ibid., Vy 12, fol. 67v, 6 *brumaire an* IV, 28 October 1795).

147

147

Broth basin and stand (*écuelle et plateau*)

1995.11[1]

Vincennes, c. 1744–1748

Soft-paste porcelain, basin: H. 3⅞ × W. 5¹⁵⁄₁₆ × D. 4⁷⁄₁₆ in.
(9.8 × 15 × 11.2 cm); stand: H. 1³⁄₁₆ × DIAM. 6¾ in. (3 × 17.1 cm)

White ground with polychrome figural decoration, iron red fillets,
brown on rim of saucer, carmine knob and handles

Marks: none

Provenance: Paris, Drouot-Richelieu, 1994;[2] Dragesco-Cramoisan,
Paris, 1995

MODEL

The shape of this broth basin and stand is taken directly from a
Meissen form made from about 1725 until about 1740.[3] The
young French factory copied the shape of the basin and the
handles, as well as the recess in the stand for the basin. Even the
size of the French version approximates that of the Meissen.[4] A
similar basin in the Musée des Arts décoratifs, Paris, has handles
like pointed ears and a different knob.[5] The Museum's cover is
topped with a berry.

There is another example of this form of *écuelle*, decorated
with landscapes, in the David Collection in Copenhagen.
Unlike the Atheneum's, it is crowned with a melon knob.[6]

COMMENTARY

The style of the decoration of the *écuelle* and *plateau* also betrays
its roots in Meissen porcelain, although, in fact, the pictorial
sources are probably French. From the 1730s the Meissen
factory began decorating wares with figures in the style of
Antoine Watteau and Nicolas Lancret, and in 1741 it purchased
engravings after these same French artists.[7] The figures sometimes were used in small vignettes and at other times as staffage
in landscapes. Throughout the 1740s Meissen produced wares
and decorative objects decorated in this fashion.

A few years later, in 1745, when the fledgling Vincennes
factory reorganized itself financially, it was granted a twenty-
year privilege to produce "la porcelaine façon de Saxe peinte et
dorée à figure humaine" [porcelain in the manner of Saxony,
painted and gilded with human figures].[8] Quite naturally
Vincennes modelers and painters looked to current Meissen
production for inspiration. It is possible that some pieces
were made available to the French factory from the personal
collection of Orry de Fulvy.[9]

147

The scenes on the broth basin and stand show charming vignettes of wooing couples, inhabiting park-like landscapes. Flowers are scattered between the scenes on the stand and a small bouquet decorates the recess. The figures are drawn somewhat naively with rounded faces, abbreviated features, rosy cheeks, and formulaic drapery. The landscape settings are dominated by washes of browns and greens, set against backdrops with smoky trees executed in semi-opaque teals surrounded by dabs of purple enamel. The same painter appears to have decorated a number of pieces of early Vincennes now in public collections, including a *lampe de nuit* and a tea cannister at the Metropolitan Museum of Art, a wine glass cooler, a covered bowl, and two *lampes de nuit* at the Musée des Arts décoratifs, Paris, a water jug in the Museum of Fine Arts, Boston, a covered bowl in the Cleveland Museum of Art, and an *étui* and a teapot in the Musée national de Céramique, Sèvres.[10]

Based on the evidence of how this broth basin and stand were fired, as well as their closeness to Meissen prototypes, it is likely that the Museum's *écuelle* was made between 1744 and 1748. Certainly it predates the introduction of gold to the factory's production, when in 1748 the marquis de Fulvy purchased the secret for gilding from a Benedictine monk Hippolyte Lefaure (Frère Hippolyte).[11]

TECHNIQUE AND CONDITION

There are four small glazed chips to the top edge of the basin, suggesting that the basin stood on its rim with four small supports when fired in the biscuit kiln. These supports, which would have been ceramic, may have adhered to the rim during the biscuit firing, at which time they would have had to be chipped off. Such difficulties were not uncommon at Vincennes before Claude-Humbert Gérin designed a new kiln for the factory in 1748 and a new style of support was subsequently introduced.[12] The way the enamel colors sit more on the surface of the glaze rather than fusing completely with it may be because of slight underfiring. The iron red used throughout the decoration is of an unusually fine quality.

NOTES

1 Credit line, Gift of J. Pierpont Morgan, by exchange.

2 Marc Ferri, Drouot-Richelieu, Paris, 9 December 1994, lot 73.

3 See Eriksen and Bellaigue, p. 225, no. 42. See also Rückert, nos. 246, 435.

4 On Meissen examples, the knob can be either fruit or flowers (see examples illustrated in Rückert, cited above).

5 No. 6298. See *Vincennes*, p. 54, no. 94.

6 Eriksen and Bellaigue, p. 225, no. 42. There was another example of this form, without its cover, with Dragesco-Cramoisan in Paris in 1991 (decorated with children playing in landscapes, unmarked). Another (also with Dragesco-Cramoisan, same year), was decorated with flowers and had a melon knob (illustrated in Dallot-Naudin, p. 208), stand marked with interlaced Ls and dots in center, above and below, and on both sides.

7 Rückert, p. 131.

8 Préaud and d'Albis, p. 22.

9 Jean-Henri-Louis Orry de Fulvy, founder of the Vincennes factory, was *intendant des finances* and half-brother of the French *contrôleur-général* Philibert Orry. See Préaud and d'Albis, pp. 7–35 for the early history of the factory. Eriksen (in Eriksen and Bellaigue, p. 225) suggests that Orry de Fulvy may have had a prototypical Meissen *écuelle* that he lent to Vincennes for copying.

10 MMA, New York, nos. 54.147.27 (see Eriksen and Bellaigue, no. 46) and 54.147.29AB (see Préaud and d'Albis, no. 81); MAD, Paris, nos. 28713 (see Préaud and d'Albis, no. 33), 36186 (see Eriksen and Bellaigue, no. 43), 409 and RI 999.7.1–2; MFA, Boston, no. 1982.776a, b (see Hawes and Corsiglia, no. 57); Cleveland, Museum of Art, no. 1944.225 (see Préaud and d'Albis, no. 79, formerly Morgan Collection); and MNC, Sèvres, nos. 26458 and 18307. Eriksen (Eriksen and Bellaigue, p. 227) also attributes a teapot in the V&A, London (no. C 131 & a. 1934) to the same hand. Another wine glass cooler was with Dragesco-Cramoisan, Paris in 1998, decorated with compositions after François Boucher.

11 See Eriksen and Bellaigue, p. 54; Préaud and d'Albis, pp. 30, 35 n. 23, 226–27. For a discussion of production in the year 1744 see d'Albis and Klein, "Scène militaire," passim.

12 See Préaud and d'Albis, pp. 223, 231.

148

Water jug and basin (*pot à la Romaine uni et jatte ovale*)

1917.965–966

Vincennes, c. 1753–1755

Soft-paste porcelain, jug: H. 9⅜ × w. 6¹¹⁄₁₆ × D. 4¾ in. (23.8 × 16.9 × 12 cm); basin: H. 2¾ × L. 14⅜ × D. 9¹³⁄₁₆ in. (7 × 36.4 × 24.9 cm)

Bleu lapis ground, polychrome birds, gilding

Marks: interlaced Ls in blue on both; incised 4 on jug;[1] another illegible incised mark; basin, incised g, 6 or 9;[2] dot in underglaze blue on jug (probably the mark of the ground-color painter)

Provenance: Cartier et Fils, Paris, 1902;[3] J. Pierpont Morgan

MODEL

The factory named this large jug and basin a *pot à la Romaine et jatte ovale*.[4] A letter from Hendrick van Hulst to Boileau dated October 1751 proves that they were designed by Duplessis.[5] There were two variations of the *pot à la Romaine*, one *uni* or plain and one with more elaborately molded decoration (*à ornements*). Plaster molds for both versions are mentioned in the October 1752 inventory.[6] In comparison to other water jugs and basins, these molds were expensive, costing 6 *livres* (*uni*) and 10 *livres* (*à ornements*). The form must have been created sometime in the second half of 1751, for Boileau in his October letter to van Hulst refers to the "pots à la romaine de M. du Plessis."[7] Even by October of 1752 no examples were ready for sale, although two were in the course of decoration, six were glazed, one was in biscuit (valued at 27 *livres*) and four molds were ready. A plaster model of the jug also survives (fig. 148-1).[8]

Once decorated a *pot à la Romaine* and its *jatte* cost between 72 *livres* (*fleurs*) and 600 *livres* (*bleu céleste fleurs*). The earliest set known to have been sold was decorated with flowers, costing 144 *livres* and bought by Hebert.[9] Sometimes the sales registers do not distinguish between *uni* and *à ornements*.[10] Examples decorated with *bleu lapis* and birds often cost 300 *livres*,[11] but could cost less on occasion.[12]

FUNCTION

Water jugs and basins were used for washing, both in the *garde-robe* or lavatory and private apartments during the *toilette*. In the *garde-robe* they were accompanied by chamber pots and close stools, and in some cases may have been part of a decorative ensemble.[13] In the private apartments or bedroom they were used for washing both the face and hands. Because the *toilette* or ritual of dressing was a lengthy process, frequently beginning at midday, food was consumed, often broth and bread. Hand washing was necessary so as not to mix powders and cosmetics with food.[14]

148

Vincennes jugs and basins were usually displayed on the dressing table, although they were sold independently of dressing-table services. Nevertheless there are examples in the sales records of jugs and basins matching broth basins and their stands.[15] When not in use the jug sat inside the basin. Thirteen water jugs were recorded in the probate inventory of Madame de Pompadour's château de Ménars.[16]

Water jugs were called either *brocs* or *pots à eau*: generally, *brocs* were uncovered and *pots à eau* were covered, except for the *pot à la Romaine*. While *pots à eau* were always sold with basins; when *brocs* were sold alone, they were probably intended for the *garde-robe*.[17] *Pots à eau* with covers often had gold or silver-gilt mounts.

COMMENTARY

The Atheneum's *pot à la Romaine et jatte* are dated about 1753 to 1755. Between 1753 and 1754 there were three recorded sales of jugs and basins fitting the description of the Museum's set, that is *bleu lapis* with polychrome birds. One sale was to Monsieur de Betz for 300 *livres*,[18] another to Lazare Duvaux in December 1753 for 220 *livres*,[19] and a third, through Duvaux, to Madame de Pompadour on 23 June 1754, for 300 *livres*.[20] Those sets delivered to Monsieur Betz and Lazare Duvaux may correspond to the ones listed in the enamel kiln records for November 1753–January 1754.[21]

Another similar jug and basin are in the Fitzwilliam Museum, Cambridge,[22] while a set with gilded birds and dated

1753–54 is at the Musée national de Céramique, Sèvres.[23] A sugar bowl with the painter's mark for Mutel, also at Sèvres, is painted with birds resembling those on the Hartford jug and basin.[24]

The birds in the reserves are birds of fancy, fat bellied, aerial acrobats conforming to the fashion of the early 1750s. Probably inspired by oriental lacquer and, by extension, furniture and *boiseries*, this type of flying bird became fixed in the repertory of the factory during this period.[25] Surrounding the reserves are gilded trellises and garlands of foliage and flowers. Elaborate gilded decoration like this was often employed in conjunction with *bleu lapis* for the blue tended to run and this could be masked by the gilding. Trellis patterns may have been inspired by the framework around some contemporary engravings,[26] although they could as easily recall rococo wood or painted molding on architectural panels or the framework around cartouches on snuff boxes of the period. The best gilders at Vincennes probably played a part in creating the designs. Flowers, foliage, and small pomegranates or rose hips were recurrent motifs at this time.[27] The trellis design seems to have gone out of vogue by 1755.

TECHNIQUE AND CONDITION

In 1753, *bleu lapis* was the only *grand feu* or high-fired color. It was applied directly on the biscuit porcelain after the biscuit had been coated with a glue mordant: the color was sieved on and then fired, producing an uneven and yet rich, dimensional blue.

The first recorded sale of a piece using this deep, underglaze blue developed in imitation of oriental porcelain was of a sugar basin sold by Lazare Duvaux to the king in March of 1752.[28] By August of that year *bleu lapis* was in full production.[29]

Both the Museum's jug and basin were molded, not thrown. The *bleu lapis* ground color used was a particular variant known as *bleu antique* or *bleu de M. Gagny*, which was put into production after October 1752. The earlier underglaze blue was duller in color.[30] The enamel colors in the birds must have been slightly underfired as the colors did not penetrate well into the glaze.[31]

Exhibition: *Morgan Loan Exhibition*, New York, 1914, not in catalogue

Literature: Chavagnac, pp. 53–54, no. 60, pl. XIV; Buckley, *Antiques*, pp. 188–89, fig. 6; Hood, *Bulletin*, p. 2, fig. 2; *Vincennes*, p. 70, no. 136[32]

NOTES

1 Savill, 3, pp. 1126–27, found on soft paste 1753–87.

2 Ibid., pp. 1127–28, found on soft paste 1754–90s.

3 APML, Cartier file, invoice, April 1902: "1 Aiguière avec son plateau en Vincennes année 1752 décor oiseaux, cartel blanc sur fond bleu," 15,000 French francs.

4 Préaud and d'Albis, p. 128, no. 55, note that the early documents did not speak of a *pot à eau* but only a *pot à la Romaine*.

5 Préaud and d'Albis, p. 128.

6 AMNS, I. 7, 8 October 1752.

Fig. 148-1 *Pot à la Romaine*, plaster model

7 AMNS, H2, letter, 26 October 1751.

8 AMNS, *casier* 766, 1814 inventory, 1740–60, no. 11. *Vincennes*, p. 70, cites plaster molds for the basin in two sizes, although Tamara Préaud notes in correspondence that there are none currently at the factory. Extant basins all appear to be one size, ranging in length from 13⅜ to 14¼ in. (34 to 36.5 cm).

9 AMNS, Vy 1, fol. 9v, 15 December 1752.

10 Préaud and d'Albis, p. 128.

11 AMNS, Vy 1, fol. 24, 26 December 1753, *1 lapis oiseau colorée*, Betz; Vy 1, fol. 47v, 30 June 1754, *1 lapis oiseau colorée*, Duvaux; Vy 1, fol. 85, 21 May 1755, Bailly; Vy 1, fol. 115, *1 lapis oiseaux*, 1 October–31 December 1755, Duvaux. Most extant examples decorated with *bleu lapis* are *uni* rather than *à ornements* but this may simply be due to an unequal survival rate.

12 One of the two sold to Duvaux in December 1753 cost only 220 *livres* (ibid., Vy 1, fol. 29, 31 December 1753, *fournée* 6, November 1753–5 January 1754), while another noted as defective sold to Bazin for 240 *livres* (Vy 1, fol. 44).

13 See cat. no. 151. See also Savill, 2, p. 691.

14 For more on their use see Savill, 2, p. 691. She quotes Mme de Sévigné's description of the *toilette* of the duchesse de Bourbon: "elle s'eveilla à midi et demi, prit sa robe de chambre, vint se coëffer et manger un pain au pot; elle se frise et se poudre elle-même, elle mange en même temps; les mesmes doigts tiennent alternativement la houppe et le pain au pot; elle mange sa poudre et graisse ses cheveux; le tout ensemble fait un fort bon déjeuner et une charmante coëffure," (Havard, 4, p. 1353).

15 Savill, 2, p. 692.

16 Eriksen and Bellaigue, pp. 77–78.

17 See Savill, 2, p. 692 for more on the terminology.

18 AMNS, Vy 1, fol. 24, 26 December 1753 (*fournée* 6, November 1753–5 January 1754): *1 Pot à la Romaine Lapis oiseaux colorés* and *1 jatte oiseaux*, 300 *livres* (Préaud and d'Albis, p. 92).

19 See note 12 (perhaps *uni* vs. *à ornements*).

20 LD, 2, p. 205, no. 1818: "Mme. la Marq. De Pompadour: (M. de Duras) Un grand pot à l'eau à la romaine & sa jatte ovale en bleu lapis & or, les cartouches peints avec oiseaux, 300 l." It is unlikely that this is the same set that Duvaux bought for 220 *livres* for the prices listed in the factory sales ledgers normally corresponded to those in Duvaux's day books. There is no entry in the factory sales records for a set costing 300 *livres* to Duvaux.

21 IF 5676, fol. 9: *2 Lapis oiseaux colorés et 2 jattes*.

22 No. C. 7 & A-1961.

23 MNC, Sèvres, no. 26318.

24 MNC, Sèvres, no. 26295, marked date letter A, three dots (above and on sides), and compass mark of Mutel, active 1754–59, 1765–67, 1771–74 (see Peters, *Marks*, p. 54). The drawing of the factory mark on the sugar bowl, in underglaze *bleu lapis*, is identical to the drawing of the factory mark on the Museum's basin. This mark was probably placed there by the ground-color painter.

25 Eriksen and Bellaigue, p. 84; Dragesco, "Oiseaux," p. 39.

26 Eriksen and Bellaigue, p. 98.

27 Compare, for example, a *seau à verre* in the MMA, New York (no. 50.211.180).

28 LD, 2, p. 118, no. 1079, 28 March 1752, "Un grand pot à sucre de Vincennes en bleu lapis, à cartouches d'oiseaux."

29 Préaud and d'Albis, p. 88.

30 Antoine d'Albis made this observation. De Gagny was one of the *actionnaires* of the Société Eloy Brichard who suggested applying Moniac's pure blue frit to the biscuit and firing it in the painting kiln (see Préaud and d'Albis, p. 218).

31 The jug has been broken around the bottom and repaired sometime before 1902.

32 Mistakenly cited as having the same decoration as the example in the Louvre being discussed.

149

149

Toilet pots (*pots à pommade*)

1917.974–975

Vincennes or Sèvres, c. 1755–1759

Soft-paste porcelain, both: H. 3 × DIAM. 2³⁄₁₆ in. (7.6 × 5.6 cm)

Bleu lapis ground with polychrome birds and gilding

Marks: on both: interlaced Ls in blue; incised 2[1]

Provenance: J. Pierpont Morgan

MODEL

At Vincennes and Sèvres, *pots à pommade* as well as *pots à pâte*—for cosmetic pastes and creams—were first recorded in 1752.[2] The difference between them was probably one of size, *pots à pâte* being the larger of the two. Of the four forms of toilet pot made at the factory, the simple cylindrical version was the most common,[3] and came in three sizes, costing between 1 and 96 *livres*.[4] Early examples were topped with flower knobs, while later ones often had fruit knobs.

FUNCTION

Pots à pommade were a dressing-table accessory for holding hair or face grease. They were among other articles made at Vincennes and Sèvres for the *toilette*. While individual cosmetic pots were made in quantity at the factory, entire toilet services were rare.[5] Other porcelain or *faïence* factories also produced such wares, especially the cosmetic pots. They were also made in gold, silver, and other valuable materials.

Like cold cream, pomade was used to moisten the skin and prevent blemishes. It often contained apples (*pommes*), from which the name *pommade* derives, and could be scented with jasmine or tuberose or other floral fragrances.[6] Sometimes it was mixed with carbonate of lead, called *céruse*, in order to hide wrinkles and other blemishes. Women—and even sometimes men—would use it to whiten their faces, necks, chests and arms. After prolonged use lead poisoning could occur, a fact duly noted in the eighteenth century.[7]

COMMENTARY

In the absence of date letters, the Museum's second-size pots traditionally have been dated about 1753 or 1754, but were more likely to have been made between 1755 and 1759, since the narrow gilded garlands around the reserves are more typical of pieces from these later years. A *bleu lapis* covered sugar bowl decorated with birds and narrow garlands and dated 1755–56 was sold in New York in 1982.[8] Two *bleu lapis* cups and saucers with birds and gilded garlands in the Museum Schloß Fasanerie, Germany, are also dated 1755–56.[9] A saucer with a gilded garland even closer in style to the Museum's toilet pots is also in the Schloß Fasanerie collection, and is dated 1758–59.[10] There is every sign that the factory decorated *bleu lapis* pieces with birds and gilded garlands throughout the 1750s.[11]

There are no entries in the sales records during the years 1755 to 1759 that may be linked definitively to the Museum's toilet pots. In December 1756 Monsieur d'Érigny purchased two toilet pots described only as *lapis* for 18 *livres* each,[12] and in the second half of 1757 Lazare Duvaux paid the factory for four *lapis pots à pommade*, one priced at 24 *livres* and three at 18 *livres*.[13] These are less expensive than examples specifically described as *lapis oiseaux colorés* in 1753, suggesting that their decoration may have been slightly simpler.[14]

TECHNIQUE AND CONDITION

Pomade pots were turned. On this pair, the covers have flower knobs; the one on 1917.975 is a modern replacement.[15]

Exhibition: *Morgan Loan Exhibition*, New York, 1914, not in catalogue

Literature: Chavagnac, p. 62, no. 74

NOTES

1 See Savill, 3, p. 1125. Found on soft paste 1753–88, most common in the 1750s.

2 AMNS I. 7, 8 October 1752; see *Vincennes*, p. 81 and Savill, 2, pp. 719 and 727 n. 15 for basic information on the form.

3 AMNS, note in file. For example, see Préaud and d'Albis, p. 142, no. 88 (with foot, c. 1748–49, private collection); Préaud and d'Albis, p. 158, no. 134 (*bombé* shape, c. 1749–52, private collection); and Savill, 2, p. 723, 1763.

4 Savill, 2, p. 727 n. 15; *Vincennes*, p. 80, notes that there were only two sizes made, although in the inventory of October 1752 a third was listed in the *magasin de ventes* (AMNS, I. 7, 8 October 1752). Extant examples suggest two sizes, approximately as follows: first size: H. 3⁹⁄₁₆–3¹⁵⁄₁₆ in (9–10 cm), second size: H. 2⅝–2¹⁵⁄₁₆ in. (6.6–7.5 cm).

5 See Savill, 2, p. 719 for a discussion of the toilet service.

6 See Chilton, pp. 87–88, and Savill, 2, p. 727 n. 28, citing Diderot, *Encyclopédie*, XIII, 1765, pp. 1–2; VI, 1756, pp. 409–10; XIV, 1765, p. 401.

7 Chilton, p. 88, citing Horace Walpole in December 1766.

8 Sotheby's, New York, 22 and 24 April 1982, lot 25.

9 Nos. FAS PE 850/a–c, *Königliches Porzellan Frankreich*, pp. 36–39, nos. 6.1–6.2.

10 No. FAS PE 850/a, ibid., no. 6.5.

11 There is no way to be certain, however, that the Museum's toilet pots were made at the later end of this tradition. Factory records indicate that two *pots à pommade bleu lapis oiseaux colorés* were sold at the factory in 1753, one to an unnamed buyer and the other to Mme de Pompadour (AMNS, Vy 1, fol. 2v, 25 April 1753, *fournée* 70, 1752, 30 *livres*, or Vy 1, fol. 7, 28 April 1753, *fournée* 70, 36 *livres*). A pair with this type of decoration is at the MAD, Paris, and shows a slightly different style of gilding than the Hartford pair, with foliate scrolls at the bottom that merge into floral garlands on the sides and top (MAD, Paris, no. GR 215a–b, in *Vincennes*, p. 81, nos. 180–81 and Préaud and d'Albis, p. 163, no. 146).

12 AMNS, Vy 2, fol. 4, 18 December 1756.

13 Ibid., fol. 50v, 1 July 1757–1 January 1758.

14 See note 11 above.

15 Treated 1993, report in Museum file.

150

Broth basin and stand (*écuelle à vignes* and *plateau à ozier*)

1917.987

Vincennes, 1755–1756

Soft-paste porcelain, basin: H. 5³⁄₁₆ × w. 9¼ × D. 6¹⁵⁄₁₆ in. (13.1 × 23.5 × 17.6 cm); stand: H. 1⅞ × w. 12⅛ × D. 9⅛ in. (4.8 × 30.7 × 23.1 cm)

White ground with relief-molded vine decoration on basin, relief-molded basketwork decoration on stand, polychrome flowers, blue fillets, gilding

Marks: on both: interlaced Ls in blue with date letter C and painter's mark H;[1] incised scrolled H under *plateau*[2]

Provenance: Cartier et Fils, Paris, 1901;[3] J. Pierpont Morgan

MODEL

The broth basin of this set was very likely called *écuelle à vignes*, because of its relief decoration of fruited vines. Molds and models with this name appear in the factory inventories of October 1752 and January 1753, although the form is not mentioned in the lists of pieces fired or glazed, nor anywhere in the sales records, nor in subsequent inventories[4] In shape it is a variant of the lobed *écuelle à 4 pans ovale*, for which a mold appears in the October 1752 inventory.[5] Some surviving examples of this *écuelle* have a fish knob like the Atheneum's and have the same entwined foliate handles.[6]

Inventories from 1752 through 1756 list *écuelles à ozier* with matching *plateaux*. Molds and models for *écuelles et plateaux à ozier*, together with glaze-fired examples, are listed in the October 1752 inventory. Three sizes are indicated, *grandes, moyennes,* and *petites*.[7] The *plateau à ozier* is a variant of the *plateau à ornements*—the standard tray for the *écuelle à 4 pans*—differing only in the molded basketwork pattern. Judging by appearances, there is every likelihood that the Museum's stand is a *plateau à ozier*. Early examples of the *écuelle à ozier* are unknown to this author, although one presumes its appearance to have been like the 1764 example at the Museum of Fine Arts in Boston.[8] The first mention of this form in the sales records was on 28 December 1753, when one decorated with flowers was sold to the dealer Bailly.[9]

FUNCTION

Handled basins with covers and stands were used for serving broth or soups.[10] By the middle of the eighteenth century, their main function was in the bedroom or boudoir to serve *bouillon* [broth] in the morning or soup with bread during the lengthy process of dressing.[11] *Écuelles* were also used in the sick room or during confinement.[12] In the Middle Ages *écuelles* were made of wood and placed on the table, shared between two diners. In fact, the word *écuelle* derives from the word *esculus,* a strong,

150

stable type of oak that was used to make these early vessels.[13] From the Renaissance, *écuelles* could be made of *faïence*, pewter, gold, silver, silver gilt, or even rock crystal.[14]

By the time *écuelles* were produced at Vincennes, they had become smaller and were meant for only one person. The cover kept the contents warm for some time, and one could sip directly from the basin using the two handles. The *plateau* held the bread. *Écuelles* with fish knobs may have been for fish soups on Fridays and other abstinence days when meat was not permitted.[15]

COMMENTARY

The marks tell us that the same painter decorated both basin and stand in 1755 with scattered bouquets of flowers, fillets and accents of blue. However, the broth basin was made some years before its date of decoration of 1755, for reasons we shall see below.[16] We may speculate that the basin was taken from the *magasin du blanc* in 1755 and put together with a newly made basket-weave stand. Unfortunately, there is no documentary evidence to prove this theory. The inventories for 1755 and 1756 do not record two such pieces being sent to the painters' studio, nor is such a pair mentioned in the sales records for those years.[17] On the contrary, the inventory of 1 January 1756 lists an *écuelle moulée* with its *plateau* (first size), and two *écuelles et plateaux à*

ozier among pieces in white, demonstrating that broth basins and stands with the same relief decoration were kept together as matched sets.[18] We could argue that the *écuelle moulée* was in fact the Hartford *écuelle à vignes* and that for some reason it was paired with one of the *plateaux à ozier*, or that—like some other known pieces of Vincennes—the Museum's pieces escaped the documents. Yet it is just as likely that there were two *écuelles et plateaux* decorated by the same painter in 1755, one *à ozier* and one *à vignes*, and that the Museum's pieces were married together much later.

The identity of the flower painter of Hartford's *écuelle* and *plateau* is unknown. Some scholars have given the mark to Pierre Houry, who was active at the factory from 1746 until his death in June of 1755.[19] As others have noted, however, this attribution is problematic, as a pair of *caisses carrées* with the painter's mark H at the Metropolitan Museum of Art is dated D for 1756, after Houry's death, and still other works with this mark exist dated as late as 1764.[20] More recently it has been suggested that either Charles-François Becquet or Michel Socquet used this mark.[21]

TECHNIQUE AND CONDITION

A new kind of kiln stand was introduced in 1752, superseding the tripod stand.[22] The new stand enabled pieces to be hung in the kiln but required a small hole to be drilled into the foot rim of a piece before biscuit firing to suspend the object. Inevitably, there would be some infilling of the hole with glaze during the next firing. In the hole in the foot rim of the Museum's basin, however, there is no infilling, only a roughly cut hole. From that we may logically conclude that the hole was gouged out after the piece had been glazed. This probably took place in 1755 when the basin was sent to the enamel kiln. The cover likewise must have been made before 1752, for it has two sets of two crudely dug-out, unglazed holes under its rim. The basketwork stand, on the other hand, seems to have been made after 1752 for it has a neatly drilled hole with glaze inside in keeping with the new method of hanging pieces in the kiln.

The stand also has a pronounced firing crack, which was filled with a mixture of biscuit and glaze, and then painted with a butterfly in an attempt to hide it. This was done at the time of manufacture. The handles and perhaps the fish knob were modeled by hand. The flowers were painted with colors that include *beau bleu no. 2*, introduced in 1751, and a poor quality iron red.

Exhibition: *Morgan Loan Exhibition*, New York, 1914, not in catalogue

Literature: Chavagnac, pp. 66–67, no. 79; Buckley, *Antiques*; Munger, *Wickes*, p. 188 n. 1[23]

NOTES

1 Perhaps either Charles-François Becquet or Michel Socquet. See Peters, *Marks*, p. 82.

2 Dauterman, *Marks*, pp. 200, 90, attributed to Michel Héricourt (or Henricourt) *jeune, cadet, façonnage* 1755–56; *répareur* 1756–62. See also Savill, 3, p. 1107, who suggests that an incised H, not scrolled, may have actually been the mark for either Michel Héricourt or his older brother Augustin.

3 APML, Cartier file 2, Paris, invoice 24 May 1901: "1 Bouillon avec son plateau, Vieux Sèvres fond blanc Louis XV, décors en relief, bleu clair et or, bouquets détachés," 6,000 French francs.

4 After 1753 some *écuelles* are described as *moulée*, which could possibly include the *écuelle à vigne*. There is no way of confirming this from the documents nor of being able to distinguish one molded broth basin from another. The *écuelle à 4 pans* might also be among the molded *écuelles* listed.

5 There were two variants of the *écuelle à 4 pans* noted in the inventory of 1752 (AMNS, I. 7, 8 October 1752), an *écuelle à 4 pans ronds à cachet* and an *écuelle à 4 pans ronds de M. Hebert*. The 1755 inventory mentions three sizes of *écuelles à 4 pans* in the *magasin du blanc*, but fails to distinguish between the above-mentioned variants. As the few lobed broth basins that survive all seem to be different variants and dimensions, it is impossible to know what each type was called or how many sizes of each variant were produced.

6 There are relatively few extant examples of the *écuelle à 4 pans*. Among them are: Louvre, Paris, c. 1750, no. TH. 1225–1226 (*Vincennes*, p. 49, no. 80, listed as oval although it is round); David Collection, Copenhagen, (Eriksen and Bellaigue, p. 238, no. 59); St. Louis Art Museum (no. 7-1945); Elton Hall, Cambridgeshire, collection of Mrs. William Proby; *écuelle* without a stand, Paris private collection, illustrated in Dallot-Naudin, p. 207; MAD, Paris, no. 1995-18 (see Arizzoli-Clémentel, no. 37, formerly in collection of the Marquis of Cholmondeley, Houghton Hall, England

[Christie's, London, 8 December 1994]); Galerie Charpentier, Paris, 24 June 1960, lot 192; Drouot, Paris, 15 December 1977, lot A; Sotheby's, New York, 26 September 1989, lot 277, later sold Ader, Tajan, Paris, 25 October 1993, lot 122; and *écuelle* and *plateau* with arms of the Stuart Kings, England, Royal Collection (*écuelle* sold Sotheby's, London, 21 April 1964, lot 42, *plateau* sold in Paris in 1996, illustrated in an advertisement for Vincent L'Herrou, *Connaissance des Arts*, September 1996). All have fish knobs and foliate handles. The *écuelle à 4 pans et plateau* with applied relief flowers and painted birds illustrated in Préaud and d'Albis, p. 149, no. 112, present location unknown, exceptionally has a knob formed of a pomegranate and has crossed handles. A later *écuelle* with basketwork decoration at the MFA, Boston (Munger, *Wickes*, pp. 187–88, no. 134) has a lemon knob and different interlaced branch handles.

7 This model is probably a variant of the *écuelle à 4 pans*. One *écuelle à ozier et plateau* with flowers was listed in the enamel kiln firing of February 1754 (IF 5676, fol. 16). Molds for this model, valued at 8 *livres* for the basin and stand together, were listed in the 8 October 1752 inventory of the factory (AMNS, I. 7, *moules en plâtre*).

8 Munger, *Wickes*, pp. 187–88, no. 134.

9 AMNS, Vy 1, fol. 25, for 60 *livres*. There is no independent citation of the *plateau à ornements* until 1755, at which time the factory would have wanted to distinguish it from the *plateau uni* just put into production (Préaud and d'Albis, pp. 147–48, no. 105). Préaud also refers to this stand as *plateau à bord de relief*.

10 Much of the following information may be found in more detail in Savill, 2, pp. 642–43.

11 The author of *Soupers de la cour* (pp. ii–v) mentions almost fifty *bouillons* and *potages*.

12 Havard, 2, p. 314. Havard states that a strong broth was served in the morning, and that traditionally one would hold the *écuelle* by the handles and inhale its fragrant vapor.

13 Ibid., p. 310.

14 Only the wealthy could own *écuelles* made of the more expensive materials. In the 18th century this included porcelain.

15 Savill, 2, p. 642.

16 See technique and condition below.

17 An *écuelle*, second size, was listed with a *plateau à ornements* as emerging from the enamel kiln in the second half of 1755, and may correspond to the Hartford example. The ensemble was decorated with flowers (IF 5676, fol. 49). An *écuelle à ozier et plateau* with flowers were in an enamel kiln firing of February 1754 (IF 5676, fol. 16) but this would have been too early for the Hartford example.

18 AMNS, I. 7, *pieces tant au dépot du blanc que dans l'attelier de Peinture et Dorure*.

19 This attribution was originally made in the 19th century, but like many attributions of marks dating from this period, it is likely that H was simplistically linked with Houry as a painter whose name began with H. (This problem occurs with other 19th-century attributions, as pointed out to the author by David Peters.) Préaud and d'Albis, p. 208, maintains the attribution to Houry.

20 See Dauterman, *Wrightsman*, p. 196, no. 79A,B. Eriksen and Bellaigue (p. 161, n. 59) lists the mark as that of an undetermined flower painter working from 1753–57. David Peters has kindly pointed out to the author that the H mark seems to belong to a highly accomplished flower painter who worked at the factory from at least 1753 to 1764 or later.

21 Peters, *Marks*, p. 82.

22 I would like to thank Antoine d'Albis for making these observations. For more on kiln supports see Préaud and d'Albis, p. 231.

23 As being mismatched with plateau.

151

151

Fountain and basin (*fontaine unie et cuvette*)

1917.993–994

Vincennes and Sèvres, 1755–56 and 1786

Soft-paste porcelain, silver-gilt spigot and hook, fountain:
H. 13¹¹⁄₁₆ × W. 8⁵⁄₁₆ × D. (less spigot) 5¹¹⁄₁₆ in. (34.7 × 21.1 × 14.4 cm);
basin: H. 3⁹⁄₁₆ × L. 13 × W. 9⁷⁄₁₆ in. (9 × 33 × 24 cm)

White ground with monochrome blue landscapes and children, the
latter also with flesh tones

Marks: fountain: interlaced Ls in blue with date letter C; incised
scrolling V;[1] basin: interlaced Ls in blue with date letters ij; painter's
mark of a hatchet for Pierre-Joseph Rosset *aîné*;[2] HP in gold for gilder
Henri-Martin Prévost;[3] incised 25

Provenance: Lazare Duvaux, 1755 (fountain);
Jacques Seligmann, London and Paris, 1903;[4]
J. Pierpont Morgan

MODEL

Plaster models and molds for both the *unie* and *à roseaux*
versions of this fountain were first made in 1754.[5] As the name
implies, the *fontaine unie* has a plain surface, while the *fontaine à
roseaux* [reeds] is more elaborate. The latter is decorated in low
relief with bulrushes and reeds, and a dolphin spout. Only the
fontaine unie came in two sizes.[6]

There is an outline drawing for the fountain inscribed
fontaine pour Mme la daufine fait du 6 Mars 1754, as well as a
drawing of the plan and profile of the basin (figs. 151-1 and
151-2).[7] The annotations are in Jean-Claude Duplessis's
hand, making it likely that it was he who designed the model,
apparently for the Dauphine, Marie-Josèphe de Saxe.[8] A plaster
model of the fountain survives in the Sèvres factory archives
(fig. 151-3).[9]

The factory made only seven or eight of these fountains and
basins, most of them between 1754 and 1758.[10] Two were sold
to Lazare Duvaux in 1755, one decorated with *fleurs guirlandes*
and one with *Enfans Cam.[aïeu] Chaires Colo.[rées] encadrés*
[children in blue with flesh tones, within a frame].[11] Each cost
600 *livres*. Duvaux bought another decorated with flowers in
1756 for 600 *livres*, and a fourth during the same period for 360
livres.[12] The latter probably was a second-size *fontaine unie*.

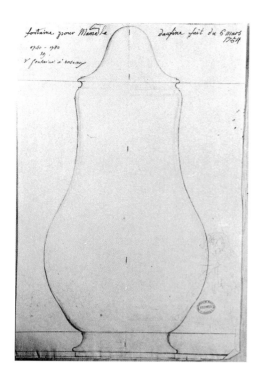

Fig. 151-1
Fontaine, drawing

(*Below*)
Fig. 151-2
Jatte de fontaine,
drawing

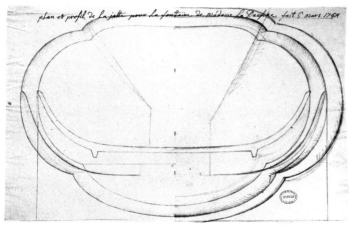

An entry in Duvaux's journal suggests the existence of a fifth fountain and basin, acquired by the Dauphine (for which there is no other mention), and mounted by him.[13] The most expensive fountain and basin in the factory records had a *bleu céleste* ground decorated with flowers, and was bought in 1758 by Louis XV for Maria-Theresa, Empress of Austria.[14] This ensemble cost 840 *livres*, the high cost attributable to the *bleu céleste* ground color. Two other fountains appeared later in the sales records, one in 1763 priced at 240 *livres* (of unspecified decoration) and one in 1788 costing 144 *livres* (with mounts costing a further 78 *livres*). The latter was bought by Madame, Louis XVI's sister.[15]

There are five fountains and basins known to survive, three of them *unies* and two *à roseaux*. Besides the Atheneum's example, there is a fountain, without its basin at the Musée national de Céramique, Sèvres, dated 1757, decorated with flowers,[16] and a fountain with its basin in the Mansfield Collection at Scone Palace, Perthshire, dated 1788.[17] A *fontaine à roseaux* is in the

David Collection, Copenhagen[18] and a recently published undated example decorated with polychrome garlands and bouquets is in the Pinacoteca Nazionale, Parma.[19]

At least four of the fountain sets made in 1755 and 1756 went to Versailles. Lazare Duvaux sold one with a white ground and flowers to Madame de Pompadour on 24 December 1755 for 600 *livres*. He had this set mounted in silver gilt for her the following month.[20] In April of the following year Duvaux supplied the silver-gilt mounts for an unspecified fountain belonging to the Dauphine.[21] Duvaux sold a fountain *de Vincennes peinte en blanc & bleu, la garniture en vermeil*, to the Dauphin on 29 August 1756, for 720 *livres*.[22] Finally, he sold a less expensive fountain, also with silver-gilt mounts, to Louis XV's sister Madame Sophie, in December 1756.[23] At least one of these fountains was still at Versailles in 1792 when a *Fontaine, à laver les mains et Sa cuvette en porcelaine de Seves [sic]* (valued at 600 *livres*) was documented as being in Louis XVI's *Cabinet de Géographie* [map-making room] on the third floor of the château.[24]

FUNCTION

Before Vincennes began making them, fountains and basins were made of *faïence* or Chinese porcelain.[25] Like jugs and basins they were used for hand washing before the widespread use of indoor plumbing.[26] Fountains and basins were often a feature of the *garde-robe*, which by the middle of the eighteenth century had begun to function like a wash closet or *cabinet de toilette*.[27] Royal *garde-robes* were commodious and finely decorated, and descriptions tell us that their furnishings often

Fig. 151-3
Fontaine à roseaux,
plaster model

matched the decoration. A treatise on varnishing written by Jean-Félix Watin in 1773 likens the painted decoration of rooms to porcelain: "[There is] nothing finer for a *salon*, an apartment, than splendid wood-paneling painted thus. In fact this painting has the sheen and freshness of porcelain: its vividness comes from its unchanging colors, from the way it reflects the light, combined in full brilliance."[28] The taste for monochrome painted paneling during the middle of the eighteenth century coincides with a taste for *camaïeu* decoration on porcelain during the same period.

COMMENTARY

Scholars have been endeavoring for some time to establish the history and ownership of the surviving fountains. We know for sure that the Atheneum's fountain was one of those sold to Lazare Duvaux since it is the only one fully matching the sales ledger description of the decoration: *enfants camaïeu chaires colorées encadrés*. We also know that the Museum's basin is dated 1786 from its date mark and from the kiln records. The sales records tell us that Louis XVI bought a basin without a fountain from Sèvres in 1786 for 192 *livres*.[29] We may reasonably suppose that his purchase was a replacement for a broken basin and that the newer basin along with the fountain, which were thus both at Versailles in 1786, may be equated with the Hartford pieces.

On the other hand, we do not know for sure to whom Lazare Duvaux sold the Museum's fountain set. Among those fountains documented there are two possibilities. The first is that the fountain set was sold to the Dauphin.[30] Lazare Duvaux's credit book informs us that he sold a fountain and basin to the Dauphin in 1756 described as blue and white with silver-gilt mounts, the latter costing 120 *livres*. This description, however, would also fit with equal validity the set of the same date in the David Collection.

The second possibility is that the fountain set was sold to the Dauphine.[31] We know from Lazare Duvaux's daybook that he mounted an unspecified fountain in 1756 for her costing 192 *livres*. We cannot tell whether it was even a Vincennes fountain, or if so, whether it was the David Collection set or the Wadsworth's since there is no way of telling why the mounts of one were dearer than those of the other.[32] If the Dauphin had been sold the set now in the David Collection, then, by a process of elimination, the Dauphine might well have been the buyer of the Hartford set. That the Hartford set was at Versailles as late as 1786 (when Louis bought a replacement basin), and in all likelihood in 1792 (when a fountain and basin were recorded in his map-making room), strengthens the case for its earlier ownership by either the Dauphin or the Dauphine.

There are strong arguments for the Dauphin's set being that in the David Collection.[33] For example the primary decoration on that fountain is an elaborate royal cipher, recalling the royal status of the heir apparent.[34] There is a parallel argument for the Dauphin owning either the David Collection or the Wadsworth's. In 1756 he had his apartments redone in blue and white, matching perfectly the color scheme of both fountains! These apartments included a *garde-robe* decorated in blue and white as well, with an *ottomane en banquette* painted blue

and white and covered in blue and white *toile*.[35] Pierre Verlet wrote that there was documentary evidence of there being a blue and white fountain listed in the *garde-robe*.[36] The papers in question are sadly now lost.

Arguments may also be posited for the Dauphine's set being that in the David Collection. A drawing at Sèvres for a fountain model depicts the molded *à roseaux* version, and bears an inscription saying that it was for the Dauphine. One might suppose, then, that the Dauphine should have received a fountain *à roseaux,* like the Copenhagen fountain, rather than a plain one, like the Museum's.

Yet a further argument proposes that neither the David Collection's nor the Atheneum's set belonged to Dauphine since neither matched the color scheme of her apartments. When the Dauphine created a new *cabinet* in 1755 and a *Pièce des Bains* in 1756,[37] she requested that her new room be painted and varnished by the Martin Brothers.[38] A plan for the room, drawn in china ink with washes of gray, red, and ochre of the *cabinet*, is in the Archives Nationales.[39] A reconstitution of the Dauphine's *cabinet* has been made at Versailles, in green, gray, yellow and rose/orange on a cream ground. It does not seem that the Dauphine's new *cabinet* was decorated in white and blue.[40] We do not know the decoration of her *Pièce des Bains*.

Is there any likelihood that the David Collection fountain and basin had belonged to Madame de Pompadour?[41] Her set was decorated with *fleurs guirlandes*, and the one in the David Collection has garlands. However her set was probably polychrome for had it been *camaïeu*, it would have been described as such. Moreover, it is unlikely that the king's mistress would have bought a fountain with the royal cipher. Might the Parma fountain have been Madame de Pompadour's? Although there is no documentary evidence to this effect, it is known that the fountain and basin were in Parma by the end of 1756.[42] It is quite plausible that Madame de Pompadour gave her set to the Infante who became the wife of the King of Parma—unless of course the Infante acquired it directly from Duvaux.

Although there are no painter's marks on the Hartford fountain, the painted decoration is undoubtedly the work of André-Vincent Vielliard, and must be regarded as one of the best achievements of this prolific painter.[43] The decoration is extremely ambitious, especially as painting with *beau bleu* was very difficult.[44] The composition is based on an engraving by Pierre Aveline after François Boucher called *Les Pescheurs*, published in 1738 (fig. 151-4).[45] Vielliard took the poses of two of the three putti in the engraving but eliminated the other putto and the fish net. The infants are older children now and no longer are naked. The landscape appears to be the invention of Vielliard, while the broken fence at the left is reminiscent of one in Aveline's engraving of *L'Été* after Boucher.[46] The gilded border around the landscape frames the image in much the same way as do the engraved borders found in some of Boucher's prints.[47] The figure of the child on the fountain's cover is in the style of Boucher but has not been traced to a known work by this artist.

The replacement basin was given to the painter Rosset on 21 April 1786 to decorate with monochrome blue figures, land-

Fig. 151-4 *Les Pescheurs*, Pierre Aveline after François Boucher

scape, and a jagged border.[48] On its exterior a boy is drawing an eel net out of a river, while his female companion holds an eel above his head.[49] Its interior is decorated with a scene of the same two children fishing, a composition drawn from Le Prince's engraving after Boucher called *La Chasse*. Here Rosset has reversed the image and replaced the string in the boy's hand with a fishing rod (fig. 151-5).[50] These may have been the same scenes that had been painted on the original 1755 basin, for in theory Rosset and the gilder Prévost would have had the broken basin to use as a model for decorating the replacement. Both the conception and the details of the landscape, especially in the clumps of foliage in the foreground, recall Vielliard, whom Rosset had to imitate in order to attain a likeness to the original. Moreover, the gilded borders are in the same style as those on the fountain, reinforcing the notion that at least the fountain went back to the factory temporarily. Rosset was not a figure painter but rather a specialist in landscapes, floral borders, and garlands. The awkwardness of the figures as against the proficiency of the landscape and floral swags bears this out.

TECHNIQUE AND CONDITION

The body of the fountain is thick and uneven with two series of faint, vertical, wave-like relief patterns going down both sides, front and back. There are two possible explanations for this unusual feature. Either the factory workers modified a cast from a *fontaine à roseaux* mold or modified a *fontaine à roseaux* mold with the same aim in view: to create a *fontaine unie*.[51]

For the decoration of the fountain Vielliard used *beau bleu no. 3*, a color created between October 1751 and June 1752.[52] There is a firing crack down the right-hand side of the back of the fountain. Floral garlands are painted to cover the crack. The basin is slightly grayish in tone indicating that it was slightly underfired in the biscuit stage, perhaps placed in back of the kiln. The finial of the fountain has been repaired.[53]

Exhibitions: *Morgan Loan Exhibition*, New York, 1914, not in catalogue; *French and English Art Treasures*, New York, 1942, no. 301; *European Porcelain*, New York, 1949, no. 160; *Morgan Treasures*, Hartford, 1960, no. 58; *Louis XV*, Paris, 1974, no. 529; *Morgan*, Hartford, 1987, no. 61

Literature: Garnier pp. 66–67, pl. XVII; Chavagnac, pp. 69–71, no. 83, pl. XXIII; *French and English Art Treasures*, no. 301; *European Porcelain*, no. 160; Verlet, *Sèvres*, p. 201; Verlet, "Historical," pp. 230–41; Gauthier, p. 175; *Handbook*, p. 98; Hood, *Connoisseur*, p. 133, fig. 5; Hood, *Bulletin*, pp. 5–7, fig. 4; Dauterman, *Sèvres*, fig. 24 (fountain only); Brunet and Préaud, p. 146; Verlet, *Versailles*, p. 413; *Morgan Treasures*, no. 58; *Louis XV*, p. 382, no. 529; Eriksen and Bellaigue, p. 298; *Floraison des arts*, no. 120; Savill, 3, p. 1066; Gonzáles-Palacios, p. 97

NOTES

1 See cat. no. 78 for this incised mark.

2 Active 1753–99. See Savill, 3, pp. 1064–65.

3 Active 1757–97.

4 APML, Seligmann file, 22 May 1903: "1 Fountain in Old Sèvres China, described in Garmais [Garnier] book, the fountain dated 1755, the basin dated 1785, and decorated by Rosset, this fountain came times passed [*sic*] from Mr. Barre." A note later in the file refers to Blarenberghe's Sèvres fountain, but I have not been able to confirm either the Barré or Blarenberghe provenances.

Fig. 151-5 *La Chasse*, Jean-Baptiste Le Prince after François Boucher

5 AMNS, I. 7, 1 January 1755 (for 1754), new models. The basic information on this model appears in de Bellaigue, "Sèvres," pp. 168–69.

6 AMNS, I. 7, *moules en Plâtre.*

7 AMNS, R. I, L. 3, d. 4, fol. 2; R. 1, L. 3, d. 17, fol. 13. The latter drawing is inscribed *plan et profil de La jatte pour La fountaine de Madame La Dauphine fait 6 Mars 1754.*

8 Marie-Josèphe de Saxe was the daughter-in-law of Louis XV, married to the Dauphin, heir to the throne. She was the daughter of Augustus III of Saxony, proprietor of the Meissen porcelain factory.

9 AMNS, 1814 inventory, 1740–80, no. 29 (Troude, pl. 88).

10 Eriksen and Bellaigue, p. 298.

11 AMNS, Vy 1, fol. 119, 1 October–31 December 1755.

12 Ibid., Vy 2, fols. 13v, 16.

13 LD, 2, p. 280, no. 2465.

14 AMNS, Vy 2, fol. 85v., December 1758. Maria-Theresa was mother of the future Queen of France, Marie-Antoinette. This is probably the fountain and basin listed among the *pièces extraordinaires* in the factory inventory (AMNS, I. 7, 1 January 1756 (for 1755), and again in I. 7, 1 January 1758 (for 1757).

15 De Bellaigue, "Sèvres," p. 168 n. 9. See AMNS, Vy 10, fol. 234v, and fol. 335v, the latter for a replacement basin sold to Mme Elisabeth for 84 *livres* on 3 June 1789 (fired 25 May 1789, Vl'3, fol. 136).

16 See *Vincennes*, p. 53, H. 12⅝ in. (32 cm), MNC, Sèvres, no. 23714.

17 See de Bellaigue, "Sèvres," p. 168 n. 4.

18 1755, with blue garlands and the royal cipher on the front. See Verlet, *Sèvres*, p. 201, pl. 20; Eriksen and Bellaigue, p. 298, no. 109.

19 Gonzáles-Palacios, pp. 93, 97, 106.

20 LD, 2, p. 266, no. 2336; p. 271, no. 2391.

21 Ibid., p. 280, no. 2465: "S.M. le Roy: La garniture en argent doré d'une fontaine de porcelaine pour Mme la Dauphine 192 l." See note 13.

22 Ibid., p. 293, no. 2575.

23 Ibid., p. 304, no. 2668 (for *300 livres*).

24 AN O' 3356, *Porcelaines,* in *Inventaire des Cabinets Interieurs du Roi.* I would like to thank Bernard Dragesco for providing me with a copy of this reference. See also de Bellaigue, "Sèvres," p. 168.

25 One could also get a blue and/or white Chinese porcelain fountain. On 4 June 1750 Lazare Duvaux (2, p. 52, no. 527) sold "cinq fontaines de porcelaines, bleu & blanc, 63 l." to the comtesse d'Egmont. This entry, which does not spell out the type of porcelain, directly follows an entry for Chinese porcelain. Considering the low price of the fountains, these five blue and white examples must have been Chinese as well.

26 For more detailed information on usage, in reference to water jugs and basins, see Savill, 2, pp. 691–92.

27 The term *garde-robe* originally described a long box used to store clothing; it evolved over the centuries into an *armoire*, then a closet or dressing area, and eventually a wash closet. See Havard, 2, pp. 934–55.

28 "Rien de plus magnifique pour un salon, un appartement, qu'une superbe boiserie peinte de cette manière. En effet, cette peinture a le brillant et la fraîcheur de la porcelaine: son éclat lui vient de ce que ses couleurs ne changent pas, de ce qu'elles reflètent bien la lumière et s'éclaircissent par son concours." Quoted in Feray, p. 225.

29 AMNS, Vy 10, fol. 49v. While several authors (Brunet and Préaud, p. 146; *Louis XV*, p. 382) have stated that Louis XVI bought the replacement basin for his aunt, de Bellaigue ("Sèvres," p. 168) thinks that the entry in sales records is ambiguous. Close reading of the sales records make it clear that the basin was not bought for Mme Louise. The items purchased for Mme Louise were two *cuvettes*, two *vases hollandois*, and two *pots-pourris*. These items are grouped together in an entry for January. The replacement basin was listed as purchased 31 May.

30 See Verlet, "Historical," p. 233; Verlet, *Versailles*, p. 413.

31 *Louis XV*, p. 382, no. 529 (says it is undoubtedly either the Dauphin's or the Dauphine's).

32 From this one can infer that the mounts on the Dauphine's fountain were more elaborate than those on the Dauphin's. The mounts on the Copenhagen example consist of a small on-off valve on the head of the dolphin and thin bands on the upper rims of the fountain and its cover. The mounts on the Atheneum's fountain consist of a simple bird's head silver-gilt spigot on the front as well as a hook in back for hanging the fountain, but no rims around the top and lid. There is also a gilt-bronze stand with the Copenhagen fountain, which does not appear to be original.

33 Eriksen, *David Collection*, p. 67.

34 Most recently Tamara Préaud has suggested that this may have been the fountain with *fleurs guirlandes* sold to Duvaux in the last third of 1755 and then sold to Mme de Pompadour.

35 AN 01 3315/3316. I would like to thank Sylvie Wallez for the information from the Archives Nationales.

36 See Verlet, *Versailles,* pp. 412-13. Documents supporting Verlet's description of the *garde-robe* with its blue and white *vernis Martin* decoration and porcelain fountain have not been found, but there is no reason to doubt that they were at one time available to that author. Verlet believed that the fountain and basin in the Dauphin's *garde-robe* is the one now in Hartford. He also notes that the Dauphin's library became a *Cabinet du midi,* decorated by the lacquerer Martin in blue and gold at the same time that the *garde-robe* became blue and white.

37 Ibid., p. 416.

38 AN 01 1070.

39 Ibid. Again, I would like to thank Sylvie Wallez for this information from the Archives Nationales.

40 According to correspondence with Claudine P. Colombo, the Dauphine did not decorate her rooms in blue and white. Ms. Colombo has identified a pair of *vases Hollandois* with a green ground and gilded trophies that were bought by Marie-Josèphe in 1758, which would have been compatible with the green, gray, yellow, and orange/rose décor on cream ground described above. These are in the Rosebery Collection at Dalmeny House, West Lothian, Scotland.

41 See note 34.

42 González-Palacios, p. 98.

43 The drawing style of both the figures and the landscape is very close to that seen on the Museum's milk jug discussed above, in cat. no. 78. The primary difference in the painting of these two objects rests in the palette used to create the flesh tones, which, in the case of the milk jug, is much pinker in tone.

44 An alkaline color, it had a tendency to dissolve in water. In order to use it easily, therefore, it was necessary to apply it with a great amount of gum arabic, which then makes a thicker application. One can see evidence of this in the occasional "bubbling" under the blue, as if the enamel did not thoroughly mix with its flux. I am grateful to Antoine d'Albis for making these observations to me.

45 See Jean-Richard, p. 84, no. 226. See also Ananoff, *Boucher*, 2, p. 387, fig. 814 (as by Fessard). Jean-Richard (p. 250, nos. 1000–3) notes that another series of engravings called *Jeux d'Enfants*, of a different format, was attributed to Étienne Fessard (1714–77) in an old inventory of the Rothschild collection of Boucher engravings.

46 See Jean-Richard, p. 81, no. 210.

47 See for example Boucher's *Pastorale* engraved by Aveline (Jean-Richard, pp. 77–78, no. 197).

48 AMNS, Vj'4, fol. 227: *1 cuvette de fontaine paysage camayeu bleu fleurs* [crossed out] *figures et dechiré.* See also enamel kiln record, Vl'3, fol. 15, 28 May 1786, *1 jatte de Fontaine camayeu bleu Rosset/Prevost.*

49 See Diderot, *Encyclopédie*, XXV (vol. 8 of plates), Pl. V, fig. 1 (pp. 748, 751) and Pl. XIII, fig. 2 (pp. 748, 753) (vol. 4 of compact reprint), for illustrations of these cone-shaped baskets used for fishing.

50 See Jean-Richard, p. 332, no. 1384. Savill mistakenly notes that Rosset uses the companion engraving of *La Pesche* for this composition (Savill, 2, p. 601). It is also possible that Vielliard used a Boucher drawing for his source, which could also have been used by Le Prince.

51 These hypotheses are fairly conjectural but may help to explain the thick, uneven back and the inexplicable appearance of the faint wave patterns. The ideas came from discussions with David Peters, Bernard Dragesco, and Tamara Préaud.

52 See Préaud and d'Albis, p. 216 for the evolution of *beau bleu. Beau bleu no. 3* was a much livelier blue than the grayer *beau bleu no. 2.*

53 Repairs were made in 1986. Old fills and discolored overpaint on the fan coral were removed and an old break reglued and inpainted. Old fills below the lip were cleaned and repainted.

152

Inkstand (*écritoire*)

1917.1013

Sèvres, 1758–1759

Soft-paste porcelain, tray: H. 2³⁄₁₆ × L. 11⅞ × W. 7⁹⁄₁₆ in.
(5.5 × 30.1 × 19.2 cm); inkwell and penholder: H. 1⅞ in. (4.8 cm); sponge pot: H. 1¹³⁄₁₆ in. (4.6 cm); sand pot: H. 2⁵⁄₁₆ in. (5.8 cm); pastille pot: H. 2³⁄₁₆ in. (5.6 cm)

White and green ground with flowers, *bleu céleste* ribbons, and gilding

Marks: interlaced Ls with date letter F and three dots below, the mark of Jean-Baptiste Tandart;[1] incised scrolling v[2]

Provenance: Edouard Chappey, Paris, 1906;[3] J. Pierpont Morgan

MODEL

The model for this five-piece inkstand may have been the *écritoire sans génie* mentioned among new designs for 1754, listed in the January 1755 inventory.[4] It seems that the first inkstand to be made from this model was an *écritoire composée de 5 pièces* that emerged from the glaze kiln in October 1755.[5] Another five-piece inkstand, taken from the biscuit kiln between 10 September and 3 December 1755, was glazed by 30 December of the same year.[6] The Sèvres factory made inkstands ranging in price from 15 to 1,200 *livres*, depending on the model and decoration.[7]

The model was probably designed by Jean-Claude Duplessis *père*.[8]

FUNCTION

It is likely that the large pot with holes around the top was meant to hold quill pens and ink, and the small pot with the pierced cover to hold sand or powdered metal for drying the wet ink.[9] The second large pot probably held a sponge for drying the pen nibs, while the second small pot might have held small sealing-wax pastilles.

COMMENTARY

The Museum's inkstand is one of only two known surviving examples of this model. The other, now at the Louvre, was made in 1755–56, and has a white ground adorned with sprays of flowers, blue fillets, and gilding. The receptacles are the same as those on the Hartford inkstand, but the two smaller pots have gilt-bronze pierced covers and one of the larger pots has a porcelain cover decorated with pastilles resembling sealing wax.[10]

While we have not found the Louvre's inkstand listed in the factory sales records, it is likely that the Atheneum's *écritoire* was the *Ecritoire verd fleurs* sold to Madame de Pompadour in December 1759 for 216 *livres*.[11] This inkstand does not appear in her probate inventory of 1764.[12]

The floral bouquets which decorate the stand and pots of the Museum's *écritoire* were painted by Jean-Baptiste Tandart *aîné*. Active from 1754 until 1800, he specialized in flowers, including sprays, bouquets, and garlands.

TECHNIQUE AND CONDITION

The tray and attendant vessels of this inkstand were molded. The green enamel used to paint the ensemble was applied rather thickly, imparting a bluish tonality. The smaller pot on the right in the photograph may have had a cover.

Exhibitions: *Morgan Loan Exhibition*, New York, 1914, not in catalogue; *French and English 18th Century Exhibition*, Montreal, 1950, no. 155; *Morgan*, Hartford, no. 62

Literature: Chavagnac, pp. 80–81, no. 96, pl. XXII; *French and English 18th Century Exhibition*, no. 155; Hood, *Bulletin*, p. 10; Eriksen and Bellaigue, p. 296; de Bellaigue, "Sèvres," p. 170; Savill, 2, pp. 721, 727 n. 23, 798, 804 n. 21

NOTES

1 See Savill, 3, pp. 1070–71, active 1754–1800. See also Peters, *Marks*, p. 69.

2 Not in Savill. See cat. nos. 78 and 151 for this mark.

3 APML, Chappey file, invoice for 2 June: "Encrier Sèvres fond vert à rubans bleus 4 godets à réserves de décor de fleurs," 27,500 French francs.

4 AMNS, I. 7, 1 January 1755 (work of 1754), *moules et modèles*, *écritoire avec un génie* and *écritoire sans génie*. See Eriksen and Bellaigue, pp. 296–97 and Préaud and d'Albis, p.189.

5 IF 5674, fol. 50, 29 October 1755. This may be the *écritoire* listed among the *pièces sculptées* in the biscuit kiln of 10 June 1755 (IF 5673, fol. 41) and perhaps may be equated with the *écritoire avec un génie* mentioned in the list of new molds and models for 1754 (see note 4 above). In correspondence with the author, Tamara Préaud postulated that if the *génie* was a sculpted figure (perhaps decorating one of the larger covers) this could explain why the inkstand was included among the sculpted pieces.

6 IF 5673, fol. 48; IF 5674, fol. 53. This inkstand may be the one in the Louvre, mentioned below.

7 De Bellaigue, "Sèvres," p. 170. See also Savill, 2, pp. 797–805 for the *écritoire à globes* and other inkstands produced at Sèvres.

8 Brunet and Préaud, p. 145, no. 67.

9 Savill, 2, p. 798.

10 Louvre, Paris, no. OA. 6502. See *Vincennes*, p. 48, Brunet and Préaud, p. 145, Eriksen and Bellaigue, p. 296, Préaud and d'Albis, p. 189. The porcelain cover does not seem to be original (also suggested by Pierre Ennès in correspondence with Geoffrey de Bellaigue). If one assumes the other covers on the Paris inkstand are original, then it is difficult to understand how the individual components functioned. Presumably both pots with pierced covers would have held sand (which seems unnecessary), and the pastilles would have been in the pot so decorated. This would leave only one pot available, while two would have been needed (one for ink, the other for a sponge). If none of the covers on the Louvre's inkstand are original, which seems more likely, then it could have been used in the same manner as the Hartford inkstand.

11 AMNS, Vy 3, fol. 7v, 28 December 1759. De Bellaigue ("Sèvres," p. 170) suggested that this may be the inkstand priced at 216 *livres* listed among the *pièces extraordinaires* in the inventories of 1 January and 1 October 1759. In the January inventory there also was another inkstand priced at 168 *livres*, which seems to have been sold by October. However, this does not take into account that two inkstands priced 168 and 216 *livres* were already listed among *pièces extraordinaires* in the inventories of January

1757 and 1758 (covering the years 1756 and 1757), precluding the possibility that one of them was the Atheneum's. Perhaps one of the two "extraordinary" inkstands of 1756 and 1757 was the one dated 1755–56 now in the Louvre.

12 De Bellaigue, "Sèvres," p. 170 n. 8. Another inkstand described as *Ecritoire ancienne forme garnie de ses pieces accessoires guirlandes de fleurs et baguettes en or* was sold in September 1773 for the very low price of 144 *livres* (AMNS, Vy 5, fol. 92v, to Mr. Terranne Bruneau, 23 September 1773). It is possible but not at all certain that this is the same model, perhaps considered out of fashion and therefore reduced in price.

153

Broth basin and stand (*écuelle ronde* and *plateau à ornements*)

1917.1015

Sèvres, basin, 1758–1759, stand 1759–1760

Soft-paste porcelain, basin: H. 4¹⁵⁄₁₆ × w. 7¹³⁄₁₆ × D. 6⅛ in. (12.5 × 19.8 × 15.5 cm); stand: H. 2 × L. 11⅜ × w. 8¹⁵⁄₁₆ in. (5 × 28.8 × 22.7 cm)

White ground with polychrome figures, blue feathering, gilding

Marks: both: interlaced Ls in blue and mark for André-Vincent Vielliard *père* above;[1] basin: date letter F, incised ND,[2] 4;[3] stand: date letter G, dot underneath factory mark

Provenance: J. Pierpont Morgan

MODEL

The model for the Hartford broth basin, the factory's most common type, was introduced before 1752.[4] The model for the stand, called a *plateau à ornements*, was not recorded before 1755 but is known to have been made earlier.[5]

The Museum's *écuelle* is of the second size. The broth basin and stand were originally paired with other pieces, and married at a later date. This accounts for the difference in date, as well as the absence of a matching blue filet with gold hatching on the *plateau*. It also explains the unwonted repetition on bowl and stand of the same girl—merely shown in a different guise.[6]

The decoration of both *écuelle* and *plateau* is by André-Vincent Vielliard, the author of a number of pieces in the 1750s with children set in landscapes. Although his figures are in the manner of François Boucher, and often were based loosely on engravings after this artist, he adapted them to his own uses and frequently changed them from babies to children.[7] He may have regularly consulted a set of working drawings, for one finds the same figure used over and over again on different pieces, as in the little girl on the Museum's basin and stand. The boy with the birdcage may be found again, with minor changes, on a 1754–55 *vase à oreilles* in the Art Institute of Chicago.[8] He is also very close to a figure on an undated *cuvette Courteille* with Dalva Brothers, New York, this time paired with a girl holding a bird.

153

The girl cutting flowers on the other side of the Hartford basin (and watering them on the stand) is also depicted on an undated triangular tray sold at Sotheby's, Zurich, 1997.[9] The boy with the walking stick on the cover of the Museum's basin appears to have been a favorite of Vielliard, who used him again on a saucer and a teapot now in the Victoria and Albert Museum and on a cup now in the David Collection, Copenhagen.[10] The girl with the bagpipes is reminiscent of a girl holding a bird on a teapot of 1754–55 in the Victoria and Albert Museum.[11]

TECHNIQUE AND CONDITION

The stand of this set appears to have been made and glazed before 1752, before a new type of kiln support was put in place at Vincennes.[12] This conclusion is based on the appearance of two indentations on the outside of the foot rim, another on the foot rim centered opposite the two. These were made for the biscuit and glaze firings. A fourth indentation inside the foot rim must have been made for the post-1752 enamel kiln firing to hold the new metal kiln support. We may surmise then that the stand was in the factory's store of glazed pieces until it was decorated in 1759–60. On the other hand, the indentation under the foot rim of the basin and the hole under the rim of the cover are indicative of firing after 1752. The basin and cover reveal wide-spread *végétations salines*. This is especially concentrated inside the bowl.[13]

Exhibition: *Morgan Loan Exhibition*, New York, 1914, not in catalogue

Literature: Chavagnac, pp. 84–85, no. 101; Buckley, *Connoisseur*, pp. 51, 53, fig. 12; Savill, 2, pp. 653, 666 n. 139

NOTES

1 See cat. no. 78 for this artist.

2 See Dauterman, *Marks*, pp. 223, 76, attributed to Nicolas Duru (I), active as a soft-paste *répareur* 1756–73.

3 Savill, 3, pp. 1126–27, found on soft paste 1753–87.

4 See cat. no. 156 for this form.

5 There is no independent citation of the *plateau à ornements* until 1755, at which time it had to be distinguished from the *plateau uni* just put into production (Préaud and d'Albis, pp. 147–48, no. 105). Préaud also refers to this stand as *plateau à bord de relief*. An example dating from c. 1750–51 is in the collection of Mrs. William Proby, Elton Hall, Cambridgeshire. Another example c. 1751–53 is in the St. Louis Art Museum (no. 7:1945a–c). See cat. no. 150 n. 6 for other examples.

6 This is the figure of the girl watering flowers on the stand and the girl cutting flowers on the bowl. These figures must have been based on a common model, probably drawings.

7 See cat. no. 151.

8 No. 1994.382. I would like to thank Ghenete Zelleke for this information.

9 9 December 1997, lot 103.

10 Saucer, 1758–59, no. C.1384&a-1919; teapot, undated (probably 1761) no. 791-1882 (King, p. 10, no. 120); cup, 1758–59, no. 8/1976 (Eriksen, *David Collection*, p. 69, no. 50).

11 No. C1430&a-1919.

12 See cat. no. 150. The fourth indentation may have been made when the stand was decorated, to accommodate the new type of kiln supports.

13 This has led some scholars to doubt its authenticity, but in comparing the painting to other similar pieces by Vielliard from the same period this author believes the decoration to be original.

154

Food warmer (*veilleuse*)

1986.178

Sèvres, c. 1759–1770

Soft-paste porcelain, H. 3¹¹⁄₁₆ × W. 3³⁄₁₆ × D. 2¾ in. (9.4 × 8 × 7 cm)

White ground, blue monochrome garlands and flowers, gilding

Marks: interlaced Ls in blue, stippled crown of Jean-Charles Sioux *aîné*[1]

Provenance: Harold and Wendy Newman, 1986

MODEL

Veilleuses or food warmers were first introduced at Sèvres in 1758. They were made with several parts: a pedestal with an aperture on one side; a covered bowl (*écuelle*) that was suspended in the pedestal; and a small oil and wick holder (*lampe* or *godet*) that sat in the aperture. In the list of new work for 1758, two molds for *veilleuses* along with four molds for its bowl and two for its *lampe* were recorded.[2] In 1759 a second-size *veilleuse* was introduced.[3] In subsequent records the model was sometimes listed as *veilleuse assortie*, meaning a *veilleuse* with its accompanying pieces.

Sèvres made two types of *veilleuses*. One version had a simple, circular form, while the other more elaborate version had a square pedestal, octagonal middle section, and either a pierced, domed cover or a pierced cover with a chicken.[4] The latter type had multiple usages, as an egg coddler and perfume burner. The two versions were not differentiated in the sales records, but kiln records did list some *veilleuses* among molded pieces and others among turned. This probably reflected the two different versions, the simpler one being turned.[5] The first time a *veilleuse* appeared in the Sèvres documents was in July 1758, when two turned examples were fired in the biscuit kiln.[6]

The first listing of a *veilleuse* in the sales records occurred in December 1758, when Madame de Pompadour purchased an example decorated with flowers for 216 *livres*.[7] Other examples with flowers sold for 168 and 192 *livres*.[8] A white example sold for 72 *livres* in 1784.[9] Other types of decoration are not specified. Madame de Pompadour had at least two Sèvres *veilleuses*, which had been purchased in 1758 and 1762.[10] Two were listed in her probate inventory of 1764, one described as "Une veilleuse fleurs, sa cuvette d'argent," [a *veilleuse* decorated with flowers, its basin of silver] and "Une veilleuse de nuit, de porcelaine à fleurs; garny de sa cuvette d'argent, d'un couvercle de porcelaine et d'une tasse à l'esprit de vin" [a night *veilleuse*, made of porcelain decorated with flowers, garnished with its silver basin, a porcelain cover, and a cup for wine spirit].[11]

FUNCTION

Veilleuses were mostly used to keep broth warm in the sick room.[12] The small flame provided by the oil lamp inside also would have given off a gentle light. Broth was put in the bowl, and air circulated through vents in the pedestal keeping the flame alive. The name *veilleuse* derived from the word *veiller*, which means to watch over.[13] These vessels were first made in pottery and porcelain in the 1750s. The introduction of this sick-room accessory at Sèvres may have coincided with the decline of Madame de Pompadour's health during the last years of her life.[14]

COMMENTARY

The Museum's *veilleuse* must simply have been used to warm broth. It was painted by Jean-Charles Sioux *aîné* who specialized in monochrome floral decoration. Another circular *veilleuse* with blue monochrome flowers dated 1758 is at Dalva Brothers, New York.[15]

TECHNIQUE AND CONDITION

The pedestal and cover should be accompanied by a bowl and *lampe* or *godet*.

Literature: Newman, *Veilleuses*, 1967, pp. 56–57, pl. III; Newman, *Connoisseur*, pp. 132–33; Newman, *Veilleuses*, 1987, p. 41, pl. IV

NOTES

1 Active 1752–92, specializing in monochrome flowers, garlands, and feathered edges. See Peters, *Marks*, p. 68. See also cat. no. 106.

2 AMNS, I. 7, 1 January 1759 (1758), molds and models (there was no model listed for the lamp, which must have been simply a small circular receptacle). Molds for the pedestal were 10 *livres*, for the bowl 4 *livres*, and for the *lampe* 1 *livre*. The model for the pedestal was valued at 20 *livres*, and for the bowl 4 *livres*. See Eriksen, *Waddesdon*, pp. 108–11, no. 37; Savill, 2, pp. 728–34.

3 AMNS, I. 7, 1 January 1760, work of the first nine months of 1759, *Moules et Contremoules de Veilleuses 2e gdr*, 9 *livres* each.

4 See Savill, 2, pp. 728–34; Eriksen, *Waddesdon*, pp. 108–11, no. 37.

5 IF 5673, fol. 135, 24 September 1759, biscuit kiln, one *veilleuse* (molded); IF 5675, fol. 3, 1 October 1759, glaze kiln, six *veilleuses assorties* (molded); IF 5673, fol. 111, 8 August 1758, three *veilleuses* (turned). See also Eriksen, *Waddesdon*, p. 108; Savill, 2, p. 728 (as possibly referring to the Wallace Collection version of the model).

6 IF 5673, fol. 110, 24 July 1758, two *veilleuses* (turned).

7 AMNS, Vy 2, fol. 77v, 30 December 1758. See also Eriksen, *Waddesdon*, p. 108; Savill, 2, pp. 728, 734 n. 21.

8 AMNS, Vy 3, fol. 13v, 5 January 1760, unnamed buyer, 192 *livres*; fol. 18, 6 May 1760, unnamed buyer, 168 *livres*; fol. 24, 22 July 1760, unnamed buyer, 168 *livres*; fol. 103v, 1 October 1762–1 January 1763, Poirier, 168 *livres*; fol. 116, 25 June 1762, Mme de Pompadour, 192 *livres*.

9 Ibid., Vy 9, fol. 150v, 26 October 1784 (Savill, 2, p. 734 n. 21).

10 See notes 7 and 8 above.

11 Corday, p. 61, no. 673 and p. 189, no. 2314. See Savill, 2, pp. 729, 734 n. 37.

12 For the most complete study of *veilleuses* see Newman, *Veilleuses*, 1987. The general information on this form is taken from this source.

13 Ibid., p. 15. See also Savill, 2, pp. 728, 734 n. 16.

14 Savill, 2, p. 729.

15 Marked interlaced Ls with date letter E, no painter's mark.

155

Inkstand (*écritoire*)

1917.1086

Sèvres, c. 1763

Soft-paste porcelain, gilt bronze, glass, oak, overall: H. 3⁵/₁₆ × L. 11¹⁵/₁₆ × D. 7⁹/₁₆ in. (8.4 × 30.3 × 19.2 cm); three sizes of plaques: H. 2⁷/₁₆ × W. 6⅞ in. (6.2 × 17.4 cm) (two); H. 2⁷/₁₆ × W. 2⅝ in. (6.2 × 6.7 cm) (two); H. 2⁷/₁₆ × W. 1⅞ in. (6.2 × 4.8 cm) (eight)

Petit verd ground with polychrome friezes, gilding

Marks: none

Provenance: probably Guillaume-François Vandenyver, Paris, 1818; Duke of Sutherland, Tretham Hall, by report; Charles Wertheimer, London, 1904;[1] J. Pierpont Morgan

MODEL

This model of inkstand probably dating from around 1760 or 1761, features a breakfronted rectangular form, canted corners, and gilt-bronze consoles. The inkstand's frame usually housed a series of porcelain plaques around all four sides. On many surviving examples there are variations in the design such as the addition of gilt-bronze bun feet or the arrangement and detailing of the gilt-bronze containers.[2] The example in the Atheneum's collection shares the same style of corner consoles, base, and top frame as an example in the Wallace Collection, but unlike the latter's and many others elsewhere, has a narrower pen tray and four rather than two gilt-bronze containers. The neoclassical design of this model is in marked contrast to the rococo inkstands attributed to Jean-Claude Duplessis of just a few years earlier.[3]

Porcelain plaques first featured on tables, coffers, and snuff-boxes. When they were first recorded at Vincennes in 1752, they were called *pièces* or *morceaux*.[4] By 1754, however, the word *plaque* was used.[5] The widespread use of plaques for mounting in furniture and inkstands, however, did not begin until 1758, when the *marchand-mercier* Simon-Philippe Poirier began buying them in quantity from the factory.[6] His shop was located on the rue Saint-Honoré in Paris and his clientele boasted members of the French court and aristocracy, as well as foreign dignitaries such as Horace Walpole.[7] Poirier went into partnership with Dominique Daguerre in 1772, and five years later retired. Daguerre took over the management of the firm, and continued to purchase Sèvres plaques for mounting. Poirier had been buying plaques since at least 1758, and come his retirement had purchased more than 1,400 plaques of various sizes.[8]

Rectangular inkstands decorated with Sèvres plaques were among the early and popular furnishing items sold by Poirier. Even though the Sèvres sales records first mention *plaques d'écritoire* in 1764,[9] we know of their being used for this purpose three years earlier (and perhaps sold as *pièces d'ornement*). The Wallace Collection's inkstand, decorated with green floral plaques dated 1761, may be considered one of the first examples of a model that was to remain popular for a number of years.[10]

155

FUNCTION

We cannot be sure how the four containers in the Hartford ink-stand were used. The small square gilt-bronze box with hinged and pierced lid surmounted with a small knob was almost certainly used to hold sand. Two containers are glass cylinders with gilt-bronze covers and acorn knobs. The fourth container is a shorter tapering glass receptacle that is suspended from a square gilt-bronze plate that fits into the gilt-bronze frame. A circular hole of about ¾ inch pierces this plate and is covered with a hinged lid. At least one of the three glass containers must have held ink, and one may have held sealing-wax pastilles. The long tray would have held quill pens, while the short tray may have been the sponge box.[11]

COMMENTARY

The Sèvres plaques on the Museum's *écritoire* are decorated with an unusual pale turquoise ground color called *petit verd*. This color was mentioned occasionally in factory records between 1761 and 1763, and then again in 1779.[12] Louis XV bought three tea sets described as *Petit Verd Et frize* in December

1761, two for 192 *livres*, and one for 204 *livres*.[13] They may have resembled the plaques on the Atheneum's piece.

Other *petit verd* plaques, dated 1763 and with almost identical frieze decoration to those on the Hartford inkstand, are mounted on a writing table by Joseph Baumhauer (called Joseph) at the Huntington Library and Art Collections (fig. 155-1).[14] Strangely enough, however, they have asymmetrical contours that are hidden by their gilt-bronze framing mounts. Still other *petit verd* plaques (one dated 1763) with the same frieze pattern, have been mounted on a filing cabinet clock (*pendule de cartonnier* or *pendule de serre papier*) now at the Louvre (fig. 155-2).[15] These appear to be en suite with the Huntington and Hartford plaques, although there are minor differences in the disposition and shape of the floral wreaths and in the laurel sprays.

It is almost certain that the Hartford inkstand was part of an ensemble comprising the Huntington Library's writing table and a filing cabinet represented now only by its clock, belonging to Guillaume-François Vandenyver, a Dutch immigrant banker living in Paris.[16] His probate inventory of 1818 listed a writing table, a filing cabinet and clock, and also an inkstand, all

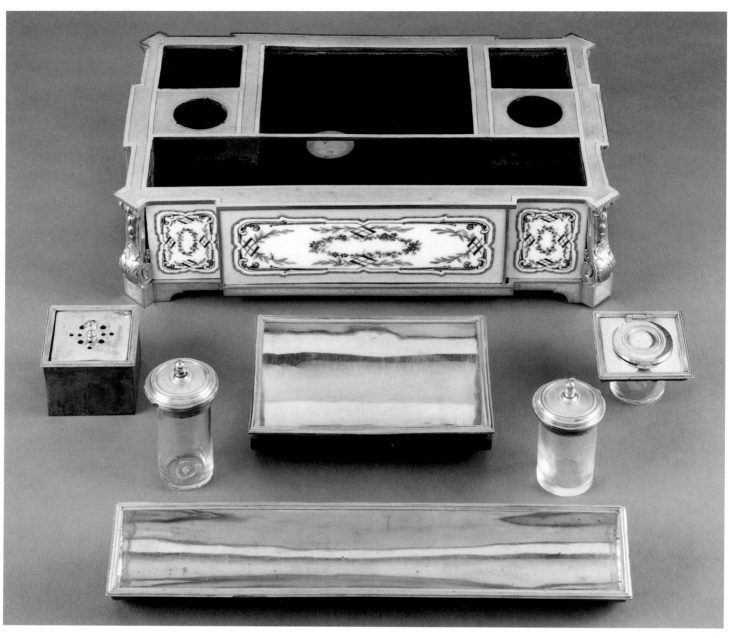

155

(*Left*) Fig. 155-1 *Bureau plat*, Joseph
Baumhauer

(*Opposite page*)
Fig. 155-2 *Pendule de cartonnier*, Julien Le Roy

with porcelain plaques.[17] This grouping of matching porcelain-mounted furniture and accessories for the *cabinet de travail* was not unique. An inventory of the duc d'Orléans of 29 November 1785 lists another ensemble comprising a writing table, filing cabinet, clock, and inkstand, all with matching porcelain plaques.[18]

There are no entries for *petit verd* plaques in the Sèvres sales records. Given the dating of the Huntington table plaques and the one dated plaque on the Louvre clock, however, we may suppose that those on the Atheneum's inkstand were made around 1763. They most probably were sold with the plaques now on the clock and the writing table.[19] Could they have been among the sixty-four plaques of various sizes described as *verd frize* bought by Poirier in the last quarter of 1763? These included four plaques at 36 *livres*, thirty-six at 24 *livres*, twelve at 18 *livres*, and ten at 9 *livres*.[20] While it may be speculative to link this entry in the sales records to the group of *petit verd* plaques

under discussion, it is not inconceivable that the word *petit* was left out when the original receipt was copied into the ledger book.[21] This appears to have happened when Madame de Pompadour bought a *petit verd* garniture in 1762.[22] Also when Madame de Pompadour sent Count Molke four *petit verd* tureens in 1761, she said that they were *d'un vert nouveau*.[23]

Technique and Condition

The plaques are glued to an oak carcass, but the central plaques on each side are bordered by a gilt-bronze strip.[24] The front left plaque has been broken and repaired. The screws holding the bottom section of gilt bronze are ferrous metal and machine made. The wooden carcass was made in the eighteenth century, as was the majority of the gilt bronze.[25] There may have been some alterations made at an undetermined later date, specifically where the glass cylinders fit in.[26] The tapered receptacle may be a later replacement, for it is shorter and lacks the pontil mark found on the other glass elements of the inkstand.[27] The gilt-bronze covers of both glass cylinders may also be later, as they are not as deeply chased as the rest of the gilt bronze, and their finials do not match that of the sand pot.

Exhibition: *Morgan Loan Exhibition*, New York, 1914, not in catalogue

Literature: Chavagnac, pp. 123–24, no. 154; Savill, 2, p. 860 n. 1e[28]

NOTES

1   APML, Wertheimer file, invoice 12 June 1904: "Louis XVI Inkstand inlaid with old Sèvres placques [*sic*], turquoise ground. From the Duke of Sutherland, Tretham Hall," £1,000.

2   Savill lists ten extant examples (2, p. 860 n. 1a–j).

3   See cat. no. 152. For more on this change from rococo to neoclassicism, see Eriksen, *Neo-classicism*, passim.

4   Savill, 2, p. 837. The following general information on plaques at Vincennes and Sèvres relies heavily on Savill, 2, pp. 837–42.

5   Ibid. See IF 5673, fol. 22, 8 May 1754.

6   Plaques of this date are mounted in a chest by Bernard II Van Risamburgh in a Paris private collection. See Verlet, *Sèvres*, pp. 206–7, pl. 39.

7   For more information on Poirier, see Dauterman, *Kress*, pp. 106–13; de Bellaigue, *Waddesdon*, 2, pp. 861–63; Eriksen, *Neo-classicism*, pp. 133–36.

8   See Eriksen, *Waddesdon*, p. 182, no. 64.

9   AMNS, Vy 4, fol. 24v, second half 1764, to Poirier. See Eriksen, *Waddesdon*, p. 182, no. 64.

10 Eriksen, *Neo-classicism*, p. 361, pl. 235. Savill (2, pp. 858–60) discusses this model in detail. See also Hughes, 2, pp. 1044–46. An example with Samson "Chinese Export" plaques, c. 1880, was with Partridge, London, in 1999 (*Vision of the East*, no. 48).

11 Savill, 2, p. 858.

12 Savill, 2, pp. 536, 541 n. 32. It may have been made from a *couleur fine* called *bleu Hellot* listed in the inventories of pigment in 1761 and 1762 (ibid., p. 536, 541 n. 34. Savill compares the stock of *bleu céleste*, *bleu pâle*, and *bleu Hellot* from 1758 to 1767 to show that the quantity of the latter increased during 1761 and 1762, coincidentally with the appearance of *petit verd* in the records. She notes, as well, that this *bleu Hellot* must differ from the term *bleu Hellot* used during the Vincennes period to describe *bleu céleste*). See also Munger, *Wickes*, p. 176, no. 122.

13 AMNS, Vy 3, fol. 82v, 24 December 1761.

14 San Marino, California. See Wark, *Huntington*, p. 79, fig. 54. See also Wilson, "Huntington," passim. Wark believed that the plaques had been

added either by the *ébéniste* Claude-Charles Saunier, whose stamp accompanies Joseph's on the table, or perhaps in the 19th century. Wilson has argued that they were mounted on the table by Joseph.

15 No. OA 10658. See *Patromoine national*, no. 82. I would like to thank Pierre Ennès for providing me with this reference. Marie-Laure de Rochebrune at the Louvre notes that the plaques have recently been removed from the clock for examination, revealing that the central plaque is marked for 1763 and with the painter's mark of Jean-Baptiste Tandart. The rest of the plaques are unmarked.

16 See Savill, 2, p. 870, and Hughes, 2, pp. 928–29 nn. 15, 19.

17 "Un bureau de bois de palissandre orné de fonte doré avec plaques de porcelaine et garni de tiroirs … Un serre papier de bois de placage avec ornemens de porcelaine et autres de cuivre doré surmonté d'une pendule à sonnerie du nom de Julien le Roy dans sa boîte avec candélabres de cuivre doré en or moulu sur lequel sont deux petits amours de cuivre bronze … Un écritoire garni in Cuivre & en porcelaine comme le Serre papier." Probate Inventory, 1818. The first two articles were published by Hughes, 2, p. 929 and before that by Lemonnier, p. 74. Lemonnier thought that the Vandenyver inventory referred to a file cabinet and clock in the Wallace Collection and a table at the MMA, New York, but Hughes has shown that these were in England by 1812 (Hughes, 2, p. 926). The reference to the inkstand is also from the 1818 Probate Inventory (fol. 2, no manuscript citation available to the author, photocopy of relevant pages very kindly provided by Patricia Lemonnier). While the clock and filing cabinet had been noted before, the inkstand had escaped attention.

18 AN, X1A 9173, 1075: "Un bureau de cinq pieds de long sur deux pieds et demi de large avec son serre-papier surmonté d'une pendule à cartel avec un groupe d'enfants de bronze et deux bras à deux branches, le tout en bronze doré d'or moulu, ledit bureau orné de carreaux de porcelaine à fleurs, une écriture aussi en porcelaine garnie d'encriers et poudriers en cuivre doré, deux groupes d'enfants en bronze de cuivre doré servant à poser sur le papier," kindly pointed out to the author by Pierre-François Dayot.

19 There are twelve plaques on the inkstand, thirty-two on the table, and nine on the clock.

20 These prices may correspond to the various size plaques in the three pieces under discussion. Savill (2, p. 859) has suggested that the green-ground plaques in the Wallace Collection inkstand were those sold to Poirier in the last quarter of 1762 (AMNS, Vy 3, fol. 103) for 18, 12, and 9 *livres*.

21 Daily transactions were noted as they occurred and then subsequently copied into the sales ledgers.

22 AMNS, Vy 3, fol. 115v: *1 Pendule petit verd / 2 Pots pourris a feuillages Verds Chinois / 2 idem a Bobeches idem*. This garniture has been identified as the clock (No. OA 10899) and a pair of *pots-pourris girandoles* or *à bobèches* (Nos. OA 11306-07) now in the Louvre, and a pair of *pots-pourris à feuillage* in the Walters Art Gallery, Baltimore, Maryland (nos. 48.590–91). See Ennès, "Pompadour," passim.

23 Letter to the Président Ogier, 22 October 1761, discussed in Dragesco, "Pompadour," pp. 79–80.

24 Savill, 2, pp. 858, 860 n. 15, remarks that 18th-century inkstands usually do not have gilt-bronze strips bordering the porcelain plaques, but instead have plaques with gilded edges. She suggests that those with gilt-bronze edges may have been assembled in the nineteenth century. This does not appear to be the case in the Museum's example.

25 The inkstand was taken apart and examined by Theodore Dell. The observations on its construction and the dating of the gilt bronze are based on this examination. The author would like to thank Mr. Dell for his assistance with this piece.

26 The holes seem to have been cut after the gilt bronze had been chased, although it is also possible that they were purposely chased beyond where the holes were going to be so that the chasing went to the very edge of the holes.

27 The pontil mark is where the pontil or iron rod used for handling the glass during manufacture was broken off after its completion.

28 Thought perhaps to be the inkstand sold Sotheby's, Monte Carlo, 25 June 1984, lot 3149. Savill must have been unaware of the fact that the Morgan inkstand was in Hartford.

156

Broth basin and stand (*écuelle ronde et plateau ovale*)

1917.1163

Sèvres, 1763

Soft-paste porcelain, basin: H. 4⅞ × W. 7¹³/₁₆ × D. 5¹⁵/₁₆ in. (12.3 × 19.8 × 15.1 cm); stand: H. 1⅝ × L. 10⅜ × W. 8⅜ in. (4.1 × 26.3 × 21.2 cm)

White ground, blue border with gilded diapers, red, pink, and purple shells and garlands, polychrome flowers

Marks: basin: incised DU;[1] stand: interlaced Ls in blue with date letter K, serif x underneath for Jacques-François Micaud *père*;[2] incised scrolling gp[3]

Provenance: J. Pierpont Morgan

MODEL

Round broth basins were made at Vincennes from the second half of the 1740s. At first the model betrayed a debt to Meissen shapes, but as was usually the case at Vincennes, it quickly lost its dependency on such German forms.[4] By 1752 four sizes of molds for *écuelles rondes* were listed in the factory inventory, although the broth basins were, in fact, turned.[5] We may surmise that from at least 1761 *écuelles* of the fifth and sixth size were being made, as *plateaux* for these sizes were listed among new models in the inventory.[6]

Two incomplete plaster models still survive.[7] There is also a drawing of a broth basin and stand dated 1753, the basin designed with branch handles and a branch knob (figs. 156-1–2). It is one of many drawings made in that year that show revisions to forms already in production.[8] Another drawing of an *écuelle ronde*, this one with feet, is dated 1755.[9]

Ecuelles rondes were the most common broth basin made and, therefore, must account for most of the references in the sales records.[10] They were sold with matching stands, which could be round, oval, or *à ornements*. The oval stand probably was made in three sizes from at least 1753, when the first *platteau ovale d'Ecuelle* appeared in the glaze kiln records.[11] A fourth-size oval stand was listed among new models for 1761, making it likely that before this date the fourth-size basin was paired with round stands.[12] The sales records rarely distinguished either the shape of the stand or the size of the basin.[13]

COMMENTARY

The Hartford broth basin and oval stand are of the second and first size, respectively.[14] They were decorated by Jacques-François Micaud with polychrome floral garlands and *frizes colorées*, the latter comprising shells, rosettes, and intertwined laurel garlands, all in shades of blue, red, and purple, and gold. In the second half of 1762 Micaud was paid 18 *livres* for

156

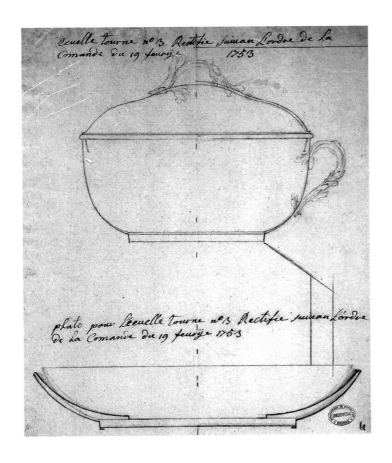

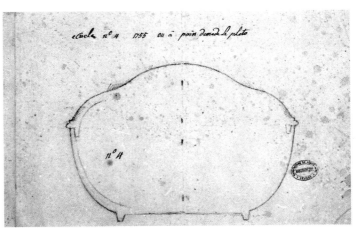

(*Left and above*) Figs. 156-1–2 *Écuelle et plateau*, drawings

decorating an *écuelle* and *plateau* of the third size, and in 1764 he was paid 24 *livres* each for two *écuelles* of the second size and their *plateaux ovales*.[15] He also decorated a broth basin with a round stand dated 1763 in the same manner.[16] In 1765 the comtesse de Brione bought an *ecuelle et plateau frizes colorées* for 216 *livres*, which must have approximated the cost of the Museum's example.[17]

Exhibition: *Morgan Loan Exhibition*, New York, 1914, not in catalogue

NOTES

1 See Savill, 3, p. 1099, found on soft paste 1756–79.

2 See cat. no. 91 for Micaud's mark.

3 See Savill, 3, p. 1106, found on soft paste primarily 1757–79.

4 See cat. no. 147 for an early model. Another early round broth basin, with striped handles and a large flower knob, is at the MAD, Paris (no. 22315, see Préaud and d'Albis, pp. 70–71, no. 1).

5 AMNS, I. 7, 8 October 1752, *48 moules d'Ecuelles rondes de 4 grandeurs avec leurs contremoules*, along with *48 platteaux idem*. For extensive information on this model see Sassoon, pp. 81–83; Savill, 2, pp. 643–66. Savill (2, p. 643) gives the following sizes: first size: H. $5\frac{3}{8}$–$5\frac{11}{16}$ × W. $8\frac{1}{4}$–$8\frac{7}{8}$ in. (13.7–14.5 × 21–22.5 cm); second size: H. $4\frac{3}{4}$–$5\frac{1}{8}$ × W. $7\frac{9}{16}$–$7\frac{7}{8}$ in. (12–13 × 19.2–19.9 cm); third size: H. $4\frac{5}{16}$–$4\frac{5}{8}$ ×W. $6\frac{1}{16}$–$6\frac{3}{4}$ in. (11–11.8 × 15.4–17.2 cm); fourth size: H. $3\frac{15}{16}$–4 × W. $4\frac{15}{16}$ in. (10–10.2 × 12.5 cm). She does not give dimensions for a fifth- or sixth-size broth basin.

6 AMNS, 1 January 1762 (work of 1761), *moules*. See Savill, 2, p. 644.

7 AMNS, 1814 inventory, 1740–80, no. 1 (see Savill, 2, p. 643 and Sassoon, p. 81; the latter citing only one model).

8 AMNS, R. 1, L. 2, d. 3, fol. 2, inscribed *Ecuelle tourne no 3 Rectifie suivan L'ordre de la comande du 19 fevrÿe 1753* and *plato pour L'ecuelle tourne no 3 Rectifie suivan L'ordre de la comande du 19 fevrÿe 1753*.

9 Ibid., fol. 4, inscribed *ecuelle no 4 1755 on à poin demande le plato*. See Savill, 2, p. 644.

10 Sales of *écuelles* are too numerous to list. Some have been noted by Savill, 2, pp. 644, 663 nn. 44–48.

11 IF 5674, fol. 10, 20 July 1753. See Savill, 2, pp. 648, 666 for a detailed account of this form of stand.

12 AMNS, I. 7, 1 January 1762, (for 1761), *modèles*. See Savill, 2, p. 648 for this hypothesis. Savill (2, p. 648 lists the sizes as follows: first size: L. $9\frac{7}{16}$–$10\frac{5}{8}$ in. (24–26.9 cm); second size: L. $8\frac{13}{16}$–$9\frac{1}{16}$ in. (22.3–23 cm); third size: L. $7\frac{11}{16}$–$7\frac{7}{8}$ in. (19.5–20 cm); fourth size: L. $7\frac{1}{16}$–$7\frac{1}{8}$ in. (17.9–18.1 cm). These increments are narrow compared to other Sèvres models.

13 See Savill, 2, p. 644. For a stand *à ornements* see cat. no. 153.

14 Savill (2, p. 648) says that generally second-size basins were paired with first-size stands, and that second-size stands were used with second- or third-size bowls, and third- and fourth-size stands with third- and fourth-size bowls.

15 AMNS, F.6.

16 See Maurice Kann sale, Galerie Georges Petit, Paris, 5–8 December 1910, lot 58. I would like to thank Clare Le Corbeiller for this information.

17 AMNS, Vy 4, fol. 51, 2 September 1765.

157

Broth basin and stand (*écuelle ronde et plateau ovale*)

1917.1164

Sèvres, 1764

Soft-paste porcelain, basin: H. $4\frac{7}{8}$ × W. $6\frac{3}{4}$ × D. $5\frac{5}{16}$ in. (12.3 × 17.1 × 13.5 cm); stand: H. $1\frac{7}{16}$ × L. $8\frac{15}{16}$ × D. $7\frac{5}{16}$ in. (3.6 × 22.6 × 18.5 cm)

White ground, blue border with *pointillé* gilding, red, blue, carmine, purple, and gold *frize coloreé* decoration, polychrome flowers

Marks: basin: interlaced Ls in blue with date letter L, painter's mark for Guillaume Noël above;[1] incised FR and O;[2] stand: partially effaced interlaced Ls in blue with date letter L and mark of Noël above, incised gc[3]

Provenance: J. Pierpont Morgan

MODEL

This is an example of an *écuelle ronde* and *plateau ovale*. It is difficult to determine the size of the broth basin for in height it falls within the second size while in width it falls within the third. The stand is of the second size.[4]

COMMENTARY

The *frize colorée* decoration was painted by Guillaume Noël, who, like Micaud and many other Sèvres painters, practiced this decorative genre in the 1760s. An *écuelle et plateau ronde* from 1764 with very similar *frizes colorées* by Noël was recently on the New York art market, and a covered cup and saucer, again with similar friezes, is now at the Wallace Collection.[5] The repetition of such specific design elements as diapered scrolls, suspended harebells, and drapery swags, makes it likely that Noël relied on shop engravings or drawings as visual guides. A smaller broth basin and oval stand also by Noël but with different *frizes colorées* is now at in the Musée des Arts décoratifs, Paris.[6]

Factory overtime records show that Noël was paid 18 *livres* in 1764 for decorating *1 écuelle 3e g. et platt. ovale*.[7] It is possible that this refers to the Museum's example.

TECHNIQUE AND CONDITION

The blue used on the Hartford basin and stand was *bleu nouveau*. The iron red was of poor quality, but the purple was extremely good. Inside the basin there is evidence that some particles dropped from inside the saggars during firing.

Exhibition: *Morgan Loan Exhibition*, New York, 1914, not in catalogue

Literature: Chavagnac, p. 98, no. 119

157

NOTES

1 Active 1755–1804. See Savill, 3, pp. 1053–54 for his biography.

2 For FR see Savill, 3, p. 1102 as possibly for François-Firmin Fresne or Dufresne. For O see ibid., p. 1117, found on soft paste 1754–82, and on *écuelles* in the 1760s.

3 Ibid., p. 1104, found on soft paste 1757–76, including *plateaux* in the 1760s.

4 For information on these forms and their standard sizes see cat. no. 156.

5 Christie's, New York, 21 May 1997, lot 95. It appears to be an *écuelle* of the first size, and shares many of the same design elements as the Hartford example, such as the opposing scrolls shaded with blue and purple and gilded with diapering, between which hang harebells topped by floral garlands, purple drapery and floral swags linking the scrolls below. The same motifs of the harebells linked together with purple drapery and floral swags may be seen on the cup and saucer in the Wallace Collection (Savill, 2, no. C439, pp. 670–72).

6 MAD, Paris, no. D36939, L. 5¹⁵⁄₁₆ × D. 4⁷⁄₁₆ in. (15 × 11.2 cm), 1765.

7 AMNS, F.7.

158

Toilet pots (*pots à pommade*)

1917.1037–1038

Sèvres, 1764

Soft-paste porcelain, both: H. 2¹⁵⁄₁₆ × DIAM. 2⁵⁄₁₆ in. (7.5 × 5.8 cm)

Bleu nouveau ground with polychrome trophies, gilding

Marks: on both: interlaced Ls in blue with date letter L, painter's mark of an anchor for Charles Buteux *père, aîné*;[1] incised I or T[2]

Provenance: Edouard Chappey, Paris, 1906;[3] J. Pierpont Morgan

MODEL

The Sèvres factory called such toilet pots *pots à pommade*.[4]

158

COMMENTARY

The trophies on these pots were painted by Charles Buteux, probably the most talented and productive painter of this genre at Sèvres. Whereas trophies in reserves were often the principal decoration of small objects like these pomade pots, large trophies frequently adorned the backs of flowerpots and vases. The factory relied on a number of engraved sources for trophies, by artists such as Antoine Watteau, Claude Gillot, J.-C. Delafosse, and J. Bernard Toro.[5] On one side of each of the Atheneum's toilet pots there are trophies of Love, complete with bow, quiver of arrows, and torch. On one pot Love is paired with Pastoral Life, represented by a plumed lady's hat, a horn, a skein of wool and a bobbin.[6] On the other pot Love is paired with Agriculture, represented by a straw flask, a sheath of wheat, grapes, a snake, and arrows.

The gilding of these *pots à pommade* is quite simple, strictly following the shape of the reserve, and punctuated only by a pattern of alternating truncated triangles created by tooling and burnishing.[7] This is in marked contrast to the rococo scrolls, trellises, and other fanciful decorative elements typical of the 1750s.[8]

TECHNIQUE AND CONDITION

The knobs were modeled by hand. The gilded rims of both lids are quite worn, and both show signs of unfired restoration. The lid of 1917.1037 is full of black specks inside as if the gilding had been renewed and refired at some later date.[9] Some of the gilding around the base of the pots has also worn away.

Exhibition: *Morgan Loan Exhibition*, New York, 1914, not in catalogue

Literature: Chavagnac, p. 97, no. 118; Buckley, *Connoisseur*, p. 52, fig. 10; Savill, 2, pp. 652, 666 n. 134

NOTES

1 Active 1756–82. See Savill, 3, pp. 1007–9.

2 See ibid., 3, pp. 1108–9.

3 APML, Chappey file, invoice for 30 April, 1906: "1 pt pot de toilette Sèvres bleu de roi attrib de musique 1250/1 pt pot de toilette Sèvres bleu de roi attrib jardinage," 950 French francs.

4 For information on the shape of these toilet pots and their use in the eighteenth century see cat. no. 149.

5 Books of ornamental designs were used by various craftsmen in the 18th century for all classes of decorative arts, including marquetry, silver, textiles, interiors. See de Bellaigue, "Engravings," p. 752. See also Belfort, "Watteau," passim. The exact source for the trophies on the Hartford toilet pots remains unidentified.

6 It is possible that there is a reference to the virtues of domestic life in this trophy. An engraving by Jean-Michel Liotard after François Boucher, entitled *La Bergère laborieuse*, depicts a shepherdess holding a bobbin of wool (Jean-Richard, pp. 335–36, no. 1399).

7 The brighter, burnished triangles are subtly tooled with linear strokes that follow the lines of the triangle, while the alternating triangles are left matte.

8 See Eriksen and Bellaigue, pp. 137–38. See also Eriksen, *Neo-classicism*, pp. 110–13.

9 Observations made by Antoine d'Albis upon examination of the pieces.

159

159

Water jug and basin (*pot à eau tourné* and probably *jatte ovale de pot à eau*)

1917.1178–1179

Sèvres, 1769

Soft-paste porcelain, silver gilt, jug: H. 6⅜ (with thumb-piece), 6¹⁄₁₆ (without thumb-piece) × W. 5¼ × D. 4¹⁄₁₆ in. (16.1/15.3 × 13.3 × 10.3 cm); basin: H. 2⅛ × L. 10⁵⁄₁₆ × D. 7³⁄₁₆ in. (5.3 × 26.2 × 18.2 cm)

White ground with monochrome blue garlands, gilding

Marks: on both: interlaced Ls in blue with date letter q below, stippled crown above for Jean-Charles Sioux *aîné*;[1] incised x within a square on jug;[2] incised 6 or 9 on basin;[3] discharge mark of *sous-fermier* Julien Alaterre (1768–75) on silver-gilt thumb-piece

Provenance: J. Pierpont Morgan

Model

This water jug, usually just called *pot à eau* in factory documents, was the most common model of its type made by Vincennes and Sèvres.[4] Based on traditional French *faïence* and Meissen porcelain shapes,[5] it was already in production in the first and fourth sizes by 1752, and in the second and third sizes by 1753.[6] Jugs of this general shape, in fact, appeared early at Vincennes, but they were characterized by a longer neck, a more

prominent foot, a more elaborate, metal-shaped handle, and an applied, molded spout, the latter sometimes with a harebell-like molding.[7] These jugs were usually paired with basins resembling round bowls. By 1752 the form seems to have evolved into the definitive, slightly squatter version with a sparrow-beak spout represented by Hartford's example, and was paired with one of seven different basins.[8]

Plaster models in three sizes were listed in the factory's 1814 inventory. They still survive at Sèvres (fig. 159-1).[9] Two drawings also remain at the factory, showing the jug and cover without a handle.[10] The form is recorded in four sizes, and was made in both soft and hard paste.[11]

Three variations of oval basin, all probably called *jatte ovale de pot à eau*, were commonly paired with the *pot à eau tourné*.[12] Documents do not distinguish between them.[13] We know from surviving examples that they were made by 1753. Two sizes were recorded in the sales ledgers in December 1752.[14]

Most jugs and basins listed in the sales ledgers were of the first or second size.[15] Prices varied widely, depending on size, decoration, and style of basin. From 1753 to 1755, first-size sets with flowers sold for 72 and 84 *livres*, while those with garlands sold for 120 and 240 *livres*.[16] A set with yellow ground and flowers cost 144 *livres*.[17] Sets in *bleu lapis* with gold or polychrome decoration cost 288 and 264 *livres*,[18] while *bleu céleste* sets with flowers ranged from 240 to 480 *livres*.[19] In one case a *bleu céleste* set decorated with children in polychrome cost 600 *livres*.[20] Second-size examples decorated with flowers sold for 48 and 60 *livres*, and *bleu lapis* sets ranged from 168 to 360.[21] *Bleu céleste* sets with flowers or birds usually cost 360 *livres*.[22]

Fig. 159-1 *Pot à eau*, plaster model

Function

Water jugs and basins were used during the ritual of dressing or while in the *garde-robe*. They sometimes matched broth basins and stands, which were also used in the same context. First- and second-size jugs were meant to contain water, but sometimes smaller sizes were used as coffee or milk pots.[23] Usually the jug came with a cover, but this was sold loose. It fell to the *marchands-merciers*—who then contracted with goldsmiths—to to provide the jug with metal hinges and mounts, often made of silver gilt or gold.

Commentary

The Museum's set probably is of the second size,[24] and in all likelihood cost between 72 and 90 *livres*.[25] In 1769 the dealer Poirier bought an unspecified jug and basin for 78 *livres*. This may have been the Museum's *pot à eau et jatte*.[26]

The Hartford jug and basin were decorated by Jean-Charles Sioux *aîné*. Other jugs or jugs and basins with kindred decoration by this painter are in the Musée des Arts décoratifs, Paris.[27] A set with similar but more accomplished decoration by Pierre-Antoine Méreaud is in the Royal Collection, England.[28] Like the Hartford example, it combines garlands of flowers, bands with gilded laurel trails, and a *pointillé* border. The same decorative scheme, including the central medallion with intersecting circles, may also be found on a two-handled cup and saucer in the Art Institute of Chicago, a tray at the Musée national de Céramique, Sèvres, and a *déjeuner Hebert* on the art market in New York in 1999.[29] Because the same decorative scheme occurs on the work of more than one painter, we may safely assume that the factory provided a common source as a model. It may have evolved from designs by Jean-Jacques Bachelier, such as one referred to in a letter by Hendrik van Hulst of the Académie des Beaux-Arts to the director of the factory Boileau in September 1751, describing "une petite guirlande roulante en haut et au bas du gobelet..." [a little rolling garland at the top and bottom of the goblet].[30]

Exhibitions: *Morgan Loan Exhibition*, New York, 1914, not in catalogue; *Morgan*, Hartford, no. 71

Literature: de Bellaigue, "Sèvres," p. 184, no. 71; Savill, 2, p. 713 n. 30p

Notes

1 See Peters, *Marks*, p. 68. Active 1752–92, specializing in monochrome flowers, garlands, patterns, and feathered edges.

2 Savill, 3, p. 1136, found on soft paste 1756–76.

3 Ibid., pp. 1127–28, found on soft paste 1754–90s.

4 Savill (2, p. 693) remarks that from 1753 this form was qualified with the description *tourné* to distinguish it from another, molded model called *lizonné*. The form is sometimes referred to as *pot à eau ordinaire* (de Bellaigue, "Sèvres," p. 184).

5 The shape was also found at Saint-Cloud and Chantilly. See cat. no. 8 for a Saint-Cloud example.

6 Savill, 2, pp. 693, 713 n. 29. These forms have been thoroughly discussed on pp. 692–718. The following information summarizes Savill's discussion.

7 See Préaud and d'Albis, p. 140, no. 83, and p. 152, no. 118.

8 Savill, 2, p. 693, who lists the seven models.

9 AMNS, 1814 inventory, 1760–80, no. 1, hts. 9⅞, 8⅝, 7½ in. (25, 22, and 19 cm). See Savill, 2, p. 692.

10 AMNS, R. 1, L. 1, d. 17, fols. 14, 20. See Savill, 2, pp. 692–93, one illustrated (fol. 14).

11 Savill breaks down the sizes as follows, with the qualification that the mounts affect the overall measurements given in various catalogues: first size: H. 7$\frac{7}{16}$–9 in. (18.8–22.8 cm); second size: without mount, H. 6⅛–6$\frac{11}{16}$ in. (15.5–16.9 cm), with mount, H. 6⅜–6¾ in. (16.2–17.2 cm); third size: about 5$\frac{13}{16}$ (14.8 cm); fourth size: 4$\frac{15}{16}$–5 (12.5–12.6 cm). She notes an exceptionally large version measuring 10⅜ in. (26.4 cm).

12 See Savill, 2, p. 698 for this form.

13 Ibid. One measures approximately H. 2¼ in. (5.7 cm), has slightly ribbed lobes in the center of the sides and ends (Wallace Collection, London, no. C451). A second is a deeper plain oval basin with curved sides, and the third is similar to the *jatte ovale à bord de relief* but without the relief decoration (see Wallace Collection, London, no. C453).

14 Ibid. First size: L. 11¼–D. 12$\frac{3}{16}$ in. (28.5–31 cm); second size: L. 10$\frac{1}{16}$–D. 10$\frac{9}{16}$ in. (25.5–26.8 cm). See AMNS, Vy 1, fol. 5v, 28 December 1752, first size, to Mme de Pompadour.

15 Savill, 2, p. 693. She notes that four examples of a third-size jug with accompanying basin are recorded.

16 AMNS, Vy 1, fol. 26, 31 December 1753, Machard; fol. 3, 9 May 1753, unnamed buyer; fol. 22, 18 December 1753, Bazin; fol. 23, 20 December 1753, Calabre.

17 Ibid., fol. 11v, 25 April 1753, M. Le Garde des Sceaux.

18 Ibid., fol. 7, 12 March 1753, Mme de Pompadour; fol. 69, 5–31 December 1754, Duvaux.

19 Ibid., fol. 11v, 25 April 1753, M. Le Garde des Sceaux; fol. 28v, 31 December 1753, Duvaux.

20 Ibid., fol. 28v, 31 December 1753, Duvaux.

21 Ibid., fol. 30v, 31 December 1753, Duvaux; fol. 40, 10 May 1754, Parseval; fol. 58, 5 December 1754, Duvaux (*lapis et or*) and (*lapis riche*).

22 Ibid., fol. 86v, 1 January–1 June 1755, Duvaux.

23 For more on the use of jugs and basins see cat. no. 148, and Savill, 2, pp. 691–92, 695.

24 The height of the jug both with and without the thumb-piece are within a millimeter of Savill's range for second-size examples. The basin corresponds to Savill's second size in length but is not as deep (high) and appears to be less wide (this measurement not given in Savill). It may be that the Hartford basin represents yet another variation of oval basin made. De Bellaigue ("Sèvres," p. 184) believed that the Museum's set was a version of the third size but his published entry preceded Savill's publication with its new information on sizes.

25 Garlands were more expensive than simple flowers, but monochrome decoration was less expensive than polychrome. In 1754 a first-size set with monochrome flowers sold for 72 *livres* (AMNS, Vy 1, fol. 45v, 30 June 1754, Duvaux), and thus one would expect a second-size set with monochrome garlands to be only slightly higher in price.

26 Ibid., Vy 4, fol. 195v, second half 1769.

27 One (no. A7803) is undated and without a basin, the other (no. A19505) is dated P on the basin. See also a *broc Roussel* and *jatte ovale*, Christie's, New York, 16–18 November 1999, lot 206.

28 *Royal Collection*, pp. 69–70, no. 63.

29 Dated 1770, Art Institute of Chicago, no. 1994.376a–b; 1770, MNC, Sèvres, no. 8497; and 1784, Christie's, New York, 16–18 November 1999, lot 258.

30 See Préaud, "Bachelier," p. 63 n. 25.

160

Broth basin and stand (*écuelle ronde et plateau ovale*)

1917.1073

Sèvres, 1772

Soft-paste porcelain, basin: H. 4^{13}/$_{16}$ × W. 6¾ × D. 5^{5}/$_{16}$ in. (12.2 × 17.2 × 13.5 cm); stand: H. 1⅜ × L. 8^{15}/$_{16}$ × W. 7^{3}/$_{16}$ in. (3.5 × 22.7 × 18.3 cm)

Bleu céleste ground with polychrome figures, gilding

Marks: basin: traces of interlaced Ls in brown, incised da or du?;[1] stand: slightly effaced interlaced Ls in brown with date letter t; partly erased m above for Jean-Louis Morin;[2] incised H;[3] scratched in the glaze the cipher WJG[4]

Provenance: William James Goode;[5] A. Wertheimer; Cartier et Fils, Paris, 1899;[6] J. Pierpont Morgan

160

MODEL

The broth basin is an *écuelle ronde*.[7] It is either of the second or third size, for in height it compares to second-size examples while in width it is closer to third-size basins.[8] The stand is a *plateau ovale* of the second size.[9]

COMMENTARY

This broth basin may have been one sold to Marie-Antoinette in December 1772. The sales ledger describes that the queen purchased an *écuelle et plateau beau bleu marine* [blue ground broth basin and stand with marine scenes] for 324 *livres*, as well as one with a *bleu céleste* ground and marine scenes (described as *idem et idem bleu céleste*) for 300 *livres*.[10] At the very least we may suppose that the Hartford broth basin and stand were comparably priced.

The quayside scenes that decorate the Atheneum's set were a specialty of the Sèvres painter Morin, who from the early 1760s depicted them on ornamental vases and wares. Morin must have had a small group of sketches at his disposal for he repeatedly used the same compositions or figures in his work.[11] We see, for example, that the reserve on the Hartford broth basin depicting three men, two of them grouped around a barrel, appears again on a cup in the Metropolitan Museum of Art,[12] and on the saucer of a socketed cup in the Victoria and Albert Museum.[13] The scene on the other side of the Atheneum's basin is found again in an abbreviated form on a cup in the Victoria and Albert Museum.[14] One of Hartford's cover reserves is repeated on a socketed cup at the Museum of Fine Arts, Boston,[15] while the other reserve may be compared to a saucer in the Royal

Collection, England.[16] The scene on the stand, showing three men with a large sack, is also on the socketed cup belonging to the Victoria and Albert Museum's saucer.[17] The scene in the other reserve is repeated on the front of a pot-pourri vase in the Metropolitan Museum of Art,[18] and on the saucer belonging to the cup in the Royal Collection.[19]

Morin's harbor scenes are akin to those of seventeenth-century Dutch marine painters such as Ludolf Backhuisen, Johann Lingelbach or eighteenth-century French painters such as Joseph Vernet or Lacroix de Marseille.[20] Comparing engravings after these artists, however, fails to reveal direct links. It may be that either Morin himself, or more likely, Genest—the head of the painter's workshop—created drawings specifically for such use.[21]

The Meissen porcelain factory made use of similar imagery on their porcelain, although usually the views were more expansive and the figures smaller in scale. Moreover, the scenes often were given an exotic flavor through the use of orientalized costumes.[22] The scenes found on the French pieces, in contrast, are more European in character and appear as if they were excerpted details from paintings.

TECHNIQUE AND CONDITION

The ground color *bleu céleste* was reformulated in 1755 to create a more uniform, more opaque, and somewhat more intense turquoise.[23] This is the color used on the Atheneum's broth basin and stand. The newer color was used throughout the 1760s and 1770s, both on vases, tea wares, and services.[24]

Exhibitions: *Morgan Loan Exhibition*, New York, 1914, not in catalogue; *Vincennes and Sèvres Porcelain,* New York, 1980, no. 56; *Morgan*, Hartford, no. 73

Literature: Chavagnac, p. 116, no. 144; Buckley, *Antiques*, p. 189, fig. 12; *Vincennes and Sèvres Porcelain*, no. 56; de Bellaigue, "Sèvres," p. 186, no. 73; Savill, 2, pp. 661, 667 n. 162

NOTES

1 See Savill, 3, p. 1097 for da, found on soft paste 1758–75, and most commonly found from 1768. Savill suggests da may be the mark of Danet *père*, active 1768–86/87. For du, see ibid., p. 1099, as found on soft paste 1756–79. Two *répareurs* are suggested for possible attribution: Gilbert-François Duponchelle, active 1754–68, and then his son, François-Philippe, active 1768–87.

2 Active 1754–87. See Savill, 3, pp. 1051–52. See also cat. no. 59.

3 See Savill, 3, pp. 1108–9.

4 According to de Bellaigue ("Sèvres," p. 186, no. 73), this cipher belonged to the collector William James Goode.

5 Probably lot 80 of the Goode sale (Christie's, London, 17 July 1895).

6 APML Cartier file, invoice 20 May 1899: "2 Ecuelles à bouillon en pâte tendre vieux Sèvres, l'une fond bleu turquoise, sujets de Marine d'apres Morin…," together 12,500 French francs.

7 See cat. no. 156 for this form.

8 Savill (2, p. 643) gives the width of the second size as 7⅝–7⅞ in. (19.2–19.9 cm). The Hartford basin is only 6¾ in. (17.2 cm) wide.

9 See cat. no. 156. De Bellaigue ("Sèvres," p. 186) states that the ensemble probably is of the third size.

10 AMNS, Vy 5, fol. 42v, December 1772.

11 Le Corbeiller, *Dodge*, p. 162. I would like to thank Clare Le Corbeiller for sharing her Morin file.

12 MMA, New York, 1775, no. 58.75.106.

13 V&A, London, no. Circ.629b-1919, dated 1776.

14 Dated 1770, no. C463.1921.

15 MFA, Boston, Wickes Collection (Munger, *Wickes*, no. 141).

16 Dated 1772. See *Royal Collection*, pp. 113–14, no. 118.

17 No. Circ.629b-1919.

18 MMA, No. 58.75.77 (illustrated in Christie's, 7 May 1910, lot 48).

19 See note 16 above.

20 Savill, 3, p. 1052.

21 This view has been suggested to the author in discussions with Clare Le Corbeiller. Savill (3, p. 1052) suggests that Genest probably adapted the engraved sources cited above for other Sèvres painters. This hypothesis warrants further investigation.

22 See for example a gold-ground dish with harbor scene dated c. 1745 in the V&A, London (J.G. Joicey Bequest, C.1455-1919).

23 Préaud and d'Albis, p. 217.

24 See for example the service made for the prince de Rohan in 1772, the same year as this broth basin (many pieces now in the MMA, New York). See Dauterman, *Wrightsman*, pp. 261–71.

161

Water jug and basin (*pot à eau tourné et jatte ovale de pot à eau*)

1917.1169–1170

Sèvres, 1773

Soft-paste porcelain, bone china (lid), silver gilt, jug: H. 7¹⁵⁄₁₆ (with hinge), 7⅞ (without hinge) × W. 5¾ × D. 4¾ in. (20.2/20 × 14.6 × 12 cm); basin: H. 2¾ × L. 11¹³⁄₁₆ × D. 9¼ in. (6.9 × 30 × 23.5 cm)

Bleu céleste ground, gilding

Marks: on both: interlaced Ls in blue with date letter u; # underneath for Michel-Barnabé Chauvaux;[1] on jug: LG in blue for Étienne-Henry Le Guay *aîné, père*;[2] and vd conjoined in blue for Jean-Baptiste-Emmanuel Vandé *père*;[3] incised JM[4]

Provenance: Duveen Brothers, London, 1904;[5] J. Pierpont Morgan

MODEL

This model was the most common water jug and basin produced by the Vincennes and Sèvres factory.[6]

COMMENTARY

The Atheneum's water jug and basin are unusual but not unique in being covered entirely in *bleu céleste*, adorned only with gilding. In the 1750s, when this ground color was introduced, a number of objects were decorated in this manner, and were listed in the documents as *bleu céleste plein*.[7] The practice continued into the 1760s and 1770s. In 1773, the year of the Museum's jug and basin, there was only one entry in the sales records listing plain turquoise pieces, when fourteen *gobelets à la Reine bleu céleste plein et filets dor* [plain turquoise cups *à la Reine* with gold fillets] without saucers were sold to the goldsmith Auguste for 18 *livres* each.[8] There were no recorded sales of a water jug and basin with this decoration.

The presence of three gilders' marks on the bottom of the Museum's jug is difficult to explain, as there does not seem to be enough gilded decoration to have occupied three artists. The only discernible difference between the gilding on the jug and the basin is in the tooling, which is slightly more detailed on the former.

TECHNIQUE AND CONDITION

The top of the jug is a later replacement, probably Minton bone china.[9] The gilt-bronze mount dates from the nineteenth century.

Exhibitions: *Morgan Loan Exhibition*, New York, 1914, not in catalogue; *French and English Art Treasures*, New York, 1942, no. 309; *Continental Table Porcelain*, San Francisco, 1965, no. 258

Literature: *French and English Art Treasures*, no. 309; *Continental Table Porcelain*, no. 258

161

NOTES

1 Gilder, active 1752–88. See Savill, 3, pp. 1020–21, Peters, *Marks*, p. 24.

2 Gilder and painter, active 1748–49, 1751–96. See Savill, 3, pp. 1045–47, Peters, *Marks*, p. 48.

3 Gilder and painter, active 1753–79. See Savill, 3, pp. 1072–73, Peters, *Marks*, p. 72.

4 Attributed by Dauterman (*Marks*, p. 208) to Joseph Martin *aîné*, *répareur* 1767–98.

5 APML, Duveen file, invoice 30 June 1904: "1 Old Sèvres soft paste Turquoise Ewer and Dish with gold decorations by Chauvaux and Le Guay (the cover is hard paste) in gilt wood vitrine," £1,850.

6 See cat. no. 159 for this model.

7 See for example a *gobelet à cuvier à cerceau* in the MAD, Paris (no. 6281), illustrated in Brunet and Préaud, p. 139, no. 49. See also AMNS, Vy 1, fols. 29, 39, 57, 64, 72v, 104v, 114, and 120v, for examples sold between 1753 and 1756. These include a wide range of objects such as cups and saucers, egg cups, water jugs, tea sets, and vases.

8 AMNS, Vy 5, fol. 121v.

9 This was known to Morgan at the time of the purchase, for it was clearly spelled out in the dealer's invoice.

162

Water jug and basin (*pot à la Romaine uni et jatte ovale*)

1917.1165–1166

Sèvres, 1775

Soft-paste porcelain, jug: H. 9¹⁄₁₆ × W. 6⁵⁄₁₆ × D. 4⁹⁄₁₆ in. (23 × 16 × 11.5 cm); basin: H. 2¹³⁄₁₆ × L. 14⁵⁄₁₆ × W. 10 in. (7.1 × 36.3 × 25.3 cm)

White ground with polychrome flowers, gilding

Marks: on both: interlaced Ls in blue with date letter X; jug: conjoined vd for Jean-Baptiste-Emmanuel Vandé;[1] basin: script b for Bertrand;[2] incised Lv[3]

Provenance: Cartier et Fils, Paris, 1902;[4] J. Pierpont Morgan

MODEL

This model of water jug and basin, known as a *pot à la Romaine et jatte ovale*, was first made by the factory in 1751.[5] Although their fluid shapes hark back to the 1750s and Jean-Claude Duplessis's rococo style, the model remained in production throughout the eighteenth century.[6] In the earlier years this type

162

Fig. 162-1 *Pot à la Romaine et jatte ovale,* Revolutionary period drawing

of set was often decorated in *bleu lapis* with gilding or polychrome birds.[7] Later examples often had a white ground decorated with either floral decoration or gilding, or had a blue ground decorated with gold.[8] We know from eight jugs and seven basins listed in the factory's inventory in 1774 that *pots à la Romaine et jattes ovale* were also made in hard-paste porcelain.[9] A Revolutionary-period drawing of this shape remains at the Sèvres factory, inscribed *trais fait dun pot a leau encienne forme du Cit. Duplessis pere* [outline drawing made of a water jug, old form, by Citizen Duplessis the elder] (fig. 162-1).[10]

COMMENTARY

The Museum's jug and basin are decorated with garlands of flowers and blue and yellow ribbons on a white ground. Surprisingly, the jug was painted by Vandé, while the basin was painted by Bertrand. This may have been the result of the death of Bertrand in January 1775,[11] probably right after he began decorating the ensemble. The Hartford jug and basin may have been one of six sets recorded in the sales ledgers in 1775, perhaps delivered either to the dealers Bazin or Poirier and Daguerre in the second half of that year. These sets were priced at 240 and 216 *livres* respectively.[12]

Other late examples of *pots à la romaine et jattes* are known today. There is an undated jug and basin set in the Musée des Arts décoratifs, Paris, decorated by Nicquet with beautiful garlands and bouquets of flowers on a white ground,[13] and another in the collection of the Earl of Mansfield at Scone Palace, Perthshire, Scotland.[14] Still another white-ground set dated 1783 painted with garlands and ribbons is in the Musée et Château, Boulogne-sur-Mer, France.[15] A set with a black ground and platinum and gold chinoiserie decoration in imitation of lacquer is in the collection of the Musée national de Céramique, Sèvres.[16]

Exhibition: *Morgan Loan Exhibition*, New York, 1914, not in catalogue

NOTES

1 Active as gilder and painter 1753–79. See Savill, 3, pp. 1072–73; Peters, *Marks*, p. 72.

2 Active as painter of flowers, 1757–75. See Savill, 3, p. 1001; Peters, *Marks*, p. 13.

3 See Dauterman, *Marks*, pp. 217–18, attributed to Pierre-Charles? Lauvergnat *jeune*, *cadet*, *oncle*, active 1754–75.

4 APML, Cartier file, invoice 23 April 1902: "1 Aiguière avec son plateau Sévres 1774, décors noeuds couronnes et guirlandes de fleurs sur fond blanc," 7,500 French francs.

5 See cat. no. 148 for this shape.

6 A set decorated with a *bleu céleste* ground and flowers was listed among old stock on 1 January 1774 valued at 360 *livres* (AMNS, I. 8, 1 January 1774). In the same inventory eight jugs and two basins were listed in the *magasin du blanc*, valued at 18 *livres* each.

7 See note 5 above.

8 A blue and gold set was sold to Versailles 22 December 1774 for 120 *livres* (AMNS, Vy 5, fol. 189v), and a white and gold set was sold to M. Gabriel 19 November 1774, also for 120 *livres* (ibid., fol. 177v).

9 AMNS, I. 8, 1 January 1774. The jugs were valued at 21 *livres* and the basins 15 *livres*.

10 AMNS, R. 1, L. 1, d. 17, fol. 23.

11 Savill, 3, p. 1001, see AMNS, Ob 1.

12 AMNS, Vy 6, fols. 51v and 63v. The other examples recorded were less costly, and probably were decorated more simply. See note 8 above.

13 MAD, Paris, no. GR 261.

14 No. 987.01–02, not dated, marked with three dots for Tandart and an unidentified gilders mark of NI. This jug is covered. I would like to thank Morag Norris for providing me with a photograph of this jug and basin and a transcription of the marks.

15 No. L. 451, attributed to Denis Levé. See *Nord-Pas-de-Calais*, p. 129, no. 102. See also a set dated 1780, decorated by Nicquet and Vincent, sold Drouot-Richelieu, Paris, 6 May 1994, lot 110, white ground, rose buds, cornflowers, and pansies.

16 MNC, Sèvres, no. 5.291, c. 1792, probably the one fired on 18 October 1792, gilding by Le Grand, AMNS, Vl'3, fol. 215v (kindly pointed out to the author by Tamara Préaud). See Pinot de Villechenon, p. 43, fig. 43.

163

Broth basin and stand (*écuelle ronde tournée et plateau ovale*)

1917.1126

Sèvres, 1780, with possible later decoration on the bowl

Soft-paste porcelain, basin: H. 4⅛ × w. 6⁄16 × D. 4⁹⁄16 in. (10.4 × 15.3 × 11.6 cm); stand: H. ¹³⁄16 × w. 7³⁄16 × D. 5⅝ in. (2 × 18.2 × 14.2 cm)

White ground with polychrome roundels, red, purple, and gold friezes, gilding

Marks: basin: interlaced Ls in blue and date letters CC, mark for André-Vincent Vielliard *père* below,[1] .... for Pierre-Théodore Buteux (Théodore);[2] incised WCC?;[3] stand: same painted marks; incised LL[4]

Provenance: possibly Cartier et Fils, Paris, 1902;[5] J. Pierpont Morgan

MODEL

The broth basin is probably a third-size *écuelle ronde tournée*, while the stand is closer to a fourth-size *plateau ovale*.[6]

COMMENTARY

The decoration of the *écuelle et plateau* with small landscape vignettes bordered by geometric friezes is typical of the later work of André-Vincent Vielliard.[7] In March 1780, an *ecuelle an[cienne] f[orme] 3g. paysage et bordure Vielliard Buteux* [old model of broth basin, third size, landscape and border, Vielliard Buteux] was fired in the kiln.[8] This probably describes the Museum's broth basin and stand. There is no entry in the artists' records that may definitively be linked to the Hartford set, but in January 1780 Vielliard is recorded as having painted one broth basin and stand of the third size with landscapes, gilding, and small borders.[9] There is a chance that this also refers to the Atheneum's broth basin.

The decorative frieze of zigzags, crescents, and dots was one of several borders favored by Vielliard in the 1780s. A white-ground cup and saucer now in the Musée national de Céramique, Sèvres, was also decorated by Vielliard, here with landscapes commemorating the first hot-air balloon ascent of 1784 but with a slightly different geometric frieze.[10] Although the factory's records sometimes used the terms *bordure de Vielliard* and *frize de Vielliard* to describe work done by other painters,[11] we cannot be sure if these terms were used for all of Vielliard's geometric borders or only for a specific kidney-shaped design found on some late services.[12]

TECHNIQUE AND CONDITION

The bowl may have been redecorated to match an existing cover and stand. There is some bubbling of the glaze on the bottom of the bowl, as well as dark bubbling around much of its exterior rim. The painting and gilding of the bowl are much more

precise and carefully executed than that of the cover and stand. The gilding around the reserves of the bowl has a scratch-like tooled pattern that does not exist on the cover and stand.

Exhibition: *Morgan Loan Exhibition*, New York, 1914, not in catalogue

Literature: Chavagnac, pp. 136–37, no. 172; Savill, 2, p. 663 n. 33z; p. 666 n. 112t

NOTES

1 Active 1752–90. See Savill, 3, pp. 1074–75; Peters, *Marks*, p. 73.

2 See Peters, *Marks*, p. 19. P. T. Buteux, known as Théodore (probably to distinguish himself in the factory records from other members of the Buteux family of painters), was active at Sèvres 1765–84 as a painter and a gilder. Earlier works on Sèvres marks (Brunet and Préaud, p. 381) list this artist under Théodore and give his dates as 1765–71, 1772–79.

3 See Dauterman, *Marks*, p. 241, who cites this broth basin but gives no other examples. It is difficult to say with certainty that the marks should actually be read as WCC.

4 Ibid., pp. 105, 215–16, noted on pieces dated 1745–79 but postulated for the *répareur* Laurent or Louis Longuet *père*, active 1769–1800.

5 APML, Cartier file, invoice 24 April 1902: "1 Bouillon avec plateau en Sèvres 1779 décor genre Saxe à medaillon," 4,000 French francs.

6 See Savill, 2, pp. 643, 648. She states that the third-size bowl is H. 4⅕₆–4⅝ × w. 6⅕₆–6¾ in. (11–11.8 × 15.4–17.2 cm), making the Hartford bowl slightly shorter and less wide. The fourth-size stand is described as ranging in length from 7⅕₆ to 7⅛ in. (17.9 to 18.1 cm).

7 Savill, 3, p. 1074.

8 AMNS, VI'1, fol. 100v, 20 March 1780.

9 Ibid., Vj'1, fol. 276, *1 Ecuelle et plateau 3e gre paysage Doré/ et Petite Bordure*.

10 MNC, Sèvres, no. 24557.

11 De Bellaigue, "Sèvres," p. 192.

12 This is according to David Peters. He points to a plate mistakenly attributed to Vincennes in the 1977 exhibition (*Vincennes*, p. 32, no. 40, MNC, Sèvres, no. 8988). Savill, 2, p. 567, suggests that the arabesque frieze underneath small landscapes on a milk jug in the Wallace Collection may have been the *frize de Vielliard* described in the records.

164

Broth basin and stand (*écuelle et plateau nouvelle forme*)

1917.1112

Sèvres, 1784

Soft-paste porcelain, basin: H. 5 × w. 7⅜ × D. 6 in. (12.7 × 18.7 × 15.2 cm); stand: H. 1⅞ × w. 9⅞ × D. 9⅛ in. (4.7 × 25 × 23.2 cm)
Bleu nouveau ground, polychrome figures, gilding

Marks: on both: interlaced Ls in blue with date letters GG; five-pointed star above for Antoine Caton;[1] on basin: incised 13 and 45;[2] on stand: LG in gold under factory mark for Étienne-Henry Le Guay;[3] incised 13 and 15[4]

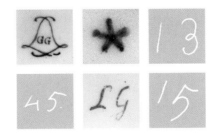

Provenance: J. Pierpont Morgan

MODEL

Factory documents referred to this broth basin and stand as *écuelle nouvelle forme et plateau*. They were made in both soft and hard paste.[5] The basin, characterized by its simple ear-shaped handles and shallow, domed cover, was an updated design of the standard round broth basin that had been produced by the factory since 1753.[6] A second updated design was also made in the 1770s, and was marked by reed handles and a cover with a broad ribbed edge and domed center. One or both

164

164

of the new basins were in production by 1773, when the factory inventory listed three *écuelles nouvelles à Rubans* and two *unies*, in the *magasin de porcelaine dure*, valued at 21 and 18 *livres* respectively.[7] There were probably six variations of round stands paired with the new basins, each distinguished by a different handle design.[8] These variations were seldom specified in the documents. Two sizes of *écuelles et plateaux nouvelles formes* were recorded, but specific versions of basin and stand were not identified.[9]

The first documented sale of an *écuelle et plateau nouvelle forme* was in 1773, although few were recorded in that year.[10] Madame du Barry, Louis XV's mistress, was among the early buyers: on 6 April she purchased a set of the first size decorated with *frize dor tres riche* for 192 *livres*.[11] In December 1773 Louis XV bought one, decoration unknown, for 144 *livres*. It probably was either of the first size with flowers or, more likely, of the second size with gold friezes.[12] First-size basins and stands with garlands of flowers on white ground were priced at 216 *livres*, while a set with garlands on a blue ground cost 240 *livres*.[13] A blue-ground set of the first size, decoration not described, sold in 1774 for 360 *livres*, and another with blue ground and children, probably of the first size, was priced at 480 *livres*.[14] Second-size sets cost 168 *livres* with garlands and trophies, 192 *livres* with birds, and probably 192 *livres* with blue ground and garlands.[15] An unspecified example of the second size, probably decorated with flowers, cost 144 *livres*.[16] Finally, an example, probably of

the first size, decorated with a textile pattern (*étoffe*), was priced at 264 *livres*.[17]

The Hartford basin is paired with a stand adorned with ribbon handles tied at the center with small bows. Several other kindred basins and stands are known. A set dated 1780 and decorated with bouquet-filled ovals and lozenges is now in the Museum of Fine Arts, Boston.[18] Another set, with an *écuelle ronde tournée* but a stand of the new shape, is in the Detroit Institute of Arts.[19] Others have been on the art market in recent years, including one dated 1778 and paired with an earlier-style basin, another dated around 1800, and a stand without its basin dated 1782.[20]

COMMENTARY

The Museum's basin and stand are of the first size, and were painted by Antoine Caton. In July 1784 he received for decoration an *écuelle nouvelle forme 1e g beau bleu mignature* [basin of the new form, first size, blue ground, figural scene] and a *couvercle en plus pour celui perdu au 1er feu mignature* [an additional cover to replace the one lost in the first firing, figural scene].[21] A basin and stand with a blue ground and figures decorated by Caton and Cornaille were recorded in the enamel kiln on 27 December 1784. Although the gilder is listed as Cornaille rather than Le Guay, this still may refer to the Museum's set.[22] In April of the following year, a first-size broth basin of the new shape with figural scenes by Caton against a blue ground was refired.[23] This also may have been the Museum's set.

It has been possible to identify the sources for four of the six scenes painted on Hartford's set. One of the basin's reserves reproduces *The Joys of Summer*, engraved by Pierre-Étienne Moitte after a painting by François Boucher of about 1770 (fig. 164-1).[24] The second reserve shows a satyr and a sleeping woman, identifiable as *Jupiter and Antiope* from a painting by Carle Vanloo as engraved by Étienne Fessard (fig. 164-2).[25] Vanloo's original painting was commissioned by the marquis de Marigny in 1752 for his *cabinet de Nudités*. It was still in his collection in 1782, and is now in the Hermitage Museum, St. Petersburg.[26] The engraving was in the factory's collection, and the composition was used repeatedly by Sèvres figure painters. The same scene may be found on a *vase ballon* from the early 1770s, formerly in the James de Rothschild Collection; on a *vase à col cylindrique* of about 1775 in the Wallace Collection; on a stand for an *écuelle* in the Musée des Arts décoratifs, Paris; and on a *compotier ovale*, part of Louis XVI's dinner and dessert service of 1783–93, now in the Royal Collection, England.[27] The

Fig. 164-2 *Jupiter et Antiope*, Étienne Fessard after Carle Vanloo

Sèvres factory also used the same engraving as inspiration for a biscuit sculpture of 1760 attributed to Étienne-Maurice Falconet.[28]

The two reserves on the Museum's stand were based on engravings by Charles-Emmanuel Patas after illustrations by Charles Monnet for Fénelons's *The Adventures of Telemachus*.[29] One scene depicts Venus bringing Cupid to the help of Calypso (fig. 164-3). It can be found repeated on a shell-shaped fruit dish from the Louis XVI service.[30] The second scene represents Telemachus recounting his adventures to Calypso (fig. 164-4). This composition also appears on this same fruit dish from Louis XVI's service.[31]

The Hartford *écuelle et plateau* must look very much like those intended for the Louis XVI service but never completed. These were to cost 720 *livres* each, which may approximate the cost of the Hartford basin and stand.[32]

Exhibitions: *Morgan Loan Exhibition*, New York, 1914, not in catalogue; *Morgan*, Hartford, no. 75

Literature: Chavagnac, p. 139, no. 175; de Bellaigue, "Sèvres," pp. 188–89, no. 75; Savill, 3, p. 1016 n. 1; Munger, *Wickes*, p. 204 n. 4; Le Corbeiller, *Dodge*, p. 175

NOTES

1 Figure painter, active 1749–97. See Savill, 3, pp. 1015–17 and Peters, *Marks*, p. 22.

2 See Savill, 3, p. 1132 for 45, found on soft paste 1767–88.

3 Active as gilder, burnisher and painter, 1742–43, 1748–49, 1751–96 (Savill, 3, pp. 1045–47). See also Peters, *Marks*, p. 48.

4 Savill, 3, pp. 1125–26, found on soft paste 1753–90s.

5 For a complete discussion of this shape of broth basin see Savill, 2, pp. 646–66. Savill also briefly discusses the specific form of stand represented by the Museum's example. See also de Bellaigue, "Sèvres," p. 189, no. 75; Munger, *Wickes*, pp. 200–1, 204; and Le Corbeiller, *Dodge*, pp. 172–75. From 1773, the earlier model of broth basin was referred to as *ancienne forme*.

Fig. 164-1 *Les Douceurs de l'été*, Pierre-Étienne Moitte after François Boucher

Fig. 164-3 *Vénus amène Cupidon au secours de Calipso*, Charles-Emmanuel Patas after Charles Monnet

Fig. 164-4 *Télémaque raconte ses avantures à Calipso*, Charles-Emmanuel Patas after Charles Monnet

6 See cat. no. 156 for this form.

7 AMNS, I. 7, 1 January 1774 (for 1773). See Savill, 2, pp. 646, 665 n. 84. According to Tamara Préaud, the Museum's version was sometimes called *à grenade* because of its pomegranate knob.

8 Savill, 2, p. 647 describes these variations, which include reed-like handles, branch-like handles, scrolling acanthus leaf handles, ribbon bows, foliage, or palm frond handles. See Savill, 2, pp. 664–65 n. 83 for examples of each style. Their approximate sizes are: first size: DIAM. 10¾–11⅛ in. (27.3–28.3 cm); second size: DIAM. 9⅝ in. (24.4 cm).

9 See AMNS, Vy 5, fol. 135v, 6 April 1773, first size; fol. 160v, 12 July 1774, second size. Savill, 2, p. 646 lists two sizes: first size: H. 4¹⁵⁄₁₆–5 × w. 7⁵⁄₁₆–7¹¹⁄₁₆ in. (12.5–12.7 × 18.3–19.5 cm); second size: H. 4¼–4⅝ × w.6⁵⁄₁₆–7⅛ in. (10.8–11.7 × 16–18.1 cm). These must refer specifically to the version with reed handles. The present author does not have enough full measurements of the version with ear-shaped handles to delineate their sizes. An example in the MFA, Boston, no. 1982.212a–b measures H. 5⅛ in.

(13 cm), which evidently is of the first size (see Eriksen and Bellaigue, pp. 342–43, no. 150).

10 AMNS, Vy 5, fol. 60, 8 January 1773, damaged hard-paste basin and stand, 27 *livres*, comte de Lowendal (Savill, pp. 647, 665 n. 89), differentiated from the earlier model which is listed as well, described as *ancienne forme*. Savill logically notes that they must have been in production by 1772 for there to have been a damaged version in the sales room by early January 1773.

11 AMNS, Vy 5, fol. 135v.

12 Ibid., fol. 133v, 23 December 1773. Compare with 1 *Ecuelle et Platteau nouvelle forme 2e frize d'or* for 144 *livres* to the duc d'Orléans (fol. 160v, 12 July 1774).

13 Ibid., fol. 165v, 22 August 1774, duchesse de Beaufort; fol. 173v, 22 October 1774, marquise de ….

14 Ibid., fol. 197, 14 December 1774, marquis de Nesle; fol. 175v, 29 October 1774, abbé de Brétheüil.

15 Ibid., fol. 171, 7 October 1774, M. Beauvais for Mr. Morgan of London; fol. 189v, 22 December 1774, to Versailles.

16 Ibid., fol. 190, 23 December 1774, to Versailles.

17 Ibid., fol. 192, 24 December 1774, to Versailles.

18 No. 65.1810. See Munger, *Wickes*, p. 204, no. 152.

19 Le Corbeiller, *Dodge*, pp. 172–75. See also a hard-paste example of 1780, with birds, in the MNC, Sèvres, no. 22 761 (illustrated in *Sèvres*, Japan, no. 28, and one of 1782 with dark blue ground and vases in landscapes (Museo Duca di Martina, Naples, Italy, in Casanova, p. 239, no. 165).

20 Drouot, Paris, 2 April 1976, lot 33; Christie's, New York, 21 May 1997, lot 78. See also Van Slyke sale, Sotheby's, New York, 26 September 1986, lot 319; Harewood sale, Christie's, London, 1 July 1965, lot 35; Christie's, Monaco, 16 June 1990, lot 82; Drouot, Paris, 8 December 1995, lot 138; Christie's, New York, 21 May 1997, lot 78; Christie's, New York, 27 May 1999, lot 151; Sotheby's, New York, 12 November 1999, lot 93.

21 AMNS, Vj'3, fol. 66, 6 July 1784. The original cover must have broken in the first firing. See de Bellaigue, "Sèvres," p. 189.

22 AMNS, Vl'2, fol. 125. See de Bellaigue, "Sèvres," p. 189 n. 5, who remarks that other inaccuracies have appeared in this register suggesting that this apparent conflict in evidence may not be terribly significant.

23 AMNS, Vl'2, fol. 136, 25 April 1785, *écuelle ne forme 1e g beau bleu mignature repassage Caton.*

24 Jean-Richard, p. 345, no. 1431. See de Bellaigue, "Sèvres," p. 189.

25 Announced in the *Mercure de France* in January 1759 (de Bellaigue, "Sèvres," p. 189).

26 Savill, 1, p. 309 n. 28.

27 Sold Palais Galliéra, Paris, 1 December 1966, lot 33, illustrated in Brunet and Préaud, p. 187, no. 190; Wallace Collection, London, no. C294 (Savill, 1, pp. 305–7); MAD, Paris, no. D.36922; de Bellaigue, *Louis XVI*, p. 134, no. 50.

28 See Brunet and Préaud, p. 230, no. 314, illustrating the plaster model for the group now in the AMNS.

29 Published between 1776 and 1782. See de Bellaigue, "Sèvres," p. 189 n. 6.

30 De Bellaigue, *Louis XVI*, p. 200, no. 125 (2).

31 Ibid., pp. 200–1, no. 125 (4).

32 It is only possible to approximate their appearance, for the specific handle style of the Louis XVI sets is not known. Their gilding would have been slightly more elaborate than that on the Hartford example, which may have impacted the price as well.

165

Broth basin and stand (*écuelle ronde tournée et plateau*)

1917.1113

Sèvres, 1785

Soft-paste porcelain, basin: H. 3⁵⁄₁₆ × w. 4¹³⁄₁₆ × D. 3¹¹⁄₁₆ in. (8.4 × 12.2 × 9.4 cm); stand: H. 1⁵⁄₁₆ × w. 6¾ × D. 6¼ in. (3.3 × 17.2 × 15.8 cm)

White ground with blue, purple, and gilded borders, purple roundels, polychrome garlands and flowers

Marks: on both: interlaced Ls in blue with date letters H·H below; stippled crown above for Jean-Charles Sioux *aîné*;[1] on basin: BD in script for François Baudouin *père*;[2] incised 45;[3] stand: incised 45 and 15;[4] inside cover in unfired black paint, etao and 9469

Provenance: probably Edouard Chappey, Paris, 1906;[5] J. Pierpont Morgan

MODEL

The broth basin is probably an example of a fourth-size *écuelle ronde tournée*, a model of the 1750s.[6] The stand, however, may be one of several new forms introduced around 1773, although it is significantly smaller than most documented examples.[7] Another example of this *écuelle*, with a double branch handle on the lid, was sold in Monaco in 1987.[8]

COMMENTARY

The decoration of the Museum's *écuelle et plateau* is by Sioux *aîné* and the gilder Baudouin. According to the artists' records, Sioux was given two basins and stands of the fourth size on 7 November 1785, which he was to paint with garlands and roses.[9] This could refer to the Hartford basin and stand, although there is no mention of the landscapes. On the other hand, Sioux may have painted this set earlier, for on 6 May 1785 a fourth-size broth basin and stand decorated by Sioux and Baudouin was listed in the enamel kiln books.[10] This is the only record of an *écuelle et plateau* of this size by these two artists to have been fired in 1785 or 1786.

TECHNIQUE AND CONDITION

The basin is extensively marked with black speckles, or *végétations salines*.[11] There are traces of blue enamel bands defining the blue zigzag and gold laurel borders above the foot of the basin and around the well of the stand, as well as under the rest of the gilded decoration. These suggest that the painter sketched in the design of the main borders with a thin wash of blue before they were painted and gilded. The gilding on both the basin and the stand is dull and grainy.

The cover is a replacement, perhaps made from an earlier cover as suggested by the flower knob, which had long gone out of fashion by 1785.[12] It does not fit precisely, and has been made of a whiter paste than the basin and stand, the latter having a slightly pink cast. Moreover, there are no traces of blue underneath the gilding, and the gilding itself is brighter and smoother. Furthermore, the green and mauve enamels are not the same as on the other two pieces, and the roses are much more

neatly drawn. The painter of the cover has more or less copied the two landscape roundels from the basin, which would have been unlikely if the cover were original. Finally, there is significant speckling inside the rim, suggesting it was refired.

Exhibition: *Morgan Loan Exhibition*, New York, 1914, not in catalogue

Literature: Chavagnac, pp. 142–43, no. 178

NOTES

1 See cat. no. 106 for this artist.

2 Peters, *Marks*, p. 12, active as gilder 1750–1800.

3 Savill, 3, p. 1132, found on soft paste 1767–88.

4 15 is not in Savill.

5 APML, Chappey file, invoice 30 April 1906: "1 Pot Bouilon décor de roses fd blanc paysge camaïeu mauve bord mauve, bleu et or," 3,750 French francs.

6 For this shape see cat. no. 156.

7 See cat. no. 164. The stand under discussion does not seem to conform to any of the new *plateaux* described by Savill (2, pp. 647, 664–65 n. 83).

8 Christie's, Monaco, 7 December 1987, lot 226, width of tray 6¹¹⁄₁₆ in. (17 cm). It is dated 1780, confirming that the model was in production at least by that date. This is the only example of a comparable basin and stand known to the author.

9 AMNS, Vj'3, fol. 240v, 7 November 1785.

10 Ibid., Vl'2, fol. 139.

11 Préaud and d'Albis, p. 232. See glossary.

12 It probably would have had a double branch handle on the lid. The cover does not appear to be an earlier sugar bowl cover, however, which would have been more domed than this one. It seems to have the same profile as later sugar bowl covers, but is just slightly too small compared with existing examples.

166

Broth basin and stand (*écuelle ronde tournée et plateau ovale*)

1917.1121

Sèvres, 1787

Soft-paste porcelain, basin: H. 3¼ (without knob) × W. 5 × D. 3¹⁵⁄₁₆ in. (8.2 × 12.6 × 10 cm); stand: H. 1⅜ × L. 7⅛ × W. 5⁹⁄₁₆ in. (3.5 × 18.1 × 14.1 cm)

Yellow ground with green, brown, and blue diaper and foliate decoration, white border with green and blue garlands, gilding

Marks: on both: interlaced Ls in blue with date letters KK, flanked by L and R for Jeanne-Joséphine Roguier, *née* Le Riche;[1] incised 29 and 27 on cup;[2] incised 34 on stand;[3] shadow of 30 # under stand, perhaps indicating a price

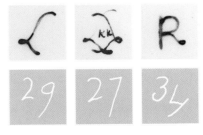

Provenance: J. Pierpont Morgan

MODEL

The basin is an example of the fourth-size *écuelle ronde tournée*. The stand is a fourth-size *plateau ovale*.[4]

COMMENTARY

The Museum's broth basin and stand were decorated by Madame Roguier, who seems to have been paid piecework in 1786 and 1787. There are no references in the kiln records for 1787 that correspond to the Hartford set, but in December of that year Madame Roguier was paid 21 *livres* for decorating an unspecified broth basin with friezes.[5]

TECHNIQUE AND CONDITION

The broth basin and stand show some signs of *végétations salines*. The lid is a later replacement, and not Sèvres porcelain. A quarter section of the cover is missing, as is the handle.

Exhibition: *Morgan Loan Exhibition*, New York, 1914, not in catalogue

Literature: Chavagnac, p. 147, no. 187; Savill, 2, pp. 1039, 1040 n. 1 (as possibly by La Roche)

NOTES

1 See Peters, *Marks*, p. 65. She was active 1782–93, painting flowers and patterns.
2 For 29 see Savill, 3, p. 1129, found on soft paste 1782–90s.
3 Ibid., found on soft paste 1781–92.
4 See cat. no. 156. See also cat. no. 165 for another basin of this size.
5 AMNS, F.29, 6 December 1787.

167

Water jug (*pot à eau tourné*)

1917.1133

Sèvres, 1788

Soft-paste porcelain, silver mounts, h. (with hinge) 8³⁄₁₆ and h. (without hinge) 7⁷⁄₁₆ × w. 5¾ × D. 4⅝ in. (20.8/18.9 × 14.6 × 11.8 cm)

Pale yellow ground with polychrome landscape and arabesque decoration directly on the ground color, blue border with polychrome flowers, gilding

Marks: interlaced Ls in blue, date letters LL to left; Y to right for Edmé-François Bouillat *père*;[1] 2000 in gold for Henry-François Vincent *jeune, père*;[2] incised 45 and 5;[3] yellow dot

Provenance: J. Pierpont Morgan

MODEL

This water jug is an example of Sèvres' most common model, produced from at least 1752.[4] It is of the second largest of four sizes made, and would have been accompanied by a round or oval basin.

COMMENTARY

The decoration was executed by Edmé-François Bouillat, who specialized in flower painting. In the late 1770s and early 1780s he and Pierre-Joseph Rosset painted numerous garden landscapes populated with antique follies and lush flowers, often on the backs of vases.[5] Bouillat frequently included large stands of hollyhocks in these settings. We see this on the Museum's jug as well as on the back of a *vase Paris* in the Wallace Collection.[6]

The garden landscape on the Hartford jug is filled with ruins, pavilions, and other architectural follies of the type found in real garden landscapes in the late eighteenth century. The pyramid depicted has Masonic emblems decorating its front, and may be linked to a similar structure in the duc de Chartres's Parc Monceau, erected in 1773 and illustrated by Louis Carrogis (called Carmontelle) in a 1779 publication on the gardens.[7] The other structures have yet to be identified, but probably derive from engravings or even watercolors of the period. The pastel palette used by Bouillat reinforces the notion that he may have been looking at a group of watercolors illustrating contemporary gardens.

Bouillat painted the same genre of garden landscape—complete with hollyhocks and architectural follies—on other wares, among them a tea set of 1787.[8] Its tray features a similar Masonic pyramid with a vase on top, and the milk jug shows a

167

167

domed building recalling the one on the Hartford jug. The cup features a stand of hollyhocks. A *plateau Hebert* with a *bleu nouveau* ground, dated 1788 and decorated by Bouillat and Philippine, shows the same pyramid with a vase on top, minus its flame, set in a pastel landscape with flowering shrubs.[9] Two turtledoves are also depicted, although they differ from the pair of doves on the Museum's jug. The presence of the same pyramid on this tray and on the Hartford jug confirms the existence of a common source.

Bouillat is known to have painted arabesques beginning in 1785, allowing us to believe that, in addition to the landscapes, he may have painted the arabesque designs on the Atheneum's *pot à eau*.[10]

TECHNIQUE AND CONDITION

The blue rim is probably an enamel color applied like a ground color. The yellow is either *jaune paille*, *jaune jonquille*, or *jaune citron*. The surface of the jug is matte, indicating that the glaze has devitrified in the firing.

Exhibition: *Morgan Loan Exhibition*, New York, 1914, not in catalogue

Literature: Chavagnac, pp. 153–54, no. 197

NOTES

1 Active 1758–1810. See Savill, 3, pp. 1002–4; Peters, *Marks*, p. 16.

2 Active 1753–1800. See Savill, 3, pp. 1076–77; Peters, *Marks*, p. 74.

3 The number 45 is found on soft paste 1767–88 (see Savill, 3, p. 1132); 5 is found on soft paste by 1753 and until the 1790s (ibid., p. 1127).

4 For this form see cat. no. 159.

5 Examples include a *vase ferré*, c. 1779, a *vase à ruban*, c. 1780, and a *vase à panneaux*, c. 1779–82, in the Royal Collection, England (Laking, p. 88, no. 123; p. 117, no. 188; p. 11, no. 176, information kindly provided by Sir Geoffrey de Bellaigue); garniture of one *vase momie à ornements* and two *vases marmites*, 1779, Walters Art Gallery, Baltimore (Brunet and Préaud, p. 199, nos. 225–26, unattributed); garniture of three *vases E de 1780*, 1781, Wallace Collection, London (nos. C334–36, Savill, 1, pp. 453–62, possibly by Bouillat); pair of *vases C de 1780*, 1781, British Museum, London (nos. 1935, 12-18, 1-2, Dawson, *British Museum*, pp. 149–52, possibly by Bouillat); garniture of three *vases C de 1780*, 1781, Huntington Library and Art Collections, San Marino, California (nos. 27.34-6, Wark, *Huntington*, p. 110, fig. 106, Bouillat).

6 Attributed to Bouillat, no. C330, see Savill, 1, pp. 438–46.

7 See Carrogis (Carmontelle), *Wood of Tombs* (Wiebenson, fig. 97). The flame on the top of the pyramid on the Museum's jug is not found on the Monceau pyramid. For Masonic imagery and the French garden see Olausson, passim.

8 Christie's, London, 1 December 1980, lot 1 (see Savill, 1, p. 461 n. 19).

9 Galerie de Chartres, Chartres, France, 21 November 1999, lot 31, decorated by Bouillat.

10 Savill, 3, p. 1003.

167

168

Bather (*La Baigneuse*)

1917.952

Vincennes, c. 1748–1752

Soft-paste porcelain, H. 4⅛ × L. 8⅟₁₆ × W. 4⁵⁄₁₆ in. (10.4 × 20.5 × 11 cm)

Glazed

Marks: none

Provenance: J. Pierpont Morgan

Model

It is not clear when the model for *La Baigneuse* was introduced at Vincennes but it was probably sometime between 1747 and 1748. Traditionally, the sculptor Fournier has been cited as the designer of the model, for in 1747 he was paid 202 *livres* for three sculptures, one of them a *Naïade*, and for repairing and finishing three River Gods and three *Nayades*.[1] More recent literature proposes that the author of the model was Jean-Joseph de Pierreux (Depierreux) who had been hired by the factory in August 1746 and created many figural groups, among them *Leda and the Swan* and six figures of gods.[2] *La Baigneuse* has been compared stylistically to the *Leda*, as well as to a figure

of a sleeping woman (*La Dormeuse*, catalogue no. 169), the *Enfants des Arts* groups, and a *Vénus accroupie* [Crouching Venus].[3]

The figure of the bather was also used at Vincennes as the model for a river goddess or *naïade*. In this group she is partially draped, her arm leaning on an urn, while resting on a bed of rock and coral.[4] Both the bather and the river goddess figure relate to a preparatory drawing of Venus by François Boucher for his composition entitled *Venus and Cupid*.[5]

Like the Museum's bather, most figural groups at Vincennes were left white. However, some of the earliest examples were decorated in enamel colors, in the manner of Meissen porcelain figures.[6]

The factory inventory of 8 October 1752 lists thirty-seven *baigneuses* in the *magasin de ventes* valued at 15 *livres* each.[7] By this period, biscuit figures were beginning to supplant glazed figures in factory production, and therefore, subsequent sales were infrequent. Four *Baigneuses* were sold in 1754 for 27 *livres*,[8] and five more were sold between 1757 and 1765.[9] It is possible that Madame de Pompadour may have had one of these bathers in her collection, for in the inventory of her goods after her death in 1764 there were "deux figures couchées, de porcelaine blanche, sur leur terreau de bronze doré" [two recumbent figures in white porcelain on their gilt-bronze stands].[10]

168

FUNCTION

La Baigneuse, along with the figure known as *La Dormeuse* (catalogue no. 169), were among the many early figures produced by the factory either singly or in pairs, primarily to serve as decoration on furniture or mantelpieces. Sometimes they featured as a part of gilt-bronze clocks or candelabra that were then embellished with Vincennes flowers.[11]

TECHNIQUE AND CONDITION

In this early period, figural groups were either entirely sculpted, or partially press-molded and then finished by sculpting. This is proven both by surviving examples and by factory documents. The sculpture workshop was described as "composé des ouvriers qui jettent en moule les pièces de porcelaine en figures humaines et animalles, et qui les perfectionnent ou même qui les font au ciseau sans moule [made up of workers who molded the pieces of porcelain into human and animal figures, and who finished them or even sculpted them without molds]."[12] *Perfectionner* in this case meant adding accessories as well as smoothing out the mold seams. Both methods of creating figures would result in noticeable differences in details, and sometimes even in dimensions, between various examples of the model. Surviving examples of *La Baigneuse* betray these differences—heads are modeled and placed differently, arms are in different positions, and the rocky formations vary.[13]

Exhibitions: *Morgan Loan Exhibition*, New York, 1914, not in catalogue; *French and English Art Treasures*, New York, 1942, no. 313; *European Porcelain*, New York, 1949, no. 158

Literature: Chavagnac, p. 40, no. 46, pl. XXI; *French and English Art Treasures*, no. 313; *European Porcelain*, no. 158; Buckley, *Connoisseur*, p. 48, fig. 1; *Vincennes*, p. 152

NOTES

1 AMNS, Vf 1, fols. 25v, 26, 27v, 28v. This probably was Louis-Antoine Fournier. See Préaud, "Biscuit," pp. 31, 36 n. 15. See also Eriksen and Bellaigue, pp. 194–95, nos. 5–6 (citing Chavagnac and Grollier, p. 261). Eriksen (Eriksen and Bellaigue, p. 64) acknowledges that there are several figures that may have been called *nayade* for which Fournier could have supplied or reworked the model.

2 Préaud and d'Albis, p. 144, no. 94.

3 Ibid.

4 See *Vincennes*, p. 152, nos. 456–57, where the figure is also called a *baigneuse* and is considered a variant of the Museum's model. See also Eriksen and Bellaigue, p. 200, no. 12.

5 Signed and dated 1742, sold 7 June 1928 (place and date not cited), reproduced in Ananoff, *Boucher*, 1, p. 366, no. 250/3, fig. 753. See *Vincennes*, p. 152. The painting was sold 19 May 1828, no. 69, Pierre-Hippolyte Lemoyne sale (see Ananoff, *Boucher*, 1, p. 366, no. 250). Boucher had painted an earlier *Venus and Cupid* in 1735, but had oriented the figures in the opposite sense of the 1742 composition (ibid., pp. 247–48, no. 122). Boucher reused the figure, in reverse, in his *Jupiter and Callisto* of 1759 (ibid., 2, pp. 188–90, no. 518). Yet another similar figure appears in an engraving by Jean-Charles Le Vasseur after Boucher entitled *Vénus sur les eaux* (Jean-Richard, p. 334, no. 1391). Differences in this figure's arms and legs indicate that it did not serve as a model for the Vincennes sculpture.

6 See Brunet and Préaud, p. 226, no. 303. At this early date Vincennes had a limited palette of soft-paste colors to work with, unlike the rich hard-paste palette of the Meissen factory. By 1748 this situation had changed and Vincennes could boast a palette of over thirty-three colors. See Préaud and d'Albis, pp. 81, 134, no. 65.

7 AMNS, I. 7.

8 Ibid., Vy 1, fols. 50v (4 September 1754, unnamed buyer) and 54v (27 November 1754, Gaudin). See *Vincennes*, pp. 152, 153 n. 1.

9 See *Vincennes*, p. 152.

10 Cordey, p. 41, no. 394.

11 See Préaud, "Biscuit," p. 31.

12 Ibid., citing *Délibération de la société des actionnaires propriétaires de la manufacture,* 8 March 1747, *instructions pour la tenue des registres* .... This register was published in Sergène, vol. 3.

13 See for example, a polychrome figure, Louvre, Paris, OA 7240 (*Vincennes*, p. 152, no. 454); London, V&A, C 360-1909 (ibid., no. 455); private collection, Paris (ibid., no. 455 *bis*); Gilbert Lévy sale, Drouot, Paris, 23 November 1967, lot 132; Christie's, London, 29 October 1973, lot 163; Palais Galliéra, Paris, 29–30 November 1976, lot 128; Sotheby's, Geneva, 10 May 1988, lot 108; Drouot-Richelieu, Paris, 6 May 1994, lot 87.

169

Sleeping woman (*La Dormeuse*)

1917.953

Vincennes, c. 1747–1752

Soft-paste porcelain, H. 5⁵⁄₁₆ × L. 8⁷⁄₈ × w. 5 in. (14.1 × 22.5 × 12.7 cm)

Glazed

Marks: none

Provenance: J. Pierpont Morgan

MODEL

The model for this sleeping woman probably was created at the same time as that of *La Baigneuse* (catalogue no. 168), with which it may sometimes have been paired. Like *La Baigneuse*, it was probably designed by Jean-Joseph de Pierreux around 1747.[1] There were two primary versions of the model. One was modeled with the head of the woman resting on a bed of foliage—as in the Atheneum's example—while the other depicted the woman resting her head on a large round pillow.[2] Some examples were decorated with colors, while many others were left white.[3] Some, like the Atheneum's *Dormeuse*, featured a carefully draped garland of flowers or leaves, cleverly creating a less-revealing image while at the same time masking prominent firing cracks.

The factory made another sculpture of a sleeping woman that may also have been called *Dormeuse*. This model is of a woman lying on a bed of plants or moss. She assumes a different position than the other *Dormeuse*, and at least once is shown with a bow and quiver, perhaps identifying her as Diana.[4]

The first mention of a *Dormeuse* occurs not in the factory records but in the account book of Lazare Duvaux. On 24 April 1749 Monsieur de Villaumont purchased "une terrasse baroque en bronze doré d'or moulu, garnie de branchages de fleurs de Vincennes, pour une dormeuse" [a baroque gilt-bronze terrace, garnished with branches of Vincennes flowers, for a Sleeping Woman], for 175 *livres*."[5] This may refer to the Museum's model. The first surviving factory documentation of *Dormeuses* is in the inventory of 8 October 1752, when twenty-eight examples valued at 15 *livres* each were listed in the *magasin de*

169

vente.[6] Another twelve figures were in the *magasin de rebuts*, in white, valued at 4 *livres* each.[7] Fifteen *dormeuses de Baillon*, also at 15 *livres*, are listed.[8] Nothing is known of this model.[9] The records show few *Dormeuses* being sold by 1752.[10] Two were purchased by an unnamed buyer in August 1753 for 27 *livres* each, three were sold to Monsieur Verdun in June 1753 for 15 *livres*, and one defective example was sold to an unnamed buyer in February 1758 for 6 *livres*.[11] The figures priced at 27 *livres* may either have been painted versions or different models altogether—simply being sold under the same name.

There is an engraving still in the Sèvres factory archives that relates to the Museum's figure, although the position of the torso differs. Entitled *Les Amusements de Cythere*, it depicts a semi-nude figure with her hand above her head in the same pose as the Hartford *Dormeuse*.[12]

Exhibitions: *Morgan Loan Exhibition*, New York, 1914, not in catalogue; *French and English Art Treasures*, New York, 1942, no. 313

Literature: Chavagnac, p. 40, no. 47; *French and English Art Treasures*, no. 313; *Vincennes*, p. 160

NOTES

1 For *La Baigneuse* see cat. no 168. See also Préaud and d'Albis, p. 144, nos. 94–95.

2 According to Tamara Préaud, there is a second version of the Museum's model, with her head and feet reversed, head on the left and feet on the right (in the exhibition *Vincennes, Les Origines de Sèvres* but not published).

3 An example in the Louvre, Paris (OA 7239, illustrated Préaud and d'Albis, no. 95) is covered with a tin glaze and then enameled. The tin glaze probably was used to mask problems of devitrification (ibid.). Another polychrome example is illustrated in *Vincennes*, p. 160, no. 473 (private collection, Paris). An example in white is in the MNC, Sèvres (no. 13 339), and another was sold from the Gilbert Lévy Collection (Hôtel George-V, Paris, 10 December 1996, lot 55). Examples with the pillow include one formerly in the Wilfred J. Sainsbury Collection, illustrated in Eriksen and Bellaigue, p. 201, no. 14 (Sotheby's, London, 21 May 1957, lot 152) and one on a gilt-bronze base in a private collection, Los Angeles.

4 See *Vincennes*, p. 160, no. 471 (V&A, London, no. C. 294-1919). While de Pierreux is known to have created six figures of gods, the authors of the *Vincennes* catalogue note that these cost between 6 and 9 *livres*, which is probably too inexpensive for this model. The price of 15 *livres* for *Dormeuses* in the *magasin de vente* in 1752 (AMNS, I. 7, 8 October 1752) seems more appropriate for this elaborate figure.

5 LD, 2, p. 19, no. 198. See also *Vincennes*, p. 160; Préaud and d'Albis, p. 144, no. 95.

6 AMNS, I. 7, 8 October 1752.

7 Ibid.

8 Ibid.

9 According to Tamara Préaud, Baillon was a Parisian cabinetmaker.

10 *Vincennes*, pp. 160–61 n. 1.

11 AMNS, Vy 1, fol. 4, 21 August 1753; fol. 13, 30 June 1753; Vy 2, fol. 55v, 4 February 1758.

12 AMNS, Tiroir D5, dossier Watteau. I would like to thank Maureen Cassidy-Geiger for bringing this engraving to my attention and for providing me with a photocopy.

170

The Grape Eaters (*Les Mangeurs de raisins*)

1917.955
Vincennes, c. 1752
Soft-paste porcelain, H. 9⁷⁄₁₆ × W. 9¾ × D. 7¹⁄₁₆ in. (24 × 24.8 × 17.9 cm)
Glazed

Marks: none

Provenance: Durlacher Brothers, London, 1900;[1] J. Pierpont Morgan

Model

This group of a shepherd feeding grapes to a shepherdess was known simply as a *groupe de Boucher* at Vincennes. It formed a pair with another *groupe de Boucher* of a shepherd teaching a shepherdess to play the flute.[2] The model for *The Grape Eaters* probably was created early in 1752.[3]

Two versions of the model were made, one glazed and one in biscuit.[4] The biscuit model must have been in production before December 1753, when the first one is mentioned in the sales ledger.[5] The figures in the biscuit version sit on a thinner rocky base than those in the glazed version, and there is no large basket behind the boy. Certain other details have been eliminated, including the staff on the ground and the drapery underneath the dog. The folds of the drapery have been significantly simplified as well. A plaster model for the biscuit survives at the factory.[6] The Boucher groups in biscuit are noteworthy for their consistency in production and quality, which may have resulted from an introduction of new and more intricate molds.[7]

Four *Groupes de Bouché à 60 l.* were listed in the October 1752 inventory of the factory. These most likely refer to the glazed version of this model and its pendant.[8] In 1753 Monsieur Verdun bought three *groupes de Bouché* for 60 *livres* each.[9] His purchase could account for three of the four examples ready to be sold in October 1752. The biscuit version of the group, first listed in the sales records in December 1753, sold for 144 *livres* on nearly every occasion.[10] It is not certain why the glazed versions of these models would have been so much less costly than the biscuit models, but another early group, *Le Jaloux*, was also less expensive in the glazed version than in biscuit.[11] Perhaps as a new and increasingly fashionable line in the factory's production, these biscuit groups could command higher prices.

Commentary

The subject of this group comes from a ballet pantomime by Charles-Siméon Favart, *Les Vendanges de Tempé* [The Grapeharvest of Tempe], first shown at the fair of Saint Laurent in Paris on 28 August 1745.[12] In 1752 Favart remade this theatrical piece into *La Vallée de Montmorency ou les amours villageois* [the Vale of Montmorency or love in the village] which was performed at the Théâtre des Italiens, Paris. Favart was director of the Opéra-Comique, where his wife was a principal dancer and played the Little Shepherd in the 1752 production. In this later version, the pantomime had additional characters and scenes and was set in a cherry orchard.[13] François Boucher, who was friendly with Favart, designed the stage sets and costumes.[14]

Favart's pantomime tells the story of the shepherdess Lisette, a shepherd (known only as the Little Shepherd), another shepherd, Corydon, and Lisette's cousin Babette. Corydon, who is courting Lisette, is sent away by his mother to gather grapes. Instead, he hides so that he can eavesdrop on Lisette. Meanwhile, the Little Shepherd espies Lisette, who has fallen asleep under a tree. He sneaks up to her, fills her basket with grapes, and then hides. She awakens and is astonished to find her basket full of grapes.[15] Hearing a bird singing in the nearby bushes, she asks her cousin Babette to help her catch it. Instead, Babette catches the Little Shepherd in her net. In return for his freedom he offers her a nest of nightingales. Corydon, who had been watching the scene from afar, offers Lisette a magpie, but she refuses his gift. Out of spite, he gives it to Babette, who lets it go free. Corydon goes off to try to catch it again.

To the strains of his flute, the Little Shepherd invites Lisette and Babette to dance. They accept, but Lisette wants him to teach her to play the flute.[16] Babette, who must then dance alone, becomes jealous and leaves in anger. As Babette goes off, the two linger behind in the fields, feeding each other grapes and cherries.[17] The Little Shepherd declares his love for Lisette. Meanwhile, Babette fetches the Little Shepherd's father and Lisette's mother, who are both angry to find the young lovers together.[18] The Little Shepherd proclaims their love for each other, and the parents are appeased. The young players all dance a *pas de quatre* [a dance for four people].[19]

Boucher based many of his compositions on Favart's original pantomime of 1745.[20] It was perhaps owing to the popularity of Favart's revised production that the Vincennes factory, in turn, based many of its figural groups on Boucher's designs.[21] The scene of the Little Shepherd and Lisette feeding grapes to each other featured in several paintings by Boucher, including two entitled *Pensent-ils au raisin?*, one now in the Art Institute of Chicago and the other in the Nationalmuseum, Stockholm.[22] These show Lisette, in a woodland setting, feeding grapes to the Little Shepherd.[23] A painting called *Les Mangeurs de raisins*, dated 1749, in the Wallace Collection, provides a more direct model for the Vincennes group. Here the Little Shepherd is feeding grapes to Lisette.[24] The sculpted figures are modeled in direct imitation of those in the 1749 painting. Hence the Vincennes factory either had direct access to Boucher's painting, or perhaps to an unknown drawing.[25]

Another glazed example of this model is in an American private collection and formerly belonged to Sir John Plumb.[26]

Technique and Condition

The individual elements were molded and then put together and finished by the sculptor, who left no visible seams.[27] The slab base provided stability during firing.

Exhibitions: *Morgan Loan Exhibition*, New York, 1914, not in catalogue; *French and English Art Treasures*, New York, 1942, no. 315; *French and English 18th Century Exhibition,* Montreal, 1950, no. 151; *Wine: Celebration and Ceremony*, New York, 1985 (no catalogue)

Literature: Chavagnac, pp. 42–43, no. 49; *French and English Art Treasures*, no. 315; *French and English 18th Century Exhibition*, no. 151;

Verlet, *Sèvres*, p. 199, pl. 12; Buckley, *Connoisseur*, pp. 47–48; *Bulletin*, pp. 3–4; Zick, "Montmorency," pp. 30–31; *Vincennes*, p. 173; Ménager, I, p. 82, ill. p. 82; Préaud and d'Albis, p. 173, no. 177

NOTES

1 APML, Durlacher file, invoice 8 June 1900, "Set of 3 old white Sèvres groups [1917.954–956, cat. nos. 170–72] with pastoral subjects by Boucher, on metal mounted tulip wood stands of the period [missing]," £2,500 [the three].

2 See cat. no. 171.

3 Its pendant was sold to Lazare Duvaux by July 1752, suggesting a *terminus ante quem* for both figures. See Eriksen and Bellaigue, p. 250, pl. 66 (photograph reproduced backward).

4 This model has been discussed in many earlier publications including: Verlet, *Sèvres*, pp. 199–200, pl. 12; *Vincennes*, p. 173; Brunet and Préaud, p. 227, no. 307; Eriksen and Bellaigue, pp. 250–51, pl. 66; Sassoon, pp. 29–35; Munger, *Wickes*, pp. 182–83, no. 129; Préaud and d'Albis, p. 173, no. 177.

5 AMNS, Vy 1, fol. 21, 21 December 1753, unnamed buyer. See Préaud and d'Albis, p. 173.

6 It measures 10¼ × 11⁷⁄₁₆ in. (26 × 29 cm). See Bourgeois, 1913, no. 398, pl. 1. See also *Vincennes*, p. 173.

7 Although molds clearly were made for parts of the glazed groups, it appears from the consistency of the surviving biscuit figures that all parts of these groups were molded, rather than some parts being fashioned by hand.

8 Eriksen and Bellaigue, p. 250.

9 AMNS, Vy 1, fol. 13, firing A (before October 1752), 30 June 1753.

10 Sassoon makes the argument that these *groupes de Boucher* were either smaller or different models than the biscuit versions of *The Grape Eaters* and *The Flute Lesson*, based on their price of 60 *livres* as compared to the 144 *livres* price that appears in the sales ledgers for the biscuit sculptures (Sassoon, p. 30). An exception is one sold to Bazin for 96 *livres* on 30 September 1754 (AMNS, Vy 1, fol. 51, firing A).

11 See cat. no. 172. The cost differential was not as great however.

12 Discussed by Zick, "Montmorency," p. 3; Ménager, I, pp. 79ff; Espinay de Saint-Luc, pp. 14–22. The earlier pantomime was performed in one act, with music by Vaud. Neither the 1745 or 1752 plays survive, but in 1756 Les Frères Parfaict published a plot summary based on both texts in *Dictionnaire des Théâtres* (Boucher, p. 234; Ménager, I, p. 79; Espinay de Saint-Luc, p. 14). Laing, in *Boucher* (pp. 234–35) believes that the two versions became somewhat muddled in Parfaict, especially with regard to the settings.

13 See *Boucher*, pp. 233–37.

14 See Sassoon, p. 29.

15 This scene was captured by Boucher in a composition called *Le panier misterieux* [sic]. See cat. no. 71.

16 See cat. no. 171.

17 This seems to be a conflation of the early and revised edition of the pantomime. See note 12 above.

18 See *Le Jaloux*, cat. no. 172.

19 This synopsis is based on the account in Zick, "Montmorency," p. 3.

20 Ménager, I, p. 79. See also Zick, "Montmorency," pp. 3–47; Espinay de Saint-Luc, passim; Savill, "Boucher," passim; and cat. nos. 171–72 for other subjects taken from Favart's work. Boucher's paintings predate the 1752 production.

21 Sassoon, p. 29. The 1752 ballet was performed thirty-one times in the course of that year.

22 See *Boucher*, p. 234, pl. 53 and p. 236, fig. 157. Both are dated 1747.

23 The grapes are the only reference to the vineyard of Favart's 1745 pantomime.

24 Again, the grapes are the only reference to Favart's vineyard. The classical fountain that provides a backdrop for the figures in this painting could

possibly be a reference to the Vale of Tempe of Favart's original title. See cat. no. 171 for a discussion of this point in reference to *The Flute Lesson*.

25 Savill, I, pp. 222–23; *François Boucher*, p. 120; Sassoon, p. 29.

26 Published in Eriksen and Bellaigue, pp. 250–51, pl. 66, formerly in the Fitzhenry Collection, bought by Mme Brasseur de Lille, Paris, then Oscar Duschendschon, Geneva, then The Antique Porcelain Company, London. See Plumb, pp. 44–54.

27 Antoine d'Albis believes that this figure and *The Flute Lesson* (see cat. no. 171) were modeled rather than molded, but there are so many exact correlations between at least two known examples that it appears that at least the major elements were molded.

171

The Flute Lesson (*Le Flûteur*)

1917.956

Vincennes, c. 1752

Soft-paste porcelain, H. 10¼ × W. 10 × D. 6½ in. (26 × 25.3 × 16.5 cm)

Glazed

Marks: none

Provenance: Durlacher Brothers, London, 1900;[1] J. Pierpont Morgan

MODEL

The factory's first inventory of October 1752 listed four *groupes de Bouché* in the *magasin de ventes*, probably describing glazed versions of either *The Flute Lesson* or *The Grape Eaters* or both. They were priced at 60 *livres* each.[2] The model must have been made before that date, however, for the Lazare Duvaux sold an example for 144 *livres* to the duchesse de Lauraguais in July

171

Fig. 171-1 *The Flute Lesson*, Vincennes

Fig. 171-2 *The Flute Lesson* (back), Vincennes

1752.[3] This high price suggests that it was a biscuit version of the model.[4]

A plaster model survives at the Sèvres factory, which corresponds to the biscuit.[5] A terracotta original, also of the biscuit version, is in the collection of the Musée national de Céramique, Sèvres.[6] In the biscuit model, the basket resting on the plinth has been eliminated, and the hair and drapery of both figures have been dramatically simplified, as have the coats of the animals. The formation of the rocky base has likewise been changed.

At least three glazed examples of this model are known. One, in the Metropolitan Museum of Art, is much like the Atheneum's group, differing only in the type of detail that would vary as the molded components were assembled and finished.[7] On the other hand, an example in a private collection, California, is quite different from both the New York and Hartford examples, and may have been created from different molds or even sculpted (figs. 171-1 and 171-2). The pedestal behind the figures has been replaced by a tree trunk,[8] the rocky base is different, and, more significantly, the modeling of the figures and animals is completely different.[9]

COMMENTARY

As with *The Grape Eaters*, the story told in *The Flute Lesson* is taken from Charles-Simon Favart's ballet-pantomime *Les Vendanges de Tempé* of 1745.[10] In Scene V, Lisette and the Little Shepherd are together with her cousin Babette. Lisette takes the Little Shepherd's flute, which she wants to play, but she does not know how. The Little Shepherd then plays the notes of the flute while Lisette blows it, and Babette dances.[11] This is exactly the moment portrayed in the Vincennes sculpture.

The porcelain model drew its inspiration from a painting of 1748 by François Boucher, now in the National Gallery of Victoria, Melbourne.[12] The poses of the figures in the painting are very close to those of the porcelain models, although in both the glazed and biscuit sculptures the boy faces forward more,

and the girl's feet are crossed.[13] In the painting, the figures are set in a pastoral landscape with classical sculpture, sheep, and flowers. Favart's original vineyard setting is nowhere to be seen in.[14] Instead, Boucher alludes to classical landscape by placing a ruined antique fountain in the background, suggesting the classical Vale of Tempe named in Favart's 1745 title.[15] On the other hand the Atheneum's porcelain group is without classical motif, but refers to the vineyard setting of Favart's 1745 play by depicting bunches of grapes.[16]

Boucher featured an earlier moment in Scene V of *Les Vendanges de Tempé* in an earlier painting of 1746, in which the Little Shepherd plays the flute for Lisette.[17]

Boucher's 1748 painting of *The Flute Lesson* was engraved in 1758 by René Gaillard as *L'Agréable Leçon*.[18] While the late date of the engraving indicates that it was not the source for the sculpture, the factory did own a copy of it, which was used as a model for painted decoration.[19]

Other European porcelain factories used Boucher's *The Flute Lesson* for inspiration. Both Frankenthal, around 1760, and Chelsea, around 1765, produced sculptural groups after this composition, as did the Vienna Porcelain Factory in the 1760s and 1770s.[20] The common source for the Frankenthal and Chelsea groups must have been the engraving by Gaillard, while the Vienna group seems to have been after an engraving by Johann Esaias Nilson after Gaillard.[21]

Boucher's design was also executed in tapestry by the Beauvais factory. Part of a series called *Noble Pastorale*, it was the last group of designs made for the factory by Boucher, and was first woven in 1755. Examples of the tapestry are in the Wadsworth Atheneum and the Huntington Library and Art Collections, California.[22]

TECHNIQUE AND CONDITION

The group has been molded in separate parts and then assembled.

Exhibitions: *Morgan Loan Exhibition*, New York, 1914, not in catalogue; *Vincennes and Sèvres Porcelain,* New York, 1980, no. 3

Literature: Chavagnac, pp. 43–44, no. 50; Buckley, *Connoisseur*, p. 49, fig. 3; *Bulletin*, pp. 3–4, cover image; Zick, "Montmorency," p. 16, fig. 21; *Vincennes*, p. 167; *Vincennes and Sèvres Porcelain*, no. 3; Ménager, 2, p. 268

NOTES

1 APML, Durlacher file, invoice 8 June 1900, "Set of 3 old white Sèvres groups [1917.954–956, cat. nos. 170–72] with pastoral subjects by Boucher, on metal mounted tulip wood stands of the period [missing]," £2,500 [the three].

2 AMNS, I. 7, 8 October 1752. See cat. no. 170.

3 LD, 2, p. 132, no. 1181, 23 July 1752. For more on this model see *Vincennes*, p. 167; Sassoon, pp. 29–35. Biscuit had been produced by the end of 1751 (see AMNS, Vy 1, fol. 11, sale of eight *enfants de Boucher* in biscuit to Courteille on 21 November 1752, which appear to have been fired at the end of 1751 in *fournée* 58).

4 The first specifically described sale of a biscuit *groupe de Bouché* did not appear until December of the next year (AMNS, Vy 1, fol. 21, 17 December 1753, to an unnamed buyer, 144 *livres*).

5 One of the plaster models is illustrated in Bourgeois, 1913, no. 313. For published examples of the biscuit, see note 3 above.

6 MNC, Sèvres, no. 7723. Illustrated by Hallé in *Boucher*, p. 356, no. 98.

7 In comparing these two, the rock base is different, but in both cases it was probably made at least partially by hand. The Metropolitan Museum's *Flute Lesson* includes a stump adorned with a basket of flowers rather than fruit, and the boy lacks the final ruffle on the cuff of his sleeve. The large basket on the plinth holds a smaller basket of flowers.

8 There is evidence that something, perhaps a basket, was on top of the trunk as there is an unglazed area in the middle.

9 The details of the drapery are different, the heads and hair of both the boy and girl are different, as are the poses and the coats of the sheep and the dog. They are not like the biscuit model, however.

10 See cat. no. 170 for the complete story of this pantomime.

11 Espinay de Saint-Luc, p. 19: "Lisette lui prend le flageolet dont elle veut jouer, mais elle n'y réussit pas. Le berger touche le flageolet pendant qu'elle souffle dedans, et que Babet danse."

12 See Ananoff, *Boucher*, 2, pp. 6–7, no. 311. See also Zick, "Montmorency," p. 16; Savill, 1, pp. 222–23.

13 It is as if the viewer of the painting is standing further to the right of the figures than the viewer of the sculpture. In the sculpture, both of the boy's legs are visible, while in the painting, one of his legs is hidden by Lisette's costume.

14 See cat. no. 170. Nor are there references to being in a cherry orchard, the setting for the 1752 version of Favart's pantomime.

15 The Vale of Tempe is the valley in Thessaly that runs between Olympus and Ossa. Laing, in *Boucher* (pp. 234–35), remarks that in the Parfaict synopsis of Favart's plays, there is no reference to the classical setting suggested in the title by the Vale of Tempe. On the one hand, it is possible that Boucher's painting is referring to such an allusion, known to him first-hand as a friend and collaborator of Favart, and omitted by the brothers Parfaict. On the other hand, it is possible that Favart never put his characters in a classical setting, but merely referenced traditional pastoral poetry in the title, perhaps ironically. It is conceivable that Boucher added the classical fountain on his own, harking back to a long-established tradition of pastoral landscape painting firmly rooted in French antecedents.

16 There are no grapes in the glazed version now in a private collection, California. Nor do they appear in the biscuit model, which instead includes a basket of flowers.

17 Sold at the Palais Galliéra, Paris, 17 June 1977, illustrated in *Boucher*, p. 236, fig. 156. Laing points out that this painting belonged to Machault d'Arnouville, *contrôleur-général* of France, who oversaw the Vincennes-Sèvres factory. See cat. no. 68 for more on Machault.

18 Jean-Richard, p. 259, no. 1027.

19 See Savill, 1, pp. 222, 228, 233 n. 44.

20 An example of the Frankenthal group is in the Wadsworth Atheneum's collection (1917.1228). See Zick, "Montmorency," pp. 17–21; Sassoon, p. 32.

21 The first two groups are oriented in the same direction as the Gaillard engraving, as opposed to the Vienna group, which is in the same direction as the Nilson engraving. See Zick, "Montmorency," pp. 17–21.

22 Wadsworth Atheneum, no. 1947.18; Huntington Library example discussed in Wark, *Huntington*, pp. 68–69, fig. 10.

172

Jealousy (*Le Jaloux* or *groupe de Vandrevolle*)

1917.954

Vincennes, c. 1752

Soft-paste porcelain, H. 11⅜ × w. 10¼ × D. 11¹⁄₁₆ in. (28.8 × 26 × 28.1 cm)

Glazed

Marks: none

Provenance: Durlacher Brothers, London, 1900;[1] J. Pierpont Morgan

MODEL

This sculpture was described by the Vincennes factory as a *groupe de Vandrevolle*. The name probably refers to Van der Voorst, the likely sculptor of the model, who was working in Paris in the middle of the century.[2] The model must have been created shortly before October 1752, when three finished sculptures were recorded in the sales room.[3]

There were two versions of the same subject. The first version was nearly always glazed, but appeared at least once in biscuit porcelain.[4] Usually a large vase on a pedestal dominates the center of the composition.[5] The second or later version, appearing in the sales records from 1756, was produced exclusively in biscuit.[6] It is smaller in scale than the glazed version and there is no vase on the top of the pedestal. The three figures assume different poses: the figure of the spying father is no longer gesturing to keep quiet but looks disapprovingly at the shepherd lovers. Moreover, the shepherd lover's hat and one of the two sheep have been eliminated, and the girl has shoes and a different hairstyle.[7] A plaster model of the second version is in the archives of the Sèvres factory, and a terracotta model is in the Musée national de Céramique, Sèvres.[8]

The Hartford sculpture is one of two glazed versions of *Jealousy* known to survive. The other group was recently sold in Paris, and differs in many details.[9] For instance, the vase in the Paris example is decorated with vertical fluting and an all-over horizontal wave design, while the vase in the Museum's group has only vertical fluting. This element must have come from a different mold. Differences attributable to modeling that occurred after the molded elements were assembled may be perceived in the foliage or in the details of costume, such as bows on the pants and shoes of the shepherd. The rocky bases, which probably were sculpted, also vary slightly.

172

The glazed version of *Jealousy* was moderately priced at either 72 or 120 *livres*. The first recorded sale was to Jean-François Verdun de Montchiroux, the factory's principal shareholder.[10] Two more groups sold to unnamed buyers on 11 September 1753 and 17 September 1754 for 120 *livres*.[11] This last group may have been the one fired in biscuit and waiting to be glazed recorded in the inventory of 1 January 1754 or one of the three examples listed in the *magasin de ventes* in 1752.[12] The revised biscuit model sold for 288 and 300 *livres*.[13]

COMMENTARY

The Museum's sculpture depicts one moment in a scene from Charles-Siméon Favart's successive pantomimes based on the same story, *Les Vendanges de Tempé* and *La Vallée de Montmorency ou les amours villageois*.[14] In this scene, and that which follows, Babette, Lisette's jealous cousin, has brought the Little Shepherd's father Mathurin to surprise Lisette and his son just as they are about to kiss.[15] At first Mathurin is angry, but in the end, the Little Shepherd proclaims his and Lisette's love for each other and the quarrel between Lisette, Babette, Corydon, and the father is resolved. The last scene of the play is a dance for four people [*pas de quatre*] in which the young couple is united in love, joined grudgingly by Corydon and Babette.[16]

The Atheneum's group of *Le Jaloux* shows Mathurin with his finger to his lips, gesturing to the audience not to reveal his presence to the lovers. In the biscuit model, Mathurin no longer gestures for silence but scowls behind the pedestal. This shift changes the tone of the sculpture, eliminating any collusion with the audience and adding a sterner note to the moment.

François Boucher was inspired by Favart's comedies to produce several different compositions. The specific derivation for *Le Jaloux* is not entirely clear. It is said to be based on a painting by Boucher entitled *Les Amants surpris*, exhibited in the Salon of 1750 and known only from an engraving by René Gaillard.[17] This composition shows a young man and a young woman seated on the edge of a wheat field, surprised by an angry man who is parting the wheat stalks with his sickle. Gabriel Huquier *père* also engraved the same composition, but he changed the angry man into a simply curious young man.[18] Neither of these engravings shows the figures in the same poses as the Vincennes sculpture, and there is nothing that defines them as being Lisette, the Little Shepherd, and Mathurin.[19]

The Vincennes sculpture has also been related to one of a suite of four Boucher pastorals, entitled *Les Amours pastorales*, engraved by Claude Duflos.[20] This composition has been dated between 1736 and 1739, and specifically relates to another play by Favart, telling the story of Silvandre and Philis.[21] The specific poses of the figures do not seem any closer to the Vincennes sculpture than do those in *Les Amants surpris*. Thus either Boucher provided a direct model to the factory for *Le Jaloux*, probably in the form of a drawing,[22] or Van der Voorst created the model himself.

TECHNIQUE AND CONDITION

The group was partially molded and then finished by hand. It was glazed with a brush rather than dipped. Some of the glaze has dripped underneath. It probably sat on three balls for support. There is a diagonal firing crack from the waist of the

172

shepherdess to the hem of her skirt. Three fingers on her right hand and the tip of her right toe were replaced. The shepherd's knee is cracked. The head of Mathurin was broken and repaired.[23]

Exhibitions: *Morgan Loan Exhibition*, New York, 1914, not in catalogue; *European Porcelain*, New York, 1949, no. 162; *Masterpieces from the Wadsworth Atheneum*, New York, 1958; *Age of Elegance*, Baltimore, 1959, no. 143; *Morgan*, Hartford, no. 60

Literature: Chavagnac, pp. 41–42, no. 48; *European Porcelain*, no. 162, pl. XXVIII; Buckley, *Connoisseur*, p. 48; *Handbook*, p. 96; *Age of Elegance*, no. 143, illus. p. 49; Hood, *Connoisseur*, p. 132, fig. 4; Hood, *Bulletin*, p. 4, fig. 3; Zick, "Montmorency," pp. 30–31; Dauterman, *Sèvres*, fig. 30; Eriksen, *Pitti*, pp. 84–85, no. 44; Eriksen and Bellaigue, pp. 248–49, pl. 65; de Bellaigue, "Sèvres," pp. 166–67, no. 60

NOTES

1 APML, Durlacher file, invoice 8 June 1900, "Set of 3 old white Sèvres groups [1917.954–956, cat. nos. 170–72] with pastoral subjects by Boucher, on metal mounted tulip wood stands of the period [missing]," £2,500 [the three].

2 De Bellaigue, "Sèvres," p. 166. A sculptor by this name was made professor at the Académie de Saint Luc in 1753. There is no record of payment by the factory to anyone by this name, however. See Préaud and d'Albis, p. 214.

3 AMNS, I. 7, *Pièces sculptées au Magasin de Ventes: 3 groupes de Vandrevolle*, at 72 *livres*. See Préaud, "Biscuit," p. 37 n. 41. See also *Vincennes*, p. 169; Eriksen and Bellaigue, pp. 348–49, pl. 65; de Bellaigue, "Sèvres," pp. 166–67, no. 60; Eriksen, *Pitti*, pp. 84–85, no. 44.

4 Christie's, London, 3 December 1984, lot 19.

5 The vase is similar to the factory's *pot-pourri à jour* (see cat. no. 56). In the biscuit example cited above, the vase has been eliminated.

6 Eriksen and Bellaigue, p. 248. See cat. no. 176 for information on biscuit porcelain.

7 For published examples in biscuit, see *Vincennes*, p. 169, no. 489 (MAD, Paris, no. 25935); Eriksen, *Pitti*, pp. 84–85, no. 44; Eriksen, *David Collection*, pp. 63–64, no. 63.

8 De Bellaigue, "Sèvres," p. 166. See also Bourgeois, 1913, no. 355, pl. 2. The terracotta in the MNC, Sèvres is inv. no. 7733.

9 Private collection, Paris (formerly Gilbert Lévy, Hôtel George-V, Paris, 10 December 1996, lot 56).

10 AMNS, Vy 1, fol. 13, 30 June 1753 (de Bellaigue, "Sèvres," p. 166).

11 AMNS, Vy 1, fols. 17, 50v.

12 Ibid., I. 7, 1 January 1754, *Pièces en Biscuit prêtes à Etre mises en couverte*, *1 Groupe de Vandrevolle à 60 l*; ibid., 8 October 1752, *Pièces Sculptées du Magasin de Vente*. Eriksen believed that the three examples listed in the 8 October 1752 inventory probably were disposed of with these three sales. He did not seem to have taken into account this unfinished example. We may speculate that the example sold at Christie's in 1984 (see note 4 above) was the one listed in biscuit ready to be glazed, which, because biscuit sculpture was just being introduced, was never glazed.

13 The revised model, after biscuit firing, was valued at 100 *livres* in the 1 January 1757 inventory (AMNS, I. 7).

14 First identified by Bourgeois, 1909, 1, p. 17. See Eriksen, *Pitti*, p. 85; Eriksen and Bellaigue, p. 248; de Bellaigue, "Sèvres," p. 166. See cat. no. 170 for more on these theatrical productions.

15 Zick, "Montmorency," p. 34. The scene (VII) recorded by Parfaict reads: "Le berger a donné la préférence à Lisette. LISETTE, LE PETIT BERGER, BABET, MATHURIN: La Bergère méprisée amène Mathurin père du petit Berger, qui surprend dans le temps qu'il veut embrasser sa maîtresse de façon qu'en se mettant entre eux deux il reçoit un baiser de l'un et de l'autre." See Espinay de Saint-Luc, p. 21, from Parfaict, pp. 79–80. Zick, in her account of the play, says that Babette

fetches both Lisette's mother and the Little Shepherd's father, but only Mathurin is mentioned in Parfaict and he alone appears in the various depictions of this scene (the porcelain and Boucher's paintings).

16 Zick, "Montmorency," p. 3.

17 Zick, "Montmorency," p. 30. See Ananoff, *Boucher*, 2, p. 41; Jean-Richard, p. 258, no. 1026.

18 Jean-Richard, pp. 281–82, no. 1152; Ananoff, *Boucher*, 2, p. 41, fig. 993.

19 The characters from *Les Vendanges de Tempé* were meant to be sitting in a vineyard and not a wheat field. In fact, in the Vincennes sculpture, the lovers are unaware of the presence of Mathurin, while in *Les Amants surpris*, they clearly react to his advance. Of course, Vincennes designers often took figures out of context for their compositions.

20 *Vincennes*, pp. 169, 154.

21 Ananoff, *Boucher*, 1, p. 276, no. 159, who transcribes the caption describing the scene and the characters: "Silvandre, heureux amant, que rien ne t'inquiète; / On n'aime point Philis sans avoir de rivaux, / En vain Lucas te suit, te guette, / Le voila qui t'écoute encore sous ses rameaux. / Mais que luy sert sa vigilence, / Il voit tes feux récompensée; / Ne cherche point d'autre vengence, / Ton bonheur le punit assés.   Favart."

22 In the 1752 inventory of the factory there were thirty-nine drawings by Boucher listed (AMNS, I. 7; see Eriksen and Bellaigue, pp. 86–87).

23 This object was treated by Echo Evetts in 1987. A report may be found in the object file at the Wadsworth Atheneum.

173

Cupid (*L'Amour Falconet*)

1917.959

Sèvres, 1762, base dated 1777[1]

Soft-paste porcelain, figure, H. 9¼ × W. 4¾ × D. 7⅞ in. (23.4 × 12.1 × 19.9 cm); base, H. 3 × DIAM. 6⁷⁄₁₆ in. (7.6 × 16.4 cm)

Figure in biscuit, base *bleu nouveau* with polychrome reserves

Marks: figure: incised T and 1762; base: interlaced Ls with date letter z and painter's mark of scrolling N for François-Joseph Aloncle;[2] script B in purple for Jean-Pierre Boulanger;[3] incised cn[4]

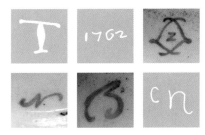

Provenance: J. Pierpont Morgan

MODEL

This biscuit figure of *Cupid* was one of the most popular of all Sèvres sculptures, and its history is well known.[5] Étienne-Maurice Falconet designed the model,[6] which he exhibited in plaster in August 1755 at the annual Salon. Documents show that the sculptor then ordered a block of marble in October 1755 to make the same model for Madame de Pompadour. This was exhibited in 1757,[7] and by 1761 it had been placed in her hôtel d'Evreux in Paris.[8] When the inventory of Madame de Pompadour's possessions was made after her death in 1764, a marble reduction was in the garden at the hôtel d'Evreux.[9] In 1781 a terracotta original was sold from the collection of Madame de Pompadour's brother, the marquis de Marigny,[10] which may also have belonged to Madame de Pompadour.

The Sèvres reduction in biscuit was introduced in 1758, and remained in production, both in soft and hard paste, until 1801 or 1802.[11] Molds and models appear in the inventory for new work of 1758, valued at 24 *livres*.[12] No molds or models survive from the eighteenth century.[13] *Cupid* probably was made in two sizes,[14] although extant examples appear to be of only one size.[15]

One of the first recorded sales of Falconet's *Cupid* was on 30 December 1758—appropriately, to Madame de Pompadour.[16] The price was 144 *livres*, but a year later the model's price was reduced to 120 *livres*, and then in 1760 to 96 *livres*.[17] An exceptional example sold for 600 *livres* in 1780 and may be a

large-scale version made in 1777.[18] Between 1760 and 1776 almost 450 biscuits of *Cupid* appear in ledgers recording payments to sculptors, the majority of them in the 1760s.[19] The sales records show that the figure was a favorite among the *marchands-merciers*, and it was sometimes included among other biscuits in the factory's dessert services.[20] *Cupid* and his female pendant, the latter introduced in 1761, were so well thought of that they were part of a diplomatic gift from the *contrôleur-général* Henry Léonard Jean-Baptiste Bertin to the envoy of China in December 1764.[21] *Cupid* was even placed on the cover of a large vase introduced at the factory by 1773.[22]

Falconet's *Cupid*, often described as *L'Amour menaçant* [Menacing Cupid], is gesturing the onlooker to be silent, presumably so that he can shoot his victim unawares.[23] In type he is a conflation of Harpocrates (the Greek name for the Egyptian god Horus) and Cupid (Amor). Harpocrates was the child of Isis, and often was represented as an infant with his finger held to his mouth.[24] Cupid, the son of Venus, was the god of Love, and usually was portrayed with wings, as well as with his attributes of a bow, quiver, and arrows. He was one of the most frequently represented mythological figures in the eighteenth century. Falconet seems to have drawn on both of these popular figures to create his 1755 *Cupid*. His model has Cupid's wings and like Harpocrates holds his finger to his mouth urging silence. Does this gesture perhaps mirror that silence advocated by Ovid in his didactic poem *Ars Amatoria*?

> Above all, Venus commands that her sacred rite
>   be kept secret.
> I am warning you, let no gossip come near them
>   [sacred rites].[25]

Falconet was probably also familiar with seventeenth-century emblem books, where silence was viewed as an attribute of friendship, as well as a virtue for lovers.[26]

The Falconet biscuit was originally sold without a pedestal. Only in 1761 was a pedestal introduced, when the factory created a pendant female figure.[27] The same model of pedestal served both figures, and cost from 18 to 108 *livres*, depending on its decoration.[28] The higher priced pedestals are only mentioned in the sales records in 1765 and 1766.[29]

COMMENTARY

The Museum's biscuit figure was made in 1762, six years after Falconet was appointed head of the sculpture workshop at the Sèvres factory. The incised T probably is the mark of the specific modeler.[30] The pedestal, which is dated 1777, is not original to the figure, and may have been decorated later to match the base of the pendant in the Museum's collection.[31] It does not bear inscriptions by Virgil and Voltaire that are often found on *Cupid's* pedestal.[32]

There are many examples of Falconet's biscuit in public collections, including the Wallace Collection, the Louvre, the Hermitage Museum, the British Museum, the Victoria and Albert Museum, and the Wrightsman Collection at the Metropolitan Museum of Art.[33] These figures frequently appear on the art market as well.

173

The popularity of the model since the eighteenth century is proven by the innumerable examples found not only in biscuit but in other mediums as well, including bronze, lead, and marble. *Cupid* was frequently depicted in paintings of the period, notably in Jean-Honoré Fragonard's *The Swing* now at the Wallace Collection, Alexandre Roslin's *Jeune fille offrant des fleurs à l'amour* at the Louvre, and Carle Vanloo's *Offering to Love* at the Wadsworth Atheneum.[34]

TECHNIQUE AND CONDITION

The big toe on the right foot of the *Cupid* has been broken off and repaired. His left wing has also been broken and repaired. The pedestal is covered with black carbon spots, suggesting that it was refired. The gilding is flaking off in many areas, which also may be the result of a later firing.

Exhibitions: *Morgan Loan Exhibition*, New York, 1914, not in catalogue; *Antique Taste*, Hartford, 1982

Literature: Chavagnac, p. 47, no. 53; Hood, *Bulletin*, p. 9; *Antique Taste*, pp. 2–3, fig. 2, p. 13; Savill, 2, pp. 826, 832 n. 1l (accession number incorrectly given as 1917.969–970), and Savill, 3, p. 996

NOTES

1 There is some evidence that the base is later decorated. See below.

2 Active 1758–81, primarily as a bird painter. See Savill, 3, pp. 995–96, and Peters, *Marks*, p. 8.

3 Active 1754–85, primarily as a gilder. See Savill, 3, pp. 1004–5, and Peters, *Marks*, p. 16.

4 Found on soft paste, 1757–67, 1771–86? See Savill, 3, p. 1096, as possibly the mark of the *répareur* Charles Cejourné (or Séjourné), active 1754–67/68 (as per Eriksen, *Waddesdon*, p. 320). Savill notes that when his mark appears on pieces that postdate 1768 they are usually earlier models that may have been decorated at a later date, either inside or outside the factory.

5 The most thorough discussion of the biscuit model and its pedestal is in Savill, 2, pp. 823–34 (with its pendant). The model has also been published recently by Dawson (*British Museum*, pp. 175–76). The information that follows is based on these earlier accounts.

6 See cat. no. 176 for more on Falconet. Falconet's *Cupid* is thoroughly discussed by Louis Réau, in *Falconet*, 1, pp. 183–91.

7 Ibid., pp. 183–84, Dauterman, *Wrightsman*, p. 290, Savill, 2, p. 832 n. 3.

8 Réau, *Falconet*, p. 187. Either this marble or another version was at one time at Mme de Pompadour's château de Bellevue. Six marble examples were documented in 1922 by Réau, four in St. Petersburg, Russia, and two in Paris. Réau believed that the one now in the Louvre Museum probably came from the hôtel d'Evreux, and that one in the collection of the comtesse Chouvalov in St. Petersburg in 1922 came from Bellevue. See also Savill, 2, p. 843 n. 59.

9 Cordey, p. 47, no. 487 (Réau, *Falconet*, p. 187).

10 Réau, *Falconet*, p. 187.

11 Dawson, *British Museum*, p. 175. She notes that it was revived in the 1850s.

12 AMNS, I. 7, 1 January 1759.

13 Troude (pl. 1) records a plaster model with its pedestal 15¾ in. (40 cm) high, which is labeled second size. Bourgeois (1913, pl. 9, no. 36) illustrates a smaller plaster, 7½ in. (19 cm) high. Savill suggests that the large plaster illustrated by Troude was labeled second size to distinguish it from an exceptionally large version produced in 1777. See Savill, 2, pp. 825, 833 n. 48. Neither of these plaster models seems to survive today. The 15¾ in. (40 cm) model relates to known examples with their pedestals, taking into account the shrinkage that occurs in firing. On the other hand,

the 7½ in. (19 cm) plaster does not correspond to surviving examples of the biscuit.

14 Dawson states that it was made in one size (*British Museum*, p. 176) but Savill feels that it was made in two or three sizes. The references to a large version made in 1777 (see note 13 above) support the notion that at least two sizes were made. Tamara Préaud kindly brought to the author's attention two entries in the factory overtime records, one for October 1775 when Chabry *père* was paid 27 *livres* for the repair of a plaster of a *grand Amour Falconet*, (AMNS, F.17), and in November 1775 (ibid.) when Perrotin was paid 120 *livres* for repairing the plaster of a *petit Amour Falconet*.

15 Many examples are known through published museum and auction catalogues. A partial listing may be found in Savill, 2, p. 832 n. 1. They range in size between 9 and 9⁵⁄₁₆ in. (22.8 and 23.6 cm), or 11⁷⁄₁₆ and 12⁵⁄₁₆ in. (29 and 31.2 cm) with their pedestals (Savill, 2, p. 823).

16 AMNS, Vy 2, fol. 78. The first sale was on 28 December, to Bouret (fol. 75v). In addition to Mme de Pompadour's, three others were sold on 30 December, another one to Bouret (fol. 76), one to Sieur (fol. 76), and one to a member of Court (78v).

17 Savill, 2, p. 823. Savill notes that from 1774 some *Cupids* sold for 72 *livres*.

18 Ibid., pp. 825, 833 n. 47. See AMNS, Vy 7, fol. 228, 17 April 1780, to Henry Léonard Jean-Baptiste Bertin, *contrôleur-général*.

19 See notes in AMNS file. Eriksen and Bellaigue mention that over 230 pairs of *Cupid* and his pendant were made between 1761 and 1770 (p. 313, no. 126).

20 See for example the Starhemberg service, 6 October 1766 (AMNS, Vy 4, fol. 86v).

21 AMNS, Vy 4, fol. 32v.

22 *Vase colonne pour l'amour* or *vase Duplessis amour Falconet*. See Troude, pl. 85, and Savill, 2, p. 826.

23 He was often called *L'amour silencieux* or *Garde à vous* as well, indicating the ambiguity of his gesture and pose. See Savill, 2, p. 823; Réau, *Falconet*, p. 185.

24 See Cary, p. 441.

25 *Praecipue Cytherea jubet sua sacra taceri: admoneo, veniat ne quis ad illa loquax*, from Ovid, *Ars Amatoria* II, 607/608, quoted by Zick, "Harpokrates," p. 238. I would like to thank James Higgenbotham for translating Ovid's quotation and Lynn Mervosh for aid in the translation of Zick's article.

26 Van Veen (see Zick, "Harpokrates," pp. 236–38, 246 nn. 93–95).

27 Savill, 2, p. 824.

28 Ibid., p. 825. The lowest priced example was probably for a biscuit version. Savill notes that blue ground pedestals cost from 72 to 96 *livres*, the latter being the same price as the figure. The more costly bases probably had expensive ground colors or elaborate inscriptions (see below), and were noticeably more expensive than the biscuits themselves.

29 Ibid. See AMNS, Vy 4, fol. 40, 25 June 1765, fol. 74, 26 June 1766.

30 For incised marks on biscuits, see Birioukova, passim. The incised T and 1762 also appear on a "Psyche" (pendant to Cupid) in the Wallace Collection, London (no. C494, in Savill, 2, p. 828). An example in the Hermitage Museum, St. Petersburg, is incised 1761 and T (see Eriksen and Bellaigue, pp. 144, 313, no. 126).

31 See cat. no. 174 for the pendant. *Cupid's* pedestal may have been decorated in the nineteenth century. See condition notes below for evidence of redecoration.

32 See cat. no. 175.

33 See respectively, Savill, 2, pp. 823–33; Brunet and Préaud, p. 229, no. 313; Eriksen and Bellaigue, p. 313, no. 126; Dawson, *British Museum*, pp. 175–76; King, p. 16, no. 139, pl. 17; Dauterman, *Wrightsman*, pp. 290–91, no. 118, pp. 292–3, no. 119.

34 See Savill, p. 834 n. 59. The Vanloo in the Atheneum's collection (1979.186) shows Cupid standing rather than sitting.

174

174

"Psyche" (*pendant de l'Amour Falconet*)

1917.960

Sèvres, c. 1761–1773

Soft-paste porcelain, figure: H. 9¼ × W. 4⁹⁄₁₆ × D. 6⅛ in.
(23.4 × 11.5 × 15.5 cm); base: H. 3¹⁄₁₆ × DIAM. 7¹⁄₁₆ in. (7.7 × 17.9 cm)

Figure in biscuit; base *bleu nouveau* with polychrome reserves

Marks: base: interlaced Ls with date letter z, scrolling N for
François-Joseph Aloncle;[1] script B in purple for Jean-Pierre
Boulanger[2]

Provenance: J. Pierpont Morgan

MODEL

This figure, although popularly called Psyche, was known at the
Sèvres factory as *Pendant de l'Amour*, or mate to *Cupid*.[3] Étienne-
Maurice Falconet designed it in 1761, specifically to be made in
biscuit porcelain. Unlike his earlier *Cupid*, it was never executed
in marble. Falconet probably exhibited a plaster model of this
figure at the Salon of 1761.[4]

Several plaster models are recorded, one in the 1814 inventory of the factory, measuring 15¾ inches (40 cm) with its
pedestal, and one in a 1913 publication measuring 7½ inches
(19 cm).[5]

The Sèvres biscuit was made in both soft and hard paste and
is known in one size. It is possible, however, that occasionally a
second or third size was made.[6] When introduced in 1761, the
figure was priced at 96 *livres*, the same as the *Cupid*. From 1775 it
usually cost 72 *livres*.[7] Although sometimes sold individually,
"Psyche" more often than not was sold with *Cupid*.[8] Pairs were
especially popular in the first two years of production, when we
know of thirty-three that were sold. Between 1763 and 1764, ten
pairs appeared in the sales ledgers, and between 1765 and 1766,
eight pairs were recorded. From this period forward, the figure
of Cupid was more often sold alone.

Falconet's pendant was frequently accompanied by a pedestal
made to match *Cupid's*. It was often decorated with an inscription, which is the second part of a line from Virgil found on
Cupid's pedestal: ET NOS CEDAMUS AMORI, or "let us
yield to love."[9]

COMMENTARY

The Museum's pedestal carries Virgil's motto on its front, and
trophies on the other three sides. It is impossible to say with
certainty that this pedestal is original to the Museum's biscuit. In
1777, the year the pedestal is dated, Louis XVI purchased a
Cupid and pendant for 72 *livres* each, and pedestals for 18 *livres*
each.[10] This low price for the pedestals leads us to think that they
were left in biscuit. On the other hand, in April 1778 the
Princess Sapicha bought a pair of figures with bases costing

84 *livres* each.[11] Since a pedestal for *Cupid* in *bleu nouveau* cost 96 *livres* in 1768, it is not difficult to believe that by 1778, a similar pedestal could cost 84 *livres*.

It is unclear when the Museum's figure of "Psyche" and its base were paired. They may have been together from 1777 when the pedestal was decorated, or else matched together at a later date. By that year, figures were usually made in hard paste, so either the Museum's figure was made earlier and matched with the pedestal in 1777 or the figure and pedestal were brought together at an unknown later date. This date may just be a year later when the Princess Sapicha bought her pair of figures with bases.[12] Nothing precludes the possibility that the pedestal could still correspond to the one sold to the princess in April 1778— and that the two were brought together at some later date. In any case, it is clear that the base of the Museum's *Cupid* was made to match that of its "Psyche," in order to create the pair as it exists today.

Exhibitions: *Morgan Loan Exhibition*, New York, 1914, not in catalogue; *Antique Taste*, Hartford, 1982

Literature: Chavagnac, p. 47, no. 53; Hood, *Bulletin*, p. 9; Verlet, *Sèvres*, p. 208; *Antique Taste*, p. 13; Savill, 2, pp. 826, 832 n. 1l

NOTES

1 Active 1758–81, primarily as a bird painter. See Savill, 3, pp. 995–96, and Peters, *Marks*, p. 8.

2 Active 1754–85, primarily as a gilder. See Savill, 3, pp. 1004–5, and Peters, *Marks*, p. 16.

3 The model has been discussed extensively by Savill, 2, pp. 823–33. For information on *Cupid*, see cat. no. 173. For convenience, the figure will sometimes be referred to as "Psyche" in this entry.

4 Ibid., p. 824. Savill (p. 833 n. 15) quotes the salon *Livrets* (*Salon de 1761*, XXI, p. 28, no. 120, and Réau, *Falconet*, p. 186) describing the model: "Une petite fille qui cache l'Arc de L'Amour. Elle a environ dix pouces de haut, & fait pendant à la figure de l'Amour en marbre, qui a été exposée aux Sallons précédens, par le même auteur." Réau states that it may never have actually been exhibited, for in an annotated copy of the Salon booklet now at the Bibliothèque nationale, Gabriel de Saint-Aubin noted that it was not seen at the Salon but was executed at Sèvres.

5 AMNS, 1814 inventory, 1760–80, 4, no. 3; Troude, pl. 1, 15¼ in. (40 cm); Bourgeois, 1913, pl. 9, no. 467, 7½ in. (19 cm). As in the case of the *Amour Falconet*, the 15¼ in. (40 cm) corresponds to surviving biscuit figures (10¹⁵⁄₁₆ in. or 27.5 cm) with their bases, allowing for shrinkage. A corresponding biscuit figure to the 7½ in. (19 cm) model is not known.

6 See cat. no. 173 for this issue. The figure usually measures 9¼–9⅜ in. (23.2–23.8 cm) without its base.

7 The inventory of 1774 (AMNS, I. 8) lists twelve *Cupids* and "Psyches" in the *magasin de vente* at 96 *livres*, and forty-five *bon rebut* examples at 72 *livres*. By the inventory of 20 January 1778, there were eight *Cupids* at 72 *livres*. It is difficult to say whether the factory was selling off the forty-five imperfect examples over the next four years or whether they dropped the price of all the figures to 72 *livres*.

8 Examples of sales of individual figures include: AMNS, Vy 3, fol. 84, 24 December 1761, member of court; fol. 111, 4 October 1762, unnamed buyer; fol. 115, December 1762, member of court; fol. 118v, 25 December 1762, duc de Choiseul; Vy 4, fol. 68v, December 1765, Bertin; fol. 142, 1 April 1768, Pallieux *frères* (two for 78 *livres*); fol. 180, 1 July 1769, supplement to the service presented by Louis XV to the Danish king. See also Savill, 2, p. 824.

9 Savill, 2, p. 824. The first part of Virgil's line reads OMNIA VINCIT AMOR or "Love conquers all."

10 AMNS, Vy 7, fol. 20, 6 June 1778, recording the king's purchases from 1777.

11 Ibid., fol. 12, 13 April 1778.

12 Thus this example would necessarily have been taken from old stock and it is unlikely that the Princess Sapicha bought such a figure.

175

Pedestal (*piédestal pour L'Amour*)

1917.1154

Sèvres, 1763

Soft-paste porcelain, H. 3¹⁄₁₆ × DIAM. 6¹⁵⁄₁₆ in. (7.7 × 17.6 cm)

Bleu nouveau ground, *vermiculé* gilding, polychrome flowers, inscription in black

Marks: interlaced Ls in blue with date letter K, PT underneath for Pierre-Nicolas Pithou *aîné*;[1] 3275 scratched in the glaze

Provenance: J. Pierpont Morgan

MODEL

This pedestal was made to support Falconet's biscuit sculpture of *Cupid*, created for the factory in 1758.[2] The first pedestal for the sculpture appeared in 1761, when a pendant for the *Cupid* was designed. The bases were produced to facilitate the creation of pairs with these two figures.

Cupid's pedestal frequently bears two inscriptions, one from Virgil's *Eclogues*,[3] and the other by Voltaire. The first reads *OMNIA VINCIT AMOR*, or "Love conquers all." The second inscription is, *QUI QUE TU SOIS, VOICI TON MAITRE/ IL L'EST, LE FUT, OU LE DOIT ETRE,* or "Who'er thou art, thy master see: He is, or was, or ought to be."[4] Voltaire composed his couplet for a sculpture of *Cupid* in the garden of the château de Maisons, northwest of Paris, the home of his

175

friend Jean René de Longueil, the marquis de Maisons.[5] The couplet also appears on an engraving of *Cupid* by Jean Daullé after Charles Coypel now in the archives of the Sèvres factory.[6]

COMMENTARY

The Museum's base is inscribed with only Voltaire's verse. The remaining reserves are decorated with flowers, with *vermiculé* gilding on the shoulder. The blue used is *bleu nouveau*, introduced at the factory a few years earlier. A pedestal for *Cupid* was sold to an unnamed buyer for 48 *livres* in October 1763.[7] An example with a *blue lapis* ground sold in that same year for 96 *livres*.[8]

Exhibition: *Morgan Loan Exhibition*, New York, 1914, not in catalogue

NOTES

1 Active 1760–90. See Peters, *Marks*, p. 61.

2 See cat. no. 173.

3 Savill, 2, p. 824.

4 Ibid.

5 Ibid. Savill goes into detail concerning these inscriptions and their presence on other pedestals of *Cupid*. I should like to thank John Curry Gay for providing me with information on the château de Maisons.

6 AMNS, Tiroir C XIII, d. 28, engraved 1755. The caption of the engraving describes the original painting as in the collection of M. de la Poplinière, Paris.

7 AMNS, Vy 3, fol. 151v, 8–13 October 1763.

8 Ibid., fol. 122, unnamed buyer, 18 March 1763.

176

Friendship (*L'Amitié*)[1]

1917.957

Vincennes, 1755

Soft-paste porcelain, sculpture: H. 10½ × W. 6¹¹⁄₁₆ × D. 3½ in. (26.6 × 17 × 8.9 cm); base: H. 1⁹⁄₁₆ × L. 7¹³⁄₁₆ × W. 5⁹⁄₁₆ in. (4 × 19.8 × 14.1 cm)

Figure in biscuit, base *bleu lapis* with *vermiculé* gilding, polychrome reserves

Marks: biscuit: incised 5 inside a right angle;[2] base: interlaced Ls with date letter G and k underneath, for Charles-Nicolas Dodin,[3] incised 5[4]

Provenance: Madame de Pompadour, 1755–1764; probably the marquis de Marigny, 1764–1781; Edouard Chappey, Paris 1904;[5] J. Pierpont Morgan

MODEL

Madame de Pompadour commissioned this figure from Vincennes in 1755.[6] The model was the first to be created for the factory by Étienne-Maurice Falconet, a sculptor who had worked for Madame de Pompadour since 1750, producing a statue of Music for her château de Bellevue, and the figure *Cupid* in 1755.[7] Madame de Pompadour probably asked that Falconet design *Friendship*.[8] It was produced only in biscuit porcelain.

The model and mold for *Friendship* appeared in the factory inventory of 1756 among new works for 1755.[9] Three examples were fired in biscuit on 3 December 1755.[10] By 29 December 1755 nineteen were completed and given as a gift from the factory to Madame de Pompadour.[11] In the margin of the sales register there is a note of explanation. "Since the figures of Friendship ordered by Madame the Marquise de Pompadour portrayed her, the company thought it ought not receive any payment for them and begged Madame de Pompadour to find that good, thereby releasing these 19 figures from the *magasin de vente*."[12]

COMMENTARY

Falconet's sculpture was one of two models he produced called *L'Amitié*. It is an allegory of friendship, a theme that was promoted by Madame de Pompadour from 1750, when her sexual relationship with Louis XV ended.[13] This changing role for Madame de Pompadour might have signaled the end of her position at court, but although she no longer shared his bed, she remained the king's official mistress, confidante, and advisor. In an effort to solidify her new position, she embarked on a campaign—frequently through artistic commissions—to announce to the world her new status as a friend to the king.[14]

The iconography of Falconet's *Friendship* follows a formula dating back at least to the the publication of Cesare Ripa's *Iconologia* in 1603.[15] Ripa depicts Friendship as a young woman dressed in white, her breast bared, her hair simply arranged, her appearance and bearing meant to denote that friendship is natural and sincere. She is accompanied by myrtle and pomegranate flowers, symbols of love and tranquility. Her arms are bare, signifying her willingness to help those she loves. She stands by an elm trunk entwined with vines, in an allusion to the constancy of friendship in adversity and prosperity. Finally, she holds her heart in her hand, and the mottos *longe et prope* [far and near], and *mors et vita* [death and life] are prominently displayed on a banner and her skirt hem, respectively.

This complex subject matter served as the basis for several eighteenth-century allegories of friendship, including an etching by Madame de Pompadour herself after a gem she engraved with the help of Jacques Guay.[16] Here, a bare-breasted young woman stands next to a column entwined with flowers. In her left hand, which seems to rest on the column, she holds her heart, while her right hand grasps Ripa's entwined elm tree. A mask lies at her feet—presumably to signify that friendship is without artifice—and Ripa's Latin mottos flank the perimeter. Both the gem and the etching should be viewed as portraits of Madame de Pompadour.[17]

Falconet's model for Vincennes appropriates much of the symbolism of the earlier allegories. The young woman, no doubt a portrait of Madame de Pompadour, is also portrayed in a simple dress, nearly bare-breasted and bare-armed, standing beside a column entwined with garlands. She holds a heart in

her right hand, as if she is offering it to the king.[18] Behind her stands the tree trunk. Clearly Falconet did not deviate from the standard iconography of Friendship.

Falconet's second model of *L'Amitié* realized in 1765 was made in both marble and biscuit porcelain.[19] The sculptor simplified the composition, eliminating the column, but retaining the motif of heart-in-hand. Although it may originally have been conceived as a portrait of Madame de Pompadour, by the time it was executed, Madame de Pompadour had died and the features no longer resembled those of the lady who had once been the king's favorite.[20]

A drawing by François Boucher of unknown date and purpose was almost certainly the inspiration for Falconet's design. We know of the drawing through the surviving engraving entitled *Offrante sincere* executed by Louis-Marin Bonnet sometime before 1767 (fig. 176-1).[21] Boucher seems to have created another similar composition, evidenced in an engraving called *Vénus appuyée sur une colonne, un cœur à la main*, by Demarteau. Published as being after Boucher, it shares many aspects of the iconography of *Offrante sincere*.[22]

Falconet's *L'Amitié* of 1755 was made for the personal use of Madame de Pompadour. Only the nineteen presented to her in 1755 were ever made, and presumably she gave most of them to family, close friends, or influential members of court.[23] At the time of her death in 1764, she still possessed four examples.[24]

Fig. 176-1 *Offrante sincere*, Louis-Marin Bonnet after François Boucher

There is only one record to indicate who received biscuit sculptures from Madame de Pompadour. In June 1757, Lazare Duvaux sold to Madame de Pompadour, "Un pied carré en bronze doré d'or moulu pour une figure de l'Amitié, pour M. Berryer" [a square gilt-bronze pedestal for a figure of Friendship, for Monsieur Berryer], for 26 *livres*.[25] Nicolas René Berryer was *lieutenant général de police* of Paris.[26] It is reasonable to suppose that at least one of the biscuits was given to Louis XV.

The Hartford *L'Amitié* sits on a rectangular Sèvres pedestal, decorated with trophies of love by one of the factory's best painters, Charles-Nicolas Dodin. One reserve, depicting Cupid's bow and quiver of arrows, a floral garland, and a flaming torch, is dominated by a shield with two hearts being pierced by Cupid's arrow. Another shows two kissing doves nestled next to a book opened to an essay entitled *TRAITE de l'amitié*. The side reserves depict, on the one hand, a lyre, a laurel crown, and a page inscribed *Anacreon,* and on the other, musical emblems, a basket of flowers, and a term.[27] It is recorded that in December 1760 Madame de Pompadour purchased two Sèvres pedestals for *L'Amitié* for 84 *livres*.[28] May we not suppose that the Museum's base for *L'Amitié* was one of them?[29] She may have given one to her brother, the marquis de Marigny, for we know that a *L'Amitié* in his collection, described as sitting on a square blue and gold porcelain socle, was sent to Paris from Ménars in 1779.[30] This figure and base seem to have been the same ones that appeared in the sale of his effects in 1781.[31]

It is interesting to note that the decorative scheme on the round base accompanying the 1770 biscuit sculpture of Louis XV (catalogue no. 177) matches *L'Amitié's*.[32]

Only three other biscuits of Falconet's 1755 model are known. One is at the Musée national de Céramique, Sèvres, another at the Bowes Museum, Durham, England, and a third was sold in 1991 from the Elizabeth Parke Firestone Collection, New York.[33]

Technique and Condition

There is a visible seam running along the shoulder of the figure, going over the head and down the back.

Exhibitions: *Morgan Loan Exhibition*, New York, 1914, not in catalogue; *Masterpieces from the Wadsworth Atheneum*, New York, 1958; *Morgan Treasures*, Hartford, 1960, no. 57

Literature: Chavagnac, p. 45, no. 51, pl. X; *Morgan Loan Exhibition*, facing p. 121, p. 124; Réau, "L'Offrande," p. 215; Réau, *Falconet*, 1, pp. 228–29; Buckley, *Connoisseur*, pp. 48, 51, fig. 6; *Handbook*, p. 82; Buckley, *Antiques*, p. 191, fig. 11; *Morgan Treasures*, p. 23, no. 57; Gauthier, p. 161; Hood, *Bulletin*, pp. 9–10, fig. 7; Gordon, p. 259, fig. 18; Levitine, p. 51, fig. 94; *Vincennes*, pp. 149–50 n. 5; Savill, 1, pp. 36, 41 n. 36; Posner, pp. 88–89, fig. 7

Notes

1 It is also commonly referred to as Friendship holding a Heart or *L'Amitié au cœur*, but this does not appear to be an eighteenth-century appellation.

2 This same right-angle mark appears under the example now in the MNC, Sèvres (no. 16057). Instead of the numeral five it is marked with the number 4. The example in the Bowes Museum, England (no. 1997.54) is

marked with a right angle and what looks to be the numeral 7. (I would like to thank Howard Coutts for sending me this information.) Another surviving example, formerly in the Firestone Collection (Elizabeth Parke Firestone sale, Christie's, New York, 21 March 1991, lot 120) is marked with an incised triangle and a plumb line mark. The five on the biscuit would seem to indicate its numerical place among the nineteen examples made, as compared with the number four on the MNC, Sèvres example and the seven on the Bowes Museum figure. However, the Firestone example does not have a number incised, which creates an incontrovertible inconsistency in this theory. Perhaps, as suggested by Bernard Dragesco in conversation with the author, one *répareur* worked on at least seven sculptures, marking each with his right-angle mark and then numbering them successively.

3   Active 1754–1802. See Savill, 3, pp. 1029–32.

4   Savill, 3, p. 1127, found on soft paste primarily 1753–90s.

5   APML, Chappey file, invoice for 27 April 1904: "1 Groupe Biscuit de Sèvres de Falconnet personnifiant Madame de Pompadour offrant son cœur au roi Louis XV socle ancienne pâte tendre de Sèvres orné de 4 médaillons à réserves représentant les attributs de l'Amour," 50,000 French francs.

6   Much information has been published on this model. In addition to those sources cited in the literature above, see Préaud and d'Albis, p. 121, no. 40.

7   For Falconet's life and work see Réau, *Falconet*, and Levitine. For the *Cupid*, see cat. no. 173.

8   Posner, pp. 88, 95.

9   AMNS, I. 7, 1 January 1756.

10   IF 5673, fol. 49. See *Vincennes*, pp. 149–50 n. 1.

11   AMNS, Vy 1, fol. 110v.

12   Ibid.: *Les figures de l'Amitié ordonnée par Madame la Marquise de Pompadour étant son portrait, la compagnie a cru ne devoir point en recevoir le paiement et en a fait prier Madame de Pompadour de le trouver bon, au moyen de quoi le magasin de vente sera déchargé de ces 19 figures*. See Réau, *Falconet*, 1, pp. 228–29. See also *Vincennes*, p. 149.

13   For the most thorough discussion of the change in relationship between Mme de Pompadour and Louis XV, and the subsequent effect it had on her personal imagery, see Gordon, passim.

14   In this context, Jean-Baptiste Pigalle was asked to sculpt four works on this theme, including a *L'Amitié* for the garden at Bellevue that was intended as a mate to a pedestrian portrait of Louis XV. See Gordon; see also Gaborit, pp. 56–61. For Mme de Pompadour's use of art to proclaim her place at court, see also Stein, passim, in which the author places Mme de Pompadour's Turkish decorations and paintings at Bellevue in this same context of her changing role at court.

15   Ripa, no. 23. See Gordon, p. 253, illustrated fig. 6 (1611 edition of Ripa).

16   Jean-Richard, pp. 356–57, no. 1482. See also Leturcq, pl. K (for drawings for the engravings). Gordon notes that Guay credits Pompadour with engraving this gem almost entirely herself (p. 255).

17   Gordon, p. 255.

18   Ibid., p. 259. Gordon equates the large column with an altar, a device found in other sculptures of Friendship, including a terracotta attributed to Falconet by Réau and recently on the art market in New York (Réau, "L'Offrande," pp. 213–18; Sotheby's, New York, 29 January 1998, lot 54). For more on the pairing of *L'Amitié* with images of Louis XV, see note 14 above (Pigalle's *L'Amitié* and *Louis XV* at Bellevue) and cat. no. 177.

19   Réau, *Falconet*, p. 228, pl. XIV; Bourgeois, 1913, p. 7, no. 16. Although the marble was not completed until after Mme de Pompadour's death in 1764, it most certainly was begun during her lifetime.

20   Réau (*Falconet*, p. 229) did not believe it to be a portrait, but Gordon (p. 259) believes that it must originally have been conceived as such.

21   Jean-Richard, pp. 106–7, no. 317.

22   Ibid., p. 215, no. 816.

23   As Gordon points out (p. 261), all of the images of Mme de Pompadour as *L'Amitié* that were produced during her lifetime were meant for a limited public audience. This is true of Pigalle's sculptures for Bellevue, her gems by Guay that she used as seals for her personal correspondence, the

etchings after the gems that she distributed to friends, and Falconet's biscuit figures.

24   Cordey, p. 43, no. 434.

25   LD, 2, p. 318, no. 2799.

26   He later was made *conseiller d'État*, *ministre d'État*, *secrétaire d'État*, and then *Garde des Sceaux de France*.

27   Referring to Rameau's ballet *Anacreon* performed at Fontainebleau on 23 October 1754 to celebrate the birth of the duc de Berri, the future Louis XVI (see Savill, 1, p. 36, who cites the base to the Atheneum's *L'Amitié*). Vincennes and Sèvres painters used this emblem in other trophies, such as a *caisse carrée* dated 1758–59 with trophies by Morin in the collection of Dalva Brothers, New York. This trophy includes the open book inscribed *Acreon* [*sic*], the kissing doves, and the arrow piercing a shield with two hearts. This proves that there must have been a drawing or engraving provided by the factory to the painters.

28   AMNS, Vy 3, fol. 45v.

29   The Museum's base is dated G, which may signify part 1759 and part 1760. See Peters, *Marks*, p. 4.

30   "La figure de l'amitié sur un socle carré de porcelaine bleu et or," Bibliothèque historique de la ville de Paris, mss. NA 105-06. This reference kindly provided by Bernard Dragesco.

31   *Catalogue des différens objets de curiosité dans le science et art qui composoient le cabinet de feu M. le Marquis de Ménars*, Paris, 1781, F. Basan and F. Ch. Joullain, p. 125, lot 650: "L'Autel de l'Amitié, aussi en biscuit de Seve, auprès duquel est une jeune fille debout tenant de la main droite deux coeurs. Hauteur 11 pouces, compris le socle quarré en porcelaine." It was purchased by Vestris for 59 *livres* 19 *sols* (handwritten note in margin of copy from the Bibliothèque d'art et d'archéologie, Paris). Although it is called *L'Autel de l'Amitié* in the sale catalogue, it should not be confused with another Sèvres model by that name (Bourgeois, 1913, pl. 22, no. 74, 1772). I would like to thank Alden Gordon for the reference in Marigny's sale.

32   See cat. no. 177.

33   See note 2.

177

Louis XV

1917.958

Sèvres, figure, c. 1770, base, c. 1770–1780

Soft-paste porcelain, figure: H. 8 1/16 × W. 7 × D. 5 5/16 in. (20.5 × 17.8 × 13.5 cm); base: H. 1 3/4 × DIAM. 8 3/8 in. (4.5 × 21.2 cm)

Biscuit figure, *bleu nouveau* base with polychrome reserves, *vermiculé* gilding

Marks: none

Provenance: possibly marquis de Marigny, c. 1770–1781; Léon André, Paris, 1906;[1] J. Pierpont Morgan

MODEL

There is a great deal of documentary evidence regarding this figure of *Louis XV*.[2] The statue is a reduction of a large-scale bronze statue by Jean-Baptiste Pigalle (1714–85), that was part of a larger monument unveiled in the Place Royale, Reims, on 26 August 1765.[3] The statue was destroyed during the French Revolution, but is known from an engraving by Pierre-Étienne Moitte after Charles-Nicolas Cochin.[4]

The Sèvres factory paid Pigalle 600 *livres* to make the model for the reduction in 1770.[5] It was to be part of an extraordinary

Fig. 177-1 *Louis XV*, Sèvres, British Museum

table decoration produced by the factory for the 16 May 1770 wedding banquet for the Dauphin (the future Louis XVI) and Marie-Antoinette. This biscuit centerpiece measured thirty by fourteen feet, and comprised an elaborate colonnade of Doric columns, with allegorical figures of the Seasons and groups of children around columns. There were fountains supported by figures of the Three Graces, others supported by Atlas, and a large series of classical gods and goddesses.[6] The statue of Louis XV stood in the center of the ensemble, on a pedestal with four allegorical figures.

Seven biscuit figures after Pigalle's model were produced in 1770.[7] The sculptors Perrotin, Mignan, Antoine Le Vaux, and Mathías are all recorded as having worked on these figures.[8] The model was made in two sizes, approximately 9⁷⁄₁₆ and 7⅞ inches (24 and 20 cm) in height. The larger version was valued at 96 *livres* in the sales room in 1778, while the smaller version sold for 72 *livres*.[9] An example of the large size with a base was listed in the stock of 1774 at 120 *livres*.[10]

The figure from the centerpiece for the Dauphin's wedding

was sold to the *marchand-mercier* Madame Lair in the second half of 1770, along with the colonnade and other components of the ensemble for a staggering 11,884 *livres*.[11] The figure of Louis XV was accompanied by its pedestal, and cost 720 *livres*. It would seem reasonable to suppose that the figure in this case was of the first size. Subsequent recorded sales over the next few years were of second-size examples. Three were sold to Versailles in December 1770, one for the king and two for the *office*.[12] Then in 1771 Madame Lair bought two more examples, both priced at 72 *livres*, one in the first half of the year and one in the second.[13] In 1777 the baron de Ros purchased still another of the smaller examples for the same price.[14] None of these purchases were recorded with either biscuit or enameled pedestals.

There are four known surviving examples of *Louis XV*, as well as the record of one in the collection of the comte de Chavagnac in 1911 (figs. 177-1–177-3).[15] The examples in the British Museum and the Musée national de Céramique, Sèvres are of the first size, while those in the Louvre and the Wadsworth Atheneum are of the second. These surviving

Fig. 177-2 *Louis XV*, Sèvres, Musée national de Céramique

biscuits display other differences, including details of costume. The Musée national de Céramique, Sèvres and Louvre examples have round bosses on the belt, while on the Atheneum's version, there are lions' heads, as in Pigalle's original design.[16] On the British Museum example, the belt has no applied ornament. The right-arm sleeve varies from example to example.[17] All these differences in detail must result from different *répareurs* assembling and finishing the figures. Even more importantly, however, the surviving biscuits differ in the modeling of the face. The figure at the Musée national de Céramique, Sèvres, has a rather young, somewhat optimistic face, while the Atheneum's example bears a decidedly older, paunchier face wearing a stern expression. The British Museum's and Louvre's sculptures, which are nearly identical, lie in between these extremes. The example formerly in the Chavagnac collection resembles the example at the Musée national de Céramique, Sèvres.[18] Could the differences in the faces simply be once again the natural result of different *répareurs* working on each sculpture,[19] or were the *répareurs* specifically instructed as to how they were to portray the king? The engraving of Pigalle's sculpture depicts a young face, more like the example at Sèvres.

In January 1771 the sculptor Mignan was paid 24 *livres* for having *reparé le plâtre du Roy*. Although we cannot be certain, this may refer to his finishing the standing figure of the king,[20] and may reflect the introduction of the second size.[21]

The Hartford *Louis XV* sits on a painted Sèvres base, decorated with *vermiculé* gilding and trophies. The latter include emblems and symbols associated with the monarchy. On the front, the trophy comprises a blue medallion with the monarch's emblem of interlaced Ls in gold, a laurel crown, a sword, the king's scepter, and the scales of justice. The reverse trophy displays another blue medallion with the royal fleur-de-lis in gold, a laurel crown, a sword in its sheath, the *bâton de justice*, a mirror, and a snake. One side reserve depicts a shield with the fleur-de-lis, horns, pikes, and foliate branches, while the other side reserve features a plumed helmet, a white banner with pale turquoise stripes, a sword, horn, and branches. The ground color and gilding pattern were designed to match those on the base of the Atheneum's *L'Amitié*, although that base is decorated with the darker *bleu lapis* (see catalogue no. 176). This difference in the blues is not immediately noticeable, the eye being distracted by the elaborate gilding. By 1770 *bleu nouveau* had superseded *bleu lapis*. The painting appears to be by the same hand as on the base of *L'Amitié*, that of Charles-Nicolas Dodin.[22]

There is every likelihood that the owner of the Museum's *Louis XV* was also the owner of its figure of *L'Amitié*. This may have been the marquis de Marigny.[23]

Technique and Condition

The right leg shows evidence of an eighteenth-century repair. The fingers on the right hand have been restored (the forefinger and third finger are not original).[24]

Fig. 177-3 *Louis XV*, Sèvres, Louvre

Exhibitions: *Morgan Loan Exhibition,* New York, 1914, not in catalogue; *Morgan*, Hartford, no. 70.

Literature: Chavagnac, p. 46, no. 52, pl. XI; *Morgan Loan Exhibition*, New York, 1914, facing p. 121, p. 124; Hood, *Bulletin*, p. 9, fig. 7; *Louis XV*, pp. 390–91, no. 540; Louvre, *Nouvelles acquisitions*, 1985, pp. 149–50;[25] Ennès, "Surtout," p. 67; de Bellaigue, "Sèvres," pp. 182–83, no. 70; Dawson, *British Museum*, pp. 188–89.

Notes

1 APML, A miscellaneous file, invoice 30 May 1906: "1 Statuette de Louis XV en biscuit de Sèvres," 125 French francs.

2 The most comprehensive study has been made by Pierre Ennès, in *Louis XV*; Louvre, *Nouvelles acquisitions*, 1985; and "Surtout." This material has been summarized by de Bellaigue ("Sèvres," p. 182) and Dawson (*British Museum*, pp. 188–89). Much of the following has been based on these published accounts.

3 See Ennès, "Surtout"; de Bellaigue, "Sèvres"; Dawson, *British Museum*; and Gaborit, pp. 12–14.

4 Gaborit, p. 13, fig. 3; Ennès, "Surtout," p. 68, fig. 14.

5 AMNS, I. 8, 1 January 1771. See Louvre, *Nouvelles acquisitions*, 1985, p. 149.

6 Ennès, "Surtout," reconstructs the centerpiece with the help of Sèvres documents, existing plaster models, and descriptions of the banquet.

7 Louvre, *Nouvelles acquisitions*, 1985, p. 149.

8 Perrotin sculpted the first in the group, including the elaborate pedestal with four allegorical figures after Pigalle's model. See ibid.; de Bellaigue, "Sèvres," p. 182; Dawson, *British Museum*, p. 188.

9 AMNS, I. 8, 1 January 1779 (Louvre, *Nouvelles acquisitions*, 1985, p. 149; Dawson, *British Museum*, p. 189).

10 AMNS, I. 8, 1 January 1775 (Louvre, *Nouvelles acquisitions*, 1985, p. 149).

11 AMNS, Vy 4, fol. 228v. In Louvre, *Nouvelles acquisitions*, 1985, Ennès suggests that there were two centerpieces made, one for the king and one purchased by Mme Lair (disputed by de Bellaigue, "Sèvres," p. 182 n. 6). In his subsequent study ("Surtout," p. 64) Ennès seems to change his opinion, believing that Mme Lair purchased the banquet centerpiece and probably recomposed it into smaller ensembles. The records support this view.

12 AMNS, Vy 4, fols. 221, 222v.

13 Ibid., Vy 5, fols. 10, 22.

14 Ibid., Vy 6, fol. 189v.

15 Sold Drouot, Paris, 19–21 June 1911, lot 283, 9⅞ in. (25 cm). See de Bellaigue, "Sèvres," p. 182 n. 8.

16 See Cochin's engraving cited above.

17 The Wadsworth Atheneum, Louvre, British Museum, and Chavagnac figures show multiple leather straps hanging from under the sleeve, which are not found on the MNC, Sèvres example. There are also differences in the sword hilts, the rope molding sometimes being vertical and sometimes being on the bias. Some but not all of these differences were mentioned by Dawson (*British Museum*, p. 189).

18 Based on the quality of the old photograph, it is difficult to be absolutely certain that the face on the Chavagnac example is like that of the MNC, Sèvres version. Like the latter figure, the eyebrows do appear to arch dramatically.

19 See note 8.

20 AMNS, F.12. It is also possible that the document refers to a bust of Louis XV introduced in 1759 (see examples in the Frick Collection, New York and the British Museum, London). I would like to thank Tamara Préaud for this information.

21 I would like to thank Bernard Dragesco for this suggestion.

22 This opinion was seconded by David Peters but doubted by Bernard Dragesco.

23 See cat. no. 176.

24 The figure was restored in 1986. A treatment report is on file at the Museum.

25 Mistakenly said to be in the MMA, New York.

178

178

Boy with a Tambourine (*Le Tambour de basque*)

1917.1077

Sèvres, 1773

Hard-paste porcelain, H. 4⁵⁄₁₆ × W. 2 × D. 2⅜ in. (11 × 5 × 6 cm)

White shirt, red pants, yellow ribbons, black hair and hat, green foliage, gilded tambourine rim and gilded base

Marks: interlaced Ls in purple with date letter u, crown above; 11⁰ and 122 in black, covering other notations, now illegible

Provenance: Edouard Chappey, Paris, 1906;[1] J. Pierpont Morgan

MODEL

This small figure of a boy with a tambourine is one of seventeen similar figures designed by Étienne-Maurice Falconet between 1764 and 1766 for the Sèvres factory.[2] In 1765 molds and models for eight *enfants Falconnet 2e grand.r* are listed among new works for 1764. The following year seven more were realized, and finally, two more appear the next year.[3] They were valued at 21 *livres* when made in biscuit. In January 1765 twenty-one were in stock.[4] By January 1766 two hundred twenty were in stock, indicating a sharp increase in production. These figures were meant to be left in biscuit state. Known examples of this figure include one in the Musée national de Céramique, Sèvres,[5] one formerly in the Maurice Fenaille collection,[6] one formerly in the W. Sainsbury collection,[7] and one sold in New York in 1992.[8] All of these figures are probably soft-paste biscuit.[9]

COMMENTARY

The Museum's figure is made of hard-paste porcelain. This new material was produced at Sèvres from 1769, although experimentation with a new kiln and several different formulas for pastes and glazes continued through much of the 1770s.[10] Hartford's *Le Tambour de basque* must have been one of the factory's earliest figures in the new paste, and may have been enameled because the results in biscuit were not entirely satisfactory. In 1772 factory documents noted that a hard-paste group of *Castor and Pollux* had emerged from the biscuit firing with a red tone, which the factory tried to mask with a light glaze.[11] It was also mentioned that any color could be applied to pieces with this light glaze, suggesting that the same thing happened with *Le Tambour de basque*. In fact, the next year the factory began using a special paste for sculpture, which must have been more successful. From then on the biscuit figures were produced in hard paste.[12]

Only one other enameled hard-paste figure is currently known. In 1774 the sculptor Chanou *fils* was paid 18 *livres* for work on a hard-paste figure of Louis XIV's doctor, Gui-Crescent Fagon.[13] While there is no mention of this figure being enameled, a painted example is now in the Philadelphia Museum of Art.[14]

There were other painted figures made in the 1770s, as shown by entries in the sales registers. In December 1773 an *enfans moissonneur colorié* was delivered to Versailles, valued at 48 *livres*.[15] Eight enameled examples of children holding candlesticks (*enfans bougeoirs coloriés*) were also delivered in 1773, two to the maréchal de Soubise, four to Madame du Barry, and two to Monsieur Bertin.[16] Nevertheless, most figures produced during the 1770s and later were left in biscuit.

While there are no references in the factory documents that can be linked with certainty to the Museum's figure, in May 1773 two *enfans de falconnet 2e* listed as *rebut peint* [painted second] were delivered to Monsieur Tristant. Perhaps the *Boy with a Tambourine*, thought to be less successful once enameled, was one of these figures.

Exhibition: *Morgan Loan Exhibition*, New York, 1914, not in catalogue

Literature: Masson, 1905, pp. 9, 31; Chavagnac, pp. 118–19, no. 148; Savill, 2, pp. 784, 788 n. 17; MNC, *Nouvelles acquisitions 1979–1989*, p. 174, no. 247

NOTES

1 APML, Chappey file, invoice 17 April 1906: "figurine Sèvres garçonnet jouait du tambourin (1772)," 6,500 French francs.

2 Although they are not listed with specific names in the 1760s, they are known from a new price list of 1787 (AMNS, Y19, fols. 48–49; see Ménager, 2, p. 291).

3 AMNS, I. 7, 1 January 1765, 1 January 1766, and 1 January 1767.

4 Ibid., 1 January 1765.

5 MNC, Sèvres, no. 25289. See MNC, *Nouvelles acquisitions 1979–1989*, p. 174, no. 247.

6 Drouot, Paris, 12 June 1941, lot 85.

7 Sotheby's, London, 14 March 1867, lot 39.

8 Christie's East, New York, 26 October 1992, lot 181.

9 The example at the MNC, Sèvres is soft paste. The example sold in 1992 carried an incised B for Bachelier, which would have appeared on pieces until 1773. It was not marked with a hard-paste crown. The example from the Fenaille collection was marked with an F for Falconet, thus dating it before 1766, when he left the Sèvres factory. This would have been too early for a hard-paste figure. The example in the Sainsbury collection probably was soft paste, for William Sainsbury wrote frequently about small biscuit sculptures and would undoubtedly have noted that his own example was hard paste if that were the case.

10 For the newest and most thorough discussion of the advent of hard paste at Sèvres see d'Albis, "Hard Paste," passim.

11 AMNS, C2/26. See d'Albis, "Hard Paste," pp. 47, 69 n. 47.

12 AMNS, C2/27, Annual register of hard-paste consumption, C2/15/1 (d'Albis, "Hard Paste," pp. 47, 69 nn. 44–45).

13 AMNS, F.16, July 1774.

14 No. 1939-041-055, H. 9½ in. (24.1 cm), marked crowned interlaced Ls in red enamel with HP for Henri-Martin Prévost, no. 119 in black enamel. This figure also comes from the Chappey Collection (Masson, p. 9). In 1776 Mme Adelaïde bought a *Dr. Fagon* for 144 *livres* (AMNS, Vy 6, fol. 67v, 27 January 1776). Information on *Dr. Fagon* kindly provided by Donna Corbin. Perhaps the numbers in black on the Philadelphia and Hartford pieces are inventory numbers from Chappey.

15 AMNS, Vy 5, fol. 126, 23 December 1773. This figure was modeled by Blondeau after Boucher and was introduced at Vincennes around 1748. An early example in the MMA, New York is enameled (see Préaud and d'Albis, p. 172, no. 174). The example delivered to Versailles in 1773 may have been hard paste.

16 AMNS, Vy 5, fol. 131, 26 December 1773, fol. 135, 26 January 1773, and fol. 136v, 23 December 1773 (see Savill, 2, pp. 783–88 for hard-paste gilded biscuit examples of this model).

179

Vase (*vase Duplessis*)

1917.981

Vincennes, c. 1750–1753 (paste), 19th-century decoration

Soft-paste porcelain, silver rim, H. 9¼ × W. 7⁵⁄₁₆ × D. 5½ in. (23.5 × 18.5 × 14 cm)

Green ground, polychrome flowers, gilding

Marks: interlaced Ls in blue with dot in center

Provenance: J. Pierpont Morgan

This vase began as a *vase Duplessis* made at Vincennes about 1753.[1] It was extensively altered in the nineteenth century.[2] Initially its upper rim was lobed, but this must have been damaged and ground down, and then covered with the silver band. The green ground and gilding were added as well.

When first made, the vase was probably decorated with a white ground and naturalistic flowers. Certain remaining sprays are in the style of early Vincennes flowers, and allow us to wonder if some of the original flower decoration still remains. This is especially true of the sprays on either side of the stem, the large spray of peach-colored flowers hanging below the clumps of fruit, the small insect next to this spray, and the peony on the other side of the vase. These bunches may have been scattered randomly across its surface, a common style of decorating at early Vincennes.[3] This would explain the strange way the later decorator applied the green ground, creating irregular and illogical "reserves." Some of the other flowers and fruit may have been added at that time to create a richer effect.

Exhibition: *Morgan Loan Exhibition*, New York, 1914, not in catalogue

Literature: Chavagnac, p. 62, pl. XVIII, no. 73; Buckley, *Antiques*, p. 190, fig. 8; Hood, *Bulletin*, p. 7, fig. 5

NOTES

1 For this shape see cat. no. 59.

2 The unglazed bottom of the vase has blackened extensively, reinforcing the aesthetic evidence of redecoration.

3 See for example a tobacco jar, V&A, London, no. C299-1927, and covered dish, MAD, Paris, no. 36186.

180

Pair of orange tubs (*caisses carrées*)

1917.991–992

Vincennes or Sèvres, 18th-century paste, 19th-century decoration

Soft-paste porcelain, both: H. 3¹¹⁄₁₆ × W. 2¾ × D. 2¹³⁄₁₆ in. (9.4 × 7 × 7.1 cm)

Turquoise ground, polychrome children, gilding

Marks: interlaced Ls in blue with date letter c on both; 1917.991: incised f;[1] 1917.992: incised c[2]

Provenance: J. Pierpont Morgan

While the porcelain is of factory origin and dates from the eighteenth century, the decoration dates from the nineteenth century. The reserves are based on figures in engravings after François Boucher,[3] and are meant to be in the manner of painters like Morin or Genest, but are not convincing as period painting.[4] The gilding has been brushed on in a pattern not found at Vincennes or Sèvres, and, uncharacteristically, has received no tooling. The large gilded chip on one foot of 1917.991, indicating that the chip occurred before the tub was decorated, is further evidence that they were redecorated.

Exhibition: *Morgan Loan Exhibition*, New York, 1914, not in catalogue

Literature: Chavagnac, p. 69, pl. XV, no. 82

NOTES

1 See Savill, 3, p. 1100, found on soft paste c. 1747, by 1753–68, c. 1788.

2 Ibid., p. 1092, found on soft paste, 1748, by 1753–79.

3 Three of the engravings have been identified as by La Rue after Boucher: *Le Printemps* (Jean-Richard, p. 310, no. 1267); *La Peinture* (ibid., p. 315, no. 1298); *L'Automne* (ibid., p. 312, no. 1271).

4 See cat. no. 73 for putti in this style.

179

180

181

Tea service with a tray, teapot, sugar bowl, milk jug, and cup and saucer (*plateau Hebert, théière Calabre, pot à sucre Hebert, pot à lait à trois pieds, gobelet litron et soucoupe*)

1917.967–971

Vincennes or Sèvres, 18th-century paste, 19th-century decoration

Soft-paste porcelain, tray: H. 1³⁄₁₆ × L. 11¼ × D. 9 in. (3 × 28.5 × 22.9 cm); teapot: H. 4³⁄₁₆ × W. 5⁵⁄₁₆ × D. 3⅛ in. (10.6 × 13.4 × 7.9 cm); sugar bowl: H. 3⁹⁄₁₆ × DIAM. 2¹³⁄₁₆ in. (9 × 7.1 cm); milk jug: H. 3³⁄₁₆ × W. 3¼ × D. 2⁷⁄₁₆ in. (8 × 8.2 × 6.2 cm); cup: H. 1⅞ W. 2⅝ × D. 1¹⁵⁄₁₆ in. (4.7 × 6.6 × 4.9 cm); saucer: H. 1 × DIAM. 4³⁄₁₆ in. (2.5 × 10.6 cm)

Yellow ground with monochrome blue children in landscapes, gilding

Marks: interlaced Ls in blue on all except milk jug; incised B in script on tray;[1] incised I or T on teapot;[2] incised pt (?) on sugar bowl;[3] incised dt[4] in script and OO[5] on cup; incised 6 (or g or 9) on saucer;[6] pseudo painter's mark for André-Vincent Vielliard *père* on all (except milk jug)[7]

Provenance: Cartier et Fils, Paris, 1905;[8] J. Pierpont Morgan

This tea service comprises a *plateau Hebert*, a *théière Calabre*, a *pot à sucre Hebert*, a *pot à lait à trois pieds*, and a *gobelet litron et soucoupe*. The tray is an example of the second size,[9] and the teapot is perhaps of the fifth size.[10] The sugar bowl represents the third size.[11] The milk jug *à trois pieds* is of the third size and the cup and saucer are of the fourth size.[12]

Each component of the tea service is decorated in *camaïeu bleu* with scenes after François Boucher. The tray shows Boucher's *La Chasse*, engraved by Le Prince after part of a panel painted between 1751 and 1755 in Madame de Pompadour's boudoir at the château de Crécy.[13] The teapot is decorated on one side with *La Petite Fille à la cage*, which had been made into a biscuit figure by the Vincennes factory in 1752 after a drawing by Boucher.[14] The other side shows Boucher's figure of a young bagpiper, which had been engraved both by François-Antoine Aveline, under the title *L'Innocence* and by Gilles Demarteau in 1770, this time called *L'Enfant berger*.[15] The sugar bowl is decorated with *Le Pêcheur*, an engraving after Boucher by Claude Duflos *jeune* and with *La Blanchisseuse*, a biscuit figure by Suzanne after Boucher dated 1755.[16] The reserve on the cup is based on a print by Marie-Madeleine Igonet after Boucher, entitled *L'Amusement de la bergère*. It is drawn in the reverse sense of the print.[17] The saucer uses a figure after Boucher called *Tailleur de pierre*, which was sculpted in biscuit for Vincennes in 1754.[18]

There is every reason to believe that this tea service was decorated in the nineteenth century. The style of the painting is imitative of André-Vincent Vielliard but the faces are not drawn with his characteristically large, round foreheads. The blue is applied more evenly than one would expect, and is somewhat pale and gray.[19] Moreover, each piece, except the milk jug,

363

181

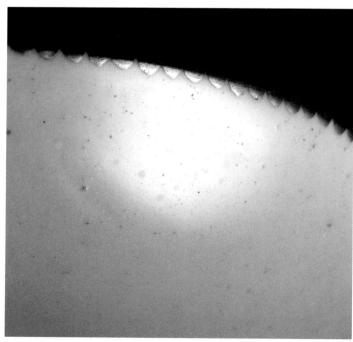

Fig. 181-1 *Plateau Hebert* (back)

is marked with a somewhat awkward version of Vielliard's mark. Legitimate examples show that the mark should be drawn with a straight line and three small vertical lines above. Here the line is more curved and the vertical lines larger than normal.

The date of 1753, as suggested by the lack of a date letter, is also problematic. Because we know when specific sizes of the components were introduced at the factory, we can say with confidence that the service could not have been decorated in 1753. The teapot was only listed in two sizes in 1753, so it is unlikely that a fifth size was being made at that early date. The sugar bowl was only made in the third size in 1754 (and not even recorded until 1755), while the milk jug was not made in the third size until 1756. The cup and saucer were not made in the fourth size until 1757.

Closer examination reveals other evidence of later decoration. For example, the feet of the sugar bowl and teapot are marked with carbon spots typical of nineteenth-century turpentine gilding. A chip on the foot of the cup also is blackened by carbon indicating that it was fired after the piece was chipped. Finally, the tray proves without a doubt that the set was redecorated: when examined in raking light it is possible to detect the shadow of the original gilded decoration around the exterior rim (fig. 181-1). The tray and its companion pieces must have been acid washed in the nineteenth century and then decorated with the then popular yellow ground and blue Vielliard children.[20] As the yellow ground on all of the pieces matches very well and the gilding is of a consistently high quality, the entire ensemble must have been redecorated at the same time.

Exhibitions: *Morgan Loan Exhibition*, New York, 1914, not in catalogue; *European Porcelain,* New York, 1949, no. 153; *French and English 18th Century Exhibition*, Montreal, 1950, no. 150 (without milk jug); *Masterpieces from the Wadsworth Atheneum*, New York, 1958; *Boucher*, no. 101 (without milk jug)

Literature: Chavagnac, p. 54, no. 61; *European Porcelain*, no. 153; *French and English 18th Century Exhibition*, no. 150 (without milk jug); Buckley, *Antiques*, pp. 189, 191; Brunet and Préaud, p. 32 (with milk jug); Savill, 2, pp. 505, 524–25, 567–69, 583–84; d'Albis, "Fond jaune," pp. 18, 21–23, figs. 1–2

NOTES

1 See Dauterman, *Marks*, p. 177. See also Savill, 3, p. 1088 (form of B not exactly the same).

2 According to Savill, 3, pp. 1108–9, probably I, used 1753–90s, although sometimes, as in this case, it is so near the rim that it looks like a T.

3 See Savill, 3, pp. 1120–21, as found on soft paste 1758–69. She proposes either Pierre-Edmond Tristant *aîné* (active 1758–87/88) or Philibert Choulet *aîné* (active 1756–79). See also Dauterman, *Marks*, pp. 229–30.

4 Attributed by Dauterman, *Marks* (pp. 190–91) to Delatre *cadet, aîné*, active c. 1752–76.

5 Savill, 3, p. 1117, found on soft paste 1756–82.

6 Savill, 3, pp. 1127–28, found on soft paste 1754–90s.

7 Ibid., pp. 1074–75, active at Sèvres 1752–90; see Peters, *Marks*, p. 73.

8 APML, Cartier file, *Composition des Colis expédiés à Monsieur J.P. Morgan*, 13 Princes Gate, London, 16 June 1905: "1 Cabaret Sévres jaune, cartels blancs et or avec paysage et sujets enfants camaieu bleu, par VIELLARD/ Composé de: no. 146: 1 Théière (avec couvercle)/147-1 Sucrier/148-1 Crémier/149-150-1 Tasse et Soucoupe/151-1 Plateau."

9 See cat. no. 85 for this shape.

10 Ibid.

11 Ibid.

12 See cat. no. 95 for this shape.

13 Jean-Richard, p. 332, no. 1384.

14 Bourgeois, 1913, pl. 2, no. 493; Eriksen and Bellaigue, p. 208.

15 Jean-Richard, pp. 77, 207, nos. 196, 780.

16 Ibid., pp. 240–41, no. 935 and Bourgeois, 1913, pl. 3, no. 113.

17 Jean-Richard, p. 294, no. 1194.

18 Bourgeois, 1913, pl. 3 , no. 569, pendant to *La Blanchisseuse*.

19 Bernard Dragesco was one of the first to observe these stylistic inconsistencies in this tea service.

20 I would like to thank Antoine d'Albis for his help in pointing out these signs of redecoration. It is possible that the tray originally was only decorated with gilding, perhaps similar to a *compotier* from c. 1759 in the MAD, Paris (Verlet, *Sèvres*, pl. 38a) or a chestnut basket from c. 1760, at the MNC, Sèvres (ibid., pl. 38b).

182

182

Cup and saucer (*gobelet litron et soucoupe*)

1917.973

Sèvres, 18th-century paste, probably 19th-century decoration

Soft-paste porcelain, cup: H. 1⅞ × W. 2¹³⁄₁₆ × D. 2 in. (4.7 × 7.1 × 5.1 cm); saucer: H. 1 × DIAM. 4¼ in. (2.5 × 10.7 cm)

Yellow ground, polychrome landscapes, gilding

Marks: both with interlaced Ls in blue; incised X and d on cup;[1] incised da on saucer[2]

Provenance: J. Pierpont Morgan

There is some evidence that this cup and saucer were redecorated in the nineteenth century. The cup is a *gobelet litron*, which was introduced at Vincennes at least by 1752. It is marked with factory marks but lacks a date letter suggesting a pre-1753 date. However, it is of the fourth of five sizes made, and this size was not introduced until 1757.[3] Furthermore, the gilding pattern around the reserves suggests a mid- to late 1760s date, as do the incised da and X.[4] At this date yellow ground would have been unusual. More importantly, perhaps, the outline of the reserve on the cup, with its odd lobed shape, is atypical of Vincennes and Sèvres and points to later decoration. Finally, there is bubbling around the outside and bottom of the saucer, again suggesting possible redecoration.[5]

Exhibition: *Morgan Loan Exhibition*, New York, 1914, not in catalogue

Literature: Chavagnac, p. 55, no. 63

NOTES

1 See Dauterman, *Marks*, p. 244 for X, on two pieces dated 1767 and 1768.

2 See Dauterman, *Marks*, p. 189, attributed to Danet *père*, active 1768–87, and Savill, 3, p. 1097.

3 See cat. no. 95 for the sizes produced.

4 See notes 1 and 2.

5 No such bubbling can be found on the cup. I would like to thank Antoine d'Albis for this information.

183

Sugar bowl (*pot à sucre à la Reine*)

1917.976

Vincennes or Sèvres, 18th-century paste, 19th-century decoration

Soft-paste porcelain, H. 4⅛ × DIAM. 4½ in. (10.4 × 11.4 cm)

Yellow ground, monochrome children, gilding

Marks: interlaced Ls in blue with five dots; inverted V with dot at point, meant to be the mark of Mutel[1]

Provenance: Cartier et Fils, Paris, 1903;[2] J. Pierpont Morgan

This tub-shaped sugar bowl was molded, not turned. It was called by the factory *pot* (or *boîte*) *à sucre à la Reine*, as evidenced in several drawings dated 19 February 1753 in the Sèvres archives.[3] Made in two sizes, the Hartford example probably is of the first size.[4] The second size was not made until June 1754.[5] The Museum's sugar bowl is like the model before it was

rectified by Duplessis in February 1753.[6] The same shape was produced with relief bands and was called *pot à sucre à cuvier à cerceaux*.[7]

The Hartford sugar bowl probably was decorated in the nineteenth century. Examination of the underside reveals black speckling consistent with refiring. Furthermore, the blue enamel used was not available in 1753.[8] The quality of the reserve painting is poor throughout, and the gilding around the reserves, with its four small indentations, is atypical of the factory. The marks also suggest that the piece was not decorated at Vincennes: while the sugar bowl appears to have been decorated in 1753, Mutel did not enter the factory's employment until May 1754 and was usually associated with landscapes or birds.[9]

Exhibition: *Morgan Loan Exhibition*, New York, 1914, not in catalogue

Literature: Chavagnac, p. 57, no. 66; Hood, *Bulletin*, p. 10

NOTES

1 Active 1754–74. See Peters, *Marks*, p. 54.

2 APML, Cartier file, invoice 30 May 1903: "1 Beurrier [*sic*] Sèvres fond jaune, amours camaïeu bleu," 10,000 French francs. See also *Colis* 3 June 1903: "1 Beurrier [*sic*] Sèvres fond jaune cartels blancs amours camaïeu bleu-par Mutel."

3 AMNS, R. I, L. 2, d. 8, fol. 3.

4 *Vincennes*, p. 82, illustrates two examples, one 4⁵⁄₁₆ in. (11 cm) in height, the other 3⅞ in. (9.8 cm).

5 Préaud and d'Albis, p. 178.

6 Eriksen and Bellaigue, p. 270, the Atheneum's example like the sugar bowl in the Pitti Palace illustrated by Eriksen, *Pitti*. See note 3 above for rectified drawings.

7 See cat. no. 76 for discussion of this variation.

8 These observations were made by Antoine d'Albis.

9 Préaud and d'Albis, p. 211.

183

184

Cup and saucer (*gobelet Bouillard et soucoupe*)

1917.1042

Sèvres, 18th-century paste, probably 19th-century decoration

Soft-paste porcelain, cup: H. 2⁷⁄₁₆ × W. 3¹¹⁄₁₆ × D. 2¹³⁄₁₆ in. (6.2 × 9.3 × 7.1 cm); saucer: H. 1³⁄₁₆ × DIAM. 5⅜ in. (3 × 13.6 cm)

Yellow ground with red *pointillé* decoration, polychrome landscapes, gilding

Marks: interlaced Ls in blue on both; cup: incised t;[1] bc;[2] saucer: incised nf (conjoined)[3]

Provenance: J. Pierpont Morgan

184

The cup is an example of the Sèvres factory's *gobelet Bouillard*.[4] Although it dates from the eighteenth century, the decoration probably is later. The saucer is especially dubious, with extensive black pitting on its exterior. Its foot has been ground down in an attempt to hide the signs of refiring. The dentil gilding is more like a shark's tooth pattern, and there is no tooling on the other areas of gilding. The landscape painting on both the cup and saucer, in the manner of two or three eighteenth-century Sèvres painters, is extremely poor, even for this type.[5] The *pointillé* ground, with its overly large dots, is also suspect, as it is unusual to find such a pattern on yellow ground.

Exhibition: *Morgan Loan Exhibition*, New York, 1914, not in catalogue

Literature: Chavagnac, p. 100, no. 122

NOTES

1 Not in Savill.

2 Dauterman, *Marks*, p. 180, different form, postulated for Nicolas Brachard, *père*.

3 Not in Savill or Dauterman.

4 See cat. no. 84 for this shape.

5 See cat. no. 67 for these painters.

185

Tray (*plat à hors d'œuvres à rubans*)

1917.1057

Vincennes, paste, 1750s, 19th-century decoration

Soft-paste porcelain, H. 1 9/16 × L. 10 11/16 × W. 8 15/16 in. (4 × 27.1 × 22.6 cm)

Blue ground with *pointillé* gilding, polychrome *incrusté* flowers

Marks: interlaced Ls in blue, indistinct incised C?[1]

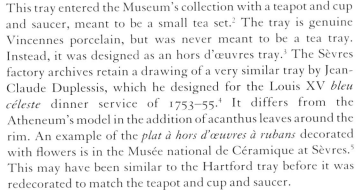

Provenance: J. Pierpont Morgan

This tray entered the Museum's collection with a teapot and cup and saucer, meant to be a small tea set.[2] The tray is genuine Vincennes porcelain, but was never meant to be a tea tray. Instead, it was designed as an hors d'œuvres tray.[3] The Sèvres factory archives retain a drawing of a very similar tray by Jean-Claude Duplessis, which he designed for the Louis XV *bleu céleste* dinner service of 1753–55.[4] It differs from the Atheneum's model in the addition of acanthus leaves around the rim. An example of the *plat à hors d'œuvres à rubans* decorated with flowers is in the Musée national de Céramique at Sèvres.[5] This may have been similar to the Hartford tray before it was redecorated to match the teapot and cup and saucer.

Evidence supporting the notion that this piece was redecorated includes blackened and pitted gilding around the rim, an orange-peel texture to the blue ground color, and a crude version of *incrusté* painting.[6] It looks as if the ground color was sprayed on the tray.

185

Exhibitions: *Morgan Loan Exhibition*, New York, 1914, not in catalogue; *Design in the Service of Tea*, New York, 1984

Literature: Chavagnac, pp. 108–9, no. 133

NOTES

1 If it is a C, this mark is noted on pieces from 1748, and by 1753–79 (Savill, 3, p. 1092). It is possible that the mark should be oriented in the opposite direction, resembling a half-moon.

2 See cat. nos. 94–95.

3 See Préaud and d'Albis, p. 150, no. 113.

4 AMNS, R. 2 (section D, § 6, N° 20, *année* 1788), fol. 24, inscribed *bon moins de façon/ H. N.° 3/ N.° 21.*

5 MNC, Sèvres, no. 25139. See note 3.

6 See note 2 above.

186

Cup and saucer (*gobelet litron et soucoupe*)

1917.1089

Sèvres, 18th-century paste, 19th-century decoration

Soft-paste porcelain, cup, H. 3 × W. 3¹⁵⁄₁₆ × D. 2¹⁵⁄₁₆ in. (7.6 × 10 × 7.5 cm); saucer, H. 1⁷⁄₁₆ × DIAM. 5¹⁵⁄₁₆ in. (3.7 × 15.1 cm)

Yellow ground with gilded garlands and scrolls, polychrome portrait figure and ciphers

Marks: on both: interlaced Ls in blue with date letter Y for 1776, k underneath for Charles-Nicolas Dodin;[1] script LG in gold on saucer for Étienne-Henry Le Guay[2] and traces of a gilded mark on the cup; cup: incised 29;[3] saucer: incised 48[4]

Provenance: A.B. Daniell & Sons, London, 1904;[5] J. Pierpont Morgan

This cup and saucer are examples of the first size *gobelet litron et soucoupe*.[6] They appear to have been redecorated in the nineteenth century. On the saucer there is an indentation and change in texture where the factory mark is drawn suggesting an earlier mark has been ground down. Furthermore, the gilded mark in the manner of Le Guay is drawn differently than other examples of his mark. There is even a subtle difference in the way the k for Dodin is drawn, noticeable in the atypical downward curve of the top-right portion of the letter. Finally, the incised mark of 29 found on the cup is usually found on pieces of the 1780s and 1790s.[7]

It is also unusual to find the same cipher in all three reserves on the saucer. Moreover, the quality of the gilding and especially the chasing is inferior to what one would expect to see on a cup and saucer of this richness.

Another cup and saucer set with a very similar portrait on the cup and almost the exact same pattern of gilding on both was sold in Stockholm in 1988.[8] Dated 1774, it was also marked with the Sèvres factory mark and the marks of Dodin and Le Guay. The reserve on the cup shows one figure from an engraving by C.-A. Littret of 1766 after Carle Vanloo's *The Grand Turk Giving a Concert to his Mistress*, now in the Wallace Collection.[9] This engraving was also used as a source for the central plaque of a *guéridon* of 1774 belonging to Madame du Barry, now in the Louvre.[10] The saucer is decorated with trophies in the reserves.

The Museum's cup depicts a woman in a very similar gown, but quite different headdress. Her identity has not yet been determined. The ciphers on the saucer, comprising the initials MLC (the M in gold, the L in roses and the C in cornflowers) match in every respect those on a set of seven porcelain plaques mounted as a table now at the Wallace Collection. These plaques date from the nineteenth century, but in 1867, when the table was shown at a Paris exhibition, were thought to have belonged to Marie-Thérèse Louise de Savoie-Carignan, the princesse de Lamballe (Turin 1748–Paris 1792).[11] She was

186

the head of Marie-Antoinette's household and the queen's devoted friend, and was executed during The Terror in September 1792. No direct engraved source for the portrait has come to light, although there are affinities in the pose of the head and especially in the formation of the mouth with known engravings of the princess.[12] We can imagine that a nineteenth-century forger would choose a well-known eighteenth-century personality to feature on a redecorated cup and saucer, creating a very marketable souvenir of the *ancien régime*. It is odd, however, that the costume of the Hartford sitter was in part taken from the Vanloo painting, as one would expect that a forger would simply copy an engraving in its entirety.

Exhibition: *Morgan Loan Exhibition*, New York, 1914, not in catalogue; *Morgan*, Hartford, no. 74

Literature: Chavagnac, p. 127, no. 160; de Bellaigue, "Sèvres," p. 187, no. 74; Savill, 3, p. 1031 n. 11

NOTES

1 See cat. no. 71 for this artist, and for an illustration of his mark.

2 See cat. no. 122 for this artist, and for an illustration of his mark.

3 Savill, 3, p. 1129, found on soft paste 1782–90s.

4 Ibid., p. 1133, found on soft paste 1761?, 1777–92.

5 APML, Daniell file, invoice 19 April 1904: "A large Cup and Saucer, rich canary ground, with painted portrait in front of cup, rich raised gold decoration, & a cypher in roses & gold, in compartments on border of Saucer," £539.

6 See cat. no. 95 for this shape.

7 This alone would not be enough to prove it was later decorated, as the incised marks are not yet fully documented or understood.

8 Bukowskis Julauktion, Stockholm, 13–16 December 1988, lot 933. A photocopy of this cup and saucer was kindly sent to me by Bernard Dragesco. He did not see the object in person, and therefore could not attest to its authenticity. The gilding differs only in the central well of the saucer, where a different starburst is surrounded by a circle and then encircled by alternating beads, and there is an additional circle of dots adjacent to the inner Vitruvian scroll.

9 Dated 1727. See Ingamells, p. 255.

10 See Eriksen and Bellaigue, pp. 328–29, no. 140.

11 Savill, 2, pp. 895–97, C509. The link with the princess de Lamballe was first suggested by Rosalind Savill, based on the ciphers on the saucer. I am very grateful for her help with this entry.

12 See an engraving by Weber after an unidentified painting (*Iconographie des Bourbon*, (LP 83-37²), image kindly provided by Joan Sussler at the Lewis Walpole Library, Yale University, and Bernard Dragesco. I would also like to thank Sylvie Wallez for searching for engraved sources for this portrait.

187

187

Cup and saucer (*gobelet litron et soucoupe*)

1917.1107

Sèvres, c. 1795–1800, with later additions

Soft-paste porcelain, cup: H. 2⁷⁄₁₆ × W. 3⁹⁄₁₆ × D. 2⅝ in. (6.2 × 9.1 × 6.7 cm); saucer: H. 1⁷⁄₁₆ × DIAM. 5⁵⁄₁₆ in. (3.7 × 13.4 cm)

Yellow ground with dark violet bands, polychrome garlands, bouquets, and patera in central well

Marks: cup: *Sevres* in blue with 9. for Charles-Nicolas Buteux *fils aîné*;[1] spurious interlaced Ls with cc for 1780; incised 4 and 51;[2] saucer: same painted marks

Provenance: J. Pierpont Morgan

The paste and glaze show many inclusions, evidence of contaminants in either the materials or in the kiln. The cup and saucer must have been left unfinished during the Revolutionary period. At some later date the purple ground and the gilded borders were added. The interlaced Ls and cc no doubt date from this time. Reglazed scratches give further proof of redecoration.

The cup and saucer are examples of the second size of the *gobelet litron et soucoupe*.[3] Chavagnac believed that the cup and saucer were made in 1780 and that the "Sèvres" in script was a fantasy of the painter Buteux.[4] In fact, from 1793, after the fall of the French monarchy, the interlaced Ls were abandoned and the factory name was used to mark the porcelain. The word Sèvres was accompanied by the letters RF for *République Française* until just before or in 1800.[5]

Exhibition: *Morgan Loan Exhibition*, New York, 1914, not in catalogue

Literature: Chavagnac, p. 136, no. 171

NOTES

1 Active 1763–1801. See Peters, *Marks*, p. 19.

2 Incised 4 found from c. 1753–87 in soft paste. Perhaps this cup and saucer were made c. 1787 and left in the white until at least 1793.

3 See cat. no. 95 for this shape.

4 Chavagnac, p. 136.

5 See Béalu, *passim*.

188

Sugar bowl (*pot à sucre Bouret*)

1917.1175

Sèvres, 18th-century paste, 19th-century decoration

Soft-paste porcelain, H. 4¼ × DIAM. 3⁹⁄₁₆ in. (10.8 × 9 cm)

Yellow ground, monochrome blue flowers around the reserves, polychrome birds, gilding

Marks: interlaced Ls in blue; incised O[1]

Provenance: A.B. Daniell & Sons, London, 1907;[2] J. Pierpont Morgan

This covered sugar bowl was called *pot à sucre Bouret* by the Sèvres factory.[3] The authenticity of its decoration has been questioned by several scholars, although there is very little

concrete evidence to cite. While there are no obvious signs of refiring, there is a gilded chip in the rim of the bowl that suggests that at least the gilding is later. Furthermore, the gilded filet on the cover is atypical of Vincennes *pots à sucre*.[4] More subjectively, perhaps, the birds are too carefully drawn in comparison to similar birds from the Vincennes period. Also disturbing is the fact that the foliage borders around the reserves are in monochrome blue, when one would expect them to be polychrome, like the birds. It is also unusual to find monochrome painting directly against a ground color, and the overlap of the blue border with the yellow serves to distort the blue.

This monochrome blue flower border is found on a few other pieces of Vincennes or Sèvres porcelain, evidently executed by the same painter, including a milk jug sold in Paris in 1994,[5] a cup and saucer formerly in the Archdeacon collection,[6] and another cup and saucer in a French private collection. According to correspondence in the Wadsworth Atheneum's files, the saucer from this last set shows evidence that an earlier mark has been ground away.[7] It seems likely that this entire group was decorated at the same time to form a tea set. The whereabouts of an accompanying tray, if it existed, is unknown.

In addition to the pieces cited above, there is a remounted chamber pot in the Ashmolean Museum at Oxford with a similar monochrome blue floral border on a yellow ground.[8] In a recent publication on the collection the decoration of this object was accepted as period. It appears to have been decorated by a different hand than the pieces described above.

Exhibitions: *Morgan Loan Exhibition*, New York, 1914, not in catalogue; *European Porcelain,* New York, 1949, no. 164; *Continental Table Porcelain*, San Francisco, 1965, no. 226

Literature: *European Porcelain,* no. 164; *Continental Table Porcelain*, no. 226

NOTES

1 Savill, 3, p. 1117, as found on soft paste 1754–82.

2 APML, Daniell file, invoice 24 July 1907: "An old Sèvres china sucrier & cover Yellow ground, with compartments of painted birds, surrounded by painted blue foliage," £432.10.

3 See cat. no. 98 for this shape.

4 As pointed out to the author by Bernard Dragesco.

5 Drouot, Paris, 9 December 1994, lot 71.

6 Illustrated in Alfassa and Guérin, pl. 49b, as in the collection of Jules Archdeacon.

7 Letter from Michel Vendermeersch, 17 February 1998.

8 Dawson, *Ashmolean*, pp. 66–67, no. 46. This piece is marked with interlaced Ls and a fleur-de-lis, attributed to the flower painter Taillandier.

189

190

189

Teapot (*théière Calabre*)

1917.1180

Sèvres, 18th-century paste, 19th-century decoration

Soft-paste porcelain, H. 4¹⁵⁄₁₆ × w. 6⅜ × D. 3¹⁵⁄₁₆ in. (12.5 × 16.2 × 9.9 cm)

Yellow ground, polychrome figures in landscapes, gilding

Marks: interlaced Ls in blue with date letter L for 1764

Provenance: A.B. Daniell & Sons, 1907;[1] J. Pierpont Morgan

The teapot probably dates from the 1750s, and was called a *théière Calabre* in the Sèvres factory records.[2] Although there is no physical evidence pointing to redecoration, the style of the painting and the strange gilded fillets on the handle and spout all suggest a nineteenth-century date.

Exhibitions: *Morgan Loan Exhibition*, New York, 1914, not in catalogue; *Design in the Service of Tea*, New York, 1984

NOTES

1　APML, Daniell file, invoice 4 July 1907: "An old Sèvres china Tea Pot, canary ground, and raised gold, with compartments on each side of finely painted figures, and landscapes A.D. 1764," £412.10.

2　See cat. no. 87 for this form.

190

Juice pot (*pot à jus ordinaire*)

1917.972

Sèvres?, 18th-century paste, decoration probably 19th century

Soft-paste porcelain, H. 3⅛ × w. 3³⁄₁₆ × D. 2½ in. (7.9 × 8 × 6.3 cm)

Yellow *pointillé* ground, polychrome landscapes, gilding

Marks: interlaced Ls in blue; incised rectangle[1]

Provenance: J. Pierpont Morgan

Juice pots were usually sold in multiples, often although not always with a tray, as part of the dinner service. They were used for serving the meat or vegetable juices that would have accompanied a roast.[2] Juice pots were being made from at least 1752, as sixty molds of different sizes appear in the October inventory.[3] They are recorded in three sizes although only two sizes appear in the sales records.[4] The factory holds two drawings dated 19 February 1753, showing four different *pots à jus*, two *ordinaires* and two *nouvelles*.[5] The earliest juice pots sold were decorated with flowers,[6] as were all but five entries in the sales records from 1753 to 1756.[7]

There has been doubt raised as to the date of the decoration of this juice pot. Several factors contribute to this suspicion, beginning with a date presumably before 1754 on an object with decoration that could not have originated before the later 1760s.

Pointillé decoration, consisting of small white circles outlined in dots of a darker enamel color on pale ground colors, usually is found from the late 1760s.[8] The gilding is also of a later style, again perhaps the mid-1760s. While these facts might merely suggest that the pot was simply undated but decorated in the 1760s, the configuration of the *pointillé* circles is unusual. On other examples the circles are much closer together so that the proportion of dots to ground is much greater.[9] Additionally, the landscape painting is labored and closer to nineteenth-century painting in style. Finally, the gilding from the foot ring sloppily spills to the underneath, which one would not expect on genuine Vincennes or Sèvres.

Exhibition: *Morgan Loan Exhibition*, New York, 1914, not in catalogue

Notes

1 See Savill, 3, p. 1134, used 1755–87.

2 See Savill, "Starhemberg," p. 28.

3 *Vincennes*, p. 160.

4 AMNS, I. 7, January 1755, lists twenty juice pots of the third size while, according to *Vincennes*, p. 160, only two sizes were sold.

5 AMNS, R. 1, L. 1, d. 4, fol. 1. On one sheet the *pots à jus ordinaires*, without handles, appear in two different sizes, the first size with more slender proportions. The second sheet, with the *pots à jus nouvelles* [*sic*], shows two sizes and different covers, one simple and one articulated. The first size has a handle with foliage at the junctures with the body, while the second size is shown without a handle. The second-size pot with the simple cover is closer to the Atheneum's example.

6 AMNS, Vy 1, fol. 9v, 1 November 1752, Cromot.

7 AMNS, files for *pot à jus*. I would like to thank Tamara Préaud for access to these notes.

8 Savill, 3, p. 1176.

9 I would like to thank Bernard Dragesco for pointing this out to me. If one looks, for example, at the cup and saucer in the Wallace Collection, London (no. C359) illustrated in Savill, 2, p. 531, as well as no. C347 (p. 506), no. C381 (a teapot, p. 583), and nos. C396–400 (a tea service, p. 611), the circles are much closer together.

191

Fruit dish (*compotier carré*)

1917.979

Vincennes or Sèvres porcelain, 18th-century paste, 19th-century decoration

Soft-paste porcelain, H. 1¾ × W. 8⁹⁄₁₆ × D. 8½ in. (4.5 × 21.7 × 21.5 cm)

Yellow ground, blue monochrome children in landscapes, gilding

Marks: interlaced Ls in blue, dot in center, painter's mark in the manner of André-Vincent Vielliard *père*[1]

Provenance: Cartier et Fils, Paris, 1904;[2] J. Pierpont Morgan

Vincennes and Sèvres called this fruit dish a *compotier carré*. The shape was introduced in 1754, when molds and models in two sizes appeared in the factory inventory.[3] Along with oval and round *compotiers*, these square dishes were used to serve compotes of fruit during the dessert service. Most dessert services at Sèvres included *compotiers,* often of more than one form.

The Museum's fruit dish is eighteenth-century porcelain, but was redecorated in the nineteenth century. The foot has been ground down in an attempt to hide the blackening that occurred during refiring, and some of the blue enamel used to paint the reserves mistakenly appears on the exterior of the dish. The factory mark suggests that it was made in 1753, just before date letters appeared at Vincennes, but there are no known or recorded yellow-ground dessert wares from this period.[4]

The painting of the reserves is meant to be by André-Vincent Vielliard, in the manner of François Boucher. A mark resembling his appears on the bottom of the dish, but it differs slightly from his autograph mark. The style of the painting also differs from Vielliard's. It is stiff and precise, and resembles the late eighteenth-century painter Greuze rather than the more appropriate Boucher. The palm and floral gilding pattern of the central reserve, more commonly found in the 1760s, is not carried through to the four smaller reserves. The tooling of the gilding is crudely executed, and not of the same standard as found on Vincennes gilding.

Exhibitions: *Morgan Loan Exhibition*, New York, 1914, not in catalogue; *French and English Art Treasures*, New York, 1942, no. 310

Literature: Chavagnac, p. 58, no. 68; *French and English Art Treasures*, no. 310; Buckley, *Connoisseur*, p. 51; Hood, *Bulletin*, p. 10

191

192

NOTES

1 See cat. no. 78.

2 APML, Cartier file, invoice 3 June 1904: "1 Plateau carré à festons, vieux Sèvres, cartels et amours camaïeu bleu sur fond jaune," 40,000 French francs.

3 AMNS, 1 January 1755, for 1754. See Préaud and d'Albis, p. 179, no. 193 for this shape.

4 The one exception found by this author is a pair of yellow-ground *seaux à verres forme du Roy* sold to Machard on 18 December 1753 (AMNS, Vy 1, fol. 21). During the 1780s the use of yellow ground became popular again, and services with this color appeared. See cat. nos. 145–46.

192

Fruit dish (*compotier ovale*)

1917.1012

Vincennes or Sèvres, 18th-century paste, 19th-century decoration

Soft-paste porcelain, H. 1⁹⁄₁₆ × L. 10⅝ × w. 7¹¹⁄₁₆ in. (4 × 26.9 × 19.5 cm)

Yellow ground, monochrome blue reserve of children in landscape, gilding

Marks: interlaced Ls in blue with date letter F for 1758–59; painter's mark in the manner of François-Joseph Aloncle;[1] incised 6[2]

Provenance: J. Pierpont Morgan

This fruit dish was called a *compotier ovale*.[3] This example is genuine eighteenth-century Sèvres porcelain, but was redecorated in the nineteenth century. The foot has been ground down to hide the discoloration of refired porcelain. Some blackening does remain, however, on the exterior, near the gilding, a sign that it was regilded using turpentine oil. Some areas of abrasion on the exterior also suggest that more blackened areas were rubbed to remove the discoloration. There are two kiln support holes, although only one would have been necessary. One of the holes is very black, another sign of redecoration.

The mark underneath the dish is off-center, and traces of the original mark are still visible in the center. The painter's mark, meant to be that of Aloncle, is incompatible with the decoration, as Aloncle was a bird painter, who is not known to have painted children. The style of the painting is typical of nineteenth-century decoration, imitating the factory painter Vielliard.[4]

Exhibition: *Morgan Loan Exhibition*, New York, 1914, not in catalogue

Literature: Chavagnac, p. 79, no. 94

NOTES

1 See cat. no. 88.

2 See Savill, 3, p. 1127. The mark appears on soft paste 1754–90s.

3 For this shape see cat. no. 141.

4 See cat. no. 78 for Vielliard. See cat. no. 191 for a similarly redecorated piece. Vielliard's children were in the style of Boucher, while these reserves are more in the style of Greuze.

193

Pair of salt cellars (*salières simples* or *salières*)

1917.1027–1028

Sèvres, 18th-century paste, 19th-century decoration

Soft-paste porcelain, 1917.1027: H. 1½ × L. 3⅜ × w. 2⅝ in. (3.8 × 8.5 × 6.6 cm); 1917.1028: H. 1⁷⁄₁₆ × L. 3⅜ × w. 2¹¹⁄₁₆ in. (3.7 × 8.6 × 6.8 cm)

Pink ground, polychrome flowers, gilding

Marks: on both: partially effaced interlaced Ls in blue, painter's mark in the style of Étienne Evans;[1] incised cl on 1917.1028[2]

Provenance: J. Pierpont Morgan

These salt cellars were called either *salières simples* or *salières*.[3] In the present examples, the porcelain dates from the eighteenth century but the decoration seems to be later. There is little physical evidence of refiring, except for small gilded chips on the rim of 1917.1027.[4] However, the decoration of the reserves and the gilding all point to a nineteenth-century date. The flower painting is inconsistent with the work of Evans, who was one of the factory's primary bird painters and would not have painted floral sprays. Moreover, the gilding is crude, and the purple outlining overwhelming. These may have been two of six pink-ground salts with flowers on the market in the 1880s.[5]

Exhibition: *Morgan Loan Exhibition*, New York, 1914, not in catalogue

Literature: Chavagnac, p. 94, no. 112

NOTES

1 Active 1752–1800. See cat. no. 88.

2 Ibid., p. 1095, found on soft paste 1770–75. This dating incompatible with the presumed decoration of the salt cellar.

3 See cat. no. 140 for this form.

4 They are not scratched inside and thus may never have been used, suggesting that they were sold by the factory undecorated, perhaps in 1800 when Alexandre Brongniart, the factory's new director, switched the production to hard paste.

5 This according to David Peters.

194

Wine glass cooler (probably *seau à verre échancré*)

1917.1071

Porcelain of unknown manufacture, 19th century

Soft-paste porcelain, H. 4⁵⁄₁₆ × w. 6⅛ × D. 5³⁄₁₆ in. (11 × 15.6 × 13.1 cm)

White ground with polychrome and gilded ciphers, polychrome garlands, pale blue and gilded urns

Marks: interlaced Ls in blue with date letter S; LB underneath meant to be Jean-Nicolas Le Bel *jeune*;[1] incised K[2]

Provenance: A.B. Daniell & Sons, London, 1900;[3] J. Pierpont Morgan

This wine glass cooler, of the same form as 1917.1070 (catalogue no. 137) and meant to be from the same service (for Madame du Barry, 1771), was probably made in the 1820s or 1830s, to extend the size of the original eighteenth-century service. The cooler is slightly larger than the original, its base has a thicker foot rim and no kiln hole, and the painting and gilding are inferior to the authentic du Barry cooler. The most noticeable difference may be seen in the pale blue vases that link the garlands. In the case of the nineteenth-century *seau* they are shaded with crude, linear dark hatchings on the right side, as compared to an additional layer of blue enamel.

The Samson porcelain factory is said to have made examples of these coolers to match the du Barry service.[4] Two *seaux échancré* in the Sèvres style with turquoise ribbons were attributed to the Minton factory in 1987.[5]

Exhibition: *Morgan Loan Exhibition*, New York, 1914, not in catalogue; *Continental Table Porcelain*, San Francisco, 1965, no. 249

Literature: Chavagnac, p. 114, no. 141;[6] *Continental Table Porcelain*, no. 249

NOTES

1 Active 1765–93. See Savill, 3, pp. 1041–42; Peters, *Marks*, p. 46.

2 Not in Savill. See Dauterman, *Marks*, p. 210, although the form is not the same as those shown in Dauterman.

3 APML, Daniell file, invoice 25 May 1900: "A pair of small shaped Seaux in finest Sèvres porcelain pâte tendre, with festoons of flowers, & initials "DB" in flowers and gold (part of service originally made for Madame Du Barri) A.D. 1771," £245.

4 Phillips, London, 4 December 1991, lot 205.

5 Sotheby's, London, 16 & 23 June 1987, lot 563. It is possible that Minton also made du Barry coolers.

6 Chavagnac illustrates 1917.1071.

193

194

195

Pair of plaques

1917.1029–1030

Possibly 18th-century Vincennes or Sèvres, with 19th-century decoration

Soft-paste porcelain, 1917.1029: W. 5½ × D. 4¹¹⁄₁₆ in. (14 × 11.9 cm); 1917.1030: W. 5⅝ × D. 4¾ in. (14.2 × 12 cm)

White ground, polychrome figures in landscapes, gilded borders

Marks: none

Provenance: J. Pierpont Morgan

The porcelain may be of factory origin from the eighteenth century, but the decoration dates from the nineteenth century.[1] The backs are unglazed and show widespread blackening from refiring. The pale colors and thinly painted enamels, as well as the gilded border around the reserves, are purely nineteenth-century in style. One scene is based on the engraving *La Fontaine d'Amour* by Pierre Aveline after François Boucher, which survives in the factory archives.[2] The other scene of two women bathing is unidentified.

Exhibition: *Morgan Loan Exhibition*, New York, 1914, not in catalogue

Literature: Chavagnac, p. 95, no. 115

NOTES

1 Antoine d'Albis believed the porcelain to be genuine, but Bernard Dragesco felt it was too glassy for factory white ware.

2 Not in Jean-Richard. It is very similar to Daullé's, *Les Charmes de la vie champêtre* (Jean-Richard, pp. 167–68, nos. 171–72) and François-Antoine Aveline's *Pastorale* (ibid., p. 77, no. 197).

196

Toilet pot (*pot à pommade*)

1917.1117

Sèvres, 18th-century paste, 19th-century decoration

Soft-paste porcelain, H. 2¹¹⁄₁₆ × DIAM. 2³⁄₁₆ in. (6.8 × 5.5 cm)

White ground with green and gold trellises, polychrome flowers

Marks: interlaced Ls in blue with date letters ii for 1786; cp below for Antoine-Joseph Chappuis *jeune, aîné*;[1] incised 41[2]

Provenance: Cartier et Fils, Paris, 1901,[3] J. Pierpont Morgan

This toilet pot and cover may have been redecorated. The green trellis design is more appropriate to the years around 1760, and the painter Antoine-Joseph Chappuis *jeune, aîné*, who became head of the kilns in October 1786, usually marked his pieces above the factory mark.[4] Moreover, the flat cover is not typical of those found on Sèvres toilet pots, which usually were domed. Flat covers do appear on *pots à confitures* but they did not have flower knobs. In the case of the Museum's cover, it does not fit the pot well and shows carbons spots that suggest redecoration. It is possible that the cover has merely been replaced, and that the pot is legitimate, although old-fashioned in its design. It is also possible that the pot is a legitimate replacement for a pot in an earlier toilet set. However, the consistency of the decoration between the pot and the lid, and the unusual placement of Chappuis's mark on the pot point more to a totally redecorated piece with a non-Sèvres cover.

195

196

Exhibition: *Morgan Loan Exhibition*, New York, 1914, not in catalogue

Literature: Chavagnac, p. 145, no. 183; Savill, 3, pp. 1018, 1020 n. 3

NOTES

1 Active 1756–87. See Savill, 3, pp. 1018–20; Peters, *Marks*, p. 23 (as beginning in 1761, when he moved from being a *répareur* to the painter's workshop).
2 Found on soft paste 1780–90s. See Savill, 3, p. 1131.
3 APML, Cartier file, invoice 24 May 1901: "1 Pot à pommade quadrille gros vert et fleurs," 750 French francs.
4 See Munger, *Wickes*, p. 202, no. 151; Casanova, p. 189, no. 116.

197

Pair of toilet pots, mounted as vases
(*pots à pommade*)

1917.1161–1162

Sèvres, 18th-century paste, 19th-century decoration and mounts

Soft-paste porcelain, gilt bronze, without mounts: 1917.1161: H. 3⅜ × DIAM. 2⅝ in. (8.5 × 6.7 cm); 1917.1162: H. 3³⁄₁₆ × DIAM. 2⅝ in. (8 × 6.6 cm); with mounts: 1917.1161: H. 7⁷⁄₁₆ × W. 3¾ × D. 3 in. (18.9 × 9.5 × 7.6 cm); 1917.1162: H. 7½ × W. 3¾ × D. 2¹⁵⁄₁₆ in. (19 × 9.5 × 7.5 cm)

Yellow ground, monochrome carmine children, gilding

Marks: on both: interlaced Ls in carmine with date letter L, and ch (inside factory mark) meant to be for Étienne-Jean Chabry *fils* or *fils aîné* or *aîné*;[1] no incised marks visible[2]

Provenance: perhaps Duveen Brothers, London, 1902;[3] J. Pierpont Morgan

These mounted vases originally were first-size Sèvres toilet pots.[4] The gilt-bronze mounts date from the nineteenth century. The covers were stripped of their original porcelain floral and foliate knobs and drilled to accommodate the gilt-bronze pine-cone finials. The porcelain itself, while dating from the eighteenth century, appears to have been redecorated, probably when the mounts were added. Fine black speckles cover all of the areas of yellow, which is the color of egg yolk and not typical of the period indicated by the date letter. The mark itself is problematic, with the highly unusual feature of having the painter's mark inside the interlaced Ls. Furthermore, the bottoms of the pots are covered with some sort of adhesive and the marks appear to have been painted on top of this material.

It is possible although by no means certain that the monochrome children are original to these toilet pots, which would have been white, and that only the yellow ground and gilding were added later. This would date the set before redecoration to the early 1750s, when monochrome decoration on white

197

197

was current.[5] The covers, with their stiff monochrome floral garlands, seem to have been entirely decorated later.

Another pair of later-mounted toilet pots was in the collection of Baron Gustav de Rothschild and then Sydney J. Laman, and sold in 1973.[6] While the mounts differ in details, their overall design is the same, suggesting a common source.

Exhibition: *Morgan Loan Exhibition*, New York, 1914, not in catalogue; *French and English Art Treasures*, New York, 1942, no. 304

Literature: Chavagnac, p. 101, no. 124; *French and English Art Treasures*, no. 304

NOTES

1 Active 1764–87. See Peters, *Marks*, p. 22.
2 Bottoms are covered with glue from mounting, obscuring the details of the paste and glaze and probably any incised marks.
3 APML, Duveen file, invoice 11 July 1902: "1 pair old Louis XVI Ormolu mounted yellow Sevres small vases," £400.
4 See cat. no. 149 for this form.
5 See cat. no. 79 for example.
6 Christie's, London, 29 November 1973, lot 43.

198

Water jug (*pot à eau tourné*)

1917.1171

Sèvres, 1769, with some later decoration

Soft-paste porcelain, H. 7⅛ × w. 5⅝ × D. 4⅝ in. (18 × 14.3 × 11.8 cm)

Pale yellow ground, polychrome birds in landscapes, gilding

Marks: interlaced Ls in blue with date letter q; cp above for Antoine-Joseph Chappuis *jeune*, *aîné*;[1] incised JS[2]

Provenance: A.B. Daniell & Sons, London, 1907;[3] J. Pierpont Morgan

This water jug would have had a cover and been accompanied by a basin. The factory almost always referred to this type of jug simply as a *pot à eau*.[4] The reserves on this example were decorated in 1769 by Antoine-Joseph Chappuis, one of the factory's more prolific bird painters. It may have been one of

198

ninety-one *sujets d'oiseaux sur différentes pièces* for which Chappuis was paid 1.10 *livres* each in overtime in 1769.[5]

The yellow ground and rococo gilding were added later. There is evidence that the foot has been ground down to hide signs of redecoration, and reglazed scratches can be found, even under the yellow ground. The gilding is thin, crude, and grainy, especially on the handle and in the dentils. It is in the manner of the 1750s rather than the late 1760s, and is not truly in the factory style.

Exhibition: *Morgan Loan Exhibition*, New York, 1914, not in catalogue

NOTES

1 Active 1761–87. See Peters, *Marks*, p. 23.

2 Not in Savill or Dauterman.

3 APML, Daniell file, invoice 1 May 1907: "An old Sèvres China Rosewater Ewer canary ground, and raised gold, with compartments on each side of finely painted birds &c: by Chapuis Senr A.D. 1769," £792.

4 For this shape see cat. no. 159.

5 AMNS, F.11. I would like to thank Geoffrey de Bellaigue for this reference.

199

199

Water jug and basin (*pot à eau tourné et jatte ovale*)

1917.1172–1173

Sèvres, 18th-century paste, 19th-century decoration

Soft-paste porcelain, silver-gilt mounts, jug: H. 7¾ × W. 5¹⁵⁄₁₆ × D. 4¾ in. (19.7 × 15.1 × 12.1 cm); basin: H. 3¹⁄₁₆ × L. 10⁹⁄₁₆ × D. 8³⁄₁₆ in. (7.7 × 26.8 × 20.7 cm)

Pink ground, polychrome flowers, gilding

Marks: interlaced Ls in blue with date letter K for 1763 and four dots below for Pierre-Théodore Buteux (Théodore);[1] jug: incised x within a rectangle;[2] basin: incised gp;[3] silver discharge mark for small works of dog's head, for 1762–1768[4]

Provenance: J. Pierpont Morgan

This jug and basin was made in the eighteenth century at the Sèvres factory but redecorated in the nineteenth century.[5] The feet of both pieces are blackened, and the kiln support hole under the basin is extremely black, all signs of refiring. There is an area under the jug that looks as if it were reglazed where an old mark was taken off. Both the marks on the jug and basin appear to have burnt off during firing. The feathered gilding on both pieces covers some kind of blue decoration, which probably was the type known as *feuille de choux*.[6] This would explain the unusual shape of the reserves. The painting of the flowers is stiff and labored, especially noticeable in the yellow bunches that resemble cauliflower. Finally, the date letter of 1763 is two years

before the painter Théodore began working at the factory. The silver-gilt mounts are genuine and may have been original to the jug and basin.

Exhibition: *Morgan Loan Exhibition*, New York, 1914, not in catalogue; *French and English 18th Century Exhibition*, Montreal, 1950, no. 159

Literature: *French and English 18th Century Exhibition*, no. 159; Hood, *Bulletin*, p. 10

NOTES

1 Active 1765–84. See Peters, *Marks*, p. 19.

2 See Savill, 3, p. 1136, as found on soft paste 1756–76.

3 Ibid., p. 1106, found on soft paste 1757–79.

4 See Dennis, 2, p. 33, no. 26d.

5 See cat. no. 159 for the model.

6 See for example the assembled dinner service pieces sold Sotheby's, New York, 9–10 October 1990, lot 368 for many objects of this type.

200

200

Two cups

1917.1039–1040

Unknown factory, unknown date

Soft-paste porcelain or possibly bone china, both:
H. 2⅜ × W. 3⅛ × D. 2½ in. (6 × 7.9 × 6.3 cm)

Yellow ground with gilded diapers, polychrome birds and laurel bands

Marks: interlaced Ls in blue, date letter G for 1759, and painter's mark of jh underneath, on both

Provenance: J. Pierpont Morgan

The cups are of a shape unknown at the Sèvres factory, and must, therefore have been made elsewhere, either in Paris or perhaps in England. They have been decorated to deceive, with the marks of Jean-François Henrion *aîné*, a flower painter at Sèvres in the 1770s and 1780s.[1] This, of course, is incompatible with the date of 1759 painted on the cups. Although it might be argued that the painter intended to date the cups GG, for 1783, the bird painting is also inconsistent with Henrion's known work.

Exhibition: *Morgan Loan Exhibition*, New York, 1914, not in catalogue

Literature: Chavagnac, p. 89, no. 108

NOTES

1 See Peters, *Marks*, p. 41, active 1770–81, 1783–84.

Glossary of Terms and Techniques[1]

Materials

Cannetille:
  gold or silver thread, of varying fineness, which was rolled on the long iron needle of a spinning wheel. It was used primarily to make embroidery and *passementerie*, especially fringe, and was the domain of the guild of *passementiers-boutonniers*.

Gilt-bronze, *ormolu*, or *bronze doré*:
  gilded bronze, made by applying a paste of gold and mercury to bronze and firing. In the 18th century this material was used to make mounts to enhance decorative objects, primarily furniture, but also porcelain.

Hard-paste porcelain (*pâte dure*):
  "true" porcelain made from white china clay (kaolin) and feldspathic rock called chinastone or *petuntse* (silicate of potassium and aluminum). These were fired together at a high temperature (2,282–2,462°F or 1,250–1,350°C) to produce a glassy matrix. It normally was covered with a feldspathic glaze before firing. Hard-paste porcelain, although first made in China in the 7th or 8th century, was only "invented" in Europe in 1709 by the Meissen factory. In France, its raw ingredients were only discovered at the end of the1760s, in the area near Limoges, and it did not become part of the production at Sèvres until the end of that decade. Hard-paste porcelain usually has a colder white color than soft paste. Enamel colors do not sink into the glaze, but tend to sit on top in very slight relief.

Silver gilt, *argent doré*, or *vermeil*:
  gilded silver, sometimes used to make hinges and other mounting devices for porcelain.

Soft-paste porcelain (*pâte tendre*):
  "artificial" porcelain consisting of ground glass of a special composition called *frit*, mixed with malleable clay, to make a pliable paste. Usually the paste was then covered with a lead (or occasionally tin glaze) and fired a second time. Painted decoration and gilding required subsequent firings. Soft-paste porcelain, although first invented by the Medici porcelain factory in the 16th century, was only produced commercially from the late 17th century in France, beginning at the Saint-Cloud factory. It was the exclusive paste used at Vincennes and Sèvres until the end of the 1760s, when the raw materials for fabricating hard-paste porcelain were discovered in France. Soft-paste porcelain is translucent, creamy-white, and incapable of withstanding high temperatures (more than 2,282°F or 1,250°C). Enamel colors tend to sink into the glaze.

Souffre or *soufre* (*modèle en souffre* or *soufre*):
  compound of sulfur (and probably other unknown ingredients) used to make models by the Vincennes-Sèvres factory in an effort to produce a model that was more durable than plaster. When a shape was introduced, a plaster model was made, from which molds were then produced. Then other working models were made, sometimes in *soufre* in the early 1750s, so that the many molds necessary for a new and popular model could be made without loss of clarity and sharpness.

Terracotta:
  a lightly fired earthenware, reddish in color, usually left unglazed. It was frequently used by sculptors to produce models or studies for more finished pieces. At Vincennes and Sèvres it sometimes preceded the plaster model for an object, the latter used to create molds for fabrication.

Process

Biscuit:
  porcelain that has gone through the first firing but has not been glazed. In the 18th century some pieces were left in this state, but the majority were subsequently glazed. The term biscuit is French and means twice fired, alluding to the fact that the *frit* in soft-paste porcelain was also fired.

Glaze (*couverte*):
  glassy coating applied to a ceramic body and fused together by firing, creating a watertight surface. Glazes were made of silica, to which various oxides (fluxes) were added to lower its melting temperature. Eighteenth-century fluxes, which gave their names to specific glazes, included lead oxide, or feldspar. Soft-paste porcelain was covered after the biscuit firing with a lead glaze that became transparent and brilliant. Hard-paste porcelain was covered before firing with a feldspathic glaze, which was capable of being fired at a high temperature. Tin glaze, although primarily used on earthenware, produced a uniform, white surface on which to place decoration, and was sometimes used on early soft-paste porcelain (primarily at Chantilly) when the paste was not of the desired purity or whiteness. Glazes could be applied to the ceramic body in the form of liquid suspension, when they would be poured over the object, used as a dip, or occasionally painted onto the object.

Grandeurs:
  sizes in which Vincennes and Sèvres pieces were made, differing among individual models. Such sizes were documented in the factory records, and were one of several factors that affected the price of object.

Grasses cuites:
  name given to pieces where blistering or bubbling has occurred on the surface of the porcelain caused by gases released by a second firing of the biscuit to try to remedy an initial underfiring.

Kiln firings (*fournées*):
  soft-paste porcelain required multiple firings, including once for biscuit, once for glazing (sometimes referred to as glost firing), at least once for enamels, and at least once for gilding. Incomplete records exist at Sèvres for the biscuit, glaze, and enamel kiln firings up to 1759. The latter covered firings for gilding as well as for enamel decoration. During the Vincennes period the final enamel kiln firing of an object was designated by a letter or number, and listed next to the object when it appeared in the sales records.

Kiln furniture:
  supports used in the kiln; usually but not always made of the same material as the objects being fired. Sometimes pads of paste were used

on unglazed bases for support. At Vincennes-Sèvres, objects were suspended on cruciform metal stands from 1752 (accounting for holes in the foot rims). Other kiln supports used for French porcelain include:

Saggars or saggers:
protective cases made of refractory clay (clay able to withstand high temperatures) in which objects were placed to protect them from ash, smoke, or gas during firing.

Pupitres:
alternative wedge-shaped forms of support for large objects, utilized after the biscuit firing. They did not use the holes in the foot rim as did traditional Sèvres kiln supports.

Leather-hard:
term used to describe ceramic bodies after some of the moisture has evaporated from the clay. Leather-hard pieces were ready to be trimmed or pierced, but required further drying before biscuit firing.

Magasin de blanc:
stock room for Vincennes and Sèvres porcelain glazed but not decorated.

Magasin de rebut:
stock room for imperfect pieces of Vincennes and Sèvres, which at times were sold as factory seconds.

Underglaze/overglaze:
terms used to describe the point at which decoration was applied to porcelain.

Végétations salines:
efflorescences that appear on the surface of unfired porcelain bodies during drying; made up of tiny crystals issued from soluble elements that did not fuse with the silica during the *frit* firing. During the biscuit firing, these elements produce tiny black spots. These speckles presented problems for the factory as early as 1751, and were caused by inadequate mixing of the minerals that made up the paste.

Vitrification/devitrification:
vitrification is the fusion of various elements to produce a glassy substance. Porcelain glazes, and some ground colors, are made of vitrified materials. Devitrification occurs when, due to multiple firings in the kiln, the glaze and ground color begin to crystallize into the original elements that made up the glaze, resulting in a dull, matte finish.

Decoration

Enamel colors:
painted colors, which on soft paste could be either transparent or opaque. They were usually derived from metallic oxides, such as cobalt (blue), copper (green), iron (brown, red), manganese (purple), and antimony (yellow).

Enamel decoration:
painted decoration, often including specific schemes such as:

Arabesques: patterns comprising scrolls, garlands, swags, small vases, and other motifs inspired by classical and Renaissance design and used at Sèvres both for borders and for all-over enamel decoration from the 1770s.

Camaïeu: monochrome enamel colors used to paint figures, landscapes, birds and flowers.

Chaires colorées or *coloriés*: decorative scheme where figures are painted in monochrome with the exception of faces, arms, and legs, which are painted in flesh tones.

Grisaille: gray and white decoration intended to imitate stone.

Kakiemon: decorative style derived from the kakiemon family of potters working in Arita, Japan. The style is characterized by the use of five colors (orange-red, blue, yellow, green or turquoise, and black), as well as specific motifs such as herons and quails, squirrels in a hedge, flowers, bamboo, tigers, dragons, and phoenix. The Japanese wares were imported into Europe in the eighteenth century and widely imitated by European porcelain makers.

Gilding:
the application of gold to porcelain, which in France during the 18th century was practiced primarily at Vincennes and Sèvres. Before 1770, powdered gold leaf either was mixed with a mordant made of garlic, onions and vinegar, and painted on the porcelain, or sieved over a mordant that was painted onto the glaze.

Burnishing: polished gilding.

Tooling: engraved decoration on gilding.

Gilding patterns:

Caillouté: pattern resembling pebbles, usually applied over *bleu lapis* ground.

Diaper pattern: trelliswork pattern, usually applied over a ground color.

Œil de perdrix: partridge-eye pattern consisting of gilded circles or circles of dots with a dot in the center.

Vermiculé: a term meaning worm tunnels, which refers to a pattern found on rusticated masonry. Like *caillouté*, it usually was applied over a ground color, frequently *bleu lapis*.

Ground color:
background color used to cover all or most of the surface of a ceramic body. Most were applied over the glaze (the exception at Vincennes-Sèvres being *bleu lapis*), some being applied as powder over a sticky coating (mordant), and others in liquid form painted onto the porcelain. For specific colors used at Vincennes-Sèvres, see index and individual catalogue entries.

Ground decoration:
term used to describe when ground colors were used to create patterns rather than applied as a plain field. At Vincennes-Sèvres, these included:

Fond Taillandier: pattern consisting of a ground (usually blue) with white circles that are edged with gilding and contain colored dots, with smaller circles of gilded dots over the ground color. It was named after the Sèvres painter Vincent Taillandier, and was current in the middle 1760s and 1770s. This pattern is often confused with the *pointillé* pattern.

Frise colorée: decoration comprising small cartouches with diaper patterns, garlands, shells, and sometimes, floral swags, found frequently on Sèvres porcelain in the first half of the 1760s. The palette often combined *beau bleu*, red, purple, and gold.

Mosaïque: term used to describe various trellis or mosaic patterns in ground colors at Vincennes and Sèvres.

Pointillé: pale ground color (blue, pink, mauve, green, yellow) with white circles outlined in darker painted dots. This pattern was popular at Sèvres from the late 1760s through the early 1780s.

Mordant:
sticky coatings made of varying materials used to bond ground colors and gold to a porcelain body.

Redecoration:
term used to describe when the original decoration on a piece of porcelain is removed and a different decoration is applied. This practice occurred frequently in the 19th century as a means of enhancing the value of simply decorated 18th-century porcelain.

Sales and Distribution

Magasin de vente:
sales room in the Vincennes and Sèvres factory where finished pieces of Vincennes and Sèvres were displayed and sold.

Marchands-merciers:
mercantile corporations that controlled and regulated commerce in luxury goods in 18th-century France. They were somewhat akin to craftsmen's guilds, each composed of merchants who dealt in one or more than one type of product. Some of the merchants or dealers who traded extensively in porcelain were considered preferred customers at Vincennes and Sèvres and were as such granted a 9% discount from the factory. We know from the daybooks of one dealer, Lazare Duvaux, that he in turn charged his customers the factory's normal retail price, making 9% gross profit. Presumably the other dealers operated in somewhat the same fashion.

Year-end sales at Versailles:
beginning in 1758, the two-week period between Christmas and New Year when Louis XV and then Louis XVI gave over three rooms in their private apartments to the Sèvres factory for use as a sale room. Most of the factory's novelties were premiered at this exhibition, and significant sales by the French aristocracy and visiting foreigners resulted. By 1789 the annual exhibitions had increased to three weeks, and in that year were transferred to the Louvre. They were abandoned in 1793.

Documentation

Date letters:
system of dating used at the Vincennes-Sèvres factory to indicate the year a piece was decorated. Date letters, which most often were placed inside the crossed Ls of the factory mark, were first used in 1753 (letter A), and continued after the onset of the French Revolution; in 1778, after the alphabet had been completed, date letters were doubled (AA, BB). Traditionally it was thought that each letter indicated one calendar year, but more recently it has been suggested that at least until 1759, each letter may have spanned part of two years (e.g. A = 1753 or part 1753 and part 1754). It has also been determined recently that in the year 1786, both ii and jj were used, and thus the letter following ii represents one year earlier than indicated in most literature on Sèvres. Dating in this catalogue follows the new scheme (see Peters, *Marks*, pp. 4–6).

Factory marks:
identifying marks applied to porcelain, usually underneath or at the bottom of an object, signifying the factory responsible for its production. In the 18th century they could be incised, impressed, or painted.

Incised marks:
at Vincennes and Sèvres, marks usually found on the base of a piece that have been inscribed in the unfired paste. They seem to be the marks of throwers, molders, and *répareurs*, and most likely were used to monitor the quality and quantity of the individual's work before firing. Incised marks usually consisted of letters, numbers, or symbols; each worker had his or her own mark, although it is possible that marks were passed down from one generation to the next.

Painters' and gilders' marks:
painted or gilded symbols or initials used by painters and gilders at Vincennes-Sèvres to identify their work. Like incised marks, these marks most likely were used as a means of allowing management to monitor production, and should not be considered equivalent to artists' signatures. Gilder's marks were not used until about 1770.

Republican calendar:
new system of dating established during the French Revolution beginning in September 1793. This calendar was used in the Sèvres documents, although especially in the first year, the factory sometimes used the Gregorian calendar as well.

Republican calendar from 1793–1800:

Years

22 September 1793–21 September 1794: *an* II

22 September 1794–22 September 1795: *an* III

23 September 1795–21 September 1796: *an* IV

22 September 1796–21 September 1797: *an* V

22 September 1797–21 September 1798: *an* VI

22 September 1798–22 September 1799: *an* VII

23 September 1799–22 September 1800: *an* VIII

23 September 1800–22 September 1801: *an* IX

Months

22/23 September–21/22 October: *vendémiaire* 1–30

22/23 October–20/21 November: *brumaire* 1–30

21/22 November–20/21 December: *frimaire* 1–30

21/22 December–19/20 January: *nivôse* 1–30

20/21 January–18/19 February: *pluviôse* 1–30

19/20 February–20/21 March: *ventôse* 1–30

21/22 March–19/20 April: *germinal* 1–30

20/21 April–19/20 May: *floréal* 1–30

20/21 May–18/19 June: *prairial* 1–30

19/20 June–18/19 July: *messidor* 1–30

19/20 July–17/18 August: *thermidor* 1–30

18/19 August–21/22 September: *fructidor* 1–30 and 1–5/6

Eighteenth-century French currency:

1 *sou* (or *sol*) = 12 *derniers*

1 *livre* = 20 *sous* (or *sols*)

1 *louis d'or* = 24 *livres*

Eighteenth-century measurements

1 *pied* = 12 *pouces* (12.79 in. or 32.49 cm)

1 *pouce* = 1.066 in. (2.71 cm)

1 *ligne* = 1/12 *pouce*

NOTE

1 Several sources were used to compile this glossary: Préaud and d'Albis, pp. 215–33; Savill, 3, pp. 1172–80; Cohen and Hess, *passim*; Fleming and Honour, *passim*.

Concordance

Accession no.	Catalogue no.	Item	French name
1913.596	11	Saucer	
1913.598	4	Saucer	
1913.599 a & b	26	Juice pot	*pot à jus*
1913.599c	25	Saucer	
1913.600	12	Cup and saucer	
1917.897–898	9	Two theatrical figures	
1917.899–900	2	Two cups and saucers	
1917.901–902	16	Two covered jars	
1917.903	17	Budai	
1917.906	21	Toilet jar	
1917.907	10	Covered bowl and stand	*écuelle*
1917.908	1	Pot-pourri	
1917.909	36	Children with a dolphin	
1917.910	43	Grotesque woman	
1917.911	35	Dwarf	
1917.912	19	Seated Chinese	
1917.913–914	22	Pair of vases	*vases à oreilles*
1917.915	28	Double salt cellar	
1917.916–917	50	Toilet jars	*pots à pommade*
1917.918	24	Covered cup and saucer	
1917.919–920	46	Girl and putto and two children	
1917.921–922	8	Ewer and basin	
1917.923	40	Child musicians	
1917.924	44	The Magic Lantern	
1917.925	52	Children with a goat	
1917.926–927	23	Pair of pots-pourris	
1917.929–930	27	Two salt cellars	
1917.931	49	Triple salt cellar	
1917.932	51	Child musicians	
1917.934	29	Covered bowl and stand	*écuelle*
1917.935	48	Snuffbox	
1917.936	33	Étui	*étui*
1917.937	30	Snuffbox	
1917.938	34	Snuffbox	
1917.939	31	Snuffbox	
1917.940	39	Child musicians	
1917.941	47	Woman playing a vielle	
1917.942	53	Harlequina	
1917.945	42	Clio(?)	
1917.947	41	Winter	

Accession no.	Catalogue no.	Item	French name
1917.948	45	Girl with a garland	
1917.949	38	Child musicians	
1917.950–951	18	Puppeteers	
1917.952	168	Bather	*La Baigneuse*
1917.953	169	Sleeping woman	*La Dormeuse*
1917.954	172	Jealousy	*Le Jaloux*
1917.955	170	The Grape Eaters	*Les Mangeurs de raisins*
1917.956	171	The Flute Lesson	*Le Flûteur*
1917.957	176	Friendship and base	*L'Amitié*
1917.958	177	Louis XV and base	
1917.959	173	Cupid	*L'Amour Falconet*
1917.960	174	"Psyche"	*pendant de l'Amour Falconet*
1917.961	76	Teapot	*théière à cuvier à cerceaux*
1917.962	57	Pot-pourri vase	*pot-pourri Pompadour*
1917.963–964	67	Pair of orange tubs	*caisses*
1917.965–966	148	Water jug and basin	*pot à la Romaine uni et jatte ovale*
1917.967–971	181	Tea service with a tray, teapot, sugar bowl, milk jug, and cup and saucer	*plateau Hebert, théière Calabre, pot à sucre Hebert, pot à lait à trois pieds, gobelet litron et soucoupe*
1917.972	190	Juice pot	*pot à jus ordinaire*
1917.973	182	Cup and saucer	*gobelet litron et soucoupe*
1917.974–975	149	Toilet pots	*pots à pommade*
1917.976	183	Sugar bowl	*pot à sucre à la Reine*
1917.977–978	54	Pair of vases	probably *urnes Duplessis*
1917.979	191	Fruit dish	*compotier carré*
1917.980	77	Cup	
1917.981	179	Vase	*vase Duplessis*
1917.982–983	56	Pair of pot-pourri vases	*pots-pourris à jour*
1917.984	78	Milk jug	perhaps *pot à lait Bouillard*
1917.985–986	58	Two vases	*vases à oreilles*
1917.987	150	Broth basin and stand	*écuelle à vignes* and *plateau à ozier*
1917.988–989	60	Pair of vases	*vases à oreilles*
1917.990	59	Vase	*vase Duplessis*
1917.991–992	180	Pair of orange tubs	*caisses carrées*
1917.993–994	151	Fountain and basin	*fontaine unie et cuvette*
1917.995–996	61	Pair of vases	*vases cannelés/vases à corset*
1917.997	62	One of a pair of orange tubs	*caisse carrée*
1917.998	80	Cup and saucer	*gobelet Hebert* and *soucoupe unie*
1917.999–1000	133	Pair of salt cellars	*salières à gondole*
1917.1001	81	Rectangular tray	*plateau tiroir*
1917.1002	82	Tray	*plateau en porte-huilier*
1917.1003	63	Flowerpot	*vase hollandois*
1917.1004–1005	64	Pair of pot-pourri vases	*pots-pourris Pompadour*
1917.1006–1009	83	Tea service with three cups and saucers	*plateau Courteille, gobelets Hebert et soucoupes unies*
1917.1010–1011	134	Pair of chestnut baskets	*marronnières à ozier* or *marronnières tenant au plateau*
1917.1012	192	Fruit dish	*compotier ovale*

Accession no.	Catalogue no.	Item	French name
1917.1013	152	Inkstand	*écritoire*
1917.1014	84	Cup and saucer	probably *gobelet Bouillard et soucoupe*
1917.1015	153	Broth basin and stand	*écuelle ronde* and *plateau à ornements*
1917.1016	135	Chestnut basket	*marronnière à ozier* or *marronnière tenant au plateau*
1917.1017–1021	85	Tea service with tray, teapot, sugar bowl, and two cups and saucers	*plateau Hebert, théière Calabre, pot à sucre Hebert, gobelets Hebert et soucoupes*
1917.1022	86	Tray	*plateau Hebert à anses*
1917.1023–1025	87	Partial tea service with teapot, sugar bowl, and milk jug	*théière Calabre, pot à sucre, pot à lait à trois pieds*
1917.1026	88	Cup and saucer	*gobelet Bouillard* and *soucoupe*
1917.1027–1028	193	Pair of salt cellars	*salières simples*
1917.1029–1030	195	Pair of plaques	
1917.1031	89	Tray	*plateau losange*
1917.1032–1036	91	Tea service with tray, teapot, sugar bowl, milk jug, and cup and saucer	*plateau octogone, théière Calabre, pot à sucre Calabre, pot à lait à trois pieds, gobelet Hebert et soucoupe*
1917.1037–1038	158	Toilet pots	*pots à pommade*
1917.1039–1040	200	Two cups	
1917.1041	92	Tray	*plateau losange*
1917.1042	184	Cup and saucer	*gobelet Bouillard*
1917.1043–1044	68	Pair of ewers	*vases en burette*
1917.1045–1046	69	Pair of vases	*vases ferrés*
1917.1047–1049	70	Garniture of three vases	*cuvettes à tombeau*
1917.1050	136	Punch bowl	*jatte à punch*
1917.1051–1056	93	Tea service with tray, teapot, sugar bowl, milk jug, and two cups and saucers	probably *plateau Duplessis, théière Calabre, pot à sucre Hebert, pot à lait à trois pieds, gobelets Hebert et soucoupes*
1917.1057	185	Tray	*plat à hors d'œuvres à ruban*
1917.1058	94	Teapot	*théière Calabre*
1917.1059	95	Cup and saucer	*gobelet litron et soucoupe*
1917.1060–1061	71	Pair of vases	*vases chinois/vases à pied de globe*
1917.1062	101	Cup and saucer	*gobelet litron et soucoupe*
1917.1063	96	Tray	*plateau à baguettes*
1917.1064	72	Vase	*vase Bachelier à anses tortillées*
1917.1065	65	Mounted vase	*vase cloche/gobelet en cloche*
1917.1066–1069	98	Tea service with tray, sugar bowl, milk jug, and cup and saucer	*plateau tiroir à jour, pot à sucre Bouret, pot à lait à trois pieds, gobelet Bouillard et soucoupe*
1917.1070	137	Wine glass cooler	probably *seau à verre échancré*
1917.1071	194	Wine glass cooler	probably *seau à verre échancré*
1917.1072	138	Triple salt cellar	*salière à trois compartiments*
1917.1073	160	Broth basin and stand	*écuelle ronde et plateau ovale*
1917.1074	139	Mustard tray	*plateau de moutardier ordinaire*
1917.1075–1076	140	Pair of salt cellars	*salières simples*
1917.1077	178	Boy with a Tambourine	*Le tambour de basque*

Accession no.	Catalogue no.	Item	French name
1917.1078–1081	99	Partial compiled tea set with tray, sugar bowl, milk jug, and cup and saucer	*plateau losange, pot à sucre Bouret, pot à lait à trois pieds*, and *gobelet Bouillard* and *soucoupe*
1917.1082–1083	141	Pair of oval fruit dishes	*compotiers ovales*
1917.1084–1085	142	Pair of sugar bowls and attached stands	*sucriers de Monsieur le Premier*
1917.1086	155	Inkstand	*écritoire*
1917.1087–1088	73	Pair of vases	*vases urne antique à ornements?*
1917.1089	186	Cup and saucer	*gobelet litron et soucoupe*
1917.1090–1094	104	Tea service with teapot, sugar bowl, two cups and saucers	*plateau à baguettes, théière Calabre, pot à sucre Bouret, gobelets litron et soucoupes*
1917.1095	144	Plate	*assiette unie*
1917.1096–1100	74	Five mounted vases	*vases et gobelets à monter*
1917.1101–1105	105	Tea service with tray, teapot, sugar bowl, milk jug, and cup and saucer	*soucoupe à pieds, théière Calabre, pot à sucre Bouret, pot à lait à trois pieds, gobelet litron et soucoupe*
1917.1106	143	Butter dish with attached stand	*beurrier tenant au plateau*
1917.1107	187	Cup and saucer	*gobelet litron et soucoupe*
1917.1108–1111	106	Tea service with tray, sugar bowl, milk jug, and cup and saucer	*plateau octogone, pot à sucre Calabre, pot à lait à trois pieds, gobelet litron et soucoupe*
1917.1112	164	Broth basin and stand	*écuelle et plateau nouvelle forme*
1917.1113	165	Broth basin and stand	*écuelle ronde tournée et plateau*
1917.1114	110	Cup and saucer	*gobelet litron et soucoupe*
1917.1115	111	Cup and saucer	*gobelet litron et soucoupe*
1917.1116	108	Cup and saucer	*gobelet litron et soucoupe*
1917.1117	196	Toilet pot	*pot à pommade*
1917.1118	109	Sugar bowl	*pot à sucre Calabre*
1917.1119	107	Cup and saucer	*gobelet litron et soucoupe*
1917.1120	120	Cup and saucer	*gobelet litron et soucoupe*
1917.1121	166	Broth basin and stand	*écuelle ronde tournée et plateau ovale*
1917.1122	123	Cup and saucer	*gobelet litron et soucoupe*
1917.1123	117	Covered cup and socketed saucer	*gobelet et soucoupe enfoncée*
1917.1124	118	Cup and saucer	*gobelet et soucoupe enfoncée*
1917.1125	119	Cup and saucer	*gobelet à anses étrusques et soucoupe*
1917.1126	163	Broth basin and stand	*écuelle ronde tournée et plateau ovale*
1917.1127	113	Cup and saucer	*gobelet litron et soucoupe*
1917.1128	114	Cup and saucer	*gobelet litron et soucoupe*
1917.1129	115	Cup and saucer	*gobelet litron et soucoupe*
1917.1130–1131	122	Cup and saucer and sugar	*gobelet litron et soucoupe, pot à sucre Bouret*
1917.1132	126	Cup and saucer	*gobelet litron et soucoupe*
1917.1133	167	Water jug	*pot à eau tourné*
1917.1134	124	Cup and saucer	*gobelet litron et soucoupe*
1917.1135	125	Cup and saucer	*gobelet litron et soucoupe*
1917.1136	127	Cup and saucer	*gobelet* or *tasse à anse Boizot et soucoupe*
1917.1137–1138	128	Two cups and saucers	*gobelets* or *tasses à anse Boizot et soucoupes*

Accession no.	Catalogue no.	Item	French name
1917.1139–1145	130	Tea service with teapot, sugar bowl, milk jug, and four cups and saucers	*théière litron, pot à sucre Calabre, pot à lait à trois pieds, gobelets litron et soucoupes*
1917.1146	131	Helmut milk jug	*pot à lait aiguière*
1917.1147–1150	145	Four plates	*assiettes unies*
1917.1151–1152	146	Two wine glass coolers	*seaux crennelés*
1917.1153	129	Cup and saucer	*gobelet litron et soucoupe*
1917.1154	175	Pedestal	*piédestal pour L'Amour*
1917.1156	97	Tea kettle	*bouillotte* or *bouillotte Chine*
1917.1157	100	Cup and saucer	*gobelet litron et soucoupe*
1917.1158	112	Cup	*gobelet litron*
1917.1159	121	Saucer	*soucoupe*
1917.1160	103	Cup and saucer	*tasse à thé et soucoupe*
1917.1161–1162	197	Pair of toilet pots, mounted as vases	*pots à pommade*
1917.1163	156	Broth basin and stand	*écuelle ronde et plateau ovale*
1917.1164	157	Broth basin and stand	*écuelle ronde et plateau ovale*
1917.1165–1166	162	Water jug and basin	*pot à la Romaine uni et jatte ovale*
1917.1167–1168	102	Two cups and saucers	*gobelets litron et soucoupes*
1917.1169–1170	161	Water jug and basin	*pot à eau tourné et jatte ovale de pot à eau*
1917.1171	198	Water jug	*pot à eau tourné*
1917.1172–1173	199	Water jug and basin	*pot à eau tourné et jatte ovale de pot à eau*
1917.1174	116	Cup and saucer	*gobelet litron* and *soucoupe*
1917.1175	188	Covered sugar bowl	*pot à sucre Bouret*
1917.1178–1179	159	Water jug and basin	*pot à eau tourné* and possibly *jatte ovale de pot à eau*
1917.1180	189	Teapot	*théière Calabre*
1917.1181–1185	90	Tea service with tray, teapot, sugar bowl, and two cups and saucers	*plateau forme de corbeille ovale* or *corbeille ovale contournée, théière Calabre, pot à sucre Hebert, gobelets Hebert et soucoupes*
1917.1234	55	Basket of flowers	
1917.1509	20	Louis XV	
1934.204	3	Cup and saucer	
1934.205	15	Plate	
1958.238–239	5	Pair of bottle coolers	*seaux à bouteille*
1961.451	14	Bowl	
1961.454	79	Tray	*plateau du roi*
1962.619	13	Cup and saucer	
1962.623	7	Covered jar	
1963.463	37	Amphitrite	
1971.52.40	32	Snuffbox	
1986.178 1	54	Food warmer	*veilleuse*
1989.84	66	Flowerpot	*caisse/cuvette à fleurs Verdun*
1990.51	62	One of a pair of orange tubs	*caisse carrée*
1991.9–10	132	Two wine bottle coolers	*seaux à bouteille ordinaires*
1991.11	6	Broth basin and cover	*écuelle*
1993.29	75	Mounted vase	*vase à monter Daguerre*
1995.11	147	Broth basin and stand	*écuelle et plateau*

Sèvres Manuscript Sources[1]

Archives, Manufacture Nationale de Sèvres

A

1   *Arrêts et ordonnances, relatifis à l'organisation de la manufacture*, 1745–89

2   *Privilège de la manufacture, et libertés de ses manufactures particulières*, 1765–84, and *Arrêts de Conseil*, 1765–77

B

Régie royale

1   *Compagnie et régie royale, administration intérieure de la manufacture*, 1745–60

2   *Régie royale, direction et régime de la manufacture*, 1760–89

3   *Régie royale, administration intérieure de la manufacture*, 1760–89

5   *Régie royale, direction financière de la manufacture*, 1755–89

C

Secrets et procédés

1   *Acquisition de procédés par la manufacture*, 1741–84

2   *Essais et expériences de la manufacture*, 1741–91

3   *Procédés non acceptés*, 1755–72

D

Personnel, États et dossiers individuels

1   1743–75

2   1776–84

3   1785–99

Eb

Travaux des ateliers

1   1746–99

Ec

1   *Matériels et matières*

F

Recettes et dépenses

Including *Travaux extraordinaires* (overtime records), *Travaux à la pièce* (piecework records) and pay rolls.

1   1741–52
2   1753–55
3   1756
4   1757–58
5   1759–60
6   1761–62
7   1763–64
8   1765–66
9   1767
10   1768
11   1769
12   1770
13   1771
14   1772
15   1773
16   1774
17   1774–75
18   1775–76
19   1777
20   1778
21   1779
22   1780
23   1781
24   1782
25   1783
26   1784
27   1785
28   1786
29   1787
30   1788
31   1789–94
32   1795

H

Correspondance

1   1746–79
2   1780–82
3   1783–86

I

2   *Pièces offertes en présents*, 1772–89

4   *Ventes publiques et expositions*, 1750–99

6   *Droits d'entrée et de circulation sur les porcelaines*, 1723–70

7   *Inventaires annuels*, 1752–70 (inventory)

8   *Inventaires annuels*, 1771–99 (inventory)

Ob

Personnel

Dossiers individuels, 1800–76, in alphabetical order

1   A
2   B
3   C
4   D
5   E–F
6   G–K
7   L
8   M
9   N–O
10   P
11   Q–S
12   T–U
13   V–Z

R

Drawings

1   l.1 Useful wares (*services, garde-robe* etc.), l.2 Tea wares (also *écuelles* etc.) and l.3 Vases

2   Drawings attributed to Duplessis *père* and *fils*

R

Recettes et dépenses, 1800–76

1	1800–5
2	1805–7
3	1808–10
4	1811–12
5	1813–14
6	1815
7	1816
8	1817
9	1818
10	1819
11	1820
12	1821
13	1822
14	1823
15	1824
16	1825

U

3 *Inventaire Brongniart*, 1814 (1814 inventory)

Va (Va')

Registres de tourneurs, mouleurs et répareurs

1 Soft and hard paste, November 1773–March 1774

2 Hard paste, July 1774–April 1777

3 (Hard paste), *Travaux extraordinaires* (overtime records), 1775–76

4 Hard paste, January 1777 – December 1779

5 Hard paste, 1779

6 (Hard paste), December 1779–80 (see also V 3)

7 (Hard paste), 1781

Vc (Vc')

Registres de couverte

1 27 November 1776 – 17 June 1785 (soft paste)

2 1 July 1785 – 3 February 1806 (paste?)

3 9 July 1785 – 9 August 1800 (21 *thermidor an* VIII) (hard paste)

Vf

Journal des recettes et dépenses, 1745–1877

Vj (Vj')

Registres de peintres (painters' records)

1	1777–80
2	1781–83
3	1784–85
4	1786–89
5	1790–19 April 1794
6	20 April 1794–15 September 1796

Vl (Vl')

Registres de fournées de peintres (painting kiln records)

1 12 April 1778 – 27 December 1781

2 1 January 1782 – 21 December 1785

3 5 February 1786 – 1 August 1794 (14 *thermidor an* II)

4 22 November 1794 (2 *frimaire an* III) – 4 November 1800 (13 *brumaire an* IX)

Vy

Registres des ventes (sales ledgers)

1 1 October 1752 – 30 July 1756

2 1 August 1756 – 30 September 1759

3 1 October 1759 – 31 December 1763

4 1 January 1764 – 31 December 1770

5 1 January 1771 – 30 June 1775

6 1 July 1775 – 31 December 1777

7 1 January 1778 – 30 September 1780 (including some earlier royal sales)

8 1 October 1780 – 31 March 1783

9 1 April 1783 – 31 December 1785

10 1 January 1786 – 31 December 1789

11 1 January 1790 – 16 September 1794 (30 *fructidor an* II)

12 22 September 1794 (1 *vendémiaire an* III) – 9 August 1801 (11 *fructidor an* IX)

V 3

Registres de tourneurs, mouleurs et répareurs, hard paste, 1780

(The reference V 3 has been used in error; the document is the second *liasse* [bundle] of Va 6)

Y

Registres du personnel

7–8	1745–58
9	1800–30

Archives Nationales, Paris

01 2060, 261
Overtime and piecework records for Sèvres workers, 1783

Bibliothèque de l'Institut de France

Ms.5673
Registre de défournements de biscuit, 18 October 1752 – 24 September 1759 (biscuit kiln records)

Ms.5674–75
Registres de défournements de couverte blanche, 19 October 1752 – 29 October 1755 and 30 December 1755 – 24 September 1759, 18 October 1759 – July 1771 (glaze kiln records)

Ms.5676
Registre de défournements de couleurs, 28 November 1752 – 31 December 1755 (enamel kiln records)

NOTE

1 This list of Sèvres manuscript sources has been taken from Savill, 3, pp. 928–31, with kind permission of the author. Not all of these sources have been directly cited in this catalogue. For fuller descriptions, see Bourgeois, *Archives*, pp. 19–29.

Exhibitions

Exhibitions which featured porcelain from the Wadsworth Atheneum (arranged by year)

1884   *Rétrospectives des Porcelaines*, Paris, 1884   *Expositions Rétrospectives des Porcelaines de Vincennes et de Sèvres*, exh. and cat., 8e Exp., Union centrale des Arts decóratifs, Paris, 1884

1914   *Morgan Loan Exhibition*, New York, 1914   *Loan Exhibition of the J. Pierpont Morgan Collection*, exh. and handlist, Metropolitan Museum of Art, New York, 1914

1942   *French and English Art Treasures*, New York, 1942   *French and English Art Treasures of the Eighteenth Century*, exh. and cat., Parke-Bernet Galleries, New York, 20–30 December 1942

1949   *European Porcelain*, New York, 1949   *Masterpieces of European Porcelain*, exh. and cat., Metropolitan Museum of Art, New York, 18 March – 15 May 1949

1950   *French and English 18th Century Exhibition*, Montreal, 1950   *French and English 18th Century Exhibition*, exh. and cat., Montreal Museum of Fine Arts, Montreal, 26 April – 31 May 1950

1958   *Masterpieces from the Wadsworth Atheneum*, New York, 1958   *Masterpieces from the Wadsworth Atheneum*, exh. and cat., Knoedler Galleries, New York, 21 January – 15 February 1958

1959   *Age of Elegance*, Baltimore, 1959   *The Age of Elegance: The Rococo and its Effects*, exh. and cat., Baltimore Museum of Art, Baltimore, Maryland, 25 April – 14 June 1959

1960   *Morgan Treasures*, Hartford, 1960   *The Pierpont Morgan Treasures*, exh. and cat., Wadsworth Atheneum, Hartford, 10 November – 18 December 1960

1965   *Continental Table Porcelains*, San Francisco, 1965   *Continental Table Porcelains of the Eighteenth Century,* exh. and cat., De Young Memorial Museum, San Francisco, 25 October – 6 December 1965

1980   *Vincennes and Sèvres Porcelain*, New York, 1980   *Vincennes and Sèvres Porcelain*, exh. and cat., The Frick Collection, New York, 4 June – 3 August 1980

1982   *Antique Taste*, Hartford, 1982   *In the Antique Taste: Carle Vanloo's "Offering to Love,"* exh. and cat., Wadsworth Atheneum, Hartford, 6 February – 4 April 1982

1984   *Design in the Service of Tea*, New York, 1984   *Design in the Service of Tea*, exh. (no cat.), The National Museum of Design, Cooper-Hewitt Museum, New York, 7 August – 8 October 1984

1985   *Wine: Celebration and Ceremony*, New York, 1985   *Wine: Celebration and Ceremony*, exh. (no cat.), The National Museum of Design, Cooper-Hewitt Museum, New York, 4 June – 13 October 1985

1986   *Boucher*, New York, 1986   *François Boucher*, exh. and cat., Metropolitan Museum of Art, New York, 17 February – 4 May 1986; Detroit Institute of Arts, 27 May – 17 August 1986

1987   *Morgan*, Hartford, 1987   *J. Pierpont Morgan, Collector: European Decorative Arts from the Wadsworth Atheneum*, exh. and cat., Hartford, 18 January – 15 March 1987, New York, 17 April – 1 August 1987, Fort Worth, 15 September – 1 December 1987, Phoenix, 8 January – 13 March 1988, Charlotte, North Carolina, 15 April – 31 July 1988, Portland, Oregon, 13 September – 6 November 1988

1988   *Makers of the American Renaissance*, Jekyll Island, Georgia, 1988   *Makers of the American Renaissance: The Jekyll Island Club Members as Patrons and Collectors*, exh. (no cat.), Jekyll Island Museum, Jekyll Island, Georgia, 19 February – 31 July 1988

1997   *Défi au goût*, Paris, 1997   *Un Défi au goût, 50 ans de création à la manufacture royale de Sèvres (1740–1793)*, exh. and cat., Musée du Louvre, Paris, 20 March – 23 June 1997

1999   *Discovering the Secrets of Soft-Paste*, New York, 1999   *Discovering the Secrets of Soft-Paste Porcelain at the Saint-Cloud Manufactory c. 1690–1766*, Bard Graduate Center, New York, exh. and cat., 15 July – 24 October 1999

Abbreviations of Sources Cited

Age of Elegance
The Age of Elegance: The Rococo and its Effects, exh. cat., Baltimore Museum of Art, Baltimore, Maryland, 25 April–14 June 1959

d'Albis, "Early years"
Antoine d'Albis, "The early years of the porcelain manufactory of Vincennes," in *The International Ceramics Fair and Seminar, London, Handbook*, June 1986, pp. 10–23

d'Albis, "Fond jaune"
Antoine d'Albis, "'Fond jaune, enfants camaïeu:' Trois remarquables contrefaçons," *Les Cahiers de Mariemont* 24/25, 1993/1994, pp. 18–27

d'Albis, "Gravant"
Antoine d'Albis, "Le Secret de Gravant ou le privilège de Vincennes," *Bulletin de la Société des Amis de Vincennes* 38, 1987, pp. 7–16

d'Albis, "Hard-paste"
Antoine d'Albis, "The Creation of Hard-paste Porcelain Production at Sèvres," *Journal of The French Porcelain Society* 13, 1998

d'Albis, "Hellot"
Antoine d'Albis, "Steps in the Manufacture of the Soft-paste Porcelain of Vincennes, According to the Books of Hellot," *Ceramics and Civilization*, 1984, pp. 257–71

d'Albis, "Inventaire"
Antoine d'Albis, "A documentary Vincennes *inventaire*," *Sotheby's Art at Auction 1987–1988*, London, 1988, p. 366–71

d'Albis, "Marchands-merciers"
"Le Marchand Mercier Lazare Duvaux et la Porcelaine de Vincennes," in *Les décors des boutiques parisiennes, Délégation à l'action Artistique de la Ville de Paris*, 1987, pp. 76–88

d'Albis, "Pourpre"
Antoine d'Albis, "Les débuts des pourpres en France, de Chantilly à Vincennes: Salomon Taunay et son fils Pierre Henri Antoine," *Sèvres: Revue de la Société des Amis du Musée National de Céramique* 3, 1994, pp. 34–39, 71

d'Albis, "Premières années"
Antoine d'Albis, "Les premières années de la manufacture de porcelaine de Vincennes," *Bulletin de la Société des Amis de Vincennes* 36, 1985, pp. 12–24

d'Albis and Klein, "Scène militaire"
Antoine d'Albis and Mireille Klein, "Un pot à scène militaire de la manufacture de Vincennes," *Sèvres, Revue de la Société des Amis du Musée National de Céramique* 6, 1997, pp. 28–35

d'Albis and Préaud, "Bouquets"
Antoine d'Albis and Tamara Préaud, "Bouquets de Sèvres," *Connaissance des Arts* 479, January 1992, pp. 69–76

d'Albis and Préaud, "Datation"
Antoine d'Albis and Tamara Préaud, "Les Éléments de datation des porcelaines de Vincennes avant 1753," *Faenza* 70, 1984, no. 5–6, pp. 479–93

Alfassa and Guérin
Paul Alfassa and Jacques Guérin, *Porcelaine Française du XVIIIe au milieu du XIXe siècles*, n.d.

Ananoff, *Boucher*
Alexandre Ananoff and Daniel Wildenstein, *François Boucher*, Lausanne, Paris, 1976, 2 vols.

Ananoff, *Drawings*
Alexandre Ananoff, *L'Œuvre dessiné de François Boucher (1703–1770)*, Paris, 1966, 2 vols.

Anderson Collection
Armin B. Allen, *Eighteenth century Meissen porcelain from the collection of Gertrude J. and Robert T. Anderson*, exh. cat., Orlando Museum of Art, Orlando, March 1988–February 1989

Antique Taste
Linda Horvitz [Roth], *In the Antique Taste: Carle Vanloo's "Offering to Love,"* exh. cat., Wadsworth Atheneum, Hartford, 1982

Antoine
Michel Antoine, *Le Gouvernement et l'administration sous Louis XV*, Paris, 1978

Arend, "Birds"
Liana Paredes Arend, "Sèvres During the Revolution: A Yellow Service with Birds," *The Post* [Bulletin of the Hillwood Museum], Autumn 1993

Arend, *Hillwood*
Liana Paredes Arend, *Sèvres Porcelain at Hillwood*, Washington, D.C., 1998

Arizzoli-Clémentel
Pierre Arizzoli-Clémentel, "Nouvelles acquisitions," *Revue du Louvre* 5/6, 1995

Art Institute of Chicago
Selected Works of 18th Century French Art in the collections of The Art Institute of Chicago, Chicago, 1976

Ballu
Nicole Ballu, *La porcelaine française*, Paris, n.d.

Ballu, "Chantilly, l'extrême-orient"
Nicole Ballu, "Influence de l'extrême-orient sur le style de Chantilly au XVIIIe siècle," *Cahiers de la céramique du verre et des arts du feu* 11, 1958, pp. 100–12

Bauer and Verfondern
Günter G. Bauer and Heinz Verfondern, *Barock Zwergenkarikaturen von Callot bis Chodowiecki*, Salzburg, 1991

Baulez, Christian
see *Louveciennes*

Béalu
Christian Béalu, "Les porcelaines révolutionnaires," *Art & Curiosité* 108, n.s., April 1989, pp. 10–39

Beaucamp-Markowsky
Barbara Beaucamp-Markowsky, *Porzellandosen des 18. Jahrhunderts*, Fribourg, 1985

Belevitch-Stankevitch
H. Belevitch-Stankevitch, *Le goût chinois en France au temps de Louis XIV*, Paris, 1910 (reprint, Geneva, 1970)

Belfort, "Boucher"
Anne-Marie Belfort, "L'œuvre de Vielliard d'après Boucher," *Cahiers de la céramique du verre et des arts du feu* 58, 1976, pp. 6–35

Belfort, "Watteau"
Anne-Marie Belfort, "Les Trophées de Watteau peints par Vielliard," *Cahiers de la céramique du verre et des arts du feu* 58, 1976, pp. 66–73

de Bellaigue, "Diplomatic Gift"
Geoffrey de Bellaigue, "A Diplomatic Gift," *Connoisseur*, June 1977, pp. 92–99

de Bellaigue, "Engravings"
Geoffrey de Bellaigue, "Sèvres artists and their sources, II: engravings," *The Burlington Magazine* 122, November 1980, pp. 748–62

de Bellaigue, *Louis XVI*
Geoffrey de Bellaigue, *Sèvres porcelain in the collection of Her Majesty the Queen: the Louis XVI service*, Cambridge, 1986

de Bellaigue, "Paintings and drawings"
Geoffrey de Bellaigue, "Sèvres artists and their and sources, I: paintings and drawings," *The Burlington Magazine* 122, October 1980, pp. 667–76

de Bellaigue, "Sèvres"
Geoffrey de Bellaigue, "Sèvres," in *J. Pierpont Morgan, Collector: European Decorative Arts from the Wadsworth Atheneum*, Hartford, 1987, pp. 162–95

de Bellaigue, *Waddesdon*
Geoffrey de Bellaigue, *The James A. de Rothschild Collection at Waddesdon Manor: furniture, clocks and gilt bronzes*, Cambridge, 1974, 2 vols.

de Bellaigue, "Woburn"
Geoffrey de Bellaigue, "Sèvres at Woburn Abbey," *Apollo* 127, no. 316, June 1988, pp. 418–24

de Bellaigue, Geoffrey
see also *Morgan*, Hartford; *Royal Collection*; *Carlton House*

Berliner and Egger
Rudolf Berliner and Gerhart Egger, *Ornamentale Vorlageblätter des 15. bis 19. Jahrhunderts*, Leipzig, 1926, (reprint, Munich, c. 1981), 2 vols.

Birioukova
Nina Birioukova, "A propos des marques sur les biscuits de Vincennes et de Sèvres," *Cahiers de la céramique du verre et des arts du feu* 40, 1968, pp. 257–61

Boltz, "Hoym, Lemaire"
Claus Boltz, "Hoym, Lemaire und Meissen, ein Beitrag zur Geschichte der Dresdner Porzellansammlung," *Keramos* 88, April 1980, pp. 3–101

Bonifas
Janine Bonifas, *Faïences du Nord de la France*, Sèvres, 1994

Bordeaux
Jean-Luc Bordeaux, "The Epitome of the Pastoral Genre in Boucher's Œuvre: *The Fountain of Love* and *The Bird Catcher* from *The Noble Pastoral*," *The J. Paul Getty Journal* 3, 1976, pp. 75–101

Böttger
Johann Friedrich Böttger zum 300. Geburtstag, Dresden, 1982

Bottineau
Yves Bottineau, *L'Art de Cour dans l'Espagne de Philippe V 1700–1746*, Bordeaux, 1962

Boucher
Alastair Laing, J. Patrice Marandel, Pierre Rosenberg, Edith A. Standen and Antoinette Faÿ-Hallé, *François Boucher 1703–1770*, exh. cat., New York, Detroit, Paris, 1986 (English edition)

Bourgeois, *Archives*
Émile Bourgeois, *Les archives d'art de la manufacture de Sèvres*, 1909

Bourgeois, 1909
Émile Bourgeois, *Le biscuit de Sèvres au XVIIIe siècle*, Paris, 1909, 2 vols.

Bourgeois, 1913
Émile Bourgeois and Georges Lechavallier-Chevignard, *Le biscuit de Sèvres, I, recueil des modèles de la Manufacture de Sèvres au XVIIIe siècle*, Paris, n.d. (1913)

Bradshaw
Peter Bradshaw, *Bow Porcelain Figures circa 1748–1774*, London, 1992

Brault-Lerch
Solange Brault-Lerch, *L'Orfèvrerie française du XVIIIe siècle*, Paris, 1959

Braütigam
Herbert Braütigam, ed., *Schätze Chinas in Museen der DDR*, Leipzig, 1989

Bremer-David
Charissa Bremer-David, *Decorative Arts, an illustrated summary catalogue of the collections of the J. Paul Getty Museum*, Malibu, California, 1993

Brulon, "Asturies"
Dorothée Guillemé-Brulon, "Service offert par Louis XV à la princesse des Asturies en 1774," in *Versailles et les tables royales en Europe*, exh. cat., Paris, 1993, p. 339

Brunet and Préaud
Marcelle Brunet and Tamara Préaud, *Sèvres, des origines à nos jours*, Fribourg, 1978

Brunet, *Frick*
Marcelle Brunet and John A. Pope, *The Frick Collection, An Illustrated Catalogue, VII, Porcelains, Oriental and French*, New York, 1974

Buckley, *Antiques*
Charles E. Buckley, "French Soft-paste Porcelain in the Wadsworth Atheneum at Hartford," *Antiques*, September 1953, pp. 188–91

Buckley, *Connoisseur*
Charles E. Buckley, "Eighteenth-Century French Porcelain in Hartford's Art Museum," *The Connoisseur Yearbook*, 1956, pp. 47–53

Buffon
Georges L. Le Clerc, comte de Buffon, *Histoire Naturelle des oiseaux*, Paris, 1770–86, 10 vols.

Bulletin Rijksmuseum
Bulletin van het Rijksmuseum 14, 2, 1966, Keuze uit de aanwinsten, pp. 86–93

Burghley Porcelains
The Burghley Porcelains, exh. cat., Japan Society, New York, May–July 1986

Burollet
   Thérèse Burollet, *Musée Cognacq-Jay*, II, *Porcelaines*, Paris, 1983

Butler, "Sèvres Imperial court"
   Kira Butler, "Sèvres from the Imperial court," *Apollo* 101, June 1975,
   pp. 452–57

Carlton House
   Carlton House: the past glories of George IV's palace, exh. cat.,
   The Queen's Gallery, Buckingham Palace, London, 1991–92

Carré
   Louis Carré, *Guide de L'Amateur D'Orfèvrerie Française*, Paris, 1930

Cary
   M. Cary et al., *The Oxford Classical Dictionary*, 1949 (1961 reprint)

Casanova
   Maria Letizia Casanova, *Le Porcellane Francesi nei Musei di Napoli*,
   Naples, 1974

Cassidy-Geiger
   Maureen Cassidy-Geiger, "Returning to 'Hoym, Lemaire und
   Meissen,'" *Keramos* 146, July 1994, pp. 3–8

Catalogue raisonné Boucher
   *Catalogue raisonné des tableaux … qui composent le Cabinet de feu
   M. Boucher*, Paris, 18ff., February 1771

Cayeux
   Jean de Cayeux, "Augustin de Saint-Aubin," in *The Dictionary of
   Art* 27, p. 531, London, 1996

Charageat, "Amphitrite"
   Marguerite Charageat, "La statue d'Amphitrite et la suite des déesses
   de Michel Anguier," *Archives de l'art français* 23, 1968, pp. 111–23

Charleston, "Althorp"
   Robert J. Charleston, "Sèvres and other French porcelain in Earl
   Spencer's collection at Althorp," *The Connoisseur* 73, no. 696, February
   1970, pp. 77–86

Charleston, *English Porcelain*
   Robert J. Charleston, *English Porcelain 1745–1850*, London and
   Toronto, 1965

Chavagnac
   Xavier de Chavagnac, *Catalogue des porcelaines française de
   M. J. Pierpont Morgan*, Paris, 1910

Chavagnac and Grollier
   Xavier de Chavagnac and Gaston de Grollier, *Histoire des Manufactures
   françaises de porcelaine*, Paris, 1906

Chilton
   Meredith Chilton, "Perfume and Porcelain in the Eighteenth Century
   Bedroom," in *The Bedroom from the Renaissance to Art Deco*, Toronto,
   1995, pp. 82–101

Chompret
   Joseph Chompret, Jean Bloch, Jean Guérin, Paul Alfassa, *Répertoire de
   la faïence française*, Paris, 1933, 8 vols.

Clarke, "Chelsea"
   T.H. Clarke, "French Influences at Chelsea," *English Ceramics Circle
   Transactions* 4, pt. 5, London, 1959, pp. 45–57

Clarke, "Pack of Hounds"
   T.H. Clarke, "Porcelain for a Pack of Hounds," *Country Life*, January,
   1987

Cohen and Hess
   David Harris Cohen and Catherine Hess, *Looking at European
   Ceramics, A Guide to Technical Terms*, Malibu and London, 1993

Cooper-Hewitt Collection
   *An American Museum of Decorative Arts and Design: Designs from the
   Cooper-Hewitt Collection*, exh. cat., Victoria and Albert Museum,
   London, 1973

Cordey
   Jean Cordey, *Inventaire des biens de Madame de Pompadour rédigé après
   son décès*, Paris, 1939

de Costa Andrade
   F.V.C. de Costa Andrade, "Collecting and study," *Keramik-Freunde der
   Schweiz* 33, December 1955, pp. 19–20, and inside back cover

Dacier
   Émile Dacier, *Catalogue de ventes et livrets de salons illustrés par Gabriel
   de Saint-Aubin*, Paris, 1909–21, 6 vols.

Dallot-Naudin
   Yvonne Dallot-Naudin and Alain Jacob, *Les Porcelaines Tendres
   Françaises*, Paris, 1983

Dam-Mikkelsen
   Bente Dam-Mikkelsen and Torben Lundbæk, *Etnografiske gentstande i
   Det Kongelige danske Kunstkammer Copenhagen 1650–1800*
   [Ethnographic Objects in the Royal Danish Kunstkammer 1650–1800],
   Copenhagen, 1980

Darblay
   Aymé Darblay, *Villeroy*, Paris, 1901

Dauget and Guillemé-Brulon
   Claire Dauget and Dorothée Guillemé-Brulon, *La porcelaine française*,
   Paris, n.d.

Dauterman, *Kress*
   Carl Christian Dauterman, James Parker, Edith Appleton
   Standen, *Decorative art from the Samuel H. Kress Collection*, New
   York, 1964

Dauterman, *Marks*
   Carl Christian Dauterman, *Sèvres porcelain: makers and marks of the
   eighteenth century*, New York, 1986

Dauterman, *Sèvres*
   Carl Christian Dauterman, *Sèvres*, New York, 1970

Dauterman, *Wrightsman*
   Carl Christian Dauterman, *The Wrightsman Collection, Vol. IV,
   Porcelain*, New York, 1970

Dawson, *Ashmolean*
   Aileen Dawson, *Eighteenth-century French porcelain in the Ashmolean
   Museum*, Oxford, 1996

Dawson, *British Museum*
   Aileen Dawson, *French Porcelain, A Catalogue of the British Museum
   Collection*, London, 1994

Dawson, "Eden service"
   Aileen Dawson, "The Eden Service: Another Diplomatic Gift,"
   Apollo 111, April 1980, pp. 288–97

Daydi
   Olivar Daydi, *La Porcelana en Europa*, Barcelona, 1953

Défi au goût
   Pierre Ennès and Brigitte Ducrot, *Un Défi au goût, 50 ans de création à
   la manufacture royale de Sèvres (1740–1793)*, exh. cat., Musée du Louvre,
   Paris, 1997

Dell
Theodore Dell, "J. Pierpont Morgan, Master Collector: Lover of the 18th-Century French Decorative Arts," in *Catalogue of the International Fine Art and Antique Dealers Show*, New York, 1995, pp. 25–34

Delplace
Lucien Delplace, *Considérations sur les porcelaines de Tournai 1750–1830*, Tournai, 1970

Dennis
Faith Dennis, *Three Centuries of French Domestic Silver*, New York, 1960, 2 vols.

Devoti
Donata Devoti, *L'Arte del Tessuto in Europa*, Milan, 1974

Diderot, *Encyclopédie*
Denis Diderot and Jean-Baptiste d'Alembert, *Encyclopédie, ou Dictionnaire raisonné des Sciences, des Arts et des Métiers*, Paris and Amsterdam, 1757–80 [compact edition, Elmsford, New York, 1969, 5 vols.]

Digard, "Museum d'histoire naturelle"
Marthe Digard, "Quelques œuvres d'art du museum d'histoire naturelle depuis la Révolution," *Bulletin de la Societé de l'Histoire de l'Art français,* 1936, pp. 155–71

Discovering the Secrets of Soft-Paste
Discovering the Secrets of Soft-Paste Porcelain at the Saint-Cloud Manufactory c. 1690–1766, exh. cat., Bard Graduate Center, New York, 15 July–24October 1999

Donnelly
P.J. Donnelly, *Blanc de Chine*, New York and Washington, 1967

Dragesco, "Oiseaux"
Bernard Dragesco, "Les décors d'oiseaux à la manufacture de Vincennes-Sèvres aux XVIIIe siècle," in *Des porcelaines et des oiseaux*, Tournai, 1994, pp. 39–53

Dragesco, "Pompadour"
Bernard Dragesco, "Une lettre inédite de Madame de Pompadour," *Mélanges en souvenir d'Elisalex d'Albis*, Paris, 1999, pp. 78–85

Duc d'Aumont
Le Cabinet du duc d'Aumont, Paris, 12ff December 1782 (1986 reprint of 1870 edition)

Duchon
Nicole Duchon, *La manufacture de porcelaine de Mennecy Villeroy*, Le Mée-sur-Seine, 1988

Duclaux
Lise Duclaux, *La statue équestre de Louis XV, Dessins de Bouchardon, sculpteur du Roi*, Paris, 1973

Dupont
Patrick Dupont, *Porcelaines françaises aux XVIIIe et XIXe siècles*, Paris, 1987

Edwards
JoLynn Edwards, "Alexandre Joseph Paillet (1743–1814): Study of a Parisian Art Dealer," dissertation, University of Washington, 1982

Eighteenth Century French Porcelain
Winifred Williams, *Eighteenth Century French Porcelain*, exh. cat., 3–20 July 1978

Elements of Style
Penelope Hunter-Stiebel, *Elements of Style*, exh. cat., Rosenberg & Stiebel, April–June 1984

Ennès, "Comte du Nord"
Pierre Ennès, "The Visit of the Comte and Comtesse du Nord to the Sèvres Factory," *Apollo* 127, March 1989, pp. 150–56, 220–22

Ennès, "Pompadour"
Pierre Ennès, "Essai de reconstitution d'une garniture de Madame de Pompadour," *The Journal of the Walters Art Gallery* 42–43, 1984–85, pp. 70–82.

Ennès, "Surtout"
Pierre Ennès, "Le surtout de mariage en porcelaine de Sèvres, du Dauphin, 1769–1770," *Revue de l'Art* 76, 1987, pp. 63–73

Ennès, Pierre
see also *Défi au goût*; Louvre, *Nouvelles Acquisitions*, 1985

Eriksen and Bellaigue
Svend Eriksen and Geoffrey de Bellaigue, *Sèvres Porcelain: Vincennes and Sèvres 1740–1800*, London, 1987

Eriksen, *David Collection*
Svend Eriksen, *The David Collection: French Porcelain*, Copenhagen, 1980

Eriksen, *Neo-classicism*
Svend Eriksen, *Early Neo-classicism in France*, London, 1974

Eriksen, *Pitti*
Svend Eriksen, *French Porcelain in Palazzo Pitti*, Florence, 1973

Eriksen, *Waddesdon*
Svend Eriksen, *Sèvres Porcelain, the James A. de Rothschild Collection at Waddesdon Manor*, Fribourg, 1968

Espinay de Saint-Luc
Michel de Espinay de Saint-Luc, "Contribution à l'iconologie du XVIIIe siècle: le biscuit de Sèvres et le théâtre italien de 1752 à 1781," unpublished thesis for the École du Louvre, 1968

Europe de la faïence
L'Europe de la faïence…, Musée des Beaux-Arts, Lille, 1991

European Porcelain
Masterpieces of European Porcelain, exh. cat., Metropolitan Museum of Art, New York, 18 March–15 May 1949

Faucheux
Louis-Étienne Faucheux, *Catalogue raisonné de toutes les estampes qui forment l'œuvre d'Israel Silvestre*, 1857 (reprinted by F. de Nobele, 1969)

Faÿ-Hallé, Antoinette
see *Boucher*; *Vincennes*

Feray
Jean Feray, *Architecture intérieure et décoration en France des origines à 1875*, Paris, 1988

Fischer
J. Fischer, *The French Bronze 1500 to 1800*, exh. cat., M. Knoedler and Co., New York, 1968

Fleming and Honour
John Fleming and Hugh Honour, *Dictionary of the Decorative Arts*, New York, 1977

Floraison des arts
Madame de Pompadour et la floraison des arts, exh. cat., David M. Stewart Museum, Montreal, 1988

Fontaine
Georges Fontaine, *La céramique française*, Paris, 1965

Forrest
Michael Forrest, "Remarkable Sèvres Porcelain," *The Antique Collector*, June 1987, pp. 108–15

Fourest, "Boîtes"
Henry-Pierre Fourest and Pierre Morel d'Arleux, "Les boîtes en porcelaine tendre au Musée Adrien Dubouché," *Cahiers de la céramique du verre et des arts du feu* 13, 1959, pp. 44–51

François Boucher
François Boucher: His Circle and Influence, exh. cat., Stair Sainty Matthiesen Gallery, New York, 30 September–25 November 1987

French and English Art Treasures
French and English Art Treasures of the Eighteenth Century, exh. cat., Parke-Bernet Galleries, New York, 1942

French and English 18th Century Exhibition
French and English 18th Century Exhibition, exh. cat., Montreal Museum of Fine Arts, Montreal, 26 April–31 May 1950

Frick, *Paintings*
The Frick Collection, II, Paintings, New York, 1968

Furcy-Raynaud, "Bâtiments du Roi"
Marc Furcy-Raynaud, "Inventaires des sculpteurs exécutées au XVIIIe siècle pour la direction des Bâtiments du Roi," *Archives de l'art français*, 14 (1925–26), 1927

Gaborit
Jean-René Gaborit, *Jean-Baptiste Pigalle 1714–1785, Sculptures du Musée du Louvre*, Paris, 1985

Gage and Marsh
Deborah Gage and Madeline Marsh, *Tobacco Containers and Accessories. Their Place in Eighteenth Century European Social History*, London, 1988

Gallet
Danielle Gallet, *Madame de Pompadour ou le pouvoir féminin*, Paris, 1985

Garnier
Edouard Garnier, *La porcelaine tendre de Sèvres*, n.d. (1889–91)

Gauthier
Serge Gauthier (preface), *Les porcelainiers du XVIIIe siècle français*, Paris, 1964

Ghidoli
Alessandra Ghidoli, *Le Vaselle: Il patrimonio artistico del Quirinale*, Milan, 1999

Gibbs
Vicary Gibbs, *The Complete Peerage*, 3, London, 1913

Gilliers
Joseph Gilliers, *Le Cannameliste François*, first edition, Nancy, 1751

Gillman
Derek Gillman, "Ming and Qing Ivories: Figure Carving," in *Chinese Ivories from the Shang to the Qing*, exh. cat., British Museum, London, May–August 1984, pp. 35–52

Gonse
Louis Gonse, *Les Chefs-d'œuvre des Musées de France, Sculpture, dessins, objets d'art*, Paris, 1904

González-Palacios
Alvar González-Palacios, *Gli arredi francesi*, Milan, c. 1995

Gordon
Katherine K. Gordon, " Madame de Pompadour, Pigalle, and the Iconography of Friendship," *The Art Bulletin* 50, no. 3, September 1968, pp. 249–62

Grand Larousse Universel
Grand Larousse Universel, 5, 1989

Grands services
Serge Grandjean and Marcelle Brunet, *Les grands services de Sèvres*, exh. cat., Musée national de Céramique, Sèvres, 1951

Granet
Solange Granet, "Images de Paris: La Place de la Concorde," *La Revue géographique et industrielle de France*, Paris, 1963, pp. 43–47

Grant
Maurice H. Grant, *Flower Paintings through four centuries*, Leigh-on-Sea, 1952

Grégory
Pierre Grégory, "Le service bleu céleste de Louis XV à Versailles: quelques pièces retrouvées," *La Revue du Louvre et des Musées de France* 31, February 1982, no. 1, pp. 40–60

Gruber
Alain Gruber, *Silverware*, New York, 1982

Guiffrey, "Académie de Saint-Luc"
Jules Guiffrey, "Histoire de l'Académie de Saint-Luc (1391–1776)," *Archives de l'art français* 9, n.s., Paris, 1915

Guiffrey, "Scellés"
Jules Guiffrey, "Scellés et inventaires d'artistes," *Nouvelles Archives de l'art français* 4, second series, 1883

Gulbenkian
Calouste Gulbenkian Museum Catalogue, Lisbon, 1982

Gunsaulus
Helen Gunsaulus, *The Clarence Buckingham collection of Japanese prints, The Primitives*, Chicago, 1955

Halfpenny
Pat Halfpenny, *English Earthenware Figures 1740–1840*, Woodbridge, Suffolk, 1991

Handbook
Wadsworth Atheneum Handbook, Hartford, Connecticut, 1958

Hansen
Günther Hansen, *Formen der Commedia dell'Arte in Deutschland*, Emsdetten, 1984

Havard
Henry Havard, *Dictionnaire de l'ameublement et de la décoration depuis le XIIIe siècle jusqu'à nos jours*, n.d. (1887–89), 4 vols.

Hawes and Corsiglia
Vivian S. Hawes and Christina S. Corsiglia, *The Rita & Fritz Markus Collection of European Ceramics & Enamels*, Boston, 1984

Hernmarck
Carl Hernmarck, *The Art of the European Silversmith 1430–1830*, London and New York, 1977

Hodgkins
Catalogue of an important collection of old Sèvres porcelain, Louis XV and Louis XVI period, belonging to E.M. Hodgkins, Paris, c. 1928

Hollstein
F.W.H. Hollstein, *Dutch and Flemish Etchings, Engravings and Woodcuts, 1450–1700*, Amsterdam, 1949, 53 vols.

Honey
W.B. Honey, *French Porcelain of the 18th Century*, London, 1950

Hood, *Apollo*
Graham Hood, "European Ceramic Masterpieces," *Apollo* 88, December, 1968, pp. 440–45

Hood, *Bulletin*
Graham Hood, "French Porcelain from the J.P. Morgan Collection at the Wadsworth Atheneum," *Wadsworth Atheneum Bulletin* I, no. 3, Winter 1965, pp. 1–14

Hood, *Connoisseur*
Graham Hood, "French Porcelain from the J.P. Morgan Collection at the Wadsworth Atheneum," *Connoisseur* 158, no. 636, February 1965, pp. 131–37

Horvitz, Linda [Roth],
see *Antique Taste*; *Morgan*, Hartford

Hozier
Louis-Pierre d'Hozier, and Antoine-Marie d'Hozier de Sérigny, *Armorial général de France*, reg. 5, second part, Paris, 1764, pp. 1–4 (Paris reprint, 1884, reg. 5, vol. 3, pp. 779–82)

Hughes
Peter Hughes, *The Wallace Collection, Catalogue of Furniture*, London, 1996, 3 vols.

Huth
Hans Huth, *Lacquer of the West*, Chicago, 1971

Hutton, "Meissen"
William Hutton, "Meissen," in *J. Pierpont Morgan, Collector: European Decorative Arts from the Wadsworth Atheneum*, Hartford, 1987, pp. 160–61

Iconographie des Bourbon
Simone Hoog, *Iconographie des Bourbon de Henri IV à Louis XVI d'après la collection de gravures de Louis-Philippe*, 42 microfiches, Paris, 1985

Ingamells
John Ingamells, *Catalogue of Pictures III, French before 1815, The Wallace Collection*, London, 1989

Inoura
Yoshinobu Inoura and Toshio Kawatake, *The Traditional Theater of Japan*, New York and Tokyo, 1981

Jacques Sarazin
Jacques Sarazin Sculpteur du Roi, 1592–1660, exh. cat., Musée du Nyonnais, Noyon, June–August 1992

Jean-Richard
Pierrette Jean-Richard, *L'œuvre gravé de François Boucher, dans la Collection Edmond Rothschild*, Paris, 1978

Jedding, *Europäisches Porzellan*
Hermann Jedding, *Europäisches Porzellan*, Munich, 1971

Jedding, *Meissener Porzellan*
Hermann Jedding, *Meissener Porzellan des 18. Jahrhunderts in Hamburger Privatbesitz*, Hamburg, 1982

de Jonge
C.H. de Jonge, *Delft ceramics*, New York, 1969

Jougla de Morenas
Henri Jougla de Morenas, *Grand armorial de France*, Paris, 1934–49, 6 vols.

King
William King, *Catalogue of the Jones Collection*, II, London, 1924

Ko-Imari
Barry Davies Oriental Art, *Ko-Imari Porcelain from The Collection of Oliver Impey*, exh. cat., London, 17–27 June 1997

Königliches Porzellan Frankreich
Königliches Porzellan aus Frankreich, Sammlerstücke und Service der Manufaktur Vincennes/Sèvres, exh. cat., Hessische Hausstiftung, Museum Schloß Fasanerie, Fulda, Germany, 12 June–31 October 1999

LD
Louis Courajod, *Livre-journal de Lazare Duvaux, marchand-bijoutier ordinaire du roy, 1748–58*, Paris, 1873, 2 vols.

La France et la Russie
La France et la Russie au Siècle des Lumières, exh. cat., Grand Palais, Paris, 1986–87

La Varenne
François-Pierre de La Varenne, *Le Confiturier François*, 1687

Lahaussois, *Delft*
Christine Lahaussois, *Faïences de Delft*, 1994

Lahaussois, *Saint-Cloud*
Christine Lahaussois, *Porcelaines de Saint-Cloud: La collection du Musée des Arts décoratifs, Paris*, Paris, 1997

Laing, Alistair
see *Boucher*

Laking
Guy Francis Laking, *Sèvres porcelain of Buckingham Palace and Windsor Castle*, London, 1907

Lami
Stanislas Lami, *Dictionnaire des sculpteurs de l'école française au dix-huitième siècle*, Paris, 1910, 2 vols.

Lang, *Burghley House*
Gordon Lang, *European Ceramics at Burghley House*, Stamford, England, 1991

Larousse Gastronomique
Larousse Gastronomique, English edition, New York, 1988 (1984 revised French edition)

Lawrence
Bishop William Lawrence, *Memoir of John Pierpont Morgan (1837–1913)*; written in the form of a letter to Herbert L. Satterlee, 6 January 1914 (Boston, 1914), mostly unpublished typescript in the archives of the Pierpont Morgan Library, printed with the kind permission of his son, the Right Reverend Frederic C. Lawrence

Lechevallier-Chevignard
Georges Lechevallier-Chevignard, *La Manufacture de porcelaine de Sévres*, 1908

Le Corbeiller, *Dodge*
Clare Le Corbeiller, "Sèvres Porcelain," in *The Dodge Collection of Eighteenth-Century French and English Art in the Detroit Institute of Arts*, Detroit, 1996, pp. 151–200

Le Corbeiller, "Tournai and Mennecy"
Clare Le Corbeiller, "Tournai and Mennecy," *Les Cahiers de Mariemont* 24/25, 1993/94, pp. 54–59

Le Duc, "Bourg-la-Reine"
Geneviève Le Duc, "La Manufacture de Bourg-la-Reine," *Cahiers de la céramique du verre et des arts du feu* 39, 1967, pp. 162–75

Le Duc, *Chantilly*
Geneviève Le Duc, *Porcelaine tendre de Chantilly au XVIIIe siècle*, Paris, 1996

Le Duc, "Chantilly, extrême orient"
Geneviève Le Duc, "Chantilly, un certain regard vers l'extrême orient 1730–1750," *Journal of the French Porcelain Society* 10, 1993

Le Duc, "Charenton"
Geneviève Le Duc, "Paris, rue de Charenton, Une manufacture royale de 'terre d'Angleterre' 1743–1749," *Sèvres, Revue de la Société des Amis du Musée National de Céramique* 2, 1993, pp. 20–28

Le Duc, "Condé"
Geneviève Le Duc, "The Porcelain of Chantilly: the collections of the Duke and Duchess of Bourbon Condé and the inventory of the factory in the middle of the 18th century," in *The International Ceramics Fair and Seminar, London, Handbook*, 1993, pp. 8–18

Le Duc, "Frédéric V"
Geneviève Le Duc, "Un buste du roi Frédéric V de Danemark en porcelaine de Copenhague par Louis-Antoine Fournier," *Les Cahiers de Mariemont* 24/5, 1993/1994, pp. 60–67

Le Duc, "Lemaire"
Geneviève Le Duc, "Rudolphe Lemaire et la manufacture de porcelaine de Meissen: Style extrême-oriental ou goût français?," *Revue de l'art* 116, 1997-2, pp. 54–60

Le Duc, "Saint-Cloud"
Geneviève Le Duc, "The Soft-Paste Porcelain Manufactory in Saint-Cloud and the so-called Saint-Cloud Porcelain Manufactory in Paris (c. 1693–1766)," in *Discovering the Secrets of Soft-Paste Porcelain at the Saint-Cloud Manufactory c. 1690–1766*, exh. cat., Bertrand Rondot, ed., Bard Graduate Center, New York, New Haven, 1999, pp. 71–82

Le Duc, *Villeroy*
Le Duc, "La Porcelaine de Villeroy," *Journal of the French Porcelain Society* 3, 1987

Le Duc and de Plinval de Guillebon, "Saint-Cloud"
Geneviève Le Duc and Régine de Plinval de Guillebon, "Contribution à l'étude de la manufacture de faïence et de porcelaine de Saint-Cloud pendant ses cinquante premières années," *Keramik-Freunde der Schweiz* 105, March 1991, pp. 3–53

Lemonnier
Patricia Lemonnier, "Jean François Leleu," *L'Estampille/L'Objet D'Art* 288, September 1989, pp. 66–75

Leturcq
Jacques Leturcq, *Notice sur Jacques Guay*, Paris, 1873

Levitine
George Levitine, *The Sculpture of Falconet*, Greenwich, Connecticut, 1972

Linsky Collection
The Jack and Belle Linsky Collection in The Metropolitan Museum of Art, New York, 1984

Louis XV
Louis XV, un moment de perfection de l'art Français, exh. cat., Musée de la Monnaie, Paris, 1974

Louveciennes
Madame Du Barry De Versailles à Louveciennes, exh. cat., Musée-promenade de Marly-le-Roi, Louveciennes, 1992

Louvre, *Nouvelles acquisitions*, 1985
Nouvelles acquisitions du Département des objets 1980–1984, Musée du Louvre, Paris, 1985

Louvre, *Nouvelles acquisitions*, 1995
Nouvelles acquisitions du Département des objets d'art: 1990–1994, exh. cat., Musée du Louvre, Paris, 1995

Luynes
Charles-Philippe d'Albert, duc de Luynes, *Mémoires du duc de Luynes sur la Cour de Louis XV, 1735–1748*, Paris, 1860–65, 14 vols.

MNC, *Nouvelles acquisitions 1979–1989*
Sèvres, Musée national de Céramique, Nouvelles acquisitions 1979–1989 (text on Vincennes and Sèvres by Antoine d'Albis and Tamara Préaud), Paris, 1989

Mallet
John Mallet, "Upton House, The Bearsted Collection: Porcelain," *Journal of the French Porcelain Society* 8, 1992 (expanded reprint of catalogue published in 1964)

Marien-Dugardin
A.M. Marien-Dugardin, *Porcelaines de Tournai*, Musées Royaux d'art et d'histoire, Brussels, 1959

Masson
Frédéric Masson, "La porcelaine de Sèvres, collection Chappey," *Les Arts* 38, 1905, pp. 1–32

Masterpieces from the Louvre
Masterpieces from the Louvre, French Bronzes and Paintings from the Renaissance to Rodin, exh. cat., Queensland Art Gallery, 1988

McCaughey
McCaughey et al., *"The Spirit of Genius": Art at the Wadsworth Atheneum*, New York, 1992

McNab
Jessie McNab, "The Legacy of a Fantastical Scot," *The Metropolitan Museum of Art Bulletin* 19, no. 6, February 1961, pp. 172–80

Meissen
Dissertation-Programme de la plus ancienne manufacture de porcelaine d'Europe à l'occasion de son deux-centième anniversaire Meissen, 1910

Meister
Peter Wilhelm Meister, *Sammlung Pauls Porzellan des 18. Jahrhunderts*, Frankfurt am Main, 1967

Ménager
Dominique Ménager, "Catalogue raisonné des biscuits de porcelaine de Vincennes et de Sèvres au XVIIIe siècle dans les collections du Musée national de Céramique, Sèvres," unpublished *mémoire* for the École du Louvre, April 1985, 2 vols.

Minneapolis, *Acquisitions*
The Minneapolis Institute of Arts, *The Art of Collecting: Acquisitions ... 1980–85*, Minneapolis, Minnesota, c. 1986

Mitchell, *Flower Painters*
Peter Mitchell, *Great Flower Painters: four centuries of floral art*, New York, 1973

Mitchell, "Van Spaendonck"
Peter Mitchell, "Gerard van Spaendonck," in *The Dictionary of Art*, 29, p. 256, London, 1996

Morgan, Hartford
Linda Horvitz Roth, ed., *J. Pierpont Morgan, Collector, European Decorative Arts from the Wadsworth Atheneum*, exh. cat., Hartford, New York, Fort Worth, Phoenix, Charlotte, Portland, 1987–88

Morley-Fletcher
Hugo Morley-Fletcher, *Early European porcelain and faience as collected by Kiyi and Edward Pflueger*, London, 1993, 2 vols.

Mottola Molfino
Alessandra Mottola Molfino, *L'Arte della porcellana in Italia*, Busto Arsizio, 1977, 2 vols.

Munger "Louis XV"
Jeffery Munger, "A Chantilly bust of Louis XV in the Museum of Fine Arts, Boston," in *The International Ceramics Fair and Seminar, London, Handbook*, 1988, pp. 29–34

Munger, "Bouillotte"
Jeffrey Munger, "A *Bouillotte* in the Museum of Fine Arts, Boston," *Mélanges en souvenir d'Elisalex d'Albis*, Paris, 1999, pp. 103–9

Munger, *Wickes*
Jeffrey Munger et al., *The Forsyth Wickes Collection in the Museum of Fine Arts, Boston*, Boston, 1992

Newman, *Connoisseur*
Harold Newman, "Sèvres veilleuses in private collections," *Connoisseur*, June 1968, pp. 132–35

Newman, *Veilleuses*, 1967
Harold Newman, *Veilleuses, A Collector's Guide, A Definitive Review of Ceramic Food and Tea Warmers, 1750–1860*, New Jersey, 1967

Newman, *Veilleuses*, 1987
Harold Newman, *Veilleuses, A Collector's Guide, A Definitive Review of Ceramic Food and Tea Warmers, 1750–1860*, revised edition, New York and London, 1987

Nocq, *Orfèvrerie*
Henry Nocq, *Orfèvrerie civile française du XVIe au début du XIXe siècle*, Paris, 1927, 2 vols.

Nocq, *Poinçon*
Henry Nocq, *Le poinçon de Paris*, 1926–1931, 5 vols.

Noël-Waldteufel
Marie-France Noël-Waldteufel, "Manger à la cour: alimentation et gastronomie aux XVIIe et XVIIIe siècles," in *Versailles et les tables royales en Europe, XVIIème et XVIIIème siècles*, exh. cat., Paris, 1993, pp. 69–84

Nord-Pas-de-Calais
Geneviève Becquart, Guy Blazy, Annic Davy, and Annie Scottez-De Wambrechies, *La porcelaine française du XVIIIe siècle dans les musées du Nord-Pas-de-Calais*, exh. cat., Saint-Omer, Lille, Arras, 1986–87

Olausson
Magnus Olausson, "Freemasonry, Occultism and the Picturesque Garden Towards the End of the Eighteenth Century," *Art History* 8, no. 4, December 1985, pp. 413–33

Ortolani
Benito Ortolani, *The Japanese Theatre from Shamanistic Ritual to Contemporary Pluralism*, Leiden, 1990

Palazzo Reale di Torino
Porcellane e argenti del Palazzo Reale di Torino, Milan, 1986

Parfaict
Les Frères Parfaict, *Dictionnaire des théâtres*, Paris, 1756, 7 vols.

Patrimoine national
Cinq années d'enrichissement du Patrimoine national 1975–1980, exh. cat., Galeries nationales du Grand Palais, Paris, November 1980–March 1981

Pavlovsk
Alexandra Vassilievna Alexeieva et al., *Pavlovsk: The Collections*, Paris, 1993, 2 vols.

Peters, "Louis XV"
David Peters, "A Service for King Louis XV," *Christie's International Magazine*, May/June 1995, pp. 64–65

Peters, "Louis XV et XVI"
David Peters, "Les Services de Porcelaine de Louis XV et Louis XVI," in *Versailles et les tables royales en Europe, XVIIème et XVIIIème siècles*, exh. cat., Paris, 1993, pp. 110–23

Peters, *Marks*
David Peters, *Decorator and Date Marks on C18th Vincennes and Sèvres Porcelain*, London, 1997

Peters, *Plates and Services*
Sèvres Plates and Services of the 18th Century (forthcoming publication)

Pinot de Villechenon
Marie-Noëlle Pinot de Villechenon, *Sèvres, 1740–1992: Une collection de porcelaines*, Paris, 1993

Place Louis XV
De la place Louis XV à la Place de la Concorde, exh. cat., Musée Carnavalet, Paris, 17 May–14 August 1982

de Plinval de Guillebon, *Faïence*
Régine de Plinval de Guillebon, *Faïence et porcelaine de Paris XVIIIe–XIXe siècles*, Dijon, 1995

de Plinval de Guillebon, *Louvre*
Régine de Plinval de Guillebon, *Musée du Louvre, Département des Objets d'art, Catalogue des Porcelaines françaises*, I, Paris, 1992

de Plinval de Guillebon, "La porcelaine tendre"
Régine de Plinval de Guillebon, "La porcelaine tendre à Paris au XVIIIe siècle," *Journal of the French Porcelain Society* 11, 1994

Plumb
Sir John Plumb, "The Intrigues of Sèvres," *House and Garden*, 1986, pp. 44–54

Porcelain for Palaces
John Ayers, Oliver Impey, and John Mallet, *Porcelain for Palaces: the fashion for Japan in Europe 1650–1750*, exh. cat., British Museum, London, July–November 1990

Porcelaine de France, 1987
Porcelaine de France: Sèvres, une manufacture protégée par Madame de Pompadour, favorite du Roi, exh. cat., Tokyo, 17–29 September 1987

Porcelaine à Saint-Cloud
Il y a 300 ans … : La Porcelaine à Saint-Cloud: une entreprise pionnière sur les bords de la Seine, exh. cat., Musée de Saint-Cloud, Saint-Cloud, September–November 1997

Porcelaines de Tournai
Porcelaines de Tournai du XVIIIe siècle, Musée royale de Mariemont, April–November 1969

Posner
Donald Posner, "Mme. de Pompadour as a Patron of the Visual Arts," *The Art Bulletin* 72, no. 1, March 1990, pp. 74–105

Pradère
Alexandre Pradère, *French Furniture Makers: The Art of the Ébéniste from Louis XIV to the Revolution*, Malibu, 1989

Préaud and d'Albis
Tamara Préaud and Antoine d'Albis, *La porcelaine de Vincennes*, Paris, 1991

Préaud, "Bachelier"
Tamara Préaud, "Bachelier and the Manufacture of Vincennes/Sèvres," in *Jean-Jacques Bachelier (1724–1806)*, exh. cat., Musée Lambinet, Versailles, 22 November 1999–20 March 2000

Préaud, "Biscuit"
Tamara Préaud, "La sculpture à Vincennes ou l'invention du biscuit," *Sèvres, Revue de la Société des Amis du Musée National de Céramique* 1, 1992, pp. 30–37

Préaud, "Sources iconographiques"
Tamara Préaud, "Recherches sur les sources iconographiques utilisées par les décorateurs de porcelaine de Vincennes (1740–1756)," *Bulletin de la Société de l'Histoire de l'Art français*, 1990 (2 December 1989), pp. 105–15

Préaud, "Vocabulaire"
Tamara Préaud,"Incertain vocabulaire," *Mélanges en souvenir d'Elisalex d'Albis*, Paris, 1999, pp. 119–23

Préaud, Tamara
see also *Vincennes*

"Le Premier fond vert"
"Vincennes 1753: Le Premier Fond Vert?" *Connaissance des Arts* 437/438, July–August 1988, pp. 82–88

Rackham
Bernard Rackham, "Sèvres and other porcelain in the collection of Mr. Lionel Faudel-Phillips," *Burlington Magazine* 99, July 1926, pp. 25–31

Réau, "L'argenterie"
Louis Réau, "L'argenterie française du XVIIIe siècle au musée de Lisbonne," *Gazette des Beaux-Arts* 773, January 1927, pp. 17–26

Réau, *Falconet*
Louis Réau, *Etienne-Maurice Falconet*, Paris, 1922, 2 vols.

Réau, *Louis XVI*
Louis Réau, *L'Art en France au XVIIIème Siècle, style Louis XVI 1760–1789*, Paris, 1952

Réau, "L'Offrande"
Louis Réau, "L'Offrande du cœur," *Gazette des Beaux Arts* 64, 1922, pp. 213–18

Reichel, *Japanese*
Friedrich Reichel, *Early Japanese Porcelain: Arita Porcelain in the Dresden Collection*, Leipzig, 1981, trans. by Barbara Beedham, London 1981

Reichel, *Rosa Familie*
Friedrich Reichel, *Die Porzellansammlung Augustus des Starken: Die Porzellankunst aus China, die Rosa Familie*, Munich, 1993

Rétrospectives des Porcelaines
O. Du Sartel and E. Williamson, *Expositions Rétrospectives des Porcelaines de Vincennes et de Sèvres*, exh. cat., 8e Exp., Union centrale des Arts décoratifs, Paris, 1884

Ripa
Cesare Ripa, *Iconologia*, Rome, 1603

Rombouts
Stephen Rombouts, "Art as Propaganda in Eighteenth-Century France: The Paradox of Edmé Bouchardon's Louis XV," *Eighteenth-Century Studies* 27, no. 2, Winter 1993–94, pp. 255–82

Rondot
Bertrand Rondot, *Discovering the Secrets of Soft-Paste Porcelain at the Saint-Cloud Manufactory c. 1690–1766*, exh. cat., Bertrand Rondot, ed., Bard Graduate Center, New York, New Haven, 1999

Rosenberg and Stewart
Pierre Rosenberg and Marion C. Stewart, *French Paintings 1500–1825 The Fine Arts Museums of San Francisco*, San Francisco, 1987

Roth, "Morgan"
Linda Horvitz Roth, "J. Pierpont Morgan, Collector," and appendix in *J. Pierpont Morgan, Collector: European Decorative Arts from the Wadsworth Atheneum*, Hartford, 1987, pp. 26–42, 196–201

Roth, Linda Horvitz
see also *Antique Taste*; *Morgan*, Hartford

Royal Collection
Geoffrey de Bellaigue, *Sèvres porcelain from the Royal Collection*, exh. cat., The Queen's Gallery, Buckingham Palace, London, 1979–80

Rückert
Rainer Rückert, *Meissener Porzellan 1710–1810*, exh. cat., Bayerisches Nationalmuseum, Munich, 1966

Samoyault, "Du Barry"
Jean-Pierre Samoyault, "L'appartement de madame Du Barry à Fontainebleau," in *Madame Du Barry: De Versailles à Louveciennes*, Paris, 1992

Sargent
William R. Sargent, *The Copeland Collection*, Salem, Massachusetts, 1991

Sargentson
Carolyn Sargentson, *Merchants and Luxury Markets: The Marchands Merciers of Eighteenth-Century Paris*, London and Malibu, 1996

Sassoon
Adrian Sassoon, *Vincennes and Sèvres Porcelain, Catalogue of the Collections, The J. Paul Getty Museum*, Malibu, 1991

Saule
Béatrix Saule, "Tables Royales à Versailles, 1682–1789," in *Versailles et les tables royales en Europe, XVIIème et XVIIIème siècles*, exh. cat., Paris, 1993, pp. 41–68

Savill
Rosalind Savill, *The Wallace Collection, Catalogue of Sèvres Porcelain, London*, London, 1988, 3 vols.

Savill, "Boucher"
Rosalind Savill, "François Boucher and the Porcelains of Vincennes and Sèvres," *Apollo* 115, March 1982, pp. 162–70

Savill, "Cameo fever"
Rosalind Savill, "Cameo fever: six pieces from the Sèvres porcelain dinner service made for Catherine II of Russia," *Apollo* 116, November 1982, pp. 304–11

Savill, "Premier service"
Rosalind Savill, " Le premier service de porcelaine de Louis XV," in *Versailles et les tables royales en Europe, XVIIème et XVIIIème siècles*, exh. cat., Paris, 1993, pp. 281–84

Savill, "Starhemberg"
Rosalind Savill, "A Sèvres Treasure house at Waddesdon: Re-assembling the Starhemberg service," *Apollo* 139, April 1994, pp. 25–33

Sceaux-Bourg la Reine
Maddy Aries et al., *Sceaux-Bourg la Reine, 150 ans de céramique des collections privées aux collections publiques*, exh. cat., Orangerie du Château de Sceaux, Sceaux, 1986

Scheurleer
D.F. Lunsingh Scheurleer, *Chinesisches und japanisches Porzellan in europäischen Fassungen*, Braunschweig, 1980

Schwartz
Selma Schwartz," The Sèvres Porcelain Service for Marie-Antoinette's Dairy at Rambouillet: An Exercise in Archaeological Neo-Classicism," *Journal of the French Porcelain Society* 9, 1992

Scott
C.M. and G.R. Scott, *Antique Porcelain Digest*, Newport (Monmouthshire), 1961

Segal
Sam Segal, *Flowers and Nature, Netherlandish Flower Painting of Four Centuries*, The Hague, 1990

Sergène
André Sergène, *La Manufacture de Sèvres sous l'Ancien Régime*, Nancy, 1974, 3 vols.

Setterwall
Åke Setterwall et al., *The Chinese Pavillion at Drottingholm*, Malmö, 1974

Severne Mackenna
F. Severne Mackenna, *Chelsea Porcelain, the Red Anchor Wares*, Leigh-on-Sea, 1951

Sèvres, Japan
Sèvres, Japan, 1998

Shono
Masako Shono, *Japanisches Aritaporzellan im sogenannten 'Kakiemonstil' als Vorbild für die Meissener Porzellanmaufaktur*, Munich, 1973

Soil de Moriamé and Delplace
Chevalier Soil de Moriamé and L. Delplace-de Fourmanoir, *La manufacture Impériale et Royale de Porcelain de Tournay*, Tournai, 1937

Solitaires Frankenthal
Die Solitaires der Manufactur Frankenthal, exh. cat., Kurpfälzisches Museum, Heidelberg, 1993

Somers Cocks
Anna Somers Cocks and Charles Truman, *The Thyssen-Bornemisza Collection: Renaissance jewels, bold boxes and objets de vertu*, London, 1984

Soupers de la cour
Les Soupers de la cour, ou l'art de travailler toutes sortes d'alimens, pour servir les meilleures tables, suivant les quatre saisons, Paris, 1755, 4 vols.

Spero
Simon Spero, *The Bowles Collection of 18th century English and French Porcelain, Fine Arts Museums of San Francisco*, San Francisco, 1995

Standen, "Country Children"
Edith A. Standen, "Country Children: Some *Enfants de Boucher* in Gobelins Tapestry," *Metropolitan Museum Journal* 29, 1994, pp. 111–33

Standen, *Tapestries*
Edith A. Standen, *European post-medieval tapestries and related hangings in The Metropolitan Museum of Art*, New York, 1985

Standen, Edith A.
see also *Boucher*

Stein
Perrin Stein, "Madame de Pompadour and the Harem Imagery at Bellevue," *Gazette des Beaux-Arts* 6, no. 113, January 1994, pp. 29–44

Strouse
Jean Strouse, *Morgan, American Financier*, New York, 1999

Tables d'Égoïstes
Tables d'Égoïstes 1750–1970, arts de la table en France, exh. cat., Musée Carnavalet, Paris, 1993

Tables royales
Béatrix Saule, Dorothée Guillemé-Brulon, David Peters, Rosalind Savill, Marie-France Noël-Waldteufel et al, *Versailles et les tables royales en Europe, XVIIème et XVIIIème siècles*, exh. cat., Musée National des Châteaux de Versailles et de Trianon, Versailles, 3 November 1993–27 February 1994

Tait, "Harewood, Early Sèvres"
Hugh Tait, "Sèvres porcelain in the collection of the Earl of Harewood. Part I: the early period: 1750–60," *Apollo* 79, June 1964, pp. 474–78

Toussaint-Samat
Maguelonne Toussaint-Samat, *A History of Food*, trans. Anthea Bell, Cambridge, Massachusetts, 1993

Troinitsky
S. Troinitsky, *Tabatières en porcelaine à l'Ermitage Impérial*, Petrograd, 1915

Troude
Albert Troude, *Choix de modèles de la Manufacture Nationale de porcelaines de Sèvres appartenant au Musée céramique*, n.d. (1897)

Tuchscherer and Sano
Jean-Michel Tuchscherer and Takahiko Sano, *Étoffes Merveilleuses du Musée Historique des Tissus, Lyon*, Tokyo, 1976, 2 vols.

Tuohy
Thomas Tuohy, "Exhibition Reviews: The St. Petersburg connection: Walpole and Angerstein," *Apollo* 145, April 1997, pp. 55–57

Van Veen
Otto van Veen, *Le théâtre moral de la vie humaine, representée en plus de cent tableaux divers, tirez du poëte Horace/ par le sieur Otho Venius; et expliquez en autant de discours moraux par le Sieur de Gomberville; avec la table du philosophe Cebes*, Brussels, 1678, revision of Philipp van Zesen, *Moralia Horatiana*, Amsterdam, 1656

Verlet, *Bronzes dorés*
Pierre Verlet, *Les bronzes dorés français du XVIIIe siècle*, Paris, 1987

Verlet, "Historical"
Pierre Verlet, "Some Historical Sèvres Porcelains Preserved in the United States," *The Art Quarterly* 17, no. 3, Autumn 1954, pp. 230–41

Verlet, "Reply"
Pierre Verlet, "Reply to Siegfried Ducret," *Cahiers de l'art céramique* 2, March 1956, p. 43

Verlet, *Sèvres*
Pierre Verlet, Serge Grandjean and Marcelle Brunet, *Sèvres, I, Le XVIIIe siècle; les XIXe et XXe siècles*, Paris, 1953

Verlet, *Versailles*
Pierre Verlet, *Versailles*, Paris, 1961, 1985

Versailles
Elaine Evans Dee and Guy Walton, *Versailles: The view from Sweden*, Cooper-Hewitt Museum, New York, 1988

di Vesme
Alessandro Baudi di Vesme, *Stefano della Bella: Catalogue raisonné*, Alexandre De Vesme; with introduction and additions by Phyllis Dearborn Massar, New York, 1971

Vesme
Schede Vesme, *L'Arte in Piemonte del XVI al XVIII secolo*, Turin, 1963–82, 4 vols.

Vincennes
Tamara Préaud and Antoinette Faÿ-Hallé, *Porcelaines de Vincennes, les origines de Sèvres*, exh. cat., Grand Palais, Paris, October 1977–January 1978

Vincennes and Sèvres Porcelain
Edgar Munhall, *Vincennes and Sèvres porcelain*, exh. cat., The Frick Collection, New York, 1980

Vision of the East
Vision of the East, Partridge Fine Arts, London, 5 November– 10 December 1999

Walcha, "Dekor"
Otto Walcha, "Wettstreit zwischen plastischem und malerischem Dekor," *Keramos* 30, October 1965, pp. 46–54

Walcha, *Meissen*
Otto Walcha, *Meissen Porcelain*, New York, 1981

Wark, *Huntington*
Robert R. Wark, *French Decorative Art in the Huntington Collection*, San Marino, California, 1979

Wark, *Meissen*
Ralph Wark, *The Wark Collection, Early Meissen Porcelain*, Jacksonville, Florida, 1984

Watney, "Prototypes"
Bernard Watney, "Some parallels and proto-types in ceramics," *English Ceramic Circle Transactions* 10, pl. 5, 1980, pp. 350–56

Watney, *Longton Hall*
Bernard Watney, *Longton Hall Porcelain*, London, 1957

Watson, "Lacquer"
Francis J. B. Watson, "Beckford, Mme De Pompadour, The Duc de Bouillon and the Taste for Japanese Lacquer in Eighteenth Century France," *Gazette des Beaux-Arts* 61, February 1963, pp. 101–27

Watson, *Oriental*
Francis J. B. Watson, *Mounted Oriental Porcelain*, exh. cat., Washington, D.C., 1986

Watson, "Walpole"
Francis J. B. Watson, "Walpole and the Taste for French Porcelain in Eighteenth-Century England," in *Horace Walpole, Writer, Politician and Connoisseur*, Warren Hunting Smith, ed., New Haven and London, 1967

Watson and Whitehead
Sir Francis J. B. Watson and John Whitehead, "An inventory dated 1689 of the Chinese porcelain in the collection of the Grand Dauphin, son of Louis XIV, at Versailles," *Journal of the History of Collections* 3, no. 1, 1991, pp. 13–52

Wees
Beth Carver Wees, *English, Irish, & Scottish Silver at the Sterling and Francine Clark Art Institute*, New York, 1997

Wendell
W. G. Wendell, "Loving Cups and Saucy Saucers," *Wadsworth Atheneum Bulletin*, Winter 1966, pp. 1–8

Wessely
J.E. Wessely, *Jan de Visscher und Lambert Visscher, Verzeichnis ihrer Kupferstiche*, Leipzig, 1866

Whitehead
John Whitehead, *The French Interior in the Eighteenth Century*, London, 1992

Wiebenson
Dora Wiebenson, *The Picturesque Garden in France*, Princeton, New Jersey, 1978

Wildenstein
Georges Wildenstein, "Simon-Philippe Poirier, fournisseur de Madame du Barry," *Gazette des Beaux-Arts* 60, 1962, 2, pp. 365–77

Wilkie
Jodie Wilkie, "Just Desserts," *Christie's International Magazine*, May 1997, pp. 64–65

Wilson, "Getty"
Gillian Wilson, Adrian Sassoon, and Charissa Brewer David, "Acquisitions Made by the Department of Decorative Arts in 1982," *The J. Paul Getty Museum Journal* 11, 1983, pp. 13–66

Wilson, "Huntington"
Gillian Wilson, "New information on French furniture at the Henry E. Huntington Library and Art Gallery," *The J. Paul Getty Museum Journal* 4, 1977, pp. 29–35

Winkler
Chryspolitus Winkler et al., *Ehemalige Hofsilber- und Tafelkammer: Silber, Bronzen, Porzellan, Glas*, Vienna, 1996

Zelleke
Ghenete Zelleke, "From Chantilly to Sèvres: French Porcelain and the Dukes of Richmond," *Journal of the French Porcelain Society* 7, 1991

Zick, "Harpokrates"
Gisela Zick, "Amor-Harpokrates: zur Wirkungsgeschichte und Ikonographischen Herleitung einer Skulptur von Etienne-Maurice Falconet," *Wallraf-Richartz-Jahrbuch* 37, Cologne, 1975, pp. 215–46

Zick, "Montmorency"
Gisela Zick, "D'après Boucher, Die 'Vallée de Montmorency' und die europäische Porzellanplastik," *Keramos* 29, July 195, pp. 3–47

Photographic Credits

The Art Institute of Chicago	18-1
Bibliothèque nationale de France, Paris	65-1, 164-2
Collection of Dr. Dale Brent, USA	36-1–2, 171-1–2
British Museum, London	177-1
Mademoiselle Yveline de Chavagnac, Paris	Introduction-2
The Huntington Library and Art Collections, San Marino, California	155-1
Manufacture nationale de Sèvres. Archives, Sèvres	*Clichés* MNS, 59-1–5, 76-1–2, 69-1, 70-1, 71-2, 61-1–2, 73-1, 79-1, 85-1, 86-1–2, 132-1, 139-1, 146-1, 151-1–3, 156-1, 159-1, 164-3–4
	photography by Jean-Loup Charmet 71-1, 85-2, 87-1, 93-1, 119-1–3, 127-1, 130-1, 131-1–2, 132-1, 133-1, 143-1, 148-1, 162-1
Metropolitan Museum of Art, New York	37-1, 44-1–2, 69-2
Musée national de porcelaine Adrien Dubouché, Limoges	52-1
Museum of Fine Arts, Boston	86-3
The New York Public Library, Astor, Lenox and Tilden Foundations, Spencer Collection, Miriam and Ira D. Wallach Division of Art, Prints and Photographs	35-1
Peabody Essex Museum	19-1
Réunion des Musées Nationaux, Paris	59-6, 59-7, 65-2, 70-2–3, 82-1, 151-4–5, 164-1, 176-1, 177-2–3
Joanna T. Steichen	Introduction-1
Trinity College, Hartford, Connecticut, Enders Ornithology Collection, Watkinson Library	128-1–4, 145-1–4, 146-2–5
Victoria and Albert Museum, London	8-1, 36-3

Wadsworth Atheneum, Hartford, all photographs of objects in the collection taken by David Stansbury, with the exception of the following, which were taken by Joseph Szaszfai: cat. nos. 21, 41, 45, 47, 55, 65, 67, 68, 91, 98, 135, 160, 194, 199

Index

Marks

Only those marks featuring on one or more pieces within a catalogue entry are given. References shown in boldface type are to catalogue entry numbers. Those for redecorated or fake pieces in the Collection are prefaced by the abbreviation "rfo."

factory marks

Bourg-la-Reine
  BR: incised, **49**, **50**
Chantilly
  hunting horn: painted, **12**, **14–16**, **21**; impressed, **15**
Crépy-en-Valois
  DCO (DC'O): incised, **51**
Saint-Cloud
  St C: incised, **5**; painted, **2–3**
  T: underglaze blue, **2–3**; incised, **5**
Sèvres
  RF: République française, **130**, **146**
  R.F.: République française, **131**
  Sèvres/Sevres, **128–31**, **146**; rfo, **187**
  crown (hard-paste mark), **178**
Villeroy and Mennecy
  DV (D.V. or D,V), incised, **22**, **24–26**, **36**, **39**, **41–42**, **45–47**, **50**, **52**
Vincennes and Sèvres
  interlaced Ls, **54**, **56–62**, **64**, **66–70**, **73–74**, **76–128**, **132–45**; **148–54**, **156–67**, **173–76**, **178**; rfo, **179–94**, **196–200**

gilders' marks

#: Chauvaux, Michel-Barnabé, *aîné*, *père*, **139**, **161**
2000: Vincent, Henry-François, *jeune*, *père*, **108**, **123**, **146**, **167**
B, script or scrolling: Boulanger, Jean-Pierre, **99**, **103**, **173–74**
BD, script: Baudouin, François, *père*, **141–42**, **165**
GI: Girard, Étienne-Gabriel, **106**, **118**, **129**
HP: Prévost, Henri-Martin, **151**
zodiacal sign for Leo (?): Weydinger family of gilders, **97**

painters' marks

9.: Buteux, Charles-Nicolas, *fils aîné* or *aîné*, **109**; rfo, **187**
AD, script: Durosey, Mademoiselle, *aînée*, **130**
anchor: Buteux, Charles, *père*, *aîné*, **158**
b, script: Bertrand, **94–95**, **162**
B.n., script: Bulidon, Nicolas, **105**, **122**, **144**

branch: Noualhier, Jean-Baptiste-Étienne-Nicolas, *fils*, **108**
ch: Chabry, Étienne-Jean, **70**; rfo, **197**
cm: Commelin, Michel-Gabriel, **121**, **146**
comma: Méreaud, Charles-Louis, *jeune*, **99**
compass mark: Mutel: rfo, **183**
cp: Chappuis, Antoine-Joseph, *jeune*, *aîné*: rfo, **196**, **198**
crescent, elaborate interlaced Ls: Armand, Louis-Denis, *aîné*, **62**
cross: Xhrouuet, Philippe, *père*, **58**, **90**
crown, stippled: Sioux, Jean-Charles, *aîné*, **106**, **154**, **159**, **165**
D: Decambos, **116**
dagger, sword: Evans, Étienne, **64**, **88**, **128**, **145**; in the style of, rfo, **193**
DT: Drouet, Gilbert, **122**
elaborate interlaced Ls: Armand, Louis-Denis, *aîné*: **62**, **66**, **86–87**
exclamation point: Thévenet, Louis-Jean, *père*, **92**
FB: Barrat, François-Marie, *oncle*, **142**
five dots in diamond form: Fontaine, Jacques, **98**, **103**, **139–40**
fleur-de-lis, stylized: Taillandier, Madame Geneviève, *née* Le Roy, **109**, **112**
fleur-de-lis: Taillandier, Vincent, **61**, **85**
four dots: Buteux, Pierre-Théodore (Théodore), **163**; rfo, **199**
fx, script: Descoins, Françoise-Philippine, *née* Le Grand, **146**
h, scrolling: Laroche, Jacques-François-Louis de, **74**, **141**
hatchet: Rosset, Pierre-Joseph, *aîné*, **145**, **151**
heraldic sign for ermine: Choisy, Cyprien-Julien Hirel de, **107**, **118**, **127**
IN: Chauvaux, Jean, *jeune* or *cadet*, **128**
jh: Henrion, Jean-François: marked to deceive, rfo, **200**
k or K: Dodin, Charles-Nicolas, **71**, **176**; rfo, **186**
L and R: Roguier, Jeanne-Joséphine, *née* Le Riche, **166**
L[.], script: Levé, Denis, **90**, **115**, **117**, **119**
LB, scrolling: Le Bel, Jean-Nicolas, *jeune*: rfo, **194**
LG: Le Guay, Étienne-Henry, *aîné*, *père*, **122**, **141–44**, **161**, **164**; rfo, **186**
LP: Parpette, Mademoiselle Louise-Thérèse (?), *aînée*, **129**
M or m: Morin, Jean-Louis, **59**, **102**, **160**
m:x: Xhrouuet, Marie-Claude-Sophie (or Secroix), **114**
N, scrolling: Aloncle, François-Joseph, **88**, **173–74**; in the manner of, rfo, **192**
nq: Nicquet, **143**

p: Buteux, Guillaume, **122**
P': Pierre, Jean-Jacques, **136**
P.B., script, or pb, script: Boucot, Jean-Joseph-Philippe, *fils*, *cadet*, **111**, **120**
phj: Philippine, Jean-François-Henry (Francisque), *cadet*, **110**
PT: Pithou, Pierre-Nicolas, *aîné*, **175**
S: Méreaud, Pierre-Antoine, *aîné*, *père*, **99**
Sc: Binet, Sophie, *née* Chanou, **126**, **145**
SS, crossed: Catrice, Nicolas, **137**
star, five-pointed: Caton, Antoine, **164**
T surmounted by a dot: Binet, François, **74**
three dots: Tandart, Jean-Baptiste, *aîné*, **101**, **131**, **152**
three small vertical lines on a horizontal line: Vielliard, André-Vincent, *père*, **60**, **78**, **80–81**, **83**, **113**, **153**, **163**; pseudo, rfo, **181**; in the manner of, rfo, **191**
three small vertical lines on a horizontal line: Vielliard, Pierre-Joseph-André, *fils*, **113**
vd, conjoined/monogrammed: Vandé, Jean-Baptiste-Emmanuel, *père*, **74**, **139**, **161–62**
vd or v..d.: Vandé, Pierre-Jean-Baptiste, *fils* or *aîné*, **107**, **112**, **123**, **131**
x: Micaud, Jacques-François, *père*, **91**, **93**, **100**, **156**
y or Y: Bouillat, Edmé-François, *père*, **124–25**, **145**, **167**
y or Y: Bouillat, Madame Geneviève-Louise, *née* Thévenet, **124–25**
zodiacal sign for Libra: Noël, Guillaume, **104**, **157**

unattributed painters' or painted marks

||, **75**, **125**
5, **79**
AN or AV, **84**
crown, **135**
dot in blue, **99**
dots (3) forming a triangle, **133**
dots (4), **103**

possible or probable attributions of other marks

G?, scrolling: Weydinger, Léopold, *père*, **74**
H: Becquet, Charles-François, or Socquet, Michel, **150**

unattributed marks on Chantilly, Saint-Cloud, Villeroy-Mennecy porcelain

painted
  A, **15**
  D^R, **15**
  L, **2**
  M., **11**
  P, **2**

General Index

Catalogue entry numbers are given for aspects of objects in the Collection. These numbers are shown in boldface type. References to redecorated or fake pieces in the Collection are prefaced by the abbreviation "rfo." Page numbers for illustrations other than of items in the Collection are shown in italics; all other page references are given in roman.

1. Soucoupe	.... gd	}	"	288.
1. Gobelet gd 2e gd ..... gd		}		
1. Soucoupe gd ..... gd		}	"	300.
1. Gobelet à lait 1e gd ..... fleur		}		
1. Soucoupe gd ..... gd		}	"	72
1 Gobelet gd 2e gd ..... gd		}		
1 Soucoupe gd ..... gd		}	"	54.
1 Gobelet gd ..... Lapis paisage		}	"	156.
1. Soucoupe ..... gd		}		
1. Gobelet gd ..... gd Enf Camaÿ		}	"	144.
1. Soucoupe ..... gd		}		
1 Pot à lait à pieds 1e gd Bleu céleste Enf colorés			"	120
1. gd ..... fleurs			"	27.
2 gd ..... Enfans camayeux ... 30.				60.
1. gd 2e gd ..... fleur			"	18.
1 gd ..... gd filet bleu			"	21.
1. gd 1e gd ..... Lapis oiseaux ...			"	60.
1 gd 2e gd ..... gd			"	42.
2 Lapis à toilette Bleu céleste oiseaux ... gd		} 72		144
2 Soucoupes gd ..... gd		}		
1 Tasse gd ..... Lapis oiseaux ...		}	"	48.
1 Soucoupe gd ..... gd		}		
1 Tasse gd ..... gd et or ...		}	"	42.
1 Soucoupe gd ..... gd		}		
1 Tasse gd ..... Blanc et or ...		}	"	30.
1 Soucoupe gd ..... gd		}		
2 Tasses gd ..... fleurs ...		} 12		24.
2 Soucoupes gd ..... gd		}		
2 Caisses quarrées 1e gd. gd 108				216.
2 gd 2e gd ..... gd 72				144.
2 gd ..... Enf Camayeux ... 96				192.
2. gd Bleu céleste oiseaux très riches ... 360.				720.

1212 Pieces.

52514.

1675. , , 50545.